James F. Stephen

A General View of the Criminal Law of England

James F. Stephen

A General View of the Criminal Law of England

ISBN/EAN: 9783337233457

Printed in Europe, USA, Canada, Australia, Japan

Cover: Foto ©Suzi / pixelio.de

More available books at **www.hansebooks.com**

A GENERAL VIEW

OF THE

CRIMINAL LAW OF ENGLAND

BY

SIR JAMES FITZJAMES STEPHEN, K.C.S.I., D.C.L.

HONORARY FELLOW OF TRINITY COLLEGE, CAMBRIDGE
A CORRESPONDING MEMBER OF THE FRENCH INSTITUTE
A JUDGE OF THE SUPREME COURT, QUEEN'S BENCH DIVISION

SECOND EDITION

London
MACMILLAN AND CO.
AND NEW YORK
1890

RICHARD CLAY AND SONS, LIMITED,
LONDON AND BUNGAY.

PREFACE.

THE first edition of this book was published in the year 1863, and I was asked for a second edition as far back as 1874; but on beginning to prepare it I found myself met at every step by the difficulty that I was unable to refer to any work in which the contents of the Criminal Law as it is, were shortly stated. This first suggested to me the scheme of writing such a work, and I accordingly wrote my *Digest of the Criminal Law, Crimes and Punishments*, which was published in 1877. In consequence of this work I proposed to the then Government to prepare a Code of Criminal Law and Procedure, and upon this I was engaged from 1877 to early in 1879, first as an independent draftsman, and afterwards as a member of the Criminal Code Commission of 1878. The Bill drawn by me, and settled by the Commission of which I was a member, has been more than once under the consideration of Parliament, but time has never been found for its full discussion. In 1883 I published a *History of the Criminal Law*, and, with the assistance of my eldest son, a *Digest of the Law of Criminal Procedure*. Of these works I think I may fairly say that collectively they constitute a pretty complete account both of the actual contents of the Criminal Law of England, and of the various circumstances which led to its assumption of its present form.

The *History* is, however, too long and elaborate for general purposes, and in particular for the purpose of an introduction to the two *Digests;* and I have been informed that my first work, the *General View of the Law of England,* is still in request, as a first book on Criminal Law, amongst students at the Universities and elsewhere, although it has become so rare as to be in practice unobtainable. I have accordingly re-written it, giving an account of the subject, which contains in a very moderate compass the essence of what I have learnt during a long and greatly varied experience of thirty-six years as a barrister, a member of the Indian Council, an author, a draftsman, and a judge.

CONTENTS.

CHAPTER VI.

CHAPTER VII.

CHAPTER VIII.

CHAPTER IX.

CHAPTER X.

CHAPTER XI.

CHAPTER XII.

CHAPTER XIII.

CHAPTER XIV.

CHAPTER XV.

CHAPTER XVI.

TRIALS.

A GENERAL VIEW

OF THE

CRIMINAL LAW OF ENGLAND.

GENERAL VIEW

OF THE

CRIMINAL LAW OF ENGLAND.

CHAPTER I.

PLAN OF THIS WORK.

A CRIME, in the strict legal sense of the word, is an act
forbidden by law under pain of punishment. Most of the
acts which fall under this definition are grossly wicked
actions, forming attacks upon person, or upon property, or
upon public order; but the definition itself includes many
actions which would not in popular language be described as
crimes. Some things which in other countries are treated as
matters of civil administration are dealt with in England as
offences against the criminal law. The law of nuisances is
perhaps the strongest illustration of this. A variety of civil
obligations—such as the obligation of repairing a road or a sea-
bank, the obligation of not interfering with erections intended
for the public convenience, and many other matters of the same
sort—are enforced by indicting those who are guilty of a trespass or a negligence which might involve punishment, but
to which no one would attach the idea of moral guilt. It
must be remembered also that, although all actions punish-

able by law may be regarded as crimes, they may also be regarded from a completely different point of view. Nearly every crime is not only a crime, but is also an individual wrong or tort, and may be dealt with as such. Assaults and some kinds of frauds are generally so dealt with. Every libel may be the subject of an indictment, but much the more usual remedy for it is a civil action. Crimes may also produce effects which bring them under the notice of courts of justice for other than criminal purposes. Bigamy, for instance, and some other crimes, are grounds for the civil remedy of divorce. Arson by a person insured would be a good defence by an insurance company to an action brought upon a policy. In these cases crimes would be judicially proved before courts of justice, but would be viewed by the court neither as crimes nor as torts, but simply as acts affecting the status or the money liability of persons other than the criminal. These illustrations show both that the consequences charged upon an act by law, and not the nature of the act itself, is the specific difference by which crimes are distinguished, and that the criminality of an act is distinct from its moral character, although, as a rule, the moral atrocity and infamy of any given action is the main reason why it is treated as a crime.

Again, there are several branches of law which cannot properly be described as a part of the criminal law, but are very nearly related to it. The most remarkable of these is the law relating to what are described as penal or *qui tam* actions.[1] These are cases in which particular matters, principally connected with the enforcement of some special Act of Parliament, are made liable to penalties which may be claimed by private persons or public authorities who choose to sue for them. Innumerable instances might be given of

---

[1] The phrase is derived from the old form of information, which ran thus: A. B. (the plaintiff's name) "*qui tam pro se quam pro domino Rege*," &c.

these. One well-known case gave rise to an action brought against Mr. Bradlaugh for having voted and sat in Parliament without taking the oaths then prescribed for a person who did sit and vote. Other instances are to be found in the Municipal Corporations Act, which imposes penalties on those who act as members of Town Councils without being duly qualified, or who, being such members, accept any contract with the Corporation.

Though closely allied with the criminal law properly so called, these enactments cannot be said to form a part of it. They all depend upon special Acts of Parliament, relating to an immense variety of subjects quite unconnected with each other, and illustrating no general theory or principle.

Many crimes in the full sense of the word are properly speaking only sanctions meant to enforce Acts of Parliament relating to subjects which have little to do with crime. Such, for instance, are sections of the various Marriage Acts, which forbid, under pain of penal servitude, certain irregular marriages; sections in numerous Acts which make certain false declarations equivalent to perjury; sections which appoint special punishments for the forgery of particular documents; and an infinite variety of others. Of these I say nothing. They belong rather to the particular subjects to which the Acts of Parliament containing them refer than to the criminal law in the common sense of the phrase.

Similar observations may be made on a large number of enactments, such as breaches of police regulations contained in particular Acts of Parliament, and enforceable in a summary manner by magistrates. Such, to mention a very few, are the series of sections of the Metropolitan and of other Police Acts; the series of sections in the Highway Act as to offences in the use of highways; sections relating to offences connected with the destruction of sea-birds and fishing in rivers; sections in the Vagrant Acts, the Public Health

Acts, and a vast number of others too various and not interesting enough to require mention here. I do not notice these.

In early times the distinction between crimes and civil injuries was even less well defined than it is now. Thus, by the Statute of Westminster the first (3 Edw. I. c. 20), it was enacted amongst other things that a trespasser in a park should pay heavy damages to the party and be imprisoned three years, besides incurring other penalties.[1]

Thus the object of this work is to give a general view of the criminal law of England, exclusive of penal actions; of offences punishable by summary proceedings before magistrates; and of special offences intended as sanctions for special statutory institutions; and including all acts commonly known as crimes. The arrangement of the work is as follows. I begin with an historical introduction, setting forth the steps by which the criminal law reached its present condition. I then proceed to give an account of certain general principles relating to crime, and of certain general exceptions which are virtually contained or implied in the definition of every crime. These may collectively be called the conditions of criminality. They include the subjects of age, sanity, compulsion, necessity, ignorance of law, and ignorance of fact. I then proceed to the question of the parties to the commission of crimes, and to the steps taken towards a crime—incitement, conspiracy, and attempts. From this I pass to the definitions of particular crimes, treating successively of crimes which affect public order, abuses and obstructions of public authority, offences which are regarded as injurious to the public at large; offences against the person, the parental and conjugal rights, or the reputation of individuals; and lastly offences against property, by way either of force or of fraud. I next give a sketch of the subject of criminal

---

[1] *History of the Criminal Law,* iii. 275.

procedure, and of that of the law of evidence in relation to criminal cases. Upon all these subjects I mention only the leading points and principles, and I give references at every point both to my *History of the Criminal Law* and to my *Digest* of those parts of it which relate respectively to crimes and punishments and to procedure. The whole contains the essence of what I have to say upon the subject, and will, I think, enable anyone who wishes to acquaint himself with the criminal law, either for professional or for other purposes, to learn all the leading details necessary to be known upon the subject, and to know where to find further information upon it.

CHAPTER II.

CHAP. II. THE history of the criminal law of England can in a certain sense be traced back to the very earliest period—certainly far beyond the Conquest; though nearly the whole of it, as it now exists, whether we look at its definitions or at the laws of procedure, is much more recent. It contains some small traces of connection with the criminal law of Rome, but they are few and unimportant, and appear to me to have been introduced into the system by English or at all events Anglo-Norman writers many centuries after all traces of the Roman authority in Britain had absolutely passed away.

The earliest body of criminal law known in England is contained in the laws of a succession of kings, beginning with King Ethelbert, and ending with the work called the *Leges Regis Henrici Primi,* a compilation made in the reign of Henry I. of the various laws and customs then in force; not a code enacted by that king. These different bodies of law vary in several important particulars, but, speaking generally, they re-enact each other with variations, and may be regarded in the light of so many new editions of a single very imperfect code, with amendments, additions, and expansions suggested by the various changes which took place in the course of about five hundred years, from Ethelbert

to Henry I., some of which were in force only in particular CHAP. II.
parts of England.

The *Leges Henrici Primi* are the latest in date, and are
the most instructive as to the general scheme and spirit
of these bodies of law. The work itself is, as I have said,
a compilation. What authority it possessed, or by whom it
was made, does not appear. It contains a great number
of matters which are to be found in the earlier laws, and
it fairly represents their spirit. A few scraps of Roman law
have found their way into it, but taking the system, such as
it is, as a whole, it seems to give a not unfair account of the
ancient English law as it was long before the Conquest. It
is a slovenly composition, full of inconsistencies, repetitions,
and unnecessary distinctions; and, like the other early laws,
it is remarkable for the complete absence of anything which
can be said to approach to the statement of a legal principle.
There is abundant reference to crimes, and to the manner
of prosecuting them, but the definitions of crime are scanty,
and no clear account of the mode in which a crime is
to be prosecuted is to be found in any part of the work.
Like all the other early laws, it assumes throughout that its
readers are acquainted with the general character of the
legal institutions and modes of trial then existing, and, with
some few exceptions, with the meaning of the various names
which are given to the different crimes; but inasmuch as these
are the very points of which we know least, and of which we
have to inform ourselves by comparing the different allusions
which are made to them, the result, on the whole, is obscure
and unsatisfactory. The following, however, may be taken as
a short description of the main points which these various
laws disclose.

The early English definitions of crime may be passed over
shortly. They can hardly be said to exist at all, and indeed
are rather names than definitions, though the names are

sometimes explained; as, "Stredbreche est si quis viam frangat concludendo vel avertendo vel fodiendo;" "Forestel [1] est si quis ex transverso incurrat vel in via expectet et assalliat inimicum suum." Sometimes no definition is given, but the meaning of the name may be inferred from the context of different places in which it is used. Thus *oſcr-hynes*, or *overseunesse*, appears to have been something in the nature of a contempt of court, or disobedience by an officer of justice to lawful orders. Some slight attempts are made to classify different kinds of homicide, but in this part of the law nothing is to be found which is on any account remarkable.

The interesting part of the early English criminal law is its procedure, which throws considerable light on the state of society in which it existed. A crime in any moderately civilized state of society is an event recognized as one which is to be if possible prevented, and, at all events, punished, by the public force upon public grounds; but in the earliest period of English history crimes seem to have been regarded as private wrongs, revenged rather than punished by those who were injured by them, first by private war, afterwards by summary execution, and then by a public administration of justice slowly organized in such a way as to bear many traces of the rough system, if so it can be called, which it gradually superseded.

Of private war it is enough to say that traces of it are to be found in many of the earlier English books of law, and in those of the Conqueror, who regarded trial by battle as a modified form of it. It is also shown by the laws which punish the breach of the king's, the lord's, or the Church's peace. These were originally confined to particular times and places, which implied that peace was the exception and war the general rule.

---

[1] *Fore*, before ; *stellan*, to leap.

The law of summary execution, or *infangthief*, was a short step nearer to the regular administration of justice. It consisted in the privilege conceded to the lords of townships of putting to death in a summary way people who committed theft or robbery in their bounds. This privilege was common, and was frequently used, certainly till the reign of Edward I., as appears by the Hundred Rolls. One or two stray instances of it survived till a much later period, especially in the forests. The Halifax "gibbet law" was enforced so lately as 1658.

These summary methods of criminal procedure, if they deserve the name, were overshadowed and greatly restrained from a very early period by a general and regular system, which, however, bore strong marks of the characteristics of the system which it superseded. This was the system which depended ultimately upon the king, and was exercised through the authorities of the shire or county, the hundred or wapentake, and the tithing, parish, or township. For each shire there was an earl or alderman, and a sheriff or viscount; in the hundreds there were chief bailiffs; every township or tithing was represented on all occasions by a reeve and four men. There were numerous exceptional "liberties," or districts which stood outside the general system, but with similar officers of their own.

The courts were held in and for the counties and hundreds, and in and for the franchises. The hundred court was simply the county court sitting in and for the hundred, as the sheriff's *tourn* or circuit. The court consisted of the representatives of the different tithings, the four men and the reeve in the jurisdiction, and the business transacted was of two kinds, administrative and judicial. The administrative business bearing on the subject of criminal law was what ultimately came to be called "view of frank pledge," which was slowly developed from that of *"borhs"* or sureties.

CHAP. II. In the maturity of the system all men were bound to combine themselves into associations of ten, each of whom was security for the good behaviour of the rest. The business of seeing that these associations were kept in order and enforced by fines was one of the chief agenda of the local courts, and was a principal means of police administration. It became obsolete many centuries ago, but a petty criminal jurisdiction which was annexed to it still survives under the same name in small manor and local courts. A full account of this jurisdiction is given in 18 Edw. II., A.D. 1325, which is called "the statute for view of frank pledge." It marks a date at which the old system of frank pledge had become so completely obsolete that the extent of the jurisdiction which inherited its name had become uncertain.

The business of prosecuting criminals was one of which it is impossible to give a perfectly distinct account for the reasons already assigned. It was unlike a modern criminal trial, both in the object aimed at and in the way in which that object was attained.

The character of the proceedings cannot be understood without an explanation of four technical terms. These are *borh, wer, bot,* and *wite.*

Borh meant a pledge or security. Everyone was bound, as early as the days of Cnut, to have "*borhs*" who would "hold and lead him to every plea," *i.e.* produce him in court when he was wanted, as a bailsman does in the present day.

Wer was a price or value set on a man according to his rank in life, and was employed for many purposes. If the man was killed, his relations were paid the amount of his *wer.* If the man was convicted of theft, he might have to pay his own *wer* to the king. If the man was outlawed, his sureties (*borhs*) had to pay his *wer.*

Bot was compensation to a person injured by a crime. The *wer* was in some cases the measure of the *bot ;* for instance, if the injury consisted in killing a relation, the persons whose relation was killed received by way of *bot* or compensation the amount of his *wer*. In many cases the *bot* was fixed according to the nature of the injury; *e.g.* in Alfred's laws, the *bot* for the loss of the great toe is twenty shillings, of the second fifteen shillings, of the middle toe nine shillings, of the fourth toe six shillings, and of the little toe five shillings.

Wite was a fine to the king for a crime. The *wer* might be the measure of the *wite* as well as of the *bot;* as, for instance, if the criminal was outlawed his *borhs* had to pay his *wer* to the king as *wite.*

The proceedings consisted of two steps—accusation and trial.

Accusation might be either by the four men and the reeve of a township, or by a sort of judicial committee of twelve—which seems to have been instituted as a representative body for judicial purposes, and may have had to do with the origin of grand juries—or by a private person.

The accused person was "led to the plea" by his *borh*, who, as well as his lord if he had one, and two thanes of the hundred, had to swear that he "had not paid thief-gild" since a certain time, which being done, he had to clear himself either by compurgation or by ordeal. Compurgation consisted in getting a number of witnesses, greater or less according to circumstances, to swear to his innocence. The compurgators were collectively called the *lad.* There were rules as to the relative value of oaths and as to their number, and there are a few traces of the existence of witnesses to facts, but nothing satisfactory can be said about them. These compurgators might be dispensed with if the accused performed the single ordeal, viz. handling a pound-weight of red-hot iron, or putting his hand up to the wrist into boiling water. If the oath "burst," *i.e.* if the witnesses were not forthcoming or

CHAP. II. would not swear, the accused went to the triple ordeal, handling three pounds-weight of red-hot iron, or plunging the arm into boiling water to the elbow.

If the ordeal failed, the accused was convicted, and had on a first conviction to pay *bot* and *wite*—compensation to the party injured, and a fine to the king—and to find *borhs* or sureties for his future good behaviour. On a second conviction he was put to death or mutilated. A certain number of offences were *bot*-less or inexpiable, and for these death or mutilation was inflicted on the first conviction.

These institutions lasted for a considerable time after the Conquest, though they were gradually superseded by others. Ordeals are mentioned in the Assizes of Clarendon (A.D. 1164) and Northampton (A.D. 1176), and their disuse formed, as will appear hereafter, a step in the history of trial by jury.

These are the main features of early English criminal law. I pass to the effects of the Conquest upon it. Remotely, the Conquest may be regarded as the origin of most of the great institutions the development of which forms the subject of the political history of England; but the Conqueror and his sons walked to a great extent upon the ancient ways, and governed by the old methods, though with a continual effort to renew and reinvigorate them. Several entirely new additions were made by the Conqueror himself to the English criminal law. [1] He separated the ecclesiastical from the temporal jurisdiction. [2] He established trial by battle, and [3] he abolished capital punishment. The first of these changes

---

[1] Stubbs's "Charters," 85.

[2] "Si Anglicus homo compellet aliquem Francigenam per bellum de furto vel homicidio vel aliqua re pro qua bellum fieri debeat vel judicium inter duos homines habeat plenam licentiam hoc faciendi."—THORPE, i. 488.

[3] "Interdico etiam ne quis occidatur aut suspendatur pro aliqua culpa sed eruantur oculi et testiculi abscidantur et hoc praeceptum non sit violatum super foris facturam meam plenam."—STUBBS, *Charters*, p. 84.

had most important effects, to be noticed hereafter. Of the
second I will at present say only that it survived nominally
till 1819, and most probably had some effect in discrediting
ordeals. The last seems merely to have expressed a personal
feeling, for if capital punishments were discontinued in
William's time they were soon afterwards resumed, and there
are instances of such punishments even under him.

The great thing, however, which the Conqueror did was to
invigorate the Royal authority in all its functions, and thus
to lay the foundation of the great judicial and administrative
reforms of Henry II., which determined the character of the
English administration of justice from his time to our own.

This was done in various ways, but in particular by two
institutions—the King's Court and the Inquest. The King's
Court, or Curia Regia, was at once a Parliament, a Supreme
Court of Justice, and a Supreme Board of Revenue and
Administration. Of the way in which these functions were
separated and distinguished it is not necessary to speak in
detail in this place. It is enough to say that the Court of
Queen's Bench, now the Queen's Bench Division of the High
Court of Justice, and the courts held before the Justices of
Assize, which to this day are the great criminal courts of
England, are directly descended from the Curia Regia. It is
owing to their influence that the criminal law of England
has always retained its uniformity, whatever other faults it
may have had, and has almost invariably been administered
to the satisfaction of the public even under the most trying
circumstances, and that the criminal courts have had sufficient
authority by their decisions to develop, with some assistance
from a few writers of law books, a crude collection of names of
offences into the most elaborate and complete body of criminal
jurisprudence in the world. This, however, was not the immediate result of the Conqueror's institutions. Henry II. had
much more influence than the Conqueror in remodelling the

CHAP. II. courts.   The hundred court, or sheriff's *tourn*, continued to be the great criminal court till Magna Charta, when it was restricted to the less important criminal cases. Ch. 24 provided, "Nullus vicecomes constabularius coronatores vel alii ballivi nostri teneant placita coronæ nostræ."

Pleas of the Crown and pleas of the sheriff are carefully distinguished by Glanville, who wrote under Henry II. Capital cases "quæ scilicet crimina ultimo puniuntur supplicio aut membrorum truncatione" were pleas of the Crown.   Thefts, though capital, were pleas of the sheriff, "pro defectu dominorum," *i.e.* unless there was some local franchise to which they belonged ; so that it is probable that in this as in some other cases Magna Charta enacted existing practice into positive law.

The Inquest, unknown, I believe, before the Norman Conquest, was in its ultimate result quite as remarkable as the Curia Regia.   It was simply an inquiry held before one or more persons appointed to make it, into facts which the king wished to know for the purposes of his government. These inquiries were taken before justices, of whom an indefinite number were attatched to the King's Court, and who were employed as occasion required for services defined by Commissions issued from time to time.

The inquests by which the information recorded in Domesday Book was collected supply the most striking and memorable illustration of the nature and working of this institution.   Commissioners were sent all over England.   The sheriffs and bailiffs brought before them people locally acquainted with the matters to be recorded.   They gave their information upon oath, probably after making inquiry of the parties interested, and their returns formed a record of all the matters on which the administration of the executive government, and particularly the collection of the feudal and territorial revenue of the

Crown, depended. These inquests were the real origin of Chap. II. trial by jury, and the intermediate position of the members of the inquest between judges and witnesses explains the history of that mode of trial and its strong and weak points.

Assizes, in our sense of the word, are the direct descendants of the *itinera* or eyres, which were first reduced to a system, by no means unlike our circuits, in the time of Henry II. The business of these eyres was to hold inquests in every part of the country as to crimes, as to civil suits, and as to a vast variety of matters connected with revenue, feudal services, &c., specified in the Commissions under which the justices sat, and varying from time to time according to circumstances.

The history of the eyres and of the different Commissions issued to them is very curious.[1] It is sufficient for my present purpose to say that the revenue and miscellaneous business being provided for in various ways, the assizes remained as an institution for the administration of criminal and civil justice by the holding of inquests, which were gradually developed into trial by jury.

It would be difficult to trace out in full detail the process by which trial by jury, as we understand it, was developed from the old inquests, but the general nature of the process may be stated with great confidence. No perfectly distinct account can be given of the proceedings before a justice in eyre as they originally were, but it is clear that the first step was to call together the principal persons of the county, and to require them to report upon the crimes which had been committed in the county since their last appearance. They would naturally present the persons who had been previously arrested or held to bail by the sheriffs, the constables, afterwards by the coroners, and at a later period still by the

[1] *History of the Criminal Law,* i. 97–111.

CHAP. II. justices of the peace, as well as those whom they knew or suspected by their own information. How the functions of the petty jury came in, or who the petty jurors originally were, is by no means clear. Whether the four men and the reeve from the particular township in which a crime was committed were originally fined for it, or whether any sort of general pannel was provided, and if so, how, are matters which cannot now be discovered, nor can I say what precise effect the accusation of a grand jury had in the very earliest times. It is also very difficult to ascertain what was the line between the functions of the grand and petty jury, and how far the justices took part in their deliberations or inquired into the reasons they had for their verdicts.

There is, however, abundant evidence to show that, however their powers may have been exercised, jurors, both grand and petty, originally were, as grand jurors still are in theory, official witnesses, upon whose sworn reports the justices acted in trying crimes. It is probable that from the very first they were aided by actual witnesses of the facts on which their reports were based, and it is certain that as time went on they ceased to be expected to testify to matters within their own knowledge only, and came to be the judges of matters of fact deposed to in their presence, and, in the case of the petty jury, in the presence and under the supervision of the justice. The question, however, occurs, How, while the grand jury acted as accusers, was the guilt of the accused person decided upon ? The answer is that at first, as appears from the Assize of Clarendon (A.D. 1164) and the Assize of Northampton (A.D. 1176), and the *Rotuli Curiæ Regis* in the reigns of Richard I. and John, the trial was, in cases in which the grand jury accused, by ordeal. and in cases in which a private appellor accused, by battle. If the prisoner was condemned by the ordeal, he lost first one foot, and after the Assize of Northampton his right hand as well, and had to abjure the .

realm. If he was acquitted by the ordeal, he nevertheless, if accused "of murder or other base felony," had to abjure the realm. Ordeals fell into disuse (probably on account of the decrees of the Lateran Council of 1216) in the course of the thirteenth century; and when this happened accusation by a grand jury became equivalent to condemnation, and no means of trial remained except in cases of private accusations or appeals, in which the trial was by combat. It is probable that in these circumstances the petty jury came into use. The first step towards it was the Great Assize, which was an inquest of persons acquainted with the facts, who returned a verdict upon oath and of their own knowledge. Even before the disuse of ordeals, the privilege of going before a petty jury instead of being tried by ordeal might be purchased from the king, and after this the petty jury came to be the regular stated means of disposing of accusations made by the grand jury.

There is abundant evidence to show first that all juries held in the thirteenth century the position of official witnesses; secondly, that they were closely examined by the justices who took the inquests as to their reasons for their accusations or verdicts; and thirdly, that they were assisted in the discharge of their functions by witnesses, in the modern sense of the word, to particular facts.[1]

The change from this antique form of trial by jury to that which still exists amongst us, in which the grand jury accuses on the evidence of witnesses heard in private, and the petty jury decides upon the accusation also on the evidence of witnesses, but under the direction of the judge, was no doubt gradual, and there would be little interest in tracing out the steps by which it came to pass; but I may

---

[1] For details and authorities see *History of the Criminal Law*, i. 251–265. The old character of juries is illustrated by the Halifax Gibbet Law, see *ibid.* 265–269, and by the Liberty of the Savoy, 270–272.

CHAP. II. shortly mention a few characteristic circumstances connected with it.

The change was substantially complete in the sixteenth century, when the first report of an important trial by jury—that of Sir Nicholas Throckmorton—is given in a form presumably more or less authentic. The account given in the reign of Elizabeth by [1] Sir Thomas Smith, Secretary of State and Ambassador to France, of criminal trials, shows that the ordinary course of criminal justice in his time was, so far as the functions of the jury were concerned, substantially what it is now.

The following matters, which it is difficult to refer to definite dates, illustrate the gradual progress of the change.

The character of the jury as witnesses is illustrated by the fact that during the early stages of the system a remedy for a corrupt verdict in criminal cases existed at the suit of the king, though not at the suit of the party, in a proceeding called an attaint. It existed in civil cases at the suit of either party. The nature of it was that a second jury of twenty-four might convict the first jury, if they thought proper, of a false verdict, the result of which was that the first jury were subjected to extremely severe penalties.

Down to the reign of Queen Elizabeth no such crime as perjury by a witness, in our sense of the word, was known to the law. The attaint obviously assumed that the jurors were witnesses, and punished them as for perjury. As they came to be recognized as judges of the fact informed by witnesses, attaints fell into disuse. Smith says that in his time they were very seldom put in use. The attaint was spoken of by Lord Mansfield as "a mere sound," and was formally abolished in 1825 (6 Geo. IV., c. 50, s. 60).

Another remarkable circumstance which illustrates the

---

[1] *Commonwealth of England*, ch. xxv. 183–201; *History of the Criminal Law*, i. 347–349.

same thing is that in ancient times the prisoner had no right to call witnesses, and though this practice was gradually relaxed, the prisoners' witnesses were not allowed to be sworn till 1st Anne, st. 2, c. 9. The explanation of this rule, which to our minds appears so monstrous as to be unintelligible, is probably that the jury were originally regarded as witnesses, who, coming from the neighbourhood where the offence was committed, were supposed to know the circumstances. Other motives, no doubt, came in to enforce this application of the principle. It saved much trouble. It prevented doubtful questions from arising, and immensely increased the powers of the prosecutor, but it was probably originally suggested by the ancient constitution of inquests, and the ancient sentiment that accusation by the grand inquest was originally almost equivalent to conviction, as its consequences could originally be averted only by ordeal or compurgation.

The last circumstance to be mentioned is that the practice of fining the jury for not finding the verdict which the king's advisers wished for or regarded as true becomes intelligible when we remember the original character of inquests. The jurors were not, as used to be assumed, constitutional judges of matters of fact. They were persons brought together to give the king information upon oath through the justices whom he sent to make inquiry into matters of fact. If they gave false or perverse information, it would be natural for the justice to fine them as for a contempt of Court. In proportion as they came to be recognized as judges of the fact, such a proceeding would be seen to be tyrannical and subversive of their position.

Sir Thomas Smith, in the sixteenth century, obviously referring to the treatment of Sir Nicholas Throckmorton's jury, who were heavily fined for acquitting him, speaks of such measures as "even then of many accounted very violent, "tyrannical, and contrary to the liberty and custom of the

CHAP. II. " realm of England." In 1670 such measures were held to be positively illegal in Bushell's case.[1] No one can question the propriety of this decision, but there was an historical explanation and foundation for the practice which it declared to be illegal.

Side by side with the development of trial by jury there existed another mode of trial, to which I have alluded in passing, which also exercised a remarkable influence over English law. This was trial by battle, which, as well as the inquest, was introduced by William the Conqueror, and was neither more nor less than private war organized and reduced to a system. The system was known by the name of appeals or private accusations, and applied to all cases in which a private person, for the sake of revenge or for any other object, wished to prosecute another for a crime. The nature of appeals differed according to the nature of the crime prosecuted. Appeals of treason were brought in Parliament, and, after having a remarkable history,[2] were abolished in 1399 by the statute 1 Hen. IV. c. 14. They were the predecessors of Parliamentary impeachments. Appeals of theft, rape, mayhem, &c., seem to have been soon disused, but appeals of murder were abolished only in the year 1819. The appeal of murder was a strange proceeding. It was originally made before the coroner, and had to be made in a highly technical, minute, and elaborate form of words, which could not be amended. The appellee was proclaimed at five County Courts, and, if he failed to appear, was outlawed, and might, by an equally elaborate process, be inlawed, and admitted to defend himself. The appeal was heard before the justices, and all manner of legal subtleties, known as " exceptiones " or pleas, might be urged by the accused. If the appellor could prove the appellee's guilt, the appellee was not allowed to wage his body—that is, to have trial by battle ;

---

[1] See *History of the Criminal Law*, i. 306.　　　[2] *Ibid.* i. 151–155.

but if all these difficulties were successfully avoided, the trial was by combat; and if the appellee was defeated, he was hanged, unless the appellor chose to pardon him.

A more barbarous practice it is difficult to imagine, or one more liable to the grossest abuses, as it made the trial and punishment of the worst of private crimes dependent upon personal caprice, malice, or avarice. It was tolerable only because elaborate technicalities inconsistent with its principles prevented it from doing much harm. Monstrous as it was, it was for some reason favoured by the judges, who in 1482 made a rule of their own authority that persons indicted for murder should not be tried for a year, " so that the suit of the party may be saved," *i.e.* that an appeal may be brought in the interval. This worked injustice, and caused an increase of murders till 1487, when it was enacted (3 Hen. VII. c. 1) that people indicted of murder should be tried as soon as possible; that if acquitted they should be either imprisoned or bailed for a year; that the acquittal at the suit of the king should be no bar to an appeal by the party; and that appellors should for the future be freed from some of the restrictions formerly imposed upon them. The effect of this statute must have been to diminish greatly the number of appeals for murder, and to substitute for them trial on an indictment as the common course. Appeals, however, were occasionally brought when for any reason an acquittal excited dissatisfaction. Horne Tooke opposed their abolition when it was proposed in 1768 or 1769, and himself promoted an appeal.[1] They continued, though with increasing rarity, to the year 1819, when the case of Ashford *v.* Thornton caused their abolition.

In the course of this sketch I have not been able to confine myself strictly to any definite period, as it is highly characteristic of English law in all its departments that laws

[1] Horne Tooke's Life, by Stephens, i. 184.

CHAP. II. continue to exist in a more or less disused condition for long periods of time, often for many centuries, after they were in actual vigour. Appeals, for instance, having been instituted by William the Conqueror, and having been nearly put an end to by Henry VII., continued to the very end of the reign of George III., more than three hundred years afterwards. Speaking generally, however, so far I have been occupied with the system of criminal law which was in the course of development down to the beginning of the reign of Edward I. It may be recapitulated in a few sentences as follows:—

Accusation was originally made by some kind of judicial committee of the County Court, or by the reeve and four men, or by private persons.

At a later period it was made by the grand jury, or what was afterwards called the grand jury, before the County Court or the justices, or after the Conquest by private persons before the coroners, when it was called an appeal.

An accusation might be answered at first either by compurgation or by ordeal.

After the Conquest, and till the thirteenth century, the accusation involved ordeal, compurgation being abolished.

Ordeals being disused, the grand assize and the petty jury were substituted as means of proof.

The juries at first were half witnesses, half judges, but it was ultimately settled, both theoretically and practically, that they were to be judges of the fact.

While this process was going on, there was published one of the earliest and the best of English law-books: this is *Bracton de Legibus Angliæ,* the second part of the third book of which is headed "De Coronâ." It is much the nearest approach to a complete account of the law of England to be found till Blackstone, and it is almost the only English law-book which is founded in most parts on the civil law. The treatise " De Coronâ " forms the second treatise of the third book, " De Actiónibus," and deals with each crime and with the procedure specially appropriate to it by itself. The result is that the impression created by the work is that it is wearisome, wandering, and indistinctly arranged. Under the head of " Homicide," for instance, accounts of the duties of coroners and of the processes of outlawry and inlawry are interposed between the general description of homicide and what is said of murder, Englishry, and homicide by misadventure. In the same way, accounts of the different kinds of appeals, and the incidents connected with them, are given in connection with the different offences in respect of which they may be brought. From this multifarious matter it is, however, possible to collect the definitions of the various crimes known in the author's time. They are eight in number :—

1. " Læsa majestas," or high treason.

This is of many kinds. One is attempting the king's death (" si quis ausu temerario *machinatus* sit in mortem domini " regis: vel aliquid egerit vel agi procuraverit ad seditionem " domini regis vel exercitus sui vel procurantibus auxilium et " consilium præbuerit vel consensum licet id quod in voluntate " habuerit non perduxerit ad effectum ").

Some kinds of the *crimen falsi*—as, for instance, forging the king's seal and making bad money—are regarded as treason. This passage was, as will appear hereafter, the foundation of the most important part of the celebrated statute of 25 Edw. 3.

2. Homicide, which is " hominis occisio ab homine facta." Homicide is classified according to the following table :—

Homicidium.

Corporale.   Spirituale.

Linguâ.   Facto.

Præcepto.   Consilio.   Defensione
sive tuitione.

Justitia.   Necessitate.   Casu.   Voluntate.

Evitabili.   Non evitabili.   Pluribus   Clanculo
astantibus   nemine vidente
et videntibus.   murdrum.

Dans operam   Dans operam
rei licitæ.   rei illicitæ.

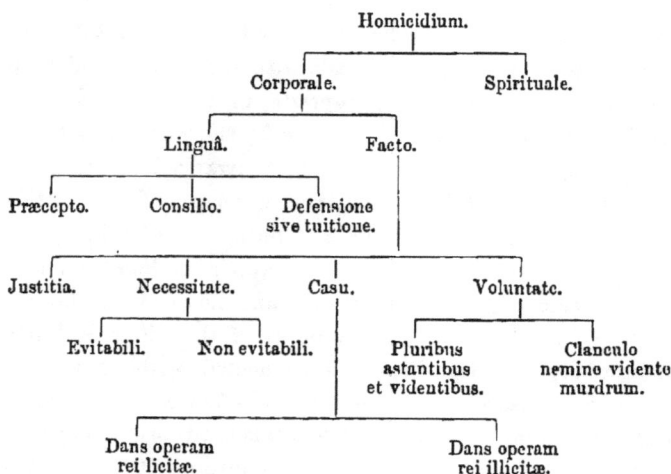

Murder is thus corporal homicide by act wilfully done in secret.

3. Wounding, which is mayhem if any part of the body is made useless for fighting, or if an eye or other member is destroyed or cut off.

4. Robbery.

5. Arson.

6. Rape.

7. Theft.

The definition of this crime is " furtum est secundum leges " contrectatio rei alienæ fraudulenta cum animo furandi " invito illo domino cujus res illa fuerit."

8. " Minora et leviora crimina," such as injuries of different kinds, are treated in the mass, and correspond partly to torts, partly to misdemeanours.

These definitions and classifications are the root, so to speak, of English criminal law, but they have had less importance in its history than this might be supposed to imply.

The definition of treason was replaced in Edward III.'s time by the well-known statute. The definition of homicide, if such it can be called, is a worthless classification of forms of killing which do not exclude each other. For instance, every killing "justitia" or "necessitate" is a killing "voluntate"; and it is absurd to distinguish killings "voluntate" according to the number of witnesses who may be present. The definition of "murdrum" as a secret homicide was no doubt given for the sake of the incident called "a presentment of Englishry." If the person killed was a Frenchman, the hundred where the body was found was liable to a fine called *murdrum.* The presentment that the dead man was an Englishman freed the hundred from this fine.[1] This practice was abolished in 1340 by 14 Ed. III. st. 1, c. 4. This swept away the old definition of murder.

The definitions of rape, robbery, and arson are mere names. Mayhem is defined, but the crime ceased to be regarded as distinguishable from other acts of violence. The definition of theft is like the one given in the Roman law,[2] but is distinguished from it by the omission of the words italicized in the note. Of the effect of these omissions I will speak further in describing the history of the law of theft. It is sufficient to say here that the distinction was very important, and it is also to be noticed that the "contrectatio" of Roman law and the "taking" of English law are by no means equivalent to each other. It is very remarkable that this slight resemblance (for it is no more) between the Roman and the English criminal law is the single trace of the former which is to be found in the latter. There is a considerable analogy between the way in which the two systems were developed, but each

---

[1] *History of the Criminal Law*, iii. 40.

[2] "Furtum est contrectatio fraudulosa *lucri faciendi gratia* vel ipsius rei *vel* " *etiam usus ejus possessionisve.*" On all these see *History of the Criminal Law*, iii. 131, &c.

CHAP. II. was home-made, and they differ at every point. This is all the more remarkable because Bracton's whole work is to a great extent founded upon Roman law as it was understood in the Universities of the thirteenth century—that is to say, rather as a branch of science which proved itself than as a set of enactments depending for their validity upon their adoption by the sovereign power of the State. His work, however, is composed to an even greater extent of a statement of English customs than of a statement of Roman law, and indeed in the treatise "De Coronâ" there is hardly anything else except the definition of theft and the description or classification of homicide.

One other matter is mentioned in Bracton which must be shortly referred to now. It is the doctrine of privilege of clergy, which had perhaps the most singular history of any part of the English criminal law, as will appear hereafter. "A clerk taken for the death of a man," says Bracton,[1] "is "if claimed, to be delivered up to the ecclesiastical authori- "ties, to be kept in safe custody either in the king's or the "bishop's prison to make purgation." If he was degraded from his orders, he was to suffer no other punishment, as degradation was considered sufficient.[2] Ecclesiastical purgation was perhaps the most absurd institution ever devised by man. There was a jury of twelve clerks; the party swore to his innocence, he produced twelve compurgators who swore that they believed him to be innocent, and he might call witnesses on his behalf, but the accuser might not call witnesses against him.[3] This statement of the law

---

[1] *De Cor.*, c. ix. ; Twiss, ii. 298.

[2] It is added, "nisi forte convictus fuerit de apostasia tunc primo degradetur "et postea per manum laicalem comburatur secundum quod accidit in Concilio "Oxon ; . . . de quodam diacono qui apostatavit pro quadam Judæâ." On this remarkable case see Mr. Maitland's article in *The Law Quarterly Review*, vol. ii. p. 153. The last words suggest a strange forgotten romance. I shall have to refer to the case again.   [3] *History of the Criminal Law*, i. 460.

was made perhaps a hundred years after the death of Thomas Becket, and before the privilege of clergy had been modified by statute. It had a long and most singular history, to which I shall return.

Such was the criminal law of England in the latter part of the thirteenth century.

As far as can be judged from such accounts of it as remain, it altered little during the reigns of Edward I. and Edward II. We have in Edward I.'s time a remarkable monument of its then condition in the Hundred Rolls, which contain the reports of Commissioners who made inquiry in all the hundreds of England into the various abuses, and especially usurpations of power, which had come into existence in the reign of Henry III. The only fact which I need notice here is that they show that, when these inquiries were taken, there were manor courts with powers of *infangthief*, summary execution, all over England. In Berkshire alone the entry "habet furcas" occurs in thirty-five places, and numerous instances occur of their use.[1]

It is not improbable that if the franchise courts had not been curbed by Edward I., and if he and his successors had been weak rulers, allowing encroachments to be made upon their power, and continuing to grant away petty local jurisdictions, the administration of justice might have been deeply and permanently degraded; but, happily, this was not the case. In the reign of Edward III. measures were taken which had deep effects, not only on the administration of criminal justice, but on many other subjects. One of these was the establishment of the officers at first called keepers and afterwards justices of the peace, who, in 1360, by the statute 34 Edw. III. c. 1, were first empowered to hold Courts of Quarter Sessions, and "hear and determine

[1] On the Hundred Rolls see *History of the Criminal Law*, i. 126-132, and also on the Statute of Quo Warranto which they occasioned.

CHAP. II.　" at the king's suit all manner of felonies and trespasses " done in the same county." [1] This is the origin of the Courts of Quarter Sessions, which, to the present day, try all minor offences. Till the end of the seventeenth century they tried capital cases as well.

The Courts of Quarter Sessions in the boroughs had a different, though analogous, origin. Charters were granted to places of all degrees of importance by all or most of our kings from Henry I., who granted the first charter now in existence to the City of London. These charters almost always made some provision or other for the local administration of justice, and from the fourteenth century the provision made consisted usually in the appointment of magistrates, who were to hold Quarter Sessions.

The jurisdiction of the town magistrates was in some cases exclusive of the county magistrates; in others, the two had concurrent powers. In some cases it extended to capital crimes, in others it was limited. In some cases there was a recorder, who was nominated in different ways; in others there was none. Most of these towns received a definite constitution under the Municipal Corporations Act of 1835 (5 and 6 Will. IV. c. 76, repealed and re-enacted with amendments in 1882, by 45 and 46 Vic. c. 50).[2] The exact extent and operation of this Act would require a long explanation, but the effect of it is that in all important towns in England there is a Court of Quarter Sessions, of which a Recorder appointed by the Crown is the judge.

The Courts of London stand on a special footing.[3] The most important of them is the Central Criminal Court, which was established in 1834 by 4 and 5 Will. IV. c. 36, and replaced the more ancient Courts of the City of London and County of Middlesex.

---

[1] *History of the Criminal Law*, i. 111–116.　　[2] *Ibid*. i. 117–121.
[3] *Ibid*. i. 118.

The result of all this is that institutions, of which the most CHAP. II. important dates from the reign of Edward III., gradually came into existence, which, with the help of the Courts held under the King's Commission and before his justices, made up the system still existing amongst us for the ordinary regular administration of criminal justice.

Another process of great interest and importance was, however, in progress during the fourteenth and fifteenth centuries, which has been memorable in two different periods of the history of England divided from each other by nearly two hundred years. This was the process of Parliamentary impeachment. In a few words, its first stage was as follows :—The old Curia Regis had a threefold character. It was the Parliament, the head of administrative business in every department, and the Supreme Court of Justice all in one. In its character of Parliament it occasionally exercised judicial functions. One of the earliest instances of such a function was the trial in 1285 at Shrewsbury, of David, the brother of Llewellyn, Prince of Wales, for high treason against Edward I. Other trials occurred in the fourteenth century, one of the most remarkable of which was that of the alleged murderers of Edward II., the record[1] of which throws great light on the functions of juries as witnesses, and on other points of the highest interest. More remarkable still are the records of appeals of treason, connected with the deposition of Richard II. In 1387 the Duke of Gloucester and others appealed or accused the Archbishop of York and others of treason on account of their bad advice, by which King Richard had been led into misgovernment, and the appellees were convicted and punished in various ways. In 1397 the appellants of 1387 were themselves appealed, convicted, and punished for "accroaching" Royal power. In 1399, Richard having been deposed, the appellants of 1397 were in their turn convicted and punished,

[1] *History of the Criminal Law,* i. 147 ; 2 *Rot. Par.,* 57.

CHAP. II. and the Parliament passed an Act, 1 Hen. IV. c. 14, which abolished appeals of treason. It was also solemnly declared [1] by the Commons that "judgments in Parliament belong only " to the King and the Lords, and not to the Commons." The reply to which was " that the Commons are petitioners and " demanders, and that the King and the Lords from all time " have had and still have by right judgment in Parliament." This put the law as to impeachments substantially on the ground on which it has rested ever since. A few impeachments took place in the fifteenth century, the last being that of Lord Stanley for not sending his troops to the battle of Bloreheath. This took place in 1459. After this, impeachments were disused till 1621, when a new and more memorable series of them began.

During the time of the Plantagenets a certain number of alterations in the definitions of crimes were made by statute. In a legal point of view, the most important of these by far was the celebrated Statute of Treasons, 25 Edw. III. st. 5, c. 3. It is still in force, and has had the singular fortune of being regarded with a sort of superstitious reverence on account of the contrast which it presented on many occasions to temporary laws punishing as treason attempts to attain certain political and religious objects, and in some cases the expression of particular religious and political opinions, but the subject is one which I cannot pursue here.[2]

Important steps were also made in the development of the law of murder and theft. These are noticed in connection with the history of the definitions of those particular crimes.

A matter of infinitely greater importance, being as it was a leading event in the history of England, happened at the beginning of the reign of Henry IV. This was the passing of the Act 2 Hen. IV. c. 15 (1400), which was followed in

---

[1] 3 *Rot. Par.*, 449.

[2] It is treated at large in my *History of the Criminal Law*, ii. 241-298.

1414 by 2 Hen. V. c. 7, which reinforced it. These Acts made heresy a capital crime, punishable by burning alive and confiscation of property. Something must be said in connection with these Acts upon the system of religious persecution which formed a leading feature in the history of England through the whole of the fifteenth and the greater part of the sixteenth centuries, and which continued to exist to a certain extent till late in the seventeenth century.

Before the Conquest the bishops took a prominent part in the ordinary administration of criminal justice as leading members of the Hundred and County Courts. At the Conquest, as I have already observed, they became the heads of separate ecclesiastical courts, which, with very various fortunes, have continued from that day to this to exercise a criminal jurisdiction over sins as distinguished from crimes. This jurisdiction was for centuries a matter of considerable importance. Persons were convened for intemperance, unchastity, all kinds of irregularity of life, and were compelled, under pain of spiritual censures, excommunication, and minor penalties, to do penance and pay fines, and if they refused obedience they might be imprisoned under writs *De Excommunicato Capiendo*. There were, however, all but no prosecutions for heresy or the like, because before the rise of the Lollards there were no heretics. A few instances of people, who were whipped in the early part of the thirteenth century, and the single case of apostasy already referred to as mentioned by Bracton, are the only instances approaching to persecution for heresy which occurred down to the fifteenth century. In the course of the fourteenth century the first motion towards the great changes of modern times was made. Wycliffe's career, in particular, excited the fiercest hostility on the part of the clergy. He was denounced and his opinions were condemned as heretical by the highest ecclesiastical authorities, but he was subjected to no temporal penalties, and died in peace in 1385. Immediately before the passing of the Act of 2 Hen. IV. c. 15, the practice of punishing heresy with death by burning was introduced by one of the most shameful acts of fraud and oppression which have ever occurred in English history.[1] This was the execution of William Sawtre without any legal warrant, and by means which bear upon their face every mark of fraud, falsehood, and lawless violence. This most wicked action was so far successful as to induce a belief, used on several subsequent occasions for wicked and cruel purposes, in the existence of a common law writ *De Hæretico Comburendo*, independent of the statutes of Henry IV. and Henry V. The most characteristic and oppressive part of the statutes referred to was that they gave the bishops the power of defining heresy. Some slight restraint over them was exercised by the Court of King's Bench, but it was very slight; and from 1400 to 1533 the bishops had and exercised from time to time the power of burning alive all of whose religious opinions they disapproved.

This was fundamentally altered by Henry VIII. He passed an Act in 1533 (25 Hen. VIII. c. 14), which, though in appearance extremely severe, nearly put an end to prosecutions for heresy, partly by giving a negative definition of heresy ("speaking against the authority of the Pope, &c., " shall not be heresy "), and partly by providing that the proceedings must begin by indictment, and not by arrest and imprisonment on suspicion, as was the law under 2 Hen. IV. c. 15. This state of things lasted for about six years, when the Act of the Six Articles (31 Hen. VIII. c. 14) was passed, which provided that everyone should be burnt who denied transubstantiation, and that the profession of certain other opinions should be felony without benefit of clergy. The grotesque and cruel side of the Act is obvious enough, but it ought to be observed that it was infinitely less cruel

[1] See the whole story of Sawtre, *History of the Criminal Law*, ii. 443–449.

than the Acts which it superseded.' The laws of the fifteenth
century enabled the bishops to burn whom they pleased for
whatever they chose to call heresy. The Act of the Six
Articles confined burning to those who denied transubstantiation.

Under Edward VI. all the statute law on the subject was
repealed, but, thanks to the fraudulent practice which had
made a precedent in Sawtre's case, Joan Bocher and a
man named Van Paar were burned in 1550 and 1551
under a Commission issued by the Protector Somerset to
the Archbishop of Canterbury. I think these executions were illegal, though probably they were not known
to be so.

Queen Mary revived the statutes of the fifteenth century,
and under them carried on her celebrated persecutions.

In 1558, Elizabeth repealed all these statutes for the last
time, but she left untouched the supposed writ *De Hærctico
Comburendo*, under which some Anabaptists (the names of
two are known, but it is uncertain whether others were burnt
or not) were burnt in 1575. The last executions under this
fictitious writ took place in James I.'s reign, in the cases of
Legate and Wightman, in circumstances of peculiar infamy.
It was abolished in 1677 by 29 Chas. II. c. 9.

The penal laws directed against the Roman Catholics and
the Protestant Dissenters belong to a different order of ideas.
The punishment of holding or expressing particular theological opinions as a sin began in 1400. It was greatly
diminished under Henry VIII., and, after a violent recrudes-
cence in Mary Tudor's time, almost entirely ceased, though
it was wrongly supposed to be theoretically possible till 1677,
and though a few, not more than six known cases, and possibly eleven others, occurred in the reigns of Elizabeth and
James I.

The third important period in the history of the criminal

CHAP. II. law begins with the reign of Henry VII., and ends with he Civil Wars of Charles I.

Trial by jury under the Plantagenets had, as I have already said, passed from the rude system of inquests, which, under the guidance and control of justices, collected and, to some extent, sifted village gossip, to a form of trial more or less similar to that to which we are accustomed; but there is great reason to believe that it was on many occasions corrupt and oppressive. Local influence was all-powerful over the jurors, and there was no effective check over them by public opinion or otherwise. Their corruption and intimidation was the most important branch of the offence of maintenance, which was the characteristic offence of the fifteenth century. The Wars of the Roses had no doubt done much to bring these evils to a head. The result is described in an emphatic manner in the preamble to 3 Hen. VII. c. 1 :—" The King remembereth how, by unlawful " maintenance, giving of liveries, signs and tokens, and " retainders, by indentures, promises, oaths, writings, or " otherwise embraceries of his subjects, untrue demeanings " of sheriffs in making of panels and other untrue returns, " by taking of money by juries, by great riots and unlawful " assemblies, the policy and good rule of this realm is " almost subdued." The Act then empowers certain high officers and Privy Councillors to call such misdoers before them and to punish them. The statute also contains regulations about appeals of murder, to which I have already referred, and requires coroners to do their duty strictly.

It is probably a mistake to suppose that this Act was the origin of the Court of Star Chamber, for there are traces of a criminal jurisdiction in the Privy Council at an earlier period; but, be this as it may, there is no doubt that from this time the jurisdiction of the Privy Council played a prominent part in the preservation of the peace throughout the whole country, or that it was highly beneficial as a supplement to the defects of the common system for the administration of criminal justice, and especially as providing means for the control of the local influences which grievously interfered with its efficiency. How long the Privy Council played with advantage to the public a part analogous in the administration of criminal justice to that which the Lord Chancellor played in the administration of civil justice would be an instructive inquiry; but, however this may be, in the process of time it became a partisan court trying with much harshness, and even cruelty, to put down the popular party, and it was abolished, together with some other local courts of a similar nature, in the year 1641.

In the course of the sixteenth century a great increase was made in the severity of the criminal law by restrictions placed upon the law as to benefit of clergy. I have already quoted a passage from Bracton which shows how this benefit stood in the thirteenth century. It was extended in the fourteenth century to all manner of clerks, as well secular as religious; that is, to all men who could read. On the other hand, it was settled in the fifteenth century that privilege of clergy could not be claimed till after conviction. The result was that benefit of clergy was extended to a great mass of people indiscriminately,[1] and that even clerks in orders could not avoid a trial by lay judges. Benefit of clergy thus ceased in the fifteenth century to be the privilege of a profession, and became a promiscuous but absurd and capricious mitigation of the cruel severity of the common law. Two truly astonishing exceptions were made to the

---

[1] The reading required extended only to reading the words, " Miserere mei " Deus " (Foster, p. 306), which, it is to be hoped, was generally known to the criminal classes. In earlier times I think it likely that the test was seriously applied. Anyone could learn " Miserere mei Deus " by heart, and repeat it on being shown the book.

CHAP. II. general rule. Women (unless they were nuns) were excluded from benefit of clergy, as being incapable of ordination; and so were " bigami," or men who had " married two wives or one widow." It applied, however, to all cases whatever except treason " interdictio viarum et depopulatio agrorum." It is hardly credible, but it is true, that till 1487 a man who could read and had not married two wives or one widow,[1] might commit murder, rape, and theft as often as he pleased without any punishment at all except the chance of being committed " absque purgatione" to the bishop's prison, which, indeed, might mean imprisonment for life.

Restrictions at length were placed upon this strange rule. In 1487 (4 Hen. VII. c. 13) it was enacted that all persons who had their clergy should be branded on the brawn of the thumb, and that no one but a clerk in orders should have clergy more than once, which the branding would prevent. Some other very special crimes were excluded from clergy in Henry VIII.'s time.

Under Edward VI. (1 Edw. VI. c. 12, s. 13) clergy was taken from murder, burglary, house-breaking, and putting the inhabitants in fear, highway robbery, horse-stealing, and robbing churches.

Under Elizabeth (8 Eliz. c. 4, 1565) stealing from the person, amounting to grand larceny, and rape and burglary in 1576 (18 Eliz. c. 7), were excluded from clergy.

These were the main points in the history of the criminal law from the earliest times to the end of the sixteenth century. From the beginning of the seventeenth century date three books : Staundford's *Plees del Corone*, Lambard's *Eirenarchia*, and Coke's *Third Institute*. They are the first detailed and systematic accounts of the criminal law since Bracton. Coke's reputation has thrown into the shade the works of Staundford and Lambard, and the fact that Staundford is written in law French is no doubt an additional reason why his book has been forgotten. It appears to me in some particulars better than the *Third Institute;* and the merits of the *Eirenarchia* are very considerable. Coke's great reputation, however, has given an importance to his work which no other can rival, unless Blackstone's *Commentaries* forms an exception. It is not by any means the best of his writings, and it appears to me to be in many ways defective. His references to Bracton and the *Year-books* are often inaccurate and sometimes unintelligent, and nothing can exceed his pedantry or his failure to reason correctly upon any sort of general grounds. His very defects, however, gave him a hold upon his contemporaries, who had been powerfully impressed by his energetic personal character and by the assurance and self-sufficiency with which he claimed exhaustive and final professional knowledge. However, whatever may be its faults, the *Third Institute* deserves to be taken as the next great literary landmark to Bracton in the history of the criminal law. It gives a full account of it as it stood at the beginning of the reign of James I.

In order to complete the sketch which I have been giving of this period, it will be necessary to say something of the principal features in the actual administration of criminal justice down to the year 1640.

I have given in my *History of the Criminal Law* an account of the most characteristic trials of which I have been able to discover reports from 1477 to 1640.[1] Of course, nearly all of them are political cases. The trials of which I have given an account are those of Nicholas Throckmorton (1537), the Duke of Norfolk (1571), Raleigh (1603), Hollis (1615), Sherfield (1632), Prynne, Bastwick, and Burton (1637), and Lilburn (1637), the last four being cases in the Star Chamber. Many other cases are referred to which illustrate the obser-

---

[1] *History of the Criminal Law,* i. 320–357.

CHAP. II. vations made. I will here confine myself to a few remarks on the general characteristics of the procedure.

The outline of the trials was, in its most general features, the same as in our own days. The jury were the judges of the fact, and they derived their information from sworn witnesses. There were counsel for the Crown, who managed the evidence for the prosecution, and the judge summed up. Unanimous verdicts were required, and an acquittal was final, even though the juries were occasionally fined for acquitting, but here the resemblance ended. The preliminary procedure was entirely in the hands of the Crown. The first step taken in a case in which the Government was interested was to put the accused into close confinement, by which he was deprived of the power of providing evidence in his own defence. He was kept in ignorance of the evidence given against him. He was himself examined as severely as a modern prisoner is examined in France and some other Continental countries by the *juge d'instruction,* and for a certain time, and in particular cases, he was liable to be tortured, though this was recognized as an abuse of power for which there never at any time was any legal excuse.

The essence of the trial lay in the examination of the prisoner upon every point of the case. If by any extraordinary chance he had witnesses, it is by no means clear that he could examine them at all. It is certain that he could not examine them upon oath. He was, in a word, placed under such circumstances that the whole course of every part of the proceedings was hostile to him, and that the jury had little more than a veto upon his conviction, and one which it required unusual courage and firmness to interpose in his favour. The rules of evidence, which gave and still give a great, though it was at one time a somewhat capricious, protection to prisoners, were unknown at the period in question. Written depositions taken in secret were often produced as evidence,

although the deponents were living; and cross-examination
was almost if not altogether unknown. In a word, the
regular procedure was to the last degree rough, imperfect,
and harsh, though it contained the essential principle of trial
by jury in a rudimentary and imperfect form.

But besides this regular system a new one was introduced
into the Star Chamber, which prevailed also in the ecclesiastical courts, and particularly in the great Court of High
Commission, and which, during the whole of the period which I
am considering, and especially during the last part of it, was
a most formidable rival to trial by jury. This was a procedure
closely analogous to that which prevailed in the Court of
Chancery. A bill was filed against the defendant, and he
put in his answer as in the Court of Chancery. He might be
examined upon interrogatories, and required to take what was
called the *ex-officio* oath. This was an oath used in the
ecclesiastical courts, also known as an oath on the *voir* (*vrai*)
dire—that is, an oath " true answer to make to such questions
" as shall be demanded of you." [1]   The evidence was given
on affidavit.

At common law a prisoner was not allowed to have counsel.
In the Star Chamber he was not allowed to put in an answer
which was not signed by counsel.   If he did not do so, he
was held to confess the indictment.   On the other hand, the
counsel incurred such serious responsibility that they were
sure not to state any defence which was likely to be in any
respect unwelcome.

If this jurisdiction had been extended, it would either have
established a despotism or caused a rebellion.   The way in
which it was used led to its abolition in 1640, and left behind
it a passionate hatred of the *ex-officio* oath, and everything

---

[1] The form is still in constant use for harmless purposes, *e.g.* if when a
prisoner has pleaded guilty the judge wishes to take evidence as to his
character.

which even remotely resembled it, which still influences our law after the lapse of nearly two hundred and fifty years.

I do not think that either the early State trials or the Star Chamber deserve the wholly unqualified censure which they have often received. For a considerable time the Star Chamber deserved some part of the applause which it received, though at last it undoubtedly became not only a partisan but a cruel tribunal. The early State trials only show of what very slow growth the sentiment of fair play is in regard of criminal law,[1] and how completely the control of the preliminary procedure puts the result of the case in the hands of the prosecutor.

One other matter must be mentioned before concluding this chapter. It is the revival of the practice of impeachments after their disuse for 161 years. All through the reigns of the Tudors the political offences of the enemies of the Tudor monarchy were punished either by the ordinary courts, which, if the offenders were peers, were the House of Lords, or, if Parliament was not sitting, the Court of the Lord High Steward with Lords Triers. These were in all essential respects like the trials of commoners, though verdicts were not required to be unanimous. All trials properly so called, however, were dispensed with in the case of bills of attainder, bills for putting to death, or otherwise punishing particular persons. They were substituted for Parliamentary impeachments during the reign of Henry VIII., and were afterwards resorted to in the case of Lord Strafford and a few other persons. In 1621, Sir Giles Mompesson, Lord Bacon, and others were impeached, and impeachment was the great weapon with which the long Parliament, and the short Parliament which preceded it, fought their early battles against

It would be easy to show that in the present day it is slight and superficial. Who, *e.g.*, is shocked at the treatment received by Shylock in the *Merchant of Venice !*

Charles I. It was used throughout the whole of the seven- teenth century by the different parties which rose in turn into power ; it was also used at intervals in the eighteenth century, especially in the memorable case of Warren Hastings, when its inherent weakness and unfitness for modern times were strikingly displayed. One impeachment only, that of Lord Melville in 1805, has taken place in the present century, and it is to be hoped that it will be disused for the future, for the House of Lords is in no degree fitted for the functions of a criminal court of first instance charged with a decision on matters of fact.

CHAPTER III.

CHAP. III.   THE principal effects of the Civil Wars of the time of
Charles I. upon the criminal law were exhibited in its
procedure.

During the Commonwealth a scheme for a deep and searching reform of the whole body of the criminal law was proposed,
and might have been carried into effect with the greatest benefit but for the Restoration; but it was laid aside, together with
other alterations then introduced. In so cursory a sketch as
this, I can only refer to them in passing, but the subject is
one of much general interest and curiosity. I have given
in my *History* some account of it, and of the great revolutionary change made by the introduction of the High Court
of Justice, which during the crisis of the establishment of
the new Government, tried capital cases without a jury,
but the tribunal lasted for only a short time, and left no
traces behind it.

One great and essential change in the spirit of English
criminal procedure was made by the Civil War. It put an
end down to the present day to the system of trial upon the
methods made so unpopular by the Star Chamber, and by the
ecclesiastical courts of all grades. The Star Chamber and
the Court of High Commission were abolished, and no one

has ever thought of reviving them. The *ex-officio* oath, which was the great weapon in the way of procedure of the ecclesiastical courts, was also abolished, and the courts were thus made nearly innocuous, though they still exist in a crippled and comparatively harmless state.

The effect on the common law courts was even more striking, though it was not caused by any definite change in the law. The old form of trial, in which the rigid examination of the prisoner formed the leading feature, was absolutely laid aside after the Civil War. There is no instance after that time of anything approaching to the disgraceful trial of Raleigh, or the harsh if not unjust State trials of the sixteenth century. In the seventeenth century, the accepted maxim, which was sometimes called the law of God, and sometimes the common law of England or common right, was "Nemo tenetur accusare seipsum," a phrase not the less influential because it rested on no definite authority.

This, no doubt, was a change for the better as far as it went. But it did not go far. The trials of the latter part of the seventeenth century, which were by jury, were perhaps even more unjust than those of the Star Chamber, under the system which prevailed in the sixteenth century.

The injustice was not confined to any one political party. The trials of the persons charged with the Popish Plot were neither more nor less scandalous than the trial of College, the joiner. The great leading defects in the state of things which then existed did not depend at all upon legal institutions. They were two: first, the prevalence of a general ignorance of or indifference to the principles on which questions of fact ought to be investigated; and secondly, the practical secrecy of the early stages of the procedure, which gave prisoners no notice of the case against them till they were put up to be tried. The remedies devised by the Legislature at the end of the seventeenth and the beginning

CHAP. III. of the eighteenth centuries for the scandals of the trials under the later Stuarts show how superficial a view was then taken of the true cause of these scandals. It was provided that in cases of treason and misprision of treason prisoners should be allowed to be defended by counsel, that their witnesses should be examined upon oath, that they should have copies of the indictment and lists of the witnesses to be called ten days before trial, and that an overt act charged in the indictment should be proved by two witnesses, or two overt acts by one witness each. These enactments, except only the one as to swearing the prisoner's witnesses, applied only to charges of treason and misprision of treason, and seemed to admit that a fair trial in cases of felony was a matter of little importance. In the second place, they left untouched the preliminary procedure, according to which the prisoner was practically kept, till his trial, to a considerable extent in the dark as to the evidence against him, and might theoretically (as indeed he still may) be put on his trial for his life upon the finding of a bill by a grand jury on evidence of which he has no notice.

A great change in the spirit of criminal procedure came about early in the eighteenth century by the combination of a variety of causes and by very gradual steps. The Revolution gave a decisive victory to one of the two great parties in the State, and the result was that they no longer fought out their differences in the law courts. The independence secured to the judges by the alteration in their tenure of their offices no doubt operated in the same direction; but, whatever was the cause, there can be no doubt of the fact that the standard of impartiality rose greatly from the year 1688 until it reached its present height. The special effects of this general change were very various. I will notice the most important of them. From this period may be dated the full though gradual acknowledgment of what I regard

as the principal characteristic of modern English criminal
jurisprudence, the adoption and full carrying out of the
doctrine that a criminal trial is to be regarded not so much
in the light of a public inquiry into the truth of the matter
alleged against the prisoner as in that of a private litigation
between the prisoner and the prosecutor. In earlier times, as
I have already shown, the two principles—which may be called
the litigious and the inquisitorial—both prevailed to a certain
extent. An appeal, in the old sense of the word, was the
strongest possible illustration of the litigious principle. It
was regulated private war, and it left to the appellant the
opportunity of compromising his proceeding for money, and
in fact of ransoming his enemy down to the last moment.
On the other hand, trial by jury as originally conceived was
emphatically a public inquiry conducted by the king's agent
for the king's purposes. By the beginning of the eighteenth
century a criminal trial came to be regarded practically as a
litigation in which the king was always plaintiff, but in which
the prisoner was entitled to the advantages of a defendant in
a civil case; and though he was prejudiced to a certain extent
by the accusation of the grand jury, the presumption of
innocence was held to be in his favour, and that to such an
extent that the king, the plaintiff, must prove his case beyond
all reasonable doubt.

This showed itself in various ways. In the first place, the
rules of evidence which were gradually developed in the civil
courts, and which are not, as a rule, older than the eighteenth
century, were, as they were developed, applied to the criminal
courts also; some, indeed, are peculiar to the criminal courts.
Of these rules probably the most general was that which
rendered a party an incompetent witness; and it appears that
very soon after the beginning of the eighteenth century the
practice of questioning the prisoner on his trial, which had
for a considerable time prevailed till then, was finally laid

aside. I doubt whether this was an advantage either for the prisoner or for the public, but no doubt it was intended to be favourable to the prisoner.

An obvious step in the same direction would have been to allow the prisoner in felony the advantage of counsel ; but the very fact that this was permitted by statute in cases of treason was enough to prevent the courts from making so great a change.[1] A long step in that direction was, however, made by the practice which grew up in the course of the eighteenth century to allow counsel to cross-examine witnesses in cases of felony—an indulgence which was certainly inconsistent with the general principle, and was not allowed by the House of Lords to Lord Ferrers[2] (in 1760), though his defence was insanity.

Only one alteration of importance was made in the eighteenth century in the law relating to indictments. In 1725 it was enacted that indictments should thenceforth be in English, but a great number of cases, reported capriciously, were decided on various points, and made its administration capricious and technical in a very high degree. These technicalities were tolerated probably because to some extent they mitigated a system which was so harsh that it never was intended to be strictly executed, and never, in fact, was so ; but much more because the notion of giving anything

---

[1] The rule against allowing counsel in cases of felony is as old as 1302. About that year a person accused of rape was thus addressed by the judge :— " Vos debetis scire quod rex est pars in casu isto, et sequitur ex officio, unde " in hoc casu jura non patiuntur quod habeatis consilium contra regem [qui] " vos sequitur ex officio. Si autem mulier ageret contra vos, haberetis adversus " eam consilium, sed contra regem non."—*Year-books*, 30 and 31 Edw. I., p. 530.

[2] 19 *State Trials*, 885–979. No application for counsel was made, but in his defence Lord Ferrers said : " I have been driven to the miserable necessity of " proving my own want of understanding, and am told the law will not allow " me the assistance of counsel in this case, in which, of all others, I should " think it most wanted," p. 944.

like system and simplicity to the criminal law, or indeed to any other part of it, did not arise till much later.

The great mass of the actual working criminal law of the present day was first enacted as law in the course of the eighteenth century; and in particular nearly all the enactments contained in the Criminal Law Consolidation Acts, passed in 1861, and drafted by the late Mr. Graves.

The general history of this legislation is as follows. One of the most striking features of the old criminal law as it stood in the seventeenth century was its extreme vagueness. For instance, the law of theft, in Hale's time, was broadly this: Theft, which was so defined as to involve a number of subtle and useless distinctions, was divided into grand and petty larceny. Grand larceny was any larceny of a thing worth more than a shilling. Its punishment was death; but this was largely qualified by the law as to benefit of clergy. Petty larceny was theft of anything worth less than a shilling, and was punishable with imprisonment and whipping. Four particular kinds of theft—namely, horse-stealing (1 Edw. VI. c. 12, s. 10), stealing from the person above the value of a shilling (8 Eliz. c. 4), and stealing the king's stores or clothes off the racks (22 Ch. II. c. 5)—were excluded from benefit of clergy. In the course of the eighteenth century this exclusion from the benefit of clergy was extended to all manner of thefts which it would be tedious to enumerate here. The most notorious instances are: 10 and 11 Will. III. c. 23 (1699), which excluded from benefit of clergy stealing to the value of five shillings in a shop; 12 Anne, c. 7 (1713), which enacted the same with regard to stealing to the value of forty shillings in a dwelling-house; and the Acts 14 Geo. II. c. 6 (1741) and 15 Geo. II. c. 34, which applied the same measure to thefts of sheep and other cattle.

Much similar legislation took place in regard to other

CHAP. III.　branches of the criminal law. For instance, I may mention what was called the Black Act (9 Geo. I. c. 22, 1722), which was directed against a set of deerstealers called the Waltham Blacks. It first provided punishments for shooting at people; sending letters "demanding money, venison, or other valuable thing"; and for many other offences of different degrees of importance all of which were made felony without benefit of clergy. A series of Acts against the forgery of particular documents, the first of which was 2 Geo. II. c. 25, were of a similar nature. Other provisions of the same kind were exceedingly numerous. These Acts resemble each other in several respects. Nearly all of them were occasioned by some particular case which attracted special attention, and most of them were restricted with almost absurd minuteness, as if the common law were proximately perfect, requiring small supplementary additions only in particular instances, instead of being, as it was, vague, imperfect, antiquated, and fragmentary to a monstrous degree. Cruel and fragmentary as this legislation was, most of the Acts which were passed did apply to real defects in the law, though it punished them with cruel severity. One instance of this will be sufficient. Till Lord Ellenborough's Act, 43 Geo. III. c. 58, passed in 1803, no special punishment at all was provided for wounding with intent to murder, or to do grievous bodily harm, or for unlawful wounding. Such acts were mere misdemeanours, punishable by fine and imprisonment. An attempt to commit murder not committed in any one of a few specified ways was a mere common law misdemeanour till 1861.

The working criminal law of England is at the present moment contained almost entirely in the Consolidation Acts of 1861, 24 and 25 Vict. cc. 95, 96, 97, 98, 99, and 100. These are composed principally, though not entirely, by consolidating the strangely narrow and imperfect legislation spread over the eighteenth century to which I have been referring. I shall say something hereafter of the way in which the alteration was made; but I must in the meanwhile make some further remarks on that legislation.

It is impossible to defend its principal characteristic, its lavish and cruel employment of the punishment of death; but it is right to say that the law was not, and was not intended to be, strictly executed. This certainly greatly modified its cruelty, but it did so at the expense of making its administration arbitrary and capricious to the last degree. A small proportion of the persons capitally convicted were executed. Most of them were pardoned conditionally on transportation, a practice recognized by the Habeas Corpus Act (31 Ch. II. c. 12. ss. 13 and 14, 1679). In 1768 (8 Geo. III. c. 15) the judges of assizes were empowered to order the transportation of persons convicted at the assizes of crimes not within the benefit of clergy. In London a list of prisoners capitally convicted was submitted after every Old Bailey sessions to the King in Council, and their fate was discussed and decided upon individually in the presence of the King upon the report of the Recorder. Much was said of the uncertainty which this practice introduced into the administration of the law; and it is perfectly true that it did make the infliction of the punishment of death so uncertain as to diminish its effect very much indeed; but a man who was capitally convicted under this system was reasonably sure that if he was not hanged he would be transported. At present he may either be sent to penal servitude or imprisoned with or without hard labour, but he cannot say which; although I have reason to believe that prisoners form an estimate of the sentences which they will receive, which, all things considered, is not very far from the truth.[1]

[1] I once sentenced a man at Bristol to penal servitude for an offence to which he had pleaded guilty. He was being removed from the dock, but he struggled

CHAP.III. Making allowance for all this, the system was a horrible one, and many dreadful instances of its nature might be given; but it prevailed throughout the whole of the eighteenth century, and was not altered till the reign of George IV., although it had long been condemned by the opinions of almost all reasonable men. The following remark from a letter of Sir James Mackintosh [1] not only shows this, but is an acute observation on the character of a remarkable man. Speaking of Windham, he says :—" Singular as it may appear, he often " opposed novelties from a love of paradox. These novelties " had long been almost established opinions among men of " speculation; and this sort of establishment had roused his " mind to resist them before they were proposed to be reduced " to practice. The mitigation of penal law had, for example, " been the system of every philosopher in Europe for the last " half-century but Paley. The principles generally received " by enlightened men on that subject had long almost " disgusted him as common-places; and he was opposing " the established creed of minds of his own class when he " appeared to be supporting an established code of law."

Besides the laws which excluded so many felonies from benefit of clergy, many others were passed which created felonies and misdemeanours not punishable with death at all, but with various terms of transportation and imprisonment. There were many of these enactments, and the punishments violently, and kept crying out, "You cannot do that ; you cannot do it." I asked him why not, for my legal power was unquestionable. He said, "I'm sure your lordship cannot know" this or that—I forget what. I said, " As you pleaded guilty and it is not in the depositions I did not know it, but " can you prove it ?" He said he could, and called a witness who proved it at once. I said this made a great difference, and altered his sentence to a term of imprisonment and hard labour, on which he said with a tone of satisfaction, "Oh, yes, that's right enough." I have always regretted that I made no note of the particulars, and I have entirely forgotten them. I have frequently observed the accuracy with which prisoners estimate the probable duration of their sentences.

[1] Quoted in Romilly's Life, vol. iv. p. 143.

which they imposed varied capriciously in many ways.
Sometimes they imposed and sometimes they did not impose
special terms of transportation, as seven, fourteen, or twenty-one
years. Sometimes there were and sometimes there were not
alternative terms of imprisonment; and these in some cases
imposed minimum terms of imprisonment, and in others left
the judge at liberty to imprison for as short a time as he
pleased. Whipping, fines, and in later times solitary imprisonment, were sometimes added, either as alternative or
cumulative punishments, and sometimes omitted.

The general result of all this was that at about 1820 the
state of the criminal law was unsatisfactory to the last degree.
It was admitted to be much too severe, especially in regard
of the punishment of death. It was immensely cumbrous. It
was utterly unsystematic. Its punishments were to the last
degree capricious, and it stood in the greatest need of compression, definition, and rearrangement, in nearly every part.
On the other hand, it had the great merits of approximate
completeness, and a solid basis of wide and long experience
—in a word it contained the materials necessary for the
construction of an excellent system. In the course of the
next forty years this system was to a great extent constructed
by the following steps.

Between 1826 and 1832 there were passed a series of Acts,
known as Sir Robert Peel's Acts, which abolished nearly all
the antiquated parts of the law, of which benefit of clergy was
practically by far the most mischievous. They also consolidated
the law relating to larceny, to offences against the person, to
forgery, and to offences against the coinage. These Acts extended only to England, and did not touch any of the common
law definitions or principles. They greatly diminished the
number of capital offences, but still left a considerable number
of offences punishable with death.

In 1837 the punishment of death was abolished in almost

CHAP. III. all the cases in which it had been retained; and after many Reports of Commissions the six Consolidation Acts were passed in 1861, which are known as Greaves's Acts, and which form a sort of imperfect Penal Code in respect of all the common offences. They contain about half of the existing working criminal law. In 1878 and 1879 Bills were introduced for establishing a complete Code both of crimes and of criminal procedure. I drew the first of these Bills, and the second consisted of the first as settled by a Commission of which I was a member.

Such has been the history of the criminal law of England. I will shortly sum it up in general terms, taking first that of the procedure, and then that of the crimes and punishments.

Before the Conquest the system of criminal procedure was essentially local. It consisted of courts in which it seems that the suitors were the judges, and which were convened by and presided over by the earl, the sheriff, or in particular places by other persons. The mode of accusation was by common report, or a sort of judicial committee of the court. The mode of trial was by compurgation or by ordeal.

At, and for a considerable time after, the Conquest, this system remained, but it was greatly invigorated by the action of the Curia Regia and the king's justices, whose authority gradually superseded that of the old County Courts.

The Courts of the Justices of Assize were first established, very nearly in their present form, by Henry II.; and the Queen's Bench Division of the High Court of Justice is of the same or nearly the same antiquity, representing as it does the Court of Queen's Bench, which represented the principal division of the original Curia Regia.

The procedure of these Courts was by means of the inquest, which was also a Norman invention.

A new mode of trial was also introduced by the Conqueror —namely, trial by battle, which was regulated private war.

Under this system accusations were made by inquests, and for about one hundred and fifty years or more the mode of trial continued to be by ordeal, or if the accuser was a private person by battle. When ordeals were disused, which was before the middle of the thirteenth century, petty juries were introduced, and they gradually became judges of the facts deposed to by witnesses, instead of official witnesses of the fact.

Trial by jury has, ever since its full development was reached, continued to be the established mode of trying criminals. The attempt to supersede it by the Star Chamber failed, and has never been renewed; but it has been to a small extent superseded in reference to the punishment of matters of comparatively trifling importance by the summary powers given to magistrates.

The preliminary proceedings by which prisoners are committed for trial have had the following history. In very early times the sheriffs, the coroners, the bailiffs of hundreds, the mayors of towns, and the constables of villes, arrested persons suspected of crimes.

In the fourteenth century justices of the peace were appointed for these and other purposes. Four times a year, they sat, and still sit, as Judges of the Courts of Quarter Sessions, but their regular duty has always been to arrest persons suspected of crime, and to confine or bail them till their trial can take place. Since the reign of Philip and Mary it has been their duty to take depositions; and this duty is now regulated principally by the Act 11 and 12 Vict. c. 43 (1848), commonly known as Jervis's Act.

Passing from procedure to the definition of crimes, the following are the principal points in their history.

Definitions of crimes can hardly be said to have existed at all before the Conquest. What answered as such were no more than names. The first approaches to definitions are

---

[1] *History of the Criminal Law*, ii. 219.

CHAP. III. those which are found in Bracton, and the most careful and elaborate of them are no more than classifications, which do not deal with the real difficulties of the subject, or show that the person who framed the definition knew where the difficulties lay. Bracton, however, imperfect as his writings were, was the only writer of importance on the subject for three hundred years.

Little was added to the substantive criminal law by Parliament for a great length of time, with the exception of the statute which defined treason in 1352. Some additions and explanations are to be found in the Yearbooks; and heresy, which the bishops were allowed to define as they pleased, became a capital crime at the beginning of the fifteenth century, and continued to be dealt with criminally till late in the seventeenth century.

From Henry VII. to the Civil Wars, the decisions of the Privy Council in the Court of Star Chamber exercised considerable influence over that part of the criminal law which punished as misdemeanours offences which, falling short of high treason, consisted in disturbances of the peace, or in conduct having a tendency to produce such disturbances; such as libels, unlawful assemblies, conspiracies, and maintenance in all its forms. The theory and practice of the Privy Council jurisdiction is to be found in the Statute 3 Hen. VII., which founded, as Mr. Hallam thinks, a statutory Court of Star Chamber, often confounded with, but in his view essentially distinct from, the common law jurisdiction of the Privy Council. When the Privy Council ceased to be a regular court of justice, a considerable number of the crimes which it used to punish fell under the jurisdiction of the Court of Queen's Bench. The extreme importance of the whole of this matter has not, I think, been duly recognized by English historians. The great services of the Court of Star Chamber have been forgotten in the abuses and oppressions of the later stage of its history. There is, however, great reason to think that it did much towards the establishment of the general supremacy of the law over the efforts which were at one time made by the aristocracy to prevent it.

Another remarkable point in the history of the criminal law is found in the increase of its severity by the legislation which excluded so large a number of crimes from benefit of clergy. This is first to be remarked in the sixteenth century, from which date it continued till the end of the eighteenth, indeed till early in the nineteenth.

It is, however, perfectly true that surprisingly little change took place in the actual substance of the criminal law for a great length of time, temporary passing legislation only being omitted. In the course of the eighteenth century it was enormously increased, and became at last so intricate and un-wieldy that the greater part of it has been codified and that attempts have been made to codify the whole.

CHAPTER IV.

THE EXTENT AND CLASSIFICATION OF THE CRIMINAL LAW—
EXTENT IN PLACE, TIME, AND PERSON; COMMON OR
STATUTE LAW, FELONIES AND MISDEMEANOURS.

Chap. IV. In the preceding chapters I have given an account of the history of the criminal law by way of introduction to the detailed consideration of its different parts, which is the subject of the present and the following chapters.

The first matter to be considered is the extent of the criminal law. Like everything else, it is limited in respect of place, time, and person.

The extent of the criminal law of England in respect of place is as follows. It includes the whole of England and Wales. Some parts of the statute law and the law relating to high treason extend to Scotland. The common law of England prevails in Ireland, but the statute law of England and of Great Britain does not, with certain exceptions, extend to Ireland, nor does the statute law of Ireland—the Acts of the Irish Parliament before the Union—extend to England. The statute law of the United Kingdom extends to both Ireland and Scotland, unless a contrary intention appears from the language of the different Acts.

The criminal law of England also extends to all land-locked waters forming part of the body of any English county, such as Plymouth Sound, Milford Haven, and probably the

whole of the Bristol Channel to an uncertain distance west;
also to the open sea adjacent to the United Kingdom,
and to all other parts of Her Majesty's dominions to the
distance of a marine league from low water mark, and to
such further distance, if any, as is deemed by international
law to be within Her Majesty's territorial dominions; but
no prosecution for an offence on board a foreign ship at sea
can be instituted without express previous sanction by a
Secretary of State.

It also extends to all British ships on the high seas or in
foreign harbours or rivers below bridges, whether a person
committing a crime is Her Majesty's subject or not.

It applies to piracy by the law of nations, committed by
any person whatever in any part of the world on any
person whatever.

It applies to high treason, misprision of treason, murder
and manslaughter, and slave-trading, and to some other
offences committed by any subject of Her Majesty in any
part of the world.

It extends to all persons whatever, except Her Majesty,
who is absolutely exempt from it, and foreign Ambassadors,
who are exempted from it to an unascertained extent.
There is some doubt as to the extent of its application
to prisoners of war, and to the officers and crews of ships
of war of a friendly power in British waters. It probably
does not apply to them so as to interfere with acts done
for the maintenance on board of naval discipline.

With respect to time, by the law of England no such
thing is known as a general term of prescription in criminal
cases, but there are a few particular crimes which must by
statute be prosecuted within a certain time after they are
committed. I have myself held a brief for the prosecution
of a theft alleged to have taken place sixty years before the
charge was made.

Many inquiries of great interest and curiosity are connected with these matters. I have given a full account of them in my *History of the Criminal Law*, vol. ii. pp. 1–71, in which will also be found some account of the law relating to the little-known subject of the Foreign Jurisdiction Act, which enables Her Majesty to enact bodies of criminal law and to give British courts jurisdiction over crimes in uncivilized countries, or countries which permit her in fact or by treaty to exercise such powers. In the same chapter I have discussed the relation between acts of State (by which I mean acts done by the military and naval forces of the Crown, by which the lives and the properties of foreigners are affected) and the criminal law, and I have given an account of the operation of the Extradition Acts. But these are matters of which the whole interest would be lost by any attempt at the compression which would be necessary in referring to them in the present work.

Such being the limits of the criminal law of England, I will now proceed to notice two important distinctions which pervade every part of it, and furnish the only approach to a general classification of the whole subject which the law itself provides.

These are the distinction between common and statute law, and the distinction between treason, felony, and misdemeanour.

The distinctions in themselves are perfectly plain. Common law is that part of the law which has never been reduced to the form of an Act of Parliament. Statute law is composed, as its name implies, of Acts of Parliament. A felony was the name of all crimes which, whether at common law or by statute, were punished with death and forfeiture of property, or were denominated as felonies whatever might be the punishment. Treason is felony, and more. All other crimes are misdemeanours. This definition is substantially, but not absolutely, accurate; as mayhem and petty larceny, being felonies, were not punishable by death, and misprision of treason was punished by forfeiture, though a misdemeanour. These distinctions do not now rest upon any assignable principle. The limits between statute and common law can be pointed out only by an enumeration of the subjects which fall under each head, and the distinction between felony and misdemeanour only by enumerating the crimes which belong to each category.

Some important consequences are, however, still attached to these distinctions. The common law is much less definite than the statute law, and its provisions are interpreted more freely, that is, with a more direct reference to expediency and other general considerations than the words of a statute. There is more to say for the counsel, and more discretion is vested in the judges, upon a question of common law than upon a question of the meaning of a statute. As to felony and misdemeanour, the fact that a crime is a felony involves these consequences: (1) a person suspected is liable to arrest without warrant; (2) he is not entitled to be bailed as a matter of right; and (3) he is entitled to twenty peremptory challenges on his trial—a right so seldom exercised as to be of little practical importance.

I ought perhaps to notice here that, besides common law and statute law, a third kind of law may be distinguished— namely, that which is contained in cases decided upon statutes, which forms a kind of secondary common law. For instance, a statute punishes everyone who "by any false "pretence obtains money," &c. So many cases have been decided on the question what is and what is not a false pretence that it takes nearly a page to give even an abstract of the result of them [1]

I will now proceed to give some account of the relation in

---

[1] See *Digest of the Criminal Law*, p. 276, Art. 330, and its ten illustrations.

CHAP. IV. which common law and statute law stand to each other, and I will in passing make a few observations upon case law.

The general principles which pervade and limit the application of the whole body of the criminal law are all, with hardly an exception, part of the common law. Those which define its extent, and which I have just stated, are, however, considerably limited by statute. It is by statute that the English courts can try cases of murder and manslaughter committed by the Queen's subjects in any part of the world, whereas by common law they cannot try them for theft or wounding committed abroad. It is by statute (the Territorial Waters Jurisdiction Act) that a crime committed on board a foreign ship within a marine league of the English coast can be tried in an English court. At the common law it was not so.

That body of law which I describe as the conditions of criminality, and which may also be regarded as constituting a set of general exceptions to every definition of crime—the law relating to the effect upon criminality of age, madness, drunkenness, marriage, compulsion, necessity, and ignorance of law and of fact—is entirely common law. The practice in the case of an acquittal on the ground of insanity, and the form of the verdict in such cases, is provided for by statute. There are also some statutory limitations upon some of the common law doctrines as to the effect of marriage upon the law relating to theft.

The law relating to principal and accessory in crimes is, as far as principle goes, entirely common law, but the common law rules as to the trial and punishment of accessories, which were extremely intricate and irrational, have been abolished by statute, and the punishment of accessories after the fact has also been regulated by statute.

Steps preparatory to crime—incitement, conspiracy, and attempts—are defined, and in most cases punished by com-

mon law, but many conspiracies and attempts, *e.g.* conspiracy CHAP. IV.
to murder, certain conspiracies in restraint of trade, attempts
to murder, attempts to burn houses, are the subject of
statutory enactments, and are in some cases made felonies,
punishable with the highest secondary punishment.

Passing from these introductory matters to substantive
crimes, the first class of offences to be noticed are those
which affect public order. Of these, high treason, treasonable felonies, inciting to mutiny, and assaulting the Queen,
are statutory crimes, but the words of the statute 25 Edw. III.
st. 5, c. 2, have been made the subject of many decisions, so
that a great amount of case law has been embodied in the
statute. Its effect, however, is for the most part given in
what is commonly called the Treason-Felony Act, 11 Vict.
c. 12, and as prosecutions under this Act have in most cases
superseded prosecutions under 25 Edw. III., these decisions
have lost much of their importance.

Disturbances of the public peace by riots are punishable
partly at common law and partly by statute. The most
important common law offences of this class are affrays,
unlawful assemblies, routs, and riots, all which are minutely
defined by common law. Some particular kinds of riots
are dealt with by statute, such as a riot continuing for an
hour after proclamation is made for its dispersal, the riotous
demolition or damage of houses, riotous smuggling, and armed
poaching at night by three or more persons together.

Forcible entry is a statutory offence, a good deal explained
by cases.

Offences against public order by illegal combinations and
confederacies are most commonly dealt with under the common law relating to seditious words, libels, or conspiracies.
Sedition itself is not, according to the law of England, the
name of a crime, as it is by the law of Scotland; but every
kind of conduct which would be included under that name in

CHAP. IV. Scotland, would, in England, be included under one or other of these heads. There are some statutes on unlawful clubs and societies, which, however, are seldom, if ever, acted upon.

Offences in which foreign countries are interested are mostly statutory, and are punishable either under the Foreign Enlistment or the Slave-Trading Acts, but piracy, by the law of nations, is an offence defined (if at all) by common law, but punished under a combination of four separate statutes.

Abuses and obstructions of public authority are generally punishable at common law, but there are elaborate statutes against bribery and the sale of offices.

Perjury was first punished by the Privy Council. It has been recognized as a crime, and its punishment is fixed by statute. Its definition is deducible from a great number of decided cases. False swearing not amounting to perjury is a misdemeanour at common law.

Maintenance and champerty are offences defined very vaguely by common law, and punished by statute.

The offences of escape, rescue, prison breach, misprision of treason, misprision and compounding of felony, are a singular jumble of common and statute law. This is perhaps the most confused part of the English criminal law.

Offences against religion consist partly of the offence of blasphemy at common law, which has been the subject of much controversy, and partly of statutes, which are practically obsolete.

Offences against morality are in several instances statutory, as in the case of unnatural offences, and offences under the Criminal Law Amendment Act of 1885. In other cases, as in the case of obscene libels and acts of public indecency, they are offences at common law, or I should perhaps say by case law, the Court of Queen's Bench having, in the seventeenth century, taken upon itself part of the powers formerly exercised by the Court of Star Chamber.

The definition of a common nuisance is part of the common law, but by many statutes particular things have been declared to be such, especially the keeping of disorderly houses of different kinds, and lotteries.

Libel is an offence at common law, though several matters connected with it are regulated by statute. The greater part of the law relating to it is very modern, consisting as it does almost entirely of decisions given in the course of the present century.

Before passing to the consideration of the part of the law codified by the Consolidation Acts of 1861, I will observe that a power has sometimes been assumed of holding acts to be misdemeanours which were considered to be injurious to the public, though there was no precedent for it. This was and is described as the elasticity of the common law. I think that it has been used practically to the utmost extent, and that it is undesirable that it should ever be used again. The fate of the attempts made to adapt to modern trade disputes certain doctrines of the common law as to conspiracy in restraint of trade is a standing warning against such an exercise of judicial power.

I come now to the part of the criminal law which has partially been codified by the Acts of 1861 and one or two others. Of these, the Malicious Mischief Act, the Act relating to offences against the coinage, and the Acts relating to fraudulent debtors and bankruptcy, have hardly any relation to the common law, except so far as it is required to interpret the word "malicious" in the Act on malicious mischief.

The Acts relating to the law of master and servant cannot be understood without reference to the common law as to conspiracies in restraint of trade.

The Act relating to offences against the person, the Larceny Act, and the Forgery Act, presuppose a considerable acquaintance with the common law, on which, indeed, each is founded.

The Act relating to offences against the person cannot be understood without reference to the law which justifies the application of force to the body of others in certain cases and to various extents. It also assumes an acquaintance with the definition of the crimes of murder, manslaughter, accidental homicide, and homicide by negligence, which, again, presupposes an acquaintance with the law relating to duties tending to the preservation of life. It also presupposes knowledge of the definitions of assault and rape, which last has to be deduced from a number of decisions, some of them not easily reconcilable. The offence of bigamy has also given rise to several difficult questions, as its statutory definition is very incomplete.

The Larceny Act is wholly unintelligible without reference to the common law definition of theft, and its rules as to things which are and things which are not capable of being stolen. Lastly, the Forgery Act depends upon the common law definition of forgery, and especially upon the common law meaning of an intent to defraud.

It thus appears that the common and statute law are mixed up in nearly equal proportions in our criminal law, and that nearly every part of it, though not to the same degree, is affected by each. It is also true that it is practically impossible to study the two apart. The statutes are unintelligible and a mere burden to the memory without the common law. The common law can be understood by itself, but unless it is studied in connection with the statutes it is, so to speak, disembodied and almost exclusively theoretical.

Of the distinction between felony and misdemeanour it

is unnecessary to say more than that the following is an CHAP. IV.
imperfect list of them :—

High treason has all the characteristics of felony and others
of its own.

Felonies.	Misdemeanours.
Offences under 11 Vict. c. 12.	Assaults on the Queen.
	Unlawful assemblies.
Inciting to mutiny.	Routs.
Felonious riots.	Riots.
Unlawful oaths.	Forcible entries.
Piratical slave-trading.	Seditious offences.
Felonious escapes.	Offences against Foreign
Unnatural crimes.	Enlistment Act.
Murder.	Extortion.
Manslaughter.	Oppression.
Attempts to murder.	Bribery.
	Perjury.
	Maintenance.
	Escapes.
	Blasphemy.
	Offences against the Criminal Law Amendment Act.
	Common nuisances.
Greater bodily injuries.	Minor bodily injuries.
Rape.	Assaults.
Connection with children under thirteen.	Assaults on girls from thirteen to sixteen, and intercourse with them by consent.
Bigamy.	
Some irregular marriages.	

Felonies.	Misdemeanours.
Abduction with intent to marry.	Abduction.
Stealing children under fourteen.	Neglect of children and not providing food for them.
Theft.	Libel.
Embezzlement.	Obtaining by false pretences.
Robbery and extortion by threats.	Cheating.
Burglary and housebreaking.	Conspiracy to defraud.
Receiving stolen goods.	Misappropriations by bankers, merchants, &c.
	Frauds by directors and trustees.
	Fraudulent false accounting.
Forgery of documents specified in Forgery Act.	Forging trade-marks, also forgery at common law.
Some personations.	Other personations.
Some coinage offences.	Other coinage offences.
Burning ships-of-war.	
Use of explosives for certain purposes.	
Arson, and some other injuries to property.	Minor injuries to property.
A bankrupt absconding.	Some other offences against the bankruptcy law, and the Fraudulent Debtors Act.
	Criminal breaches of contracts of service.
	Offences against Merchant Shipping Acts.

In the Draft Code of 1379 the distinction between felony Chap. IV.
and misdemeanour was laid aside, but the distinction between
crimes which do and do not render the offender liable to
summary arrest, and in respect of which he has a right to be,
bailed absolutely or only at discretion, is inherent in the
nature of things, and must in some form be preserved. The
confused state of the present law upon this subject is set
forth in my *Digest of the Law of Criminal Procedure*, chap.
xii. Articles 96–98, pp. 59–62 ; as to bail, see pp. 88–92.

CHAPTER V.

CONDITIONS OF CRIMINALITY.

ACCORDING to the law of England, in order to be a crime an act—

(1) Must be done by a person of competent age.

(2) It must be voluntary, and the person who does it must also be free from certain forms of compulsion.

(3) It must be intentional.

(4) It must be accompanied by knowledge, the nature and amount of which differs according to the nature of the crime.

(5) In many cases, malice, fraud, or negligence, enter into the definition of offences.

(6) Each of these general conditions (except the condition of age) may be affected by the madness of the offender.

AGE.—A child under seven years of age is not criminally responsible for its actions. From seven to fourteen a child is presumed to be irresponsible, but may be proved to have sufficient knowledge of right and wrong to make him responsible. In practice this rule is tacitly passed over. A child of ten or twelve would be unusually dull if it did not know that it might be punished for stealing.

VOLUNTARY ACTS.—A voluntary action is a group of bodily motions accompanied or preceded by volition, and directed to some object. Every such action involves, the following elements: knowledge, motive, choice, volition, intention, and thoughts, feelings, and motions adapted to the execution of the intention.

These states of mind occur in the order in which I have named them.

The intention is the direction of conduct towards the object chosen upon considering the motives which suggest the choice. The word properly means aim, and involves a metaphor taken from shooting with a bow. In the absence of any one of these elements, action ceases to be voluntary.

Involuntary action is action in which there is no choice or no intention. A man in a convulsion fit, a person walking in his sleep, a person whose face changes its expression and whose heart beats violently under the influence of passion supply cases of involuntary action. No involuntary action is a crime.

Voluntary and involuntary actions are contradictory, but voluntary action may be either compulsory or free. To walk to the gallows is a voluntary act done under the strongest compulsion. When a thirsty man drinks, he acts freely. It will thus be seen that in the case of voluntary actions freedom is the general rule, and compulsion the rare exception, for no one would be said to be compelled unless he was under the influence of motives at once terrible and powerful, which is rarely the case. On the other hand, freedom means only the absence of such motives. It is a word, indeed, which has no definite meaning, unless we are told who is free from what, and from what restraints which might apply to him he is free.

The effect of compulsion thus understood is, according to the law of England, as I understand it, narrowly limited and somewhat capricious. Two cases of it only need be mentioned. The first is the rule that a married woman who commits a crime in her husband's presence is deemed, unless the contrary appears, to act under his compulsion, and to be thereby entitled to an acquittal. It is not certain how far this rule applies, for it certainly does not apply to high treason or murder. An historical explanation of it may, I think, be given, but this is a subject which I need not discuss here.[1]

The second case is when a body of rebels or rioters have, by fear of death or instant bodily harm, compelled unwilling persons to take a subordinate part in an insurrection or other disturbance.

There would be a strong objection to carrying the law further on this point, as it would afford a ready excuse for systematic crime. Criminals might commit offences with impunity by threatening others. Criminal law itself is a system of compulsion, and ought not to withdraw its threats on account of counter-threats. It would be foolish to say, "I "will hang you if you commit murder, unless you can show "that some one else threatened to shoot you if you did not." Besides this, the fact of compulsion may always be taken into account in reduction of punishment.

INTENTION.—I have said that an act to be a crime must be intentional. I have already explained what I mean by intention, but several explanations are required to avoid natural misconceptions.

First, I do not mean that the accused person must intend to commit the crime which he actually does commit, but that he must intend to do the act which constitutes the crime. A man, for instance, may not intend to kill by some act of intentional violence, and may yet be guilty of murder or manslaughter by reason of it; but if he did not intend to do the act which caused the death, he would be guilty of no crime at all unless the act was accompanied by negligence.

[1] See *Digest of the Criminal Law*, Art. 30 and note.

Secondly, it is important to distinguish between motives and intentions. An intention to do anything is consistent with any number of different motives, and may remain unchanged while the motives vary. In the crime of publishing a libel the intention must always be to give more or less publicity to a certain libel. The motives for this may be infinite, and may vary from time to time. So an intention to kill may be the result of all sorts of motives. It may be the act of an executioner, of a soldier in time of war, of a man defending his own life, of a murderer. The intent to kill is the same in all these and many other cases. Intention is a much more definite thing than motive, and is usually of much greater importance in criminal cases.

Thirdly, it is important to observe that one intention does not exclude another. A man intending to escape from custody intentionally disables an officer who has him in custody. He intends both to escape and to disable.

Fourthly, I may observe that in many cases the existence of a particular definite intention forms part of the definition of a crime. Wounding with intent to murder or do grievous bodily harm, abduction with intent to marry, are instances. In these cases the presence of that particular intention is, of course, essential to the crime.

Fifthly, I may point out that the rule is so worded as not to include the case of crimes by omission. Where an omission is criminal, it may in some cases be unintentional, as, for instance, if a drunken engine-driver were to forget to notice the signals for the train, and so to cause death, he would be guilty of manslaughter. The state of mind, which in such a case would be criminal, would be a default of due attention in the discharge of legal duties. Crimes by omission are exceptional.

These remarks are of use because they display the falsehood of certain popular common-places about intention. Of the nature of these common-places I will say only that the most conspicuous example of them is to be found in Lord Erskine's celebrated arguments about the law of libel. I have examined this matter minutely in my *History of the Criminal Law.*[1]

I may remark in conclusion, on the maxim that a man is presumed to intend the natural consequences of his acts, that the rule is quite as much a rule of common-sense as of law, and that it is a rule of which the application has, after all, to be left to juries with reference to the particular circumstances of particular cases.

KNOWLEDGE.—Knowledge is always an element of criminality of more or less importance. Whatever controversies have arisen about the effects of madness, it has never been doubted by anyone that it destroys all responsibility if it is of such a nature as to prevent the person affected by it from knowing the nature and quality of his acts. But the question remains, What is the degree of knowledge which is essential to criminality in different cases?

The answer is that knowledge of the law is never required at all. This is a blunt and possibly ungracious equivalent for the well-known statement that everyone is conclusively presumed to know the law, a presumption opposed to notorious facts, and closely resembling a forged release to a forged bond. The degree of knowledge of fact which is necessary to criminality varies according to the different crimes which may be committed.

Generally, everyone is presumed, and the presumption is usually correct, to have a capacity of knowing the nature and consequences of his conduct, and the common opinions of his own time and country about morality and crime; to know that knives cut or stab, that gunpowder explodes, that

---

[1] Vol. ii. c. xxiv. ; and see particularly my account of Shipley's case and Fox's Libel Act, pp. 330–356, and in particular p. 351, &c.

murder, theft, robbery, &c., are the names of wicked and punishable acts; nor is any excuse for the want of such knowledge accepted, speaking generally, except madness, the effects of which I shall consider separately. If, however, such ignorance should really exist, *e.g.* if a person did not know that a loaded gun would go off if the trigger were pulled, such ignorance, if proved, would be a good defence to a charge of shooting with intent to murder.

The question how far ignorance or mistake as to a particular matter of fact connected with a crime is important or not depends upon the definition of the crime. For instance, the definition of theft includes as its mental element an intention to deprive the owner of his property permanently, fraudulently, and without claim of right. Hence it is not theft to take the property of another under a real belief that it belongs to the taker. Burglary is breaking and entering a house between 9 P.M. and 6 A.M. with intent to commit a felony. A.'s watch is wrong, and he breaks into a house at 9.5 P.M honestly believing that it is 8.35. Does A. commit burglary or not? Would it make any difference if he committed the crime by railway time instead of local mean time—a little before 6 by local mean time, and a little after by railway time? These questions may be decided when they arise, but others of more importance may and actually do occur. A woman marries a second husband believing in good faith and on reasonable grounds that her first husband is dead. He is in fact alive. Has she committed bigamy?[1] This depends on the construction of the section of the Act relating to offences against the person which punishes the offence of bigamy. Similar questions have arisen on other statutes, and they are in some instances expressly provided for, particularly in the Criminal Law Amendment Act of 1885. Many questions

---

[1] It has been very recently decided that she has not (see R. *v.* Jobson, *Law Reports* 28, Queen's Bench Division, p. 163).

may be raised as to the effect of mistakes of fact upon the lawfulness of summary arrests, and acts intended as acts of resistance to crimes of violence. Their nature may be understood by reference to a variety of clauses drawn by Lord Blackburn in the Draft Criminal Code of 1879.

The consideration of these conditions of criminality may properly end with a reference to the saying, "*Non est reus nisi mens sit rea*," which is said by some to be the fundamental maxim of the criminal law. It appears to me to be neither more nor less valuable than the other scraps of Latin which have found their way into it, and which are generally used when counsel do not clearly know their own meaning. It would be just ast rue and just as important to say, "*Non est reus nisi corpus sit reum.*" I have never been able to discover anything like the expression about *mens rea* in the *Pandects*, though something ot the kind is to be found in the *Leges Henrici Primi*. It is a mischievous phrase, because it is usually understood to mean that legal guilt cannot exist in the absence of moral guilt, and that a man may break the law if he is actuated by virtuous motives. The only true meaning which can be attached to it is that every definition of a crime involves some mental element. This is true, and now that all crimes have been more or less carefully defined it is easy to say what that mental element is in any particular case. In murder, for instance, the mental element is malice aforethought, a phrase which has itself been reduced to certainty. In theft, it is an intent to take away property permanently, and without claim of right, and so on. The only doubtful cases are those in which there is a question how much knowledge and what knowledge is required to constitute a given offence; or, in other words, whether the word knowingly or the like is to be understood in an Act of Parliament. On this the maxim, as it is called, throws no light; for the question commonly is whether or not the Legislature meant to compel peeple to act at their peril in taking certain steps. Did it mean that a person who abducts a girl is to take his chance of her being under sixteen? that a person who does, in fact, keep a house in which people are treated as lunatics is to take his chance of their actually being lunatics? that a woman who marries within seven years of the disappearance of her first husband is to take her chance of his being dead? These questions must all be decided according to circumstances, which differ from case to case.

There are three words which form the mental element of a number of crimes, on which it will be well to say something here. They are "malice," "fraud," and "negligence," and the corresponding adjectives and adverbs.

MALICE.—This word is objectionable, partly because it has to do with motives rather than intentions, and so is at once vague and an appeal to popular feeling. It was on these accounts omitted entirely from the Draft Code of 1879, and from the Indian Penal Code. It has, however, been rendered sufficiently definite for practical purposes in the principal cases in which it is used in the criminal law. These are three. In each the meaning of the word is different; nor would it in any case be safe to give to it the meaning which it bears in common popular use.

(1) The definition of murder is " killing with malice afore- " thought." The word malice here means a variety of totally different states of mind. I shall comment on them in connection with the history and the definition of the crime of murder.

(2) "Malice" is an element of the crime of libel. By a number of subtle fictions it has at last come to mean that written blame is always criminal unless it is justified or excused on one or another of some six or seven different grounds which are said to rebut the presumption of malice.

(3) The word "malice" is introduced into nearly every section of the Act which punishes malicious mischief.

CHAP. V. Throughout this Act it means intentional, and without justification or excuse or claim of right.

FRAUD is very nearly equivalent to deceiving a man so as to injure him or expose him to the risk of injury. This definition supplies an answer to the common saying, " I did not " mean to defraud him, because I meant to pay the money " back." To which the answer is, " You did mean to expose " him to the risk of your not paying it back." " Falsehood " profitable to the author " is perhaps as good a definition of fraud as could be given in a word, for such falsehood must, in order to be profitable to A., involve an equivalent loss to B.

NEGLIGENCE means the omission to perform a duty imposed by law. The word is used in criminal law principally in reference to the infliction of bodily injury by neglecting to perform one of the duties which are by law imposed on various persons for the preservation of human life. Questions of some nicety may occur in reference to this.

NECESSITY.—I may add a few words on the defence of necessity, which is the strongest possible form of compulsion. It is a question which, in fact, is hardly ever raised, and which, when it is raised, is always, as it ought to be, dealt with exceptionally. The only case of the kind of which I am aware was the case of R. *v.* Dudley and Stephens,[1] in which certain sailors in danger of death by starvation killed one of their number and ate him. This was held to be murder on grounds which appear from the judgment, and on which I have made some remarks in the last edition of my *Digest* (pp. 24-25, note). I think, on the whole, the judgment was right, but I disagree with part of it, which appears to me to " base a legal conclusion upon a questionable moral and " theological foundation, and to be rhetorically expressed." There is not, and I think there cannot be, any principle

---

[1] *Law Reports,* 14 Queen's Bench Division, p. 273.

involved in cases of this kind. It is, in my judgment, one of the very few cases in which a pardon might properly have been granted before trial. I can imagine somewhat similar cases, in which, notwithstanding R. *v.* Dudley, necessity might be an excuse. Suppose a man is so situated that he must either leave two persons to die, or kill one. You must either run over a boat, or have a fatal collision with a ship. You must leave both mother and child to die, or effect the delivery in such a way as to sacrifice at least one life. The subject is one on which it is useless to argue.

CHAPTER VI

THE RELATION OF MADNESS TO CRIMINAL RESPONSIBILITY.

CHAP. VI.   I HAVE considered this subject in the fullest possible
manner in my *History of the Criminal Law*,[1] and I refer to
that chapter for a full statement of all my views on the subject. I will content myself here with a very short statement
of my understanding of the law. It is, as I believe, correctly
expressed in the 27th Article of my *Digest*, which is as
follows.[2]

No act is a crime if the person who does it is at the time
when it is done prevented, either by defective mental power,
or by any disease affecting his mind—

(*a*) From knowing the nature and quality of his act ;

(*b*) From knowing that either the act is illegal or that it is
morally wrong ; or

(*c*) From controlling his own conduct, unless the absence
of the power of control has been produced by his own
default.

But an act may be a crime although the mind of the
person who does it is affected by disease, if such disease does

---

[1] Vol. ii. chap. xix. pp. 124–186.

[2] I have in the *Digest* inclosed in brackets certain parts of this statement,
because some persons have regarded them as doubtful on the authority of the
opinions of the judges in MacNaghton's case. I print in the text what, in my
opinion, is the law as it exists. In my *History* I have minutely examined both
the authority and the meaning of MacNaghton's case.

not in fact produce upon the mind one or other of the effects Chap. VI.
above mentioned, in reference to that act.

By "knowing either that an act is illegal or that it is morally wrong" I understand being able to judge calmly and reasonably of the moral or legal character of a proposed action; and "by controlling his own conduct" I mean ability to refer calmly and reasonably to those motives which would lead men in general to resist temptations to crime and to allow proper weight to them. A man may be aware as a general proposition that murder is a crime, but if his mind is haunted by delusions, which, even if they are not immediately connected with the killing of any particular person, vitiate the sufferer's mental operations, and are inconsistent with such an appreciation of the facts as a sane man has, this is strong evidence to show that he does not know the moral character of the act of killing any particular person. It is equally strong evidence to show that he has not the ordinary power of control over his actions; for how does anyone ever control his actions except by attending to the various considerations, moral, legal, and religious, which make him resist temptation? There may be no definite connection between the delusion, say, that a man's finger is made of glass and the murder of his wife; but if it was shown of anyone that he was under the delusion that his finger was made of glass when he murdered his wife, a long step would be taken towards showing that he was not in a position to know that to murder his wife was wrong, or to appreciate correctly the moral nature of any action whatever, or to perform that process of deliberation or comparison of conflicting considerations which is necessary to the control of conduct in any circumstances of temptation.

The law thus stated and explained is not, I think, open to objection, nor is it difficult to understand or to administer; but the subject has been made the occasion of great controversy between the legal and medical professions. Of this

CHAP. VI. I have in my *History* said all that I think it necessary to say. I will, however, indicate the principal points on which it has turned.

It has been thought that the law of England is that the fact that a man is disabled from controlling his conduct by madness is not, if proved, a good defence to a charge of crime in respect of an act so done.

This appears to me to be a mistake traceable in part to a misunderstanding of the meaning, and in part to an exaggeration of the authority, of the answers of the judges in Mac-Naghten's case. I have considered this matter at large in the chapter already referred to, and shall not return to it here. I think that the answers in question are unfortunately expressed, and imperfect. They do not explain that the knowledge that an act is wrong, which is the test not of insanity but of responsibility—that is, liability to punishment—means, not knowledge of the truth of the general proposition that a particular class of actions are wrong, but a power of appreciating the moral quality of a particular action. This power may be disturbed by delusions or impulses of various kinds not immediately connected with crime by any link apparent to a sane mind unacquainted with the way in which madness works, and in spite of the retention by the madman of a power of appreciating the difference between moral good and evil in cases with which he is not personally concerned.

I have tried many cases of murder in which the defence was insanity, and I do not think that I ever found the least difficulty in disposing of them in a way which was not complained of by medical men. I do not think I have ever had occasion to check a medical man in giving any evidence which he wished to give, nor have I found any difficulty in pointing out to the jury the way in which it bore on the issue to be tried by them according to my understanding of the law of England; and for these reasons I think that the controversy supposed to exist between the medical and legal professions on this subject is merely a misunderstanding arising partly from the circumstance that the two professions look at the matter from different points of view, and partly from the fact that the nature of the disease was till lately very imperfectly understood.

Practically, there is no doubt that as a general rule madness in any of its forms is inconsistent with liability to legal punishment or responsibility, but this is not strictly true. It is the usual but not the invariable or necessary result of madness to destroy responsibility ; and it is important to bear this in mind, for cases might occur in which a man might be both mad and responsible. Suppose, for instance, a very wicked man were to be slightly affected with a curable form of madness, so much so that it was thought desirable not at once to restore him to complete liberty, and suppose that, presuming on his supposed irresponsibility, he were with every circumstance of premeditation and contrivance to poison some person on whose death he would inherit a fortune. Surely such a person ought, as by law he would be, to be guilty of murder, and responsible for his act.

In connection with the subject of madness, the effects of drunkenness and anger may be noticed, each of which has something in common with madness. Neither drunkenness nor anger can in any case be an excuse for crime, but each may have, under certain circumstances, the effect in certain cases of affecting the degree of a criminal's guilt. Certain forms of provocation have the effect of reducing murder to manslaughter, and when any particular intention is essential to the commission of a crime, the fact that a person charged with the crime was drunk when he committed it is to be taken into account in considering whether he had the intention or not.

CHAPTER VII.

PRINCIPAL AND ACCESSORY. STEPS TOWARDS CRIME—INCITEMENT; CONSPIRACIES; ATTEMPT.

IN former times the law relating to principal and accessory was one of the most intricate parts of the law. It was attended with one very singular circumstance: the law applied only to cases of felony. In cases of treason, the object was to include as many as possible in guilt, and all were accordingly held to be principals. In cases of misdemeanour, all were regarded as principals, because it was not thought worth while to make the distinction. In cases of felony, there were anciently four degrees in crime. Principals in the first degree—those who actually committed the offence; principals in the second degree—those who were present aiding or abetting at the actual commission of the offence; accessories before the fact—being all who directly or indirectly counselled, procured, or commanded the crime; and accessories after the fact—those who received or comforted a criminal knowingly, and in order to procure his escape. Consequences, all of which have since ceased to follow, depended upon the conviction or liability to justice of the principal at the time when it was sought to make the accessory also liable. It is now sufficient to remark that every person who would have been a principal in the second degree, or an accessory before the fact, is now a principal felon, and is liable to be tried and convicted as a principal felon, whatever may become of the principal felon himself.

An accessory after the fact is one who receives, comforts, or assists a felon in his attempt to escape punishment. Such a person is, in all cases whatever, punishable by the law as it stands with a maximum punishment of two years' imprisonment and hard labour. In the case of murder alone, the maximum punishment is ten years' penal servitude.

There is little interest or curiosity in the law as it stands, except in one respect. It affords a strong instance of the injury formerly done to the law by its extreme severity. When all the parties to a crime were nominally felons, and as such were liable to death, it was natural to resort to all sorts of quibbles in order to avoid so terrible a consequence. The nature of the old subtleties, so far as I regarded the matter as likely to be interesting, is set forth in my *History.*[1] It is a curious instance of the reasons which made our old criminal law intricate and complicated. Every alteration in it was made for some unavowed reason, and had some effect other than that which was its professed object. Essentially the subject has no special interest.

I pass now towards those imperfect crimes which constitute the first steps, so to speak, in criminality. These are— incitement to a crime, conspiracy to commit a crime, and attempts to commit crimes which are not in fact committed. All such preliminary steps towards crime are, according to the law of England, themselves criminal. The exact point at which they become criminal cannot, in the nature of things, be precisely ascertained, nor is it desirable that such a matter should be made the subject of great precision. There is more harm than good in telling people precisely how far they may go without risking punishment in the pursuit of an unlawful object.

[1] Vol. ii. pp. 231-240.

The bare formation of a criminal intention is not in itself criminal, but this is the last step towards crime of which this can be affirmed.

To incite another to commit a crime is a misdemeanour. To agree with another to commit it is a conspiracy. To attempt to commit a crime is to do an act intended to form part of a series of acts which, if actually done, would complete the crime, but it may be difficult to say precisely what is the first step in such a series. A conspiracy is often, perhaps generally inferred from a course of conduct which shows concerted action on the part of a variety of persons who unite in the pursuance of some common object.

In regard to conspiracy, it must be observed that in these days all objects of importance are obtained by combination. Every trading association, every club, every literary or artistic society, is in many respects a conspiracy, and would be criminal if the persons concerned in it had in view any common illegal object, either as an end in itself, or as a means of gaining other ends, themselves legal or illegal. The case of trade unions and the different laws relating to them is a standing illustration of the weight and interest attaching to this class of offences. I know of no more remarkable instance of many of the most interesting features of English common and statute law, and of the way in which they are called upon to complete each other in different states of opinion and under different circumstances.[1]

---

[1] *History of the Criminal Law*, iii. 209-227, but see the whole chapter.

CHAPTER VIII.

POLITICAL OFFENCES BY VIOLENCE.

POLITICAL offences may be divided into two classes— namely, first, political offences by open force; secondly, political offences not committed by open force.

Of political offences committed by open force the principal is high treason, an offence which if it is fully successful constitutes to a greater or less extent a new departure in politics, according to the nature of the objects which the traitors have in view. These may of course vary as widely as those of the authors of the English Revolution of 1688 and those of the authors cf the various French Revolutions which took place at the end of the last century and in the course of the present one. In all these, however, and in a vast number of more or less analogous cases, new systems of government have been erected or attempted to be erected by open force in a variety of different ways.

The history and the present condition of the law relating to treason and analogous offences can hardly be understood without reference to nearly the whole of the political history of England.

The law can be traced back to the Norman Conquest, or at least to the reign of Henry II. Glanville, who lived in that reign, uses language upon the subject repeated with some expansions by Bracton in the reign of Henry III. This, again, is no doubt closely connected with the language of the statute of 25 Edw. III., st. 5, c. 3, which has ever since it was passed been the standard authority upon the law of treason.

The statute of 25 Edw. III. appears to have been passed at a time when Edward III. was at the very height of his power, when his title was undisputed, and when no question likely to produce excitement of any sort was in agitation. It distinguishes only three kinds of treason : (1) compassing and imagining the king's death ; (2) levying war against the king ; (3) adhering to the king's enemies. Some minor offences of rare occurrence, such as compassing and imagining the death of the Prince of Wales, were also declared to be treason, but they are now mere historical curiosities.

Treasonable offences falling short of attempts on the king's life are not within the statute, whatever may be their gravity. An attempt to depose the king, to imprison him, or even to blind or mutilate him, or compel him by threats of such treatment to submit to deposition or minor restraints upon his power, are not within the statute, and the same may be said of attempts to obtain political objects by attacks upon his advisers, counsellors, and ministers. In a word, if the statute of Edward III. were construed as extending to the plain natural meaning of the words only, it would afford no protection to the sovereign in his political capacity unless his life was exposed to manifest danger, or unless an army were actually brought into the field against him. It is hardly too much, indeed, to say that such assistance as the statute would give must, if it were strictly construed, be useful only for the purpose of punishing either an assassination plot or an unsuccessful rebellion after it was over. Preparations for civil war in every shape are unmentioned in the statute, and this is all the more remarkable as great parts of the reigns of Henry III. and Edward II. had been occupied by civil wars.

It may be that the statute was mild because the Government was unusually strong. The Statute of Treasons was nearly (A.D. 1352) contemporary with the Statutes of Labourers and Præmunire (1351—1353), and the establishment of Justices of the Quarter Sessions, the most important legislative measures of the time.

The subsequent history of the law on this subject must here be very concisely referred to. A full account of it is to be found in my *History of the Criminal Law*. It may be summed up in a few words as follows.

At every important crisis in our history, at the Reformation, in the time of Elizabeth, in the time of James I., at the Restoration, at the Revolution of 1688, at all periods of political excitement—in 1730, in 1794, in 1848, for instance—in a word, whenever there was any cause to apprehend a revolution, the definition of treason given in the 25th Edw. III., has either been enlarged by construction or has been reinforced by statutes intended to meet temporary purposes. The enlarged constructions given to the statute must still be regarded as theoretically law, but they have been practically superseded by the statute 11 Vict. c. 12 (1848), which makes them statutory felonies punishable with penal servitude for life as a maximum punishment; and it is by this statute that of late years such offences have been usually punished. The result is that the law has fallen into this shape, speaking roughly :—High treason is divided into three heads—

First, compassing and imagining the Queen's death, taking the words in a wide but not unnatural sense—that is, as including every conspiracy, the natural effect of which may probably be to cause personal danger to the Queen.

Second, actual levying of war against the Queen for the attainment by open force of public objects.

Third, political plots and conspiracies intended to bring

about the deposition of the Queen, or levying of war against her, or the invasion of her territories. These last offences are usually punished not as treason but as felony under 11 Vict. c. 12.

I pass over with a bare mention, such an unusual form of treason as adhering to the Queen's enemies ; I may observe, however, that its vagueness is a curious proof of the small experience which we have had of war. The French and German Codes are on this subject much fuller.

The provisions as to imagining the death of the Prince of Wales, the violation of a queen-consort or the wife of the heir-apparent, and the killing of the Chancellor and the judges in the actual exercise of their duties, are worth bare mention only.

The next most important acts of disturbance of the public peace are riots, which are of different degrees of importance. If they are committed by a number of persons riotously assembled to the number of twelve at least, who continue so assembled for an hour after being commanded by proclamation to disperse ; or if the rioters demolish or begin to demolish any building, they are liable to the most severe secondary punishment. If these aggravating circumstances do not exist, the offence is a misdemeanour, punishable, as a rule, with a maximum punishment of two years' imprisonment and hard labour.

These laws are sufficient for the suppression of attacks by main force upon the public peace, especially when it is borne in mind that the law not only sanctions, but requires the use of any necessary degree of force, involving, if required, military power in its most terrible form for the restoration of the peace. Partly from a misunderstanding of the Riot Act, partly from the repugnance which for a great part of the last century was felt to a standing army, a notion prevailed at that time that it was illegal to use military force for the dispersion of a mob till after a proclamation made and the lapse of an hour, but this has been declared on the highest authority and on several memorable occasions to be a mistake.

Minor attacks on the public peace are dealt with as constituting the common law crimes of unlawful assembly, rout, and riot. I have given the definition of these offences in my *Digest*. The crime of unlawful assembly is not difficult to define, but it is by no means easy to apply the definition to particular facts, for it is not always easy to decide whether the conduct of a public meeting is such as to give firm-minded observers reasonable grounds to believe that it will lead to a breach of the peace.

Of political offences not committed by open force, the only ones of much interest are those which are compre-hended in Scotland under the single name of sedition. In England they are distinguished as seditious words, seditious conspiracies, and seditious libel. In each case the words spoken or written, or the agreement entered into, must be with a seditious intent. The definition given of a seditious intent in my *Digest* is taken principally from a statute still in force (60 Geo. III. and 1 Geo. IV. c. 8), and partly from other standard authorities, and was accepted by the Criminal Code Commissioners of 1878–79 as a sound state-ment of the law as it stands. Perhaps the most interesting chapter in the whole history of the criminal law is that which relates to the steps by which the doctrine that a seditious intent is essential to seditious libel was introduced into the law ; and not the least interesting part of the subject is that which relates to the difference between seditious motives and seditious intentions. A mere abstract of it would convey little instruction. I have gone into the whole matter at length in my *History of the Criminal Law.*[1] I hope that what is

[1] Vol. ii. c. xxiv. pp. 298–395.

CHAP. VIII. there said exhibits in full detail the development of a striking
part of the law of England. It is certainly a curious instance
(if I am right in my view of the subject) of the way in which
either a legal fiction, or at least a misconception of the principles of the law, may be of service in first disguising and
ultimately removing its harshness.

CHAPTER IX.

OF OFFENCES IN WHICH THE NATIVES OF FOREIGN COUNTRIES ARE INTERESTED.

NEXT to offences in which internal domestic tranquillity is principally concerned are offences in which the natives of foreign countries are principally interested.

Of these, the principal are the violation of the privileges of ambassadors, interference in foreign hostilities by the equipment of expeditions against a friendly Power, equipping ships for such purposes, and in other ways taking part in them. To these must be added piracy, slave-trading, and the kidnapping of the Pacific Islanders. Most of these offences are created by statute, and to all of them a history of more or less interest attaches. I have given in my *History* some account of the circumstances which led to each of them. Piracy at common law, or by the law of nations, is the only one of the offences mentioned which is not created by statute. There are singularities connected with the offence which I do not think it necessary to go into. The most authoritative definition of piracy in English law is " robbery at sea," but I think it is easy to show that this is too wide in one direction and too narrow in another. If a foreign sailor on a foreign ship were to rob another sailor of the same nation on the same ship, it would be absurd to call him a pirate, yet such an act would be a robbery at sea ; and if a piratical vessel were to attempt to capture a lawful ship and to be captured herself, it would be strange to describe her crew as anything but pirates, yet they would have committed, not what on shore would have been a robbery, but what would have been an assault with intent to rob.

Many of the statutes relating to piracy are curious relics of a past time, especially of the early part of the eighteenth century, when the cessation of a war, by throwing privateers out of employment, naturally led to piracy; a consequence which followed, it is to be hoped for the last time, at the end of the great war in 1815, when there was an outburst of piracy in the West Indies.

These are the principal offences which can be committed against public and private tranquillity by open force, or without open force, at home and abroad.

CHAPTER X.

ABUSES AND OBSTRUCTIONS OF PUBLIC AUTHORITY.

DIRECT attacks upon public authority must, from their nature, be exceptional crimes, and can hardly be committed without raising exciting questions arising out of passionate controversies—political, social, and religious. This is not the case with abuses and obstructions of public authority. Such offences have definite degrees of importance, and may be viewed as the irregularities naturally to be expected in the working of all human institutions. They arise in one or the other of the following ways.

A person invested with public authority may abuse it by oppression, by extortion, or by fraud. He may also neglect his duty, or refuse to use his authority when he is required to do so. On the other hand, his lawful orders may be disobeyed. A public officer may be corrupted by bribery. He may be misled by falsehood, the most aggravated form of which is perjury. The execution of lawful orders, especially of sentences of courts of justice, may be frustrated by various means, such as escapes or rescues, and may be anticipated by illegal agreements for compounding offences.

No very minute detail is required in describing these various offences. They are fully defined in my *Digest*, Arts. 118–159. I will make a few remarks on them.

Extortion and oppression by public servants is a crime which in our days is difficult to commit and is unlikely to be committed, for public officers have no longer the individual influence necessary to its commission, and what they do is for the most part done under the fullest possible publicity. An unlawful association may, and such associations sometimes do, oppress individuals, but it is difficult to believe that the sort of acts of oppression recorded in old times could now occur, except under very exceptional circumstances.

Frauds by public officers may, of course, occur from time to time, but since the time when this was decided to be criminal the number of frauds punished in private persons has been so much increased that the special liability of public servants to such punishment has become comparatively unimportant. Thus in the case of Bembridge, which early in the century attracted great attention, it was held to be criminal in a public servant to make fraudulent entries in his accounts, whereby he was enabled to retain large sums of money in his own custody, and to appropriate the interest on them to his own purposes, after they ought to have been paid over to the Crown. This would now be a crime in a private person under 38 and 39 Vict. c. 24, s. 2, an enactment suggested by a somewhat similar fraud committed by one of the clerks of a well-known London bank

A neglect or refusal to discharge an official duty may be a misdemeanour, as, for example, a neglect to take proper steps to put a stop to a riot. These, and the rules that it is a misdemeanour to disobey a lawful order of a competent authority, or to disobey a statutory prohibition, or neglect a statutory command, are only the equivalents of the principle that the law must be obeyed expressed in terms of criminal law.

I may observe in passing that these offences often afford the only means of testing certain rights. A dispute, for instance, arose as to the liability of a particular sheriff to execute particular criminals. It was decided by an indictment against him for refusing to do so.

Passing from abuses by public officers and disobedience to them, the next class of offences are those which consist of corruption by bribery. It is an honourable feature of English public life that judicial or other official corruption has been in practice almost unknown in nearly every period of English history. The occasional character of English law gives it one remarkable peculiarity. When no statutes are passed for the punishment of a particular crime, it is always probable that the crime has never attracted sufficient attention to provoke special legislation; and this is certainly the case with every form of corruption except one—namely, the corruption of voters in Parliamentary, and more recently in municipal, elections. The sale of offices and the sale of interest for the procurement of offices it has been found necessary to condemn by statute, but no traces of habitual corruption amongst either political or executive officers are to be found in the statute-book. A certain number of instances of such offences have certainly occurred from a time long before the famous case of Lord Bacon.

The statutes against Parliamentary corruption in all its forms have, on the contrary, become so elaborate and minute that they afford a nearly perfect specimen of what can be done by careful legislation seriously directed against habits confessedly injurious to the public, and which the public has really decided to put down.

Justice may be misled as well as corrupted. The principal crime of this kind is in the present day perjury, which is closely connected with a curious though almost forgotten branch of the history of the criminal law.

One of the great leading heads of crime in the latter part of the Middle Ages was what was known by the general name of "maintenance." It has now dwindled down to an offence of little importance, and seldom committed. I have defined it in my *Digest* as "the act of assisting the "plaintiff in any legal proceeding in which the person "giving the assistance has no valuable interest, or in which "he acts from any improper motive." The definition is necessarily vague, because the crime is hardly known, but it was of the first importance. I have given in my *History*[1] an account of maintenance in the fourteenth and fifteenth centuries. The general character of crimes of this class appears from one of the recitals in the celebrated statute 3 Hen. VII. c. i. It is quoted above. "The King re- "membereth how by unlawful maintenances, giving of liveries, "signs and tokens, and attainders, by indentures, pro- "mises, oaths, writings, or other embraceries of his subjects, "untrue demeanings of sheriffs in making of panels and "other untrue returns, by taking of moneys, by fines, by "great riots and unlawful assemblies, the policy and "good rule of this realm is almost subdued." The effect of this is declared to be "the increase of murders, robberies, "perjuries, and unsureties of all men living." The statute then proceeds to empower either the Star Chamber or a new body of the same nature to deal with these offences. The fact that the Star Chamber did deal with them vigorously, and put a powerful check on maintenance, is its title to respect and gratitude.

Maintenance was greatly facilitated and promoted by the fact that down to the passing of this Act there was by the law of England no such crime as perjury by a witness; though Hallam justly describes perjury as "more universal and more characteristic than others"[1] in the Middle Ages. The only form of perjury which was punishable at all was perjury by a juror, which was in some cases punishable

---

[1] Vol. iii. pp. 234-240.   [2] *Middle Ages*, iii. 30, 1855.

by the process of attaint, as I have already said. The witness seems hardly to have been regarded by the theory of the law as before the court at all. For the satisfaction of the jurors no doubt he was sworn, but the jurors continued to a singular extent to be both judges and witnesses long after they had ceased, in fact, to be witnesses at all.

The Star Chamber, or the statutory court of Henry VII., by an usurpation founded upon an obvious misinterpretation of the statute of Henry VII., first assumed, though by slow degrees, the power of treating as a common law crime perjury by witnesses. The process is described in detail . in Hudson's treatise of the Star Chamber, and the authorities are collected in my *History*.[1] This has long since been confirmed by statute, and the maximum punishment of the offence is now penal servitude, or imprisonment with hard labour for seven years. It is the only crime for which such a term of imprisonment can now be given.

The details of this useful and successful usurpation of legislative power by the Court of Star Chamber, which was afterwards supported by the Court of King's Bench, are very curious. They will be found in my *History*.[2] The offence as now understood is defined in my *Digest*, Art. 135. The doctrine of materiality in perjury deserves particular notice. It was, I have no doubt, a relic of the ancient law of attaint ignorantly parodied by Coke. Its intrinsic absurdity, the stupid way in which it was introduced into the law, and the skill with which it was rendered inoffensive by judicial construction, are all characteristic and instructive.

The offence of escape is, oddly enough, one of the most intricate branches of the law, which, as it stands, is a good illustration of its strangely occasional unsystematic

---

[1] Vol. i. pp. 244-248.   [2] Vol. iii. pp. 230-250.

H

CHAP. X. character, by which the same thing is provided for many times over. I will give a single illustration of the result. A, by helping B, confined for murder, to break out of Millbank Prison, would be—

(1) An accessory after the fact to the murder, for which, by 24 and 25 Vict. c. 100–101, he would be liable to ten years' penal servitude.

(2) He would be a principal in the second degree in prison-breaking, and liable in respect thereof to seven years' penal servitude (see authorities, *Digest,* p. 153, and Art. 18).

(3) He would commit the offence of rescuing a person committed for murder, and would be liable to penal servitude for life, 25 Geo. II. c. 37, s. 9.

(4) He would be guilty of an offence against the Millbank Prison Act, 6 and 7 Vict. c, 26, s. 22.

(5) He would be guilty of an offence under 28 and 29 Vict. c. 126, s. 37, and liable therefor to two years' imprisonment and hard labour.

These are the principal offences against public officers and against the administration of justice.

CHAPTER XI.

IN a general sense, all offences may be said to be against CHAP. XI the public interest, but most of them are directed against some particular person, who is injured in his person, reputation, or property in some direct manner; as, for instances by the infliction of a bodily injury, by robbery, or by arson. The crimes of which I am now about to speak do not, as a rule, affect anyone in particular, but are punished because of the harm they are considered to do to some of the great interests of life.

The first, and in some respects the most curious of all, are what I have classed under the head of undefined misdemeanours,[1] a name which I have employed to designate acts mischievous to the public, which are punishable by no known or express law, but which appear to be such violations of the public interest or the public sense of propriety, or such outrages upon the great principles on which society is founded, that impunity should not be permitted to them. Such acts are usually done by several persons acting in concert, and are indicted as conspiracies; and instances have occurred in which the *quasi*-legislative power, which is exercised in declaring such conduct for the first time to be criminal, has been well and

[1] *Digest*, Art. 160.

H 2

wisely exercised. The creation of the offences of perjury and obscene libel are instances; but it appears to me that such a power ought to be exercised with the greatest reluctance and caution, and I have acted on this view on several occasions of some interest. For instance, I held in the case of a man who burnt his child's body in a manner not amounting to a public nuisance, that he was guilty of no legal offence, and I should fully have accepted the consequence, which was put by way of a *reductio ad absurdum* in a Parliamentary discussion on the subject, that cannibalism was not a crime. I also was of opinion that a man who wilfully infected his wife with a foul disease could not be convicted of unlawfully inflicting grievous bodily harm upon her, or of any other offence known to the law.

I will not dwell upon the subject, but will content myself with a reference to the authorities referred to in the note on Art. 160 of my *Digest*, and to some observations in my *History* [1] on the elasticity of the common law.

The first great interest which the criminal law protects or tries to protect is religion. The efforts which have been made to do so are of the deepest historical interest. A full account of them will be found in my *History of the Criminal Law.* [2] A statement of the existing law, which however, consists of a few obsolete statutes and a common law doctrine to the last degree doubtful, and which I think is capable of being used only for bad purposes, will be found in my *Digest*, Arts 161–167. The only offence against religion which can be described as a living part of the criminal law is the offence of disturbing public worship.

The history of these offences is, in a highly condensed form, as follows.

The ecclesiastical courts were at the Conquest separated from the temporal courts and made independ-

[1] Vol. iii. p. 351, &c.   [2] Vol. ii. pp. 396–407.

ent in their own sphere, the most important part of which was dealing with sins as such by punishments intended for the good of the souls of the persons punished —the infliction, namely, of different forms of penance. This system was worked by putting suspected persons upon their oaths as to the matters to be inquired into, and sentencing them on conviction. It applied specially to all sexual immorality. This ordinary well-established ecclesiastical jurisdiction continued in full force down to the year 1640, and for reasons which can still be explained and illustrated, at length excited passionate hatred, which was much intensified by the proceedings of the different Courts of High Commission from the time of Queen Elizabeth till the reign of Charles I. The final result was the Act of 16 Chas. I. c. 11 (A.D. 1640), which put an end for twenty-one years to the ecclesiastical jurisdiction, though on the Restoration it was re-established in a much milder form, in which it still retains a shadowy existence.

To some small extent the old ecclesiastical courts were superseded by statute law, as in particular in dealing with witchcraft, which was the subject of punishment by Act of Parliament from 33 Hen. VIII. c. 8 (1541) till 9 Geo. II. c. 5 (1736). Witchcraft then ceased to be even an ecclesiastical offence.

The ordinary ecclesiastical courts were, however, far too weak to deal with the tremendous question of heresy, which fell *primâ facie* under their jurisdiction. One well-known case is mentioned by Bracton in the thirteenth century, of a deacon "qui se apostatavit pro quadam Judæâ," and was burnt; but heresy was all but absolutely unknown in England till the latter part of the fourteenth century. At that time, in consequence of the preaching of Wicliffe's doctrines, passionate efforts were made to find legal means of burning persons adjudged by the clerical power to be heretics.

These efforts were carried so far as to bring about the forgery of an Act of Parliament,[1] and to procure the burning of William Sawtre as for heresy by a writ called the writ *De Hæretico Comburendo*, which I believe to have been a wholly unauthorized exercise of a prerogative invented for the occasion.[2]

These disgraceful measures were followed by two statutes, 2 Hen. IV. c. 15 (1400) and 2 Hen. V. c. 7 (1414), the effect of which was that the bishops' courts obtained authority to declare anyone to be a heretic of whose doctrines they disapproved, and to call upon the sheriff to burn him. These Acts continued in force till 1533, when various changes (the Act of the Six Articles, 31 Hen. VIII. c. 14 (1539), for one) were introduced. In some ways the last-mentioned Act was severe, but it greatly narrowed the powers given by the Acts of 1400 and 1410, which allowed the ecclesiastical judges to define heresy as they pleased, whereas Henry VIII.'s statutes, strange and harsh as they are, do give a sort of definition of it as consisting in certain definite opinions. They also substituted a mode of procedure, of which Hale describes the effect as being to make heresy "in a great measure a secular offence."

Edward VI. restored what was understood after the burning of Sawtre to be the common law—that is to say, the common law with the addition of the supposed writ *De Hæretico Comburendo*, under which two executions at least, those of Jean Bocher and George Van Paar, took place in Edward's reign. Mary restored the Acts of 1400 and 1410, and it was under their provisions that the great persecution of 1555 and the following years took place; and Elizabeth repealed the whole of both her sister's and her father's legislation. When the High Commission was established,

---

[1] *History of the Criminal Law*, vol. ii. p. 443.
[2] *Ibid.*, vol. ii. pp. 447–448.

its powers as to defining heresy were practically almost taken away,[1] but the writ *De Hæretico Comburendo* was still kept alive for the suppression of Anabaptists or Unitarians, a few of whom were burnt in the sixteenth century, and two as late as 1610—one, Legate, by an act of shameful illegality, and merely to please the fanatical or, rather, pedantic animosity of James I.; and another, Wightman, at about the same time, of whom little is known. These were the last executions for heresy in England. The writ *De Hæretico Comburendo* was expressly abolished in 1677 by 29 Chas. II. c. 9.

The old offences against religion thus became obsolete by the year 1677, but a new one of some importance was invented at about the same time. This was the offence of blasphemous libel, to which may be added that of blasphemous words. These offences were originally punishable either by the ecclesiastical courts or by the Star Chamber, or Court of High Commission, but the ecclesiastical courts were disabled by the abolition of the *ex-officio* oath. The Courts of High Commission and Star Chamber were abolished; the Court of King's Bench took up some of their principles and practices, and treated on several occasions blasphemous words and libels (as also obscene libels) as offences against good order and good manners, and also as attacks upon religion, which was to be protected as one of the safeguards of society. The extent to which the law as it stands does in fact condemn the denial of the fundamental doctrines of religion, and the extent to which it is confined to the prohibition of indecency of language, is a matter of dispute on which I have expressed my views elsewhere. It is not necessary here to give any minute account of the matter.[2]

---

[1] *History of the Criminal Law*, vol. ii. p. 461.

[2] *Ibid.*, vol. ii. pp. 469–473; see also note 2 in my *Digest*, Art. 161.

The Acts which at different times were passed for the security and maintenance of the Established Church, and for the restriction by tests and disabilities of Dissenters and Roman Catholics, belong rather to the political history of the country than to the history of the criminal law. Some account of them, however, will be found in my *History*.[1]

OFFENCES AGAINST MORALITY.—Crimes are, as a general rule, immoral actions, but it is only in a few cases that they are punished because they are immoral. In the great majority of cases an immoral act is punished as a crime only when it involves an outrage on some particular person.

The subject is not a pleasant one, and it involves little curiosity or interest. The offences referred to in Arts. 169 and 169A were, I believe, originally of ecclesiastical cognizance, and were first legislated against in 1533 by 25 Hen. VIII. c. 6.[2] Public acts of indecency and obscene libel were formerly punished by the ecclesiastical courts, but more lately by the Court of King's Bench. By far the most important Act of this kind is the Criminal Law Amendment Act of 1885 (48 and 49 Vict. c. 49). To what extent it has effected any improvement in morality is a matter of great doubt, but it has been in operation for only five years, and opinions must naturally differ. That it has in some important respects amended the previous procedure in such matters does not admit of a doubt.

COMMON NUISANCES.—Nuisance *nocumentum* is etymologically a word of the widest possible meaning. It might be used so as to cover all manner of crimes, and might so have been nearly as useful to lawyers desirous of giving a wide sweep to the criminal law as the words libel or con-

---

[1] Vol. ii. pp. 476–494.
[2] *History of the Criminal Law*, vol. ii. pp. 429–430.

spiracy. In fact, the word has been practically harmless,
its ordinary meaning having been fairly maintained. It is
an act not warranted by law, or an omission to discharge
a legal duty, which inconveniences the public in the exercise of rights common to all Her Majesty's subjects.
The following familiar instances set the matter in a clearer
light. The public have a right to breathe the air in a
natural and unpolluted state. A man who makes foul or un-
wholesome smells commits a nuisance unless he can justify
or excuse himself. The public have a right to pass safely
along public highways without danger or interruption. A
person whose duty it is to repair the roads, and who fails
to do so, whereby their safety or convenience is seriously
diminished, commits a nuisance. The public have a right
to be undisturbed by riotous or disorderly proceedings
and collections of ill-conducted people. Those, therefore, who gather together collections of disorderly persons
commit a nuisance. In accordance with this principle,
brothels, gaming-houses, betting-houses, and disorderly
places of entertainment are declared by statute to be
common nuisances. Acts tending to spread infectious
diseases and the like are common nuisances. On the
other hand, an interference with a private right of way, or
noises made by a man in his own house to the annoyance
of his neighbour only, are not public nuisances, which are the
subject of indictment, but only private wrongs, for which the
remedy is by an action for a nuisance or by injunction.

It is highly characteristic of our law that the common
method of deciding upon the existence of a considerable body
of liabilities is by indictments for the offence of not discharging them. An indictment for not repairing a road, for
instance, is the common way of deciding whether the liability
to repair it exists. This is the point at which the criminal
law and the law which protects civil rights practically

run into each other. It is also the appropriate manner of deciding upon questions which in some countries would depend upon the discretion of the police authorities. I have known of a case in which it was proposed to hold a great dog show, which, no doubt, would have pleased and interested a large number of persons; but the scheme was given up because a lawyer's clerk threatened an indictment for nuisance, because 'the dogs would disturb his night's rest. This, again, is very characteristic of the way in which English law protects on occasion the rights of poor and obscure people by decisive means.

Another remarkable matter in connection with the law of nuisances is the nature and extent of the limitations upon it. To a considerable extent the law upon the subject is made up of compromises. It is said in an old case in regard to candle-making in a town, "Le utility del "chose excusera le noisomeness del stink"; and a law which required in a large town the quietness and purity of air which may be fairly expected in the country would be absurd, and inconsistent with the common interest. This principle is unquestionable law, but it requires great care and consideration in its application, for it is limited by others which are not obviously and perhaps not really, consistent with it on all occasions.

In considering whether a thing is or is not a public nuisance, the following principles must, amongst others, be borne in mind. A jury is not entitled to sum up the conveniences and inconveniences to the public of a given act or omission, and to pronounce it to be or not to be a nuisance according to the result. Striking illustrations of this are given in the two well-known cases of the telegraph-pole and a tramway not authorized by Parliament. A telegraph-pole which occupied a certain part of a public highway caused no perceptible inconvenience to anyone, and was a necessary part of an apparatus which was, no doubt, as a whole, highly convenient. In the absence of express Parliamentary sanction, it was, however, held to be a nuisance because it was inconsistent with an unqualified right possessed by every member of the public to pass and repass over the space which it occupied.[1] So of the tramway, which, though it may have been a convenience on the whole to passengers, interfered with the unqualified right of every person to use every part of the road for traffic at all times.[2]

The question whether the use of a road or river is interfered with, in fact, may have light thrown upon it by the effect of staiths, embankments, and the like; but if the interference is admitted, Parliamentary sanction for them is required.

It is also to be remembered that it is part of the definition of a nuisance that the act or omission by which it is constituted must be unlawful. Parliament frequently authorizes what, without its authority, would be unlawful acts. Such, however, as are authorized cease to be nuisances. A strong illustration is to be found in the case of a railway which was authorized by statute, and frightened horses and otherwise interfered with the ordinary traffic on a neighbouring road. This was held not to be a nuisance.

---

[1] R. *v.* United Kingdom Telegraph Company, 3 *F. and F.*, 73.
[2] R. *v.* Train, 2 *B. and S.*, 640.

CHAPTER XII.

OFFENCES AGAINST THE PERSON—CASES OF JUSTIFIABLE AND EXCUSABLE FORCE AGAINST THE PERSON; CASES OF NEGLIGENT OFFENCES AGAINST THE PERSON.

CHAP. XII.

In the previous chapters I have given an account of what appeared to me to require notice in regard to crimes against public tranquillity, by violence or without violence; crimes in which foreign countries are interested; crimes committed by and against public officers; crimes against religion and morals; and public nuisances,—all of which have the common character of being directed against the public, or some part of it, rather than against particular individuals.

I now come to consider common offences against individuals. Nearly all of these—I think I may say all of any importance or of ordinary occurrence—are punished by the 24 and 25 Vict. c. 100, c. 96, c. 97, c. 98, c. 99, or c. 100, the five Consolidation Acts which form the nearest approach contained in our law to a Criminal Code.[1] In general, these Acts speak for themselves, and need little explanation. This is particularly true of c. 97, relating to offences of which arson may be taken as the type; c. 98, relating to forgery; and c. 99, relating to offences against the coinage; but the

---

[1] 24 and 25 Vict. c. 96, theft; c. 97, malicious injuries to property; c. 98, forgery; c. 99, coinage; c. 100, the person.

law which deals with offences against the person (c. 100) assumes in the reader a previous knowledge of the doctrines of the common law relating to the employment of force against the person of another, and of the common law definitions of certain crimes which the Act punishes but does not define. I proceed to consider the principles by which these matters are regulated.

The first general principle which runs through the whole law on this subject is that any interference whatever with the person of another, or with his personal liberty, requires special justification. The general rule is that everyone is entitled to be free from all bodily harm voluntarily inflicted, and from all restraint, either by mechanical means or by threats or the show of force, from going to any place to which he has a lawful right to go, or being in any place in which he has a lawful right to be. The protection of the law extends to some cases in which negligence, and even to cases in which accident, causes bodily harm.

This general principle is accompanied by another equally general. It is that, even in cases in which the application of force to the person of another is on any ground justifiable, such force as is reasonably necessary for the purpose which justifies it is all that can be justified, and that any excess is unlawful.

These principles are assumed in all cases, but are nowhere explicitly stated in an authoritative shape; but it is necessary to state them explicitly, in order to state in a clear and systematic way the principles which apply to the subject.

There are two general heads under which all cases of the justifiable employment of force against the person of another may be classed. The first is force used either in the execution of legal process or in the prevention of crime in various forms. The second is the case of private defence in the large sense of the word—that is to say, in a sense which includes not merely the defence of the person from violence, but the assertion by force of any right which is allowed by law to be so asserted or protected. I include under the expression, for instance, not only the act of a man who forcibly resists a trespasser seeking to enter upon his land, but also the act of an owner who forcibly ejects a trespasser who has entered upon it.

For the sake of brevity, the two may be called force in aid of justice and force in private defence. These two forms of lawful force to a considerable extent run into each other, for an act may fall under both heads. Thus, summary arrest is for certain crimes a form of legal process. A man who arrests a burglar is at once preventing a crime, arresting a criminal, and, it may be, defending himself from violence ; and of course the effect of the union of these different characters is to give the person in whom they are united all the rights which he would have in any one of them. In order to be understood, however, they must be considered separately.

FORCE JUSTIFIABLE IN AID OF JUSTICE.—This is of two kinds—namely, (1) force used in the execution of the law, and (2) force used for the suppression of violent crime.

(1) Force used in the execution of the law may be used for a great variety of purposes. Common illustrations are the execution on criminals of legal sentences, and the enforcement of legal decisions in civil cases, as, for instance, by giving possession of land to the successful party in a lawsuit, or by the removal of a structure decided to be a public nuisance. But all these cases depend upon one plain principle : whatever may be the object to be obtained, the right and duty of the proper executive officer is to obtain it

by the use of any kind and amount of force which may be necessary for that purpose. The amount and kind of force to be used can be limited only by the resistance opposed to it. The plain duty of the executive power is to overcome that resistance at whatever risk.

(2) The use of force for the suppression of crimes of violence has given rise to many questions of interest connected principally with cases in which the crimes suppressed were regarded with sympathy, and in some cases with approval, by those who were opposed to their suppression. Unlawful assemblies and riots are judged of in a very different way by people of different political and social views. I have considered the most important of these questions as carefully as I could in different parts of my *History of the Criminal Law,* where I have traced the history of the law on the subject and the legislation relating to it from the first institution of watchmen to the organization of the modern police force, and the gradual establishment of what is, in fact though not in form, a standing army.

The following pages are partly quoted and partly condensed from my *History.*

The common law right and duty, not only of the conservators of the peace, but of all private persons (according to their power), to keep the peace and to disperse and, if necessary, to arrest those who break it, is obvious and well settled, but it is also obvious that it can hardly be discharged to advantage without special statutory power. In the earlier stages of our history the power and turbulence of the nobility was so great that private war was all but continual, and the preservation of the peace by force of arms was the first duty of all rulers. Violence in all its forms was so common, and the suppression of force by force so simple a matter, that special legislation did not appear

¹ *History of the Criminal Law,* vol. i. pp. 184–200.

CHAP. XII. necessary in very early times.[1] The earliest express recognition by statute of this state of things to which I can refer occurs in the Statute of Treasons. After defining treason positively, the statute proceeds to say what shall not be held to be treason. "And if percase any man of "this realm ride armed covertly" (it should be translated "openly," the French is "descovert") "or secretly with "men of arms against any other to slay him, or rob "him, or take him, or retain him till he hath made fine "or ransom for to have his deliverance, it is not the "mind of the king nor his council that in such case it "shall be judged treason, but shall be judged felony or "trespass according to the laws of the land of old time "used, and according as the case requireth." In other words, private war, whatever else it may be, is not treason.[2]

A history of the legislation of the fifteenth and sixteenth centuries, is followed by an account of the existing law on the subject.

At the beginning of the eighteenth century was passed the famous Act, 1 Geo. I. st. 2, c. 5, still in force, and commonly known as the Riot Act. It increases the severity of the Tudor Acts (which expired at the death of Elizabeth) by making it felony without benefit of clergy for twelve rioters to continue together for one hour after the making by a magistrate of a proclamation[3] to them to

---

[1] See, however, 7 Edw. I. st. 1 (1279), as to coming armed to Parliament, and 33 Edw. I. st. 2 (1304), a definition of conspirators.

[2] *History of the Criminal Law*, vol. i. p. 201.

[3] " Our Sovereign Lady the Queen chargeth and commandeth all persons " being assembled immediately to disperse themselves, and peaceably to de- " part to their habitations or to their lawful business, upon the pains con- " tained in the Act made in the first year of King George for preventing " tumults and riotous assemblies. God save the Queen." The making of this proclamation is commonly, but very incorrectly, called reading the Riot Act.

disperse. It then requires the magistrates to seize and apprehend all persons so continuing together, and it provides that if the persons so assembled, or any of them, "happen to be killed, maimed, or hurt, in dispersing, "seizing, or apprehending, or endeavouring to disperse, "seize, or apprehend them," the magistrates and those who act under their orders shall be indemnified. As a standing army had come into existence before this Act passed, the effect of it was that after making the proclamation and waiting for an hour the magistrates might order the troops to fire upon the rioters or to charge them sword in hand. To say so in so many words would, no doubt, have given great offence, but the effect of the indirect hint at the employment of armed force given by the statute was singular. It seems to have been generally understood that the enactment was negative as well as positive; that troops not only might be ordered to act against a mob if the conditions of the Act were complied with, but that they might not be so employed without the fulfilment of such conditions. This view of the law has been on several occasions decided to be altogether erroneous. The true doctrine on the subject was much considered, both in the case of Lord George Gordon's Riots in 1780, and in the case of the Bristol Riots in 1831. It may be shortly stated as follows. The fact that soldiers are permanently embodied and subjected by the Mutiny Act to military discipline, and bound to obey the lawful orders of their superior officers, does not in any degree exempt them from the obligation incumbent on all Her Majesty's subjects to keep the peace and disperse unlawful assemblies. On the contrary, it gives them special and peculiar facilities for discharging that duty. In a case of extreme emergency they may lawfully do so without being required by the magistrates. In the words of Lord

CHAP. XII. Chief Justice Tindal,[1] in his charge to the grand jury at Bristol, January 2nd, 1832 :—"The law acknowledges "no distinction between the soldier and the private in- "dividual. The soldier is still a citizen, lying under the "same obligation and invested with the same autho- "rity to preserve the peace of the king as any other "subject. If the one is bound to attend the call of the "civil magistrate, so also is the other. If the one may "interfere for that purpose when the occasion demands "it, without the requisition of the magistrate, so may "the other too. If the one may employ arms for that "purpose when arms are necessary, the soldier may do the "same. Undoubtedly, the same exercise of discretion which "requires the private subject to act in subordination to "and in aid of, the magistrate rather than upon his own "authority before recourse is had to arms, ought to operate "in a still stronger degree with a military force. But "where the danger is pressing and immediate ; where a "felony has actually been committed or cannot otherwise "be prevented, and from the circumstances of the case "no opportunity is offered of obtaining a requisition from "the proper authorities, the military subjects of the king, "like his civil subjects, not only may but are bound, "to do their utmost of their own authority to prevent "the perpetration of outrage, to put down riot and tumult, "and to preserve the lives and property of the people. "Still further, by the common law not only is each private "subject bound to exert himself to the utmost, but every "sheriff, constable, and other peace officer is called upon "to do all that in them lies for the suppression of riot, "and each has authority to command all other subjects "of the king to assist them in that under the king."

The result of this view of the subject is to put soldiers

[1] 5 *C. and P.*, 261, &c.

acting under the orders of their military superiors in an awkward position. By the ordinary principles of the common law they are, speaking generally, justified only in using such force as is reasonably necessary for the suppression of a riot. By the Mutiny Act and the Articles of War they are bound to execute any lawful order which they may receive from their military superior, and an order to fire upon a mob is lawful if such an act is reasonably necessary for the dispersion of rioters. If not reasonably necessary, it would not be a lawful order. The hardship upon soldiers is, that, if a soldier kills a man in obedience to his officer's orders, the question whether what was done was more than was reasonably necessary has to be decided by a jury, probably upon a trial for murder; whereas, if he disobeys his officer's orders to fire because he regards them as unlawful, the question whether they were unlawful as having commanded something not reasonably necessary would have to be decided by a court-martial upon the trial of the soldier for disobeying orders, and for obvious reasons the jury and the court-martial are likely to take different views as to the reasonable necessity, and therefore as to the lawfulness, of such an order.

I do not think, however, that the question how far superior orders would justify soldiers or sailors in making an attack upon civilians has ever been brought before the courts of law in such a manner as to be fully considered and determined. Probably upon such an argument it would be found that the order of a military superior would justify his inferiors in executing any orders for giving which they might fairly suppose their superior officer to have good reasons. Soldiers might reasonably think that their officer had good grounds for ordering them to fire into a disorderly crowd which to them might not appear to be at that moment engaged in acts of dangerous violence, but soldiers could hardly suppose that their officer could have any good grounds for ordering them to fire a volley down a crowded street when no disturbance of any kind was either in progress or apprehended. The doctrine that a soldier is bound under all circumstances whatever to obey his superior officer would be fatal to military discipline itself; for it would justify the private in shooting the colonel by the orders of the captain, or in deserting to the enemy on the field of battle on the order of his immediate superior. I think it is not less monstrous to suppose that superior orders would justify a soldier in the massacre of unoffending civilians in time of peace, or in the exercise of inhuman cruelties, such as the slaughter of women and children during a rebellion. The only line that presents itself to my mind is that a soldier should be protected by orders for which he might reasonably believe his officer to have good grounds. The inconvenience of being subject to two jurisdictions, the sympathies of which are not unlikely to be opposed to each other, is an inevitable consequence of the double necessity of preserving on the one hand the supremacy of the law and on the other the discipline of the army.[1]

Beyond the employment of the ordinary forces of the Crown for the suppression of a riot lies a proclamation of martial law. This has never occurred in England since the Civil Wars in Charles I.'s time; but the prerogative of proclaiming it has been asserted in Ireland on several occasions, for the last time, I think, in 1833 (3 and 4 Will. IV. c. 4), and it was used in the most vigorous way for the suppression of the Rebellion of 1798. It has also taken place on several occasions in the colonies and in India. Of the legal effects of a proclamation of martial law I have given a full account in my *History*.[2]

[1] *History of the Criminal Law,* vol. i. pp. 202–206.   [2] Vol. i. pp. 207–216.

The result of it is thus summed up on p. 215 :—

(1) Martial law is the assumption by officers of the Crown of absolute power, exercised by military force, for the suppression of an insurrection, and the restoration of order and lawful authority.

(2) The officers of the Crown are justified in any exertion of physical force, extending to the destruction of life and property to any extent, and in any manner that may be required for the purpose. They are not justified in the use of cruel and excessive means, but are liable civilly or criminally for such excess. They are not justified in inflicting punishment after resistance is suppressed, and after the ordinary courts of justice can be reopened.

The principle by which their responsibility is measured is well expressed in the case of Wright *v.* Fitzgerald.[1] Wright was a French master of Clonmel, who, after the suppression of the Irish Rebellion in 1798, brought an action against Mr. Fitzgerald, the sheriff of Tipperary, for having cruelly flogged him without due inquiry. Martial law was in full force at that time, and an Act of Indemnity had afterwards been passed to excuse all breaches of the law committed in the suppression of the rebellion. In summing up, Mr. Justice Chamberlain, with whom Lord Yelverton agreed, said :—

"The jury were not to imagine that the Legisla-
"ture, by enabling magistrates to justify under the In-
"demnity Bill, had released them from the feelings
"of humanity, or permitted them wantonly to exercise
"power, even though it were to put down rebellion.
"They expected that in all cases there should be a
"grave and serious examination into the conduct of the
"supposed criminal, and every act should show a mind
"intent to discover guilt, not to inflict torture. By exami-

[1] 27 *St. Tr.* 765.

"nation and trial he did not mean that sort of examina-
"tion and trial which they were now engaged in, but
"such examination and trial the best the nature of the
"case and existing circumstances should allow of. That
"this must have been the intention of the Legislature was
"manifest from the expression 'magistrates and all other
"'persons,' which provides that as every man, whether magis-
"trate or not, was authorized to suppress rebellion, and
"was to be justified by that law for his acts, it is required
"that he should not exceed the necessity which gave him that
"power, and that he should show in his justification that he
"had used every possible means to ascertain the guilt which
"he had punished, and, above all, no deviation from the com-
"mon principles of humanity should appear in his conduct."

Wright recovered £500 damages, and when Mr. Fitzgerald applied to the Irish Parliament for an indemnity
he could not get one.

(3) The courts-martial, as they are called, by which
martial law, in this sense of the word, is administered,
are not, properly speaking, courts-martial or courts at
all. They are merely committees formed for the purpose
of carrying into execution the discretionary power assumed
by the Government. On the one hand, they are not
obliged to proceed in the manner pointed out by the Mutiny
Act and Articles of War. On the other hand, if they do
so proceed, they are not protected by them as the members
of a real court-martial might be, except so far as such
proceedings are evidence of good faith. They are justified
in doing, with any forms and in any manner, whatever
is necessary to suppress insurrection, and to restore peace
and the authority of the law. They are personally liable for
any acts which they may commit in excess of that power,
even if they act in strict accordance with the Mutiny Act
and Articles of War.

As for the use of force for the purpose of preventing crimes of violence of the common kind, and for the purpose of apprehending persons who commit them, the law requires an historical as well as a systematic explanation. I have mentioned in my *History* [1] the steps by which the great prerogative of keeping the peace was at first exercised locally by the sheriffs and constables; how the coroners were added about the end of the twelfth century; and how the ancient system was completed by the appointment of justices of the peace under various statutes passed in the reign of Edward III. I have also referred to the ancient institutions of frankpledge, hue and cry, the Assizes of Northampton (A.D. 1166) and Clarendon (A.D. 1176), the Assize of Arms (A.D. 1181), and the eyres of the justices, as described by Bracton. All these laws and institutions are proofs that from the very earliest period of English history one of the first objects of the law was to secure the instant and summary arrest of criminals by the force of the neighbourhood, which was justified in using violence to any extent in arresting them or preventing their escape. The various institutions which I have mentioned became superannuated, and are now superseded by the police system established by numerous statutes, the first of which was passed in 1829, viz. 10 Geo. IV. c. 44, which constitutes the Metropolitan Police District.

Every one of these laws and institutions assumes and rests upon the principle that everyone may, and that all officers of justice must, arrest a felon in a summary way as soon as he has notice of his crime, using any required degree of force for that purpose, and for the purpose of preventing his escape, even if it extends to the use of deadly violence, and actually kills. Of course, in the present day, such extreme cases do not occur, but the language used by Hale

[1] Vol. i. pp. 184–200.

and other authorities, and justified by a consideration of the institutions with reference to which it was used, would justify a person whose pocket was picked, or indeed anyone who tried to arrest the thief, in shooting or stabbing him if he could not otherwise be prevented from getting into a crowd in which he would escape.

I do not think it necessary to enter minutely upon the question what are the offences for which summary arrest is permitted. They are enumerated, and the authorities respecting them are given, in my *Digest of Procedure*, Arts. 96–98. They show in what respect a police-constable's position differs from that of an ordinary person. I do not think it has ever been decided that a summary arrest under the provisions of a statute for misdemeanour may be executed with the same unrestricted violence as an arrest for felony. Granting that it is lawful to fire a rifle at a boy who steals a handkerchief and runs away too quickly to be otherwise stopped, I am not sure that this would be held to be true of a boy found by the owner unlawfully and maliciously cutting a stick from his hedge or taking his gate off its hinges.[1] The law as to felonies might advantageously, I think, be limited in several ways, and it might possibly be held that some such limitations would be recognized if the case arose.

THE RIGHT OF PRIVATE DEFENCE.—Many cases of private defence are, as I have already pointed out, cases of violence in support of justice ; and in cases where the two coincide, the justification of violence being in support of justice is the best to be relied upon, as it is the more emphatic and peremptory of the two. If a man attempts to rob another by violence, and the person assaulted shoots him, the fact that the shooting was for the prevention of a felony and for the arrest of the felon is a complete defence ; though on a variety

[1] 24 and 25 Vict. c. 97, ss. 25 and 61.

of possible grounds it might be difficult to prove that if the act were regarded as one of mere self-defence it was not excessive.

For this reason it will be unnecessary to deal in this place with those acts of private defence which may be justified on the ground that the person against whom violence is used is a criminal. It will be enough to say something of acts of private defence in cases which do not arise out of crime. They may be divided into three classes :—

(1) Defence against violence to the person of the man who defends himself.

(2) Defence against the invasion of his proprietary rights.

(3) Forcible assertion of his proprietary rights.

Private defence against personal violence can very rarely occur except in cases of crime, for it is difficult to put a case of personal violence which is neither justifiable nor criminal. The only one at all likely to happen which occurs to me are cases of mistake or madness. A man might, no doubt, attack another under the impression that he was a robber, or a madman might attack another in a frenzy. In each of these cases the right of the person assaulted would be the same—namely, to defend himself as circumstances might require, using such violence only as was reasonably necessary for effecting his purpose. Thus, if a man were assaulted by a madman in such a way as to endanger his life, he might kill him if necessary to save his own life. If he were similarly assaulted by a robber, he might not only kill him to prevent the robbery, but might kill him if he could not otherwise prevent his escape. He might justify such violence only to the madman as might be necessary to prevent him from harming others; but even for that purpose he might not do him any deadly injury, unless possibly as the only means of saving another from immediate death or deadly injury. The only remark on this subject which need be made is that in all cases, even in the case of a crime against a man's own person, it is his duty, if reasonably possible, to avoid a breach of the peace by appealing, if he can, to the protection of the law; to call in a constable, if it can be done, before defending yourself against threats of violence; to retreat as far as can be reasonably done before a blow is returned. This is stated more pointedly and harshly by Hale and others than would now, I think, be correct, because people in those times carried arms and fought with them upon trifling occasions. There is reason and wisdom in the doctrine that, if A draws his sword to provoke B to a duel, B must retreat, as was said, "to the wall" before he draws and defends himself; but I should not be prepared to hold without argument that a man is bound to run away from a drunken bully who strikes him, if the person attacked is fortunate enough to be able to knock down his assailant. I have, on several occasions, allowed, and even more or less invited, juries to acquit people of manslaughter who unintentionally and unexpectedly caused death by returning a blow in what the jury regarded as reasonable self-defence. The greatest caution ought, however, to be used in regard to this matter. A deliberate fight, even with fists, is in all cases unlawful; and self-defence against a slight assault must, if justifiable at all, be confined within the narrowest limits—that is, it must be confined to what is reasonably necessary to avoid personal injury or to stop, not to punish, the grossest personal insult.

(2) DEFENCE AGAINST THE INVASION OF PROPRIETARY RIGHTS AND IN THEIR ASSERTION.—The leading principle in cases of this kind is that in nearly all cases rights of all kinds should be protected, not by the person entitled to them, but by the law of the land and its executive officers. In some cases, however, private defence is, to a limited extent, permissible. Generally speaking, the principle is this :—The person injured may prevent the wrong-doer, by force not ex-

tending to blows or wounding, from pursuing or effecting his
unlawful purpose, but may not strike or wound him, either
in order to prevent his unlawful act or in order to punish
him for having acted unlawfully. For instance, he may put
a trespasser out of his house or out of his field by force, but
he may not strike him, still less may he shoot or stab him.
If the wrong-doer resists, the person who is on the defensive
may overcome his resistance, and may proportion his efforts
to the violence which the wrong-doer uses. If the wrong-
doer assaults the person who is defending his property, that
person is in the position of a man wrongfully assaulted, and
may use whatever violence may become necessary for the
protection of his person. It must be added that an attack
upon a man's dwelling-house is always regarded as almost as
strong a justification for violence in defence as an attack on his
person. In the assertion of a proprietary right, force is less
frequently justifiable, and to a smaller degree, than in its
defence. This is not so much a matter of law as a wise
and necessary rule of evidence in appreciating the nature
and extent of the force used, for such forcible assertions of
right usually border, at all events, on criminal offences, such
as riot, unlawful assembly, forcible entry, and wilful damage.
If a large number of persons pull down inclosures, or walk
along a disputed road, or the like, there is great danger
of their doing so in such numbers, or with the accom-
paniment of such speeches or other proceedings, as are
likely to cause a breach of the peace; and there can be
no doubt that all such proceedings are unlawful. For
instance, if two parties of men set out, the one to exercise and the other to resist the exercise of an alleged
right to abate a nuisance, or to pass along a disputed tho-
roughfare, the justices of the peace would be justified in
preventing each party from taking such steps, and the
meetings, if held, would be unlawful assemblies if shown

to be likely to cause a breach of the peace, irrespectively of the merits of the question whether the alleged right existed or not.

There are some other cases in which the use of private force may be justified, as, for instance, the right of a schoolmaster to correct his scholars, the rights of the captain of a merchantman incidental to the maintenance of discipline, and some others; but I do not think these involve any principles of interest.

MISTAKES.—The employment of force against the person of another is the part of the law in which the question of the effect of mistakes most frequently arises. These mistakes may be mistakes of fact or of law, and they may be made either by a constable or other officer of justice, or by a private person; so that the question is divided into mistakes of law made by an officer, mistakes of law made by a private person, mistakes of fact made by an officer, and mistakes of fact made by a private person. Regard must also be had in all these cases to the distinction between the civil and criminal consequences of all these mistakes.

In all cases of mistake it must be assumed that the mistake is made in good faith and without culpable negligence, the meaning and effect of which will be explained further on. Speaking generally, the effect of such a mistake is, in reference to penal consequences at least, the same as if the facts supposed to exist had really existed. A man who kills a person breaking into his house because he mistakenly believes him to be a robber is justified as if he had been a robber, whether he is a constable or a private person; but there is in some cases an important distinction between them, especially in reference to civil consequences. A man who mistakenly supposes that the law imposes a duty upon him, and upon whom such a duty would be imposed by the facts which he believes to be true, is in a better position with regard to civil consequences than a man who merely supposes himself to have a right, but not to be under a duty, to act as he does. Thus it is a good plea on an action for false imprisonment that the defendant being a constable reasonably suspected that the prisoner committed felony ; but if the defendant is a private person he must prove in addition that a felony was actually committed. If an action for false imprisonment is brought against two persons—namely, A, a policeman, and B, a private person ; and it is proved that B gave the plaintiff in charge to A for picking a pocket, as B thought, in his sight, A is justified and entitled to a verdict if he proves that he acted on B's information, but B is not justified unless he proves that some one did pick a pocket, and that he was mistaken only in the identity of the man. I believe, though I cannot prove it by any definite authority, that if a policeman is ordered by his superior officer to disperse a crowd under such circumstances that he may, and does, naturally and reasonably believe that the order was lawful, he would be protected at all events from criminal consequences by the order, even if it were illegal as not being justified by the circumstances. The rule as to the particular case of false imprisonment is exceptionally favourable to a defendant who has mistakenly arrested a man without a warrant, for it certainly results in the consequence that one person may suffer for the mistake of another, although the sufferer is completely innocent. I do not quite understand why, because my pocket is picked, a private person who takes it into his head that A B, an honest man, who was miles off at the time, was the person who picked it, is with impunity to cause him to be arrested and imprisoned from Saturday till Monday. I suppose the answer is that it is desirable to protect *bonâ fide* prosecutors. For the purposes of civil consequences the general rule is that a volunteer acts at his peril.

As to mistakes in law, the only cases in which they are likely to cause difficulty are cases in which constables and other executive officers act under irregular warrants.

NEGLIGENT OFFENCES AGAINST THE PERSON.—I have now gone through the principal cases of justifiable and excusable violence against the person, though I do not pretend, and it is not the object of this book, to treat completely of all the cases which may arise in connection with the subject. I now pass to the subject of negligence, which is the omission to discharge a legal duty of whatever kind, and such an omission may be either (1) intentional, (2) culpable, or (3) not culpable.

There are four cases in which the negligent infliction of bodily harm is criminal. The only statutory offences of the sort known to me are defined by 24 and 25 Vict. c. 100, s. 31.[1] They consist of negligence endangering a person conveyed on a railway, and the causing of bodily harm by misconduct or neglect in driving. These offences are not often prosecuted, and are of no special interest. The only cases of criminal negligence which are at once common and important are cases in which death is caused by it.

Upon intentional negligence I have only one remark to make. If it is the neglect of a legal duty, it does not differ, as far as criminal or civil consequences are concerned, from an act. A mother who, having the means to do so, wilfully omits to feed her infant child, and so starves it to death, is both legally and morally in the same position as if she put it to death by the means which caused its death; and the same might be said of a man who, in order to prevent the proper ventilation of a mine, wilfully omitted to open air-ways necessary for that purpose. Negligence of this kind may accordingly be regarded as being, for all purposes, on the same footing as an act, and must always be culpable when an act would be criminal. No further notice need be taken of

[1] *Digest*, Art. 240.

it. Indeed, I use the words intentional negligence solely in order to mark the fact that in some cases acts and omissions stand on the same footing.

It is, however, to be remarked that the omission must be an omission to discharge a legal duty. An omission to do what it is not a legal duty to do is no crime at all, even if the omission causes, and is intended to cause, death. It is not a criminal offence to refuse to throw a rope to a drowning man, or to allow a man to walk over a cliff or into a quicksand when a word of advice would save him.[1]

The difficult matter to deal with is to define the nature of negligence which is culpable, though not intentional, and to distinguish it from that which is not culpable, though it may be actionable as a wrong. The best mode of understanding this subject is to begin by considering what are the duties which are imposed by law on persons whose conduct may preserve or destroy human life. I think these duties may all be reduced under three heads, which, stated in a summary way, are these. It is a legal duty, incumbent on every person, who, by law, or by contract, or by the act of taking charge, wrongfully or not, is in charge of any other person, to provide such last-mentioned person with the necessaries of life, if he cannot provide for himself or withdraw from the care of the person first mentioned. It is the duty of everyone who does any act which is or may be dangerous to life to employ proper precautions in doing it. It is the duty of every person who undertakes to administer surgical or medical treatment, or to do any other lawful act of a dangerous kind which requires special knowledge, skill, attention, or caution, to employ in doing it a common

---

[1] Lord Macaulay has some curious remarks on this in his notes on the Indian Penal Code. I lent the book to Mrs. Cross (George Eliot) for her novel of *Middlemarch*. It approaches the subject, but in *Daniel Deronda* a much more striking illustration of the principle is given.

amount of such knowledge, skill, attention, and caution, or at all events, if he acts as a matter of necessity, to do his best. The omission to discharge these duties and others of the same kind, if any such there are, is criminal, unless it is so slight that the jury do not regard it as such. I do not think it is possible to be more precise than this, or that the attempt to be so would really be of any advantage. It is easy to give instances which fall on different sides of the line between culpable and not culpable negligence, but I do not think it possible to lay down any principle on which such cases can be decided. An engine-driver causes the death of passengers by omitting to notice signals because he went drunk on to his engine. No one would doubt this was culpable negligence. A signalman causes death by omitting to make proper signals. He proves that his hours of work were very long, and his duties were extremely arduous. This is evidence which may be worth more or less according to circumstances, to show that his negligence was not culpable so as to make him guilty of manslaughter, though both the company and he (if he were worth suing) might be liable in damages. Juries, in my experience, have no difficulty in dealing with this question. The only general observation I can make upon it is that in this, as in all cases in which the criminal law is brought into play, the connection between law and morals ought, as far as possible, to be maintained when it is possible; and it may often be a guide to a proper conclusion in this matter to consider whether the negligence of which the accused person was guilty was morally blamable or not, it being always borne in mind that it is a moral duty to appreciate the extreme importance of duties on the due discharge of which the safety of many persons depends, and to be alert, active, and attentive in their discharge. If a man is to be a surgeon, a station-master, or the captain of a ship, it

is his duty to know his business fairly well, to have reasonably steady nerves, and not to lose his head in a difficulty. If he has a specially weak or foolish head, or
specially sensitive nerves, he ought to know it, and not try
to discharge duties for which he is not competent.

ACCIDENT.—I will conclude this chapter by a short account
of accidental bodily harm. The history of the subject is exceedingly curious, and was much misunderstood even while
the old law upon the subject was still in force. Upon this
I must refer to my history of the law relating to murder and
manslaughter,[1] which contains a full account of a number of
matters which it would be uninteresting and uninstructive
to abridge. What is said of accident is as follows [2]:—The
cases in which homicide is excusable may all be reduced
under the head of accident—that is to say, killing without any
intention to kill or hurt—and upon this the law of England
recognizes two distinctions. Death may be caused accidentally or, which is the same thing, unintentionally, in the doing
of an act in itself lawful or in itself unlawful. It may also
occur by reason of the omission to perform a legal duty
tending to the preservation of life. The following are typical
instances of these four classes of accidental death :—

1. A fires a gun at a mark. The gun bursts and kills B.

2. A fires a gun at a mark without giving proper warning
or taking proper care in placing the mark, and kills B.

3. A fires a gun at C with intent to murder him. The
gun bursts and kills B, A's accomplice.

4. A fires a gun at B, intending to murder him, and kills
C, whom A did not warn to stand out of the way.

I may add that in the four cases referred to under the
law as it stands, A would, in Case 1, be guilty of no crime
at all. In Case 2 he would be guilty of manslaughter;
but if B had been dangerously wounded instead of dying, A

[1] Vol. iii. pp. 1–107.   [2] *Hist.* vol. iii. pp. 15–16.

K

CHAP. XII. would be liable only civilly. In Cases 3 and 4, A would be guilty of murder at common law, and under 24 and 25 Vict. c. 100, s. 18, would be guilty of felonious wounding, if B had been only wounded (slightly or dangerously) instead of being killed; or if A intended only to wound C slightly and wounded B, whether slightly or severely, A would have been guilty only of unlawful and malicious wounding. The Act says (s. 18), "who with intent to do grievous bodily harm to *any person* "wounds *any person,*" and (s. 20) "unlawfully and maliciously "wounds any person";[1] words which take in the wounding of one with intent to wound another, or by the wounding of one by an act which is malicious and unlawful as against another.

This is a striking instance of the advantage of statute over common law, though I think the common law in this case is rational and well understood.

[1] See Regina *v.* Latimer, 17 Queen's Bench Division, 359 ; and my *Digest,* Art. 239 (2).

CHAPTER XIII.

OFFENCES AGAINST THE PERSON (*continued*)—DEFINITIONS ASSUMED IN 24 AND 25 VICT. C. 100.

THE bulk of the criminal law as to offences against the person is contained in 24 and 25 Vict. c. 100 (1861), "An "Act to consolidate and amend the Statute Law of England "and Ireland relating to Offences against the Person."

The greater part of it requires no explanation or remark whatever; but as the most important of the crimes which it punishes are defined by the common law, it presupposes an acquaintance with the common law definitions, and this presupposes some historical observations on their gradual development.

The first series of sections (1–10) deal with murder and manslaughter. After a judicial experience of ten years, in the course of which I must, I should think, have disposed of at least a hundred cases of murder or manslaughter, I am, I think, entitled to say that I have never found reason to doubt the accuracy and completeness either of the distribution of the subject of homicide, or of the definitions of the various crimes and common law doctrines stated in chapters xxiii. and xxiv. of my *Digest*. To this there is one exception. I doubt whether Art. 223 (*e*) is law. It is generally supposed to be so. But for reasons given in my *History*, vol. iii. pp. 57, 58, and 69, I have doubts about it. It is

K 2

founded on the well-known dictum of Foster, that shooting at a fowl with intent to steal it and killing a man is murder, because of the felonious intent, whereas if the thing shot at were a wild bird the accidental killing of a man would be but barely manslaughter. In the passages already referred to, I suggest some reasons for thinking that this doctrine is as much mistaken in law as it is repugnant to common-sense and humanity.

For this reason I shall content myself with giving an account of the reasons why the subject of homicide is arranged and defined as it is in my *Digest*, with as much historical matter as is necessary to show how the distinction between murder and manslaughter came to be made, and what it means.

I will first explain the grounds on which my systematic exposition of the existing law is founded.

Having stated the propositions already explained or referred to as to the justifiable, excusable, negligent, and accidental application of force to the human body, I proceed to the consideration of homicide. This is not now a technical legal term, though the word is used and defined with perfect correctness and completeness by Bracton. "Homicidium est " hominis occisio ab homine facta." Though this definition is simplicity itself, it involves questions of principle not at all obvious. They are—At what period, for the purpose of the definition, does a person become a human being? What acts amount to killing? These questions are answered in full detail, and the authorities for the answers are given, in Art. 218–222 of my *Digest*. They require considerable detail. For common purposes, it is enough to say that a child becomes a human being as soon as it issues in a living state from its mother's body, and not before; and that killing is causing death by an act or omission without which the person killed would not have died when he did, and which is directly and immediately connected with his death. This may appear at first sight a merely pedantic substitution of many words for one, but it is necessary in order to show the necessity for something closer and more definite than the mere word "killing" would imply. The illustrations to Art. 219 show the necessity for the definition. Such a phrase as " He killed his wife ; he broke her heart and killed her by his " infamous behaviour," might be a natural way of expressing the real belief of the speaker, but it would not necessarily mean that the person spoken of had killed his wife in the sense of Art. 219. I give my reasons in the illustrations for thinking that Iago and Fagin did not in this sense kill Desdemona and Charlotte.

I have also dealt with the cases of an act being the remote cause or one of several causes of death (Art. 220), and with some cases in which the causing of death is not regarded as homicide. These cases involve matters of a good deal of curiosity which I here pass over.

Passing from these preliminary matters, I come to the classification of homicide as being unlawful or not unlawful, in the sense of not being punishable by law. Upon considering the contents of the last chapter, it will be found that all cases of homicide may be classified according to the following table, the distinctions contained in which are inherent in the nature of things, and ought to be, and I believe are, in a clumsy way provided for by all bodies of criminal law :—

Homicide must be committed either

By an act ——————— or by an
omission

Accompanied by
an intention to
kill or hurt

or not accompanied
by an intention to
kill or hurt

Such intention
being lawful
(1)

or such inten-
tion being un-
lawful
(2)

The act
itself being
lawful
(3)

or the act
itself being
unlawful
(4)

To discharge
a legal duty

Amounting to
culpable negli-
gence
(5)

or not amounting
to culpable negli-
gence
(6)

To do an act not
amounting to a
legal duty [1]
(7)

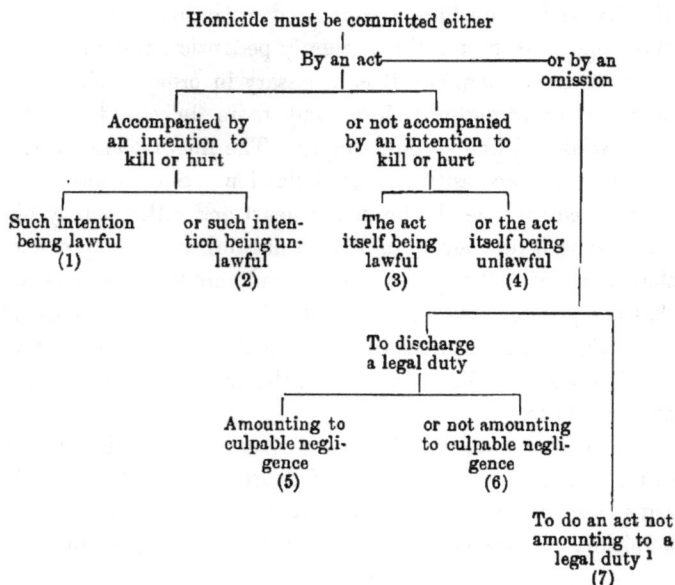

Of these seven kinds of homicide three involve the legal guilt of either murder or manslaughter as the case may be. Four involve no legal guilt at all, though one

[1] The construction of this table caused me greater labour than almost any part of the book. It is implied in s. 222 of my *Digest,* and the main difficulty of constructing it lay in perceiving that the unlawfulness of homicide by an act done depends upon the intention with which the act is accompanied and its lawful or unlawful character, whereas the lawfulness or unlawfulness of homicide by an omission depends on the question whether the act left undone is a legal duty or not. An act is almost always intentional, an omission as a rule is unintentional, and in this particular case the intention of the negligent person does not always measure his fault. Not to stretch out a stick to a drowning man, with the intention of causing his death, involves as much moral guilt as the intentional omission of a sick-nurse to administer medicine which she has contracted to administer ; but the one is a legal duty and the other is not. The difficulty of forming distinct coherent schemes on this subject can be fairly appreciated by those only who know in full detail the history of it. See my *History,* vol. iii. pp. 23-107.

of them may involve the blackest kind of moral guilt. Chap. XIII.
The four which involve no legal guilt are—

Homicide (1) committed by an act accompanied by a lawful intention to kill or hurt;

(2) Committed by an act not accompanied by an intention to kill or hurt, such act being lawful; or

(3) By an omission to discharge a legal duty, such omission not amounting to culpable negligence; or

(4) By an omission to do an act not amounting to a legal duty, however wicked may have been the intention with which such omission was made.

But homicide

(1) By an act accompanied by an unlawful intention to kill or hurt; or

(2) By an unlawful act unaccompanied by an intention to kill or hurt; or

(3) By an omission amounting to culpable negligence to perform a legal duty, must be either murder or manslaughter. It is to be understood that an intentional omission to perform a legal duty is always culpable negligence.

The distinction between murder and manslaughter is a different matter from this, depends upon different considerations, and has a different history.

The history of the law relating to homicide so far as it is necessary to be known for the purpose of taking a general view of the existing system of criminal law, consists of two parts—namely, first, the history of the formation of the general conception that all culpable homicide is either murder or manslaughter; and secondly, the history of the different meanings which gradually came to be attached to the words "malice aforethought," the presence or absence of which forms the test by which the two crimes are distinguished. I do not think a better illustration could be given of the slow and gradual way in which all general legal conceptions are formed. Mr. Pollock has shown the same thing in relation to both contract and tort, and I think the same may be said of the way in which fictions are at a certain stage of legal history not merely useful but practically indispensable aids to the reform of the law.

GENERAL CONCEPTION OF HOMICIDE AS CONSISTING OF MURDER AND MANSLAUGHTER.

Till the days of Bracton, nothing in the nature of legal theory upon this subject deserves notice, except the explanation given by Glanville (*temp.* Henry II.) of the word murder—*murdrum.* He contrasts it with *simplex homicidium.* " Duo sunt genera homicidii : murdrum quod nullo vidente " nullo sciente clam perpetratur præter solum interfectorem " et ejus complices, et aliud homicidium quod constat in " generali vocabulo et dicitur simplex homicidium."

Bracton gives a much more elaborate definition, dividing homicide into twelve different kinds, which produce an utterly confused, hardly intelligible, and almost wholly useless network of divisions which do not exclude each other, or depend upon any coherent principles.[1] He does, however, hit upon one principle of importance, viz. that in the case of homicide *casu* a distinction must be made between "dans operam rei " licitæ," and " dans operam rei illicitæ." He also explains murder as done "clanculo nemine vidente." As appears from other places in Bracton, and from the statute-book, the practical difference between homicide and murder was that in cases of murder a presentment of Englishry was required, in the absence of which the person found killed was presumed to be a Frenchman (Norman), and the township was

---

[1] See it *supra.*

fined. The fine was called *murdrum* as well as the offence. CHAP. XIII.
Englishry was abolished in 1340 by the 14 Edw. III. st. 1,
c. 4;[1] but there is evidence that in the course of the 274
years which had then elapsed since the Conquest its meaning
and the meaning of the word "*murdrum*" in connection
with it had become almost forgotten.[2] The abolition of
Englishry took away all distinction between murder and
other forms of homicide, but the name of murder was
not discontinued, probably because it had become well
known and popular. Assassinations usually are secret, and
the words "morth" and "morth works" continually occur in
the laws before the Conquest. The word "murder" was
thus in all probability preserved by accident as a name
of the worst kind of homicide, though it had no longer
any distinctive meaning. Murder subjected the offender to
the same punishment as other kinds of homicide, and persons guilty of it were entitled like others to the benefit
of clergy.

There were from the days of Bracton some forms of
homicide which were regarded in a different light from the
rest. Some homicides were always regarded as strictly
justifiable, as, for instance, the execution of a felon or the
killing a felon who refused to be arrested. These involved

[1] *History of the Criminal Law*, vol. iii. p. 40.

[2] The evidence is this. In 1267 the Statute of Marlbridge (52 Hen. III.
c. 25) enacted : "Murdrum de cetero non adjudicetur coram justiciariis ubi im-
" fortunium tantummodo adjudicatum est sed locum habeat murdrum in inter-
" fectis per feloniam et non aliter. ' The fine called *murdrum* is not to be adjudged
before the justices henceforth in cases adjudged to be misadventure. *Murdrum*
is to take place only in case of people killed by felony and not otherwise. In
Year-book, 21 Edw. III. p. 17 B (A.D. 1348), the reporter says that a person
found guilty of killing another in self-defence lost his chattels but was not
hanged, "la cause fut parce qu'al comon ley home fut pendu in cet cas aux
" avant si come il eat ce fait felonisement." The reporter no doubt construed
" murdrum " murder, and not the fine for murder, with which Coke is quite
satisfied, so utterly had lawyers even forgotten all about Englishry between
1267 and 1348. *History of the Criminal Law*, vol. iii. pp. 36 and 41.

no penal consequences at all, but if a man killed another by accident or in self-defence or when mad ("si home tue autre "par misadventure ou soy defendant ou en deverie") the jury found a special verdict to that effect, and he was entitled to his pardon, apparently forfeiting his chattels and probably paying fees. The effect of this no doubt was to provide something in the nature of a punishment for manslaughter by negligence, and some small profit for the casual revenue of the Crown. Deodands had much the same effect. The thing which "moved to the death of a man" was forfeited, and at one time was in a sort of way punished by being burnt. Thus from the reign of Henry III. till nearly the end of the fourteenth century homicide consisted practically of—

(1) Strictly justifiable killing, as the execution of criminals.

(2) Homicides by misadventure, in self-defence, and by madmen, which were regarded as in some degree blamable, on the principle that in a deadly brawl both are more or less blamable, and that misadventure generally involves carelessness, and that a man who kills another ought at least to be pardoned and to pay for his pardon.

(3) Homicide by felony, which was punished by death, subject to the law of benefit of clergy, and which used, if it was secret, to be called murder. Murder ceased to be distinguishable from other criminal homicides when, under Edward III., Englishry was abolished, but it is probable that all punishable homicides came to be popularly known as murders.

This, I think, is the real meaning of Bracton's involved and elaborate account of the whole subject. I may add that the obscure learning about homicide in self-defence and by misadventure hung about the law in an obsolete and much misunderstood condition till 1828, when by 9 Geo. IV. c. 31, s. 10, it was enacted that no punishment or forfeiture shall be incurred by any person who shall kill another by mis- fortune, or in his own defence, or in any other manner without felony.

MALICE AFORETHOUGHT.

The next question is as to the history of the phrase " malice aforethought," and the way in which it came to be adopted as the test by which it was to be determined whether a given homicide was murder or manslaughter, understanding by each word the name of a distinct crime.

Very shortly the history is this. In 1389 (13 Rich. II.) it appears from entries in the Parliament Rolls[1] that the prerogative of pardoning was much abused, pardons for the most heinous crimes being frequently pleaded in bar of trials, the pardons being procured by the interest of great men. The king promised that if a general pardon for murder was granted and pleaded, a jury should be charged to try whether the murdered man " fuist mourdrez ou occis par agait assaut or malice purpense." If he was, the pardon was to be void.[2] This is a step towards a new definition of murder, though it is no more than a step. Murder might after 1389 have been defined as a kind of homicide in defence of which a pardon for murder in general terms could not be pleaded. That the pardon might be good it must state that the murder pardoned was by assault, waylaying, or malice prepense. Murder of all kinds was still clergyable.

This distinction was deepened and made the specific difference between murder and other forms of homicide or manslaughter by the statutes (there were four of them) which excluded murderers from the benefit of clergy. They were passed between 1496 (12 Hen. VII. c. 7) and 1547 (1 Edw. VI. c. 1, 2, 7, 10) ; the words used are—" wilfully prepensed

[1] See these, *History of the Criminal Law,* vol. iii. pp. 42-44.
[2] See 13 Rich. II. st. 2, c. 1.

CHAP. XIII.   " murders," " prepensed by murder," " murder upon malice " prepensed," " wilful murder of malice prepensed," " murder of " malice prepensed." [1] The result of these Acts no doubt was to divide homicide thus :—

(1) Murder, killing with malice aforethought—a felony without benefit of clergy.

(2) Wilful killing without malice aforethought, then and since called manslaughter—a clergyable felony.

(3) Homicide in self-defence or by misadventure, which included many cases of what would now be called manslaughter by negligence—not a felony, but an act requiring pardon, and involving forfeiture of chattels.

(4) Justifiable homicide, which was not criminal at all.

Petty treason was an aggravated kind of murder, and murder by poison was for a short time punishable by boiling alive.

We may thus consider the present definitions of murder and manslaughter as settled by the year 1547, but though the words " malice aforethought " thus became part of the law, the questions, What amounted to " malice " ? and What satisfied the word " aforethought " ? were not decided till long afterwards.

The subsequent arrangements of the subject by Lambard Staundforde, Coke, and Hale, are all, I think, bad, for they are all based upon Bracton, which is radically vicious and confused. Coke's is very bad, much worse than those of Lambard and Staundforde; Hale's is, I think, the worst of all.[2] All these writers with more or less skill tried to explain the words " malice aforethought " by distinguishing between express or implied malice. Lambard and Staundforde showed most

---

[1] *History of the Criminal Law*, vol. iii. p. 44.

[2] Homicide he says is "purely voluntary," "purely involuntary," or "mixed." How can voluntary and involuntary be mixed? How can it be said that to kill a man " se defendendo " is partly purely voluntary and partly purely involuntary? There is a great deal of downright nonsense in Hale.

skill in this, Coke is nearly as bad as bad can be, but Hale is
worse. At a later date several of the judges of the eighteenth century, in particular Holt and Lord Raymond, and one eminent writer, Foster, appear to me to have succeeded much better; and an enormous number of decisions, to be seen in *Russell on Crimes,* Roscoe, Archbold, and other books of practice, have at last made the meaning of the phrase sufficiently plain for practical purposes. Omitting refinements and qualifications " malice aforethought" may now be described thus. It means killing with any one of the following intentions or states of mind :—

(*a*) An intent to kill or do grievous bodily injury.

(*b*) Knowledge that the act done will probably kill or do grievous bodily harm, although the offender hopes that the consequence will not follow.

(*c*) An intent to commit any felony.[1]

(*d*) An intent to oppose by force any officer of justice in discharging certain of his duties.

All other culpable homicide is manslaughter.

The law as to the effect of provocation is traceable as far back as Coke, but not much further. It anciently had much the same effect as it has now, but in another way. If malice aforethought is construed in a popular sense, killing on a sudden provocation is not killing on malice aforethought. When murder meant only secret killing, and when both murder and manslaughter were clergyable, the doctrine had little importance.

All these matters are set out with the fullest detail in my *History of the Criminal Law,* vol. iii. pp. 23–87.

After disposing of the subject of homicide, the Offences against the Person Act deals with attempts to murder (ss. 11–15). The sections on this subject are a remarkable

---

[1] As to this I have great doubts, unless the felony is in itself an act of such a kind as to fall within (*a*) or (*b*).

instance of timidity in drafting, for, instead of providing for the punishment of all attempts to murder, they provide in four sections for different ways of attempting to commit murder, and in a fifth for attempts by any means other than those specified, which is as if, after providing in four sections for assaults by each arm and each leg, a fifth section were added to include all other assaults. The explanation is that till 1861 a certain number of ways of attempting murder were capital crimes, and that the rest were misdemeanours at common law. In 1861 all attempts at murder which were till then capital crimes ceased to be capital, and all attempts which used to be misdemeanours were made felonies punishable with the severest secondary punishment. The details of all this legislation have a good deal of historical curiosity, and illustrate the gradual and fragmentary character of English legislation, but it is not my purpose to say anything of them here. A full account of the matter will be found in my *History*, vol. iii., chap. xxvii., pp. 108–120. The strongest illustration known to me of what I have said is that till 1803 (43 Geo. III. c. 58) the administration of poison with intent to murder was only a misdemeanour at common law as an attempt to commit a felony. It was not even an assault.

The remainder of the Act needs only a few words.[1]

RAPE.—Trials for this offence have given rise to a few disputed points, which will be found in my *Digest;* and the Criminal Law Amendment Act of 1885 (48 and 49 Vict. c. 69) has made considerable additions to the law relating to this and other offences against women; but it is sufficient to mention this, and to refer for such details as are required in practice to my *Digest*.

BIGAMY.—This offence is punished by s. 57 of the Offences against the Person Act. It would be more appropriate to

---

[1] *Digest*, Arts. 253A ; *ib.* Arts. 257, 258.

call it an offence against conjugal rights, for no violence is used in committing it; but an offence against rights insepar-ably annexed to the person is closely connected with an attack on the person. Several most singular questions have been raised in connection with trials for bigamy. I may mention the great case of R. *v.* Millis (10 *C. and F.*, 534), when it was decided by the House of Lords in 1844—very strangely, as most people thought, and in virtue only of the maxim "præsumitur pro neganti," for the Court was equally divided—that at common law the presence of a priest in episcopal orders was necessary, at least in the British Islands [1] outside Scotland, to a valid marriage; for the decision was that a man who had been married in Ireland by a Presby-terian minister did not commit bigamy by a subsequent marriage otherwise unquestionably valid. Several other questions of great interest have arisen in the same way, but upon these I have said all that is necessary in my *Digest.*

LIBEL.—A libel on a private person may be referred to here, as it is an attack on a right inseparable from his person —his right to his reputation. I have already made such reference as I thought necessary to seditious libels under the head of political offences without violence. Of libels on private persons I will only say that I think it would be a great mistake to relax the criminal law in regard to them. When a man wishes to defend his character against a serious and plausible attack, it is usually best on all grounds that he should take the civil rather than the criminal remedy, and this most people are usually ready to do if a defendant can pay costs and damages; but I do not know of a meaner class of criminals than those who, either for money or to gratify personal spite, make a man's life a burden to him by constant

---

[1] It appears that the principle does not apply to India. I doubt whether it would apply to a British ship at sea, or a barbarous country.

libelling, when they cannot pay a farthing of any damages awarded against them or of any costs which they compel their victim to incur. The crime is by no means an uncommon one, and appropriate punishments, such, *e.g.*, as taking a plea of guilty and allowing the defendant to go free on recognizances to come up and receive judgment if called upon, will generally stop the annoyance.

CHAPTER XIV.

OFFENCES AGAINST PROPERTY.

In my *History of the Criminal Law*[1] will be found a full history of the law of theft from Glanville to the present day I do not propose here to do more than state such parts of it as must be known in order to understand the enactments of 24 and 25 Vict. c. 96. The law must in the nature of things deal with the following matters :—

(1) The question what is theft.

(2) The question what things can be stolen.

(3) The question how the crime may be committed, and by whom.

(1) What is theft ? Omitting one or two matters of little interest, Bracton's definition of theft, which is the root of the whole law, is this : " Furtum est secundum leges con-" trectatio rei alienæ fraudulenta cum animo furandi." The definition of the Roman law was : " Furtum est contrectatio " fraudulenta *lucri faciendi causa vel ipsius rei vel etiam usus* " *ejus possessionisve.*" The omission in English law of the words italicized is remarkable, and may throw some light on the source of most of the difficulties of the subject for instan of the " lucri faciendi causa " is of little im-stolen. C It expresses the principle that the motives of laid down by our law of no importance. The omission of

[1] Vol. iii. pp. 128–166.

"usus ejus .possessionisve" indicates that, from Bracton's time, a taking, to be felonious, must be an absolute misappropriation of the thing itself. The words in the definition "cum animo furandi" are awkward, as they include the word to be defined, but the meaning, no doubt is to exclude the case of taking under a claim of right. Theft in English law has always meant taking a thing with intent to deprive its owner of it permanently and without claim of right, and no change has been introduced into this principle from the earliest times.

(2) What things can be stolen? The answers given to this question will be regarded with continually increasing surprise and disapproval the more they are studied. I have given in my *History* [1] an account of the cases in the *Year-books* and other ancient authorities on this subject, and I add the following remarks :—[2]

In order that a thing might be the subject of larceny, it must fulfil three conditions : it must be the subject of property ; it must be movable personal property ; it must have a definite value of its own. These conditions were supposed to exclude several classes of things from the possibility of being stolen, but neither the classes of things nor the ground on which they were incapable of being stolen were at all definitely settled. Three classes of things were in one way or another decided to be incapable of being stolen—namely, things growing out of the earth, deeds, and certain animals. Things of the first and second classes were regarded as not being movable chattels, but as either realty or savouring of realty. Deeds were also regarded as having no definite independent value of their own ; and the same was said of some animals. Animals were regarded as in the proper sense of the word, property. Eac three principles thus applied to more than one of tl

---

[1] Vol. iii. pp. 134–142.   [2] Vol. iii.

of things, and the extracts given from the *Year-books* show
how very ill-defined the old law was down to the time of
Henry VIII. The last case I have quoted, for instance,
shows that in 1528 it was doubtful whether a peacock could
be stolen. It was not quite clear whether it was tame, or
whether it had real value. The meaning of "value" seems not
to have been the same in earlier times as it is in our own days.
We should describe anything which would command a price as
valuable, but in earlier times it seems to have been thought
that "valuable" implied serious practical importance as opposed to mere fancy or amusement. Thus it was argued in
the case of the peacock that mastiffs, hounds, and spaniels, and
tame goshawks, are not the subject of larceny, "Car ils sont
"proprement choses de plaisir plus que de profit. Et aussi le
"peacock est un oiseau plus pur plaisir que pour profit."
This view was carried to an extreme length by Hales, J.,
who is said [1] "to have thought it no felony to take a dia-
"mond, rubie, or other such stone (not set in gold or other-
"wise), because they be not of price with all men, however
"some do hold them dear and precious." The common
law on this subject was thus extremely uncertain both in its
principles and in their application. I may conclude my account
of it by noticing its further application. The most irrational
case which I have quoted from the *Year-books* is that of the
deeds and the boxes in which they were contained. It depended on two principles: first, that the deeds savoured of
the realty, and that the boxes were merely appurtenant to
the deeds; and, secondly, that the deeds had no definite independent value. The *Year-books* do not refer to "choses in
action" other than deeds. There is no decision that a bond,
for instance, which did not affect land was incapable of being
stolen. Coke, however, who accepted any sort of principle
laid down in the *Year-books* as if it was a law of Nature,

[1] Stanford, p. 275.

accepted this principle, and applied it to all " choses in action " whatever. In Caly's case he gives an elaborate commentary on the writ in the register which defines the liability of innkeepers for the goods of their guests. Some of its words, he says, extend to all movable goods, although of them felony cannot be committed, as of charters, evidences, obligations, deeds, specialties, &c. The only authority quoted for this incidental remark is the case in the *Year-book*, 10 Edwd. IV. c. 14, already referred to, and references to it in Broke and FitzHerbert. Hence the doctrine that a "chose in action" cannot be stolen rests upon an unauthorized extension made by Coke, in treating of a different subject, of a case in the *Year-books* which depends on a wholly different principle.

A long series of statutes has been passed, by which these so-called common law principles—for they really did not deserve the name—have been repealed by the cumbrous method of denying in detail what they approved in general; with this strange result, that nearly everything which can physically be stolen and which is worth stealing—even water in a pipe, gas, and, what is still stranger, electricity—is the subject of larceny, except, perhaps, ferrets, pigeons flying at liberty, and the dead bodies of human beings.

It is necessary shortly to observe that the things which, according to what was supposed to be the common law, were not the objects of larceny, were—

(1) Land, because it was not physically movable, whence it was inferred that parts of it or of its fruits which were made movable could not be stolen.

(2) Rights, because it was physically impossible to steal them, as they had no physical existence; whence it was inferred that the evidence of their existence could not be stolen, though they might easily be moved, and do certainly exist.

(3) A number of animals, for various reasons, some good, as in the case of wild animals, some absurd, as in the case of dogs.

(3) How can theft be committed? The full answer to this question is given in my *Digest*, Arts. 295–312. I may, however, point out that all the forms of theft there described depend upon one principle—namely, that in all cases of theft there must be a fraudulent taking. An innocent taking, followed by a fraudulent conversion, is not theft. The most striking instance of this is to be found in the case of finding (Art. 302). A man who picks up something which he sees dropped by another, intending to keep it for himself steals it. If he takes it with intent to return it, and afterwards changes his mind and determines to and does keep it, he does not commit theft.

This principle runs through all the cases. The commonest form of theft is by taking and carrying away. If this form of the offence is committed in the presence of the owner, and by actual violence or the threat of violence, the crime is robbery.

Theft may be committed by a servant or other person who has charge of a thing for a special limited purpose. Thus a groom may steal his master's horse while riding it on his master's service. A guest at an inn may steal plate which he is using at table. A clerk or servant who commits such an offence is guilty of embezzlement, which is a statutory form of theft.

Theft may also be committed by obtaining the possession of a thing by a trick; but if the property and not merely the possession is obtained, the offence is not theft, but obtaining goods by false pretences.

Theft may be committed by converting property received from the owner under a mistake which the offender knows to be such when it is made, but the distinctions here are fine, and not quite perfectly ascertained (see Art. 299).

The old common law rule that there must in all cases of theft be a felonious taking is still maintained to a considerable extent; indeed, the bad results to which it led have been remedied to such a great extent by the creation of special statutory offences, which in themselves are so many recognitions of the principle, that it will no doubt be maintained unless the whole of the law upon the subject should ever be recast.

There were only two exceptions of much importance to the old common law rule. It was always held that if a bailee determined the bailment made to him by breaking bulk, and then misappropriated the goods, he was guilty of theft; and it was always the law that if a servant who had the custody of goods for his master, or a guest at an inn who had a cup or plate for use at a meal, misappropriated them, he was guilty of theft; but this was because it was considered that the servant or guest was not properly in possession of such things, but had a mere custody or charge, and that the possession still remained in the master or the host, and so the thing when stolen was feloniously taken. These exceptions were construed so strictly, that when, in Bazeley's case,[1] a banker's clerk was tried for theft for having put in his own pocket a note for £100 which a customer gave him to be carried to his credit, it was held that he could not be convicted; and a statute was passed which enacted that clerks and servants who embezzled money received on their masters' account should be deemed to have stolen it. This statute, though it considerably extended the law as to one particular class of offenders—namely, clerks and servants, made no fundamental alteration in it, and much increased its difficulty by raising a long series of questions as to the technical meaning of "clerk" and "servant." The Act which punished it introduced other technicalities, which I need not here point out.

By degrees, attention was called to the fact (the neglect

[1] Leach, 835; and see *History of the Criminal Law*, vol. iii. p. 152.

of which is pointed out and ridiculed by Swift in *Gulliver's Travels*) that a breach of trust deserves punishment as much as a felonious taking; and a variety of statutes were passed upon this subject, which constituted new offences, like theft, but differing from it in the circumstance that each of them treats as a crime a fraudulent dealing with property innocently received. The first of these statutes was suggested by the case of a stockbroker,[1] who stole £22,000, the proceeds of a cheque with which he was intrusted to buy securities for Sir T. Plumer. This occasioned an Act for the punishment of bankers, brokers, merchants, solicitors, and other agents who misappropriated securities, &c., with which they were intrusted. The first Act passed for this purpose was 52 Geo. III. c. 63.

A still further inroad was made upon the principle that a felonious taking was essential to larceny by the enactment that all bailees, whether they had or had not broken bulk, who stole anything bailed to them, should be guilty of theft. This was in 1857. These two enactments practically repealed the old common law doctrine that a person who stole property intrusted to him was liable to no punishment, though cases may be put in which it still applies; but it did not reach the case of trustees, in whom the whole legal interest in property is vested for the benefit of *cestui que trustent*, who are beneficial owners. If, *e.g.*, the trustee of a marriage settlement sold all the securities in which the settled funds were invested, and spent the proceeds, he was, till 1857, guilty only of a civil wrong.

These offences, however, have since been dealt with, though in an exceedingly clumsy and imperfect way,[2] but the result of the whole may thus be summarized :—

The fraudulent misappropriation of property is not a

---

[1] R. *v.* Walsh, January 4, 258.
[2] *History of the Criminal Law*, vol. iii. pp. 156–157.

criminal offence, if the possession of it was originally honestly acquired, except in the case of—

(1) Servants embezzling their master's property, who were first excepted in 1799.

(2) Brokers, merchants, bankers, attorneys, and other agents misappropriating property intrusted to them, who were first excepted in 1812.

(3) Factors fraudulently pledging goods intrusted to them for sale, who were first excepted in 1857.

(4) Trustees under express trusts fraudulently disposing of trust funds, who were first excepted in 1857.

(5) Bailees stealing the goods bailed to them, who also were first excepted in 1857.

Before passing to the exposition of the Larceny Act, the following observation must be added. Many of its enactments differ from each other only in varying the maximum punishments for different kinds of theft; *e.g.* stealing a horse may be punished by fourteen years' penal servitude. Stealing an ass only by five years' penal servitude. Theft by a servant is punishable by penal servitude for fourteen years, whereas if the offender were not a servant he might not be liable to a sentence exceeding five years. These provisions appear, and indeed are, capricious. The historical explanation of their existence is this. The old division of larceny was into grand larceny (stealing over the value of a shilling), which was punishable with death, and petty larceny (stealing the value of less than a shilling), which involved minor punishments. Grand larceny, however, was clergyable. In the course of the eighteenth century many larcenies were excluded from clergy, sometimes in an arbitrary way. When the punishment of death was abolished in cases of larceny, those offences which had been excluded from clergy were punished with greater severity than the rest, and felonies which were not otherwise specially provided for were subjected to seven years' transportation as a maximum punishment. In the case of theft, five years' penal servitude is now the maximum punishment in cases not otherwise provided for.

I now proceed to the arrangement of the Larceny Act. It is wretchedly ill-arranged, though the Act is drawn with the most complete knowledge of the law which it consolidates, and shows a servile respect for the mass of intricate and irrational technicalities which I have tried to explain.

Section 1 gives the Act its title. Section 2 abolishes the distinction between grand and petty larceny, which had been abolished forty-six years before. Section 3 (which ought to come in before Section 67) re-enacts the Act which made larceny by a bailee a crime.

Some confused sections about punishments and indictments (4–9 inclusive) follow. Then come a series of exceptions to the common law rules as to things which are not the subject of larceny at common law, and as to the rule that a felonious taking is essential to theft.

Sections 10–26 are principally exceptions from and qualifications of the common law rules about stealing animals; Sections 27–30, exceptions to the common law rules as to stealing written instruments; Sections 31–39, exceptions to the common law rule that land or things growing out of or fixed to land cannot be stolen; Sections 67–87, exceptions to the common law rules that fraudulent breach of a common law trust is not a crime, and that a trustee possessed of the whole legal interest in property commits no offence when he defrauds his *cestui que trust*.

The Act would be rather less unintelligible if Section 3 and Sections 67–87 followed Section 39, as this would keep together all the exceptions made to the common law rule as to a felonious taking; but for some reason not apparent Sections 40–49 relate to robbery and extortion by threats; Sections 50–59 to burglary and housebreaking, which are defined in a very intricate way; and Sections 60–66 to some special forms of larceny are interposed. Sections 88–90 relate to obtaining goods, &c., by false pretences; and Sections 91–99 to the receiving of stolen goods, and to various matters connected with the procedure relating to it.

The rest of the Act relates to procedure.

I have arranged all this matter on a different principle in my *Digest.* I first (chap. xxxiii. Arts. 279–285*a*) deal with the definition of the terms and of the common law doctrines which pervade the subject, viz. property, possession, ownership general and special, taking and carrying away, or asportation, and bailment.

I next (chap. xxxiv. Arts. 286–294) state the law as to what is the subject of larceny, and what not, putting together the common law rules and the statutory exceptions.

In chap. xxxv. Arts. 295–308, I state the ways in which theft may be committed, the law as to finding, and the distinctions between theft and other fraudulent conversions, of which some are and others are not criminal.

In chap. xxxvi. Arts. 309–312, I state the law as to embezzlement.

I then proceed to define different kinds of theft, taking the most serious first, and stating the punishments. Chap. xxxvii. Arts. 313–314, defines robbery and extortion; chap. xxxviii. Arts. 315–320, burglary and similar offences; chap. xxxix. Arts. 321–328, deals with thefts for which no special punishment is provided, or after a previous conviction, and with thefts punishable with a maximum punishment of penal servitude for life, for fourteen years, for seven years, for five years, and with various terms of imprisonment; in chap. xl. Arts. 329–342, I deal with obtaining goods by false pretences and some other frauds like theft; I deal in chap. xli. Arts. 343–352, with frauds by bankers, brokers, agents, trustees, &c., and with the new offence of fraudulent false accounting ; and finally, in chap. xlii. Arts. 353–354, with the receiving of property unlawfully obtained. In these chapters I have included several offences punished otherwise than under the Larceny Act, *e.g.* those which are defined by the Post Office Act.

Of the remaining Consolidation Acts, 24 and 25 Vict. c. 97, which relates to malicious injury; c. 98, which relates to forgery ; and c. 99, which deals with offences relating to coin, I have nothing to say beyond what is said in the Acts themselves. The common law definition of forgery involves questions of some difficulty, but I need add nothing to what I have said on this subject in my *Digest*, Arts. 355 and 356.

The law as to offences against trade has a history of the greatest interest, which I have related to the best of my ability in vol. iii. of my *History* (chap. xxx. pp. 192–234) ; but as to the actually existing law, which consists principally of enactments relating to fraudulent debtors, criminal breaches of contract, and certain statutes as to navigation, I have nothing to add to what is said in chap. xlix. Arts. 387–398 of my *Digest*.

CHAPTER XV.

CRIMINAL PROCEDURE.

In the earlier chapters of this book I have given an historical account of the gradual development of the law of criminal procedure, which shows the steps by which the present most elaborate and complete system has been gradually formed. Referring to the statements there made, I propose in the present chapter to draw a sketch of the system as it stands, avoiding all the details which, though absolutely necessary for practical purposes, are too minute to be accurately remembered, unless they are learnt by long practice, and interfere with the unity of impression which it is the great object of a general view to communicate. The authorities for each statement contained in this chapter, and the details which for purposes of practice require to be known, will be found in my *Digest of Criminal Procedure*, at the articles referred to in the foot-notes. The first, the most general, and perhaps the most characteristic principle of the law of England on this subject is that every-one, without exception, has the right to use the Queen's name for the purpose of prosecuting any person for any crime. This is subject only to the condition that the Attorney-General has power on his own authority to stop any prosecution by entering a *nolle prosequi*.

Prosecutions are, in fact, usually instituted by the police, and in cases of importance they are not unfrequently carried on by the Public Prosecutor, in which character the Solicitor to the Treasury acts. He has, however, no legal authority whatever as such. He cannot require any person to attend before him or to answer questions. He can, in a word, do nothing whatever which may not equally be done by any private person through his private solicitor.

This is one of the most marked distinctions between the criminal procedure of this and, I believe, almost all other countries.

I have already said what appeared to be necessary on the subject of the local extent of the criminal law of England in regard to place, time, and person.[1] I begin my sketch accordingly with the constitution of the criminal courts.[2] They consist of—

(1) The House of Lords and the Court of the Lord High Steward, for peers accused of treason or felony and for commoners impeached by the House of Commons. These courts have not been called upon to act since the trial of Lord Cardigan in 1841.

(2) The High Court of Justice (Queen's Bench Division), which usually sits only in cases of special magnitude or interest—principally misdemeanours removed into it by *certiorari*.

(3) The Courts of the Commissioners of Assize, Oyer and Terminer, and Gaol Delivery, which sit in every county in England for the trial of all crimes committed there.

(4) The Central Criminal Court, which sits in London for the trial of all cases occurring in London and the neighbourhood.

These are the superior criminal courts, in which all offences may be, and in which all serious offences usually are, tried.

[1] *Digest of Procedure*, Part I.   [2] *Ibid.*, Part II.

CHAP. XV. The judges are the judges of the High Court of Justice. Many other persons of eminence are honorary members of these Courts, and the Recorder of London, the Common Serjeant and the Judge of the Sheriff's Court try the less important cases at the Central Criminal Court, and the Queen's Counsel on the several circuits may try the less important cases on circuit if asked by the judge to do so. Criminal, like all other courts, have also ministerial officers, of whom it is not necessary to speak in detail, though in the Commissions of Assize and Gaol Delivery they hold a somewhat peculiar position under what is called a Commission of Association.[1]

The other criminal courts are courts of limited jurisdiction in respect of the crimes which they are competent to try. These are the Courts of Quarter Sessions. They are courts either for counties or parts of counties, or for boroughs. Each county or part of a county has a separate Commission of the Peace,[2] and the magistrates of each Commission are the judges of the Court of Quarter Sessions. They elect their own Chairman, who exercises most of the functions of a judge, though only as *primus inter pares.* In all boroughs having Courts of Quarter Sessions, and all such boroughs have a separate Commission of the Peace, there is a Recorder who is appointed by the Crown, and is sole judge.

The limits of the criminal jurisdiction of the Courts of Quarter Sessions are fixed by statute,[3] and in general may be

---

[1] See *Digest of Procedure*, Art. 24.

[2] There is one for each county except York and Lincoln   50

York, one for each Riding	...	...	...	...	3
Lincoln, one for each part	...	...	...	...	3
Liberties	...	...	...	...	9
Counties of towns ...	...	...	...	...	18

In all   83

Commissions for England and Wales.

—*History of the Criminal Law*, vol. i. p. 115.

[3] 5 and 6 Vict. c. 38, s. 1   *Digest of Procedure*, Art. 39.

said to exclude all capital crimes, all crimes which may be punished on a first conviction by penal servitude for life, and all cases which are likely to give rise to important questions of law, or to cause local prejudice.

Various property qualifications [1] are required of county and borough magistrates. There are also in London (outside the City), and in many other populous places, stipendiary magistrates appointed by the Crown.

Such is the organization of the criminal courts. To complete the subject I may mention the coroners, though only in a few words. The coroners are the most ancient of English officers of justice, excepting only the judges.[2] They are at present in almost all cases elective, and their duties connected with criminal justice consist in holding inquiries by the aid of coroners' juries into the causes of all deaths by violence or accident or under suspicious circumstances. There is much in the discharge of their duties which is historically interesting, but nothing which, in such a statement of our system of criminal procedure as I am now giving, requires notice.

The next point to be mentioned is as to the place where a crime committed within the jurisdiction of the English criminal courts is to be tried.[3] As a general rule, they are tried where they are committed; but there are many exceptions, which can hardly be stated correctly in fewer words than are used in the articles of my *Digest* referred to below.[4] One principle may, I think, be suggested which is omitted in it. A crime, I think, may be said to be committed in any place in which anything essential to its commission is done. This is expressly enacted in the obvious case of a fatal wound given in one place and the death of the person

---

[1] *Digest of Procedure*, Art. 30.
[2] *History of the Criminal Law*, vol. i. pp. 216-245.
[3] *Digest of Procedure*, Arts. 67-87   [4] Arts. 79-87.

CHAP. XV. wounded taking place in a different jurisdiction, and it is more or less implied in several decided cases. Thus, a man posts at Leicester a libellous letter to a newspaper which publishes it in London.[1] He commits the offence of publishing a libel both in Leicester and London. A writes at Nottingham a letter to B in France, making a false pretence, whereby B is persuaded to send to A at Nottingham a bill of exchange, which A receives and discounts at Nottingham. A commits an offence at Nottingham.[2] A man who steals goods is held to go on stealing them as long as he has them, and may be tried for the theft in any county where he has them. A variety of special provisions are made with regard to offences on journeys, to offences near the boundary of a county, to bigamy, forgery, offences connected with the coinage, &c.

In some few cases the High Court of Justice has power to vary the usual place of trial: as, for instance, if a fair trial cannot be otherwise conveniently had; if it is desired to try a criminal case on the civil side; and in a few special cases, as, for instance, when a soldier is accused of the murder of a soldier. This is commonly done by the issue of a writ of *certiorari* upon terms fixed by statute. The *certiorari* may in some cases be issued by the High Court, or any judge, including the Recorder of London, to the counties of Middlesex, Essex, Kent, and Surrey, for the trial of any prisoner therein at the Central Criminal Court.

Passing from the organization of the criminal courts, I now come to the course taken upon the commission of a crime to bring the criminal to justice. The first step is the arrest of the criminal. This may in many cases be done either in a summary way by any person, whether a police constable or not in many cases, and in some additional cases

---

[1] Regina v. Burdett, 4 *B. and A.*, p. 95.
[2] Regina v. Holmes, *Law Reports*, 12 Queen's Bench Division, p. 23.

by a constable without a warrant. These are set out in my *Digest.*[1] An arrest may also be made for any offence on a summons or on a warrant on the first instance, and such a warrant must be issued on an information in writing and on oath, or on a warrant issued on a failure to appear to a summons. A warrant issued by any magistrate in England, Scotland, Ireland, or the Channel Islands, must be backed by a magistrate having local jurisdiction in the county where it is executed,[2] and the case of Indian and colonial warrants is similarly provided for, but with more elaboration.[3]

It is a peculiarity of English criminal procedure that till some person charged with an offence appears before a magistrate, either on arrest, summons, or warrant, no official inquiry into the crime can be held except in the single case of a coroner's inquest. This has always appeared to me one of the most irrational defects in the criminal law, and one of which the removal has by experience been shown most to increase its efficiency.

When a suspected person appears before the magistrates, the witnesses against him are heard in his presence, and he is allowed to call witnesses. If the magistrates are of opinion that the evidence is not sufficient to put the prisoner on his trial, it is their duty to discharge him. If it is in their opinion sufficient for that purpose, they must commit him. If the case cannot be finished at one hearing, the prisoner may be remanded for periods of not exceeding eight days till it is completed.

If the prisoner is committed, the clerk to the magistrates forwards the depositions as to the taking of which there are various enactments, to the clerk of assize, clerk of the peace or other principal ministerial officer of the court by which the prisoner is to be tried. In all cases, except murder

---

[1] *Digest of Procedure*, Arts. 96–98. [2] *Ibid.*, Arts. 105–107.
[3] *Ibid.*, Arts. 164–166.

M

and treason, the justices may bail a prisoner till he is tried. In the case of misdemeanours which border on felony they have a discretion.[1] A judge, or the Queen's Bench Division, may bail in all cases, but it admits of a doubt whether the Habeas Corpus Act does not enable a prisoner to claim to be bailed in all cases of misdemeanour.[2] As a general rule, it may be said that till sentence is passed prisoners may be bailed ; as, for instance, during remands, during adjournments of the court at or after commitment for trial. The committing magistrate has power to compel the attendance of witnesses both at his own inquiry and at the assizes, to issue search warrants, and to do some other necessary things which I pass over.

There is one case in which a man may be committed for trial without going before a magistrate. This is the case in which a witness appears to the judge to perjure himself at a trial ; the judge may thereupon direct him in a summary way to be prosecuted for perjury, and either commit or bail him till trial. This course is hardly ever taken, and is most unwise. If the judge were authorized to direct such a person to be taken in the usual way before a police magistrate, it would be much better. In the only two cases in which I have thought it desirable to interfere, I contented myself with saying in open court that I thought a particular witness ought to be prosecuted. In the case of crimes incidentally brought to notice in a different proceeding, it is generally sufficient for the presiding judge to write to the Public Prosecutor. In the case of bankruptcy misdemeanours, the county court judge can commit for trial.[4] A series of provisions to be found in several Acts of Parlia-

---

[1] *Digest of Procedure*, Art. 137. The misdemeanours are enumerated in the note.

[2] *Ibid.*, Art. 136.　　　　　　　　[3] *Ibid.*, Arts. 122-128.

[4] 46 and 47 Vict. c. 52, s. 165. The Act was passed since my *Digest of Procedure* was published.

ment called the Extradition Acts, the important one being the Extradition Act of 1870, 33 and 34 Vict. c. 52, provide for the case of the extradition of criminals, for the verification of the evidence against them, and for some other matters, such as the return of criminals to distant parts of Her Majesty's dominions. Of all these things an account will be found in my *Digest*.[1] The history of the subject is related and its principles are stated in my *History*.[2]

The next question to be considered is that of accusation. Substantially, a committal for trial is an accusation ; but formally, a prisoner is regarded as being detained or bailed only for the purpose of being accused, and this may be done in various ways. An accusation may be, and generally is, made, (1) by a grand jury, (2) by a coroner's inquest in the case of murder or manslaughter ; (3) by a criminal information. Other ways in which accusations may be made are said to exist, but are obsolete.

All criminal courts summon a grand jury for the purpose of receiving indictments preferred before them. They are charged by the judge. The indictments, which are usually drawn by the clerk of assize, or other officer, are laid before them in turn by the various prosecutors, and the witnesses in support of them are examined in private by the grand jury, who indorse upon each indictment " A true bill," if they think there is a case for inquiry, and " No true bill " if they think there is none.

It is a curious feature of the English law that any person may present a bill of indictment against any person whatever for any crime whatever, except a few,[3] without having given notice to the accused, or going before a magistrate.

---

[1] *Digest of Procedure*, Arts. 141–184.

[2] *History of the Criminal Law*, vol. ii. pp. 65–74.

[3] Perjury and subornation, conspiracy, false pretences, keeping a gaming-house, keeping a disorderly house, indecent assault, libel, and certain offences under the Newspaper Libel Act. *Digest of Procedure*, Art. 192.

CHAP. XV. It would be perfectly lawful for any man to accuse the most distinguished person of treason, murder, rape, or any other crime except those mentioned, by false witnesses, without notice, without any previous authority or inquiry whatever ; and to have the accused arrested and locked up in prison under circumstances in which he might find it difficult to get bail, and in which he would find it impossible to know what was the evidence given against him. It has often surprised me that this is not, in fact, done, and it is still more surprising that the remedy which is applied in the excepted cases is not applied in all cases. I think that all persons charged with crimes should be taken before a magistrate before committal, especially persons charged on a coroner's inquisition ; and that if the magistrate refuses to commit, the accuser should not be allowed to send up a bill unless he causes himself to be bound over to prosecute, and makes himself liable to costs. I should like him to be liable to be made to find security for them. Prisoners are usually in custody or on bail when indictments are found against them. If not, they may be arrested on a certificate[1] or Bench warrant.[2]

CORONER'S INQUISITION.—A coroner's inquisition is equivalent to an indictment in cases of manslaughter and murder. Coroners' juries have very loose notions about manslaughter by negligence, and often return verdicts of manslaughter where there is no real ground for them.

CRIMINAL INFORMATIONS.—The Attorney or Solicitor General has a right to put a person on his trial for any misdemeanour without an indictment. This right was formerly used for purposes and in a way which made it a stock subject of denunciation. It is now of little importance.[3] The procedure is described in my *Digest*.[4]

---

[1] *Digest of Procedure*, Art. 196.   [2] *Ibid.*, Art. 195.
[3] *History of the Criminal Law*, vol. i. pp. 294-296.
[4] *Digest of Procedure*, Arts. 197-208.

Criminal informations will in some particular cases be ordered, upon a motion made in court, to be issued by the Master of the Crown Office, on affidavits showing that certain offences have been committed, filed by persons aggrieved by such offences.[1] The power is, however, used very sparingly —chiefly in cases of misdemeanour by or against official persons, or libels on public men.

The most important topic connected with accusation is the contents of indictments and criminal pleading generally. The subject is one which I shall treat very concisely. The principles, when rightly understood, are extremely simple, but a full statement of the law is and must be intricate and qualified, especially because it must, so to speak, describe what may be called a forged release to a forged bond. By the forged bond I mean the intricate technical rules of the old common law. By the forged release I mean the many statutory enactments which have partially, but not entirely, blotted them out. A full exposition of the whole system will be found in my *Digest of Procedure*, Arts. 236–255. It will be found that the result of the whole is that the words of Art. 244 describe an indictment with substantial accuracy,[2] though some exceptions to part of it have been made by statute with a view to brevity, and though many irrational rules which formerly obtained in relation to it, and which were intended, to a greater or less extent, to provide means for evading the cruelty of the old criminal law by quibbles, are now removed, or at least neutralized by being allowed by statute to be amended.

An indictment may be quashed; demurred to, if the facts alleged, being admitted, are denied to amount to a crime; or may be pleaded to. The common pleas are guilty, not guilty, *autrefois* acquit, *autrefois* convict or pardon, and a

---

[1] *Digest of Procedure*, Arts. 206-207.
[2] "An indictment must be consistent with each."—*Ibid.*, Art. 244.

special plea is allowed in the case of an indictment for libel.[1] There are several rules of practice connected with this which I need not notice; a full account of them is given in my *Digest*.

The next step is the trial, which used in early times to be called the arraignment, though the expression is now applied rather to taking the plea than to the actual trial. The effect of the Habeas Corpus Act is to give a person accused of treason or felony a right to be indicted on his trial at the first sessions after his committal, or if he is not tried to be bailed, unless the witnesses for the Crown cannot appear. If he is not tried after being bailed, he can at the second sessions insist on his release without bail. The arraignment usually occupies only a few minutes, as the prisoners are usually arraigned in groups, and plead at once either guilty or not guilty. There is, however, a legal possibility of a challenge to the array which alleges default or partiality on the part of the sheriff in returning the panel; or a challenge to the individuals or polls, who may be challenged either peremptorily or for cause. In cases of felony, twenty peremptory challenges and any number of challenges for cause are allowed; but there are no peremptory challenges in cases of misdemeanour.

It is remarkable that for centuries challenges have been uncommon in England. I cannot remember more than two cases in which any considerable number have been made in thirty-five years. There are, however, elaborate rules about them, and about the rare incident of standing mute, which, however, operates now only as a plea of not guilty.

In the common course of things this is followed by the trial.[3]

---

[1] *Digest of Procedure*, Arts. 256–268.   [2] *Ibid.*, Arts. 270–275.

[3] The following is condensed from my *History*, vol. i. pp. 428–456.

The first step in the trial, properly so called, is the opening speech of the counsel for the Crown. He is expected to confine himself—except under very special and unusual circumstances—to a quiet account of the different facts to be proved, and of their bearing upon each other, and on the guilt of the prisoner. This statement is often of decisive importance, for it produces the first impression made upon the minds of the judge and jury, the indictment being a neutral, formal document, wholly unlike a Continental *acte d'accusation*. It is pleasant to be able to say that, as a rule, subject only to rare exceptions, extreme calmness and impartiality in opening criminal cases is characteristic of the English Bar. It is very rare to hear arguments pressed against prisoners with any special warmth of feeling or of language : one reason for which no doubt is, that any counsel who did so would probably defeat his own object. Apart, however, from this, it is worthy of observation that eloquence either in prosecuting or defending prisoners is almost unknown and unattempted at the bar.

The opening speech for the prosecution is followed by the examination of the witnesses, who are first examined in chief by the counsel for the Crown, then cross-examined by the counsel for the prisoner, if he is defended by counsel, or by the prisoner himself if he is not, and then re-examined by the counsel for the Crown. The judge and the jury can also ask such questions as they may think necessary. The object of examination-in-chief is to make the witness tell what he knows relevant to the issue in a consecutive manner and without wandering from the point. The object of cross-examination is twofold—namely, to prove any facts favourable to the prisoner which may not have been stated by the witness when examined in chief, and to bring to light any matter calculated to shake the weight of his evidence by damaging his character, or by showing that he has made inconsistent statements on former occasions, or that his opportunities of observation, or his memory as to what passed were defective. The object of re-examination is to clear up any matter brought out in cross-examination which admits of explanation.

The main rule as to the manner in which the examination of a witness must be conducted is, that leading questions—that is, questions which suggest the desired answer—must not be asked by the side which calls the witness, and to which he is presumed to be favourable, but that they may be asked by the party against whom he is called, and to whom he is presumed to be unfavourable; in other words, leading questions may not be asked in an examination-in-chief or in a re-examination, but they may be asked in cross-examination.

This rule, however, is liable to be modified at the discretion of the judge, if the witness appears to be, in fact, unfavourable to the party by whom he is called, and to be keeping back matter with which he is acquainted. A common instance of this is when a witness refuses or hesitates to state at the trial what he stated in his depositions before the magistrate. The great care bestowed upon the examination of the witnesses, and the importance attached to such rules as these, are characteristic features in an English trial; and though they are sometimes carried to an apparently pedantic length, there can be no doubt of their substantial value.

Their proper application requires experience and skill. It is not easy to question a person in such a way as to draw from him the knowledge which he possesses on a given subject in the form of a continuous statement in the order of time, the questions being so contrived as to keep alive the attention and memory of the witness without being open to the objection that they suggest the answer which he is to give.

The examination-in-chief is followed by the cross-examination. Cross-examination is a highly characteristic part of an English trial, whether criminal or civil; and hardly any of the contrasts between the English and Continental systems strikes an English lawyer as forcibly as its absence in the Continental systems. Its history may be collected from the particulars given in my *History.* So long as prisoners were really undefended by counsel in serious cases, their cross-examination of the witnesses against them was trifling and of little or no importance, though they did cross-examine to a greater or less extent. When they were allowed to have counsel to cross-examine, but not to speak for them, the cross-examination tended to become a speech thrown into the form of questions, and it has ever since retained this character to a greater or less extent. Cross-examination is, no doubt, an absolutely indispensable instrument for the discovery of truth, but it is the part of the whole system which is most liable to abuse, and which, in my opinion, ought to be kept most carefully under control by the judge; but I do not think that the unfavourable criticisms often made upon it by unprofessional persons are well founded.

Few stronger proofs are to be found of the simplicity of English taste in the matter of making speeches than the exceedingly prosaic character of speeches in defence of prisoners. Even when the circumstances of crimes are pathetic or terrible in the highest degree, the counsel on both sides are usually as quiet as if the case was an action on a bill of exchange. This way of doing business is greatly to be commended. It is impossible to be eloquent in the sense of appealing to the feelings without more or less falsehood; and an unsuccessful attempt at passionate eloquence is of all things the most contemptible and ludicrous, besides being usually vulgar. The critical temper of the age has exercised an excellent influence on speaking in the courts. Most barristers are justly afraid of being laughed at and looking silly if they aim at eloquence, and generally avoid it by keeping quiet.

The defence is followed by the examination of the prisoner's witnesses, if any, the summing up of his counsel, and the reply of the counsel for the Crown, if he is entitled to a reply. But upon these matters I need add nothing to what I have already said.

The trial concludes by the summing up of the judge.

This, again, is a highly characteristic part of the proceedings, but it is one on which I feel it difficult to write. I think, however, that a judge who merely states to the jury certain propositions of law, and then reads over his notes, does not discharge his duty. This course was commoner in former times [1] than it is now. I also think that a judge who forms a decided opinion before he has heard the whole case, or who allows himself to be in any degree actuated by an advocate's feelings in regulating the proceedings, altogether fails to discharge his duty; but I further think that he ought not to conceal his opinion from the jury, nor do I see how it is possible for him to do so if he arranges the evidence in the order in which it strikes his mind. The mere effort to see what is essential to a story, in what order the important events happened, and in what relation they stand to each other, must of necessity point to some conclusion. The act of stating for the jury the questions which they have to answer, and of stating the evidence bearing on those questions and showing in what respects it is important, generally goes a considerable way towards suggesting an answer to them; and if a judge does not do as much at least as this, he does almost nothing.

The judge's position is thus one of great delicacy, and

---

[1] It was followed, to take one instance in a thousand, by Lord Mansfield in Lord George Gordon's case.

it is not, I think, too much to say that to discharge the duties which it involves as well as they are capable of being discharged, demands the strenuous use of uncommon faculties, both intellectual and moral. It is not easy to form and suggest to others an opinion founded upon the whole of the evidence without on the one hand shrinking from it, or on the other closing the mind to considerations which make against it. It is not easy to treat fairly arguments urged in an unwelcome or unskilful manner. It is not easy for a man to do his best, and yet to avoid the temptation to choose that view of a subject which enables him to show off his special gifts. In short, it is not easy to be true and just. That the problem is capable of an eminently satisfactory solution there can, I think, be no doubt. Speaking only of those who are long since dead, it may be truly said that, to hear in their happiest moments the summing up of such judges as Lord Campbell, Lord Chief Justice Erle, or Baron Parke, was like listening not only (to use Hobbes's famous expression), to " law living and armed," but to the voice of Justice itself.

A verdict of guilty or not guilty concludes the whole matter, and the prisoner is in the one case sentenced and in the other is at once discharged, unless there are other charges against him. But the jury may not agree. Various accidents (such as the death or illness of a judge or juryman) may occur. These are all enumerated, and the way of disposing of such occurrences are stated, in my *Digest*.[1]

There is no appeal in criminal cases, but there are three modes of procedure which are more or less analogous to it. In cases of error in the form of the proceedings, a writ of error may be brought if the Attorney-General consents. In cases of law arising upon the trial, a case may in the judge's discretion be reserved for the Court for the Consideration of Crown Cases Reserved ; and in misdemeanours tried upon the civil

[1] *Digest of Procedure*, Arts. 296–302.

side of the Queen's Bench Division, a new trial may be moved for. Many rather technical questions arise upon these points, of which I need not here speak in detail. Punishments of all kinds may be either wholly remitted or commuted in any case whatever. This is done, if at all, on the advice of the Home, Secretary, who, I believe, invariably consults the judge who tried the case, if there is a question of the guilt of the prisoner or of over-severity in his sentence. In cases where a man is pardoned on account of his health, *e.g.,* the judge is not consulted.

On the question of costs and of rewards, compensation, and restitution of goods in criminal cases,[1] I can only refer to my *Digest.*

Upon the question whether there ought to be an appeal in criminal cases there has been much discussion. I was at one time in favour of such an appeal. The Report of the Criminal Code Commission, of which I was a member, contained a recommendation of a scheme for such a court, which I concurred in. Subsequent experience, however, has led me entirely to change my opinion, and to think that substantially the existing system cannot be improved, and that such defects as exist in it are inevitable consequences of the nature of trial by jury, or are easily removable.

Put very shortly, the principal argument in favour of admitting an appeal upon matters of fact is this :—

(1) Appeals are admitted in nearly all civil cases, sometimes absolutely, sometimes under restrictions. Why allow an appeal on a question of a small sum of money, which the parties may, if they please, carry up to the House of Lords, and yet allow no appeal on a question of life, liberty, and character ?

(2) Why pardon a man admitted to be innocent, and on the ground of his innocence ? Pardon implies guilt.

---

[1] *Digest of Procedure,* Arts. 318–329.

The shortest and most general answer to the question is that to admit appeals in criminal cases upon matters of fact is to overlook the essential distinction between criminal and civil proceedings, and to carry out the principle of assimilating them beyond the point which reason or expediency warrant. A civil proceeding is meant to decide a question as to a right to property or a right to compensation for an injury between party and party. Appeals are admitted (I think too freely) not so much for the purpose of arriving at truth as for the purpose of satisfying the parties. A man appeals if he can afford it and thinks he will succeed, and his willingness to embark in an appeal and to carry it on depends, to a great extent, upon the importance to him of the interests at stake. In a criminal case the question is one in which the public is almost as much interested as the party, and in which an appeal is reasonable only in cases where granting it is desirable for the sake of truth.

It must in the first place be borne in mind that the diminution of the decisiveness of a criminal trial is in itself a great evil, which should be incurred only for the sake of avoiding injustice, and to such an extent as is required for that purpose only. The vigour of the criminal law depends to a great extent upon its deciding finally upon matters brought before it, and appeals from it have beyond all doubt the effect of breaking its point and blunting its edge. The possibility of evading it, and all unnecessary delay in carrying it into execution is so much taken away from its capacity of preventing crime. It is therefore essential, in considering the present question, to try to form something like a fair estimate of the extent of its failures, in the way of wrong convictions. I have one piece of evidence on this point to give, which I believe would be corroborated by most of my brethren. In the course of the last five years (January,

1885, to September, 1889) 1,216 criminal cases came before me.

Of these, there ended in a plea of guilty . .   199
Bills were thrown out in   38
And there were tried   979
——————
1,216

Practically one case out of a thousand was proved to be a case of a false conviction. In twenty-eight of these, references have been made to me by the Home Office. In one case only was a convict pardoned on the ground of his innocence. He was convicted of a burglary, and the mistress of the house came out of her room, met the burglar, and swore to the prisoner as the man. It was afterwards discovered that she was mistaken in his identity, though there were some other suspicious circumstances in the case. One of the cases was that of Mrs. Maybrick, which attracted so much attention, in the summer circuit of 1889. I mention it not in order to say anything about it, but merely in order to remark that it was the only case in which there could be any doubt about the facts. In the remaining twenty-six cases there was more or less of a question as to the severity of the punishment inflicted, but little as to the facts. There was one famous case in which a certain number of newspapers made a great noise, but the prisoner made a full confession before his execution. He was a man called Lipski, a Polish Jew.

I have no knowledge of the experience of others, but from my own I feel entitled to say that the number of wrong convictions must be very small, and that it is not worth while to provide for such cases at the expense of establishing any institution at variance with the established principles of trial by jury and of diminishing the efficacy of the criminal law. The less need be said about this because, when a few years ago an attempt to frame a scheme for a Court of Appeal was made, these very difficulties caused it to be given up.

Taking for granted, then, that trial by jury is to retain its present position as the stated regular method of disposing of criminal cases, the following observations as regards a Court of Criminal Appeal as to matters of fact appear to me to follow.

First, such cases must be regarded as exceptional, and must be treated exceptionally. This, in itself, appears to me to be a conclusive objection to the proposal which was the basis of the last Bill introduced into Parliament.

The proposal was to permit motions for a new trial on any ground on which a new trial may be moved for in a civil case, and on several other grounds besides, of which the following were instances. There was to be no limit of time within which a new trial might be moved for. It was not to be an objection to such a motion that the new trial was moved for on the ground that witnesses had not been called at the trial who might have been called, or on the ground that a defence which had not been raised might have been raised. A defence might be kept back till the witnesses against it were dead.

It appears to me that all such proposals are in reality opposed to the principle of trial by jury, for reasons which may be put in various shapes, but which may be illustrated by two special remarks as well as by a finished essay. In the first place, it is an elementary and indisputable principle of trial by jury that a jury are bound to give a prisoner the benefit of every reasonable doubt. Therefore, before a new trial can be granted, it must be established, to the satisfaction of the Court which grants the new trial, that the jury which gave their verdict did not fulfil their duty in this respect, but such a decision would entitle the prisoner, not to a new trial, but to an acquittal. In every case in which the complaint was grounded on any cause other than the discovery subsequently to the first trial of new evidence, the result would be that the judges and not the jury would have the last word on the final result.

The same thing is perhaps even more strongly illustrated by a second remark.   It is an undoubted principle as to trial by jury, approved by recent decisions of the highest authority, that to grant a new trial on the ground that the verdict is against the weight of evidence, the Court must be of opinion, not merely that the verdict is wrong, but that it is so wrong that the jury could not reasonably hold it.   If this rule were observed by a Court of Appeal in criminal cases, the Court of Appeal would, by the act of granting a new trial, effectually prejudge the case at that trial.   If the doctrine is given up in such cases, all steady administration of criminal law is at an end.   If it is maintained, it will be found in practice that the supposed advantages of a Court of Criminal Appeal will not be gained.   The true reason for wishing for such a Court is that exceptional cases occur to which the attention of the public is directed, it may be by some picturesque circumstance or person.   The newspapers take a leading part in the matter, and a quantity of bitter, ill-informed, and often most ignorant controversy arises ; and such scenes, which are objectionable on all possible grounds, lead to the demand for a Court of Appeal, as if by that means they might be avoided. I do not believe it is possible to avoid them.   Much occurs on such occasions which is to be regretted, but popular manifestations on such a subject are only the manifestations under an absurd form of that interest in public affairs which is the mainspring of modern political life.   It is a grotesque but a powerful security against injustice and oppression, though it is as unequal to doing justice in any given case as to expressing itself in a rational form, with reasonable modesty and without foolish exaggeration.

The present system appears to me to deal with such occasional exhibitions of public feeling in the best possible manner. The Home Secretary has facilities for testing the truth of every conclusion arrived at, and for forming an opinion upon the correctness of verdicts after a trial, which can be equalled by no one else. He can and does see the judge, the principal witnesses, especially those on whose testimony special discussions have arisen, and, in fact, all persons who really know anything about the matter, in a perfectly easy natural way, and with entire freedom from the disturbing causes which may always arise from a trial. The Secretary of State is, as a rule, himself a distinguished lawyer. The Under-Secretary is, I think, always chosen with special reference to his qualifications in this matter, and the Secretary of State can, of course, command any special assistance he thinks proper. My belief, from personal experience during ten years, is, that any change which could be made would necessarily be for the worse.

It must be borne in mind that it is only in a small minority of cases that questions of law and fact are the only questions to be considered in such matters as these. Questions of popular feeling have, and ought to have, their importance. Assume that a person is capitally convicted upon evidence in which the jury have given an unpopular verdict, and suppose further that he contends both that he ought to be pardoned upon some general ground and also on the ground that the proof against him is deficient—it is hard not to allow him to rely upon both grounds at once, and to appeal to their combined effect. This he can do at present. Under the proposed system he would, I suppose, be obliged to rely upon the defects of the evidence before the Court of Appeal, on the other ground before the Secretary of State.

One suggestion as to the nature and powers of a Court of Appeal has been made which appears to me to deserve consideration. It was made by Lord Esher, and is to the effect that there should be a Court of five or seven judges which

N

should be able to do all kinds of things—set aside the verdict, order a new trial, mitigate the sentence; in a word, do all that the Secretary of State can do and a great deal more besides. To this I say only that it appears to me that it would be to the last degree mischievous to create such a Court for such a purpose; that a Court of five or seven judges would be far too large, and that in practice a difference between the members would be far more awkward than anything which can be said to exist at present; that it would be practically impossible either to execute a man who had in his favour two or even one powerfully expressed judgment, and absurd to acquit a man convicted by a jury and by a majority of members of the Court of Appeal ; that, after all, the only result would be to substitute five or seven Secretaries of State who are wholly irresponsible, for one who has always to think of the political effect of his decision. I can hardly imagine, in short, a proposal more unconstitutional and dangerous in all ways.

I do not say that the present system might not be improved, though I should not myself think it worth while to try to do so. I think it is true that a man ought not to be pardoned for being innocent. This anomaly might be set right by empowering Her Majesty to set aside a verdict on the express ground of the convict's innocence. I think the Secretary of State might have power, if he thought proper, to compel the attendance of witnesses who might be sworn and cross-examined. I do not attach much importance to this. Evidence can now be taken on a statutory declaration, which is much the same as an oath.

Where new evidence is discovered, or where perjury, is suspected, or where inconsistent verdicts have been delivered, but in no other cases, I would allow the Secretary of State to direct a new trial.

CHAPTER XVI.

ON EVIDENCE IN CRIMINAL CASES.

I FIND much difficulty in writing on this subject in a manner altogether satisfactory to myself. In the first edition of this work, I entered, with what now strikes me as youthful enthusiasm, upon a variety of subjects connected with it which I should like to discuss at far greater length, and without special reference to law if I discussed them at all. I had also at that time failed to devise any arrangement of the purely legal part of the subject which deserved to be regarded as at all satisfactory. I have since that time thought and learnt much on the subject, having been called to legislate about it in India, and having written on it in England. The subject is far too interesting and characteristic a part of the criminal law to be completely passed over; and as it is always difficult to give an account of part of a system without giving some notion of the whole of which it is a part, I will say a few words of the nature of English rules of evidence as a whole before I go on to discuss the particular rules which apply more particularly to criminal proceedings.

The object—I believe for the most part the unconscious or half-conscious object—of English rules of evidence is to provide that conclusions in judicial cases should be founded on solid grounds. The leading principle of Bentham's specula-

N 2

tions on this subject, and none were ever in their own line more influential, was that all objections to evidence ought to be objections not to its admissibility but to its weight. This, I think, was a not wholly unnatural exaggeration of the indignation excited in Bentham by the rules of evidence as he knew them, encumbered as they were with all manner of irrational matter from which they are now happily set free. His notice was never directed to the fact, that, in the first place, inexperienced persons continually mistake suspicions of all kinds for proof, and that in the absence of rules of evidence they have no sure test by which to distinguish them ; that, in the second place, doubt is so unwelcome to the mass of mankind that in most cases there is more danger of believing too much than of believing too little; and thirdly, that in judicial affairs fraud, or at all events want of candour, is always to be carefully guarded against, and that for this purpose it is necessary to understand what is the nature of the real securities against fraud and want of candour—when they ought to be rigorously enforced, and when and to what extent they may be safely relaxed. The result of a long history, the principal points of which I have given in my *History*,[1] is that most of the rules of evidence now existing may be to a considerable extent justified on these grounds, though they have come into existence gradually and in spite of every sort of obstruction, arising from misapprehension of their nature, and from all the other causes, from which legal errors generally do arise.

The common accounts of the law of evidence are in many cases made impenetrably obscure by the non-recognition of the double meaning of the word "evidence," which is sometimes used in the sense (*a*) of testimony given orally by witnesses, and sometimes in the sense (*b*) of a fact taken to be

---

[1] See especially vol. i. chaps. viii.-xii., and the trials at the end of vol. iii.

true and used as an argument to show the existence of a fact the truth of which is in question.

The word is sometimes used in both senses at once. Thus, according to the *evidence* of A, the money was paid. In this phrase "evidence" means testimony, it means that A says he saw the money paid, and is used in sense (*a*). In the phrase "Recent possession of stolen goods is *evidence* of theft," the word is used in sense (*b*). The meaning is, the one fact makes the other probable. In the phrase "Hearsay is no evidence," the word means both things at once. The witness is not to be allowed to repeat what was said, and if it is repeated, no inference is to be drawn from the fact that it was said. Of such facts it is commonly said that they are not evidence—that is, they are not evidence in sense (*b*).

This ambiguity in expression has for certain purposes its conveniences; but I here confine myself to the use of the word "evidence" in the sense of testimony. It will be found that the whole law of evidence may be thrown, by recognizing this distinction, into the following perfectly simple shape.

It supplies answers to three great questions :—

(1) What facts may be proved to be true upon a legal proceeding having for its object the ascertainment of any legal right or liability ?

The answer is (1) All facts which, if proved, would establish or rebut the existence of any such right or liability ; and (2) any facts which alone or with others render probable or improbable the existence of any such fact.

Facts of the first class I describe as facts in issue—they may always be proved, and the pleadings in each particular case show what they are ; facts of the second class I describe as facts relevant, or deemed to be relevant, to the issue. But certain facts which might naturally be considered relevant to the issue are not considered as being so. These all fall under one of the following heads :—

(*a*) The fact that a person not sworn as a witness asserted something to be true. This is also called hearsay.

(*b*) The fact that something was asserted in a document not regarded as authoritative for the particular purpose.

(*c*) The fact that things similar to, but not specifically connected with, the matter inquired into occurred.

(*d*) The fact that any person had an opinion about its having occurred or not.

To each of these rules there are exceptions of great importance. I pass over the details, but I will give an illustration to show the form of the law.

Let the question be whether A committed a crime. The commission of the crime by A is the fact in issue. Evidence is tendered to show that A confessed that he committed the crime. This is a fact relevant to the issue, and evidence of it is admissible. It appears that the confession was preceded by an exhortation to confess made by B. This excludes the evidence of the confession if B was a person in authority in reference to the case. B was a person wholly unconnected with the case, and A did not suppose him to be so. The confession may be proved.

Thus the principal part of the working law of evidence consists of the application to particular cases of exceptions to exceptions to general rules which I was the first writer to state expressly.

(2) If a fact can be proved, how is it to be proved?.

The answer is: The fact may be so notorious as to be judicially noticed, which dispenses with all proof; but if it requires proof at all, whatever the fact may be, and on whatever ground it can be proved, it must be proved by direct evidence. If it was a fact which could be seen, heard, or otherwise directly perceived by any of the senses, it must be proved by some one who directly perceived it by that sense—who saw, or heard, or touched it. If it is the contents of a document, it must be proved by the production and verification of that document, or by a copy fulfilling the conditions of the law upon the subject of the proof of documents by copies.

(3) Lastly, who is to prove it?

The answer is, as a rule, that he who affirms must prove ; but this rule is varied by presumptions—especially in criminal cases, by the presumption of innocence. There are many subordinate rules as to the manner in which evidence is to be given, &c., which I need not notice. Of all these matters a short but full, I believe I may say a practically complete, account may be found in my *Digest of the Law of Evidence*, to which I refer for fuller information.

Confining myself to the rules of evidence which are practically confined to criminal cases, I will refer to the following only.

In the first place, I may mention the general presumption of innocence, which, though by no means confined to the criminal law, pervades the whole of its administration. This rule is thus expressed in my *Digest of the Law of Evidence* [1] :—

" If the commission of a crime is directly in issue in any " proceeding, civil or criminal, it must be proved beyond all " reasonable doubt. The burden of proving that any person " has been guilty of a crime or wrongful act is on the person " who asserts it, whether the commission of such act is or is " not directly in issue in the action."

This is otherwise stated by saying that the prisoner is entitled to the benefit of every reasonable doubt. The word " reasonable " is indefinite, but a rule is not worthless because it is vague. Its real meaning, and I think its practical operation, is that it is an emphatic caution against haste in coming to a conclusion adverse to a prisoner. It may

[1] Art. 94.

be stated otherwise, but not, I think, more definitely, by saying that before a man is convicted of a crime every supposition not in itself improbable which is consistent with his innocence ought to be negatived. But I do not know that "improbable" is more precise than "reasonable." Another way of stating it is that in order to justify a conviction, a jury ought to be in a state of moral certainty caused by legal evidence; but this, like the rest, is indefinite, for the phrase "moral certainty" is as vague as "no reasonable doubt." It is also closely connected with the saying that it is better that ten guilty men should escape than that one innocent man should suffer, an observation which appears to me to be open to two decisive objections. In the first place, it assumes, in opposition to the fact, that modes of procedure likely to convict the guilty are equally likely to convict the innocent, and it thus resembles a suggestion that soldiers should be armed with bad guns because it is better that they should miss ten enemies than that they should hit one friend. In fact, the rule which acquits a guilty man is likely to convict an innocent one; just as the gun which misses the object at which it is aimed is likely to hit an object at which it is not aimed. In the second place, it is by no means true that under all circumstances it is better that ten guilty men should escape than that one innocent man should suffer. Everything depends on what the guilty man has been doing, and something depends on the way in which the innocent man came to be suspected. I think it probable that the length to which this sentiment has been carried in our criminal courts is due to a considerable extent to the extreme severity of the old criminal law, and even more to the capriciousness of its severity, and the element of chance which, as I have already shown, was introduced into its administration by technical rules. In the Report

already quoted,[1] M. Cottu remarks that, the English "not
" thinking it for the advantage of the public to punish every
" crime committed, lest the effect of example should be
" weakened by the frequency of executions, they reserve the
" full measure of their severity for the more hardened
" offenders, and dismiss unpunished those whose guilt is not
" proved by the most positive testimony. They are indifferent
" whether among the really guilty such be convicted or
" acquitted.[2] So much the worse for him against whom the
" proofs are too evident, so much the better for the other
" in whose favour there may exist some faint doubts;
" they look upon the former as singled out by a sort
" of fatality to serve as an example to the people, and
" inspire them with a wholesome terror of the vengeance
" of the law; the other as a wretch whose chastisement
" Heaven has reserved in" (? for) "the other world." He
adds that none of the English with whom he was in company
" ever positively expressed such a sentiment, but they act as
" if they thought so." There may be some exaggeration
in this, but the sentiment here described is not altogether
unlike the practical result to be expected from the maxim
" *Timor in omnes, pœna in paucos,*" a sentiment not unnatural
when the practice and the theory of the law differed so widely
as they did sixty years ago. It was natural that a convicted
prisoner should be looked upon as a victim, chosen more or
less by chance, when the whole law was in such a state that
public sentiment would not permit of its being carried even
proximately into effect.

I know of only four rules of evidence which can be said
to be peculiar to criminal proceedings.

(1) The first, and by far the most important, is the rule
that the prisoner and his wife are incompetent witnesses.

---

[1] *Cottu's Report*, p. 91, &c.

[2] This clumsy sentence is obviously the fault of the translator.

The history of this rule is as follows :—The husbands or wives of prisoners were never, so far as I know, compelled to testify against their wives or husbands. But down to the Civil Wars, as I have already shown, the interrogation of the prisoner on his arraignment formed the most important part of the trial. Under the Stuarts, questions were still asked of the prisoner, though the extreme unpopularity of the *ex-officio* oath, and of the Star Chamber procedure founded upon it, had led to the assertion that the maxim " *Nemo tenetur accusare scipsum,*" was part of the law of God and of nature (to use the language of the day), an assertion which was all the more popular because it condemned the practice of torture for purposes of evidence then in full use both on the Continent and in Scotland.

Soon after the Revolution of 1688, the practice of questioning the prisoner died out, and as the rules of evidence passed from the civil to the criminal courts, the rule that a party was incompetent as a witness, which (subject to occasional and partial evasion by bills of discovery in equity) prevailed in civil cases till 1853,[1] was held to apply to criminal cases. This, however, was subject to two important qualifications. First, the prisoner in cases of felony could not be defended by counsel, and had therefore to speak for himself. He was thus unable to say, as his counsel sometimes still says for him, that his mouth was closed. On the contrary, his mouth was not only open, but the evidence given against him operated as so much indirect questioning, and if he omitted to answer the questions it suggested he was very likely to be convicted. This was considerably altered by the Act which allowed prisoners accused of felony the benefit of counsel. The counsel was always able to say, " My client's mouth is closed. If he could speak, he might say so and so."

[1] It was repealed by 16 and 17 Vict. c. 83.

For some years past, and by some judges, prisoners have been allowed to make whatever statements they please in their defence. I have done so for the last six or seven years, and I believe that course to be in accordance with principle, and not opposed to any enactment. I have, however, held that such a statement, if the prisoner is defended, gives a right of reply.

Secondly, the statutes of Philip and Mary already referred to, repealed and re-enacted in 1826 by 7 Geo. IV., c. 64, authorized committing magistrates to " take the examination " of the person suspected. This examination (unless it was taken upon oath, which was regarded as moral compulsion [1]) might be given in evidence against the prisoner.

This state of the law continued till the year 1848, when, by the 11 and 12 Vict., c. 42, the present system was established, under which the prisoner is asked whether he wishes to say anything, and is warned that if he chooses to do so what he says will be taken down and may be given in evidence on his trial. The result of the whole is that as matters stand the prisoner is absolutely protected against all judicial questioning before or at the trial, and that, on the other hand, he and his wife are prevented from giving evidence in their own behalf. He is often permitted, however, to make any statement he pleases at the very end of the trial, when it is difficult to test the correctness of what is said. I may just add that statutory exceptions to the general rule have been made in so many cases as to reduce the law to an absurdity. What can be more inconsistent than to prevent a man from contradicting an accusation of an unnatural crime and to allow him to contradict an accusation of rape ?

This is one of the most characteristic features of English criminal procedure, and it presents a marked contrast to that

---

[1] See my *Digest of the Law of Evidence*, Art. 23, and note xvi.

which is common to, I believe, all Continental countries. It is, I think, highly advantageous to the guilty. It contributes greatly to the dignity and apparent humanity of a criminal trial. It effectually avoids the appearance of harshness, not to say cruelty, which often shocks an English spectator in a French court of justice,[1] and I think that the fact that the prisoner cannot be questioned stimulates the search for independent evidence.[2] The evidence in an English trial[3] is I think, usually much fuller and more satisfactory than the evidence in such French trials as I have been able to study.

Such are the rules of evidence, the most celebrated and characteristic part of English criminal trials. I proceed to make some observations on their nature and value.

I do not think anyone at all acquainted with the subject practically can doubt their immense value as securities

---

[1] The contrast is described by M. Cottu in a singular passage, pp. 103–104. "The courts of England offer an aspect of impartiality and humanity which "ours, it must be acknowledged, are far from presenting to the eyes of the "stranger. In England everything breathes an air of lenity and mildness ; "the judge looks like a father in the midst of his family occupied in trying "one of his children" (an extraordinary position certainly for a man to be placed in). "His countenance has nothing threatening in it. According to "an ancient custom, flowers are strewed upon his desk and upon the clerk's. "The sheriff and officers of the court wear each a nosegay. . . .

"Everything among us, on the contrary, appears in hostility to the prisoner. "He is often treated by the public officers with a harshness, not to say cruelty, "at which an Englishman would shudder. Even our presiding judge, instead "of showing that concern for the prisoner to which the latter might appear "entitled from the character of impartiality in the functions of a judge whose "duty is to direct the examination and to establish the indictment, too "often becomes a party against the prisoner, and would seem sometimes to "think it less a duty than an honour to procure his conviction."

[2] During the discussions which took place on the Indian Code of Criminal Procedure in 1872, some observations were made on the reasons which occasionally lead native police officers to apply torture to prisoners. An experienced civil officer observed :—"There is a great deal of laziness in it. "It is far pleasanter to sit comfortably in the shade rubbing red pepper into a "poor devil's eyes than to go about in the sun hunting up evidence." This was a new view to me, but I have no doubt of its truth.

[3] See the trials at the end of this work.

for a healthy scepticism, as checks upon haste to convict, as being productive of industry in searching for evidence deserving of the name, and so preventing a vast amount of injustice. If anyone really doubts this, let them suppose what would have happened if the trials in Titus Oates's plot, or the cases tried before the French Revolutionary tribunal, had been subject to the modern rules of evidence. I doubt whether any equally valuable security for innocent people can be devised, except, perhaps, the necessity for a specific definite charge amounting to a known crime, which is secured by the law as to indictments.

Passing from this, however, what is the value of these rules, and of the evidence produced under them, with reference to securing a true result? This is quite a different question, and ought to receive a different answer. Laying aside all that can be described as speculation on a subject which at every turn suggests it, I think this much may be said with confidence.

All inquiries into assertions as to matters of fact rest upon the same foundations as assertions about physical science. At bottom they rest upon the same great assumptions—the general uniformity of Nature, and the general trustworthiness of the senses. The logic on which each proceeds is the same. In each case certain conclusions are drawn from certain facts, and in each case it is easy to err, either because any given premiss is false, or any given conclusion is incorrect. The certainty of the conclusions reached in each is proportional to the strength of the evidence.

But what is strong and what is weak evidence? Its strength is only a metaphorical way of asserting either that the assertions made by the witnesses are true, or that the inferences from them are highly probable: that it is true that the moon appeared at a certain hour to form a given angle with a given star, and that it is rightly inferred from that fact that the observer was then in a certain longitude; that a particular man actually was the person seen at a given time and place, and that it follows from thence that he committed such a crime.

Though science and law have this in common, there are also great differences between the sort of evidence on which scientific and legal inquiries depend.

The leading differences between them are as follows :—

(1) In physical inquiries the number of relevant facts is generally unlimited, and is capable of indefinite increase by experiments.

In judicial investigations the number of relevant facts is limited by circumstances, and is incapable of being increased.

(2) Physical inquiries can be prolonged for any time that may be required in order to obtain full proof of the conclusion reached ; and when a conclusion has been reached, it is always liable to review if fresh facts are discovered, or if any objection is made to the process by which it was arrived at.

In judicial investigations it is necesary to arrive at a definite result in a limited time; and when that result is arrived at, it is final and unalterable, with exceptions too rare to require notice.

(3) In physical inquiries the relevant facts are usually established by testimony open to no doubt, because they relate to simple facts which do not affect the passions, which are observed by trained observers, who are exposed to detection if they make mistakes, and who could not tell the effect of misrepresentation if they were disposed to be fraudulent.

In judicial inquiries the relevant facts are generally complex. They affect the passions in the highest degree. They are testified to by untrained observers, who are generally not open to contradiction, and are aware of the bearing of the facts which they allege upon the conclusion to be established.

(4) On the other hand, approximate generalizations are more useful in judicial than they are in scientific inquiries, because in the case of judicial inquiries every man's individual experience supplies the qualifications and exceptions necessary to adjust general rules to particular facts, which is not the case in regard to scientific inquiries.

(5) Judicial inquiries being limited in extent, the process of reaching as good a conclusion as is to be got out of the materials is far easier than the process of establishing a scientific conclusion with complete certainty, though the conclusion arrived at is less satisfactory.

It follows from what precedes that the utmost result that can in any case be produced by judicial evidence is a very high degree of probability. Whether upon any subject whatever more than this is possible—whether the highest form of scientific proof amounts to more than an assertion that a certain order in nature has hitherto been observed to take place, and that if that order continues to take place such and such events will happen—are questions which have been much discussed, but which lie beyond the sphere of the present inquiry. However this may be the reasons given above show why courts of justice have to be contented with a lower degree of probability than is rightly demanded in scientific investigation. The highest probability at which a court of justice can, under ordinary circumstances, arrive is the probability that a witness or a set of witnesses tell the truth when they affirm the existence of a fact which they say they perceived by their own eyes, and upon which they could not be mistaken. It is difficult to measure the value of such a probability against those which the theories of physical inquiries produce, nor would it serve any practical purpose to attempt to do so. It is enough to say that the process, by which a comparatively low degree of probability is shown to exist in the one case, is identical in principle with that by which a much higher degree of probability is shown to exist in the other case.

There is thus in all verdicts in criminal cases a perceptible degree of doubt. Whether that doubt is " reason-" able " or not is a question not of law, but of prudence ; the danger of opposite mistakes being put in the two scales. If a neat phrase on such a subject were of any use, I should say that a verdict of guilty can be justified only by a moral certainty of guilt founded upon legal evidence, but I do not much like such phrases. I usually tell a jury that a reasonable doubt means a doubt which they feel it reasonable to act upon, and that the great object for which they are empanelled is to find out whether they have such doubts or not. I have never thought or heard of a better direction, and I believe that no one ever misunderstands it.

It is principally with reference to questions of evidence that I have inserted the accounts of trials which conclude this work. They show, as nothing else can, the characteristic features and the most important results of two judicial systems, each of which has had its own principles, history, and results. Accounts of the French system of procedure will be found in my *History ;* [1] and the Code Pénal and other systems are compared in that work with our own on the principal subjects to which they relate.

It would be impossible to do anything like justice to the subject of evidence without treating of the most important parts of the great subject of the nature of knowledge, and of the conditions upon which its increase depends. That probability is the guide of life is an obvious truth. But though the expression has been a commonplace for more

---

[1] Vol. i. pp. 504–565.

than a century and a half, and though there has been abundant discussion of the nature of probability, I do not think that more can well be said on this great subject than that a statement is probable to whatever extent it generically resembles the common course of human conduct and of physical nature, that it is improbable to whatever extent it involves any deviation therefrom, and that it is impossible if it contradicts the conceptions upon which all language and thought rest, as, if it were affirmed that a thing could be in two places at once, and that twice two could ever be more or less than four, that it is nonsense unless it can be in some way represented to the mind so as to be the object of thought ; but I do not know that any rules wide enough to be valuable have been established, unless it is in relation to special themes or subjects of inquiry which are of much value in measuring the amount of it which ought to be ascribed to different propositions of fact. Who, for instance, can say how far a common proposition is made probable by the direct assertion of its truth by an unknown person ? By what rule can anyone be required to believe a person who describes correctly the operations of the electric telegraph, and yet be justified in refusing to listen to a ghost story ? Why is a judge required to listen with gravity to conflicting medical theories of the cause of a death, and to state to a jury the grounds on which they are to decide whether a man died of this disease or that, and yet to treat with contempt the notion that he died of witchcraft, and to reject all evidence tendered to prove it ? Probably no more difficult question can be asked, and I doubt whether there is any which, if fully solved, would be of greater practical importance. To offer any opinion on this great problem as an incident in a general view of the criminal law of England would be idle presumption. Something, however, must be said, if not on these subjects, at all events on subjects cognate to these, in order to explain the prin-

o

ciples on which the law of evidence is founded, and the circumstances which distinguish strong evidence from weak.

The law of evidence, like so many other parts of English law, has grown up to, and not out of, the general principles on which it may now be said to be founded. The oldest parts of it are simple practical rules from which inferences of gradually increasing width and importance have been drawn. It has been said that the oldest of all rules of evidence is that an attesting witness to a deed must always be called.[1]   The rule now extends only to cases in which a document is required by law to be attested, and goes back to times when the parties to an attested document were supposed to contract that it should be proved by those witnesses only. It afterwards connected itself with other rules, each of which in its turn was established because it was found by experience to be convenient, and the whole at present admits, as I have tried to show elsewhere, of being stated in a clear systematic way, and is being continually tested by practical use.[2]

Indeed, the whole scheme, and the fundamental propositions of my *Digest of the Law of Evidence*, are only a scheme of the law as it stands, devised by myself for the purposes of the Indian Evidence Act (Act I. of 1872), which, with little if any alteration, has, since 1872, been the Act by which the law of evidence is regulated throughout the whole of the Indian Empire. So far as I can judge, it had occurred to no other writer on the subject that it is impossible to understand refined distinctions upon exceptions to exceptions of which the working part of the law of evidence is composed, until the positive qualities of a fact which entitle it to be called evidence at all are ascertained and stated.   To be

---

[1] See my *Digest of the Law of Evidence*, Arts. 66 and 67, and see Note xxviii. for a statement of the rule and its history.

[2] *Ibid.*, chap. ix. Arts. 63-72.

told that hearsay is not evidence is to be told nothing until you know what is evidence. It is like being told that a cat is not a lion without any account of a lion. Let a lion be produced, and it is easy at once to say in what respects a cat differs from a lion, and what are the similarities which make it worth while to insist upon the differences.

To be told that evidence in any given case means the proof of facts in issue between the parties, and of facts relevant, or by law deemed to be relevant, to such facts, is to rescue the whole subject from confusion. Bentham, I think, remarks that, where the power and the will to speak the truth co-exist, truth will necessarily be spoken ; and I think it cannot be denied that whenever anyone speaks falsely either his power or his will to speak truly must be defective. Hence the probability of a witness's telling the truth varies according to his power and his will to do so, and the strength or the weight of his evidence varies according to these two variables; and if any rule for weighing evidence can be devised it must be done by noting the circumstances which increase or diminish the power or the will of witnesses to speak the truth. The importance of the evidence given varies according to a different set of considerations according to the nature of the crime under trial and the place which the fact alleged to be proved occupies in the theory that the accused person committed it.

First, then, as to the power of speaking the truth on any given subject. The first requisite of power to speak the truth is knowlege of it ; and knowledge depends upon the power of observing, the power of recollecting, and the power of expressing what is recollected. I think few people are aware of the extremely imperfect way in which each of the operations in question is usually performed. Most persons observe partially and very incorrectly ; their memories usually are still more imperfect ; and their powers of expression, especially if they have to testify in a public Court, are often very bad indeed.

I have been told that it is a part of the discipline of the German cavalry to make the men take rides of a considerable length, and to receive on their arrival at their destination a message which is read to them, and carried back by them to the place whence they came. They are then required to repeat the message from memory, besides giving an account of the road they took and of the things and people they saw on the way. The game of Russian scandal is a well-known illustration of the same thing, and there are innumerable others. The simplest experiments will convince almost anyone of the imperfection both of his own memory and that of other people. Let anyone, for instance, after reading with common attention a paragraph in a newspaper, try to write down the substance of it, and see how much he will remember of it, or let him take a good look at a table, and then try to write a list of the things upon it.

There is no probability that the amount to be allowed in respect of the deviations from truth caused by these defects will ever be much varied, or that any rules will ever be devised by which it will become in any reasonable degree measurable, for it varies according to time, place, individual character, and also according to the subject spoken of.

Deductions to be made because of a deficiency in will to speak the truth are, I think, much more considerable than is usually supposed, but it is so difficult to specify or measure them that it is impossible to value them at all. The fullest and best marked form of want of will to speak the truth is to be found in wilful perjury. I believe it is very common—much commoner than people in general suppose it to be. In a very large proportion of civil cases, and in most of the criminal cases in which witnesses are called for the defence, contradictions occur, and in these cases it is certain that both sides cannot be right, and probable that on one side, at least, there is perjury, unless we extend defective powers of memory, observation, and expression to an incredible degree. It must be remembered that very little perjury is all that is wanted, in most cases, and that the chance of detection is in many cases exceedingly slight. It is frequently not required of a false witness that he should invent and stand to a false story. All that is required of him may often be to forget or falsely remember a few words in a conversation at which no one except his interlocutor and himself were present, or to change the time at which a real incident occurred. That this constantly happens I have no sort of doubt, and it greatly diminishes the value of all human testimony to matters of fact.

As the impediments to the power of speaking the truth arise from imperfect observation, recollection, and description, so circumstances favourable to speaking the truth are that the matters described would be easy to be observed, recollected, and described ; and such facilities and difficulties suggest themselves upon any given set of circumstances. In the trials at the end of this book, of which I have given an account, it will be found that at least in the English trials, notwithstanding the very minute details given, hardly any incident is mentioned which might not be readily observed, remembered, and described by anyone who observed it. The only striking exception which occurs to me is in the case of Donellan, where Lady Boughton, the mother of the man supposed to be poisoned, swore, of the medicine which she gave her son, that she " observed it was very like the taste of " bitter almonds." This was one of the most important pieces of evidence in the case. Its importance was, however, much diminished by the fact being capable of being observed only for a very short time, and by the least trustworthy of all the senses. This is not noticed in the report of the summing up of Mr. Justice Buller. Apart from this, according to traditions still remembered, it is said that Lady Boughton was an extremely foolish person.

As to want of will to speak the truth, the causes of it are infinitely various. They are, indeed, as many as the causes which may lead people to wish for one result or another of any trial, and they operate to an extent which depends upon the strength of the wish felt and the character of the person by whom it is felt. The results are so various that no general observation upon them is worth making. I believe, however, that several observations may be made. In regard to perjury, and in regard also to those approaches to it which cover the distance between falsehood on oath and the complete candour which complies literally with the terms of the witness's oath to speak the truth, the whole truth, and nothing but the truth, I believe it to be strictly true that every witness has his price. I do not, of course, mean a price payable in money, but a price payable in a thousand other ways. When people think themselves incapable of perjury, or regard themselves as being so, they generally omit to think of cases of real temptation. I greatly doubt whether any large number of people would withstand such a temptation as that presented to Jeanie Deans in the *Heart of Midlothian.* Early in the present century, juries in criminal cases habitually perjured themselves to avoid a capital conviction, by finding goods stolen in a shop to be worth 39s. when they were really notoriously worth much more. From a perjury of this kind the step was short, in some cases it was almost imperceptible, to a perjury committed to save an innocent man or a man supposed by the perjurer to be innocent, or to save another from loss of character by making public circumstances which the witness is under the strongest moral obligation to conceal. An infinitely weaker temptation would be nearly sure to cause, if it did not altogether excuse, some of the minor reticences or defects in complete candour which would be inconsistent with telling the whole truth and nothing but the truth. The case of experts is as strong a one as can be mentioned. No one expects an expert, except in the rarest possible cases, to be quite candid. Most of them—for there are a few exceptions—are all but avowedly advocates, and speak for the side which calls them.

To take as an illustration of the limits within which perjury is all but inevitable, and would hardly be considered as blamable by people in general, the oaths of co-respondents in the Divorce Court are continually disbelieved—whatever, apart from the particular case, might be their character for truthfulness and candour. It is, indeed, not unfrequently maintained that a man in such circumstances is bound in honour to perjure himself. I do not mean in any degree to favour such an opinion: I merely refer to a notorious fact, to prove the essential weakness of a bare unsupported oath taken under a temptation to lie.

I must, however, point out that these remarks apply only to cases in which an oath is taken where the witness has a known interest in the result. Where no such interest can be pointed out, a direct positive oath has, as a fact, great weight. Many years ago a series of trials took place in which a will was supposed to have been forged, and many circumstances were proved which in themselves were highly suspicious. One of the alleged witnesses, however, a man of a good position in life, and as far as appeared wholly indifferent in the matter, swore most positively and circumstantially to its execution, and in the first and I think the second trial—for there were three—his oath was believed by the jury.

It will appear on the fullest investigation that all defects whatever in the truthfulness of evidence may be ascribed either to a defect of power or of will to tell the truth. I may add that some degree of oral evidence is necessary in all cases whatever, though admissions by the parties may often supersede the necessity for giving it. If the identity of any person or thing is disputed, it must be proved, unless it belongs to the small list of matters of which judicial notice is taken.

This consideration of the more general topics which affect the credibility of evidence naturally suggests the means which are available for testing its truth.

These are two—namely, first, corroboration and contradiction, and secondly, cross-examination, the process by which corroborations and contradictions are most frequently put forward and tested.

As to evidence in confirmation or in contradiction of a statement made, it is open, of course, to the same general observations as have been made already upon the general deductions to be made from the credibility of all oral evidence arising from want of power or want of will on the part of a witness to speak the truth.

Cross-examination requires some further remarks. It is a process by which the most severe of all tests may be applied to the witness under examination, and if he sustains it satisfactorily it may usually be said that nothing which makes his story improbable, or which would, if true, injure his character or shake his credit, is known to or has been heard of by those who represent the accused. So much is this the case, that, on a trial for felony, the fact that a witness is not cross-examined is almost always in practice equivalent to an admission that that to which he testifies is not contested by the other side.

Cross-examination is the part of a trial which gives rise to more popular misconception and misrepresentation, and which is more completely misunderstood, than any other part of it. A specially successful cross-examination is often supposed to arise from some singular gift of sagacity, knowledge of the world, or presence of mind, on the part of the cross-examiner. No one can know this from merely hearing a cross-examination. Counsel in such cases speak from instructions, and the effectiveness or otherwise of his instructions is the main source of the efficiency of a cross-examination, though to make a really good use even of good instructions, makes a great demand on all the lively and showy qualities of the mind.

In each of the accounts of English trials given at the end of this work, the importance of cross-examination was strikingly illustrated, if we except that of Donellan, which took place many years before counsel were allowed to the prisoner in cases of felony. If counsel had been employed to speak for the prisoner in that case, he might, I think, have easily pointed out and emphasized the difficulty under which the medical witnesses·for the prosecution lay, of proving that Sir Th. Boughton was murdered at all, by distinguishing between the symptoms of poisoning by laurel-water and those of death by a fit of epilepsy or apoplexy, suggested as possible by John Hunter.

The most brilliant instances of cross-examination to be met with anywhere are to be found in the parts of Palmer's trial in which Sir Alexander Cockburn dealt with the medical witnesses for the defence, and reduced them all to the admission that, if their own particular solution of the question "What did Cook die of?" was rejected, the answer that he died of strychnine was the next most probable solution; and in the way in which, by taking them through the various symptoms, he showed that nothing that could be called a difference could be established between the symptoms of strychnine and those of which Cook admittedly died. Sir Alexander Cockburn's cross-examination of Smith was all the more remarkable, because notwithstanding the fact that Smith was right on a point on which

the prosecution was mistaken, he was shown to be so in-
famously connected with the prisoner's admittedly criminal
and fraudulent proceedings, that he must be regarded almost
as an accomplice who thought that, by taking advantage of a
mistake made by witnesses on the other side, he could prove
a fact inconsistent with a great part of their case.

One great use of cross-examination is the fear which it
excites, which must prevent many attempts to impose upon
the Court.

The abuses of cross-examination are notorious. It may be
conducted in a manner and carried to a length which make it
an instrument of the worst kind of oppression ; but if this is
done, and I think it is done very seldom, it is, as a rule, the
fault of the judge who permits it, instead of taking whatever responsibility is involved in keeping it within proper
bounds. Its entire absence in a French Court is one of the
most striking differences between French and English procedure. In every one of the French trials described at the
end of this book, the proceedings suggest at every point that
anything like an efficient cross-examination might have
destroyed the case for the prosecution. Thus, for instance,
the whole case against the monk Léotade was based upon
inferences from the result of general inquiries made by official
and judicial inquirers. Great weight, for instance, was laid
upon the assertion that Léotade on the night of the crime
wore a certain shirt. The proof that he did so was that all
the shirts were used in common by all the monks, and were
changed every Saturday. The judge of instruction is said, in
the *acte d'accusation,* to have examined all the persons present
in the monastery at the time (about 200) as to their dirty
shirts. It is also said that each of the monks recalled with
precision the particular marks which he had remarked on his
shirt, and none of them resembled the shirt supposed to have
been worn by the murderer. In England all the shirts

would have had to be produced and identified in open Court by the persons who wore them. Practically this could not be done, but if the matter was handed over to a judge of instruction, the inevitable result was to put the greater part of the responsibility for the result of the trial upon him, and practically to relieve the jury of the responsibility which is supposed to belong to them.

The only attempt, which has attracted any attention, of which I am aware, to classify evidence at all with reference to its nature as evidence, is contained in the well-known expression which divides all evidence into direct and circumstantial. These are phrases which appear to me to be most objectionable on a variety of grounds, and especially on the following grounds :—

1. Evidence, as I have pointed out already, is itself an ambiguous word, meaning (1) testimony actually given ; and (2) facts alleged to be proved by such evidence, and used as arguments to show the existence of other facts. Thus the evidence of A proves that B was in possession of goods recently stolen. Here evidence is used in sense (1). Recent possession of stolen goods is evidence of theft. Here evidence is used in sense (2).

In the phrases direct and circumstantial evidence, the word evidence is used in both senses. Direct evidence means an assertion that the witness actually perceived a fact. Circumstantial evidence means a fact alleged to exist, and to be relevant to the issue. Therefore, to distinguish between direct and circumstantial evidence is like distinguishing between hares with four legs and hairs which grow on the head. One illustration of the practical inconvenience of this division is that it conceals or denies the fundamental principle that all evidence without distinction or exception must be direct. If the thing to be proved is something seen, heard, felt, tasted, or smelt, it must be proved by some person who says he has seen, heard, felt, tasted, or smelled it. According to this principle, which is unquestionably true, there can be no such thing as circumstantial evidence at all. It would be correct, if this view is taken, to say, All circumstantial evidence must always be proved by direct evidence. Evidence is given that a man suspected of robbery sold shortly after the robbery part of the property obtained by it. The fact that he did so must be proved by an eye-witness, or must be direct.

The most serious practical objection to the use of the phrase is that it implies, and is generally used in order to imply, a distinction which does not really exist—namely, the distinction that circumstantial evidence, or the proof of a crime by facts which are not in issue, but are relevant to the issue itself, must in all cases be weaker than proof by an alleged eye-witness of the crime itself which is in issue. This is wholly untrue, and has a plausibility about it which is very apt to mislead. The fact that A had B's purse in his pocket is far less likely to mislead in considering A's guilt than the fact that someone says that he saw him take it. The most direct evidence imaginable of a crime would in many cases not be accepted in proof of it unless it were confirmed by circumstantial evidence of it. Suppose several persons swore that they had seen the prisoner push a man into the river above the falls of Niagara, and suppose no body was found, no one was missed, no one had been seen in the neighbourhood, and nothing was found upon the accused person to create suspicion, how many witnesses would it require to secure a conviction? I do not say that the expression circumstantial evidence is unmeaning, though I think it incorrect and misleading, and used mostly for the purpose of supporting commonplaces of the most fallacious kind. I think that the division between direct and circumstantial is an idle one—a distinction without a

difference—and therefore a phrase which it would be well to
discard.

There is a sense in which the more circumstantial evidence
is the better and stronger it is, and that sense, I think, is the
original and natural sense of the word. Circumstantial evidence
in this sense means evidence in which a variety of circumstances are minutely detailed. "He broke open this door
"standing at a place where are two footmarks minutely
"corresponding with those of his shoes. The instrument
"used to break open the door must have been this crowbar.
"Here are the marks it made, and it was also used on this
"plate-chest, as appears by similar marks," is a highly
circumstantial statement, and each circumstance offers an
opportunity for confirmation or refutation. In proportion
as a statement is in this sense circumstantial, it is easy to
prove or disprove.

A full classification of evidence so made as to explain fully
the rules of evidence ought, I think, to have reference to the
nature of crimes. It should, I think, be somewhat of the
following kind. Every act and therefore every crime has its
history, from the time when it is first conceived in the mind,
if not, indeed, from the time when the circumstances occur
which cause it to be conceived, till it is completed, and has
produced its effects. It is first conceived or imagined; the
occasion arises for its execution; it is executed; and certain
consequences follow. It may, according to circumstances, be
connected with an infinite variety of other matters, any or
all of which it may be necessary to follow out to a greater or
less extent. A complete sketch of a crime may be given in
a very few words, marking these steps in it, such as motive,
preparation, execution, consequences. The whole of the
evidence will arrange itself in order of time according to
the circumstances of each case. On the width of these
inquiries, and on the way in which one bears upon another,

it is easier to give specimens than rules. I do not think a more perfect one could be found than is afforded by Palmer's trial.

These few observations sum up what I have to say upon the nature of the English rules of evidence, which contribute perhaps the most characteristic part to the English criminal law regarded as a whole. I will conclude with a few words on their practical effect.

In his famous *Rationale of Judicial Evidence*, Jeremy Bentham wrote such an attack on the system of the then existing English law on the subject as was hardly ever written on any existing system whatever. It might be compared to a shell bursting in the powder-magazine of a fortress, the fragments of the shell being lost in the ruins which it has made. The main object of the book is to show that rules tending to the exclusion of evidence must be pernicious, and with some exceptions Bentham proved his point, and with immense advantage to the cause of truth and justice. One only of the rules which he attacked still survives, and I do not think it will do so long. This is the rule which excludes the evidence of accused persons in most cases, but the exceptions already made to it are fatal to its principle. I have dealt, however, with this matter separately.

One observation, however, must be made upon Bentham's book which applies to all his works in different ways. He assumes the existence of wholly imaginary states of fact to which the rules he proposes are to be applied, and his assumptions are often the very opposite of the truth. With reference to judicial evidence, for instance, it ought never to be forgotten that one of their great objects is to prevent fraud and oppression in their worst forms, to keep out prejudices which would be fatal to the administration of justice, and to protect character except in those cases in which justice demands that it should be exposed to attack. Criminal justice may be so administered as to make it a subject of universal horror, and to cause people to fear any connection with it like the plague. Rules of evidence which prevent these evils are not to be lightly tampered with. In Léotade's case, Conte, who brought the girl said to have been murdered into the monastery in which the crime was said to have been committed, and who said he saw Léotade in the passage to which he brought her, had, says the *acte d'accusation,* " the whole of his life explored with the greatest care." It was discovered that six years before he had seduced his wife's sister—a fact not even alleged to have the most remote connection with the crime. In England the counsel for the defence might possibly ask such a question, but the judge might, and probably would, disallow it.[1]

I believe that as they now stand the rules of evidence are consistent with, and to a great extent embody, the essential conditions of all careful inquiry upon all subjects, and I also think that they form the greatest protection against the principal abuses of judicial evidence which has ever been devised.

---

[1] *Digest of the Law of Evidence,* Arts. 129, 139A. At all events in a civil case. I think he might in a criminal case also, p. 196.

TRIALS.

TRIALS.

THE following accounts of trials are intended to display the practical working of the institutions, rules, and principles described in earlier parts of the work, and in particular to enable the reader to compare the practical results of the system adopted in England, and in countries which derive their laws from England, with those of the system adopted in France and in many other parts of the continent of Europe.

[1] THE CASE OF JOHN DONELLAN.

John Donellan was tried at Warwick Assizes on the 30th March, 1781, before Mr. Justice Buller, for the murder by poison of his brother-in-law, Sir Theodosius Edward Allesley Boughton.

[2] Sir Theodosius Boughton was a young man of twenty, who, on attaining his majority, would have come into the possession of an estate of about £2,000 a year. In August, 1780, he was living with his mother, Lady Boughton, at

---

[1] The references are to "The Proceedings at large in the Trial of John "Donellan, Esq., for the wilful Murder (by Poison) of Sir The. Edward Allesley "Boughton, Bart., late of Lawford Hall, in the County of Warwick. Tried "before Mr. Justice Buller, at the Assizes at Warwick, on Friday, the 30th day "of March, 1781, taken in Short-hand by the permission of the Judge, by "W. Blanchard." London. There is also a folio report by Gurney which I have compared.   [2] P. 33.

Lawford Hall, in Warwickshire. [1] His brother-in-law, Captain Donellan, and his sister, Mrs. Donellan—who had been married in 1777—also formed part of the family. [2] They had lived in the house from about the month of June, 1778. [3] Sir Theodosius Boughton had returned to his mother's, from the house of a tutor (Mr. Jones) about Michaelmas in the same year. [4] In the event of his death, unmarried and without issue, the greater part of his fortune would descend to Mrs. Donellan; [5] but it was stated by the prisoner in his defence that he, on his marriage, entered into articles for the immediate settling of her whole fortune on herself and children, and deprived himself of the possibility of enjoying even a life-estate in case of her death; and that this settlement extended not only to the fortune, but to expectancies. It does not appear that the articles themselves were put in.

[6] Whilst Sir Theodosius Boughton was at Mr. Jones's he appears to have had an important complaint, for which he was attended by Mr. Kerr, of Northampton. He was under treatment for a disorder of the same kind in the summer of 1780. In all other respects, he appeared perfectly well to his mother, to his apothecary, and to other witnesses. Donellan, however, had for some time before been speaking of his health as bad. [7] Lady Boughton said, "Several times "before the deceased's death Mr. Donellan mentioned to me, "when I wished him to go to the country, that I did not "know what might happen in the family, and made several "observations on the bad state of his health. . . . When I "was talking about going to Bath, he said, 'Don't think of "'leaving Lawford; something or other may happen before "'you come back, for he is in a very bad state of health.' "I thought he might mean something of his being very "venturous in his going a hunting, or going into the water,

---

[1] P. 123. [2] P. 34. [3] P. 34. [4] P. 33.
[5] P. 123. [6] P. 60. [7] P. 34.

" which might occasion his death." [1] It appeared, on cross-
examination, that Lady Boughton went to Bath on the 1st
of November, 1778 ; and that, when she was at Bath, she
wrote to the Donellans to say that she was afraid her son
was in a bad way, and that his fine complexion was gone.
[2] A clergyman, Mr. Piers Newsam, proved that he had a
conversation with Donellan about Sir Theodosius Boughton's
health on the 26th August, the Saturday before his death.
" On that occasion," said Mr. Newsam, "he (Donellan) in-
" formed me that Sir Theodosius Boughton was in a very ill
" state of health, that he had never got rid of the disorder
" he had brought with him from school, and had been con-
" tinually adding to it ; that he had made such frequent use
" of mercury outwardly that his blood was a mass of mer-
" cury and corruption." He added some other particulars,
which led Mr. Newsam to say that, " If that was the case,
" I did not apprehend his life was worth two years' purchase ;
" he replied, ' Not one.' " At this time the deceased looked
very well to Mr. Newsam, though not so florid as formerly.

[3] On Tuesday, the 29th of August, 1780, Mr. Powell, an
apothecary of Rugby, sent him a draught composed of jalap,
lavender water, nutmeg water, syrup of saffron, and plain
water. He had sent him a similar draught on the preceding
Sunday. With the exception of the complaint under which
he suffered, and which was slight, he was "in very good
" health and great spirits." [4] The draught was delivered to Sir
Theodosius Boughton himself, by a servant named Samuel
Frost, about five or six on the Tuesday evening, and he took
it up stairs with him. [5] He went out fishing after the
medicine had been delivered to him ; and Frost, who delivered it, joined him about seven, and stayed with him till
he returned home about nine in the evening. He was on

---

[1] P. 47.   [2] P. 58.   [3] Pp. 28-29.
[4] Pp. 101-102.   [5] Pp. 102-107.

horseback all the time (the fishing was probably with nets), and had on a pair of boots; nor did he, during the whole time he was fishing, get his feet wet. Donellan was not there while the fishing was going on. [1] The family dined early that afternoon; and after dinner Lady Boughton and Mrs. Donellan went to take a walk in the garden: about seven the prisoner joined them, and said Sir Theodosius should have his physic, and that he had been to see them fishing, and he had endeavoured to persuade Sir Theodosius to come in—he was afraid he should catch cold—which appeared from the other evidence to be untrue. Sir Theodosius came in a little after nine, had his supper, and went to bed. His servant Frost went to his room at six next morning to ask for some straps for a net, which he was to take to Dunchurch, and Sir Theodosius got out of bed and gave them to him. He then appeared quite well. [2] On the preceding evening he had arranged with Lady Boughton to come to him at seven in the morning and give him his medicine. Some time before his death he used to keep it locked up in an inner room, and he had forgotten to take one dose. [3] Donellan said, "Why don't you set it in the outer room, " then you will not so soon forget it." After this the bottles were put on a shelf in the outer room, where, it would seem, any one would have access to them.

[4] At seven on the Wednesday morning, Lady Boughton accordingly came to give the medicine. She took particular notice of the bottle, shook it at her son's request, and, on his complaining that it was very nauseous, smelt it. She said, " I smelt it, and I observed it was very like the taste " of bitter almonds. Says I, 'Don't mind the taste of it,' " and he upon that drank the whole of it up." On smelling a bottle prepared with similar ingredients, but mixed with laurel water for the purpose of the trial, Lady Boughton said

---

[1] P. 37.   [2] P. 37.   [3] P. 35.   [4] Pp. 38–39.

that the smell was very like that of the medicine which her son had taken. After taking the draught, Sir Theodosius said he thought he should not be able to keep it on his stomach, and washed out his mouth. In "about two minutes, " or less," he struggled violently, appeared convulsed, "and " made a prodigious rattling in his throat and stomach, " and a gurgling, and seemed to me" (Lady Boughton) "to " make very great efforts to keep it down." This went on for about ten minutes, when he became quiet, and seemed disposed to sleep; and his mother went out to complete her dress, [1] intending to go with Donellan to a place called Newnham Wells. In about five minutes she returned to her son's room, and found him lying with his eyes fixed, his teeth clenched, and froth running out of his mouth. She immediately sent for the doctor; and on Donellan's coming in, shortly after, said, [2] "Here is a terrible affair! I have been " giving my son something wrong instead of what the apothe- " cary should have sent. I said it was an unaccountable " thing in the doctor to have sent such a medicine; for if it " had been taken by a dog, it would have killed him." On this Donellan asked where the physic bottle was, and, on its being pointed out, took it and held it up, and poured some water into it; he shook it and emptied it out into some dirty water in the wash-hand basin. Lady Boughton said, "Good " God! what are you about? You should not have meddled " with the bottle." He then put some water in the other bottle (probably the bottle sent on the Sunday), and put his finger to it to taste it. Lady Boughton said again, "What " are you about? you ought not to meddle with the bottle." He said he did it to taste it.

After this, two servants, Sarah Blundell (who died before the trial) and Catherine Amos, came in. Donellan ordered Blundell to take away the bottles and the basin, and put the

[1] P. 100. [2] P. 40.

bottles into her hand. Lady Boughton took them away, and
bid her let them alone. Donellan then told her to take away
the clothes, so that the room might be cleared, and a moment
after Lady Boughton, whose back had been turned for a
minute, saw Blundell with the bottles in her hand, and saw
her take them away. At the time when this happened Sir
Theodosius was in the act of dying. While the things were
being put away, [1] Donellan said to the maid, " Take his stock-
" ings, they have been wet; he has caught cold, to be sure,
" and that may have occasioned his death." Lady Boughton
upon this examined the stockings, and there was no mark or
appearance of their having been wet.

Some time in the morning—and it would seem shortly
after Sir Theodosius's death—[2] Donellan went to the gardener
and told him to get two pigeons directly to put to his
master's feet, as " he lies in sad agonies now with that nasty
" distemper; it will be the death of him." [3] In the afternoon of the same day he told his wife, in Lady Boughton's
presence, that she (Lady Boughton) had been pleased to take
notice of his washing the bottles out; and he did not know
what he should have done if he had not thought of putting
in the water, and putting his finger to it to taste. He afterwards called up the coachman, and having reminded him that
he had seen him go out that morning about seven, observed
that was the first time of his going out; and he had never
been on the other side of the house that morning, and
having insisted on this, said, " You are my evidence?" to
which the man replied, " Yes, sir." [4] In the evening he said
to the gardener, Francis Amos, " Now, gardener, you shall
" live at your ease and work at your ease; it shall not be
" as it was in Sir Theodosius's days; I wanted before to be
" master. I have got master now, and I shall be master."

On the day of Sir Theodosius Boughton's death, Donellan

[1] P. 45.   [2] P. 108.   [3] P. 43.   [4] P. 107.

announced it to his guardian, Sir William Wheler, in a letter which mentioned none of the circumstances, but observed merely that he had been for some time past under the care of Mr. Powell for a complaint similar to that which he had at Eton, and had died that morning. Sir William Wheler returned a civil answer; but on the following Sunday he saw Mr. Newsam, and in consequence of what he heard from him, he wrote to Donellan on the 4th September, saying that there was a report that the death was very sudden, that there was great reason to believe the physic was improper, and might be the cause of the death; that he had inquired of Mr. Powell, whose reputation was at stake, and that it would be a great satisfaction to Mr. Powell to have the body opened. The letter proceeded to say :—" Though it is very late to do " it now, yet it will appear from the stomach whether there " is anything corrosive in it. As a friend to you, I must say " that it will be a great satisfaction to me, and I am sure it " must be so to you, Lady Boughton, and Mrs. Donellan, " when I assure you it is reported all over the country " that he was killed either by medicine or by poison. The " country will never be convinced to the contrary unless the " body is opened, and we shall all be very much blamed; " therefore I must request it of you and the family that " the body may be immediately opened by Mr. Wilmer " of Coventry, or Mr. Snow of Southam, in the presence of " Dr. Rattray, or any other physician that you and the family " may think proper." [1] Donellan answered this on the same day by a note, in which he said, "We most cheerfully wish " to have the body of Sir Theodosius opened for the general " satisfaction, and the sooner it is done the better; therefore " I wish you could be here at the time." To this Sir William Wheler replied, " I am very happy to find that Lady Bough- " ton, Mrs. Donellan, and yourself approve of having the body

[1] Pp. 113-115.

" opened." He went on to say that it would not be proper for him to attend, or any one else, except the doctors.

In consequence of these letters, Dr. Rattray and Mr. Wilmer were sent for, and came to Lawford Hall about eight o'clock the same evening. [1] Donellan received them, and told them that he wished the body opened for the satisfaction of the family, producing to them Sir William Wheler's second letter—not the one about the suspicion of poison, but the one which contained a mere general expression of satisfaction at the willingness of the family to have the body opened, and excused himself from attending. He said nothing of any suspicion of poison. The body was found in a high state of putrefaction, and the two medical men, disgusted at the business, and not knowing of any special reason for inquiry, said that they thought at so late a period nothing could be discovered, declined to open the body, and left the house.

On the following morning (Tuesday, September 5) Donellan wrote to Sir W. Wheler a letter in which he said that Dr. Rattray and Mr. Wilmer and another medical man had been at the house, and that Mr. Powell had met them there. He then proceeded :—[2] " Upon the receipt of your last letter I gave " it them to peruse, and act as it directed ; the four gentlemen " proceeded accordingly, and I am happy to inform you they " fully satisfied us, and I wish you would hear from them the " state they found the body in, as it would be an additional " satisfaction to me that you should hear the account from " themselves."

These expressions naturally led Sir W. Wheler to believe that the body had actually been opened, though in fact this was not the case.

On the same day [3] Mr. Bucknill, a surgeon at Rugby, came and offered to open the body, but Donellan said that as Dr. Rattray and Mr. Wilmer had declined, it would

---

[1] Pp. 63–64.   [2] P. 116.   [3] P. 97.

be disrespectful to them to allow any one else to take their
place.

On the next day, the 6tL September, [1] Sir William Wheler heard that the body had not been opened, and heard also of Bucknill's offer. He accordingly wrote again to Donellan, saying, that from his last letter he had inferred that the body had been opened, but now found that the doctors had not thought it safe, and that Bucknill's offer to do so had been refused. He added that if Bucknill and Mr. Snow would do it they ought by all means to be allowed. [2] Donellan replied by a letter on the day of the funeral, in which he offered to have the funeral put off, if Sir W. Wheler wished, till after he (Sir W. Wheler) had seen Dr. Rattray and Mr. Wilmer. [3] He did not offer to have the body opened. In the meantime Sir W. Wheler had sent to Bucknill and Snow to go over to open the body, and Bucknill went for the purpose, and arrived at the house about two in the afternoon of Thursday, the 6th September, the day of the funeral. Snow had not then arrived. Bucknill was sent for to a patient who was supposed to be dying, and went away, saying he should be back in an hour or an hour and a half. He came back in an hour, and [4] Donellan said " he was gone, and he had given his orders " what to do, and they were proceeding according to those " orders; and I am sorry you should have given yourself " this trouble." [5] Bucknill then left, and the body was buried without being opened.

These incidents prove that Donellan did all he could to destroy all evidence as to the cause of the death of the deceased. After Lady Boughton had said she thought there

---

[1] P. 118.
[2] P. 21. This letter was read in the opening speech of Mr. Howarth, the counsel for the Crown. It does not appear in the report of the evidence.
[3] P. 93.   [4] It appears from the summing up that *he* meant Snow.
[5] Pp. 99-100.

was something wrong about the draught, he threw it away. After Sir William Wheler said there was a report of poisoning, he kept the doctors in ignorance of it, and so prevented their opening the body. He then ingeniously contrived to lead Sir William Wheler into the belief that they had opened it, and also parried and put aside Bucknill's offer to do so.

The suspicions of poisoning which prevailed were so strong that the body was taken up and opened by Mr. Bucknill in the presence of Dr. Rattray, Mr. Wilmer, Mr. Powell, and Mr. Snow. It was in an advanced state of decomposition, and none of the appearances which presented themselves required to be explained by any other cause. There was, however, one exception, and it is remarkable that this piece of evidence was not given on the examination of the witness in chief, but was got out of Dr. Rattray—injudiciously and needlessly, it would seem—by questions asked by the prisoner's counsel in cross-examination. It was as follows :—

[1] " *Q.* Did you ever smell at that liquor that was in the " stomach ? *A.* Ay, smell ; I could not avoid smelling. " *Q.* Was it the same offensive smell ? *A.* It in general had ; " one could not expect any smell but partaking of that general " putrefaction of the body ; but I had a particular taste in " my mouth at that time, a kind of biting acrimony upon my " tongue. And I have, in all the experiments I have made " with laurel-water, always had the same taste from breathing " over the water, a biting upon my tongue, and sometimes a " bitter taste upon the upper part of the fauces."

Having got out this evidence against his client whilst feeling his way towards the suggestion that putrefaction accounted for the whole, the counsel could not let it alone, but pursued his questions, and made matters worse.

[1] P. 83.

" *Q.* Did you impute it to that cause, then ? *A.* No ; I " imputed it to the volatile salts escaping the body."

If the questions had stopped here, it would have left Dr. Rattray in the wrong, but, apparently encouraged by this advantage, the prisoner's counsel went a step further.

" *Q.* Were not the volatile salts likely to occasion that ? " *A.* No. I complained to Mr. Wilmer, ' I have a very odd " ' taste in my mouth—my gums bleed.' *Q.* You attributed it " to the volatility of the salts ? *A.* At that time I could not " account for it ; but, in my experiments afterwards with the " laurel-water, the effluvia of it constantly and uniformly " produced the same kind of taste ; there is a very volatile " oil in it, I am persuaded."

The *post-mortem* examination was followed by an inquest. At the inquest, [1] Lady Boughton gave an account of Donellan's washing the bottle. When she did so, [2] he laid hold of her arm and gave her a twitch, and on their return home (said Lady Boughton), " he said to his wife, before me, that I had " no occasion to have told of the circumstance of his washing " the bottle. I was only to answer such questions as had " been put to me, and that question had not been asked me." At or after the inquest, [3] Donellan wrote a letter to the coroner and jury, of which the following passage was the most important part :—" During the time Sir Theodosius was here, " great part of it was spent in procuring things to kill rats, " with which this house swarms remarkably ; he used to " have arsenic by the pound weight at a time, and laid the " same in and about the house in various places, and in as " many forms. We often expostulated with him about the " continued careless manner in which he acted respecting " himself and the family in general. His answer to us was, " that the men-servants knew where he laid the arsenic, " and for us, we had no business with it. At table, we

[1] P. 45. [2] P. 109. [3] P. 24.

" have not knowingly eaten anything for many months past
" which we perceived him to touch, as we well knew his
" extreme inattention to the bad effects of the various things
" he frequently used to send for for the above purposes, as
" well as for making up horse-medicines." [1] It was true that
Sir Theodosius had bought a pound of arsenic for the purpose
of poisoning fish and rats, as appeared on the cross-examination
of his mother.

[2] Besides these circumstances, it was shown that Donellan
had a still, in which he distilled roses. He kept the still in
a room which he called his own, and in which he slept when
Mrs. Donellan was confined. [3] Two or three days after Sir
Theodosius's death, he brought out the still to the gardener
to clean. It was full of lime, and the lime was wet. He
said he used the lime to kill the fleas. [4] About a fortnight
after the death, he brought the still to Catherine Amos, the
cook, and asked her to put it in the oven and dry it, that it
might not rust. It was dry, but had been washed. The
cook said it would unsolder the tin to put it in the oven. [5] It
was suggested by the prosecution that the object of this might
be to take off the smell of laurel water.

[6] After Donellan was in custody, he had many conversations

---

[1] P. 51.   [2] P. 106.   [3] P. 107.   [4] P. 57.

[5] In the observations on Donellan's case contained in Mr. Townsend's Life
of Justice Buller (*Lives of English Judges*, p. 14), the following statement is
made :—" In his [Donellan's] library there happened to be a single number of
" the *Philosophical Transactions ;* and of this single number the leaves had
" been cut only in one place, and this place happened to contain an account
" of the making of laurel water by distillation." Nothing is said of this in
the reports of the trial. It is something like the evidence in Palmer's case
(*post*, p. 253) about the note on strychnine in the book, though much stronger.

[6] The following anecdote forms a curious addition to the evidence given at
the trial :— My grandfather, well known as one of the leading members of the
Anti-Slavery Society, took great interest in Donellan's case, and wrote a
pamphlet against the verdict, which attracted much notice at the time. He
was thus introduced to Donellan's attorney, who told him that he always
believed in his client's innocence, till one day he (the attorney) proposed to
Donellan to retain Mr. Dunning specially to defend him. Donellan agreed,

on the subject of the charge with a man named Darbyshire, a debtor. In these conversations, he frequently expressed his opinion that his brother-in-law had been poisoned. He said, " It was done amongst themselves,—himself " (the deceased), " Lady Boughton, the footman, and the apothecary." He also said that Lady Boughton was very covetous ; that she had received an anonymous letter the day after Sir Theodosius's death, charging her plump with the poisoning of Sir Theodosius, that she called him, and told it to him, and trembled.

The medical evidence given against the prisoner was that of Dr. Rattray, Mr. Wilmer, Dr. Ash, and Professor Parsons, Professor of Anatomy at Oxford. They substantially agreed in their opinions ; but the way in which they were allowed to give them differed much from what would be permitted in the present day, as their answers embodied their view of the evidence, with their opinion of the nature of the symptoms described. In the present day great pains are taken to prevent this, and to oblige skilled witnesses to give scientific opinions only, leaving the evidence to the jury.

Dr. Rattray said, ¹ " Independent of the appearances of the " body, I am of opinion that draught, in consequence of the " symptoms which followed the swallowing of it, as described " by Lady Boughton, was poison, and the immediate cause of " his death."

and referred the attorney to Mrs. Donellan for authority to incur the necessary expense. Mrs. Donellan said she thought it needless to pay so high a fee. When the attorney reported this to Donellan, he burst into a rage, and cried out passionately,—" And who got it for her ! " Then, seeing he had committed himself, he suddenly stopped. I have heard this story related by two of my grandfather's children, in nearly the same form, with the addition, that he was fond of telling it. At the time of the trial, Dunning was still in practice. He was raised to the peerage in the following year. The story itself is hearsay at the fifth remove as to a conversation more than 100 years ago. I, in 1889, say that my uncle and an aunt told me that my grandfather told them that an attorney told him that Donellan said, &c., in 1781.

¹ P. 67.

Dr. Ash was asked, [1] " What is your opinion of the death of " Sir Theodosius Boughton ?

" *A.*—I answer, he died in consequence of taking that " draught administered to him in the morning. He died in " so extraordinary a manner. It does not appear, from any part " of the evidence that has been this day given, that Sir Theo- " dosius had any disease upon him of a nature, either likely " or in any degree sufficient, to produce those violent conse- " quences which happened to him in the morning, when he " was seized in that extraordinary manner, nor do I know of " any medicine, properly so called, administered in any dose " or form, which could produce the same effects. I know " nothing but a poison, immediate in its operation, that could " be attended with such terrible consequences." He then went on to say that the *post-mortem* appearances in some degree resembled those of animals poisoned by vegetable poisons.

Dr. Parsons said, [2] " I have no difficulty in declaring it to " be my opinion, that he died in consequence of taking that " draught, instead of the medicine of jalap and rhubarb. " The nature of that poison appears sufficiently described by " Lady Boughton, in the account she gives of the smell of " the medicine when she poured it out in order to give it to " her son."

[3] Donellan, according to the practice of that time, delivered a written defence to the officer of the court, by whom it was read. It affords a good illustration of the fact that when counsel are refused to a prisoner every statement made by the prose- cution amounts to an indirect interrogation of the prisoner. He does not attempt to explain the washing of the bottles. He does attempt to explain the transactions about the doctors ; but, in doing so, he contradicts the witnesses. He says, " These gentlemen arrived about nine o'clock at night,

[1] P. 92.   [2] P. 95.   [3] Pp. 123–126.

" when I produced to their Sir William's letter, and desired
" they would pursue his instructions." The letter he produced
was the second letter, not the first. In the preceding part of
his defence, he mentioned only one letter from Sir William
Wheler. In reference to Bucknill's visit on the day of the
funeral, he said that after Bucknill was called away, Snow
came and waited for Bucknill a considerable time ; and, on
making inquiry of the plumber and others as to the state of
the body, said he would not be concerned in opening it for
Sir Theodosius's estate, and went away ; after which the body
was buried, " but not by my directions or desire." It is
remarkable that Snow was not called on either side. According to our modern practice, he ought to have been called by
the Crown, unless there were strong reasons to the contrary.

On the whole, it appears that the defence contains one
false suggestion, and one unproved suggestion which, if true,
could have been proved ; and that, on all the other parts
of the prisoner's behaviour, it maintains a most significant
silence. This is most important, as, being in writing, it must
have been prepared before the trial.

Evidence for the prisoner was given [1] which showed that
in June, 1778, two years before the alleged murder, he
acted in such a way as to prevent his brother-in-law from
fighting a duel, [2] and that, about a year afterwards, he was
sent for as second on another occasion, though the quarrel
was arranged before he arrived. This went to show that, if he
was guilty, his design was not formed in 1778.

He also called the famous John Hunter to contradict the
medical evidence for the prosecution.

In Palmer's case, the witnesses were confined in the closest
way to speaking of the symptoms in general terms, and
were not permitted to give any sort of opinion as to the
means by which they were produced. So far was this

---

[1] Pp. 47, 127.   [2] P. 128.

distinction from being understood, or at least favoured, in Donellan's case, that Hunter was hardly permitted to confine himself to an opinion on the symptoms. The gist of his evidence was, that all the symptoms were consistent with epilepsy or apoplexy, though also consistent with poisoning by laurel water. The greatness of John Hunter's name, and the curious difference between the practice of that day and our own, will excuse an extract of some length from his evidence. After being examined as to some of the circumstances of the case, he was asked :—

[1]" *Q.* Do you consider yourself as called upon by such " appearances to impute the death of the subject to poison ?

" *A.* Certainly not. I should rather suspect it to be an " apoplexy, and I wish the head had been opened. It might " have removed all doubts.

" *Q.* From the appearances of the body . . . no inference " can be drawn for me to say he died of poison ?

" *A.* Certainly not ; it does not give the least suspicion."
He was then cross-examined.

[2]" *Q.* Having heard before to-day that a person, apparently " in health, had swallowed a draught which had produced the " symptoms described—I ask you whether any reasonable man " can entertain a doubt that that draught, whatever it was " produced those appearances ?

" *A.* I don't know well what answer to make to that " question.

" *Q.* I will therefore ask your opinion. Having heard the " account given of the health of this young gentleman, pre- " vious to the taking of the draught that morning, and the " symptoms that were produced immediately upon taking " the draught—I ask your opinion, as a man of judgment,

---

[1] P. 131.

[2] Pp. 131–132. The phraseology is very ungrammatical ; but it always is so in shorthand reports. The meaning is plain enough. Gurney's report is less incorrect as to language, but hardly so vivid.

" whether you do not think that draught was the occasion of
" his death ?

" *A.* With regard to the first part of the question, his being
" in health, that explains nothing. Some healthy people, and
" generally healthy people, die suddenly, and therefore I shall
" lay no stress upon that. As to the circumstances, I own
" there are suspicions. Every man is as good a judge as
" I am.

[1] " *Court.*—You are to give your opinion upon the symptoms
" only, not upon any other evidence given.

" *Q.* Upon the symptoms immediately produced upon the
" swallowing of the draught, I ask your judgment and opinion,
" whether that draught did not occasion his death ?

" *Prisoner's Counsel.*—I object to that question, if it is put
" in that form ; if it is put ' after the swallowing it,' I have no
" objection." (Probably the objection was that the words
" produced *upon*" implied causation.)

" *Q.* Then ' after' swallowing it. What is your opinion,
" allowing he had swallowed it ?

" *A.* I can only say that is a circumstance in favour of such
" opinion.

" *Court.*—That the draught was the occasion of his
" death ?

" *A.* No : because the symptoms afterwards are those of a
" man dying, who was before in perfect health ; a man dying
" of an epilepsy or apoplexy. The symptoms would give one
" those general ideas.

" *Court.*—It is the general idea you are asked about now ;
" from the symptoms which appeared upon Sir Theodosius
" Boughton immediately after he took the draught, followed
" by his death so very soon after—whether, upon that part of
" the case, you are of opinion that the draught was the cause
" of his death ?

---

[1] *See* in Gurney's report.

" *A*. If I knew the draught was poison, I should say, most
" probably, that the symptoms arose from that; but when I
" don't know that that draught was poison, when I consider
" that a number of other things might occasion his death, I
" can't answer positively to it."

Here more questioning followed, the most important part of
which was an inquiry whether laurel-water, if taken, would
not have produced the symptoms; to which the answer was,
" I suppose it would." At last, the judge asked the following
question :—

" *Q*. I wish you would be so good as to give me your opinion,
" in the best manner you can, one way or the other, whether,
" upon the whole—you have heard of the symptoms described
" —it is your opinion the death proceeded from that medicine
" or from any other cause ?

" *A*. That question is distressing. I don't mean to equivo-
" cate when I tell the sentiments of my own mind—what I
" feel at the time. I can give nothing decisive."

Upon this evidence, the judge observed as follows :—

[1] " For the prisoner you have had one gentleman called who
" is likewise of the faculty, and a very able man. One can
" hardly say what his opinion is; he does not seem to form
" any opinion at all of the matter; he at first said he could
" not form an opinion whether the death was occasioned by
" that poison or not, because he could conceive it might be
" ascribed to other causes. I wished very much to have got
" another answer from Mr. Hunter if I could,—What, upon
" the whole, was the result of his attention to this case ?
" what his present opinion was ? But he says he can say
" nothing decisive. So that, on this point, if you are deter-
" mining in the case upon the evidence of the gentlemen who
" are skilled in the faculty, why, you have a very positive
" opinion of four or five gentlemen of the faculty, on the one

[1] P. 139.

" side, that the deceased did die of poison; and, upon the
" other side, what I really cannot myself call more than the
" doubt of another—that is, Mr. Hunter."

The rest of the summing up was equally unfavourable to
the prisoner. After observing that the two questions were,
whether the deceased was poisoned, and, if so, by whom—and
after concluding the consideration of the first question by
the remarks just quoted—the judge went through every
particular of the prisoner's conduct, showing how they suggested that he was the poisoner. Describing Donellan's false
statement that the deceased had taken cold, he asked, " Is
" that truth? . . . What was there that called upon the
" prisoner, unnecessarily, to tell such a story? If you can
" find an answer to that that does not impute guilt to the
" prisoner, you will adopt it; but on this fact, and many others
" that I must point out to your attention, I can only say, that
" unnecessary, strange, and contradictory declarations cannot
" be accounted for otherwise than by such fatality, which
" only portends guilt." He then went through the other
circumstances with a dexterity to which an abstract cannot
do justice, here and there qualifying the points against the
prisoner by suggestions in his favour. For instance, after
remarking on the keeping back of Sir W. Wheler's letter,
he says, " It is possible the prisoner might suppose Sir
" W. Wheler's ideas were sufficiently communicated to the
" physicians and surgeons by the last letter, and therefore
" unnecessary to show the first." On the whole, however,
every observation made the other way.

Upon this evidence and summing up, Donellan was almost
immediately convicted, and was afterwards hung.

Few cases have given rise to more discussion. Both the
conduct of the judge and the verdict of the jury were warmly
censured at the time.

In the present day, I doubt whether the prisoner would

Donellan's Case.

have been convicted, because the medical evidence certainly is far less strong than it might have been. John Hunter's evidence obviously comes to this. Epilepsy or apoplexy or poison are equally probable solutions of the facts proved if we look only at the symptoms, and there is in the nature of things no reason why a man apparently in perfect health should not have a fatal attack of epilepsy or apoplexy a few minutes after drinking a glass of medicine as well as at any other time. On the other hand, the symptoms were precisely those which would be caused by poisoning with laurel-water. The evidence as to the smell of the medicine, and as to the smell perceived by the doctors who examined the body, points directly to the conclusion that laurel-water was used. Every incident in Donellan's conduct pointed to his guilt. He took every step which a guilty man would naturally take. Before the death he did all he could to prevent surprise at its occurrence and to lead people to expect it. After the death he did his best to destroy all evidence as to its cause and to prevent the examination of the body. He also prepared means by which he obtained an opportunity for committing the crime, and he had the means by which he might prepare the poison supposed to have been used if he were so disposed. Moreover, he entirely failed to give any plausible explanation of the course which he was proved to have taken. To my mind, all this taken together raises so strong a probability of his guilt, that I think the jury were right in rejecting the possibility that the death might have been caused by apoplexy or epilepsy happening to follow close upon the administration of the medicine. No doubt the case is near the indeterminate and indeterminable line at which reasonable doubt would begin. It forms a curious contrast to the case of Belany, tried and acquitted for the murder of his wife, on evidence which was rather stronger, in 1844.

[1] THE CASE OF WILLIAM PALMER.

O<small>N</small> the 14th May, 1856, William Palmer was tried at the Old Bailey, under the powers conferred on the Court of Queen's Bench by 19 Vict. c. 16, for the murder of John Parsons Cook at Rugeley, in Staffordshire. The trial lasted for twelve days, and ended on the 27th May, when the prisoner was convicted, and received sentence of death, on which he was afterwards executed at Stafford.

Palmer was a general medical practitioner at Rugeley, much engaged in sporting transactions. Cook, his intimate friend, also a sporting man, after attending Shrewsbury races with Palmer on the 13th November, 1855, returned in his company to Rugeley, and died at the Talbot Arms Hotel, at that place, soon after midnight, on the 21st November, 1855, under circumstances which raised a suspicion that he had been poisoned by Palmer. The case against Palmer was, that he had a strong motive to murder his friend, and that his conduct before, at the time of, and after his death, coupled with the circumstances of the death itself, left no reasonable doubt that he did murder him, by poisoning him with antimony and strychnine.

The evidence stood as follows. At the time of Cook's death, Palmer was involved in bill transactions, which appear to have begun in the year 1853. [2] His wife died in September,

---

[1] The authority referred to is "A Verbatim Report of the Trial of William " Palmer, &c., transcribed from the Shorthand Notes of W. Angelo Bennett." London : Allen. 1856.

[2] A true bill for her murder was returned against the prisoner; but as he was convicted in Cook's case, it was not proceeded with.

1854, and on her death he received £13,000 on policies on her life, nearly the whole of which was applied to the discharge of his liabilities. In the course of the year 1855 he raised other large sums, amounting in all to £13,500, on what purported to be acceptances of his mother's. The bills were renewed from time to time at enormous interest (usually sixty per cent. per annum) by a money-lender named Pratt, who, at the time of Cook's death. held eight bills—four on his own account and four on account of his client; two already overdue and six others falling due—some in November and others in January. About £1,000 had been paid off in the course of the year so that the total amount then due, or shortly to fall due, to Pratt, was £12,500. The only means which Palmer had by which these bills could be provided for was a policy on the life of his brother, Walter Palmer, for £13,000. [1] Walter Palmer died in August, 1855, and William Palmer had instructed Pratt to recover the amount from the insurance office, but the office refused to pay. [2] In consequence of this difficulty, Pratt earnestly pressed Palmer to pay something in order to keep down the interest or diminish the principal due on the bills. He issued writs against him and his mother on the 6th November, and informed him in substance that they would be served at once, unless he would pay something on account. Shortly before the Shrewsbury races he had accordingly paid three sums, amounting in all to £800, of which £600 went in reduction of the principal, and £200 was deducted for interest. It was understood that more money was to be raised as early as possible.

[3] Besides the money due to Pratt, Mr. Wright, of Birmingham, held bills for £10,400. Part of these, amounting to £6,500, purported to be accepted by Mrs. Palmer; part were

---

[1] A bill for his murder also was returned against William Palmer ; but, in consequence of his conviction, was not proceeded with.

[2] Pratt, 165–166.   [3] Wright, 169–170.

collaterally secured by a bill of sale of the whole of William
Palmer's property. These bills would fall due in the first
or second week of November. Mr. Padwick also held a bill of
the same kind for £2,000, on which £1,000 remained unpaid,
and which was twelve months overdue on the 6th October,
1855. [1] Palmer, on the 12th November, had given Espin a
cheque antedated on the 28th November, for the other £1,000.
[2] Mrs. Sarah Palmer's acceptance was on nearly all these
bills, and in every instance was forged.

The result is that, about the time of the Shrewsbury races,
Palmer was being pressed for payment on forged acceptances
to the amount of nearly £20,000, and that his only resources
were a certain amount of personal property over which
Wright held a bill of sale, and a policy for £13,000, the payment of which was refused by the office. Should he succeed
in obtaining payment, he might no doubt struggle through
his difficulties, but there still remained the £1,000 antedated
cheque given to Espin, which it was necessary to provide for
at once by some means or other. That he had no funds of
his own was proved by the fact that [3] his balance at the bank
on the 19th November was £9 6s., [4] and that he had to borrow
£25 of a farmer, named Wallbank, to go to Shrewsbury races.
It follows that he was under the most pressing necessity to
obtain a considerable sum of money, as even a short delay in
obtaining it might involve him not only in insolvency, but in
a prosecution for uttering forged acceptances.

[5] Besides the embarrassment arising from the bills in the
hands of Pratt, Wright, and Padwick, Palmer was involved in
a transaction with Cook, which had a bearing on the rest of
the case. Cook and he were parties to a bill for £500, which
Pratt had discounted, giving £375 in cash, and a wine warrant for £65, and charging £60 for discount and expenses.

---

[1] Espin, 164. [2] Strawbridge, 104, 169–170. [3] Strawbridge, 169.
[4] Wallbank, 169. [5] Pratt, 167.

He also required an assignment of two racehorses of Cook's —Polestar and Sirius—as a collateral security. By Palmer's request, the £375, in the shape of a cheque payable to Cook's order, and the wine warrant, were sent by post to Palmer at Doncaster. Palmer wrote Cook's indorsement on the cheque, and paid the amount to his own credit at the bank at Rugeley. On the part of the prosecution it was said that this transaction afforded a reason why Palmer should desire to be rid of Cook, inasmuch as it amounted to a forgery by which Cook was defrauded of £375. It appeared, however, on the other side, that there were £300 worth of notes, relating to some other transaction, in the letter which inclosed the cheque; and as it did not appear that Cook had complained of getting no consideration for his acceptance, it was suggested that he had authorized Palmer to write his name on the back of the cheque, and had taken the notes himself. This arrangement seems not improbable, as it would otherwise be hard to explain why Cook acquiesced in receiving nothing for his acceptance, and there was evidence that he meant to provide for the bill when it became due. [1] It also appeared late in the case that there was another bill for £500, in which Cook and Palmer were jointly interested.

[2] Such was Palmer's position when he went to Shrewsbury races, ·on Monday, the 12th November, 1855. Cook was there also; and on Tuesday, the 13th, his mare Polestar won the Shrewsbury Handicap, by which he became entitled to the stakes, worth about £380, and bets to the amount of nearly £2,000. Of these bets he received £700 or £800 on the course at Shrewsbury. The rest was to be paid at Tattersall's on the following Monday, the 19th November. After the race Cook invited some of his friends to dinner at the Raven Hotel, and on that occasion and on the following day

---

[1] Pp. 307, 310.
[2] Fisher, 25–26. Read, 30. Gibson, 31. Thos. Jones, 29.

he was both sober and well. On the Wednesday night, a man named Ishmael Fisher came into the sitting-room which Palmer shared with Cook, and found them in company with some other men drinking brandy-and-water. Cook complained that the brandy "burned his throat dreadfully," and put down his glass with a small quantity remaining in it. Palmer drank up what was left, and, handing the glass to Read, asked him if he thought there was anything in it; to which Read replied, "What's the use of handing me the glass "when it's empty?" Cook shortly afterwards left the room, called out Fisher, and told him that he had been very sick, and "he thought that damned Palmer had dosed him." He also handed over to Fisher £700 or £800 in notes to keep for him. He then became sick again, and was ill all night, and had to be attended by a doctor. He told the doctor, Mr. Gibson, that he thought he had been poisoned, and he was treated on that supposition. Next day, Palmer told Fisher that Cook had said that he (Palmer) had been putting something into his brandy. He added that he did not play such tricks with people, and that Cook had been drunk the night before—which appeared not to be the case. Fisher did not expressly say that he returned the money to Cook, but from the course of the evidence it seems that he did, for Cook asked him to pay Pratt £200 at once, and to repay himself on the following Monday out of the bets which he would receive on Cook's account at the settling at Tattersall's.

[1] About half-past ten on the Wednesday, and apparently shortly before Cook drank the brandy-and-water which he complained of, Palmer was seen by a Mrs. Brooks in the passage, looking at a glass lamp through a tumbler which contained some clear fluid like water, and which he was shaking and turning in his hand. There appears, however, to have been no secrecy in this, as he spoke to Mrs. Brooks,

[1] P. 52.

and continued to hold and shake the tumbler as he did so.
[1] George Myatt was called to contradict this for the prisoner.
He said that he was in the room when Palmer and Cook
came in; that Cook made a remark about the brandy, though
he gave a different version of it from Fisher and Read; that
he did not see anything put in it, and that if anything had
been put in it he should have seen. He also swore that
Palmer never left the room from the time he came in till
Cook went to bed. He also put the time later than Fisher
and Read. All this, however, came to very little. It was
the sort of difference which always arises in the details of
evidence. As Myatt was a friend of Palmer's, he probably
remembered the matter (perhaps honestly enough) in a way
more favourable to him than the other witnesses.

It appeared from the evidence of Mrs. Brooks, and also
from that of a man named Herring, that other persons besides
Cook were taken ill at Shrewsbury, on the evening in question, with similar symptoms. [3] Mrs. Brooks said, " We made
" an observation we thought the water might have been
" poisoned in Shrewsbury." [4] Palmer himself vomited on
his way back to Rugeley, according to Myatt.

The evidence as to what passed at Shrewsbury clearly
proves that, Palmer being then in great want of money, Cook
was to his knowledge in possession of £700 or £800 in
bank-notes, and was also entitled to receive on the following Monday about £1,400 more. It also shows that Palmer
may have given him a dose of antimony, though the weight
of the evidence to this effect is weakened by the proof that
diarrhœa and vomiting were prevalent in Shrewsbury at the
time. It is, however, important in connection with subsequent
events.

On Thursday, November 15th, Palmer and Cook returned

---

[1] G. Myatt, 264.　　　　　　　　　[2] Herring, 105.
[3] Brooks, 54:　　　　　　　　　　　[4] Myatt, 264.

together to Rugeley, which they reached about ten at night. Cook went to the Talbot Arms, and Palmer to his own house immediately opposite. Cook still complained of being unwell. On the Friday he dined with Palmer, in company with an attorney, Mr. Jeremiah Smith, and returned perfectly sober about ten in the evening. At eight on the following morning (November 17th) Palmer came over, and ordered a cup of coffee for him. The coffee was given to Cook by Mills the chambermaid, in Palmer's presence. When she next went to his room, an hour or two afterwards, it had been vomited. [1] In the course of the day, and apparently about the middle of the day, Palmer sent a charwoman, named Rowley, to get some broth for Cook at an inn called the Albion. She brought it to Palmer's house, put it by the fire to warm, and left the room. Soon after, Palmer brought it out, poured it into a cup, and sent it to the Talbot Arms with a message that it came from Mr. Jeremiah Smith. [3] The broth was given to Cook, who at first refused to take it. Palmer, however, came in, and said he must have it. [4] The chambermaid brought back the broth, which she had taken down stairs, and left it in the room. It also was thrown up. [5] In the course of the afternoon, Palmer called in Mr. Bamford, a surgeon eighty years of age, to see Cook, and told him that when Cook dined at his (Palmer's) house he had taken too much champagne. Mr. Bamford, however, found no bilious symptoms about him, and he said he had drunk only two glasses. On the Saturday night, Mr. Jeremiah Smith slept in Cook's room, as he was still ill. [6] On the Sunday, between twelve and one, Palmer sent over his gardener, Hawley, with some more broth for Cook. [7] Elizabeth Mills, the servant at the Talbot Arms, tasted it, taking two or three spoonfuls. She became

[1] Mills, 32-33.   [2] Rowley, 59.   [3] G. T. Barnes, 54.   Mills, 34.
[4] Mills, 34.   [5] Bamford, Dep. 114.   Evidence, 164.
[6] Hawley, 59.   [7] Mills, 34.   Barnes, 54.

exceedingly sick about half an hour afterwards, and vomited till five o'clock in the afternoon. She was so ill that she had to go to bed. [1] This broth also was taken to Cook, and the cup afterwards returned to Palmer. It appears to have been taken and vomited, though the evidence is not quite explicit on that point. [2] By the Sunday's post Palmer wrote to Mr. Jones, an apothecary, and Cook's most intimate friend, to come and see him. He said that Cook was " confined to his " bed with a severe bilious attack, combined with diarrhœa." [3] The servant Mills said there was no diarrhœa. It was observed on the part of the defence that this letter was strong proof of innocence. [4] The prosecution suggested that it was " part of a deep design, and was meant to make " evidence in the prisoner's favour." The fair conclusion seems to be, that it was an ambiguous act which ought to weigh neither way, though the falsehood about Cook's symptoms is suspicious as far as it goes.

[5] On the night between Sunday and Monday, Cook had some sort of attack. When the servant Mills went into his room on the Monday, he said, " I was just mad for two " minutes." She said, " Why did you not ring the bell ? " He said, " I thought that you would be all fast asleep, and " not hear it." He also said he was disturbed by a quarrel in the street. It might have waked and disturbed him, but he was not sure. This incident was not mentioned at first by Barnes and Mills, but was brought out on their being recalled at the request of Serjeant Shee. It was considered important for the defence, as proving that Cook had had an attack of some kind before it was suggested that any strychnine was administered; and the principal medical witness for the defence, [6] Mr. Nunneley, referred to it with this view.

[1] Barnes, 54. Mills, 34.   [2] W. H. Jones, 61 62.   [3] Mills, 35.
[4] Compare Smethurst's calling in Dr. Todd, *post*, p. 445.
[5] Barnes, 70. Mills, 70.   [6] P. 217.

[1] On the Monday, about a quarter-past or half-past seven, Palmer again visited Cook; but as he was in London about half-past two, he must have gone to town by an early train. During the whole of the Monday Cook was much better. He dressed himself, saw a jockey and his trainer, and the sickness ceased.

In the meantime Palmer was in London. [2] He met by appointment a man named Herring, who was connected with the turf. Palmer told him he wished to settle Cook's account, and read to him from a list, which Herring copied as Palmer read it, the particulars of the bets which he was to receive. They amounted to £984 clear. Of this sum Palmer instructed Herring to pay £450 to Pratt and £350 to Padwick. The nature of the debt to Padwick was not proved in evidence, as Padwick himself was not called. Palmer told Herring the £450 was to settle the bill for which Cook had assigned his horses. [3] He wrote Pratt on the same day a letter in these words: "Dear Sir,—You will place the £50 I have just paid "you and the £450 you will receive from Mr. Herring, to- "gether £500, and the £200 you received on Saturday" (from Fisher) "towards payment of my mother's acceptance for "£2,000 due 25th October."

Herring received upwards of £800, and paid part of it away according to Palmer's directions. [4] Pratt gave Palmer credit for the £450; but the £350 was not paid to Padwick, according to Palmer's directions, as part was retained by Mr. Herring for some debts due from Cook to him, and Herring received less than he expected. [5] In his reply, the Attorney-General said that the £350 intended to be paid to Padwick was on account of a bet, and suggested that the motive was to keep Padwick quiet as to the antedated cheque for £1,000 given to Espin on Padwick's account. There was no evidence of this, and it is not of much importance. It was clearly intended to be paid to Padwick on account, not of Cook (except possibly as to a small part), but of Palmer. Palmer thus disposed, or attempted to dispose, in the course of Monday, November 19th, of the whole of Cook's winnings for his own advantage.

This is a convenient place to mention the final result of the transaction relating to the bill for £500, in which Cook and Palmer were jointly interested. [1] On the Friday when Cook and Palmer dined together (November 16), Cook wrote to Fisher (his agent) in these words : " It is of very great im-
" portance to both Palmer and myself that the sum of £500
" should be paid to a Mr. Pratt, of 5 Queen Street, Mayfair ;
" £300 *has been sent up to-night,* and if you would be kind
" enough to pay the other £200 to-morrow, on the receipt of
" this, you will greatly oblige me. I will settle it on Monday
" at Tattersall's." [2] Fisher did pay the £200, expecting, as he said, to settle Cook's account on the Monday, and repay himself. [3] On the Saturday, November 17th (the day after the date of the letter), " a person," said Pratt, " whose name I
" did not know, called on me with a cheque, and paid me
" £300 on account of *the prisoner ;* that " [apparently the cheque, not the £300] " was a cheque of Mr. Fisher's."
[4] When Pratt heard of Cook's death, he wrote to Palmer, saying, " The death of Mr. Cook will now compel you to look
" about as to the payment of the bill for £500 due the 2nd
" of December."

Great use was made of these letters by the defence. It was argued that they proved that Cook was helping Palmer, and was eager to relieve him from the pressure put on him by Pratt; that in consequence of this he not only took up the £500 bill, but authorized Palmer to apply the £800 to similar purposes, and to get the amount settled by Herring, instead

[1] Fisher, 29.　　[2] Fisher, 27.　　[3] P. 166.　　[4] Read by Serjeant Shee, p. 181.

of Fisher, so that Fisher might not stop out of it the £200 which he had advanced to Pratt. It was asked how it could be Palmer's interest, on this supposition, that Cook should die, especially as the first consequence of his death was Pratt's application for the money due on the £500 bill.

These arguments were, no doubt, plausible; and the fact that Cook's death compelled Pratt to look to Palmer for the payment of the £500 lends them weight; but it may be asked, on the other hand, why should Cook give away the whole of his winnings to Palmer? Why should Cook allow Palmer to appropriate to the diminution of his own liabilities the £200 which Fisher had advanced to the credit of the bill on which both were liable? Why should he join with Palmer in a plan for defrauding Fisher of his security for this advance? No answer to any of these questions was suggested. As to the £300, Cook's letter to Fisher says, " £300 *has been* sent up this " evening." There was evidence that Pratt never received it, for he applied to Palmer for the money on Cook's death. Moreover, [1] Pratt said that, on the Saturday, he did receive £300 *on account of Palmer*, which he placed to the account of the forged acceptance for £2,000. Where did Palmer get the money? The suggestion of the prosecution was, that Cook gave it him to pay to Pratt on account of their joint bill, and that he paid it on his own account. This was probably the true view of the case. The observation that Pratt, on hearing of Cook's death, applied to Palmer to pay the £500 bill is met by the reflection that that bill was genuine, and collaterally secured by the assignment of the racehorses, and that the other bill bore a forged acceptance, and must be satisfied at all hazards. The result is, that on the Monday evening, Palmer had the most imperious interest in Cook's death, for he had robbed him of all he had in the world, except the equity of redemption in his two horses.

[1] Pratt, 166.

R

[1] On Monday evening (November 19th), Palmer returned to Rugeley, and went to the shop of Mr. Salt, a surgeon there, about 9 P.M. He saw Newton, Salt's assistant, and asked him for three grains of strychnine, which were accordingly given to him. Newton never mentioned this transaction till a day or two before his examination as a witness in London, though he was examined on the inquest. He explained this by saying that there had been a quarrel between Palmer and Salt, his (Newton's) master, and that he thought Salt would be displeased with him for having given Palmer anything. No doubt, the concealment was improper, but nothing appeared on cross-examination to suggest that the witness was wilfully perjured.

[2] Cook had been much better throughout Monday, and on Monday evening, [3] Mr. Bamford, who was attending him, brought some pills for him, which he left at the hotel. They contained neither antimony nor strychnine. [4] They were taken up in the box in which they came to Cook's room by the chambermaid, and were left there on the dressing-table, about eight o'clock. [5] Palmer came (according to Barnes, the waitress) between eight and nine, and [6] Mills said she saw him sitting by the fire between nine and ten.

If this evidence were believed, he would have had an opportunity of substituting poisoned pills for those sent by Mr. Bamford, just after he had, according to Newton, procured strychnine. The evidence, however, [7] was contradicted by a witness called for the prisoner, Jeremiah Smith, the attorney. He said that on the Monday evening, about ten minutes past ten, he saw Palmer coming in a car from the direction of Stafford; that they then went up to Cook's room together, stayed two or three minutes, and went with Smith to the house of old Mrs. Palmer, his mother. Cook said, "Bamford

---

[1] Newton, 71-72. [2] Mills, 35. [3] Bamford, 165. [4] Mills, 35-36.
[5] Barnes, 55. [6] Mills, 36. [7] J. Smith, 271.

" had sent him some pills, and he had taken them, and
" Palmer was late, intimating that he should not have taken
" them if he had thought Palmer would have called in
" before." If this evidence were believed, it would, of course,
have proved that Cook took the pills which Bamford sent as
he sent them.   [1] Smith, however, was cross-examined by the
Attorney-General at great length. He admitted, with the
greatest reluctance, that he had witnessed the assignment
of a policy for £13,000 by Walter to William Palmer; that
he wrote to an office to effect an insurance for £10,000 on the
life of Bates, who was Palmer's groom at £1 a week; that he
tried, after Walter Palmer's death, to get his widow to give
up her claim on the policy; that he was applied to to attest
other proposals for insurances on Walter Palmer's life for
similar amounts; and that he had got a cheque for £5 for
attesting the assignment.

[2] Lord Campbell said of this witness, in summing up, " Can
" you believe a man who so disgraces himself in the witness-
" box? It is for you to say what faith you can place in
" a witness who, by his own admission, engaged in such
" fraudulent proceedings."

It is curious that, though the credit of this witness was so
much shaken in cross-examination, and though he was contradicted both by Mills and Newton, he must have been right,
and they wrong, as to the time when Palmer came down to
Rugeley that evening. [3] Mr. Matthews, the inspector of police
at the Euston Station, proved that the only train by which
Palmer could have left London after half-past two ([4] when he
met Herring) started at five, and reached Stafford on the night

---

[1] Smith, 275-277. No abbreviation can give the effect of this cross-examination. The witness's efforts to gain time, and his distress as the various answers
were extorted from him by degrees, may be faintly traced in the report. The
witness's face was covered with sweat, and the papers put into his hands
shook and rustled.
[2] P. 323.   [3] P. 263.   [4] Herring, 102.

in question at a quarter to nine. It is about ten miles from Stafford to Rugeley, so that he could not have got across by the road in much less than an hour; yet Newton said he saw him "about nine," and Mills saw him "between nine and "ten." Nothing, however, is more difficult than to speak accurately as to time; on the other hand, if Smith spoke the truth, Newton could not have seen him at all that night, and Mills, if at all, must have seen him for a moment only in Smith's company. Mills never mentioned Smith, and Smith would not venture to swear she or anyone else saw him at the Talbot Arms. It was a suspicious circumstance that Serjeant Shee did not open Smith's evidence to the jury. An opportunity for perjury was afforded by the mistake made by the witnesses as to the time, which the defence were able to prove by the evidence of the police inspector. If Smith were disposed to tell an untruth, the knowledge of this fact would enable him to do so with an appearance of plausibility.

Whatever view is taken as to the effect of this evidence,[1] it was clearly proved that, about the middle of the night between Monday and Tuesday, Cook had a violent attack of some sort. About twelve, or a little before, his bell rang; he screamed violently. When Mills, the servant, came in, he was sitting up in bed, and asked that Palmer might be fetched at once. He was beating the bedclothes; he said he should suffocate if he lay down. His head and neck and his whole body jumped and jerked. He had great difficulty in breathing, and his eyes protruded. His hand was stiff, and he asked to have it rubbed. Palmer came in, and gave him a draught and some pills. He snapped at the glass, and got both it and the spoon between his teeth. He had also great difficulty in swallowing the pills. After this he got more easy, and Palmer stayed by him some time, sleeping in an easy-chair.

[2] Great efforts were made, in cross-examination, to shake

[1] Mills, 37.   Barnes, 55.   [2] Pp. 41–45.

the evidence of Mills by showing that she had altered the evidence which she gave before the coroner, so as to make her description of the symptoms tally with those of poisoning by strychnine, and also by showing that she had been drilled as to the evidence which she was to give by persons connected with the prosecution. She denied most of the suggestions conveyed by the questions asked her, and explained others. As to the differences between her evidence before the coroner and at the trial, a witness ([1] Mr. Gardner, an attorney) was called to show that the depositions were not properly taken at the inquest.

On the following day, Tuesday, the 20th, Cook was a good deal better. [2] In the middle of the day, he sent the boots to ask Palmer if he might have a cup of coffee. Palmer said he might, and came over, tasted a cup made by the servant, and took it from her hands to give it to Cook. This coffee was afterwards thrown up.

[3] A little before or after this, the exact hour is not important, Palmer went to the shop of Hawkins, a druggist at Rugeley, and was there served by his apprentice, Roberts, with two drachms of prussic acid, six grains of strychnine, and two drachms of Batley's sedative. Whilst he was making the purchase, Newton, from whom he had obtained the other strychnine the night before, came in: Palmer took him to the door, saying he wished to speak to him, and when he was there asked him a question about the farm of a Mr. Edwin Salt—a matter with which he had nothing at all to do. Whilst they were there, a third person came up and spoke to Newton, on which Palmer went back into Hawkins's shop and took away the things, Newton not seeing what he took. The obvious suggestion upon this is that Palmer wanted to prevent Newton from seeing what he was about. No attempt even was made to shake, or in any way discredit, Roberts the apprentice.

---

[1] P. 50. As to the coroner's conduct, see below.
[2] Mills, 39. [3] Roberts, 76. Newton, 72.

[1] At about four P.M., Mr. Jones, the friend to whom Palmer had written, arrived from Lutterworth. He examined Cook in Palmer's presence, and remarked that he had not the tongue of a bilious patient, to which Palmer replied, " You " should have seen it before." Cook appeared to be better during the Tuesday, and was in good spirits. At about seven P.M., Mr. Bamford came in, and Cook told him in Palmer's presence that he objected to the pills as they had made him ill the night before. The three medical men then had a private consultation. Palmer proposed that Bamford should make up the pills as on the night before, and that Jones should not tell Cook what they were made of, as he objected to the morphine which they contained. [2] Bamford agreed, and Palmer went up to his house with him and got the pills, and was present whilst they were made up, put into a pill-box, and directed. He took them away with him between seven and eight. Cook was well and comfortable all the evening ; he had no bilious symptoms, no vomiting, and no diarrhœa.

[3] Towards eleven, Palmer came with a box of pills directed in Bamford's hand. He called Jones's attention to the goodness of the handwriting for a man of eighty. It was suggested by the prosecution that the reason for this was to impress Jones with the fact that the pills had been made up by Bamford. With reference to Smith's evidence, it is remarkable that Bamford on the second night sent the pills, not " between nine and ten," but at eleven. [3] Palmer pressed Cook to take the pills, which at first he refused to do, as they had made him so ill the night before. At last he did so, and immediately afterwards vomited. Jones and Palmer both examined to see whether the pills had been thrown up, and they found that they had not. This was about eleven. Jones then had his supper, and went to bed in Cook's room about twelve. When he had been in bed a short time, perhaps ten

[1] W. H. Jones, 62–63.   [2] Bamford, 164- 165.   [3] W. H. Jones, 63-64

minutes, Cook started up, and called out, "Doctor, get up; I am going to be ill; ring the bell for Mr. Palmer." He also said, "Rub my neck." The back of his neck was stiff and hard. [1] Mills ran across the road to Palmer's, and rang the bell. Palmer immediately came to the bedroom window, and said he would come at once. Two minutes afterwards he was in Cook's room, and said he had never dressed so quickly in his life. He was dressed as usual. The suggestion upon this was that he had been sitting up expecting to be called.

[2] By the time of Palmer's arrival Cook was very ill. Jones, Elizabeth Mills, and Palmer were in the room, and [3] Barnes stood at the door. The muscles of his neck were stiff; he screamed loudly. Palmer gave him what he said were two ammonia pills. Immediately afterwards—too soon for the pills to have any effect—he was dreadfully convulsed. [4] He said, when he began to be convulsed, "Raise me up, or I shall " be suffocated." Palmer and Jones tried to do so, but could not, as the limbs were rigid. He then asked to be turned over, which was done. His heart began to beat weakly. Jones asked Palmer to get some ammonia to try to stimulate it. He fetched a bottle, and was absent about a minute for the purpose. When he came back, Cook was almost dead, and he died in a few minutes, quite quietly. The whole attack lasted about ten minutes. The body was twisted back into the shape of a bow, and would have rested on the head and heels, had it been laid on its back. [5] When the body was laid out it was very stiff. The arms could not be kept down by the sides till they were tied behind the back with tape. The feet also had to be tied, and the fingers of one hand were very stiff, the hand being clenched. This was about one A.M., half or three-quarters of an hour after the death.

Deferring for the present the inferences drawn by the

---

[1] Mills, 40.　　[2] W. H. Jones, 64.　　[3] Barnes, 56.
[4] W. H. Jones, 64-65.　　[5] Keeling, 84-85.

medical men from these symptoms, I proceed to describe the subsequent occurrences. As soon as Cook was dead, [1] Jones went out to speak to the housekeeper, leaving Palmer alone with the body. When Jones left the room, he sent the servant [2] Mills in, and she saw Palmer searching the pockets of Cook's coat, and searching also under the pillow and bolster. [3] Jones shortly afterwards returned, and Palmer told him that, as Cook's nearest friend, he (Jones) ought to take possession of his property. He accordingly took possession of his watch and purse, containing five sovereigns and five shillings. He found no other money. Palmer said, " Mr. " Cook's death is a bad thing for me, as I am responsible for " £3,000 or £4,000; and I hope Mr. Cook's friends will not " let me lose it. If they do not assist me, all my horses will " be seized." The betting-book was mentioned. Palmer said, " It will be no use to anyone," and added that it would probably be found.

[4] On Wednesday, 21st November, Mr. Wetherby, the London racing agent, who kept a sort of bank for sporting men, received from Palmer a letter inclosing a cheque for £350 against the amount of the Shrewsbury stakes (£381), which Wetherby was to receive for him. This cheque had been drawn on the Tuesday, about seven o'clock in the evening, under peculiar circumstances. [5] Palmer sent for Mr. Cheshire, the postmaster at Rugeley, telling him to bring a receipt-stamp, and when he arrived asked him to write out, from a copy which he produced, a cheque by Cook on Wetherby. He said it was for money which Cook owed him, and that he was going to take it over for Cook to sign. Cheshire wrote out the body of the cheque, and Palmer took it away. [6] When Mr. Wetherby received the cheque, the stakes had not been paid to Cook's credit. He accordingly returned the

---

[1] W. H. Jones, 66. [2] Mills, 41–42. [3] W. H. Jones, 65–66.
[4] Wetherby, 96. [5] Cheshire, 95–96. [6] Wetherby, 96.

cheque to Palmer, [1] to whom the prosecution gave notice to produce it at the trial. [2] It was called for, but not produced. This was one of the strongest facts against Palmer in the whole of the case. If he had produced the cheque, and if it had appeared to have been really signed by Cook, it would have shown that Cook, for some reason or other, had made over his stakes to Palmer, and this would have destroyed the strong presumption arising from Palmer's appropriation of the bets to his own purposes. In fact, it would have greatly weakened and almost upset the case as to motive. On the other hand, the non-production of the cheque amounted to an admission that it was a forgery; and, if that were so, Palmer was forging his friend's name for the purpose of stealing his stakes at the time when there was every prospect of his speedy recovery, which must result in the detection of the fraud. If he knew that Cook would die that night, this was natural. On any other supposition, it was inconceivable rashness.

[3] Either on Thursday, 22nd, or Friday, 23rd, Palmer sent for Cheshire again, and produced a paper which he said Cook had given to him some days before. The paper purported to be an acknowledgment that certain bills—the particulars of which were stated—were all for Cook's benefit, and not for Palmer's. The amount was considerable, as at least one item was for £1,000 and another for £500. This document purported to be signed by Cook, and Palmer wished Cheshire to attest Cook's execution of it, which he refused to do. This document was called for at the trial, and not produced. The same observations apply to it as to the cheque.

[4] Evidence was further given to show that Palmer, who, shortly before, had but £9 6s. at the bank, and had borrowed £25 to go to Shrewsbury, paid away large sums of money

[1] Boycott, 96.   [2] 97.   [3] Cheshire, 97-98.
[4] Strawbridge, 169.

soon after Cook's death. [1] He paid Pratt £100 on the 24th; [2] he paid a farmer named Spilsbury £46 2s. with a Bank of England note for £50 on the 22nd; [3] and Bown, a draper, a sum of £60 or thereabouts, in two £50 notes, on the 20th. The general result of these money transactions is that Palmer appropriated to his own use all Cook's bets; that he tried to appropriate his stakes; and that, shortly before or just after his death, he was in possession of between £500 and £600, of which he paid Pratt £400, though very shortly before he was being pressed for money.

[4] On Wednesday, November 21st, Mr. Jones went up to London, and informed Mr. Stephens, Cook's stepfather, of his stepson's death. Mr. Stephens went to Lutterworth, found a will by which Cook appointed him his executor, and then went on to Rugeley, where he arrived about the middle of the day on Thursday. He asked Palmer for information about Cook's affairs, and he replied, " There are £4,000 worth of bills out of his, and I am sorry to say my name is to them; but I have got a paper drawn up by a lawyer and signed by Mr. Cook to show that I never had any benefit from them." Mr. Stephens said that at all events he must be buried. Palmer offered to do so himself, and said that the body ought to be fastened up as soon as possible. The conversation then ended for the time. Palmer went out, and, without authority from Mr. Stephens, ordered a shell and a strong oak coffin.

[5] In the afternoon, Mr. Stephens, Palmer, Jones, and Mr. Bradford, Cook's brother-in-law, dined together; and after dinner Mr. Stephens desired Mr. Jones to fetch Cook's betting-book. Jones went to look for it, but was unable to find it. The betting-book had last been seen by the chambermaid Mills, who gave it to Cook in bed on the Monday night, when he took a stamp from a pocket at the end of it. [6] On hearing

---

[1] Pratt, 167.   [2] Spilsbury, 169.   [3] Armshaw, 168.
[4] Stephens, 78–80.   [5] Mills, 41.   [6] Stephens, 81.

that the book could not be found, Palmer said it was of no manner of use. Mr. Stephens said he understood Cook had won a great deal of money at Shrewsbury, to which Palmer replied, "It's no use, I assure you ; when a man dies, his bets "are done with." He did not mention the fact that Cook's bets had been paid to Herring on the Monday. Mr. Stephens then said that the book must be found, and Palmer answered that no doubt it would be. Before leaving the inn, Mr. Stephens went to look at the body, before the coffin was fastened, and observed that both hands were clenched. He returned at once to town, and went to his attorney. He returned to Rugeley on Saturday, the 24th, and informed Palmer of his intention to have a *post-mortem* examination, which took place on Monday, the 26th.

[1] The *post-mortem* examination was conducted in the presence of Palmer by Dr. Harland, [2] Mr. Devonshire, a medical student assisting Dr. Monkton, and Mr. Newton. The heart was contracted and empty. There were numerous small yellowish white spots, about the size of mustard-seed, at the larger end of the stomach. The upper part of the spinal cord was in its natural state ; the lower part was not examined till the 25th of January, when certain granules were found. There were many follicles on the tongue, apparently of long standing. The lungs appeared healthy to Dr. Harland, but Mr. Devonshire thought that there was some congestion. Some points in Palmer's behaviour, both before and after the *post-mortem* examination, attracted notice. [3] Newton said that on the Sunday night he sent for him, and asked what dose of strychnine would kill a dog; Newton said a grain. He asked whether it would be found in the stomach, and what would be the appearance of the stomach after death. Newton said there would be no inflammation, and he did not think it would

---

[1] Harland, 85–86.   [2] Devonshire, 92.
[3] Newton, 73.

be found. Newton thought he replied, " It's all right," as if speaking to himself, and added that he snapped his fingers. [1] Whilst Devonshire was opening the stomach, Palmer pushed against him and part of the contents of the stomach was spilt. Nothing particular being found in the stomach, Palmer observed to Bamford, " They will not hang us yet." As they were all crowding together to see what passed, the push might have been an accident ; and, as Mr. Stephens's suspicions were well known, the remark was natural, though coarse. [2] After the examination was completed, the intestines, &c., were put into a jar, over the top of which were tied two bladders. Palmer removed the jar from the table to a place near the door, and when it was missed said he thought it would be more convenient. When replaced, it was found that a slit had been cut through both the bladders.

[3] After the examination, Mr. Stephens and an attorney's clerk took the jars containing the viscera, &c., in a fly to Stafford. [4] Palmer asked the postboy if he was going to drive them to Stafford. The postboy said, "I believe I am." Palmer said, "Is it Mr. Stephens you are going to take ?" He said, " I believe it is." Palmer said, " I suppose you are " going to take the jars ? " He said, " I am." Palmer asked if he would upset them ? He said, "I shall not." Palmer said if he would there was a £10 note for him. He also said something about its being " a humbugging concern." Some confusion was introduced into this evidence by the cross-examination, which tended to show that Palmer's object was to upset Mr. Stephens and not the jars, but at last the post-boy (J. Myatt) repeated it as given above. Indeed, it makes little difference whether Palmer wished to upset Stephens or the jars, as they were all in one fly, and must be upset together if at all.

---

[1] Harland, 88.　Devonshire, 92.　　　[2] Harland, 88.
[3] Boycott, 93.　　　　　　　　　　　[4] J. Myatt, 94.

[1] Shortly after the *post-mortem* examination, an inquest was held before Mr. Ward, the coroner. It began on the 29th of November and ended on the 5th of December. On Sunday, 3rd December, Palmer asked Cheshire, the postmaster, " if he " had anything fresh ? " Cheshire replied that he could not open a letter. Afterwards, however, he did open a letter from Dr. Alfred Taylor, who had analyzed the contents of the stomach, &c., to Mr. Gardiner, the attorney for the prosecution, and informed Palmer that Dr. Taylor said in that letter that no traces of strychnia were found. Palmer said he knew they would not, and he was quite innocent. Soon afterwards Palmer wrote to Mr. Ward, suggesting various questions to be put to witnesses at the inquest, and saying that he knew Dr. Taylor had told Mr. Gardiner there were no traces of strychnia, prussic acid, or opium. A few days before this, on the 1st of December, Palmer had sent Mr. Ward, as a present, a codfish, a barrel of oysters, a brace of pheasants, and a turkey. These circumstances certainly prove improper and even criminal conduct. Cheshire was imprisoned for his offence, and Lord Campbell spoke in severe terms of the conduct of the coroner; but a bad and unscrupulous man, as Palmer evidently was, might act in the manner described even though he was innocent of the particular offence charged.

[2] A medical book found in Palmer's possession had in it some manuscript notes on the subject of strychnine, one of which was, " It kills by causing tetanic contraction of the " respiratory muscles." It was not suggested that this memorandum was made for any particular purpose. It was used merely to show that Palmer was acquainted with the properties and effects of strychnine.

This completes the evidence as to Palmer's behaviour before, at, and after the death of Cook. It proves beyond all ques-

---

[1] Cheshire, 97-98. Hatton, 98-99. As to the presents, Hawkes, 100. Stack, 106.   [2] Bergen, 100.

tion that, having the strongest possible motive to obtain at once a considerable sum of money, he robbed his friend of the whole of the bets paid to Herring on the Monday by a series of ingenious devices, and that he tried to rob him of the stakes; it raises the strongest presumption that he robbed Cook of the £300 which, as Cook supposed, were sent up to Pratt on the 16th, and that he stole the money which he had on his person, and had received at Shrewsbury; it proves that he forged his name the night before he died, and that he tried to procure a fraudulent attestation to another forged document relating to his affairs the day after he died. It also proves that he had every opportunity of administering poison to Cook, that he told repeated lies about his state of health, and that he purchased deadly poison, for which he had no lawful occasion, on two separate occasions, shortly before two paroxysms of a similar character to each other, the second of which deprived him of life.

The rest of the evidence was directed to prove that the symptoms of which Cook died were those of poisoning by strychnine, and that antimony, which was never prescribed for him, was found in his body. Evidence was also given in the course of the trial as to the state of Cook's health. It may be conveniently introduced here.

[1] At the time of his death, Cook was about twenty-eight years of age. Both his father and mother died young, and his sister and half-brother were not robust. He inherited from his father about £12,000, and was articled to a solicitor. Instead of following up that profession, he betook himself to sporting pursuits, and appears to have led a dissipated life. He suffered from syphilis, and was in the habit of occasionally consulting Dr. Savage on the state of his health. [2] Dr. Savage saw him in November, 1854, in May, in June, towards the end of October, and again early in November, 1855, about a

---

[1] Stephens, 78.   [2] Savage, 70 71.

fortnight before his death, so that he had ample means of giving satisfactory evidence on the subject, especially as he examined him carefully whenever he came. Dr. Savage said that he had two shallow ulcers on the tongue, corresponding to bad teeth, that he had also a sore throat, one of his tonsils being very large, red, and tender, and the other very small. Cook himself was afraid that these symptoms were syphilitic, but Dr. Savage thought decidedly that they were not. He also noticed "an indication of pulmonary affection under the "left lung." Wishing to get him away from his turf associates, Dr. Savage recommended him to go abroad for the winter. His general health Dr. Savage considered good for a man who was not robust. [1] Mr. Stephens said that when he last saw him alive he was looking better than he had looked for some time, and on his remarking, "You do not look anything of an invalid now," Cook struck himself on the breast, and said he was quite well. [2] His friend, Mr. Jones, also said that his health was generally good, though he was not very robust, and that he both hunted and played at cricket.

On the other hand, witnesses were called for the prisoner who gave a different account of his health. [3] A Mr. Sargent said he was with him at Liverpool, a week before the Shrewsbury races, that he called his attention to the state of his mouth and throat, and the back part of his tongue was in a complete state of ulcer. " I said," added the witness, " I was " surprised he could eat and drink in the state his mouth was " in. He said he had been in that state for weeks and months, " and now he did not take notice of it." This was certainly not consistent with Dr. Savage's evidence.

Such being the state of health of Cook at the time of his death, the next question was as to its cause. The prosecution contended that the symptoms which attended it proved that

---

[1] Stephens, 78.   [2] W. H. Jones, 62.   [3] Sargent, 269.

he was poisoned by strychnia. Several eminent physicians and surgeons—Mr. Curling, Dr. Todd, Sir Benjamin Brodie, Mr. Daniel, and Mr. Solly—gave an account of the general character and causes of the disease of tetanus. [1] Mr. Curling said that tetanus consists of spasmodic affection of the voluntary muscles of the body which at last end in death, produced either by suffocation caused by the closing of the windpipe or by the wearing effect of the severe and painful struggles which the muscular spasms produce. Of this disease there are three forms : idiopathic tetanus, which is produced without any assignable external cause; traumatic tetanus, which results from wounds; and the tetanus which is produced by the administration of strychnia, bruchsia, and nux vomica, all of which are different forms of the same poison. Idiopathic tetanus is a very rare disease in this country. [2] Sir Benjamin Brodie had seen only one doubtful case of it. [3] Mr. Daniel who for twenty-eight years was surgeon to the Bristol Hospital, saw only two. [4] Mr. Nunneley, Professor of Surgery at Leeds, had seen four. In India, however, it is comparatively common : [5] Mr. Jackson, in twenty-five years' practice there, saw about forty cases. It was agreed on all hands that though the exciting cause of the two diseases is different their symptoms are the same. They were described in similar terms by several of the witnesses. [6] Dr. Todd said the disease begins with stiffness about the jaw, the symptoms then extend themselves to the other muscles of the trunk and body. They gradually develop themselves. When once the disease has begun, there are remissions of severity, but not complete intermissions of the symptoms. In acute cases the disease terminates in three or four days. In chronic cases it will go on for as much as three weeks. There was some question as to what was the shortest case upon record. In a case mentioned

---

[1] Curling, 110-111. [2] Brodie, 120. [3] Daniel, 121. [4] Nunneley, 215.
[5] Jackson, 161. [6] Todd, 113. Compare Sir B. Brodie, 119–120.

by one of the prisoner's witnesses, [1] Mr. Ross, the patient was said to have been attacked in the morning, either at eleven or some hours earlier, it did not clearly appear which, and to have died at half-past seven in the evening. This was the shortest case specified on either side, though its duration was not accurately determined. As a rule, however, tetanus, whether traumatic or idiopathic, was said to be a matter, not of minutes or even of hours, but of days.

Such being the nature of tetanus, traumatic and idiopathic, four questions arose. Did Cook die of tetanus? Did he die of traumatic tetanus? Did he die of idiopathic tetanus? Did he die of the tetanus produced by strychnia? The case for the prosecution upon these questions was, first, that he did die of tetanus. [2] Mr. Curling said no doubt there was spasmodic action of the muscles (which was his definition of tetanus) in Cook's case; and even [3] Mr. Nunneley, the principal witness for the prisoner, who contended that the death of Cook was caused neither by tetanus in its ordinary forms nor by the tetanus of strychnia, admitted that the paroxysm described by Mr. Jones was "very like" the paroxysm of tetanus. The close general resemblance of the symptoms to those of tetanus was indeed assumed by all the witnesses on both sides, as was proved by the various distinctions which were stated on the side of the Crown between Cook's symptoms and those of traumatic and idiopathic tetanus, and on the side of the prisoner between Cook's symptoms and the symptoms of the tetanus of strychnia. It might, therefore, be considered to be established that he died of tetanus in some form or other.

The next point asserted by the prosecution was, that he did not die of traumatic or idiopathic tetanus, because there was no wound on his body, and also because the course of the symptoms was different. They further asserted that the

---

[1] Ross, 239. [2] Curling, 109–111. [3] Nunneley, 227.

S

symptoms were those of poison by strychnia. Upon these points the evidence was as follows :—[1] Mr. Curling was asked, " *Q.* Were the symptoms consistent with any form of trau- " matic tetanus which has ever come under your knowledge " or observation ? " He answered " No."

" *Q.* What distinguished them from the cases of traumatic " tetanus which you have described ? *A.* There was the " sudden onset of the fatal symptoms. In all cases that have " fallen under my notice the disease has been preceded by the " milder symptoms of tetanus. *Q.* Gradually progressing to " their complete development, and completion, and death ? " *A.* Yes." He also mentioned " the sudden onset and rapid " subsidence of the spasms " as inconsistent with the theory of either traumatic or idiopathic tetanus ; and he said he had never known a case of tetanus which ran its course in less than eight or ten hours. In the one case which occupied so short a time, the true period could not be ascertained. In general, the time required was from one to several days. [2] Sir Benjamin Brodie was asked, " In your opinion, are the " symptoms those of traumatic tetanus or not ? " He replied, " As far as the spasmodic contraction of the muscles goes, the " symptoms resemble those of traumatic tetanus ; as to the " course which the symptoms took, that was entirely dif- " ferent." He added, " The symptoms of traumatic tetanus " always begin, as far as I have seen, very gradually, the " stiffness of the lower jaw being, I believe, the symptom " first complained of—at least, so it has been in my experi- " ence ; then the contraction of the muscles of the back is " always a later symptom, generally much later ; the muscles " of the extremities are affected in a much less degree than " those of the neck and trunk, except in some cases where " the injury has been in a limb and an early symptom has " been a contraction of the muscles of that limb. I do not

[1] Curling, 110–111.   Brodie, 119–120

" myself recollect a case in which in ordinary tetanus there
" was that contraction of the muscles of the hand which I
" understand was stated to have existed in this instance. The
" ordinary tetanus rarely runs its course in less than two or
" three days, and often is protracted to a much longer period;
" I know one case only in which the disease was said to
" have terminated in twelve hours." He said, in conclusion,
" I never saw a case in which the symptoms described arose
" from any disease; when I say that, of course I refer not to
" the particular symptoms, but to the general course which
" the symptoms took." [1] Mr. Daniel, being asked whether the
symptoms of Cook could be referred to idiopathic or traumatic tetanus, said, " In my judgment they could not." He
also said that he should repeat Sir Benjamin Brodie's words
if he were to enumerate the distinctions. [2] Mr. Solly said
that the symptoms were not referable to any disease he ever
witnessed, and [3] Dr. Todd said, " I think the symptoms were
" those of strychnia." The same opinion was expressed with
equal confidence by [4] Dr. Alfred Taylor, [5] Dr. Rees, and [6] Mr.
Christison.

In order to support this general evidence, witnesses were
called who gave accounts of three fatal cases of poisoning by
strychnia, and of one case in which the patient recovered.
[7] The first of the fatal cases was that of Agnes French, or
Senet, who was accidentally poisoned at Glasgow Infirmary,
in 1845, by some pills which she took, and which were intended for a paralytic patient. According to the nurse, the
girl was taken ill three-quarters of an hour, according to one
of the physicians (who, however, was not present) twenty
minutes, after she swallowed the pills. She fell suddenly
back on the floor; when her clothes were cut off she was stiff,

[1] Daniel, 121.   [2] Solly, 123.   [3] Todd, 116.
[4] Taylor, 110.   [5] Rees, 155.   [6] Christison, 159.
[7] Dr. Corbett, 124.   Dr. Watson, 125.   Dr. Patterson, 126.   Mary Kell
(nurse), 126.

"just like a poker," her arms were stretched out, her hands
clenched ; she vomited slightly ; she had no lockjaw ; there
was a retraction of the mouth and face, the head was bent
back, the spine curved. She went into severe paroxysms
every few seconds, and died about an hour after the symptoms began. She was perfectly conscious. The heart was
found empty on examination.

[1] The second case described was that of Mrs. Serjeantson
Smyth, who was accidentally poisoned at Romsey in 1848, by
strychnine put into a dose of ordinary medicine instead of
salicine. She took the dose about five or ten minutes after
seven ; in five or ten minutes more the servant was alarmed
by a violent ringing of the bell. She found her mistress
leaning on a chair, went out to send for a doctor, and on her
return found her on the floor. She screamed loudly. She
asked to have her legs pulled straight and to have water
thrown over her. A few minutes before she died she said,
"Turn me over ;" she was turned over, and died very quietly
almost immediately. The fit lasted about an hour. The
hands were clenched, the feet contracted, and on a *post-
mortem* examination the heart was found empty.

[2] The third case was that of Mrs. Dove, who was poisoned
at Leeds by her husband ([3] for which he was afterwards hung),
in February, 1856. She had five attacks on the Monday,
Wednesday, Thursday, Friday, and Saturday of the week
beginning February 24th. She had prickings in the legs and
twitchings in the hands ; she asked her husband to rub her
arms and legs before the spasms came on, but when they
were strong she could not bear her legs to be touched. The
fatal attack in her case lasted two hours and a half. The
hands were semi-bent, the feet strongly arched. The lungs

[1] Caroline Hickson, 127.   W. F. Taylor (surgeon), 128.   R. Broxam
(chemist), 129.
[2] J. Williams, 129.   Mr. Morley, 130.
[3] See the next case for an account of his trial.

were congested, the spinal cord was also much congested. The
head being opened first, a good deal of blood flowed out, part
of which might flow from the heart.

[1] The case in which the patient recovered was that of a
paralytic patient of Mr. Moore's. He took an overdose of
strychnia, and in about three-quarters of an hour Mr. Moore
found him stiffened in every limb. His head was drawn
back; he was screaming and "frequently requesting that we
"should turn him, move him, rub him." His spine was drawn
back. He snapped at a spoon with which an attempt was
made to administer medicine, and was perfectly conscious
during the whole time.

[2] Dr. Taylor and Dr. Owen Rees examined Cook's body.
They found no strychnia, but they found antimony in the
liver, the left kidney, the spleen, and also in the blood.

The case for the prosecution upon this evidence was that
the symptoms were those of tetanus, and of tetanus produced by strychnia. The case for the prisoner was, first,
that several of the symptoms observed were inconsistent with
strychnia; and, secondly, that all of them might be explained on other hypotheses. Their evidence was given in
part by their own witnesses and in part by the witnesses for
the Crown in cross-examination. The replies suggested by
the Crown were founded partly on the evidence of their
own witnesses given by way of anticipation, and partly by
the evidence elicited from the witnesses for the prisoner on
cross-examination.

The first and most conspicuous argument on behalf of the
prisoner was that the fact that no strychnia was discovered
by Dr. Taylor and Dr. Rees was inconsistent with the theory
that any had been administered. The material part of Dr.
Taylor's evidence upon this point was that he had examined
the stomach and intestines of Cook for a variety of poisons,

[1] Mr. Moore, 133.   [2] A. S. Taylor, 138-139   Rees, 154-155.

strychnia among others, without success. The contents of
the stomach were gone, though the contents of the intestines
remained, and the stomach itself had been cut open from end
to end, and turned inside out, and the mucous surface, on
which poison, if present, would have been found, was rubbing
against the surface of the intestines. [1] This Dr. Taylor considered a most unfavourable condition for the discovery of
poison, [2] and Mr. Christison agreed with him. Several of
the prisoner's witnesses, on the contrary—[3] Mr. Nunneley,
[4] Dr. Letheby, and [5] Mr. Rogers—thought that it would only
increase the difficulty of the operation and not destroy its
chance of success.

Apart from this, Dr. Taylor expressed his opinion that,
from the way in which strychnia acts, it might be impossible to discover it even if the circumstances were favourable.
The mode of testing its presence in the stomach is to treat
the stomach in various ways, until at last a residue is
obtained which, upon the application of certain chemical
ingredients, changes its colour if strychnia is present. All
the witnesses agreed that strychnia acts by absorption—that
is, it is taken up from the stomach by the absorbents, thence
it passes into the blood, thence into the solid part of the
body, and at some stage of its progress causes death by its
action on the nerves and muscles. Its noxious effects do
not begin till it has left the stomach. From this Dr. Taylor
argued that, if a minimum dose were administered, none
would be left in the stomach at the time of death, and therefore none could be discovered there. He also said that, if the
strychnia got into the blood before examination, it would be
diffused over the whole mass, and so no more than an extremely
minute portion would be present in any given quantity. If
the dose were half a grain, and there were twenty-five pounds

[1] A. S. Taylor, 139.   [2] Christison, 159.   [3] Nunneley, 222.
[4] Letheby, 235.   [5] Rogers, 233.

of blood in the body, each pound of blood would contain only one-fiftieth of a grain. He was also of opinion that the strychnia undergoes some chemical change by reason of which its presence in small quantities in the tissues cannot be detected. In short, the result of his evidence was, that if a minimum dose were administered, it was uncertain whether strychnia would be present in the stomach after death, and that if it was not in the stomach, there was no certainty that it could be found at all. [1] He added, that he considered the colour test fallacious, because the colours might be produced by other substances.

[2] Dr. Taylor further detailed some experiments which he had tried upon animals jointly with Dr. Rees, for the purpose of ascertaining whether strychnia could always be detected. He poisoned four rabbits with strychnia, and applied the tests for strychnia to their bodies. In one case, where two grains had been administered at intervals, he obtained proof of the presence of strychnia both by a bitter taste and by the colour. In a case where one grain was administered, he obtained the taste but not the colour. In the other two cases, where he administered one grain and half a grain respectively, he obtained no indications at all of the presence of strychnia. These experiments proved to demonstration that the fact that *he* did not discover strychnia did not prove that no strychnia was present in Cook's body ; and as this was the only way in which the non-discovery of strychnia was material to the case, great part of the evidence given on behalf of the prisoner became superfluous. It ought, however, to be noticed, as it formed a very prominent feature in the case.

[3] Mr. Nunneley, [4] Mr. Herapath, [5] Mr. Rogers, [6] Dr. Letheby, and [7] Mr. Wrightson, contradicted Dr. Taylor and Dr. Rees

---

[1] A. S. Taylor, 138-9.   [2] A. S. Taylor, 138 ; Rees, 154.
[3] Nunneley, 222.   [4] Herapath, 230-231.   [5] Rogers, 532.
[6] Letheby, 233-234.   [7] Wrightson, 241.

upon this part of their evidence. They denied the theory
that strychnine undergoes any change in the blood, and they
professed their own ability to discover its presence even in
most minute quantities in any body into which it had been
introduced, and their belief that the colour tests were satisfactory. Mr. Herapath said that he had found strychnine in
the blood and in a small part of the liver of a dog poisoned
by it ; and he also said that he could detect the fifty-thousandth
part of a grain if it were unmixed with organic matter. Mr.
Wrightson (who was highly complimented by Lord Campbell
for the way in which he gave his evidence) also said that he
should expect to find strychnia if it were present, and that he
had found it in the tissues of an animal poisoned by it.

Here, no doubt, there was a considerable conflict of evidence upon a point of which it was very difficult for un-
scientific persons to pretend to have any opinion. The
controversy, however, was foreign to the merits of the case,
inasmuch as the evidence given for the prisoner tended to
prove, not that there was no strychnia in Cook's body, but that
Dr. Taylor ought to have found it if there was. In other
words, it was relevant not so much to the guilt or innocence
of the prisoner, as to the question whether Mr. Nunneley and
Mr. Herapath were or were not better analytical chemists
than Dr. Taylor. The evidence could not even be considered
relevant as·shaking Dr. Taylor's credit, for no part of the case
rested on his evidence except the discovery of the antimony, as to which he was corroborated by Mr. Brande, and
was not contradicted by prisoner's witnesses. His opinion
as to the nature of Cook's symptoms was shared by many
other medical witnesses of the highest eminence, whose credit
was altogether unimpeached. The prisoner's counsel were
placed in a curious difficulty by this state of the question.
They had to attack and did attack Dr. Taylor's credit vigorously, for the purpose of rebutting his conclusion that Cook

might have been poisoned by strychnine; yet they had also
to maintain his credit as a skilful analytical chemist, for, if
they destroyed it, the fact that he did not find strychnine
went for nothing. This dilemma was fatal. To admit his
skill was to admit their client's guilt. To deny it was to
destroy the value of nearly all their own evidence, which, in
reality, was for the most part irrelevant. The only possible
course was to admit his skill and deny his good faith, but
this, too, was useless, for the reason just mentioned.

Another argument used on behalf of the prisoner was, that
some of the symptoms of Cook's death were inconsistent with
poisoning by strychnine. [1] Mr. Nunneley and [2] Dr. Letheby
thought that the facts that Cook sat up in bed when the
attack came on, that he moved his hands, and swallowed, and
asked to be rubbed and moved, showed more power of voluntary motion than was consistent with poisoning by strychnia.
But Mrs. Serjeantson Smyth got out of bed and rang the bell,
and both she, Mrs. Dove, and Mr. Moore's patient begged to
be rubbed and moved before the spasms came on. Cook's
movements were before the paroxysm set in, and the first
paroxysm ended his life.

[3] Mr. Nunneley referred to the fact that the heart was
empty, and said that, in his experiments, he always found that
the right side of the heart of the poisoned animals was full.
Both in Mrs. Smyth's case, however, and in that of the girl
Senet, the heart was found empty; [4] and in Mrs. Smyth's case
the chest and abdomen were opened first, so that the heart
was not emptied by the opening of the head. [5] Mr. Christison
said that if a man died of spasms of the heart, the heart
would be emptied by them, and would be found empty after
death; so that the presence or absence of the blood proved
nothing.

[1] Nunneley, 221.   [2] Letheby, 234.   [3] Nunneley, 220.
          [4] F. Taylor, 128-129.   [5] Christison, 159.

[1] Mr. Nunneley and [2] Dr. Letheby also referred to the length
of time before the symptoms appeared as inconsistent with
poisoning by strychnine. The time between the administration of the pills and the paroxysm was not accurately
measured; it might have been an hour, or a little less or
more; but the poison, if present at all, was administered in
pills, which would not begin to operate till they were broken
up, and the rapidity with which they would be broken up
would depend upon the materials of which they were made.
Mr. Christison said that if the pills were made up with re-
sinous materials, such as are within the knowledge of every
medical man, their operation would be delayed. He added,
" I do not think we can fix, with our present knowledge, the
" precise time for the poison beginning to operate." [4] According to the account of one witness in Agnes French's case,
the poison did not operate for three-quarters of an hour,
though, probably, her recollection of the time was not very
accurate after ten years. [5] Dr. Taylor also referred (in cross-
examination) to cases in which an hour and a half, or even
two hours, elapsed, before the symptoms showed themselves.

These were the principal points, in Cook's symptoms, said
to be inconsistent with the administration of strychnia. All
of them appear to have been satisfactorily answered. Indeed,
the inconsistency of the symptoms with strychnia was faintly
maintained. The defence turned rather on the possibility of
showing that they were consistent with some other disease.

In order to make out this point, various suggestions were
made in the cross-examination of the different witnesses for
the Crown. It was frequently suggested that the case was
one of traumatic tetanus, caused by syphilitic sores; but to
this there were three fatal objections. In the first place, there
were no syphilitic sores; in the second place, no witness for

[1] Nunneley, 219.   [2] Letheby, 233.   [3] Christison, 158.
[4] Mary Kelly, 126.   [5] A. S. Taylor, 150.

the prisoner said that he thought that it was a case of traumatic tetanus; and, in the third place, several doctors of great experience in respect of syphilis—especially [1] Dr. Lee, the physician to the Lock Hospital—declared that they never heard of syphilitic sores producing tetanus. [2] Two witnesses for the prisoner were called to show that a man died of tetanus who had sores on his elbows and elsewhere which were possibly syphilitic; but it did not appear whether he had rubbed or hurt them, and Cook had no symptoms of the sort.

Another theory was, that the death was caused by general convulsions. This was advanced by [3] Mr. Nunneley; but he was unable to mention any case in which general convulsions had produced death without destroying consciousness. [4] He said vaguely he had heard of such cases, but had never met with one. [5] Dr. McDonald, of Garnkirk, near Glasgow, said that he considered the case to be one of "epileptic convulsions "with tetanic complications." But he also failed to mention an instance in which epilepsy did not destroy consciousness. This witness assigned the most extraordinary reasons for supposing that it was a case of this form of epilepsy. He said that the fit might have been caused by sexual excitement, though the man was ill at Rugeley for nearly a week before his death; [6] and that it was within the range of possibility that sexual intercourse might produce a convulsion fit after an interval of a fortnight.

Both Mr. Nunneley and Dr. McDonald were cross-examined with great closeness. Each of them was taken separately through all the various symptoms of the case, and asked to point out how they differed from those of poisoning by strychnia, and what were the reasons why they should be supposed to arise from anything else. After a great deal of trouble, Mr. Nunneley was forced to admit that the symptoms

---

[1] Lee, 124.   [2] Dr. Corbett, 239. Mr. Mantell, 241.   [3] Nunneley, 227.
[4] Nunneley, 217-218.   [5] McDonald, 252-253.   [6] McDonald, 253-254.

Palmer's Case.

of the paroxysm were "very like" those of strychnia, and that the various predisposing causes which he mentioned as likely to bring on convulsions could not be shown to have existed. He said, for instance, that excitement and depression of spirits might predispose to convulsions; but the only excitement under which Cook had laboured was on winning the race a week before; and as for depression of spirits, he was laughing and joking with Mr. Jones a few hours before his death. Dr. McDonald was equally unable to give a satisfactory explanation of these difficulties. It is impossible, by any abridgment, to convey the full effect which these cross-examinations produced. They deserve to be carefully studied by anyone who cares to understand the full effect of this great instrument for the manifestation not merely of truth, but of accuracy and fairness.

Of the other witnesses for the prisoner, [1] Mr. Herapath admitted that he had said that he thought that there was strychnine in the body, but that Dr. Taylor did not know how to find it. He added that he got this impression from newspaper reports; but it did not appear that they differed from the evidence given at the trial. [2] Dr. Letheby said that the symptoms of Cook were irreconcilable with everything that he was acquainted with—strychnia poison included. He admitted, however, that they were not inconsistent with what he had heard of the symptoms of Mrs. Serjeantson Smyth, who was undoubtedly poisoned by strychnine. [3] Mr. Partridge was called to show that the case might be one of arachnitis, or inflammation of one of the membranes of the spinal cord, caused by two granules discovered there. In cross-examination he instantly admitted, with perfect frankness, that he did not think the case one of arachnitis, as the symptoms were not the same. Moreover, on being asked whether the symptoms described by Mr. Jones were consistent

[1] Herapath, 231.   [2] Letheby 237.   [3] Partridge, 244-245.

with poisoning by strychnia, he said, "Quite"; and he concluded by saying that, in the whole course of his experience and knowledge, he had never seen such a death proceed from natural causes. [1] Dr. Robinson, from Newcastle, was called to show that tetanic convulsions preceded by epilepsy were the cause of death. He, however, expressly admitted in cross-examination that the symptoms were consistent with strychnia, and that some of them were inconsistent with epilepsy. He said that, in the absence of any other cause, if he "put aside "the hypothesis of strychnia," he would ascribe it to epilepsy; and that he thought the granules in the spinal cord might have produced epilepsy. The degree of importance attached to these granules by different witnesses varied. Several of the witnesses for the Crown considered them unimportant. [2] The last of the prisoner's witnesses was Dr. Richardson, who said the disease might have been angina pectoris. He said, however, that the symptoms of angina pectoris were so like those of strychnine that he should have great difficulty in distinguishing them from each other.

The fact that antimony was found was never seriously disputed, nor could it be denied that its administration would account for all the symptoms of sickness, &c., which occurred during the week before Cook's death. No one but the prisoner could have administered it.

I was present throughout the greater part of this celebrated trial, and it made an impression on my mind which the experience of thirty-four subsequent years, during which I have witnessed, studied, and taken part, both as counsel and as judge, in many important cases, has rather strengthened than weakened. It is impossible to give an adequate idea of the manner in which it exhibited in its very best and strongest light the good side of English criminal procedure. No more horrible villain than Palmer ever stood in a dock. The pre-

---

[1] Robinson, 258-259.   [2] Richardson, 249-260.

judice against him was so strong that it was considered necessary to pass an Act of Parliament to authorize his trial in London. He was actually indicted for the murder of his wife, and for that of his brother, and it was commonly reported at the time that he had murdered in the same way many other persons. Under the French system, the *acte d'accusation* would have paraded these, with all the other discreditable incidents of his life, before the eyes of the jury. He would have been questioned by the president, probably for days, about them ; and it would have been practically impossible for the jury to consider, calmly and impartially, whether the fact that he had murdered Cook was properly proved. As it was, no one of these matters was introduced or referred to, except so far as it directly bore upon the case of Cook. Thus, Mrs. Palmer's death, and the way in which he disposed of the £13,000 for which he had insured her life, were referred to only in order to show his money position at the time of Cook's death. The suggestion that he had murdered his wife (as he most unquestionably had) was never made or hinted at. So the fact that on Walter Palmer's death the policy for which Palmer had insured his life was disputed by the office was referred to only for the same purpose, and the same remark applies to the forged acceptances of his mother's which Palmer had uttered. The evidence on all these matters was confined to what was absolutely necessary for the purpose of showing motive.

Not less remarkable than the careful way in which all topics of prejudice were avoided was the extreme fullness and completeness of the evidence as to facts which were really relevant to the case. Nothing was omitted which the jury could properly want to know, nor anything which the prisoner could possibly wish to say. No case could set in a clearer light the advantage of two characteristic features of English criminal law—namely, its essentially litigious

character, and the way in which it deals with scientific
evidence. A study of the case will show, first, that evidence
could not be more condensed, more complete, more closely
directed to the very point at issue ; secondly, that the subjec-
tion of all witnesses, and especially of all skilled witnesses, to
the most rigorous cross-examination is absolutely essential to
the trustworthiness of their evidence. The closeness and the
skill with which the various witnesses, especially those for
the defence, were cross-examined, and compelled to admit
that they could not really distinguish the symptoms of Cook
from those of poisoning by strychnine, were such an illustration of the efficiency of cross-examination as is rarely indeed
afforded.

The defence was by far the least impressive part of the
trial, but that was mainly because there was in reality
nothing to say. It was impossible to suggest any innocent
explanation of Palmer's conduct. It was proved to demonstration that he was in dire need of money in order to avoid
a prosecution for forgery, that he robbed his friend of all
he had by a series of devices which he must instantly
have discovered if he had lived, that he provided himself
with the means of committing the murder just before Cook's
death, and that he could neither produce the poison he had
bought nor suggest any innocent reason for buying it.
There must have been some mystery in the case which was
never discovered. Palmer, at and before his execution, was
repeatedly pressed to say whether he was guilty or not, and
was told that everyone would believe him to admit his guilt
if he did not emphatically deny it. He would say only, " He
" was not poisoned by strychnine ; " and I have reason to
know that he was anxious that Dr. Herapath should examine
the body for strychnine, though aware that he said he could
detect the fifty-thousandth part of a grain. He may have
discovered some way of administering it which would render

discovery impossible, but it is difficult to doubt that he used it, for, if not, why did he buy it ?

The best points for the defence were that the descriptions given by the maid-servants of Cook's symptoms were coloured by what they afterwards read in the newspapers about the symptoms of Mrs. Dove and could not be trusted, and that the evidence as to the purchase of the strychnine was unsatisfactory. To some extent this no doubt weakened the evidence, but not so much as to raise a reasonable doubt as to what it proved.

I am tempted to make one other observation on Palmer's case. His career supplied one of the proofs of a fact which many kind-hearted people seem to doubt—namely, the fact that such a thing as atrocious wickedness is consistent with good education, perfect sanity, and everything, in a word, which deprives men of all excuse for crime. Palmer was respectably brought up; apart from his extravagance and vice, he might have lived comfortably enough. He was a model of physical health and strength, and was courageous, determined, and energetic. No one ever suggested that there was even a disposition towards madness in him; yet he was as cruel, as treacherous, as greedy of money and pleasure, as brutally hard-hearted and sensual a wretch as it is possible even to imagine. If he had been the lowest and most ignorant ruffian that ever sprung from a long line of criminal ancestors, he could not have been worse than he was. He was by no means unlike Rush, Thurtell, and many other persons whom I have known. The fact that the world contains an appreciable number of wretches, who ought to be exterminated without mercy when an opportunity occurs, is not quite so generally understood as it ought to be, and many common ways of thinking and feeling virtually deny it.

[1]THE CASE OF WILLIAM DOVE.

ON the 16th of July, 1856, William Dove was indicted at York for the murder of his wife, Harriet Dove, and, after a trial before Baron Bramwell which occupied four days, was convicted. His case is remarkable as an illustration of the practical application of the principles of law relating to the criminal responsibility of madmen discussed in a preceding chapter.

Dove was a man of about thirty, and had been married to his wife, at the time of her death, between four and five years. He had about £100 a year of his own, and lived with his wife at various places. At the time of her death (Saturday, March 1, 1856), they had been living at Leeds since a few days before the previous Christmas. A servant, Elizabeth Fisher, who lived with them for about a year before Mrs. Dove's death, proved that for some time they had lived very unhappily. He was often drunk and violent, and they had quarrels in consequence. On one occasion he was so violent that the servant went out for help, and he threw a bottle at her on her return. Another time, the servant saw him holding Mrs. Dove with one hand and threatening to kill her with a knife which he had in the other. Afterwards, when she asked for a part of some money which he had got, he said " he would rather give " it to anyone than her, and he would give her a pill that

[1] This account is taken from the notes of Lord Bramwell, who was so kind as to lend them to me for the purpose. I have followed throughout their very words, though the form in which they are taken is of course at times elliptical, and though there are one or two obvious slips of the pen.

T

Dove's Case.

" would do for her." This made so much impression on Mrs. Dove, that she told the servant (in Dove's presence) that he had said so ; and also said to her, on the morning when she left their service, "Elizabeth, if I should die and you are " away at the time, it is my wish that you tell my friends to " have my body examined." Elizabeth Fisher went home on Tuesday, February 19th, and on the following Saturday (the 23rd) her mother, Anne Fisher, came to take her place. On the Monday, before breakfast, Mrs. Dove was quite well. After breakfast, she went upstairs to make the beds, and complained of feeling very strange. In a short time, symptoms came on which, no doubt, were those of poisoning by strychnine. The attack went off, but she remained in bed, and was attended by Mr. Morley, who was fetched for the purpose by Dove.

She had similar attacks on the Wednesday, the Thursday, and a very bad one on the Friday night. Through the early part of Saturday (March 1) she was better, but, about half-past eight in the evening, another attack came on, and she died at about twenty minutes to eleven. A *post-mortem* examination made by Mr. Morley and Mr. Nunneley proved, beyond all doubt, that she had died of strychnine. Substances extracted from the body poisoned several animals, which died from symptoms identical with those which were produced in other animals poisoned with strychnine procured for the purpose elsewhere.

It was equally clear that the poison was administered with the intention of destroying life, with premeditation, and with precautions intended to conceal it. Mrs. Dove had been unwell, though not seriously, for some time before her death, and had been attended by Mr. Morley for about three months. Dove used to go to his surgery for medicines. " He came " (said Elletson, a pupil of Mr. Morley's) "a month before her " death. We talked about [1] Palmer's trial. He said Palmer

---

[1] See last case.

" had poisoned his wife by repeated doses of antimony. It
" was mentioned Cook had been poisoned by strychnine.
" Dove said strychnine could not be detected after death. I
" said it could. I mentioned nitric acid as a test. I showed
" him the amount in Pereira's *Materia Medica*. He took it
" in his hand and read it, page 903, &c. He said his house
" was infested with wild cats, which he wished to destroy. He
" said he thought laying poison would be the best way. I
" said I thought it would. He asked me for some strychnine.
" I gave him some, about ten grains, wrapped as a powder
in " a piece of foolscap paper. I wrote 'poison' on it." He
afterwards got from three to five grains more in the same
manner, and he was seen by Mr. Morley's coachman in the
surgery when no one was there. As he had observed, in the
course of his conversation with Elletson, the place where the
strychnine bottle was kept, he had, on this occasion, an opportunity of obtaining a further supply if he chose. He did poison
two cats with the strychnine thus obtained, and also a mouse,
thus giving colour to his possession of the poison.

Besides the circumstances which showed that Dove lived
on bad terms with his wife and had threatened her, evidence
was given to show that he had formed designs upon her
life. During her illness, he told Mrs. Thornhill, a widow, that
he had been to the witchman, who said Mrs. Dove had not
long to live. He added that, as soon as she died, he would
make an offer to the lady next door. In the course of her
illness, he repeatedly told Mr. Morley, the surgeon, that he
thought she would not recover, notwithstanding Mr. Morley's
opinion to the contrary. He also told a woman named Hicks
that she would not get over the disease, and that he should
most likely marry again, as no one could expect him, a young
man, to remain single. He told the same witness, on the day
of Mrs. Dove's death, that Mrs. Dove would not have another
attack till half-past ten or eleven ; and on being asked whether

the attacks came on periodically made no answer. Lastly, on the evening of her death, he gave her a dose of medicine. She complained of the taste being very hot, and in about a quarter of an hour was seized with all the symptoms of strychnine poisoning, which continued till her death.

Some other evidence upon the subject was given, but it is needless to go into it. It is enough to say that it was proved beyond the possibility of doubt on the part of the prosecution, whilst it was hardly denied on the part of the prisoner, that he caused her death by the repeated administration of doses of strychnine, which he had procured for that purpose under false pretences, and which he administered in order to destroy her life, partly because he was on bad terms with her, partly because he wished to marry again.

The substantial defence which gives the case its interest was, that the act was either not wilful or not malicious; and the evidence of this was, that Dove was insane, and was thus either prevented by mental disease from knowing that the act was wrong, or constrained by an irresistible impulse to do it. The evidence as to the state of his mind was given partly by the witnesses for the prosecution, and partly by the witnesses called by his own counsel. The most convenient way of describing its effect will be to throw it into the shape of a continuous account of his life, from the sixth year of his age down to the time of his trial.

The first witness upon the subject was his nurse, who had known him from the sixth to about the twentieth year of his age. She said, "I never thought him right in his mind." The proof of this seemed to consist principally in his habit of playing exceedingly mischievous and ill-natured tricks. For example, he tried to set the bed-curtains on fire ; he chased his sisters with a red-hot poker ; he cut open a wound on his arm which had healed, saying it had healed false.   The nurse added : " His father and family were very pious and regular

" Wesleyans. Great pains were taken to instruct the child.
" He could not regularly be taught his lessons and duties.
" That is one reason for thinking he was not in his right
" mind." Mr. Charles Harrison, who had been usher at a
school where Dove was from ten to thirteen years of age, spoke
of him as follows : " I regarded him as a youth of a very low
" order of intellect. I never remember to have met with a
" similar case—great imbecility of mind and great want of
" moral power, [1] evil and vicious propensities." He added,
that once Dove got a pistol, and told the boys that he meant
to shoot his father with it. The father was told of it, and
said he should flog him. In cross-examination, Mr. Harrison
said : " He was a dull boy and a bad boy. I then thought
" him insane. I did not feel myself in a position to object
" to him being flogged. I never sent him from my class to
" be flogged. He was frequently flogged for incapacity."
Mr. Highley, the schoolmaster, spoke strongly of his bad conduct, and said : " His reasoning powers were extremely limited.
" He appeared to have no idea of any consequences. He
" appeared to be deprived of reason. I am satisfied he was
" labouring under an aberration of intellect." These strong
expressions, however, were not supported by any specific proof
worth repeating. Mr. Highley admitted that he used to flog
him, but he added : " I flogged him till I was satisfied there
" was a want of reason, but not after." He admitted, however
that he flogged him slightly (" perhaps a stroke or two ") the
day before he left.

Dove having been expelled from Mr. Highley's school, his
father took the opinion of Mr. Lord, who was also a schoolmaster, as to what was to be done with him. Mr. Lord said :
" I, at his father's request, invited him into my study, to give
" him religious instruction. I made myself acquainted with
" the character of his mind. I could make no impression on

---

[1] *Sic* in the notes.

" his heart or his head. He would not at all appreciate what
" I said. He listened, but I could make no impression—get
" no rational answer. His father consulted me as to what
" provision [1] I should make for him. I advised him. He was
" not then capable of disposing of property to any amount
" rationally. I never forbade him my house. I did not invite
" him in consequence of his deficiency and perverseness. I
" should say he was not of sound mind." In cross-examination,
Mr. Lord said that, when he heard of Dove's engagement, he
told his future wife's brother that inquiry ought to be made
about Dove, "on account of his unaccountable irrational con-
" duct." In answer to further questions, he repeated several
times his strong conviction of his being "irrational" in conversation and behaviour, though he could give no particular
instance of it.

In consequence, apparently, or at any rate soon after his
reference to Mr. Lord, Dove's father sent him to a Mr.
Frankish to learn farming. He stayed with Mr. Frankish
for five years and a half. Mr. Frankish said : " I think there
" were certain seasons when he was not of sound mind. That
" was frequent. He never could learn farming." He also
mentioned a number of instances of the sort of conduct on
which this opinion was founded. Thus, he put vitriol on the
tails of some cows. He at first denied, but afterwards confessed
it, and was sorry for what he had done. He also burnt two
half-grown kittens with vitriol. He put vitriol into the horse-
trough, and set fire to the gorse on the farm, doing considerable
damage. After leaving Frankish, he went for a year as a pupil
to a Mr. Gibson, also a farmer. Gibson's account of him was
as follows : " I did not consider him one of the brightest and
" most powerful minds. I tried to teach him practically, as
" far as farming went, as stock and the rotation of crops. I
" was not as successful as I should like."

---

[1] *Sic.*   Obviously it should be "he."

After this he seems to have gone to America, for what purpose does not appear. He went alone, and he seems not to have stayed there long; and he told wild stories about his adventures there on his return. He was next established on a farm taken for him at a place called Whitwell. It was about this time that he married. James Shaw, Mary Peek, and Robert and William Tomlinson, Emma Spence, and Emma and Fanny Wilson, who had been in his service, all gave evidence of his extravagant behaviour whilst he held the farm. He used to point loaded fire-arms at his servants, and threaten to shoot people who had given him no offence. He told strange stories about his having been attacked or followed by robbers. He cut a maid-servant's cap to pieces. He and his wife often quarrelled, and sometimes played like children. Some of the servants spoke of having seen him crying, wandering about his fields without an object. Shaw said : " I many " times used to think he did things different from what a man " would do if he had his right mind." Tomlinson said : " I do " not think he was a sound-minded man at all times." Several other witnesses—two schoolmasters, a postman, a Wesleyan preacher, who had lodged at his father's, and a friend of his wife's—all deposed to a variety of extravagant acts and conversations somewhat similar to those already stated. They spoke of his conversation as being unusually incoherent, " flying " about from one subject to another,"—of his lying on the ground and crying without a cause, of his complaining of noises in his house, and of his reaping part of his own corn while it was green because, he said, others had reaped theirs and he would not be later than they, and of his telling wild stories about his adventures in America, as if he believed them. In addition to this, whilst he was in gaol, he wrote in his own blood a letter to the devil. It was suggested that this might be for the purpose of making evidence of his insanity.

In addition to the evidence as to facts, three medical witnesses were called, who had been physicians to lunatic asylums or otherwise specially occupied with the subject of madness for many years. They all agreed in describing Dove as of unsound mind. Two of them, Dr. Pyeman Smith, proprietor of a lunatic asylum at Leeds, and Dr. Kitchen, of York, at once admitted, on cross-examination, that they thought he knew right from wrong during the week which he passed in poisoning his wife. Dr. Pyeman Smith added that many mad people do know right from wrong; that a madman having that knowledge might be regardless of consequences, and might be wholly unable to refrain from doing what was wrong. He then said, "I cannot say that of the prisoner during " that week ; circumstances might have made him refrain. " Other circumstances. Not the greater chance of detection. " His not possessing the poison. Slight circumstances might " have [? made] him defer it to another time. In my opinion " possessing [? the means] he was regardless of the conse- " quences." Mr. Kitchen said : "I think it probable that he " had some knowledge of the difference between right and " wrong during the fatal week. If he did it, I have no doubt " he knew he was committing murder, and that if found out " he would be likely to be punished for it." On re-examina- tion, he added, " I consider his conduct that week the natural " consequence of what had gone before. All his previous life " justified the expectation. I believe he has been insane all " his life. When I say he knew if he did it he was commit- " ting murder, I mean he knew he was killing his wife. I " do not mean he knew he was doing wrong. I think he " would know that in proportion as he knew the difference " between right and wrong."

Dr. Williams, who had been medical attendant of a lunatic asylum at York for thirty years, gave evidence on the subject at great length. The most important parts of his evidence are as follows. After stating his conviction that Dove's

letter to the devil was genuine, and that he believed himself
to be under supernatural influences, he said : " During the
" fatal week, from all I have heard, I should say that, while
" impelled by a propensity to injure or take life, his mind
" was probably influenced by his notions regarding super-
" natural agency, and therefore he was the subject of delusion.
" A person labouring under such delusion might retain his
" power of judging in adopting means to an end, and as to
" consequences as regards the object he had in view.   Under
" those delusions he could not have the power of resisting
" any impulse."   On cross-examination, Dr. Williams said :
" I know of no case of a man " (obviously meaning a man
under the influence of madness) " giving poison in small and
" repeated doses.   Insanity to take away life by poison is
" rare.   If poison were administered six or seven times run-
" ning, I should not call it an impulse ; I should call it an
" uncontrollable propensity to destroy, give pain, or take life.
" The propensity might continue as a permanent condition of
" the mind.   It might select a special object and not injure
" any body or thing else.   I think such a person would not
" know he was doing wrong.   He might fear the consequences
" of punishment.   He would probably know that he was break-
" ing the law.   He would not know at the time he did it he
" would be hanged for murder.   I found that opinion on the
" occupation of the mind by the insane propensity.   It is
" uncertain if he would know it before he did it.   He might
" afterwards."

After several questions pointing to the conclusion that vice
as well as insanity might be the cause of crime in men so
constituted, Dr. Williams was asked the following question :
" If a person lived with his wife and hated her, and deter-
" mined to and did kill her, what is the difference between
" that determination which is vice and the propensity which
" is insanity ? "   He answered : " The prisoner's previous his-

" tory would be required to determine whether it was vice
" or insanity." He then proceeded, in answer to other questions : " A man by nourishing an idea may become diseased
" in his mind, and then he cannot control it. This is moral
" insanity. It does apply to other cases : it might apply to
" rape ; as, if a man nourished the desire to possess a particular
" woman till the desire became uncontrollable, and then he
" committed the rape, that would be moral insanity. So of
" theft. If a man permits himself to contemplate the grati-
" fication of any passion or desire till it becomes uncontrol-
" lable, that is moral insanity." On re-examination, he gave
the following evidence :—[1] " *Q.* Suppose the man had from his
" childhood been excitable, used fire-arms when no danger,
" threatened to shoot his father and mother, complained of
" sounds in his house, and the other things proved by wit-
" nesses yesterday, treating his wife kindly and weeping ?
" *A.* I have no doubt that man is insane, and not fit to be
" trusted abroad. I would have certified him a lunatic before
" the fatal week."

The jury returned the following verdict :—" Guilty, but we
" recommend him to mercy on the ground of his defective
" intellect." He was sentenced to death, and executed at
York in pursuance of his sentence.

I have entered minutely into the details of this case, because it furnishes a perfect illustration of the state of mind
which Erskine [2] alluded to, though it was unnecessary for
him to discuss it minutely, in his celebrated speech on the

---

[1] Verbatim from the notes.

[2] "You will have to decide whether you attribute it wholly to mischief
" and malice, or wholly to insanity or to the one mixing itself with the other.
" . . . *If you consider it as conscious malice and mischief mixing itself with
" insanity,* I leave him in the hands of the court to say how he is to be dealt
" with. It is a question too difficult for me."—27 *State Trials,* 1328. This
remark is characteristic of Erskine. The great logical capacity, which was one of
the principal characteristics of his mind, led him to say that malice and insanity
might mix. His excessive caution as an advocate admonished him to point

trial of Hadfield. It is impossible to resist the conclusion, which the evidence given above suggests, that Dove was not a sane man. It is equally impossible to doubt that he wilfully, maliciously, and of his malice aforethought, in the full and proper sense of those words, murdered his wife. The result of the whole history appears to be, that he was from infancy predisposed (to say the least) to madness ; that symptoms indicating that disease displayed themselves at frequent intervals through the whole course of his life, but that they never reached such a pitch as to induce those about him to treat him as a madman. He was allowed to go by himself to America, to occupy and manage a farm, to marry, though his wife's brother was warned of his character, to live on his means without interference at Leeds, and generally to conduct himself as a sane person. This being so, he appears to have allowed his mind to dwell with a horrible prurience on the prospect of his wife's death and of his own marriage to another person, to have formed the design of putting her to death, and to have carried out that design with every mark of deliberate contrivance and precaution. In this state of things, can he be said to have known, in the wider sense of the words, that his act was wrong ? He obviously knew that the act was wrong in the sense that people in general would so consider it ; but was he capable of thinking like an ordinary man of the reasons why murder is wrong, and of applying those reasons to his conduct ?

Undoubtedly there was evidence both ways. Looking at the whole account of his life, it cannot be denied that his language and conduct appear at times to have been inconsecutive, capricious, and not capable of being accounted for on any common principles of action. His lying down on the

to the difficulty and leave it on one side, but I know of nothing in his speeches or writings to lead to the supposition that he could have done much towards solving it had he tried.

ground to cry, his wandering in the fields, the noises he supposed himself to hear, are all strong illustrations. On the other hand, this was only an occasional state of things. He appears to have acted, as a rule, rationally enough, and to have transacted all the common affairs of life. Did, then, this killing of his wife belong to the rational or to the irrational part of his conduct? Every circumstance connected with it referred it to the former. Its circumstances presented every conceivable mark of motive and design. It was a continued series of deliberate and repeated attempts, fully accomplished at last.

The suggestion of Dr. Williams, that Dove had allowed his mind to dwell on his wife's death till at last he became the victim of an uncontrollable propensity to kill her, if correct, would not prove that his act was not voluntary. It is the setting and keeping the mind in motion towards an object plainly conceived that constitutes the mental part of an act. Every act becomes irrevocable by the agent before it is consummated. If a man, for example, strikes another, he may repent while his arm is actually falling, but there is a point at which he can no more deprive his arm of the impetus with which he has animated it than he can divert from its course a bullet which he has fired from a rifle. Suppose he deals with his mind in this manner at an earlier stage of the proceeding, and so fills himself with a passionate, intense longing for the forbidden object, or result, that he becomes as it were a mere machine in his own hands. Is not the case precisely similar, and does not the action continue to be voluntary and wilful, although the act of volition which made it irrevocable preceded its completion by a longer interval than usual?

It must, however, be remembered that the proof that Dove's propensity was uncontrollable is very defective. An uncontrollable propensity which accidental difficulties, or the

fear of detection, constantly control and divert for a time, is an
inconceivable state of mind. Is there the smallest reason to
suppose that, if Mrs. Dove had met with a fatal accident, and
had been lying in bed dying before her husband gave her any
poison at all, his uncontrollable propensity to kill her would
have induced him to administer the poison nevertheless? If
not, the propensity was like any other wicked feeling. It
was certainly uncontrolled, and may probably have been
strong, but that is different from being uncontrollable.

It is easy, no doubt, to imagine circumstances which
would have justified the jury in returning a different verdict.
If Dove had always treated his wife kindly, and lived on
good terms with her, and if he had killed her in a sudden,
unaccountable fury, the evidence as to the state of his mind
would, no doubt, have suggested the conclusion that the act
was not part of the regular and ordinary course of his life;
that it was not planned, settled, and executed as rational men
carry out their purposes, but that it was one of those occurrences which rebut the presumption of will or malice on the
part of the agent, and was, therefore, not within the province
of the criminal law. This conclusion might have been
rendered more or less probable by an infinite variety of
collateral circumstances. Concealment, for example, would
have diminished its probability. Openness would have increased it, and so would independent traces of excitement.

[1] THE CASE OF THOMAS SMETHURST.

THOMAS SMETHURST was indicted for the wilful murder of Isabella Bankes at the Old Bailey Sessions, on the 7th of July, 1859. After the case had proceeded for a considerable time, one of the jury was taken ill, and the court adjourned till Monday, the 15th of August. A trial, which occupied four days, before the Lord Chief Baron of the Exchequer, then took place; the prisoner was convicted and sentenced to death, but he subsequently received a free pardon on the ground that his guilt had not been sufficiently proved.

Smethurst, who had been for many years married to a person much older than himself, was living with his wife, in November, 1858, at a boarding-house in Bayswater, where he became acquainted with Miss Bankes, the deceased. On the 9th of December he went through the ceremony of marriage with her, and they went to live together at Richmond, Smethurst's real wife being left at the boarding-house at Bayswater. There he visited her once or twice after he left, and he also transmitted money on her account to the mistress of the house. There was no evidence to show that Mrs. Smethurst was aware of the relations between her husband and Miss Bankes, though it is hardly possible that her suspi-

---

[1] This account is founded on the notes of Lord Chief Baron Pollock, who was kind enough to lend them to me for that purpose, and also to give me a copy of his communication to Sir G. C. Lewis on the subject. The quotations of the evidence are taken from the Lord Chief Baron's notes. I have compared the Report in the 50th Volume of the Old Bailey Sessions Papers, and the references are to the pages of that volume.

cions should not have been roused by their leaving the house within a fortnight of each other, [1] especially as Miss Bankes's departure was caused by the representations of the landlady as to the impropriety of her conduct.

After the sham marriage, the prisoner and the deceased went to live at Richmond, where they stayed for four months. [2] From the 4th February to the 15th April they lodged at Old Palace Gardens. From the 15th April to Miss Bankes's death, on the 3rd May, they lodged at 10 Alma Villas; Miss Bankes was taken ill towards the end of March, or beginning of April, and grew rapidly worse. [3] Dr. Julius, of Richmond, was called in on the 3rd of April, by the direction of the prisoner, on the recommendation of the landlady of the first set of lodgings. [4] In the midst of her illness Miss Bankes was removed to another lodging at 10 Alma Villas, the motive of the change being the raising of the rent of the first lodgings. [5] Dr. Bird, the partner of Dr. Julius, attended her from the 18th April, and by the prisoner's desire she was visited by Dr. Todd, on the 28th. [6] On Sunday, the 1st May, a will was made for Miss Bankes by a Richmond solicitor, named Senior, who was applied to on the subject by Dr. Smethurst, and by this will the whole of her property, with the exception of a brooch, was left to him absolutely. The property consisted of £1,740 lent on mortgage. [7] The deceased had, also, a life interest in £5,000, the dividend on which she had just received and handed to the prisoner. [8] On May 1st, being Sunday, the will was executed, and on May 2nd the prisoner was brought before the Richmond magistrates on a charge of administering poison to the deceased. [9] He was liberated on his own recognizances the same evening, and Miss Bankes died on the morning of the

[1] P. 504. [2] P. 505. [3] P. 505. [4] P. 530.
[5] P. 524. [6] Pp. 520-521. [7] Pp. 522, 547, 513.
[8] P. 545. [9] P. 513-517.

3rd. [1] Her sister, Miss Louisa Bankes, had visited her on the 19th April. She also visited her on the 30th, and attended her from the time of Dr. Smethurst's liberation to her death. On the *post-mortem* examination, it appeared that the deceased was between five and seven weeks advanced in pregnancy. On the prisoner's second apprehension, which took place immediately after the death of Miss Bankes, a letter was found upon him addressed to his real wife.

The first question suggested by these facts was whether they disclosed any motive on the part of the prisoner for the murder of the deceased.

The consequences of the death of Miss Bankes to Smethurst, measured in money, would be a gain of £1,740 lent on mortgage, and a loss of the chance of receiving the dividend to accrue on the principal sum of £5,000 during her life. His chance of receiving the dividend depended entirely on the continuance of their connection and of his influence over her. Now, the connection was one which involved not merely immorality, but crime. If Mrs. Smethurst had become aware of its character, she might at any moment have punished her husband's desertion and neglect by imprisonment; and, so long as the connection continued, his liberty and character were at the mercy of anyone who might discover the circumstances bearing on it. There was also the chance that he himself might become tired of his mistress, or that she, from motives which might readily arise, might wish to leave him. His hold over her dividends would terminate in any of these cases, and was thus uncertain. Besides this, it must be remembered that the dividends, whilst he received them, would have to be applied to their joint support. He could not apply them to his own purposes and turn her out of doors, for, if he had done so, she would have retained them for herself. [2] A precarious hold over £150 a year, for the

---

[1] P. 539.   [2] The dividend was £71 5s., probably for a half-year.

life of a person who was to be supported as a lady out of that sum, and who was likely to become a mother, was certainly not worth the right to receive a gross amount of £1,740, unfettered by any condition whatever. It thus seems clear that Smethurst had a money interest in the death of Miss Bankes; but there is nothing to show that he was in pressing want of money, whilst there is some evidence to show that he was not. In Palmer's case the possession of a large sum of money at the very time of Cook's death was a matter of vital importance; but [1] Smethurst had a considerable balance at his banker's at the time in question, and appears to have lived upon his means at Richmond without any visible mode of earning a living.

A consideration which weighed more heavily, in respect to the existence of a motive for murder, arose out of the nature of the connection between the prisoner and the deceased. It is sometimes said that there is no need to look further for a motive when the parties are man and wife. The harshness of the expression ought not to be allowed to conceal the truth which it contains. Married people usually treat each other with external decency, good humour, and cordiality, but what lies under that veil is known only to themselves; and the relation may produce hatred, bitter in proportion to the intimacy which it involves. In the particular case in question, the relation which existed between the parties was one which could hardly fail to abound in sources of dislike and discomfort. Both were doing wrong; both (if Miss Bankes knew of Smethurst's first marriage) had committed a legal as well as a moral offence; and at the very period when the illness of the deceased commenced she had become pregnant.

To a man in Smethurst's position, that circumstance (if he were aware of it) would in itself furnish some motive for the

[1] P. 547.

U

crime with which he was charged, for the birth of a child could hardly have failed to increase the difficulties and embarrassments incidental to the position in which he had placed himself.

Some expressions occurred in a conversation between Miss Bankes and her sister, Miss Louisa Bankes, which have an important bearing on this part of the subject. Miss Louisa Bankes saw her sister for the first time after the ceremony of December 9th at Richmond, on the 19th April. Her evidence as to what passed was as follows: [1] "I was taken into the " deceased's bedroom. She was rather agitated. She said, " if I would be quiet it would be all right. He said, 'Yes, " ' it would be all right.' " These expressions suggest a doubt whether Miss Bankes was fully aware of the true nature of her connection with Dr. Smethurst, and whether she may not have supposed that she was his lawful wife, though there was another person passing by the same name.

[2] If Smethurst had deceived her on this point, and if he was aware of her pregnancy, his position would be most distressing, and would explain a wish on his part to be freed from it at all hazards.

In opposition to this it must be observed that the will was executed in her maiden name, which implies a knowledge on her part that she was not married, though, as there is nothing to show that she had any particular acquaintance with business, and as the will was executed only forty-eight hours before she died of exhaustion, too much weight must not be attached to this. The letter found in Smethurst's pocket on his second arrest, and addressed to his wife, is deserving of attention in reference to this part of the subject. It was as follows:—

---

[1] P. 513.

[2] This suggestion was negatived by subsequent proceedings (see note, *post*).

"K. W. C.
"Monday, May 2, 1859.

" MY DEAREST MARY,—I have not been able to leave for
" town as I expected, in consequence of my medical aid being
" required in a case of illness. I shall, however, see you as
" soon as possible ; and should any unforeseen event prevent
" my leaving for town before the 11th, I will send you a cheque
" for Smith's money and extras. I will send £5. I am quite
" well, and sincerely hope you are the same, and that I shall
" find you so when I see you, which I trust will not be long
" first. Present my kind regards to the Smiths and all old
" friends in the house. I heard from James the other day ;
" he said he had called on you, but that you had gone out for
" a walk. With love,

"Believe me,
"Yours most affectionately,
" T. SMETHURST."

This letter contains several expressions which raise a doubt
whether Mrs. Smethurst was aware of her husband's relations
with Miss Bankes. Though the writer was staying at Richmond, the letter is dated, " K. W. C.," as if it had been written
at some place, the name of which began with a K., in the
West Central district. It also appears as if Smethurst had
arranged with his wife to "leave for town" before the 11th,
and was intending to return to her ; and there is an indis-
tinctness and an incompleteness about the letter which looks
as if it were one of a series, and as if Mrs. Smethurst had had
reason to believe that her husband was absent from her only
for a time, and was shortly intending to return. If she had
known of his connection with Miss Bankes, it is hardly conceivable that some explicit mention of her state should not
have been made in the letter, as she died on the following
day, and Smethurst had procured her will to be made on the
Sunday (the day before), lest Monday should be too late. If

U 2

Mrs. Smethurst was in correspondence with her husband, but did not know of his position, and had reason to expect his return, his relations with Miss Bankes would be most painful. This, however, is little more than conjecture.

The result of the inquiry into the question of motive would thus seem to be that Smethurst had a money interest in Miss Bankes's death, but that he was not proved to be in any particular want of money ; that their relation was one which may probably have caused enmity in various ways. There is no proof, but there are not unreasonable grounds for conjecturing, that it did so in point of fact.

Two points were urged against Smethurst at his trial arising out of his conduct. They were, that he had allowed no one to see Miss Bankes during her illness except himself and the medical men, and in particular that he prevented her sister from seeing her ; and that he acted in a suspicious manner in relation to the preparation of her will. The evidence upon these points was as follows :—[1]At the first set of lodgings, Miss Bankes was waited on by the landlady and her daughter ; Smethurst went repeatedly to town, and Dr. Julius saw Miss Bankes in his absence ; but this was not so at the second set of lodgings, where the deceased passed the last three weeks of her life. [2] During this period Smethurst waited on Miss Bankes himself, declining to employ a sick-nurse on the ground that he could not afford it, though he had in his hands about £70, the amount of the dividend handed over to him by her. This in itself is remarkable, for the offices which it was necessary that he should render to her were not such as a man ought to discharge for a woman, if it is possible that they should be discharged by one of her own sex. His conduct towards Miss Louisa Bankes, it was argued, was of the same character. [3] He invited her to see her sister twice, but on neither occasion did he voluntarily leave

---

[1] Pp. 506–507.   [2] P. 509.   [3] P. 513.

them alone together, and he wrote four letters in the interval, in two of which he dissuaded her from repeating her visit on the ground that the doctors had prohibited it on account of the excitement produced by the first visit. [1] Dr. Julius said, " I never gave directions she should not see her sister. I " never heard the subject alluded to." [2] Dr. Bird said, " To " the best of my belief the prisoner mentioned the visit of " Miss Louisa Bankes on the 19th. He told me the patient " had been excited by the visit of her sister, and it had done " her a great deal of harm. On which I said, ' Perhaps she " ' had better not come again.' "

The circumstances which attended the execution of the will were detailed by Mr. Senior, an attorney at Richmond. [3] His evidence was that Smethurst, who was a complete stranger, came to him on the Saturday and asked whether he would make a will for Miss Bankes on the Sunday, which Mr. Senior with some reluctance agreed to do. Smethurst said, " This is what the will would be," and produced a draft will in his own favour, saying that the draft had been prepared by a barrister in London, a statement which, if true, might easily have been proved, but which was not proved. He also gratuitously informed Mr. Senior of the state of his relations with the deceased, and endeavoured to persuade him to allow a witness to attest the execution of the document under a false impression as to its nature. It is true that the will was as much the act of the deceased as his own ; but it is also true that its execution was, according to Mr. Senior's evidence, attended with falsehood on his part, and with a want of decency which showed a temper very greedy after the property to be disposed of.

These are the suspicious parts of the prisoner's conduct towards the deceased. [4] His having written for Miss Louisa Bankes to come down on the Sunday, and his suggestion that

[1] P. 525.   [2] P. 552.   [3] P. 520.   [4] P. 516.

she should take a.lodging in the neighbourhood, may perhaps weigh in the other scale; [1] and it is no doubt possible to take a similar view as to his having called in Dr. Todd. The weight of each of these circumstances is, however, diminished by several considerations. When Miss Louisa Bankes came down on the Sunday to see the deceased, Smethurst appears, from the evidence, to have objected to every proposal she made to attend on her sister. [2] He told her once that she could not bear her in the room; [3] another time (on her proposing to sit up with her all night), that he would rather attend upon her himself; [4] and on the Monday he persuaded her to go up to London to have a prescription made up, which occasioned her absence from the house for two or three hours. [5] With respect to Dr. Todd's visit, it should be borne in mind that Miss Louisa Bankes had suggested that Mr. Lane, a relation, should be consulted. Smethurst objected to this. " The deceased lady," says Dr. Bird, "more than once, in " the presence of the prisoner, expressed a wish for further " medical assistance, and it was after this that Dr. Todd " was called in." It is not, therefore, true that Smethurst spontaneously called in Dr. Todd. But even if he did, the suggestion presents itself that his object was to make evidence in his own favour. This, however, appears needlessly harsh. The fair conclusion would seem to be that the reference to Dr. Todd, under the circumstances of the case, proves nothing either for or against the prisoner. When Dr. Julius and Dr. Bird were freely admitted to watch every stage of the case, the visit of an additional physician, however eminent, could hardly entail much additional risk. It was also urged that Smethurst supplied Dr. Bird with matter for the purpose of analysis. That is true; but to have refused Dr. Bird's application would have been suspicious in the extreme; and it

---

[1] Bird, p. 532. [2] P. 516. [3] P. 516.
[4] P. 517. [5] P. 513. [6] P. 532.

would probably have had no other effect than that of inducing
him to obtain what he required by other means. Indeed, Dr.
Bird, [1] with an artifice which under the circumstances was
natural and probably justifiable, gave a false account of the
purpose for which he wanted it. This point, therefore, may
be left out of the case.

No poison was traced to the prisoner's possession, and this
is usually one of the facts relied on in trials for poisoning.
It must, however, be remembered that, as a medical man,
Smethurst could have no difficulty in getting poison ; and he
would appear to have been left at liberty in his lodgings for
some time after his arrest. It does not, however, clearly
appear from the Lord Chief Baron's notes of the evidence
what opportunities he had during this interval of making
away with poison unobserved. Dr. Bird said, " He was taken
" into custody about 5 P.M., and admitted to bail on his
" own recognizance. I returned to his house with McIntyre "
(the superintendent of police) " and prisoner, all three to-
" gether. McIntyre took possession of all " [2 the bottles and
vessels about the deceased's room]. " They were handed
" out to McIntyre, who stood at the door." McIntyre says,
" He " (Smethurst) " was allowed to go at large on his own
" recognizances. I returned with him and Bird to Alma
" Villas. They handed out bottles and vials ; I handed them
" to Dr. Taylor. [3] I saw the secretary." (This was a secretary
belonging to the landlord of the house, which stood outside
Miss Bankes's room, and of which Smethurst had been
allowed to make use and to keep the keys.) " The whole
" of the evening he was at liberty, and till eleven o'clock "
(11 A.M., May 3rd), " when, hearing of Miss Bankes's death,
" I took him into custody." If the meaning of this is that
Smethurst was alone in the house all night, and at liberty,

---

[1] P. 533.   [2] These words are omitted in the Judge's note.
[3] " *Examined* the secretary." *Sess. Pap.* 546.

the non-discovery of poison proves nothing. If he was watched by McIntyre, and if McIntyre's evidence means that he not only saw the secretary, but saw what was in it, the fact that no poison was found would be in his favour.[1]

The fair conclusions upon the whole of this part of the evidence would seem to be that Smethurst would gain in respect of money, and might in other respects derive advantage from the death of Miss Bankes, and that his conduct towards her was suspicious in several material particulars, and that he was the only person who had the opportunity of poisoning her, if she was poisoned at all.

The next division of the evidence was the medical testimony, and this again divided itself into two parts—the evidence of the medical men who actually attended the deceased, and the opinions pronounced by others as to the cause to which the symptoms reported by them were to be referred. [2] In considering this part of the case, it must be remembered that Smethurst himself acted as a medical man throughout Miss Bankes's illness. He constantly administered food and medicine to her, and repeatedly discussed with the other physicians about the course to be taken, and they appear to have relied principally on his reports as to the symptoms of the disease.

The course of the symptoms and treatment was as follows :— [3] Dr. Julius was called in on the 3rd of April, and was told by Smethurst that Miss Bankes was suffering from diarrhœa and vomiting; on the 5th he said she was bilious, and that there was much bile to come away. The vomiting and purging continued, the colour of the vomit being grass-green. She began to pass blood on the 8th, and the symptoms con-

---

[1] The Report in the *Sessions Papers* seems to show that the secretary was examined, but does not show whether the prisoner had the control of the lodgings at night. McIntyre found bottles on a second search which he had not seen the first time.

[2] P. 531. [3] Pp. 522-523.

tinued to increase. She complained of heat and burning in the throat and through the bowels. [1] When Dr. Todd examined her he observed " a remarkable hardness and rigidity " of the abdomen, suggesting great irritation, and a very " peculiar expression of countenance, as if she was under " some influence or terror which did not result from any " disease." He prescribed opium and sulphate of copper. [2] Smethurst afterwards, according to Dr. Bird and Dr. Julius, stated to them that these pills produced " violent palpitations, " as if her heart were jumping out of her body, and intense " burning in the throat, constant vomiting, and fifteen bloody " motions." He said ([3] said Dr. Julius), " the burning was " throughout the whole canal. His expression was " from the " mouth to the anus," an effect which, [4] according to Dr. Julius, Dr. Bird, and Dr. Todd, could not have been so produced. [5] During the last day and a half of life she twice vomited medicine, and was purged three times before twelve on the Monday night; after that she retained both food and medicine, and died of exhaustion on the Tuesday, at 10.55 A.M.

Such was the course of the symptoms. The opinions formed on them by the medical men were as follows :—

Dr. Julius first, and Dr. Bird afterwards, came independently to the conclusion that, whatever was the complaint of Miss Bankes, the natural effect of the medicines which they administered was perverted by the administration of some irritant poison. Dr. Julius's words are, [6] " I tried a variety " of remedies ; whatever was given, the result was the same. " No medicine produced any of the effects I expected in " arresting the disease. The symptoms continued the same " after every medicine. On the 18th" (of April), " I had " formed an opinion as to the reason of the sufferings. I

[1] P. 543.　　　　[2] P. 532.　　　　[3] P. 524.
[4] Pp. 524, 532, 543.　　[5] Pp. 533, 519.　　[6] P. 523.

" thought there was something being administered which had
" a tendency to keep up the irritation in the stomach and
" bowels, and now I am unable to account in any other way
" for the continued irritation. In consequence of this opinion,
" I requested my partner, Mr. Bird, to see her, and I left him
" to form an unbiased opinion." Mr. Bird said, [1] " I formed an
" opinion that some irritant was being administered that coun-
" teracted the effect of the medicines we were giving. I had
" a conversation with Dr. Julius about it three days after I
" began to attend, about the 21st of April. He asked me my
" opinion of the case before he told me his own." Dr. Todd
said, [2] " I inquired of Dr. Julius the symptoms of the treat-
" ment," and after describing the peculiar expression of
countenance already referred to, he added, " I was very
" strongly impressed with the opinion that she was suffering
" from some irritant poison. It was by my desire that part
" of a motion " (which was afterwards analyzed by Dr. Taylor)
" was obtained. I suggested sulphate of copper and opium."
Thus, the medical evidence begins with this fact, that three
medical men who saw the deceased whilst living came independently to the conclusion that she was then being
poisoned. [3] So strongly were the two Richmond doctors
impressed with this, that they thought it their duty to go
before a magistrate, whilst Dr. Todd suggested the chemical
examination of the evacuation.

After the death of Miss Bankes, her body was examined by
Mr. Barwell, who found a large black patch of blood near the
cardiac, or upper end of the stomach, redness in the small
intestines in several places ; and in the cæcum, or first division
of the large intestine, appearances indicating serious disease
—namely, inflammation, sloughing, ulceration, suppuration.
In the rectum there were three ulcerations. Of these, and
some other *post-mortem* appearances, and of the symptoms

[1] P. 532.   [2] P. 543.   [3] P. 525.

presented during life, [1] Mr. Barwell said, "They are not
"reconcilable with any natural disease with which I am
"acquainted;" and he added, "The conclusion that I drew
"is that the symptoms have resulted from the administration
"of some irritant poison frequently during life." [2] Dr. Wilkes
said, "I should ascribe her death to an irritant. I am not
"familiar with any form of disease which would account for
"the symptoms and appearances." [3] Dr. Babington, [4] Dr.
Bowerbank, [5] Dr. Taylor, and [6] Dr. Copland, all expressed the
same opinion.

In opposition to this evidence, it was contended on the part
of the prisoner that the symptoms were not those of slow
poisoning; and the evidence in support of this opinion consisted, first, of proof of inconsistencies between the symptoms
observed and those of slow poisoning by arsenic or antimony;
and, secondly, of explanations of the symptoms on the theory
that they were due to some other disease. The evidence to
show that the symptoms were inconsistent with arsenical
poisoning was that several symptoms were absent which
might have been expected on that hypothesis.

The most important of these, according to Dr. Richardson,
were nervous symptoms, especially convulsions and tremor of
the whole of the limbs; also inflammation of the membrane
of the eye, soreness of the nostrils and other mucous orifices,
and an eruption on the skin peculiar to arsenical poisoning.
It appeared, however, that none of the witnesses, either for
the Crown or for the prisoner, had ever seen a case of slow
poisoning by arsenic. [7] Their opinions were formed partly
from experiments on animals, and it also seemed clear that
the symptoms of arsenical poisoning varied considerably in
different cases [8] Dr. Taylor said, "We never find two cases
"alike in all particulars;" and [9] Dr. Richardson said that

[1] Pp. 539-540.   [2] P. 542.   [3] P. 549.   [4] P. 550.
[5] P. 556.   [6] P. 551.   [7] P. 563.   [8] P. 560.   [9] P. 563.

he should not expect to find all the symptoms to which he referred in any one case, though he did not think it possible they should all be absent.

The evidence that antimonial poisoning was not the cause of death was fainter than the evidence against arsenical poisoning. [1] Dr. Richardson, one of the prisoner's witnesses, said that he should have expected to find congestion of the lungs and a cold sweat, if death had been caused by anti-monial poisoning. Mr. Rogers (who, however, said that he knew little of pathology, having attended principally to chemistry) added, he should have expected in addition softening of the liver, and Dr. Thudichum agreed with them. Dr. Richardson, however, admitted that he knew very little about antimonial poisoning, and his evidence upon the subject was cautious and qualified. [2] He said, " The symptoms " in Miss Bankes's case are not altogether reconcilable with " slow poisoning by antimony. With respect to the effect of " antimony on the human liver, there are no data. The " evidence is very scanty."

This is the principal part of the evidence as to whether or no the symptoms were those of slow poisoning. It is obvious that the evidence for the prisoner did not exactly meet the evidence for the Crown. The witnesses for the Crown all spoke indefinitely of " some irritant." The medical witnesses for the prisoner did not negative the general resemblance between the symptoms and those of poisoning by an irritant poison, but testified to the absence of some of the symptoms which might be expected to arise from two specific poisons—namely, arsenic and antimony. That there was a general resem-blance between the symptoms and those of some irritant seems to have been proved beyond all reasonable doubt, not only by the fact that the three doctors who saw the deceased during her life formed that opinion independently

[1] P. 566.
[2] P. 566.

of each other, but by the evidence of the seven other medical witnesses for the prosecution, and by a statement made by Dr. Tyler Smith, who was called for the prisoner. [1] He said that if a pregnant woman were affected with diarrhœa it might degenerate into dysentery, and that he had known a case of the kind which was supposed to be a case of poisoning. The medical witnesses for the prisoner attributed Miss Bankes's death to dysentery, aggravated by pregnancy; and it thus appears, from Dr. Tyler Smith's evidence, that they attributed it to a disease which may closely resemble the symptoms produced by the administration of irritant poisons.

The prisoner opposed the theory of the prosecution, not only by denying that the symptoms were those of slow poisoning, but by asserting that they were those of dysentery. [2] All the medical witnesses whom he called swore to their belief that all the symptoms were consistent with this theory. On the other hand ([3] with one exception), they all agreed with the witnesses for the prosecution that dysentery was a very rare disease in this country, and their experience of it was in no case great. Dr. Richardson said, [4] "The word is used very "loosely;" and he added, "I have seen a few cases of dysen-"tery—two or three in this country; I have suffered from it " myself." [5] Dr. Thudichum had seen two cases in London of what he called diphtheritic dysentery, to which he attributed the death of the deceased. [6] Dr. Girdwood said, "Dysentery "is not very common;" and he added, "The dysentery I allude "to is one which I know to exist in this country." [7] Dr. Webbe, on the contrary, said, "Dysentery is a very common disease " in this country." Both he and Dr. Girdwood appear, however,

---

[1] P. 586.

[2] Richardson, 565–571. Thudichum, 574. Webbe, 578. Girdwood, 582. Edmunds, 583. Tyler Smith, 585–586. Mr. Rogers was a chemist and not a practising physician.

[3] Richardson, 567.   [4] P. 567.   [5] P. 575.

[6] P. 583.   [7] P. 578.

to have been speaking of a form of the disease differing in various particulars from that which in hot countries is described as dysentery.

The experience of some of the witnesses for the prosecution as to dysentery proper was much more extensive. [1] Dr. Bird had seen many cases of it in the Crimea. [2] Dr. Bowerbank was twenty-three years in practice in Jamaica, where acute dysentery is a common disease. He said, " The symptoms, " mode of treatment, and appearances *post-mortem,* are not " reconcilable with any form of dysentery." [3] Dr. Copland saw many cases in 1815 and 1816, and in Africa in 1817. He said, " Her death is not referable to acute dysentery." [4] Dr. Babington saw six or eight epidemic cases in Chelsea, and two more in Hammersmith. He said, " I have heard " the symptoms and remedies, and also the *post-mortem* ex- " amination ; taking all those circumstances, I do not think " she died of acute dysentery."

[5] On the other hand, Dr. Todd, after giving his opinion that slow poisoning was the cause of death, said, " Acute dysentery " alone would account for the worst symptoms." It appeared, however, that he had never seen a case of that disease. Two of the prisoner's witnesses, whose evidence in the event was very important, described cases similar in many particulars to Miss Bankes's, in which women had died of dysentery combined with pregnancy. [6] Mr. Edmunds had a patient who miscarried at the seventh month of her pregnancy, and ultimately died of dysentery ; and [7] Dr. Tyler Smith said he had known cases in which the sickness often incidental to preg-

---

[1] P. 534.   [2] P. 550.   [3] P. 551.   [4] P. 549.

[5] The emphasis lies on *acute* and *alone.* In the *Sessions Papers* the answer is, " The only form of dysentery that would account for any portion of these " grave symptoms would be what is called acute dysentery."—P. 545.

[6] P. 534.

[7] P. 586. He referred in particular to the case of Mrs. Nicholls, the authoress of *Jane Eyre,* &c.

nancy, especially during its early stages, had caused death; and he added that this sickness "might be accompanied by " diarrhœa, and that might degenerate into dysentery." [1] It appeared that two years before Miss Bankes had had a complaint of the womb, which, in Dr. Tyler Smith's opinion, would aggravate the sickness consequent on pregnancy. There was also some evidence that she was bilious, which would have a similar effect.

Dr. Tyler Smith and Mr. Edmunds were called after the rest of the prisoner's witnesses, and till they were called the question as to the effect of pregnancy was passed over somewhat lightly on both sides. Most of the witnesses deposed to the well-known fact that sickness is very common in the early stages of pregnancy, and some of them added that they had known the sickness to be attended with diarrhœa, though they all spoke of that as an uncommon circumstance. Of the witnesses for the prosecution, [2] Dr. Julius and [3] Dr. Bird said that the opinion which they had formed of the case was not altered by the fact of pregnancy. [4] Dr. Todd thought that pregnancy would not account for the extensive ulceration of the bowels: and [5] Dr. Babington, whose experience in midwifery was large, said, "I do not consider her death in any " way to have been occasioned by incipient pregnancy. I do " not remember any case in the early stage (of pregnancy) " where the life of the mother has been saved by abortion." The case of abortion referred to by Mr. Edmunds was in the seventh month

The general result of the medical evidence appears to be—

First.—As to the connection of the symptoms of Miss Bankes's illness with poisoning—

That the symptoms which preceded Miss Bankes's death so much resembled those of slow poisoning by some irritant,

---

[1] Pp. 517-518.   [2] P. 528.   [3] P. 534.   [4] P. 513.   [5] P. 549.

that the three doctors who saw her during her life independently arrived at the conclusion that they must be attributed
to that cause; that two of them acted upon this impression
by going before a magistrate; and that eight other doctors,
who judged from the accounts which they heard of the
symptoms, treatment, and *post-mortem* appearances, came to
the same conclusion. On the other hand, some of the
symptoms which might have been expected in slow poisoning
by arsenic or antimony were wanting, but there was evidence
that these symptoms are not invariable.

Secondly.—As to the connection of the symptoms with
dysentery—

That there is much general resemblance between the
symptoms of dysentery and those of poisoning; that dysentery proper is an extremely rare disease in this country; that
there was a difference of opinion between the witnesses for
the Crown and those for the prisoner on the question whether
dysentery alone would produce the symptoms observed, but
that the witnesses for the Crown had had much greater
experience of the disease.

Thirdly.—As to the pregnancy of the deceased—

That there was some evidence that it was possible that the
symptoms which occurred in Miss Bankes's case might be
produced by a complication of pregnancy and dysentery.

Taking all these three conclusions together, the medical
evidence seems to establish that Miss Bankes's symptoms
were not only consistent with slow poisoning by some irritant, but that they actually convinced the doctors who
attended her that they were caused by that means.

This is the proper place to notice a circumstance respecting
the pregnancy of Miss Bankes which assumed more importance after the prisoner's conviction than it had at the trial,
though it was even then important. [1] Dr. Julius said, " Early

---

[1] P. 523.

" in the visits I inquired about her being in the family way.
" Dr. Smethurst said she was unwell ([1] usual period on her).
" It was within five or six days of my first attendance "—*i.e.*
about the 10th of April.   As she was in the fifth or seventh
week of her pregnancy at the time of her death (May 3rd), it
was highly improbable that this should have been the case.
[2] Dr. Tyler Smith said, " In some cases, the periods occur after
" pregnancy, once in a hundred times—certainly as often as
" that."   A medical man would hardly have made the assertion which Dr. Julius swore that Smethurst made without
knowledge as to its truth ; and Dr. Tyler Smith's evidence
shows that, apart from the value of his assertion, there was
(at the time of the trial) a chance—perhaps not less than a
hundred to one—that it was untrue.   Therefore (at the trial)
the evidence, if believed, showed that Smethurst had made
a statement which, if false, was probably false to his knowledge, and the chance of the falsehood of which (apart from
the value of his assertion) was as a hundred to one.

The third and last division of the evidence is the chemical
evidence.   [3] Dr. Taylor deposed that he had discovered arsenic
in an evacuation procured for the purpose by Dr. Bird on the
1st of May, three days before the death of Miss Bankes ; and
antimony in two places in the small intestine, in the cæcum
or upper division of the large intestine, in one of the kidneys,
in the blood from the heart, and in the liquor which had
drained from part of the viscera into the jar which contained
them.   He calculated that four ounces of the evacuation contained less than one-fourth of a grain of arsenic.   As to the
antimony, Dr. Taylor was corroborated by [4] Dr. Odling, who
assisted in the examination of those parts of the body in which
it was alleged to be found.

This evidence was opposed, first, by an attack on Dr. Taylor's
credit.   The first objection made to his evidence related to the

---

[1] *Sic* in judge's notes.   [2] P. 585.   [3] Pp. 553–554.   [4] P. 561.

arsenic. [1] It appeared that amongst other things he examined for arsenic a bottle containing chlorate of potass, a mixture which the prisoner had been recommended by Mr. Pedley, a dentist, to use for foulness of breath. In testing it, Dr. Taylor used copper gauze, which was dissolved by the chlorate of potass, and on the dissolution of which a certain quantity of arsenic which it contained was set free. After exhausting the chlorate of potass by dissolving the copper gauze, he introduced other copper, and upon this crystals of arsenic were deposited. He thus extracted from the liquid arsenic which he had himself introduced into it. The inference drawn from this was that Dr. Taylor's evidence generally, and especially as to the arsenic in the evacuation, could not be relied on.

As to its bearing on the general value of his evidence, Mr. Brande, a very eminent chemist, said that he should have fallen into the same error: [2] "The fact," he said, "is new to "the chemical world." As to the bearing of the mistake upon the discovery of arsenic specially, two observations occur. In the examination both of the draught and of the evacuation, Reinsch's test was employed, and it was also employed in more than seventy other experiments, and is a well-known and established process for separating arsenic and some other minerals from matter in which they are contained. Copper gauze is introduced into the liquid to be tested, and by chemical means the metal is deposited on it in a crystalline form. In the case of the draught, the arsenic deposited on the gauze may, no doubt, have been that which was contained in the other gauze which had been previously dissolved. [3] Altogether there were seventy-seven experiments conducted by the same process. In

---

[1] P. 587.

[2] Somewhat less strongly in the *Sessions Paper:* "The matter that has "appeared since is to a certain extent new to the chemical world."—P. 562.

[3] P. 557. It is not quite clear whether there were seventy-seven or seventy-eight, nor is it material.

one, copper was dissolved, and arsenic found. In seventy-four, no copper was dissolved, and no arsenic was found; in two, (on the evacuation), no copper was dissolved, and arsenic was found. The first experiment confirms the general doctrine that the test will detect arsenic, as it extracted arsenic from a liquid into which arsenic had been introduced. The seventy-four cases in which arsenic was not found showed that the process was not so conducted as of itself to produce arsenic; and both the first experiment and the other seventy-four taken together confirm the impression that the two remaining experiments proved both that there was arsenic in the evacuation and that it was not put there by Dr. Taylor.

The second argument against Dr. Taylor's evidence as to arsenic was brought forward by the three chemical witnesses for the prisoner—Dr. Richardson, Mr. Rogers, and Dr. Thudichum. Dr. Richardson said, "It is quite impossible that "a person should die of arsenical poisoning without some being found in the tissues. It makes no difference in [1] what-"ever way or under whatever combination the arsenic was "introduced." He also referred to the case of three dogs which he had poisoned by repeated small doses of arsenic and antimony. To one of them he administered eighteen grains in sixteen days, and killed him twelve hours after the last meal. He found some arsenic in his liver, lungs, and heart, and a trace in the spleen and kidneys,—the greater part by far in the liver. He said, "I cannot now say how "much arsenic I found altogether. I will not venture to "say I found half a grain or a grain. [2] I think," he after-wards added, "I could venture to say I found a quarter of a "grain."

This evidence was hardly opposed to the theory of the

---

[1] *I.e.* by the mouth or by injection.—P. 564.

[2] P. 565. A word or two have dropped out of the judge's note in the answer quoted.

prosecution. The account of the matter appears to be this. Arsenic on administration passes into the stomach; it is there taken up into the circulation; thence it passes with the blood through the organs which separate the various fluids secreted from the blood—in the same manner it passes into the flesh—and it finally leaves the body by the skin, or by the ordinary channels. When the patient dies, all vital functions being arrested, the poison will be found at that point of the process which it happened to have reached at the moment of death. The poison, however, is continually passing through the body, and this goes on to such an extent that Dr. Richardson could not venture to say he found more than a quarter of a grain of arsenic in the dog to which he had administered eighteen grains; but as, in order to try the effects of chlorate of potass in eliminating the arsenic, a large quantity of that substance was administered, this was a peculiar case. If the dog had been left to die from the effects of the poison, it is not improbable that a smaller quantity, or even none at all, might have been discovered. The evidence of Dr. Richardson seems to prove that, upon the supposition of poisoning by arsenic, arsenic must have been present in various parts of Miss Bankes's body at the time when the arsenic discovered by Dr. Taylor passed from her, rather than that it must have been present after her death. It might have passed away in the interval; and thus the absence of arsenic in the tissues after death would go to prove, not that no arsenic had been administered during life, but that none had been administered during the last two or three days of life.

Indeed, Dr. Richardson's experiments do not support the strong opinion he gave as to the impossibility of death by arsenic without arsenic being found in the tissues, unless it be restricted to the direct as distinguished from the secondary effects of arsenic. It was agreed on all hands that the proximate cause of Miss Bankes's death was exhaustion.

With regard to the antimony, the only evidence offered in opposition to Dr. Taylor was that of Dr. Richardson and Mr. Rogers. [1] Dr. Richardson said he should have expected to find antimony in the liver, but he spoke with hesitation upon the subject. Mr. Rogers's evidence was to the same effect, but he said, [2] " My speciality is chemistry and not pathology." Upon this evidence, it must be observed that there is the direct assertion of a fact on the one side, against an expression of opinion on the other. Dr. Taylor said, " I found " antimony in the intestines." Dr. Richardson and Mr. Rogers replied, " It should have been in the liver." Dr. Taylor was not cross-examined, nor was any substantive evidence offered to show that there was any fallacy in the tests by which he alleged that he had discovered antimony in Miss Bankes's intestines.

With respect to the antimony, it should be mentioned that, after Smethurst had been committed, it appears from the evidence that he wrote three letters to Dr. Julius, asking him for copies of the prescriptions dispensed by him for Miss Bankes. The first letter, dated May 5th, was as follows : " Dr. Smethurst will feel much obliged by forward- " ing as above, by return of post, prescriptions of the following " medicines, prescribed and dispensed by the firm of Dr. Julius " and Mr. Bird, required for defence—the sulphate of copper " and opium pills (Dr. Todd) ; 2nd, the nitrate of silver pills ; " 3rd, the bismuth mixture." On the 6th he wrote to the same effect, stating the medicine as follows : "Acetate of lead " and opium, the nitrate of silver pills, the bismuth mixture, " the pills with sulphate of copper." On the 9th he wrote a third time, heading his letter " Second application," in these words, [3] " Sir, I made application for the acetate of lead pre-

---

[1] Pp. 525 526.   [2] P. 551.   [3] P. 506.

" scription, prescribed by you or Mr. Bird, with date ; also the
" dates of prescriptions sent, which were wanting—*namely,* 1*st,*
" *antimony* ; 2nd, sulphate of copper; 3rd, nitrate of silver."
Antimony was never prescribed nor mentioned till this third
letter.[1] It does not appear, from Dr. Taylor's evidence, that
at that time he had found any antimony.

An attempt was made to account for the presence of the
antimony and arsenic alleged to be discovered by Dr. Taylor
by the suggestion that it might have been contained in
the medicines administered to Miss Bankes during her life.
Arsenic is generally found in bismuth, and [2] for three or four
days doses of bismuth, containing five or six grains, were
administered to Miss Bankes. [3] Dr. Richardson put the proportion of arsenic in bismuth at half a grain in an ounce,
and, as an ounce contains 480 grains, each dose would have
contained about $\frac{1}{140}$ of a grain of arsenic. If, therefore, Miss
Banks took twelve doses of bismuth, she would have taken
between one-eleventh and one-twelfth of a grain of arsenic in
four days. This seems (for it is not perfectly clear), from Dr.
Bird's evidence, to have been more than a week before the
day on which he obtained the evacuation analyzed by Dr.
Taylor, and in four ounces of which he said he found nearly
one-fourth of a grain.

[4] Upon the question of the credit due to the chemical witnesses for the defence, it was brought out on cross-examination that all of them, as well as Dr. Webbe, were connected
with the Grosvenor School of Medicine; and that two,
Dr. Richardson and Mr. Rogers, had given evidence for the
prisoner in Palmer's trial,—the object of Dr. Richardson's
evidence being to show that Cook's symptoms were those of

[1] P. 572.   [2] P. 535.
[3] P. 567. " The quantity varies very materially. The largest quantity
" that I am acquainted with is very nearly half a grain in one ounce."
[4] Dr. Richardson, 568 ; Mr. Rogers, 574. His connection with the school
had ceased at the time of the trial. Dr. Thudichum, 575.

angina pectoris, and the object of Mr. Rogers's being to show that, if he died of strychnine, it ought to have been found in his body.

The result of the chemical evidence seems to be that there was evidence to go to the jury, both that arsenic passed from Miss Bankes, and that antimony was found in her body after death; the evidence as to the antimony being the stronger of the two. There was also evidence for their consideration affecting the credit of Dr. Taylor as an analyst, and suggesting the presence of a professional *esprit de corps* amongst the witnesses for the prisoner, which, if it existed, might affect their impartiality.

Combining the inferences deducible from each separate division of the evidence, which, of course, strengthen each other, there can be little doubt that, if the jury believed that poison was found in Miss Bankes's body, they were bound to convict the prisoner. Even if the whole of the chemical evidence on both sides were struck out, there was evidence on which, if it satisfied them of his guilt, they might have convicted him, though such a conviction would have proceeded on weaker grounds than juries of the present day usually require in cases which attract great public attention and involve capital punishment. As it was they convicted him, and he received sentence of death.

The trial at any time would have excited great public attention; and as it took place in the latter part of August, after Parliament had risen, it excited a degree of attention almost unexampled. The newspapers were filled with letters upon the subject, and one or two papers constituted themselves amateur champions of the convict, claiming openly the right of what they called popular instinct to overrule the verdict of the jury. Petitions were presented on the subject, and communications of all kinds relating to it were addressed to Sir George Lewis, Secretary of State for the Home Depart-

ment. All these were forwarded to the Lord Chief Baron
for his opinion, and were considered by him in an elaborate
report to the Home Secretary. Some of the letters were
of great importance; but the majority were nothing more
than clamorous expressions of opinion, founded upon no real
study of the case; for which, indeed, those who took their
notions of it exclusively from newspaper reports had not
sufficient materials. A considerable number of the communications were simply imbecile. One man, for example, wrote
in pencil, from the Post Office, Putney, in favour of the
execution of the sentence; another, "a lover of justice,"
thought that, if the voice of the nation was not attended
to, by respiting the convict, we had better be under the sway
of a despot. Many other letters, equally childish and absurd,
were received, and all appear to have been considered. I
refer to them merely as illustrations of the ignorance, folly,
and presumption, with which people often interfere with the
administration of public affairs. The same sort of thing
happened in August 1889, on the conviction for murder of
a woman named Maybrick before me at Liverpool.

Upon a full examination of the various points submitted to
him, including in particular a notice of an important, though
somewhat hastily prepared, communication from Dr. Baly and
Dr. Jenner, and after commenting on the medical evidence
given at the trial, the Lord Chief Baron said:—

"The medical communications which have since reached
" you put the matter in a very different light, and tend very
" strongly to show that the medical part of the inquiry did
" not go to the jury in so favourable a way as it might, and
" indeed ought to have done, and in two respects—

" 1. That more weight was due to the pregnant condition
" of Miss Bankes (a fact admitting, after the *post-mortem*, of
" no doubt) than was ascribed to it by the medical witnesses
" for the prosecution.

" 2. That, in the opinion of a considerable number of
" medical men of eminence and experience, the symptoms of
" the *post-mortem* appearances were ambiguous, and might
" be referred either to natural causes or to poison. Many also
" have gone so far as to say that the symptoms and appear-
" ances were inconsistent and incompatible with poison."

On the other hand, the Lord Chief Baron referred to
" disclosures made since the trial," which, in his opinion,
" confirmed the prisoner's guilt." These were, first, a statement in a memorial from Smethurst to the Prince Consort,
stating that " a lady friend of deceased was a witness " to her
knowledge of the fact that he was married already, and that
she (Miss Bankes) wished the ceremony to be gone through.
This lady " was to have been called, but Mr. Parry deemed it
" unnecessary." Upon this the Chief Baron observes : " I do
" not believe Mr. Serjeant Parry gave any such advice ; but,
" if it be true that any such evidence was ready, why is not
" the lady friend named, and why is not her statement or
" declaration now offered and laid before you ? Such evidence
" would, in my opinion, much alter the complexion of the
" case."

[1] Secondly, the report refers to certain entries in a diary said
to be the prisoner's, of which no notice was taken at the trial.
These entries appeared to the Lord Chief Baron to show that
one of Smethurst's statements as to Miss Bankes's symptoms
was wilfully false. This would, of course, be a most import-

---

[1] After Dr. Smethurst's pardon, he was convicted for bigamy, and sentenced
to a year's imprisonment. On the expiration of his imprisonment, he commenced proceedings in the Court of Probate to have the will executed by
Miss Bankes established. It was contested by her family ; and one of the
points raised was, that it was obtained by fraud, as she was under a mistake
as to her true position, and supposed herself to be Smethurst's true wife at the
time of the execution of the will. The question whether this was so was specifically left to the jury, and found by them in Smethurst's favour. This would,
of course, strengthen the conclusion that further inquiry was necessary, and
weaken the case against Smethurst.

ant fact; but the report does not show how Smethurst was connected with the diary, when it was discovered, or why it was not given in evidence at the trial.

The report concluded in the following words :—" I think " there is no communication before you in all or any of the " papers I have seen upon which you can rely and act. That " from Dr. Baly and Dr. Jenner seemed to me to be the most " trustworthy and respectable ; but there is an unaccountable " but undoubted mistake in it which must be rectified before " it can be taken as the basis of any decision. If you have " been favourably impressed by any of the documents, so as " to entertain the proposition of granting a pardon, or of " commuting the sentence to a short period of penal servi- " tude, I think it ought to be founded upon the judgment " of medical and scientific persons selected by yourself for " the purpose of considering the effect of the symptoms and " appearances, and the result of the analysis, and I think, " for the prisoner's sake, you ought to have the points " arising out of Herapath's letter further inquired into and " considered. I forbear to speculate upon facts not ascer- " tained ; but, if Dr. Taylor had been cross-examined to this, " and had given no satisfactory explanation, the result of the " trial might have been quite different."

The meaning of the allusion to a mistake in the communi- cation of Dr. Baly and Dr. Jenner is that their letter contained this passage : " We would further remark, with regard to the " symptoms present, that Dr. Julius appeared to have been " in attendance on Isabella Bankes five days before he heard " of vomiting as a symptom ; this absence of vomiting at " the commencement is quite inconsistent with the belief " that an irritant poison was the original cause of the illness." This was completely opposed to Dr. Julius's evidence, who spoke of " diarrhœa *and vomiting* " as present from his very first visit throughout the whole course of the illness.

The " points arising out of Herapath's letter " were these :—
Mr. Herapath addressed a letter to the *Times*, in which he
asserted that Dr. Taylor had extracted from the draught
containing chlorate of potass a larger quantity of arsenic
than could have been set free by the copper gauze which
he dissolved in it. If this had been substantiated, it would
have no doubt diminished the weight of Dr. Taylor's evidence ;
but, on the other hand, it would have led to the conclusion
that the draught contained arsenic which Dr. Taylor had not
put there—an inference which, if true, would have been
fatal to the prisoner.

Upon receiving this report, Sir George Lewis took steps
which he described in a letter to the Lord Chief Baron, a
copy of which was communicated to the *Times*, and published
on the 17th of November, 1859. After referring to the Lord
Chief Baron's recommendation, Sir George Lewis says :—

" I have sent the evidence, your Lordship's report, and all
" the papers bearing upon the medical points of the case, to Sir
" Benjamin Brodie, from whom I have received a letter, of
" which I inclose a copy, and who is of opinion that, although
" the facts are full of suspicion against Smethurst, there is
" not absolute and complete evidence of his guilt.

" After a very careful and anxious consideration of all the
" facts of this very peculiar case, I have come to the con-
" clusion that there is sufficient doubt of the prisoner's guilt
" to render it my duty to advise the grant to him of a free
" pardon. . . . The necessity which I have felt for advising
" Her Majesty to grant a free pardon in this case has not, as
" it appears to me, risen from any defect in the constitution or
" proceedings of our criminal tribunals; it has risen from the
" imperfection of medical science, and from fallibility of judg-
" ment, in an obscure malady, even of skilful and experienced
" practitioners."

Sir Benjamin Brodie's letter, founded on a consideration

of the whole of the materials submitted to him, consists of six reasons for believing that Smethurst was guilty, and eight reasons for doubting his guilt; and it concludes in these words : " Taking into consideration all that I have now " stated, I own that the impression on my mind is that there " is not absolute and complete evidence of Smethurst's guilt." The reasons given are by no means confined to the medical points of the case, but range over every part of it, including inferences from the behaviour and moral character of the prisoner; and, indeed, of the six reasons against the prisoner, two only, and of the eight reasons in his favour, four only, proceed upon medical and chemical points. These opinions are expressed with a cautious moderation which, however creditable to the understanding and candour of the writer, excite regret at the absence of that opportunity which cross-examination would have afforded of testing his opinions fully, and of ascertaining the extent of his special acquaintance with the subjects on which his opinion was requested.

The great interest of this trial lies in its bearing on the question of new trials in criminal cases. The jury convicted Smethurst on the evidence as it stood, and if it had remained unaltered their verdict would undoubtedly have been justified. After the trial it appeared that, on the points mentioned by the Lord Chief Baron, further information appeared to be requisite. The Secretary of State thereupon asks a very eminent surgeon what he thinks of the whole case, and receives from him an opinion that, " although the facts are full " of suspicion against Smethurst, there is not absolute and " complete evidence of his guilt." Sharing this view, the Secretary of State advises the grant of a free pardon. It is difficult to imagine anything less satisfactory than this course of procedure. It put all the parties concerned—the Secretary of State, Sir Benjamin Brodie, and the Lord Chief Baron—in a false position. Virtually they had to re-try the man without the proper facilities for that purpose. The result was substantially that Smethurst, after being convicted of a most cruel and treacherous murder by the verdict of a jury after an elaborate trial, was pardoned, because Sir Benjamin Brodie had some doubts as to his guilt after reading the evidence and other papers, one of which was a report from the judge expressing his opinion that, owing to circumstances, the evidence had not been left to the jury as favourably for the prisoner as it ought to have been. The responsibility of the decision was thus shifted from those on whom it properly rested on to a man who, however skilful and learned as a surgeon, was neither a juryman nor a judge. It appears to me that, whatever would have been the proper course, nothing but specific medical questions should have been referred to Sir Benjamin Brodie. The final question ought to have been determined by Sir George Lewis himself. He might perfectly well have directed the execution of Smethurst or have advised his pardon, or might even have commuted his sentence if he thought it wrong to take his life on account of the doubts thrown on his guilt, thus reserving an opportunity for remitting his sentence if his innocence had been proved.

[1]THE CASE OF THE MONK LÉOTADE.

LOUIS BONAFOUS, known in his convent as Brother Léotade, was tried at Toulouse, in 1848, for rape and murder committed on the 15th April, 1847, on a girl of fourteen, named Cecile Combettes. The trial lasted from the 7th till the 26th February, 1848, when it was adjourned in consequence of the revolution. It was resumed on the 16th March, before a different jury, and ended on the 4th April. The case was as follows :—

Cecil Combettes, a girl in her fifteenth year, was apprenticed to a bookbinder named Conte, who was much employed by the monks known as the *Frères de la Doctrine Chrétienne*, at Toulouse. On the 15th April, at about nine, Conte set out to carry to the monastery some books which the monks wanted to have bound. He put them in two baskets, of which the apprentice carried the smaller, and he and a woman called Marion, the larger. When he was let into the convent he saw, as he declared, two monks in the passage. One, Jubrien, wore a hat, the other, Léotade, who faced him, wore a hood. Conte wished Jubrien good day, left his umbrella by the porter's lodge, laid down the baskets, and sent home the servant Marion with the sheepskins in which they had been covered. He went upstairs to take the books to the

[1] The authority referred to in this case is entitled, *Procès du Frère Léotade, accusé du double crime de viol et d'assassinat sur la personne de Cecile Combettes.* (Leipzig, 1851.) The report of the first trial is full, though not so full as English reports usually are. The report of the second trial is a mere outline, but the two appear to have been substantially the same. The same witnesses were called, and the same evidence given.

director, and the porter went with him. He left Cecile to take
care of his umbrella and to help to bring back the baskets.
He stayed for three-quarters of an hour with the director,
and then returned. Cecile was gone, but the umbrella was
standing against the wall. Conte asked the porter for Cecile.
He said he did not know where she was; she might be gone,
or might be at the *pensionnat*. The establishment consisted
of two buildings, the *pensionnat* and the *noviciat*. They stood
on different sides of a street, and communicated by a tunnel
which passed under it Behind the *noviciat* was a large
garden.

Not finding Cecile, Conte went to see his uncle. [1] He afterwards bargained for a pair of wheels, went to a place called
Auch, where he slept, and returned next day to Toulouse.
As Cecile was not heard of in the course of the day, various
inquiries were made for her. [2] Her aunt, Mme. Baylac, inquired for her at the convent, but in vain. Her parents
applied to the police, and they searched for her unsuccessfully.
She was never seen alive again.

Early on the following morning a grave-digger, named
Raspaud, had occasion to go to a cemetery bounded on two
sides by the wall of the garden of the monastery, and on a
third (its figure was irregular) by a wall of its own, which
divided it from a street called the Rue Riquet. The two
walls met at right angles. On the ground in the corner
formed by their meeting, Raspaud found the body of the girl.
It was lying on the knees and the extremity of the feet. Its
feet were directed towards the garden of the monks, its head
in the opposite direction. [3] Over the place where the body
lay and on the wall of the Rue Riquet, was a handkerchief suspended on a peg. When the commissary of police
(M. Lamarle) arrived, several persons, attracted by curiosity,
had come up and were standing round the body, and they

---

[1] Pp. 171-174.   [2] P. 183.   [3] Pp. 105-106.

were in the act of getting over the wall by a breach at the corner. They had made footmarks all about, so that it was impossible to say whether or not there were other footmarks before they came. The commissary sent for the soldiers and had the public turned out, after which he walked round the cemetery inside. [1] There were no marks of scaling the walls or of footsteps. At eight the judge of instruction arrived. [2] He was called as a witness at the trial, but on his appearance the president said, " It is well understood, sir, that you have " obeyed the citation served on you only because you thought " proper," and he replied, " To begin with, and as a general " principle, I refer to my *procès-verbaux*, and to all that I have " registered in the procedure."

[3] The *procès-verbaux* are not printed in the trial, but the *acte d'accusation* professes to state their purport. According to this document, the judge of instruction found on the side of the monastery wall next to the cemetery a place from which a sort of damp mossy crust had lately been knocked off. This might, from its position, have been done by the rubbing of the branches of certain cypresses which over-hung the wall of the Rue Riquet and touched the wall of the monastery garden. In the hair of the dead body were particles of earth of the same kind. On the top of the monastery wall were some plants of groundsel a little faded, also a wild geranium, one of the flowers of which had lost all its petals. In the hair of the dead body was one petal which the experts declared was a petal of the same kind. There was also a thread of tow which might have come from a cord, and there was a similar thread on the cypress branches. There were no marks on the wall of the Rue Riquet except that near the junction of the two walls, and about one foot eight inches (fifty centimetres) from the top, there was a tuft of groundsel which looked as if it had been pulled by a hand.

[1] P. 107.   P. 263.   [3] P. 268.

Near the junction of the two walls was a small plant nearly rooted up, and on the point of the junction at the top was a small branch of cypress lately broken off. The wall between the Rue Riquet itself and the monastery garden was undisturbed, though there were plants upon it, and especially a peg of fir loosely inserted which would probably have been disturbed if a body had been passed along it. The left cheek of the body and the left side of its dress were covered with dirt. As the head was away from the monastery wall, and the wall of the Rue Riquet was on the left hand of the body as it lay, the dirt would have been on the right if the body had fallen over the wall of the Rue Riquet.

From these circumstances, the *acte d'accusation* infers that the body could not have come into the cemetery over the wall of the Rue Riquet, and that it did come over the wall of the monastery garden. [1] To clench this argument the *acte* adds: " Lastly the impossibilities which we have pointed out are " increased " (the energy of this phrase as against the accused is highly characteristic) " by the existence of a lamp on the " wall of the orangery of the monks which throws its light " against the surface of the wall of the Rue Riquet, precisely " at the place where the murderer would have had to place " himself to throw the body of Cecile into the cemetery. Let " us add, that at a short distance from this amp are the " Lignières barracks, and in front of them a sentinel." It adds that these circumstances made it very unlikely that the body should have been thrown over at this point. [2] It does not add, though it appeared in the evidence of Lamarle, the commissary of police, that it was very rainy during the night before, and that the judge of instruction himself remarked, or at least that the remark was made in his presence (*il fut dit*, it does not appear by whom) that if the corpse had been thrown

[1] P. 30.   [2] P. 108.

Y

over from the Rue Riquet the sentinel would have seen it, because he must have been in his box owing to the rain. The *acte* also contradicts the evidence in another particular to the disadvantage of the prisoner. [1] It says of the breach in the corner of the wall, "the breach, already" (*i.e.* when the judge of instruction arrived) "enlarged by the inquisitive " persons who got over, or leant on it, cannot favour the notion " that the body of Cecile may have traversed it to be trans- " ported to the place where it was found. The ground at the " foot of the wall, covered with damp herbs, is free from the " footmarks which must have been remarked if the murderer " had passed over and trodden on this part of the ground." [2] M. Lamarle said that when he fetched the troops the crowd had got over the breach, come within two or three feet of the body, and made footmarks.

These inconsistencies give good grounds for suspicion that if the commissary and the judge of instruction had been pro- perly cross-examined by the prisoner's counsel, the effect of much of this evidence might have been entirely removed. As it stands, it fails to supply conclusive proof that the body came over the monastery wall. The earth might have been knocked off by the scraping of the boughs against the wall as the wind shook them, or it might have fallen off of itself, as such a crust naturally would when it became damp beyond a certain degree. That a geranium should lose its petals in a rainy night is nothing extraordinary; and it is perfectly natural that one of them should fall on the hair of a dead body lying close under it. The other circumstances—the threads of tow, the broken twig, the faded groundsel—cer- tainly tend to support the conclusion of the *acte* as far as they go, but they are very slight circumstances, and if a single man had really thrown the body of a girl of fourteen from the top of a wall covered with plants and earthy matter, it would

[1] P. 25.   [2] P. 108.

be natural to expect to find unequivocal marks of his having done so. It would indeed be a remarkable feat of strength.

These indications, slight as they were, naturally and properly led the authorities to make further investigations in the monastery itself. [1] Accordingly, Coumes, a brigadier of *gendarmerie*, went to examine the garden. Two monks went with him. He found footmarks leading before the orangery and near to the wall before which was the body. The marks were fresh. Some conversation took place between the monks and the brigadier on the subject, as to the nature of which there was a great conflict of evidence, to be noticed hereafter.

The *post-mortem* examination of the body showed that death had been caused by great violence to the head, which was bruised in various parts so seriously that the brain had received injuries which must have caused death almost immediately. [2] This appears from the extracts given in the *acte d'accusation* from the report of the medical experts. [3] The injuries to the head appear to have been inflicted by a broad blunt instrument, and might have been caused by knocking the head against the wall or against a pavement. There were marks on the person showing a violent attempt to ravish, which had not succeeded (the girl had not reached maturity). The underclothing was covered with fæcal matter, and from the contents of the stomach it appeared that death must have taken place one or two hours after the last meal. The fæces contained some grains of figs. On the folds of the underclothing was a stalk of fodder, a piece of barley-straw, other bits of straw, and a feather. The stalks of fodder appeared, on being examined, to be clover grass (*trèflc*).

These facts suggested the thought that the state of the linen of the monks might throw some light on the commission of the crime. There were about [4] 200 inmates altogether in the monastery, which was divided into two

---

[1] P. 120. [2] P. 40. [3] P. 115. [4] So stated, *Proc.-Gen.*, 327

parts, the *pensionnat* and the *noviciat*. The linen of each
establishment was used in common by the members of that
establishment. The shirts of the *noviciat* were numbered ;
the shirts of the *pensionnat* were marked F + P (*frères du
pensionnat*). The division, however, was not kept up strictly,
some of the shirts properly belonging to each division being
occasionally used in the other. The shirts were changed
every Saturday. On making a search a shirt was found
numbered 562, and consequently belonging to the *noviciat*.
It was very dirty, having many spots of fæcal matter in
different places, especially on the sleeves, on the outside of
the back part and inside of the front. On the inside of the
tail of the shirt were certain grains which the experts first
took for the seed of clover-grass, but which, on more careful
examination, they declared to be the grains of figs. A careful
comparison was made between these grains and those which
were found on the clothing of the dead body : the experts
declared that they corresponded ; and one of them, [1] M. Noulet
(called for the first time at the second trial), declared the
resemblance was so close between the two sets of fig-grains
that, though he had made 200 different experiments on figs
bought for the purpose, he had not found any such resemblance elsewhere. M. Fillol, a professor of chemistry, was
less positive. Being asked whether he could say that the figs
were of absolutely the same quality, he replied that to say so
would be a mere conjecture. [2] M. Fillol examined all the
other dirty shirts in the monastery (about 200), and found no
fig-grains on them.

[3] It is asserted in the *acte d'accusation*, though no other
evidence of the assertion appears in the report of the trial,
that the judge of instruction separately and individually
examined all the persons present in the monastery at the
time as to the state of their linen, and particularly as to the

[1] P. 299.   [2] Pp. 117–119.   [3] Pp. 67–68.

shirt which they took off on the 17th of April, two days after the murder, and that " each of the monks recalled with pre-
" cision the particulars which he had remarked on his shirt,
" but none of these resembled those which appeared on the
" shirt seized." The inference from this was that the shirt was worn by the murderer. The points as to the dirt and the seeds of figs were no doubt important, and the alleged result of the examination of all the 200 monks as to their recollection of the particular spots on their dirty shirts would have been vitally important if it were trustworthy; but no one could pretend to form an opinion on the question whether or not it was proved by the method of exhaustion that the shirt in question was the shirt of the murderer, unless he had either heard their evidence, or read a full report of it. All that was proved was, that the judge of instruction was satis-fied upon the subject. Anyone who has seen the way in which professional zeal generates conviction of the guilt of a person accused will attach to this no importance at all.

Whether or not the shirt had been worn by the murderer was an irrelevant question, unless it was shown to have been worn by Léotade. The proof of this consisted entirely of his answers when under interrogation. [1] It does not appear from the report when he was arrested, nor when the shirt was seized; but, according to the *acte d'accusation*, he said, before it was shown to him, that he had not changed his shirt on Sunday, the 18th, and that he had returned the clean shirt served out to him to the monk who managed the linen. His reason for keeping the dirty shirt was that he had on his arm a blister, and that the sleeve of the dirty shirt was wider, and so more commodious than the sleeve of the clean one. If this were false there would be a motive for the falsehood, as, if believed, it would have exempted Léotade from the necessity of owning one of the shirts. On the other hand, it

[1] P. 66.

was unlikely that he should tell a lie which exposed him to contradiction by the monk who managed the linen, who is said to have declared that he had no recollection of the fact mentioned by Léotade. The *acte d'accusation* adds, that Léotade " wishing to give colour to the explanation which he " had invented," asked, when in prison, and after he had seen the shirt seized, for shirts with wider sleeves than those supplied to him, and that the monk who managed the linen deposed that he had never made any such application before. All this is consistent with the notion of a timid man losing his presence of mind when in solitary confinement under pressure, and inventing false excuses in mere terror.

The only other circumstance directly connected with the commission of the crime was that the garden of the monastery contained several outhouses, in some of which were contained a considerable quantity of hay, straw, and other fodder of the same kind as the few straws found on the body. Léotade had access to these places, and it was suggested that he enticed the girl into one of them, and there committed the crime. [1] No marks were found to show that this had been done, though the *acte d'accusation* observes : " These barns " appear predestined for a crime committed under the " conditions of that of April 15th."

[2] It was also mentioned as a matter of suspicion, that, after the murder was committed, the judge of instruction asked Léotade to show him where he slept. Léotade took him to a room behind one of the large dormitories. This room was so situated that the judge of instruction thought that he could not possibly have got out at night for the purpose of disposing of the body. The judge of instruction afterwards asked where he had slept on the night in question, and Léotade showed him at once a room on the first floor. From this room, which Léotade occupied alone, he might have got

[1] P. 63. [2] P. 64.

out and reached the garden by opening two doors which had the same lock. It is said in the *acte d'accusation* that a key found in his possession would open these doors. He had thus an opportunity of getting to the garden if he pleased. The change of bed was made on the 17th, two days after the murder ; and inquiry was made into the reasons for it. Another monk, called Brother Luke, was moved into the room into which Léotade was moved on the 17th. [1] It would appear that the two had previously slept each in a room by himself, but the reason given for their being removed into the room behind the dormitory was that Brother Luke was frightened at the crime, and did not wish to sleep alone. It was, indeed, an irregularity to allow a monk to do so. Upon this the *acte d'accusation* remarks that it is difficult to see how a man of Brother Luke's age could be alarmed by such a crime as the one committed on Cecile Combettes, and it adds :—" The futility of these reasons " suggests the existence of more serious ones, which the " director hides from justice. We must see in this (*il faut* " *y voir*) a measure of internal discipline, destined to isolate " from the other members of the community a brother stained " with a double crime." One objection to this is that the measure consisted in removing the person supposed to be a criminal from a room where he slept alone in an isolated situation, to a room where he slept with another person, close to the principal dormitory of the establishment. The suggestion was, therefore, not only very harsh, but absurd and contradictory.

This was the case against Léotade, as it was established by other evidence than his own statements on interrogation : the principal items added to it by that process consisted of differences between the accounts which he gave at different

---

[1] Cf. *acte d'accusation*, p. 65 ; evidence of Irlide, p. 199 ; evidence of Luc, p. 244.

Léotade's Case.

times of the way in which he had spent his time on the morning in question. The exact date of his apprehension does not appear, but it appears to have taken place some time in April, and from that time till his trial in the following February he appears to have been constantly examined, cross-examined, and re-examined, and confronted with other witnesses, always in secret. [1] At the trial, after the *acte d'accusation* had been read, and the President had pointed out to him the manner in which it bore upon him, he was again cross-examined at great length, and the argument for the prosecution was that he must be guilty because his answers on different occasions were in some degree inconsistent, and because on one or two points he was contradicted by other witnesses. The chief inconsistencies in his answers related to the way in which he disposed of his time on the day in question. His final account of the matter was that he went to mass on getting up, and came out at eight or a quarter-past eight; after mass he went to the *pensionnat,* and thence to another part of the monastery. He stayed there from nine to half-past nine, and then breakfasted. After this he gave the pupils some things which they wanted, and he then finished a *lettre de conscience* to his superior at Paris. He gave the letter to the director of the establishment at about a quarter-past ten, and then went through various other occupations, which he enumerated at length. A great point made against the prisoner was that he did not mention his *lettre de conscience*, the writing of which took up half an hour, from a quarter to ten to a quarter-past ten, when he was first examined on the subject, and that in all his numerous examinations he mentioned it only once before his trial. [2] A commission was sent to Paris to examine the superior to whom the letter was addressed, and it appeared from his evidence, and also from that of the clerks at the diligence office, that a parcel was sent on the 15th April from

[1] Pp. 81-105. [2] P. 243.

Toulouse to the superior at Paris, that the superior received it in due course, and that it contained a letter from Léotade. To an ordinary understanding this would appear, as far as it went, to corroborate Léotade's account. The corroboration would, indeed, be of little importance, because it would prove nothing as to the time when the letter was written, which was the important point; but the President cross-examined the prisoner upon it with great severity, suggesting that, notwithstanding the solitary confinement (*le secret*) in which he had been placed, he had contrived to learn this fact from the monks, and had altered his evidence accordingly. [1] It would seem, however, that the concert between them, if there was one, was not complete; for the director of the establishment, Brother Irlide, said that Léotade gave him his *lettre de conscience* about nine, after which he sent him to the infirmary to wait upon a boy who had the scarlet fever. It must be observed that Léotade was not contradicted on this matter. As far as the evidence went it confirmed his story. The argument for the prosecution would seem to have been that the statement must be false, because it was not made at once, and that, if false, the motive for the falsehood must have been to conceal the fact that the time was really passed in committing the murder.

Another point in his interrogatory related to his shirt. The President read over the interrogatory of the 15th of May. The effect of it was that he had not changed his shirt on the Saturday; that he had given the clean shirt to the monk who managed the infirmary, and that he had pointed out to the doctor who examined him on the 18th that his shirt was dirty. [2] The *acte d'accusation* declares that on all these points he was contradicted, but there was only one contradiction. [3] The doctor said he had remarked that the shirt was not dirty, but he remembered nothing about the conversation; and

[1] P. 207.   [2] P. 17.   [3] P. 114.

the infirmary monk declared only that he did not remember receiving back the shirt.

[1]Another alleged contradiction extracted by the interrogatory was, that Léotade said on one occasion that a pair of drawers he had worn would be found in his breeches, when, in fact, he had them on. He explained this by saying that he was confused at the accusation.

[2] Léotade was also interrogated at great length as to whether he had been with Jubrien in the passage at the time mentioned by Conte. He positively denied it. When first he was questioned on the subject, he said he did not recollect having been there; but when Conte described their position, dress, &c., circumstantially, both Léotade and Jubrien declared that it was not so; and Léotade added that he had not been in the *noviciat* during the whole day.

[3] Lastly, on being asked whether he had told the brigadier of *gendarmerie* that he had made certain footmarks in the monastery garden, he said he had not. He was somewhat roughly cross-examined about this; but he was right, and the President wrong. [4] The *acte d'accusation* charges such a conversation, not with the brigadier, but with one of the doctors, Estevenet, who said in his evidence: " On seeing " the footmarks, Léotade said, Probably some of our monks, " with the gardener, have made the footprints." Léotade admitted that he might have said this, though on a different day from that mentioned at first by the witness, and the witness owned that he might be mistaken as to the day. This shows at once the harshness and inaccuracy both of the judge and of the *acte d'accusation*.

These were the principal points in the case against Léotade. There were several others, for some sort of issue was raised or inference suggested upon almost every word that he said, and upon every trifling discrepancy that could be detected between

[1] P. 92.   [2] P. 97.   [3] P. 101.   [4] P. 33.

his answers in any of his numerous interrogatories. Assuming that Conte spoke the truth, and taking every item of the evidence to be proved in a manner most unfavourable to him, it appears to me that there was barely a case of suspicion against him. The fact that he saw the girl in the passage proves no more than a possibility that he might have committed the crime. The marks and the fig-seeds on the shirt are the strongest evidence in the case ; but the proof that he wore the shirt is altogether unsatisfactory. The inconsistencies in his accounts of the way in which his time was passed are trifling in the extreme. The only wonder is that, when kept in solitary confinement for many months, and interrogated every day, he did not fall into many more. Two of his observations on this subject are very remarkable. On being closely pressed to give a reason why he did not mention his *lettre de conscience* earlier, he said, " It is because the " judge of instruction and the *Procureur-Général* treated me " as a man who could not be innocent—they browbeat me " (*violentaient*), they tortured me ; it was not till I came to this " prison that I found a judge and a father. You, M. le Prési- " dent—yes ! you alone—have not tormented me. [1] The others " treated me as a poor wretch already condemned to death." [2] At the close of the proceedings, on being asked whether he wished to add anything to his defence, Léotade observed, " I " declare that I have not lied before justice. There is nothing " but sincerity in my words. If there are some contradictions " in my deposition, it is owing to the solitary confinement " (*le secret*) which I have undergone. Ah ! gentlemen, if " you knew what solitary confinement is ! Yesterday I saw " a scene which pained me. I saw a man who was being " brought out of solitary confinement to hear the mass—it " was terrible !—he was as thin as a skeleton. How he must " have suffered ! "

[1] P. 87.   [2] P. 359.

The President ridiculed the notion of these tortures, but
his own conduct showed that they were both possible and
probable. His interrogatory is full of rebukes and sneers
which, to a man on trial for his life, are most indecent. [1] For
instance, he asked Léotade if he ever saw workwomen at
Conte's. "*Léotade.* Not as far as I remember. *President.*
" Stay. You already employ an expression which indicates
" reticence." So, again : "I pass to your interrogatory of the
" 3rd of May, and there I find a series of contradictions and
" reticences." [2] So, " Brother Irlide will be examined directly.
" He will remember, he will admit, that you have had several
" communications with the establishment, and especially
" with him." (When Irlide was called he was never questioned on the subject.) " You would do better, perhaps, to
" confess the truth." [3] Again, Léotade explained a mistake by
saying that he was troubled at the accusation. The President
said : " This time, at all events, your trouble is not referred to
" the pretended violence of which you say you were the victim.
" That is better."

As for the judge of instruction, his own account of his
proceedings supersedes all criticism. [4] After a long examination, the President said : "I will now profit by your
" presence here to ask you whether you do not think it
" proper to tell us, in order to throw as much light as possible
" on this debate, those facts which are not introduced into
" *procès-verbaux*, but which are not unimportant to judges ? "
" *Judge of Instruction.* You mean the impressions which
" have resulted from my unofficial " (*en dehors de mes fonctions*)
" conversations with the accused? I often went to see the
" accused, to persuade him to submit patiently to his long
" detention, and also to try to inspire him, as is my duty,
" with the thought of making sincere and complete con-
" fessions. I generally found Brother Léotade kneeling in

[1] P. 81.   [2] P. 89.   [3] P. 92.   [4] P. 266.

" prayer in his chamber, and appearing so much absorbed in
" his meditations that he did not perceive my arrival, and
" that I was obliged to speak first to get a word from him.
" He got up, and then long conversations between us began.
" I made every effort to make him see that, in a religious
" point of view, the way to expiate his crime was to tell the
" whole truth to justice. One day he said to me, ' Yes, I
" understand ; and accordingly, if I had been guilty, I should
" have already thrown myself at your feet.' ' My God !' said
" I, ' you must not exaggerate your crime ; it is, no doubt,
" ' enormous ; but human justice takes everything into account.
" ' Perhaps they will think that you acted in one of those
" ' movements of accidental fortuitous passion when reason
" ' yields and the will almost disappears. God, who appreciates
" ' all, will inspire your judges, and they will measure equitably
" ' the proportions of your crime.' He listened with great
" attention, and looking at me fixedly, said, ' Admit for a
" ' moment . . . but death.' ' Well,' said I, ' who knows that
" ' the perpetrator of the first crime was the perpetrator of the
" ' second ? The girl may have thrown herself down. The
" ' death may have been accidental.' He reflected, and then
" said, ' No ; I am not guilty.' However, if I must say all I
" think, I thought, and I still think, Léotade was on the point
" of making a confession "

" *President.* What sense did you attach to the words, ' but
" ' death ' ? "

" ' Oh, my God !' I thought he meant to say, ' if they
" ' excuse the first crime, will not they be inexorable for the
" ' second ! ' "

Upon this, says the report, " Léotade energetically protests
" against the sense put on his words."

To a mind accustomed to English notions of justice, these
artful attempts to entice the prisoner into a confession,
mixed as they are with suggestions which are palpably

false—like that about the girl having caused her own death —are unworthy, not merely of an officer of justice, but of any man who has honour enough to refuse the functions of the vilest prison-spy. It is viewed differently in France. [1] The advocate of the *partie civile* used this incident as follows, without reproof : " Will you appeal, Léotade, to your " demeanour—to your demeanour before Dr. Estevenet, who " remarked your trouble and your incoherent words, or " before the judge of instruction, when, pushed by remorse, " you were on the point of confessing ? Well, I demand " that confession from you now. I adjure you in the name " of all that is most sacred ; I adjure you in the name of " this family, in tears, for whom I speak ; I adjure you in " the name of this wretched girl, on whom the tomb is " closed ; I adjure you in the name of religion, of which " you are one of the representatives, speak, confess. . . . ! " He is silent. He is the criminal. Human justice is " about to condemn him, as a prelude to the sentence of " Divine justice." What would he have said if Léotade had confessed ?

Léotade was found guilty, with extenuating circumstances, and sentenced to the galleys for life ; he died there after two or three years' confinement. It is obvious that, if guilty at all, he was guilty of one of the most cruel and treacherous crimes on record ; and it is difficult not to believe that the extenuation was rather in the evidence than in the guilt.

I have attempted to extract the pith of this case from the long, intricate, and yet imperfect report of it ; but in order to do so I have passed over a vast mass of evidence by which the case was swollen to unmanageable and almost unintelligible proportions. It will, however, be necessary to give a general description of its character in order to show the practical result of doing without rules of evidence, and

[1] P. 314.

investigating to the bottom every collateral issue which has any relation, however remote, to the question to be tried.

The case affords numerous illustrations of this, which it would be tedious and useless to describe in detail. A few may be referred to for the sake of illustration. The *acte d'accusation* is divided into two main parts; one intended to show that the crime was committed in the monastery, and the other intended to show that it was committed by Léotade. The first point was dwelt upon much more fully than the second. The monks were of course anxious to free themselves from the charge that their establishment had been the scene of rape and murder, and tried to find evidence by which it might be shown that the crime was committed elsewhere. With this object they made inquiries amongst the other persons who had been in the corridor when Conte and his two servants arrived. [1] It appeared that some young men were at that very time in the parlour which opened out of the corridor; and shortly after the arrest of Léotade "a " deposition," says the *acte d'accusation*, "which tended to give " a different direction to the procedure had been announced " through the newspapers." It was said in effect that a lad of the name of Vidal, who was one of the party, had seen the girl going towards the door to go out. This was a mere newspaper paragraph. It did not even appear that the monks were in any way connected with it, but "the judge of in- " struction prepared to receive this deposition and to provide " means for checking it."

Vidal and Rudel were accordingly examined, and it appeared from their account that they had been sent for by the director of the monastery, to see whether they could prove that the girl had left it. Both of them said at first that they had not seen the girl go out; but on a second visit to the monastery, and on being shown the place, Vidal "thought that

[1] Pp. 45–46.

" he could remember that he seemed to have seen the girl pass
" behind him, though he could not say he had seen her go
" out, as at the moment he had his back towards the street."
[1] Rudel, three novices, Navarre, Laphien, and Janissien, and
the porter, who were all with Vidal at the time, are said in
the *acte d'accusation* to have said that they had not seen the
girl. The *acte d'accusation* accordingly declares that " the
" *Court* has not hesitated to declare that Vidal's deposition is
" unworthy of credit." Instead of leaving it to the prisoner
to call him if he thought fit, he was called by the prosecution
for the purpose apparently of being contradicted. [2] His first
observation on giving his evidence was : " When I was called
" before the judge of instruction I said that I thought I had
" seen this young girl in the neighbourhood, but some days
" afterwards I saw and was persuaded that that was impossible."
This of course destroyed any value which his evidence might
have had in favour of the prisoner, but this was far from
satisfying the prosecution. They went at length into the
question how he came to say that he thought he had
seen the girl. He then said that the monks had succeeded
in persuading him that he had really seen her, and that
they held a sort of rehearsal in which the persons who
had been present were put in the positions which they
had occupied in the corridor, and discussed the evidence
which they were to give. They afterwards went upstairs into
another part of the convent, and there consulted on it
further. Vidal declared that he allowed himself at these
conferences to be persuaded into saying that he thought he
had seen the girl go out, though he also stated that he said
he *thought* he had seen her in the first instance, and before
any persuasion at all.

This was represented on the part of the prosecution as
organized perjury, and every effort was made to make Vidal's

[1] P. 47.   [2] P. 186.

evidence go to that length. [1] For instance, the President
said: "Did not they reason like this—did not they say.
" 'The girl must have passed at this instant, and you will
" 'say that you saw her slip out as the chaplain entered;'
" and did not they add, 'that will agree perfectly with the
" 'deposition of Madeleine Sabatier, who will say that she
" 'met the girl near la Moulinade'?

" *Vidal.* No, sir; Madeleine Sabatier was not mentioned.

" *President.* Well, but as to the rest, did not they reason in
" this way?

" *Vidal.* They asked me if I had seen the girl go out, and
" I said it seemed so to me.

" *President.* That is, to please them (*par complaisance*) you
" said you would say that it seemed so?

" *Vidal.* No. I had already said that it did seem so to me."

The two directors, Irlide and Floride, were also examined
upon this point. [2] They both admitted that they had talked
over the matter with Vidal, but declared that Vidal positively asserted that he had seen the girl go out, and that
they told him to tell the truth. [3] There was, however, a contradiction between Vidal and Floride as to the place where
the conversation took place; Vidal said it was in a place called
the *Procure.* Floride at first denied it, but another monk
confirming Vidal, he admitted that it might have been so.

The other persons present in the corridor said that the chaplain came in while they were talking, and in this the chaplain
to some extent confirmed them, and three of them swore that
they saw something or some one pass by the door as the chaplain came in. [4] The porter said that after Conte came in, he
let out the servant Marion, and he then went up with Conte
to the director, that on coming down again he saw several
monks in the passage, but he did not observe whether or not
the girl was there, and that he afterwards opened the door

[1] P. 253. [2] Pp. 200 207. [3] P. 206. [4] P. 156-160.

Léotade's Case.

for the chaplain. From the way in which his evidence was given it is difficult to state shortly its effect, but the general result of it was that he wished to show that the girl might have left the convent without his seeing her, whilst the President cross-examined him with great strictness and asperity to show that he must have seen her if she had left it. Jubrien, whom Conte said he saw with Léotade, was examined at great length and with frequent rebukes. He asserted that he was not with Léotade at the time and place mentioned, but he appears to have replied to almost every other question on the subject, that he did not remember or could not tell. The report is considerably abridged, but it indicates that Jubrien's deposition ran into a sort of argument between himself, the prisoner, the President, and the *Procureur-Général,* of which it is difficult to form any distinct notion.

From the way in which the whole of this evidence was taken it was put before the jury in an inverted order, and a great part of it was utterly irrelevant. The question was, whether Léotade had murdered the girl in the convent. If Vidal could prove that she left it, the case was at an end. His first answer showed that he could not prove that, and it also showed that he was either too weak or too false to be trusted at all, because it contradicted his previous deposition. To show that he had been tampered with was altogether unimportant even if it were true, for Léotade was in prison and could not tamper with him, and he could not be responsible for the indiscretion or even for the dishonesty of unwise partisans. There was, however, no evidence of any subornation except Vidal's own statement, and as the case for the prosecution was that he was weak and dishonest, his statement was worth nothing. It was contradictory to say that when it made against the prisoner it was valid, and when it made in his favour it was worthless. The other witnesses, no doubt, gave their evidence in an unsatisfactory way; and if they had been called by the prisoner to prove his innocence by establishing the fact that the girl had left the convent, the degree of credit to which they would have been entitled would have been very questionable ; but to argue that their disingenuous way of affirming that the girl did leave the convent amounted to proof that she did not leave it, was equivalent to affirming that if the partisans of an accused person are indiscreet or fraudulent, he must be guilty. The fair result of the whole controversy seems to be, that it was not proved on the one hand that the girl did leave the convent, and that it was not proved on the other that she could not have left it unnoticed, though it does not seem probable that she could.

The intricacy and clumsiness of the way in which the evidence was given is indescribable. Vidal was recalled seven times, and was constantly confronted with the other witnesses, when warm disputes and contradictions took place. Every sort of gossip was introduced into the evidence. For instance, a witness, Evrard, said that Vidal had told him that he had seen the girl talking to two monks. Vidal, on being asked, said, he had not seen anything of the sort, nor had he said so. [1] Evrard maintained that he had. Vidal declared that Evrard had retracted his statement on another occasion. Evrard owned that he had retracted because one Lambert had threatened him, but declared that, notwithstanding this, it was true, and that Vidal had told the same story to the *Procureur du Roi* at Lavaur. Hereupon the *Procureur du Roi* of Lavaur [2] was sent for. He said that Evrard had told him that Vidal had said that he had seen the girl speak to two monks, and one of them make a sign to her; that Evrard came back next day, and said that his evidence was all false ; that he returned in the evening and said it was true, and the retractation false, and that Lambert had

---

[1] P. 212.   [2] P. 213.

threatened him. Hereupon the *Procureur* sent for Lambert, who said Evrard was a liar. Lastly, upon being asked whether or not he thought Vidal had said what Evrard said he said, the *Procureur* answered, "I do not know what to " think," on which the President answered, "No more do I." This is a good instance of the labyrinths of contradictions and nonsense which have to be explored if every question is discussed which is in any way connected with the main point at issue.

I will mention one more illustration of the same thing. Conte, upon whose assertion that he had seen Léotade in the passage all this mass of evidence was founded, was himself suspected, and the prosecution at once "explored his " whole life with the greatest care." [1] They found out that seven years before he had seduced his wife's sister, and a bookseller named Alazar, [2] to whom she was engaged, was called to prove that he had broken off the engagement in consequence, and to produce a letter from her (she had been dead six years), excusing her conduct. Hereupon Conte wished to give his version of the affair, but the President at last interfered. "*Mon Dieu!*" he exclaimed; "*où cela nous "menera-t-il?*" The question should have been asked long before.

The evidence of Madeleine Sabatier, already alluded to, was another instance of one of these incidents, as the French call them. Early in the proceedings, and long before the trial, she declared that on a day in April—she could not say which day, but she thought the 8th or 9th (*i.e.* a week before the murder) —she had seen the deceased standing at a window in a house not far from the cemetery. "It might be questioned," says the *acte d'accusation*, "whether the day when Sabatier said " she saw Cecile was the 15th," which is certainly true, as she said herself she thought it was the 9th; "but other facts,

" still more peremptory, demonstrate the lie of the witness."
There is a wonderful refinement of harshness in arguing that
a witness must have been suborned to commit perjury, because
something which she did not say might have been of use to
the prisoner, and would have been a lie if she had said it.
[1] The *acte* then proceeds to prove that Sabatier's story was altogether false, if it asserted that the girl had been seen at the
place mentioned on the 15th, and in a particular dress, &c.
Under these circumstances the natural course would have
been to leave this woman and her story out of the case,
or to allow the prisoner to call her if he thought proper ;
but it appears to have been considered that, if she were
called for the purpose of being contradicted, the exposure
of her falsehood would raise a presumption that she had
been suborned by persons who were aware of Léotade's guilt.
She was called accordingly, and repeated her deposition, which
was then contradicted by six other witnesses, some of whom
got into supplementary contradictions amongst themselves.
Sabatier was committed on the spot for perjury.

Another large division of the evidence had reference to
certain footmarks discovered by the brigadier of the
gendarmerie in the monastery garden. A monk, called
Laurien, the gardener, said he had made them ; and the
brigadier and he contradicted each other as to the circumstances of a conversation between them on the subject.
As Léotade had nothing whatever to do with the conversation,
and as no attempt was made to connect him with the
footmarks (except to the extent already mentioned), this
was altogether irrelevant. It might have some tendency to
show that one of the monks wanted to make evidence in
favour of his convent, but it had no tendency to show the
prisoner's guilt. Laurien, however, was committed to prison
for perjury, and strong remarks were made on him. It

[1] Pp. 154-155.

is impossible not to see that the arrest of two witnesses favourable to the prisoner on the ground of perjury, simply because their evidence was contradicted by other witnesses, must have prejudiced the case for the prisoner fearfully, and terrified every witness whose evidence was favourable to him. The effect of this was obvious in Vidal's case. Whenever he seemed disposed to say that he thought the girl had left the convent he was threatened with arrest, and when so threatened he immediately became confused and indistinct.

A single illustration will show the brutal ferocity with which witnesses are liable to be used if their evidence is unwelcome to the authorities. A man named Lassus, [1] having given evidence to prove an *alibi* for Léotade, the *Procureur-Général* made the following observation on him: " To com-" plete your edification, gentlemen of the jury, as to this " witness, we think we ought to read you a letter from his " father, which will enable you to judge of his morality. The " presence of this witness at the trial is the height of im-" morality : it proves that not merely have they abused " religion, but they have gone so far as to practise with vice. " To produce such evidence is the last degree of depravity " and baseness." This appears to have roused at last the counsel for the prisoner, who began : " If such anathemas as " these are kept for all the prisoner's witnesses——" The President, however, interrupting him, observed : "In con-" science, this witness deserves what he has got."

A third series of witnesses was produced to rebut the possible suggestion that Conte had committed the crime, by establishing an *alibi* on his part. There appears to have been no reason to suppose he did commit it, except the suspicion which crossed the mind of the authorities in the first instance.

[1] P. 272.

Many other witnesses were called to give an account of all sorts of rumours, conjectures, and incidents, which appear to have no connection with the subject. For instance, [1] Bazergue, a trunk-maker, declared that, when he heard that the girl was missing in the convent, he told his informant that if Cecile had entered the monastery, she would not leave it alive. " I " had," he said, " a sort of presentiment ; and I added that, " if she had remained, their interest alone would be enough " to prevent her from being allowed to leave it alive." " This," said the President, "may be called a rather prophetic " appreciation if the fact is true." [2] Muraive, a painter, said that on the 20th April a man bought some rose-coloured paint of him, burned his face with a lucifer match, and rubbed the paint on it, so as to disguise himself. " *J'ai mon idée*," said the witness, " he was a monk in disguise." [3] M. Guilbert, who had kept a journal for twenty-nine years of everything that occurred in Toulouse, produced it in court, and read an entry to the effect that the body of a young girl had been found, and that there were many rumours on the subject. [4] Another witness saw some cabbages trampled on in a garden.

A number of witnesses for the defence were called, of whom some proved an *alibi* on behalf of Léotade, and others on behalf of Jubrien. The evidence as to Léotade was that he was engaged elsewhere in the convent at the time when Conte said he saw him in the corridor. The evidence as to Jubrien was, that he went from the corridor to the stable to sell a horse to a man named Bouhours, who was accompanied by Saligner. [5] Bouhours declaring that he had seen Vidal and Rudel, who declaring that they had not seen him, he was immediately arrested. This part of the evidence is given in such an unsatisfactory manner in the report that it is difficult to make much out of it. [6] It appears, however, that Jubrien

---

[1] P. 182.   [2] P. 285.   [3] P. 284.

[4] P. 285.   [5] P. 269.   [6] P. 281.

himself never mentioned the sale of the horse, and that he had declared that he had never been in the stable at all.

I do not pretend to have stated the whole of the evidence in this case. It would be almost impossible, and altogether unimportant to do so ; but this account of the trial seems to be correct, as far as it goes, and is sufficiently complete to give some notion of the practical working of the French system of criminal procedure.

[1]THE AFFAIR OF ST. CYR.

IN June, 1860, Jean Joanon, Antoine Dechamps, and Jean François Chretien, were tried at Lyons for the murder of Marie Desfarges ; the murder and rape of her daughter-in-law, Jeanne Marie Gayet, and her granddaughter, Pierrette Gayet; and the robbery of the house in which the murders and rapes were committed. The wives of Dechamps and Chretien were tried at the same time for receiving the goods stolen from the house. The trial began on the 7th of June, and on the 12th it was adjourned till the following session, which began on the 10th of July. On the 15th of July, it ended in the conviction of Joanon, Dechamps, and Chretien, all of whom were condemned to death, and executed in pursuance of their sentence. Chretien's wife was convicted of receiving, and sentenced to six years' *reclusion,* and Dechamps's wife was acquitted. The circumstances were as follows :—

[2] Marie Desfarges, an old woman of seventy, lived with her daughter-in-law, Madame Gayet, aged thirty-eight, and her granddaughter, Pierrette Gayet, aged thirteen years and three months, in a house belonging to Madame Gayet, at St. Cyr-au-Mont-d'Or, near Lyons. The family owned property worth upwards of 64,000 francs, besides jewellery and ready money. They lived alone, and had no domestic servant, employing labourers to cultivate their land. On the 15th of October, 1859,

---

[1] The authority quoted is a report of the trials published at Lyons in 1860, and apparently edited by M. Grand, an advocate. It is in two parts, separately paged, referred to as I. and II.

[2] *Acte d'accusation,* I. 14.

their house was shut up all day. On the 16th, it was still shut, and Benet, a neighbour, being alarmed, looked in at the bedroom window. The beds were made, but the boxes were open, and the room in great disorder. On going downstairs, the three women were found lying dead on the kitchen floor. The grandmother had contused wounds on her head which had broken the skull, and one of which formed a hole through which a person could put his finger into the brain : besides this, her throat had been chopped, apparently with a hatchet. The mother was stabbed to the heart, and had a second stab on the right breast. She had also an injury which had parted the temporal artery in front of the right ear, and bruises on the arm. On her throat were marks of strangulation, such as might have been made by a knee. The daughter had a contused wound on her thumb, and a stab to the heart, which might have been produced by the same instrument as that which had been used against her mother. The bodies of the mother and daughter showed marks of rape. There were two wooden vessels near the bodies which contained bloody water, as if the murderers had washed their hands. The house had been plundered.

Of the three prisoners, Dechamps and Chretien were relations of the murdered women. Chretien's mother-in-law was the paternal aunt of Madame Gayet, and Chretien acted as her agent and trustee (*mandataire*). Dechamps is stated to have claimed an interest in the inheritance ; it does not appear in what capacity. [1] Joanon was no relation to any of them, but he had been in the employment of Madame Gayet as a labourer, and had some years before made her an offer of marriage. Madame Bouchard, who made the offer for him, said that Madame Gayet refused, "saying that she did not " wish to unite herself with the family of Joanon, and that she

[1] II. 54.

" thought Joanon himself idle, drunken, and gluttonous." It appears, however, that Madame Bouchard did not consider the refusal final, as she told Joanon that the marriage might come about after all. [1] It also appeared that he continued in the service of Madame Gayet, as his advocate stated, for as much as two years. [2] The *acte d'accusation* says that, after the refusal, his mistresses sought an opportunity of discharging him ; but this is not intelligible, for they might have done so at any moment without giving a reason.

A good deal of evidence was given to prove that, in con-sequence of Madame Gayet's refusal, Joanon had expressed ill-will towards her, that she and her daughter had expressed terror of him, and that his general character was bad. None of it, however, was very pointed. The principal evidence as to Joanon's expressions was, [3] that he said to a woman named Lhopital, " These women make a god of their money ; but no " one knows what may happen to women living alone." This was seven months before the crime. [4] He told a man named Bernard, about eighteen months before the crime, that he had taken liberties with Madame Gayet, of whom he used a coarse expression, [5] but that she resisted him ; [6] and he said something of the same sort to Madame Lauras. [7] He also said to Ber-thaud, " I made an offer of marriage to the widow Gayet : she " refused ; but she shall repent it," using an oath. [8] A woman named Delorme came into Madame Gayet's house four years before the crime. She found her crying, and her cap in some disorder. She made a sign for her to stay when she was about to leave. All this comes to next to nothing. [9] The evidence that the Gayets went in fear of Joanon is thus described in the *acte d'accusation :* " The Gayets were under " no illusion as to the bad disposition of Joanon towards " them. Timid, and knowing that the man was capable of

[1] II. 120.   [2] I. 17.   [3] I. 65.   [4] I. 74.   [5] II. 55.
[6] I. 76.   [7] I. 78.   [8] I. 78.   [9] I. 17

" everything, they *hardly dared to allow their most intimate*
" *friends to have a glimpse of their suspicions.*   Pierrette, being
" less reserved, mentioned them to several persons."   It was
hard on the prisoner to make even the silence of the murdered
women evidence against him by this ingenious suggestion.

There was little evidence that Madame Gayet ever complained of him.   [1] One witness, Ducharme, said that, eight
days before the crime, she told him of her vexations at
Joanon's nocturnal visits and annoyances, and added, that he
advised her to apply to the mayor or the police.   [2] The President also said, in Joanon's interrogatory, that Madame
Gayet had complained to the mayor of the *commune* of his
annoying her.   [3] The mayor himself, however, said that when
she was at his office on other business she *was going to talk*
about Joanon, but had said only *Il m'ennuie*, when the conversation was interrupted.   The girl Pierrette had made
some complaints.   She told one witness that Joanon climbed
over their walls and frightened them all, except her mother.
It so happened that this witness was for once asked a question in the nature of cross-examination : [4] " Was it a serious
" alarm, or merely something vague, that Pierrette expressed ? "
" Not precisely " (*i.e.* not precisely serious) ; " she said, only
" that they feared to be assassinated some day, without re-
" ferring these fears to Joanon.   However, they were afraid
" of him."   This shows the real value of gossip of this sort.
[5] Pierrette told another witness, Dupont, that they were afraid
of being murdered.   [6] A girl called Marie Vignat, who was
intimate with Pierrette, said that Pierrette told her also
that she was afraid of being assassinated.   " The evening
" before the crime, I said to her, ' Good-bye till to-morrow.'
" She answered, ' We cannot answer for to-morrow.   You
" ' sometimes come to see us in the evening, but you had
" ' better come in the morning—at least, you would give the

---

[1] II. 59.   [2] II. 36.   [3] I. 47.   [4] I. 64.   [5] I. 66.   [6] I. 68.

' ' alarm if we were murdered.' " She does not appear to have said that she feared Joanon would murder them ; but she spoke strongly against him to Marie Vignat. [1] She said : " It " is said you are going to marry Joanon. You had better " jump into the Saône with a stone round your neck. He is " a man to be feared. My mother and I are afraid of him, " and we would not for all the world meet him in a road."

None of this evidence could have been given in an English court : but it would, perhaps, be going too far to say that it ought to have no weight at all. The fact that people are on bad terms may be proved quite as well, and generally better, by what each says of the other in his absence, than by what they say in each other's presence. It goes, however, a very little way towards showing the probability that a crime will be committed. It was clear that Pierrette Gayet disliked and feared Joanon ; but it does not follow that he had given her reasonable grounds for fear. If she disliked him, and knew that he wanted to marry her mother, her language would be natural enough. Her fears of assassination in general prove little more than timidity, not unnatural in a girl living alone with her mother and grandmother.

The consequence of these circumstances is thus described in the *acte d'accusation* : [2] " After the 16th of October " (the date of the discovery of the bodies), " public opinion pro- " nounced violently against Joanon. He had fixed himself " at St. Cyr for some years. His house is hardly two hundred " paces from that of the Gayets. Though the eldest son of a " family in easy circumstances, Joanon seems to have been, " so to speak, repudiated by his relations. His maternal " grandfather, in excluding him from the inheritance by his " holograph will, dated February 21, 1857, inflicted on him a " sort of curse in these words : ' I give and I leave to my

[1] I. 68.   [2] II. 58.

" ' grandson Joanny Joanon, the eldest boy, the sum of ten
" ' francs for the whole of his legacy, because he has behaved
" ' very ill.'   Signalized by the witnesses as a man without
" morality, of a sombre, false, and wicked character, Joanon
" lived in isolation." The principal witnesses to this effect
were the mayor and the *juge de paix*. [2]The mayor said at
the first hearing, Joanon "was feared, and little liked. . . ."
" I never, however, heard that he was debauched." At the
adjourned hearing, however, he spoke very differently. [3]" *Pr.*
" Give us some information as to Joanon's morality? *A.* It
" was very bad at St. Cyr. Twice I heard of follies (*niai-*
" *series*) which ended before the *juge de paix*. He went with
" idiot girls and women of bad character." The *juge de
paix* gave him a very bad character. He owed five francs
" to the *garde champêtre*, and refused to pay them; he stole
" luzern, either from avarice, or cupidity, or bad faith;
" he contested a debt of fifty francs to his baker. I know
" he was debauched, and reputed to be connected with
" women of bad character." He also referred to the idiot
girls. When Joanon was asked what he said to this, he
replied, [4]" The *juge de paix* has listened to the scandal (*les
" mauvaises langues*) of St. Cyr "—a sensible remark.

I have given this part of the evidence in detail, because it
shows what sort of matter is excluded by the operation of our
own rules of evidence.

On the 19th of October, Joanon was called as a witness, and
examined as to where he had been at the time of the crime,
" like many others." [5]He said first that he had come to his
own house at 8.30 P.M., and that he had then gone to a
baker's. He went next day to the baker, Pionchon, and
asked him to say that he had bought his bread that evening,
and had passed the evening with him. This was Pionchon's
account at the trial, which differed to some extent from what

[1] I. 17.   [2] I. 59.   [3] II. 47.   [4] I. 95.   [5] I. 77.

he had said previously. Joanon said in explanation : " I told " him I had made a mistake before the judge of instruction " but I did not mean to ask for false evidence." He had, in fact, been at Pionchon's the day before. At his next examination (October 20), he said he might be mistaken as to the baker, but that he had been at Vignat's, and had come home at 7.30. On the 21st, he said he had stayed at Vignat's till 7.30, and then gone home. Madame Vignat and her daughter both said he had left about 4. He added, that three persons, Mandaroux, Lauras, and Lenoir, must have seen him. [1] Mandaroux said he saw him about 5 ; [2] H. Lauras had heard a voice in his house at 7 or 7.15 ; [3] and two women, Noir and Dury, met him thirty or forty yards from the house of the Gayets at about 7.30. One of them, Dury, heard the clock strike as she passed the house of a neighbour. Joanon declared at the trial that it was 6.30 and not 7.30 when he met them. His advocate said that it appeared from the evidence of J. L. Lauras that the two women, Noir and Dury, left his house, at which they had been washing, at 5.45, and that it was 1,748 metres, or less than one mile and a quarter, from that house to the place where they met Joanon ; whence [4] he argued that Joanon must have been right as to the time. The difficulty of fixing time accurately is notorious ; nor did it in this case make much difference. The murder was probably committed between 6.30 and 7.30. Joanon's house was only 200 yards from the house of the Gayets. Hence, whether he returned home at 6.30 or 7.30, he was close by the spot at the time.

In his interrogatory at the trial, he said he had been at a piece of land belonging to him, had returned at nightfall, and not gone out again. Hereupon the President said : [5] " You gave " a number of versions during the instruction ; you make new " ones to-day. *A.* They said so many things to me—they

[1] I. 75. [2] I. 76. [3] I. 77. [4] I. 122. [5] I. 44.

" bothered me so dreadfully (*ils m'ont si péniblement retourné*) " that I do not know what I said. . . ." The general result seems to have been that, though he did not establish an *alibi*, he did not attempt to do so, for his conversation with Pionchon would account for part only of the evening ; and that, on the one hand, he was close to the place where the crime was committed at the time, though, on the other hand, he naturally would be there, as it was his home. To me, the fact that he gave different accounts when he was re-examined five or six times over, seems to prove nothing at all. A weak or confused memory, that amount of severity in the magistrate which would provoke the exercise of petty and short-sighted cunning and falsehood, fright at being the object of suspicion, would account for such confusion as well as guilt : indeed, they would account for it better. A guilty man would hardly have mentioned the persons who saw him, and would, probably, have seen the necessity of inventing one story and sticking to it. This is a good instance of the perplexity which may be produced by putting too great a stress on a man's memory. It is more difficult to say what was the precise amount of discrepancy between Joanon's different statements, and what is the fair inference to be drawn from those discrepancies, under all the circumstances, than to form an opinion of his innocence or guilt apart from his statements on this subject. Evidence treated thus is like handwriting scratched out and altered so often as to become, at last, one unintelligible mass of blots and scratches. It shows that too much inquiry may produce darkness instead of light.

Notwithstanding the suspicion thus excited against Joanon, he was not arrested, and no further information on the subject of the crime was obtained for several months. At last, on the 14th of February, four months after the murder, Joanon was drinking with the *garde champêtre* of St. Cyr at a cabaret.

The *garde* asked him to pay five francs which he owed him.
Joanon said, [1] "I will give you them, but I must first have an
"apology." I answered, "Everyone in the neighbourhood
"accuses you." I pressed him, saying, "You ought at least to
"have spared the girl." He answered, "I did my best; I
"could not prevent it; but I will not sign."

It is in relation to evidence of this sort that cross-
examination is most important. It is quite possible that,
on proper cross-examination, a very different turn might have
been given to this expression from the one attached to it by a
man who was obviously fishing for a confession. The report
(like most reports of French trials) is not full, and no cross-
examination is given. Another witness, Bizayon, heard the
same words, and reported them quite differently. "You would
"like to make me talk, but I won't sign." Two others, Gerard
and Clement, made it a little stronger. Gerard said it was,
"I tried to prevent the crime;" Clement, "I tried to prevent
"the crime of the Gayet family." Clement also complained
that Joanon had tried to cheat him of fifty franes by a false
receipt. [2] Gerard added, that Joanon was pressed with questions as to the part he had taken in the crime, and that
he spoke on the faith of a declaration that the prosecution
against him had been abandoned. [3] Joanon himself said that
he said what he did to get rid of the *garde*, who was plaguing
him with questions. However this may be, he was immediately arrested, and when before the mayor he observed that
he had better have broken his leg than have said what he did.
Joanon denied having said this, but it proved nothing against
him. Whether he was innocent or guilty, the remark was
perfectly true.

This was the whole of the evidence against Joanon, with
the exception of the confessions of the other two prisoners,
obtained under the following circumstances. On the 16th of

[1] I. 61.   [2] I. 79.   [3] I. 62.

February, two days after Joanon's arrest, Chretien offered for sale, at Lyons, two old gold watches. The watchmaker found spots on them, which he thought were blood, and took them to the commissary of police. Upon examination it appeared that the spots were not blood, but that the watches had belonged to the Gayets. Hereupon Chretien was arrested. He said at first that he had stolen the watches, when the property was removed after the sale, having found them on the top of a piece of furniture. This, however, was contradicted by persons to whom he referred, and his house was searched. On the first search there were found 670f., for the possession of which he accounted; but on a further search a purse was discovered, containing 1,380f. in gold, in a purse set with pearls, and various small articles, which were identified as the property of the Gayets. Chretien declared that he knew nothing of the money, and that it belonged to his wife.

[1] She said that at her marriage she had 600f., which she had concealed from her husband; that for twelve years past she had had a lover (who said he gave her about 120f. a year—a sum which the President described as enormous), and that she saved on the poultry. She said that as soon as she got a piece of gold she put it into this purse, and never took any out. She had been married twenty years. On examining the dates of the coins, it appeared that 220f. only were earlier than 1839, when she said she had 600f., 200f. between 1839 and 1852, and 960f. between 1852 and 1859. [2] This ingenious argument silenced her. [3] Chretien had a difficulty in accounting for his time. He was seen coming home at eight, and he left his work at half-past five.

As Chretien was supposed to have committed the murder

---

[1] " Dans la situation pécuniaire où vous êtes à raison de vos dettes cette " somme de 120f. était énorme."—I. 89.

[2] *Acte d'accusation*, I. 22, 23.   [3] I. 90.

for the sake of the inheritance, Dechamps was arrested also as a party interested in the same way. [1] Some articles are said in the *acte d'accusation* to have been found in his house, and his father was seen digging in a field, for the purpose, as he afterwards said, of hiding a cock and some copper articles given him by his son. He also was arrested, but, on the cock being found, was set at liberty, and immediately drowned himself. [2] Dechamps had the same sort of difficulty in proving an *alibi* as Chretien and Joanon, and his wife asked a neighbour to say she had seen her between five and eight. [3] On searching a well at Dechamps's house, a hatchet, such as is used for vine-dressing, was found. The handle was cut off, the end of the handle was charred, and the head had been in the fire ; and Dechamps's wife tried to bribe the persons who made the search not to find it. This hatchet had belonged to the Gayets, and might have been used to make the wounds on the throat of the grandmother and granddaughter. It had been seen in the house after the murder hidden behind some faggots in the cellar, and had afterwards disappeared. It was, no doubt, the height of folly in Dechamps to meddle with it ; but it was just the sort of folly which criminals often commit, and his wife's conduct left no doubt that it was purposely concealed in the well. This is a case in which the English rules would have excluded material evidence. Her statements in his absence would not have been admissible against him, but they were clearly important.

Chretien and Dechamps being both arrested, and taken to Lyons, Chretien, on the 3rd of April, sent for the judge of instruction, and made a full confession to him. The substance of it was that the murder was planned by Joanon, out of revenge because Madame Gayet had refused him. That he suggested to Dechamps to take part in the crime, on the

[1] I. 24.   [2] I. 25.   [3] I. 82.

The Affair of St. Cyr.

ground that by doing so he would inherit part of the property, and that Dechamps mentioned the matter to him
(Chretien) about a fortnight before the crime. Joanon was
to choose the day. On the 14th of October, at about six, Dechamps fetched Chretien, and they went to a mulberry wood
close by the house of the Gayets, where they found Joanon.
They then got into the house, which was not locked up, and
found the Gayets at supper. They received them kindly, and
talked for a few minutes, when Joanon gave the signal by
crying "*Allons,*" on which Chretien, who was armed with a
flint-stone, knocked down the grandmother, and killed her
with a single blow, Dechamps stabbed the girl with a knife,
and Joanon attacked the mother. She got the hatchet, afterwards found in the well; but Dechamps pulled it from her,
on which Joanon stabbed her. Joanon and Dechamps then
committed the rapes. [1] It is not stated what account he gave
of the wounds in the neck.

On being confronted with Dechamps and Joanon, Dechamps contradicted Chretien; as for Joanon, a remarkable
scene took place. [2] The *acte d'accusation* says: "As to
" Joanon, to give an account " (*pour faire connaître*) " of his
" attitude and strange words during this confrontation, it
" would be necessary to transcribe verbatim the *procès-verbal*
" of the judge of instruction." (If the jury were to form an
opinion it would have been just as well to take this amount
of trouble.) "After their first confrontation he pretends
" that he has not seen Chretien, and demands to be again
" brought into his presence. Chretien was brought before
" him several times. Sometimes Joanon declared that he
" did not know the man; that he was then speaking to him
" for the first time; then he begs to be left alone with him
" for an hour, that he would soon confess him and make
" him change his language; sometimes he tries to seduce

[1] I. 27.　　　　　　　　　[2] I. 28.

" him, by declaring that he will take care of his wife and
" children, by talking of the wealth of his own family, by
" saying that he attaches himself to him like a brother, and
" that he wishes to render him every sort of service.

" Chretien does not allow himself to be shaken ; he recalls
" to his accomplice, one by one, all the circumstances of their
" crime ; then Joanon insults him, calls him a hypocrite and
" a man possessed, and accuses him of dissembling his crime,
" of hiding his true accomplices to save his friends, his re-
" lations, and his son ; then abruptly changing his tone, he
" becomes again soft and coaxing ; he tells Chretien that he
" takes an interest in him, that he does not think him
" malicious, and he begs him to be reasonable. He talks,
" also, of the money of which he himself can dispose ; of the
" services he can render his wife and children, if on his part
" he will make the confessions he ought to make, whereas
" if he causes his (Joanon's) death he will be able to do
" nothing for him."

The way in which Joanon behaved on hearing Chretien's
statement was, no doubt, important evidence either for or
against him. According to English notions it would be
the only part of the evidence which in strictness would be
admissible against him. The degree in which the French
system of procedure takes the case out of the hands of the
jury, and commits it to the authorities, is well illustrated by
the fact, that as far as this most important evidence was
concerned they had in this instance to be guided entirely by
the impression of the *Procureur-Général* who drew up the
acte d'accusation as to the purport of the *procès-verbal* of the
judge of instruction. It is as if an English jury were asked
to act upon the impression made on the mind of the counsel
for the Crown by reading the depositions.

At a later stage of the case, the *Procureur-Général* thought
fit to read the *procès-verbal* in full. It is so characteristic

and curious that I translate verbatim that part of it which describes the confrontation of Chretien and Joanon.

"*Judge of Instruction to Chretien.* Do you persist in " maintaining that you have no further revelations to make " to justice?

" *A.* No, sir, I have no more to say. I adhere to my " confessions, which are the expression of the truth.

" We, judge of instruction, caused the prisoner Joanon " to be brought from the house of detention to our office. " Chretien renewed his confessions in his presence, to which " Joanon answered only : ' What! Chretien, can you accuse " ' me of sharing in this crime?' To which Chretien an- " swered, with energy, ' YES, YES, Joanon, I accuse you " ' because you are guilty, and it is you who led us into " ' the crime.'

" The same day, at four o'clock, Joanon, having asked to " speak to us, we had him brought from the house of deten- " tion to our cabinet, when he said only, ' I am innocent ; I " ' am innocent.'

" *Q.* Yet you have been in the presence of Chretien, who " recalled to you all the circumstances of the crime of which " you were the instigator? *A.* I certainly heard Chretien " accuse me, but I did not see him. I was troubled.

" *Q.* Your trouble cannot have prevented you from seeing " Chretien. He was only four paces from you in my office. " *A.* Still my trouble did prevent me from seeing him.

" *Q.* You saw him well enough to speak to him. *A.* I " own I spoke to him, but I did not see him.

" We, the judge of instruction, had Chretien brought into " our office again.

" *Q.* (to Joanon). You see Chretien now. Do you recog- " nize him? *A.* I have never seen that man.

" *Chretien* (of his own accord). Scoundrel! (*canaille*). You " saw me well enough in the mulberry garden, and I saw you

" too, unluckily. You did it all, and but for you I should
" not be here.

" *Joanon.* I never spoke to you till to-day.

" *Chretien.* I have not seen you often, but I saw you ·
" only too well, and spoke to you too much, the 14th October
" last, in the mulberry garden, in the evening about seven
" o'clock."

These answers are very important, and their effect is not
given in the abstract contained in the *acte d'accusation.* They
are an admission by Chretien that he was a stranger to the
man, on a mere message from whom he was willing as he
said to commit a horrible murder on his own relations.

" *Joanon.* Sir, you will search the criminals and you will
" find them.

" *Q.* (to Chretien). In what place in the mulberry garden
" was Joanon ? *A.* In front of the little window outside the
" drain of the kitchen, by which you can see what goes on
" in that room. Joanon told us that the two widows, Des-
" farges and Gayet, were at supper, and pointed out to each
" his victim.

" *Q.* What do you say to that, Joanon ? *A.* This man
" wants to make his confession better and more complete ;
" put us together in the same cell for an hour, and I answer
" for it that he will say something else.

" *Q.* Why do you want to see Chretien alone ? *A.* Because
" when I have confessed (*confessé*) Chretien, he won't accuse
" me. That man does not know all the services that I can do
" to him and his children ; he does not know that my family
" is rich, poor fellow ; he does not know how I attach myself
" to him like a brother. I will do him all sorts of services,
" grant me what I ask to throw light on this affair.

" *Q.* (to Chretien). You hear what he says. *A.* I hear and
" stand to my confession, because it is true. There were three
" of us, Joanon, Dechamps, and I. Joanon said that we must

" present ourselves to these women as if to ask shelter from
" the storm " [there was a violent storm at the time], " and
" that at the word '*Allons*' which he, Joanon, would give,
" each should take his victim.

" *Joanon* (interrupting). I did not say so. (After a short
" pause) I was at home.

" *Chretien* (in continuation). Joanon, addressing himself to
" Dechamps said, ' You will kill Pierrette ; Chretien, widow
" 'Desfarges ; and I take charge of widow Gayet.'

" *Joanon* (interrupting). Allow me, sir, to take an hour
" with him. I will make him retract. (To Chretien) My
" lad, you think you are improving your position, but you are
" mistaken. We can only die once. Reflect ; this man wants
" to save his son, who, no doubt, is his accomplice.

" *Chretien.* My son has been absent from St. Cyr for three
" years, and on the 14th October was one hundred and sixty
" leagues off. (This has been verified by the instruction, and
" is true.)

" *Joanon.* I hope Dechamps will make a better confession.

" *Q.* Then you know that Dechamps is guilty ? " (The
eagerness to catch at an admission is very characteristic.)
" *A.* I said that Dechamps will confess if he is guilty.

" *Q.* (to Chretien). Continue your account of the events of
" the evening of the 14th October ? *A.* After receiving
" Joanon's instructions we scaled together the boundary wall
" which separates the court from the mulberry garden, and
" when we came to the kitchen door, Joanon entered first.

" *Joanon* (interrupting). You always put me first !

" *Chretien.* Dechamps entered second, and I third. As we
" entered Joanon said that we came to ask shelter from the
" storm. The women were at supper ; they rose and offered us
" their chairs. They received us well, poor women.

" *Joanon.* This is all a lie. I was at home.

" *Q.* (to Joanon). You have heard all these details, what

"do you say to them ? *A.* I take an interest in Chretien, he "is not a bad fellow, no more am I : he will be reasonable, "and I will take care of his wife and children if he makes "such confessions as he ought to make.

"*Chretien.* Scoundrel! my wife and children don't want "you for that.

"*Q.* If you are innocent, why does Chretien accuse you at "the expense of accusing himself? *A.* I don't know; per-"haps he hopes to screen a friend (*un des siens*) ; poor fellow, "he thinks he is freeing himself, but he is making his position "worse.

"*Q.* Chretien, go on with your story. *A.* After a few "moments, during which we talked about the storm, Joanon "got up, saying, '*Allons*'; at this signal we each threw "ourselves on our victims, as we had agreed in the mulberry "garden. I killed widow Desfarges with the stone ; the poor "woman fell at my feet. Joanon and Dechamps, armed with "a knife, threw themselves on the widow Gayet and her "daughter Pierrette. The widow Gayet, trying to save her-"self from Joanon, took from the cupboard the hatchet which "you have shown me, to use it. Dechamps, seeing this, came "to the assistance of Joanon and disarmed the widow Gayet." The women were then stabbed and ravished. "Dechamps "and Joanon washed their hands; they then went with me "into the next room, where I took from the wardrobe the two "watches which I afterwards came to Lyons to sell. Joanon "and Dechamps took the jewellery, which I believe they "afterwards shared at Joanon's house; as for me, I went "straight home, as I have already told you.

"*Q.* Well, Joanon, you have heard Chretien ; what do you "say to these precise details ? *A.* Chretien can say what he "likes; I am innocent. Oh, Mr. Judge, leave me alone an 'hour with Chretien—I will clear it all up for you over a "bottle of wine ; he knows that my family is rich ; there is

The Affair of St. Cyr.

"no want of money; my relations must have left some for "me at the prison. Pray leave us alone an hour, I want to "enlighten justice." Then he said, "Let Chretien say how I "was dressed."

"*Chretien.* [1] I can't say, I took no notice."

This last question is very remarkable. It looks like a gleam of common-sense and presence of mind in the midst of mad and abject terror; and, the instant that Chretien found himself upon a subject where he might be contradicted, his memory failed. Confrontation is in French procedure a substitute for our cross-examination. The one is as appropriate to the inquisitorial as the other to the litigious theory of criminal procedure. It is obvious that to a student who examines criminals in the spirit of a scientific inquirer, confrontation is likely to be most instructive, but for the purposes of attack and defence it is far less efficient than cross-examination.

At the trial Chretien was brought up first, the other prisoners being removed from the court after answering formal questions as to their age and residence. Chretien repeated, in answer to the President's questions, the story he had already told in prison. [2] He maintained, however, that the purse of 1,380f. was not part of the plunder. Joanon was then introduced, and taken through all the circumstances of the case. He contradicted nearly every assertion of every witness, constantly repeating that he was as innocent as a new-born child, at which the audience repeatedly laughed. [3] Judging merely from the report, it would seem that his behaviour throughout, though no doubt consistent with guilt, and to some extent suggestive of it, was also consistent with the bewilderment and terror of a man who had utterly lost his presence of mind and self-command by a long imprisonment, repeated interrogations, and the pressure of

[1] I. 110–112.   [2] I. 39.   [3] I. 42.

odium and suspicion. He was treated with the harshness
habitual to French judges. [1] For instance, in his second trial,
he said, "I am the victim of two wretches. I swear before
"God that I am innocent." The President replied, "Don't
"add blasphemy" (*un outrage*) "to your abominable crimes."
[2] Dechamps in the same way, though with more calmness and
gravity, denied all that was laid to his charge. He could not
explain the presence of the hatchet in his well, or of the property in his house. On the night between the fourth and
fifth days' trial, Dechamps tried to hang himself in prison.
The turnkey found him in bed with a cord round his neck.
[3] The advocates then addressed the jury; after which Chretien
was again examined. He then said that the whole of his
previous statement was false; that he knew nothing of the
murder; that he had made up his circumstantial account of
it from what he saw and heard at St. Cyr. He was, however, unable to give any satisfactory, or even intelligible,
account of his reasons for confessing, or of his acquaintance
with the details of the offence. Upon this the *Procureur-
Général* said that, as there was a mystery in the case, he
wished for a "supplementary instruction" to clear it up, and
requested the court to adjourn the case till the next session.
This was accordingly done.

[4] During the adjournment, each of the prisoners underwent
several interrogatories by the President of the *Cour d'Assises.*
Chretien at once withdrew his retractation, and repeated the
confession which he had originally made, saying that Dechamps had first mentioned the matter to him, that he
mentioned it once only, and that he had never had any
communication on the subject with Joanon on that, or as it
would appear on any other, subject, either before or after

---

[1] II. 38.
[2] I. 47. For the sake of brevity, I omit the case against the two women.
[3] I. 12. [4] II. 71.

the crime. Dechamps, on his second interrogatory, began to confess. He said that Joanon had suggested the crime to him months before it was executed, that he at the time took no notice of the suggestion; that Chretien mentioned it to him about a fortnight before the crime, and that on the evening when it was committed he came to him again and said that the time was come, and that he had made arrangements with Joanon. Dechamps at first refused, but, Chretien insisting, "in a moment of madness" he agreed to go. They found Joanon in the mulberry garden, entered the house, and committed the crime. [1] Dechamps murdered the grandmother with a flint-stone, Chretien the girl, and Joanon the mother. A disgusting controversy arose between Chretien and Dechamps on this subject, each wishing to throw upon the other the imputation of having murdered the girl and committed the rape. Dechamps had the advantage in it, as the state of his health rendered it unlikely that he should have been guilty of the most disgusting part of the offence. [2] In one of his interrogatories, Chretien admitted that this was so. Dechamps declared that Chretien took the money and Joanon the jewels, that he got nothing except 15f. 85c., and that when he asked Chretien to divide the plunder with him the next day, Chretien refused, saying that he might sue him for it if he pleased. Chretien, on the other hand, declared that Joanon took the money. Each declared that the other cut the women's throats with the hatchet.

[3] Joanon declared on his interrogatory that he had nothing to do with the murder, but that he was passing on his way to his own house, and that he saw Chretien Dechamps, and a man named Champion, go into the house together. He also said that he heard Champion make suspicious remarks to Dechamps afterwards.

At the trial, which took place on the 10th of July, and the

---

[1] II. 73.   [2] II. 85.   [3] II. 75.

following days, the three prisoners substantially adhered to these statements, though in the course of the proceedings Joanon retracted the charges against Champion, whose innocence, it is said in the *acte d'accusation*, was established by a satisfactory *alibi*. Little was added to the case by the numerous witnesses who were examined. Most of them repeated the statements they had made before. The three prisoners were condemned to death, and executed in accordance with their sentence.

There can be no doubt as to the guilt of Chretien and Dechamps, though it must be admitted that under our system they would probably have escaped. The only evidence against them was the possession of part of the property, and the discovery of the hatchet in Dechamps's well. The property, however, might have been stolen after the murder, and, as the hatchet was seen at the house of the Gayets after the crime was committed, the fact that Dechamps stole and concealed it, even if proved, would have been no more than ground for suspicion. No stronger case in favour of interrogating a suspected person can be put than one in which he is proved to be in possession of the goods stolen from a murdered man. So far as they were concerned, there can be no doubt that the result was creditable to French procedure; but with regard to Joanon it was very different. Not only was there nothing against him which an English judge would have left to a jury, but it is surely very doubtful whether he was guilty. To the assertions of such wretches as Chretien and Dechamps, no one who knows what a murderer is would pay the faintest attention. The passion for lying which great criminals display is a strange, though a distorted and inverted, testimony to the virtue of truth. It is difficult to assign any logical connection between lying and murder; but a murderer is always a liar. His very confession almost always contains lies, and he generally goes to the gallows with his mouth full of cant and hypocrisy.

Putting aside their evidence, there was really nothing against Joanon, except the expression which he incautiously used to the *garde champêtre,* and his statement about Champion. It would be dangerous to rely upon either of these pieces of evidence. The remark to the *garde champêtre* may have meant anything or nothing. The statement about Champion may have been, and probably was, a mere lie, invented under some foolish notion of saving himself. There are, moreover, considerable improbabilities in the stories of Chretien and Dechamps. [1] There was nothing to show that Joanon even knew Chretien, and as to Dechamps, the only connection between them stated in the *acte d'accusation* was that in the summer of 1859, some months before the crime, Joanon had threshed corn for him and his father. It was added, however, and this was described as " a fact of the highest importance, " throwing great light on the relations of the two prisoners," that Joanon carried on an adulterous intercourse with Dechamps's wife. It is remarkable that Dechamps and Chretien contradicted each other in their confessions. Each said that the other suggested the crime to him as from Joanon. It seems barely credible that he should have sent a message either to or by a man whom he did not know, by or to a man almost equally unknown, on whose honour he had inflicted a deadly injury, to come to help him to commit a murder from which both of them were to receive advantage, whilst he was to receive none. The motives imputed to him were vengeance and lust. As to the first, he must have waited a long time for his vengeance, for the refusal to marry him had taken place some years before, and he had remained in the woman's service for some time afterwards. It seems, too, that he had got over his disappointment, such as it was. In his inter-

---

[1] I. 25.

rogatory on the adjourned trial, the President charged him with various acts of immorality, and then said, "You were "making offers to three young girls at once—Vignat, Benson, "and Tardy. *A.* There is no harm in making offers of "marriage." He admitted immoral conduct with other women. All this is opposed to the notion that he could have cared much for the widow Gayet's refusal, or have entertained that sort of passion for her which would be likely to produce the crime with which he was charged. Besides, if lust were his motive, it is hardly conceivable that he should beforehand associate others with him in the offence. There is an unnatural and hardly conceivable complication of wickedness and folly, which requires strong proof, in the notion of a man's inducing two others to help him in committing a triple murder, in order that he might have the opportunity of committing a rape.

It must also be remarked that there is no necessity for supposing that more than two persons were concerned in the crime. Two modes of murder only were employed, stabbing and striking with a stone, and the stabs might all have been inflicted with the same knife. Two of the women, indeed, were struck with the hatchet, but the hatchet belonged to the house, and both Chretien and Dechamps admitted that this was done after the rest of the crime. There were two rapes, and the presence of a man not sharing in such an infamy would, it might be supposed, have been some sort of restraint to anyone who had about him any traces of human nature. On the other hand, Dechamps was one of the criminals, and the state of his health made it improbable that he should commit that part of the crime, and this would, to some extent, point to the inference that a third person was engaged.

When the whole matter is impartially weighed, the inference seems to be that as against Dechamps and Chretien the case was proved conclusively, for the confession in each case was made circumstantially, with deliberation, and without any particular pressure. It was also persisted in, and was corroborated by the possession of the property of the persons murdered ; to which it must be added, that the two men were friends and neighbours and connections, and that they had the same interest in the perpetration of the crime. As against Joanon, I think there was nothing more than suspicion, and not strong suspicion. Chretien knew that he was suspected, and was thus likely to mention his name in his confession. Dechamps heard the evidence at the first trial, and thus had an opportunity of making his confession agree with Chretien's. He also heard at that trial, possibly for the first time, of the relations between Joanon and his wife, and this would be a strong motive for his wishing to involve him in his destruction.

If it be asked what motive Chretien could have had in the first instance for adding to his other crimes that of murder by false testimony, the answer is supplied by the speech of his advocate, who pressed the jury to find him guilty with extenuating circumstances. After dwelling on the notion that the lives of Joanon, Dechamps, and Dechamps's father, might be set off against those of the three murdered women ; and on the fact that without Chretien's confession it would have been difficult, if not impossible, to convict the others, he said, " If you are without pity, take care lest some " day, under similar circumstances, after a similar crime, " after suspicions, arrests, and accusing circumstances, some " criminal, shaken at first, but confirmed by reflection in his " silence, may say, ' I confess ? [1] I destroy myself deliberately ? " ' Remember Chretien, and what he got by it. No, no con- " ' fessions.' " The possibility that such arguments might be used in his favour, and that the jury might listen to them, is enough to account for any lie that a murderer might tell, if such a circumstance as his lying required to be accounted for at all.

[1] II. 103.

[1] THE CASE OF FRANÇOIS LESNIER.

THE case of François Lesnier is remarkable as an illustration of the provisions of the French *Code d'Instruction Criminelle* as to inconsistent convictions.

In July, 1848, François Lesnier was convicted, with extenuating circumstances, at Bordeaux, of the murder of Claude Gay, and of arson on his house.

On the 16th of March, 1855, Pierre Lespagne was convicted at Bordeaux of the same murder, and Daignaud and Mme. Lespagne of having given false evidence against Lesnier.

These convictions being considered by the Court of Cassation to be contradictory, were both quashed, and a third trial was directed to take place at Toulouse to re-try each of the prisoners on the acts of accusation already found against them.

At the third trial, the act of accusation against Lesnier on the first trial formed part of the proceedings. It constitutes the only record of the evidence on which he was then convicted. Reports of the second and third trials were published at Bordeaux and Toulouse in 1855. In order to give a full account of the proceedings, which, taken as a whole, were extremely curious, I shall translate verbatim the act of accusation of 1848, and describe so much of the trials of 1855 as appears material.

---

[1] See the "Affaire Lesnier," Bordeaux, 1855. It is in two parts, separately paged.

ACT OF ACCUSATION.

The *Procureur-Général* of the Court of Appeal of Bordeaux states that the Chamber of Accusation of the Court of Appeal, on an information made before the tribunal of first instance sitting at Libourne, by an order dated May 24, 1848, has sent Jean and François Lesnier, father and son, before the Court of Assize of the Department of the Gironde, there to be judged according to law.

In execution of the order above dated, in virtue of Article 241 of the Code of Criminal Procedure, the undersigned draws up this act of accusation, and declares that the following facts result from a new examination of the documents of procedure:—

Claude Gay, an old man of seventy, lived alone in an isolated house in the *commune* of Fieu, in a place called Petit-Massé. In the night between the 15th and 16th of November last, a fire broke out in this house. Some inhabitants of the *commune* of Fieu, having perceived the flames, hurried to the scene of the accident. The door of the house and the outside shutter of the window of the single room of which the house consisted were open. The fire had already almost entirely destroyed a lean-to, or shed, built against the back of Gay's room.

Drouhau junior, trying to enter the house, struck his foot against something, which turned out to be the corpse, still warm, of Pierre Claude Gay. It lay on the back, its feet turned towards the threshold, the arms hanging by the side of the body. A plate, containing food, was on the thighs, a spoon was near the right hand, and not far from this spoon was another empty plate.

The fire was soon confined and put out by pulling down the shed which was the seat of it.

The authorities arrived: the facts which they collected proved that Gay had been assassinated, and that, to conceal the traces of the assassination, the criminals had set fire to the house. It was also proved that three or four barrels of wine, which were in the burnt shed, had been previously carried off.

Marks which appeared to have been made by a bloody hand were observed on one of the wooden sides of the bed of Claude Gay. A pruning-knife found in Gay's house had a blood-stain on its extremity.

The head of the deceased rested on a cap (*serre-tête*), also marked with blood.

The doctors—Emery and Soulé—were called to examine the body. They found a wound on the back and side of the head, made by a cutting and striking instrument, and were of opinion that death was caused by it.

Three or four barrels and a tub, which Gay's neighbours knew were in his possession, were not to be seen amongst the ruins of the shed. In the place where the barrels stood no remains of burnt casks were seen, and the ground was dry and firm.

A pine-wood almost touched the house of Gay. The witness Dubreuil, remarked that the broom was laid over a width of about a yard to a point outside the wood, where a pine broken at the root was laid in the same direction as the broom, and where a cart seemed to have been lifted. The marks of this cart could be traced towards the village of Fieu, the ground which borders the public road reaching to the track through the wood. Dubreuil perceived by the form of the foot-marks that the cart had been drawn by cows. These circumstances left no doubt that the barrels had been carried off.

Justice at first did not know who were the guilty persons. It afterwards discovered that the terror which they inspired had for some time put down public clamour. It was only

Lesnier's Case.

in the month of December that Lesnier the father and Lesnier the son, each domiciled in the *commune* of Fieu, and at last pointed out to the investigations of justice, were put under arrest.

On the 21st of September, 1847, Lesnier the son had become the purchaser of the landed property of Claude Gay, for a life annuity of 6f. 75c. a month (5s. 7½d. a month, or 3l. 7s. 6d. a year).

He had not treated Claude Gay with as much care and attention as he ought. The old man complained bitterly of his proceedings to all the persons to whom he talked about his position. In the course of October, 1847, he said to Barbaron, " I thought I should be happy in my last days. Lesnier ought " to take care of me; but instead of trying to prolong my " life he would like to take it away. Ay ! these people are " not men," he added, speaking of the father and son; "they " are tigers."

Another day Gay said to the *curé*, " Lesnier the son lets " me want bread, and does not come to see me." Indeed, such was Gay's poverty, that to buy bread he sold M. Laboinière agricultural tools. On this occasion he said, " Young Lesnier is a rogue, a wretch; he would like to " know I was dead."

On the 9th and 14th of October, Gay said to Pierre Lacoude that he had to do with thorough blackguards (*canaille à pot et à plat*), and that he should like to go to the hospital.

Young Lesnier had asked Barbaron to go and take down Gay's barrels, adding that Gay had given him half his wine on condition that he should pay the expense of the vintage. Barbaron repeated this to Gay, who answered, " I have " never given him my wine ; you see he wants everything " for himself."

It is not out of place to observe, that, on the 12th of

September, at Petit-Massé, young Lesnier came to Barbaron and asked him if he should know Gay's barrels again.

The complaints of Claude Gay were but too well justified by the murderous language of Lesnier against the unfortunate old man. A few days after the sale of the 21st of September, he [" *on*," probably a misprint for "*il* "] said to Jacques Gautey, that when Gay died he would have a debauch. Jacques Gautey observed that Gay would, perhaps, survive him. [1] " No," he answered, " he is as good as dead ; and be-" sides, M. Lamothe, the doctor, has assured me that he will soon die."

He said also to Jacques Magère, " I bet twenty-five francs " that he has not six months to live ; " and to Guillaume Drouhau junior, " I bet he will be dead in three months."

Leonard Constant heard Lesnier say these words : " I am " going to send Gay to the hospital at Bordeaux ; I must beg " one of my friends, a student, to give him a strong dose ; in " fifteen days he will be no more. After his death I will " have a house built at Petit-Massé, and there I will keep " my school."

Afterwards, Jean Bernard, the cartwright, spoke to him of a plan of Gay's to go to the hospital. " He will not go," said young Lesnier ; " I think before long you will have to make " him a coffin."

In the beginning of November, Lesnier said to Mme. Lespagne, that Gay was ill, and that in eight days he would be no more.

Eight days afterwards Gay was assassinated. During the night of the 15th—16th, Jacques Gautey, the sexton, hearing a cry of fire, got up. He tried to wake young Lesnier, who, it is said, sleeps very lightly, and struck three hard blows at his door at different intervals. Lesnier got up before answering ; but, instead of running to the scene of the accident, he

---

[1] " Il est mort là où il est."

waited till several of his neighbours joined him. Jacques Gautey, as sexton, was going to ring the alarm-bell; Lesnier told him he had, perhaps, better wait till the mayor ordered him, adding, however, that he could do as he pleased. The *curé* of Fieu, coming up at the moment, told the sexton to go and ring the alarm-bell.

On the scene of the accident Lesnier took no part in the efforts made to put out the fire. He said to the persons who expressed surprise at his indifference, " What do you want of " me ? I can do no more." He asked a witness if Gay was dead ; and on his replying that he was, observed, " All the " better ; God has been gracious to him." As he went back to the village, Lesnier was in a state of high spirits, which struck everyone who was with him. He played with two girls, Catherine Robin and Séconde Bireau, and made them laugh.

Marguerite Mothe heard him say, " I saw the first fire, but " hearing no one give the alarm I went to bed." He also said that he had executed the deed of the 29th of September with Gay ; that he was sure to be accused of having assassinated him. He begged the sexton to go and fetch his father. " I " want him," he said, " to guide me."

On the morning after the crime, Lesnier the son returned to Petit-Massé. Whilst the *juge de paix* was making investigations, Pierre Reynaud, who was standing by Lesnier, said, on perceiving blood on the chairs, " I think Gay was assas- " sinated. Look, there is blood !" " It is a trifle," said Lesnier. " We are the only people who have seen it, we must say " nothing." The same morning, David Viardon, a *gendarme,* remarked footsteps in a field of Gay's ; and seeing at the same moment the steps of Lesnier, he was struck with their identity with the first.

On the 16th, Lesnier senior came to the place of the accident with his servant, Jean Frappier, who pointed out a bit of rubbish from the fire. His master said, "Touch "nothing, and put your tongue in your pocket."

On the 15th, two witnesses, Guillaume Drouhau and Pierre Reynaud, remarked, at Petit-Massé, spots of blood on the breast of the shirt of Lesnier senior. On the same day Lesnier went to Coutras. On his way, he met Joseph Chenaut, a country agent, to whom he said, "A great mis-"fortune has happened. Gay is dead, and his house is burnt. It seems he must have been into his shed to get wine, set it on fire, and died of fright." As he said this, Joseph Chenaut saw spots of blood on his shirt at the place mentioned.

Jean Frappier declared at first before the judge of instruc-tion that Lesnier, his master, had changed his shirt on his return from Petit-Massé, and before he went to Coutras; but he (Lesnier) had advised him to say so if he was questioned on the subject. Besides, Lesnier himself admitted that he had not changed his linen. We must add this important fact, that the three witnesses agree on the number of the marks of blood, on their place on the shirt, and on their extent.

After the burial of Gay, several persons met at young Lesnier's. Lesnier, the father, and Lesnier, the son, talked together in a low voice near the fire. Two witnesses heard the father say to the son, "The great misfortune is that all "was not burnt; the trial would be at an end. You did right "in putting the money into Gay's chest. You see, my boy, "that all has happened as I told you. I know as much "of it as these gentlemen." A moment after old Lesnier went out.

Young Lesnier came to Barbaron, and said, " A man has "gone to my father, and said this and that to him, and "has invited him, on the strength of his investigations, to "summons so-and-so. My father has quieted him. I was

" unwell yesterday ; I am well to-day. Do you know this is
" a matter which might get my head cut off ? "

Lesnier senior and junior tried to misdirect the suspicions
of justice by turning them upon an honourable man. They
already began to point him out, as they have themselves
admitted, by the obscure and lying remarks just mentioned.

After the crime, Lesnier senior asked Magère what he
thought of the affair of Gay ? He kept silent. " It must,"
said old Lesnier, " be either the Lesniers themselves or else
" their enemies who have done the job." Lesnier junior at
the same time spoke in the same way to Jacques Santez.
" Our enemies," he said, " have assassinated Gay and have
" burnt his house to compromise us."

Lesnier junior also said to Lamothe, " The rascals who
" killed him knew that I had granted him an annuity :
" thinking to destroy me they killed him : but I have just
" come from Libourne, whither I was summoned. They are
" on the track of the culprits. Ah, the rogues, they will be
" found out ! " On another occasion young Lesnier pointed
out clearly the person whom he wished to submit to the
action of the law. He told Guillaume Canbroche and Lagarde
that, on the evening of Gay's murder, Lespagne had brought
wine to St. Médard, and that it was supposed that this wine
belonged to Gay. It is needless to observe that Lesnier
senior and junior alone accused Lespagne, and that all those
whose suspicions they tried to rouse vigorously repelled their
imprudent accusations.

Lesnier expressed himself thus on the assassination of Gay,
in the presence of Mme. Lespagne : " Bah ! if I had killed a
" man, I should not care a curse. I belong to the Government
" [he was Government schoolmaster]. I should be pardoned."

Another time, Lesnier said to Michael Lafon that he could
kill a man and be pardoned ; that the Government to whom
he belonged protected him.

After his arrest he said to the brigadier (Viardon), that in some days the barrels would be brought back empty to Gay's house.

After Gay's assassination, Lesnier senior and junior appeared preoccupied and troubled before several witnesses.

The evidence which we have described was assuredly very weighty. However, a witness of capital importance, Mme. Lespagne, with whom young Lesnier publicly held criminal relations, had not at first revealed all that she had learnt. Pressed by the mayor of the *commune* of Fieu, and by several persons, to tell the truth without reserve, she presented herself twice before the judge of instruction, and declared the following facts.

Terror had prevented her from speaking. She was not ignorant that the Lesniers were in prison, but she feared their return. One day, profiting by the absence of her husband, young Lesnier forced her to comply with his criminal wishes. Afterwards he ordered her to poison her husband in these terms :— "You must go to an apothecary, you must buy " arsenic, and, to avoid your husband's suspicions, you must " first eat your own soup, and then put his into your dish, in " which you will have put the poison."

Some time after he compelled her to leave her husband's house. He wished to force her to sue for judicial separation, and to make to him (Lesnier) a donation of all she possessed.

One day he was talking with Mme. Lespagne of what he intended to do for her. She said, "You are much embar- " rassed ; you have many people to support ; you will have " a bad bargain of Gay's land." "Ah, the rogue !" said Lesnier, " he won't embarrass me long."

In the beginning of November, Mme. Lespagne was think- ing of the misery which threatened her. Lesnier junior, to reassure her, said, " I will have Gay's house rebuilt, and you

" shall go and live with my father and mother." " What will
" you do with Gay ? " answered Mme. Lespagne. " Gay ? he
" won't be alive in eight days. I'll teach him to do without
" bread. I'll make him turn his eyes as he never turned
" them yet."

There was a report that Gay was selling his furniture.
Mme. Lespagne told Lesnier of it, who said, " Gay is an old
" rogue ! It appears that he won't go to the hospital. He
" will see what will happen to him." " Well, what will you
" do with him ? " said Mme. Lespagne. " I will kill him,"
said Lesnier in a low voice.

He said another time to this woman, " Gay is an old good-
" for-nothing rascal. My father told me that if he could not
" get him out one way he would another."

Mme. Lespagne said, " What do you want to do with the
" old man ? " " He is not strong," said Lesnier ; " a good blow
" with a hammer will soon lay him on the ground." " The
" man, then, is very much in your way ? " said Mme. Lespagne.
" He will see—he will see," said Lesnier, shaking his head.

Mme. Lespagne had sold bread to Gay to the value of 43f.,
which he owed her. Gay agreed, on the 16th of November,
to give her his wine in payment. Mme. Lespagne mentioned
this to Lesnier junior, who said to her, " Don't count on the
" wine to pay yourself; it won't stay long where it is. You
" can scratch that debt out of your book ; you will never have
" anything." He added, as if to console Mme. Lespagne, " I
" will make up half a barrel for you."

In fact, on the 14th of November, at four in the afternoon,
Mme. Lespagne was in front of her father's house. Lesnier
junior came along the road, and she asked him where he was
going, " I am going to Grave-d'Or, to settle with my father
" about carrying off Gay's wine." She asked what teamster
would carry the wine. " I do not want a teamster. Has not
" my father a cart and cows ? " She observed that it would be

difficult for him to drive the cart near to Gay's house. He added that he and his father would roll the barrels through Chatard's pine wood, and pointed out to her the road which he would follow with the cart. Young Lesnier had already told the same witness several times that his father and he were to carry the wine to Grave-d'Or.

Next day, towards seven in the evening, Mme. Lespagne again saw young Lesnier on the footpath which goes to Petit-Massé. Mme. Lespagne was in front of her father's house, which is by the side of the path. In passing by her Lesnier said, " I am very tired ! I am waiting for my father, " and he does not come " He then went towards Gay's house.

On the morning of the 16th, at six or seven, this witness went to get water at M. Chatard's well. She had to pass before the house of Lesnier junior ; she saw him on the threshold. His arms were crossed, and his face was pale and sad. He had *sabots* on his feet, and they were spotted with blood. In the course of the day, Mme. Lespagne went to Petit-Massé. Lesnier was there ; he wore the same *sabots*, but she no longer saw the marks which she had observed some hours before.

The same day, Lesnier junior told Mme. Lespagne that he had been the first to see the fire, but that, hearing no noise, he had called no one, but gone into his own house and gone to bed.

The same day, again, Mme. Lespagne asked young Lesnier why neither he nor his father had approached the corpse. " We had no need," said he, " to approach it ; we had knocked " it about quite enough."

Three days after the crime, young Lesnier met Mme. Lespagne near her own house. He seemed anxious. She asked him what was the matter. He said, " I have passed " two bad nights, but the last has been better, I was afraid

" they should look for Gay's wine; but I think now the " search is given up, and I am less anxious."

She remarked that the inquiry was not over. " That be " damned," said he. " Let them do what they like. I don't " answer for Gay. Besides, they will find no evidence." The day he came to this woman, who had seen him in a ditch near the church of Fieu, he asked her if she was summoned. " Before you give your evidence I want to speak to you. I " cannot speak to you here, for we are seen." (In fact, Pellerin, a mason, was at work on the roof of the *curé's* house.) " No one " must hear what I have to say." Having a fowl of his son's, old Lesnier said, " Take that fowl and bring it to my house."

Eight or ten days before his arrest, young Lesnier came to Mme. Lespagne, and giving her a piece of soft cotton-stuff, said, " You will be summoned; and take care not to mention " my name, and speak much of your husband."

Lastly, on another occasion young Lesnier expressed in these terms the hope he had to escape the danger of his trial : "I am now comfortable ; I shall get out of it." After some other remarks, Lesnier was, for a moment, silent; then he continued : " Don't repeat my confidences. You would " repent of it ; you don't know what would happen."

Such, shortly, are the most important points in the crushing evidence of Mme. Lespagne.

Old and young Lesnier denied all the charges made against them. They pretended, before the authorities, that the assassination of Gay and the burning of his house had been committed by enemies who had resolved to destroy them ; that the witnesses who deposed against them were bought, or gave their evidence from malice.

Young Lesnier went so far as to deny his relations with Mme. Lespagne, in the face of public notoriety. The two prisoners are surrounded by a reputation of malice, which makes them feared in the district where they live. This reputation is justified by the murderous remarks which they have made of the *curé* of the *commune* of Fieu, of Drouhau and Lespagne, a landowner,—remarks attested by trustworthy witnesses. Daignaud was stopped at night on a public road by two persons. He fully recognized young Lesnier; he only thought he recognized his father.

After the arrest of the two prisoners, the wife of old Lesnier announced that she received letters from her son and her husband every day; that both were going to return; that they knew the witnesses who were examined against them; and that on their return those witnesses would repent of it.

This terror which old and young Lesnier tried to inspire had obviously no other object than to prevent the manifestation of a truth which must be fatal to them.

In consequence, Lesnier the elder and the younger are accused—

(1) Of having, together and in concert, fraudulently carried off from the place called Petit-Massé, in the *commune* of Fieu, on the 15th of November, 1847, a certain quantity of wine, to the prejudice of Claude Gay.

(2) Of having, during the night between the 15th and 16th of November, wilfully set fire to the house inhabited by and belonging to the said Claude Gay.

(3) Of having, under the same circumstances and at the same place, wilfully put to death the said Claude Gay.

Of having committed this *meurtre* with premeditation— the homicide having preceded, accompanied, or followed the crimes of theft and arson qualified as above.

On which the jury will have to decide whether the prisoners are guilty.

Done at the bar (*parquet*) of the Court of Appeal, the 4th of June, 1848.

The *Procureur-Général*,
(Signed) TROPLONG.

I have translated this document in full, both because it is the only report of the trial of 1848, and in order to give a complete specimen of an act of accusation.

The evidence which it states is of the weakest description possible; for, with exceptions too trifling to mention, it consists entirely of reports of conversations, of which all the important ones rested upon the evidence of single witnesses Not a single fact was proved in the case which it is possible to represent upon any theory as having formed part either of the preparation for or execution of the crime, or as conduct caused by it and connected with it. The whole case rested, in fact, on the evidence of Mme. Lespagne, who was a woman of notoriously bad character, and who never opened her mouth on the subject till Lesnier was in prison. Daignaud's evidence as to the robbery by the two Lesniers—which, according to English law, would have been irrelevant and inadmissible—is introduced at the end of the act of accusation as a sort of make-weight. The act says nothing of the occasion on which either it or the evidence of Mme. Lespagne was given. The vital importance of these circumstances and the iniquity of suppressing all mention of them, appears from the subsequent proceedings.

Lesnier the father was acquitted; Lesnier the son was convicted, with extenuating circumstances—which are to be found in abundance in the evidence, but nowhere else—and sentenced to the galleys for life. His father, dissatisfied with the conviction, made every effort to obtain new information on the subject, and, in the summer of 1854, he succeeded in doing so. The result of his inquiries was, that Lespagne was accused of the murder and arson; Mme. Lespagne and Daignaud of perjury in relation to the Lesniers. Lespagne was also accused of subornation of perjury. The trial lasted for a long time, and a great mass of evidence was produced, which it is not worth while to state. The chief points in the evidence are enumerated in the act of accusation, which adds to the statements made in the act of accusation against Lesnier several facts of the utmost importance, and which must have been known to the authorities at the time of the first trial, but which they did not think fit to put forward.

The most important of these points related to the manner in which Mme. Lespagne made her revelations. Her first statement was made on the 20th of December, 1847, the next on the 4th of January, 1848, the next on the 1st of February, the next on the 10th. She had been examined before, and had then said nothing important. On each occasion she brought out a little more than the time before, and reserved for the last the strongest of her statements—that Lesnier had said that he and his father had no occasion to approach the body because they had "knocked it about enough already." It also was stated that, before the trial of Lesnier, Mme. Lespagne was reconciled to her husband. "She had been driven " by her husband from his home," says the act. "She returned " after the arrest of young Lesnier. Then began the series " of her lying declarations against the Lesniers. [1] This coin- " cidence alone is worth a whole demonstration." This remark is perfectly just, but it might and ought to have been made seven years before. If, instead of being in solitary confinement undergoing interrogatories, Lesnier had had an attorney to prepare his defence, and counsel to cross-examine the witnesses on the other side, the infamy of the woman would have been clearly proved. As soon as the least inquiry was made, it appeared that her story about Lesnier's seducing her by violence was ridiculously false. Various eye-witnesses deposed to acts of the greatest indecency and provocation on her part towards him. She admitted, as soon as she was strictly examined on the subject, that all she had said was false; she said that she had been suborned to say what she said by the

[1] I. 40.

curé of the parish, who was charged by Lesnier with courting his sister, and who made up what she was to say, and taught it her like a lesson, and threatened to refuse her the sacrament if she did not do as he wished. She also said that her husband had confessed his guilt to her. Daignaud admitted that his story about being robbed by the Lesniers was altogether false; and he added that his reason for telling it was that he owed Lespagne fifteen francs, and that Lespagne forgave him the debt, in consideration of his evidence.

These retractations appear to have been obtained by collecting a variety of remarks, made partly by Mme. Lespagne, and partly by other persons, implying that Lesnier was innocent and Lespagne guilty. A young man, in particular, of the name of Malefille, who lived with Lespagne at the time of the murder, and died before the second trial, was said to have said that Lespagne and his brother-in-law, Beaumaine, had committed the crime, that Lespagne was to take Gay's wine for a debt of 45f., that there was a dispute about one of the barrels, that Gay resisted its removal, and that Lespagne thereupon struck him a fatal blow on the head with a hammer—an account consistent with the position of the wounds and other circumstances. Lespagne was seen, with his brother-in-law and another man, taking wine along the road on the day after the murder; and evidence was given of a considerable number of broken hints, and more or less suspicious remarks, by his wife and himself. With regard to Daignaud's evidence, several witnesses proved an *alibi* on behalf of each of the Lesniers.

Lespagne was arrested and charged with the murder. The case against him rested on the evidence of his wife and Daignaud. His wife was an adulteress, a perjured woman, and had attempted to commit murder by perjury. Daignaud, according to his own account, had agreed to swear away another man's life for 15f. The evidence in itself was utterly worthless. The way in which the prisoner was dealt with gives an instructive illustration of the practical working of the French criminal procedure. He was arrested, and after a time brought to confess. On his trial he retracted his confession, declaring that it had been obtained from him by violence. This was treated as an impossibility, but the account given by the witnesses is as follows:—"On the "fourth day," said M. Nadal, [1] Commissary of Police, "Les-"pagne was interrogated. The *Procureur-Impérial* informed "him of the numerous charges against him. He vigorously "denied for more than an hour that he was guilty. At last "disconcerted by the evidence collected against him, he "asked me to go and find his relations, as he would tell all "before them. I went to his house for the purpose, but I "had hardly gone fifty paces before the brigadier of *gen-*"*darmerie* ran after me and said it was no use, as he had "confessed everything." After some further evidence, the *Procureur-Général* asked : "Is it true that the *Procureur-*"*Impérial* threatened Lespagne with the scaffold ? *A.* Alto-"gether untrue. On the contrary, they always tried to coax "him (*prendre par le douceur*). The [2] *Procureur-Impérial* "confined himself to begging Lespagne to tell the truth, and "confess all if he was guilty ; *he made him understand that* "*if he kept silence he exposed himself to having his conduct* "*judged more severely.*" Another *gendarme*, Bernadou, was asked, "The accused says that he made these confessions "because he was frightened ? [3] *A.* No one threatened him ; " *on the contrary, they spoke of his family, and told him that* " *the only way to obtain some indulgence was to tell the whole* "*truth.*" The degree of pressure which is considered legiti-mate under this system is curiously exemplified by these answers, and by the fact that when Lespagne retracted his

[1] I. 78. [2] I. 80. [3] I. 124.

confessions, his advocate, the *juge de paix*, his brother-in-law, and the President, all in open court begged Lespagne to confess. He refused to do so, but was convicted, and sentenced to twenty years of the galleys.

The result of this conviction was that a third trial took place, which was a repetition of the second. During the interval fresh efforts were made to obtain a confession from Lespagne. They are thus described by the *juge de paix* who made them :—[1] "As *juge de paix*, and on account of " the influence which I thought I ought to exert over the "accused, when I saw that he constantly retracted, during " the hearings of the 12th, 13th, and 14th, the confessions " which he had made at the time of his arrest, I thought it " my duty to visit him in prison, to get him to tell the truth. " M. Princeteau, his advocate, who had preceded me, had in " vain tried to bring him to do so. I found him immovable " myself. Soon after, I told his relations to try new efforts " for this purpose, and I went with them and M. Princeteau " again to the prison. Being then pressed very closely, " he at last said, "Well, yes, you will have it; I shall lose " my head ; I am forced to own that I was the involuntary "cause of his death. I pushed him, he fell backwards, and " his head must have struck upon some farming tool or other, " which made his wound."

The degree of terror and prejudice which is produced by the zeal of *gendarmes* and the other local agents of the central power—that is, by the practical working of the inquisitorial theory of criminal law—is well shown by the fact that all the witnesses who proved the perjury of Daignaud, on being asked why they had not come forward at the first trial, answered, that they were afraid because the guilt of Lesnier was the established theory. [2] One man,

[1] II. 33.　　　　　　　　　　[2] I. 90.

who proved an *alibi* on behalf of old Lesnier, as to the
robbery on Daignaud, was asked, " Why did not you speak
"of this in 1848? *A.* I was afraid, because I thought I
"should be alone." Another [1] said, " I was afraid because I
"was alone, and everyone said that Lesnier was guilty." The
practical application of the system is described with great
point and vigour by the *Procureur-Général,* in his summing
up to the jury. His language supplies a better vindication
of the practical sagacity of many of the rules and principles
of English criminal procedure than the most elaborate
arguments on the subject. After describing the way in
which Lespagne was connected with the mayor, the *curé,*
and the other important personages of the *commune,*
he says : —

" You understand now, gentlemen of the jury, what passed
"in 1847. Justice pursued its usual routine (*ses errements*
"*ordinaires*). It did what it inevitably must do when it
"informs itself of a crime. As it has not the gift of
"divination, it took its first instructions from the local
"authorities, influenced by their impressions, and, circum-
"vented and abused by them, it has unhappily allowed
"itself to be drawn into their ways of thinking. To its eyes
"as theirs, the evidence against Lesnier came to light, the
" guilt of Lespagne remained in the shade.

" In this state of affairs, and in this state of feeling, there
"suddenly appeared two crushing depositions against Lesnier,
"received with a sort of acclamation by the factitious opinion
"of the country, and, combined with detestable skill, they
"easily surprised the confidence of the judge."

On his second trial, Lespagne was sentenced to the galleys
for life. He made other confessions, which appear more
trustworthy than those already mentioned, but, on the whole,

[1] I. 88.

his guilt was not much more satisfactorily proved than that of Lesnier. It would be tedious to enter minutely into the evidence in this case. . Its value lies in the illustration which it affords of the spirit of the inquisitorial system of procedure.

INDEX OF CASES AND STATUTES CITED.

CASES CITED.

STATUTES CITED.

GENERAL INDEX.

THE END.

RICHARD CLAY AND SONS, LIMITED,
LONDON AND BUNGAY.

Catalogue of Books

PUBLISHED BY

MACMILLAN AND CO.

BEDFORD STREET, COVENT GARDEN, LONDON

February, 1890.

ABBOT (Francis).—SCIENTIFIC THEISM. Crown 8vo. 7s. 6d.

ABBOTT (Rev. E. A.).—A SHAKESPEARIAN GRAMMAR. Extra fcp. 8vo. 6s.

—— CAMBRIDGE SERMONS. 8vo. 6s.

—— OXFORD SERMONS. 8vo. 7s. 6d.

—— FRANCIS BACON: AN ACCOUNT OF HIS LIFE AND WORKS. 8vo. 14s.

ABBOTT (Rev. E. A.) and RUSHBROOKE (W. G.).—THE COMMON TRADITION OF THE SYNOPTIC GOSPELS, IN THE TEXT OF THE REVISED VERSION. Crown 8vo. 3s. 6d.

ACLAND (Sir H. W.).—THE ARMY MEDICAL SCHOOL. An Address delivered at Netley Hospital. 8vo. 1s.

ACTS OF THE APOSTLES. The Greek Text of Drs. Westcott and Hort. With Notes by T. E. PAGE, M.A. Fcp. 8vo. 3s. 6d.

ADAMS (Sir F. O.) and CUNNINGHAM (C.)—THE SWISS CONFEDERATION. 8vo. 14s.

ADDISON.—By W. J. COURTHOPE. Crown 8vo. 1s. 6d.; sewed, 1s.

ADDISON, SELECTIONS FROM. Chosen and Edited by J. R. GREEN. 18mo. 4s. 6d.

ÆSCHYLUS.—PERSÆ. Edited by A. O. PRICKARD, M.A. Fcp. 8vo. 3s. 6d.

—— EUMENIDES. With Notes and Introduction, by BERNARD DRAKE, M.A. 8vo. 5s.

—— PROMETHEUS VINCTUS. With Introduction, Notes, and Vocabulary, by Rev H. M. STEPHENSON, M.A. 18mo. 1s. 6d.

—— THE "SEVEN AGAINST THEBES." With Introduction, Commentary, and Translation, by A. W. VERRALL, Litt.D. 8vo. 7s. 6d.

—— THE "SEVEN AGAINST THEBES." With Introduction and Notes, by A. W. VERRALL and M. A. BAYFIELD. Fcp. 8vo. 3s. 6d.

—— AGAMEMNON. With Introduction, Commentary, and Translation, by A. W. VERRALL, Litt.D. 8vo. 12s.

—— THE SUPPLICES. Text, Introduction, Notes, Commentary, and Translation, by Prof. T. G. TUCKER. 8vo. 10s. 6d.

ÆSOP—CALDECOTT.—SOME OF Æsop's FABLES, with Modern Instances, shown in Designs by RANDOLPH CALDECOTT. 4to. 5s.

AGASSIZ (Louis): HIS LIFE AND CORRESPONDENCE. Edited by ELIZABETH CARY AGASSIZ. 2 vols. Crown 8vo. 18s.

AINGER (Rev. Alfred).—SERMONS PREACHED IN THE TEMPLE CHURCH. Extra fcp. 8vo. 6s.

AINGER (Rev. A.).—CHARLES LAMB. Crn. 8vo. 1s. 6d.; sewed 1s.

AIRY (Sir G. B.).—TREATISE ON THE ALGEBRAICAL AND NUMERICAL THEORY OF ERRORS OF OBSERVATION AND THE COMBINATION OF OBSERVATIONS. Cr. 8vo. 6s. 6d.

—— POPULAR ASTRONOMY. With Illustrations. Fcp. 8vo. 4s. 6d.

—— AN ELEMENTARY TREATISE ON PARTIAL DIFFERENTIAL EQUATIONS. Cr. 8vo. 5s. 6d.

—— ON SOUND AND ATMOSPHERIC VIBRATIONS. With the Mathematical Elements of Music. 2nd Edition. Crown 8vo. 9s.

—— GRAVITATION. An Elementary Explanation of the Principal Perturbations in the Solar System. 2nd Edition. Cr. 8vo. 7s. 6d.

AITKEN (Mary Carlyle).—SCOTTISH SONG. A Selection of the Choicest Lyrics of Scotland. 18mo. 4s. 6d.

AITKEN (Sir W.).—THE GROWTH OF THE RECRUIT AND YOUNG SOLDIER. With a view to the selection of "Growing Lads" for the Army, and a Regulated System of Training for Recruits. Crown 8vo. 8s. 6d.

ALBEMARLE (Earl of).—FIFTY YEARS OF MY LIFE. 3rd Ed., revised. Cr. 8vo. 7s. 6d.

ALDIS (Mary Steadman).—THE GREAT GIANT ARITHMOS. A MOST ELEMENTARY ARITHMETIC. Illustrated. Globe 8vo. 2s. 6d.

ALEXANDER (C. F.).—THE SUNDAY BOOK OF POETRY FOR THE YOUNG. 18mo. 4s. 6d.

ALEXANDER (T.) and THOMPSON (A.).—ELEMENTARY APPLIED MECHANICS. Part II. Transverse Stress; upwards of 150 Diagrams, and 200 Examples carefully worked out. Crown 8vo. 10s. 6d.

ALLBUTT (Dr. T. Clifford).—ON THE USE OF THE OPHTHALMOSCOPE. 8vo. 15s.

ALLEN (Grant).—ON THE COLOURS OF FLOWERS, as Illustrated in the British Flora. With Illustrations. Crown 8vo. 3s. 6d.

ALLINGHAM (William).—THE BALLAD BOOK. 18mo. 4s. 6d.

AMERICAN JOURNAL OF PHILOLOGY. Edited by BASIL L. GILDERSLEEVE. Quarterly Parts. 4s. 6d. each.

AMIEL (Henri Frederic).—THE JOURNAL INTIME. Translated by Mrs. HUMPHRY WARD. 2nd Edition. Crown 8vo. 6s.

AN ANCIENT CITY, AND OTHER POEMS. Extra fcp. 8vo. 6s.

AN AUTHOR'S LOVE. Being the Unpublished Letters of PROSPER MÉRIMÉE'S "Inconnue." 2 vols. Ex. cr. 8vo. 12s.

ANDERSON (A.).—BALLADS AND SONNETS. Crown 8vo. 5s.

ANDERSON (Dr. McCall).—LECTURES ON CLINICAL MEDICINE. Illustrated. 8vo. 10s. 6d.

ANDERSON (L.).—LINEAR PERSPECTIVE AND MODEL DRAWING. Royal 8vo. 2s.

ANDOCIDES.—DE MYSTERIIS. Edited by W. J. HICKIE, M.A. Fcp. 8vo. 2s. 6d.

ANDREWS (Dr. Thomas), THE SCIENTIFIC PAPERS OF THE LATE. With a Memoir by Profs. TAIT and CRUM BROWN. 8vo. 18s.

ANGLO-SAXON LAW : ESSAYS ON. Med. 8vo. 18s.

ANTONINUS, MARCUS AURELIUS.— BOOK IV. OF THE MEDITATIONS. The Greek Text Revised. With Translation and Commentary, by HASTINGS CROSSLEY, M.A. 8vo. 6s.

APPLETON (T. G.).—A NILE JOURNAL. Illustrated by EUGENE BENSON. Cr. 8vo. 6s.

ARATUS.—THE SKIES AND WEATHER FORECASTS OF ARATUS. Translated by E. POSTE M.A. Crown 8vo. 3s. 6d.

ARIOSTO.—PALADIN AND SARACEN. Stories from Ariosto. By H. C. HOLLWAY-CALTHROP. Illustrated. Crown 8vo. 6s.

ARISTOPHANES.—THE BIRDS. Translated into English Verse, with Introduction, Notes, and Appendices. By Prof. B. H. KENNEDY, D.D. Crown 8vo. 6s.

—— HELP NOTES FOR THE USE OF STUDENTS. Crown 8vo. 1s. 6d.

ARISTOTLE ON FALLACIES; OR, THE SOPHISTICI ELENCHI. With Translation and Notes by E. POSTE, M.A. 8vo. 8s. 6d.

ARISTOTLE.—THE FIRST BOOK OF THE METAPHYSICS OF ARISTOTLE. Translated into English Prose, with marginal Analysis and Summary of each Chapter. By a Cambridge Graduate. 8vo. 5s.

—— THE POLITICS. Translated with an Analysis and Critical Notes by J. E. C. WELLDON, M.A. 2nd Edition. 10s. 6d.

—— THE RHETORIC. By the same Translator. Crown 8vo. 7s. 6d.

ARMY PRELIMINARY EXAMINATION, Specimens of Papers set at the, 1882-88. With Answers to the Mathematical Questions. Crown 8vo. 3s. 6d.

ARNOLD (Matthew).—THE COMPLETE POETICAL WORKS. New Edition. 3 vols. Crown 8vo. 7s. 6d. each.—Vol. I. Early Poems, Narrative Poems, and Sonnets. —Vol. II. Lyric and Elegiac Poems.—Vol. III. Dramatic and Later Poems.

—— ESSAYS IN CRITICISM. 6th Edition. Crown 8vo. 9s.

—— ESSAYS IN CRITICISM. Second Series. With an Introductory Note by LORD COLERIDGE. Crown 8vo. 7s. 6d.

—— ISAIAH XL.—LXVI. WITH THE SHORTER PROPHECIES ALLIED TO IT. With Notes Crown 8vo. 5s.

ARNOLD (Matthew).—ISAIAH OF JERUSALEM. In the Authorised English Version, with Introduction, Corrections, and Notes. Crown 8vo. 4s. 6d.

—— A BIBLE-READING FOR SCHOOLS. The Great Prophecy of Israel's Restoration (Isaiah xl.-lxvi.) Arranged and Edited for Young Learners. 4th Edition. 18mo. 1s.

—— HIGHER SCHOOLS AND UNIVERSITIES IN GERMANY. Crown 8vo. 6s.

—— SELECTED POEMS. 18mo. 4s. 6d.

—— POEMS OF WORDSWORTH. Chosen and Edited by MATTHEW ARNOLD. With Portrait. 18mo. 4s. 6d. Large Paper Edition. 9s.

—— POETRY OF BYRON. Chosen and arranged by MATTHEW ARNOLD. With Vignette. 18mo. 4s. 6d. Large Paper Edition. 9s.

—— DISCOURSES IN AMERICA. Cr. 8vo. 4s. 6d.

—— JOHNSON'S LIVES OF THE POETS, THE SIX CHIEF LIVES FROM. With MACAULAY'S "Life of Johnson." With Preface and Notes by MATTHEW ARNOLD. Crown 8vo. 4s. 6d.

—— EDMUND BURKE'S LETTERS, TRACTS AND SPEECHES ON IRISH AFFAIRS. Edited by MATTHEW ARNOLD. Crown 8vo. 6s.

—— REPORTS ON ELEMENTARY SCHOOLS, 1852-82. Edited by the Right Hon. Sir FRANCIS SANDFORD, K.C.B. Cr. 8vo. 3s. 6d.

ARNOLD (T.)—THE SECOND PUNIC WAR. By the late THOMAS ARNOLD, D.D. Edited by WILLIAM T. ARNOLD, M.A. With Eight Maps. Crown 8vo. 8s. 6d.

ARNOLD (W. T.).—THE ROMAN SYSTEM OF PROVINCIAL ADMINISTRATION TO THE ACCESSION OF CONSTANTINE THE GREAT. Crown 8vo. 6s.

ARRIAN.—SELECTIONS. Edited by J. BOND, M.A., and A. S. WALPOLE, M.A. 18mo. 1s. 6d.

ART AT HOME SERIES. Edited by W. J. LOFTIE, B.A.

MUSIC IN THE HOUSE. By JOHN HULLAH. Fourth Edition. Crown 8vo. 2s. 6d.

THE DINING-ROOM. By Mrs. LOFTIE. With Illustrations. 2nd Ed. Cr. 8vo. 2s. 6d.

THE BEDROOM AND BOUDOIR. By Lady BARKER. With numerous Illustrations. 2nd Edition. Crown 8vo. 2s. 6d.

AMATEUR THEATRICALS. By WALTER H. POLLOCK and LADY POLLOCK. Illustrated by KATE GREENAWAY. Crown 8vo. 2s. 6d.

NEEDLEWORK. By ELIZABETH GLAISTER. Illustrated. Crown 8vo. 2s. 6d.

THE LIBRARY. By ANDREW LANG, with a Chapter on English Illustrated Books, by AUSTIN DOBSON. Crown 8vo. 3s. 6d.

ARNAULD, ANGELIQUE. By FRANCES MARTIN. Crown 8vo. 4s. 6d.

ARTEVELDE—ASHLEY.—JAMES AND PHILIP VAN ARTEVELDE. By W. J. ASHLEY, B.A. Crown 8vo. 6s.

ATKINSON (J. Beavington).—AN ART TOUR TO NORTHERN CAPITALS OF EUROPE. 8vo. 12s.

ATTIC ORATORS, SELECTIONS FROM THE. Antiphon, Andocides, Lysias, Isocrates, and Isaeus. Edited, with Notes, by Prof. R. C. JEBB, Litt.D. 2nd Edition. Fcp. 8vo. 6s.

ATTWELL (H.)—A BOOK OF GOLDEN THOUGHTS. 18mo. 4s. 6d.

AULUS GELLIUS (STORIES FROM). Edited by Rev. G. H. NALL, M.A. 18mo. 1s. 6d.

AUSTIN (Alfred).—SAVONAROLA: A TRAGEDY. Crown 8vo. 7s. 6d.

—— SOLILOQUIES IN SONG. Crown 8vo. 6s.

—— AT THE GATE OF THE CONVENT; AND OTHER POEMS. Crown 8vo. 6s.

—— PRINCE LUCIFER. Crown 8vo. 6s.

—— MADONNA'S CHILD. Crown 4to. 3s. 6d.

—— THE TOWER OF BABEL. Crown 4to. 9s.

—— ROME OR DEATH. Crown 4to. 9s.

—— THE GOLDEN AGE. Crown 8vo. 5s.

—— THE SEASON. Crown 8vo. 5s.

—— LOVE'S WIDOWHOOD: AND OTHER POEMS. Crown 8vo. 6s.

—— THE HUMAN TRAGEDY. Cr. 8vo. 7s. 6d.

AUTENRIETH (Dr. G.)—AN HOMERIC DICTIONARY. Translated from the German, by R. P. KEEP, Ph.D. Crown 8vo. 6s.

AWDRY (Frances).—THE STORY OF A FELLOW SOLDIER. (A Life of Bishop Patteson for the Young.) With a Preface by CHARLOTTE M. YONGE. Globe 8vo. 2s.

BABRIUS. With Introductory Dissertations, Critical Notes, Commentary, and Lexicon, by W. G. RUTHERFORD, LL.D. 8vo. 12s. 6d.

"BACCHANTE." THE CRUISE OF H.M.S. "BACCHANTE," 1879-1882. Compiled from the private Journals, Letters and Note-books of PRINCE ALBERT VICTOR and PRINCE GEORGE OF WALES. With Maps, Plans, Illustrations, and Additions, by the Rev. JOHN N. DALTON, Canon of Windsor. 2 vols. Medium 8vo. 2l. 12s. 6d.

BACON.—By the Very Rev. Dean CHURCH, Globe 8vo. 5s.; Crn. 8vo. 1s. 6d. : swd., 1s.

BACON'S ESSAYS AND COLOURS OF GOOD AND EVIL With Notes and Glossarial Index, by W. ALDIS WRIGHT, M.A. With Vignette. 18mo. 4s. 5d.

—— ESSAYS. Edited by Prof. F. G. SELBY, M.A. Globe 8vo. 3s. 6d.

BACON (Francis).—AN ACCOUNT OF HIS LIFE AND WORKS. By E. A. ABBOTT. 8vo. 14s.

BAINES (Rev. Edward).—SERMONS: Preached mainly to Country Congregations. With a Preface and Memoir, by ALFRED BARRY, D.D., Bishop of Sydney. Cr. 8vo. 6s.

BAKER (Sir Samuel White).—ISMAILIA. A Narrative of the Expedition to Central Africa for the Suppression of the Slave Trade, organised by ISMAIL, Khedive of Egypt. Crown 8vo. 6s.

—— THE NILE TRIBUTARIES OF ABYSSINIA, AND THE SWORD HUNTERS OF THE HAMRAN ARABS. Crown 8vo. 6s.

—— THE ALBERT N'VANZA GREAT BASIN OF THE NILE AND EXPLORATION OF THE NILE SOURCES. Crown 8vo. 6s.

—— CYPRUS AS I SAW IT IN 1879. 8vo. 12s. 6d.

BAKER (Sir Samuel White).—CAST UP BY THE SEA : OR, THE ADVENTURES OF NED GRAY. With Illustrations by HUARD. Crown 8vo. 6s.

—— THE EGYPTIAN QUESTION. Letters to the Times and the Pall Mall Gazette. 8vo. 2s.

—— TRUE TALES FOR MY GRANDSONS. Illustrated by W. J. HENNESSY. Cr. 8vo. 7s. 6d.

BALFOUR (The Right Hon. A. J.)—A DEFENCE OF PHILOSOPHIC DOUBT. Being an Essay on the Foundations of Belief. 8vo. 12s.

BALFOUR (Prof. F. M.).—ELASMOBRANCH FISHES. With Plates. 8vo. 21s.

—— COMPARATIVE EMBRYOLOGY. With Illustrations. 2 vols. 2nd Edition. 8vo.—Vol. I. 18s.—Vol. II. 21s.

—— THE COLLECTED WORKS. Memorial Edition. Edited by M. FOSTER, F.R.S., and ADAM SEDGWICK, M.A. 4 vols. 8vo. 6l. 6s. Vols. I. and IV. Special Memoirs. May be had separately. Price 73s. 6d.

BALL (Sir R. S.).—EXPERIMENTAL MECHANICS. Illustrated. New Ed. Cr. 8vo. 6s.

BALL (W. W. R.).—THE STUDENT'S GUIDE TO THE BAR. 5th Ed. revised. Cr. 8vo. 2s. 6d.

—— A SHORT ACCOUNT OF THE HISTORY OF MATHEMATICS. Crown 8vo. 10s. 6d.

BALLIOL COLLEGE. PSALMS AND HYMNS FOR BALLIOL COLLEGE. 18mo. 2s. 6d.

BARKER (Lady).—FIRST LESSONS IN THE PRINCIPLES OF COOKING. 3rd Ed. 18mo. 1s.

—— A YEAR'S HOUSEKEEPING IN SOUTH AFRICA. Illustrated. Crown 8vo. 3s. 6d.

—— STATION LIFE IN NEW ZEALAND. Crown 8vo. 3s. 6d.

—— LETTERS TO GUY. Crown 8vo. 5s.

—— THE BED ROOM AND BOUDOIR. With numerous Illustrations. Crown 8vo. 2s. 6d.

BARNES.—LIFE OF WILLIAM BARNES, POET AND PHILOLOGIST. By his Daughter, LUCY BAXTER ("Leader Scott"). Cr. 8vo. 7s. 6d.

BARRY (Bishop).—FIRST WORDS IN AUSTRALIA. Sermons preached in April and May, 1884. Crown 8vo. 5s.

BARTHOLOMEW (J. G.).—ELEMENTARY SCHOOL ATLAS. 4to. 1s.

—— LIBRARY REFERENCE ATLAS OF THE WORLD. With Index to 100,000 places. Folio. 2l. 12s. 6d. net.

—— PHYSICAL AND POLITICAL SCHOOL ATLAS. Royal 4to. [In the Press.

BARWELL (Richard, F.R.C.S.).—THE CAUSES AND TREATMENT OF LATERAL CURVATURE OF THE SPINE. Crown 8vo. 5s.

—— ON ANEURISM, ESPECIALLY OF THE THORAX AND ROOT OF THE NECK. 3s. 6d.

BASTIAN (H. Charlton).—THE BEGINNINGS OF LIFE. 2 vols. Crown 8vo. 28s.

—— EVOLUTION AND THE ORIGIN OF LIFE. Crown 8vo. 6s. 6d.

—— ON PARALYSIS FROM BRAIN DISEASE IN ITS COMMON FORMS. Crown 8vo. 10s. 6d.

BATHER (Archdeacon).—ON SOME MINISTERIAL DUTIES, CATECHISING, PREACHING, &c. Edited, with a Preface, by C. J. VAUGHAN, D.D. Fcp. 8vo. 4s. 6d.

BATH (Marquis of).—OBSERVATIONS ON BULGARIAN AFFAIRS. Crown 8vo. 3*s*. 6*d*.

BEASLEY (R. D.)—AN ELEMENTARY TREATISE ON PLANE TRIGONOMETRY. With numerous Examples. 9th Ed. Cr. 8vo. 3*s*. 6*d*.

BEAUMARCHAIS. LE BARBIER DE SEVILLE, ou LE PRÉCAUTION INUTILE. Comedie en Quatre Actes. Edited by L. P. BLOUET, B.A., Univ. Gallic. Fcp. 8vo. 3*s*. 6*d*.

BECKER (B. H.).—DISTURBED IRELAND. Being Letters written during the winter 1880-81. Crown 8vo. 6*s*.

BEESLY (Mrs.).—STORIES FROM THE HISTORY OF ROME. Fcp. 8vo. 2*s*. 6*d*.

BELCHER (Rev. H.).—SHORT EXERCISES IN LATIN PROSE COMPOSITION AND EXAMINATION PAPERS IN LATIN GRAMMAR ; WITH A CHAPTER ON ANALYSIS OF SENTENCES. 18mo. 1*s*. 6*d*.
    KEY (supplied to Teachers only). 3*s*. 6*d*.

—— SHORT EXERCISES IN LATIN PROSE COMPOSITION.—Part II. On the Syntax of Sentences. With an Appendix. 18mo. 2*s*.
    KEY (supplied to Teachers only). 18mo. 3*s*.

BENHAM (Rev. W.).—A COMPANION TO THE LECTIONARY. Crown 8vo. 4*s*. 6*d*.

BENTLEY.—By Professor JEBB. Crown 8vo. 1*s*. 6*d*. ; sewed, 1*s*.

BERLIOZ (Hector).—AUTOBIOGRAPHY OF. Translated by RACHEL (Scott Russell) HOLMES and ELEANOR HOLMES. 2 vols. Crown 8vo. 21*s*.

BERNARD (M.).—FOUR LECTURES ON SUBJECTS CONNECTED WITH DIPLOMACY. 8vo. 9*s*.

BERNARD (St.)—THE LIFE AND TIMES OF ST. BERNARD, ABBOT OF CLAIRVAUX. By J. C. MORISON, M.A. Crown 8vo. 6*s*.

BERNERS (J.)—FIRST LESSONS ON HEALTH. 18mo. 1*s*.

BETHUNE-BAKER (J. F.).—THE INFLUENCE OF CHRISTIANITY ON WAR. 8vo. 5*s*.

—— THE STERNNESS OF CHRIST'S TEACHING, AND ITS RELATION TO THE LAW OF FORGIVENESS. Crown 8vo. 2*s*. 6*d*.

BETSY LEE : A FO'C'S'LE YARN, AND OTHER POEMS. Crown 8vo. 7*s*. 6*d*.

BETTANY (G. T.).—FIRST LESSONS IN PRACTICAL BOTANY. 18mo. 1*s*.

BIGELOW (M. M.).—HISTORY OF PROCEDURE IN ENGLAND FROM THE NORMAN CONQUEST. The Norman Period, 1066-1204. 8vo. 16*s*.

BIKÉLAS.—LOUKIS LARAS ; OR, THE REMINISCENCES OF A CHIOTE MERCHANT DURING THE GREEK WAR OF INDEPENDENCE. Translated by J. GENNADIUS, Greek Minister in London. Crown 8vo. 7*s*. 6*d*.

BINNIE (the late Rev. William).—SERMONS. Crown 8vo. 6*s*.

BIRKBECK (William Lloyd).—HISTORICAL SKETCH OF THE DISTRIBUTION OF LAND IN ENGLAND. With Suggestions for some Improvement in the Law. Crown 8vo. 4*s*. 6*d*.

BIRKS (Thomas Rawson, M.A.).—FIRST PRINCIPLES OF MORAL SCIENCE ; OR, FIRST COURSE OF LECTURES DELIVERED IN THE UNIVERSITY OF CAMBRIDGE. Cr. 8vo. 8*s*. 6*d*.

BIRKS (Thomas Rawson).—MODERN UTILITARIANISM ; OR, THE SYSTEMS OF PALEY, BENTHAM, AND MILL EXAMINED AND COMPARED. Crown 8vo. 6*s*. 6*d*.

—— THE DIFFICULTIES OF BELIEF IN CONNECTION WITH THE CREATION AND THE FALL, REDEMPTION AND JUDGMENT. 2nd Edition. Crown 8vo. 5*s*.

—— COMMENTARY ON THE BOOK OF ISAIAH, CRITICAL, HISTORICAL, AND PROPHETICAL; INCLUDING A REVISED ENGLISH TRANSLATION. 2nd Edition. 8vo. 12*s*. 6*d*.

—— THE NEW TESTAMENT. Essay on the Right Estimation of MS. Evidence in the Text of the New Testament. Cr. 8vo. 3*s*. 6*d*.

—— SUPERNATURAL REVELATION ; OR, FIRST PRINCIPLES OF MORAL THEOLOGY. 8vo. 8*s*.

—— MODERN PHYSICAL FATALISM, AND THE DOCTRINE OF EVOLUTION. Including an Examination of Mr. Herbert Spencer's " First Principles." Crown 8vo. 6*s*.

—— JUSTIFICATION AND IMPUTED RIGHTEOUSNESS. Being a Review of Ten Sermons on the Nature and Effects of Faith by JAMES THOMAS O'BRIEN, D.D., late Bishop of Ossory, Ferns, and Leighlin. Cr. 8vo. 6*s*.

BJÖRNSON.—SYNNÖVÉ SOLBAKKEN. Translated from the Norwegian, by JULIE SUTTER. Crown 8vo. 6*s*.

BLACK (William).—THE STRANGE ADVENTURES OF A PHAETON. Illustrated. Cr. 8vo. 6*s*.

—— A PRINCESS OF THULE. Crown 8vo. 6*s*.

—— THE MAID OF KILLEENA, AND OTHER TALES. Crown 8vo. 6*s*.

—— MADCAP VIOLET. Crown 8vo. 6*s*.

—— GREEN PASTURES AND PICCADILLY. Crown 8vo. 6*s*.

—— MACLEOD OF DARE. With Illustrations by eminent Artists. Crown 8vo. 6*s*.

—— WHITE WINGS : A YACHTING ROMANCE. Crown 8vo. 6*s*.

—— THE BEAUTIFUL WRETCH : THE FOUR MACNICOLS : THE PUPIL OF AURELIUS. Crown 8vo. 6*s*.

—— SHANDON BELLS. Crown 8vo. 6*s*.

—— YOLANDE. Crown 8vo. 6*s*.

—— JUDITH SHAKESPEARE. Crown 8vo. 6*s*.

—— GOLDSMITH. Cr. 8vo. 1*s*. 6*d*. ; sewed, 1*s*.

—— THE WISE WOMEN OF INVERNESS : A TALE. And OTHER MISCELLANIES. Cr. 8vo. 6*s*.

—— WHITE HEATHER. Crown 8vo. 6*s*.

—— SABINA ZEMBRA. Crown 8vo. 6*s*.

BLACKBURNE.—LIFE OF THE RIGHT HON. FRANCIS BLACKBURNE, late Lord Chancellor of Ireland, by his son, EDWARD BLACKBURNE, one of Her Majesty's Counsel in Ireland. With Portrait. 8vo. 12*s*.

BLACKIE (Prof. John Stuart.).—GREEK AND ENGLISH DIALOGUES FOR USE IN SCHOOLS AND COLLEGES. 3rd Edition. Fcp. 8vo. 2*s*. 6*d*.

—— HORÆ HELLENICÆ. 8vo. 12*s*.

—— THE WISE MEN OF GREECE : IN A SERIES OF DRAMATIC DIALOGUES. Cr. 8vo. 9*s*.

—— GOETHE'S FAUST. Translated into English Verse. 2nd Edition. Crown 8vo. 9*s*.

BLACKIE (Prof. John S.).—LAY SERMONS. Crown 8vo. 6s.

—— MESSIS VITAE : Gleanings of Song from a Happy Life. Crown 8vo. 4s. 6d.

—— WHAT DOES HISTORY TEACH? Two Edinburgh Lectures. Globe 8vo. 2s. 6d.

BLAKE (J. F.).—ASTRONOMICAL MYTHS. With Illustrations. Crown 8vo. 9s.

BLAKE.—LIFE OF WILLIAM BLAKE. With Selections from his Poems and other Writings. Illustrated from Blake's own Works. By ALEXANDER GILCHRIST. New and Enlarged Edition. 2 vols. cloth gilt. Mec. 8vo. 2l. 2s.

BLAKISTON (J. R.).—THE TEACHER: HINTS ON SCHOOL MANAGEMENT. Cr. 8vo. 2s. 6d.

BLANFORD (H. F.).—THE RUDIMENTS OF PHYSICAL GEOGRAPHY FOR THE USE OF INDIAN SCHOOLS. 12th Edition. Illustrated. Globe 8vo. 2s. 6d.

—— A PRACTICAL GUIDE TO THE CLIMATES AND WEATHER OF INDIA, CEYLON AND BURMAH, AND THE STORMS OF INDIAN SEAS. 8vo. 12s. 6d.

BLANFORD (W. T.).—GEOLOGY AND ZOOLOGY OF ABYSSINIA. 8vo. 21s.

BÖHM-BAWERK (Prof.).—CAPITAL AND INTEREST. Translated by W. SMART. 8vo.

BOLDREWOOD (Rolf).—ROBBERY UNDER ARMS: A STORY OF LIFE AND ADVENTURE IN THE BUSH AND IN THE GOLDFIELDS OF AUSTRALIA. Crown 8vo. 3s. 6d.

—— THE MINER'S RIGHT. 3 vols. 31s. 6d.

BOLEYN (ANNE): A Chapter of English History, 1527-1536. By PAUL FRIEDMANN. 2 vols. 8vo. 28s.

BONAR (James).—MALTHUS AND HIS WORK. 8vo. 12s. 6d.

BOOK OF GOLDEN DEEDS OF ALL TIMES AND ALL LANDS. By CHARLOTTE M. YONGE. 18mo. 4s. 6d. Edition for Schools. Globe 8vo. 2s. Abridged Edition. 18mo. 1s.

BOOLE (George).—A TREATISE ON THE CALCULUS OF FINITE DIFFERENCES. Edited by J. F. MOULTON. 3rd Edition. Cr. 8vo. 10s. 6d.

—— THE MATHEMATICAL ANALYSIS OF LOGIC. 8vo. Sewed, 5s.

BOTTOMLEY (J. T.). — FOUR-FIGURE MATHEMATICAL TABLES. Comprising Logarithmic and Trigonometrical Tables, and Tables of Squares, Square Roots and Reciprocals. 2s. 6d.

BOUGHTON (G. H.) and ABBEY (E. A.).— SKETCHING RAMBLES IN HOLLAND. With Illustrations. Fcp. 4to. 21s.

BOWEN (H. Courthope).—FIRST LESSONS IN FRENCH. 18mo. 1s.

BOWER (Prof. F. O.).—A COURSE OF PRACTICAL INSTRUCTION IN BOTANY. Cr. 8vo. 10s. 6d.

BRADSHAW (J. G.).—A COURSE OF EASY ARITHMETICAL EXAMPLES FOR BEGINNERS. Globe 8vo. 2s. With Answers. 2s. 6d.

BRAIN. A JOURNAL OF NEUROLOGY. Edited for the Neurological Society of London, by A. DE WATTEVILLE. Published Quarterly. 8vo. 3s. 6d. (Part I. in January, 1878.) Yearly Vols. I. to XII. 8vo. cloth. 15s. each.

BREYMANN (Prof. H.)—A FRENCH GRAMMAR BASED ON PHILOLOGICAL PRINCIPLES. 3rd Edition. Extra fcp. 8vo. 4s. 6d.

—— FIRST FRENCH EXERCISE BOOK. 2nd Edition. Extra fcp. 8vo. 4s. 6d.

—— SECOND FRENCH EXERCISE BOOK. Extra fcp. 8vo. 2s. 6d.

BRIDGES (John A.).—IDYLLS OF A LOST VILLAGE. Crown 8vo. 7s. 6d.

BRIGHT (John).—SPEECHES ON QUESTIONS OF PUBLIC POLICY. Edited by Professor THOROLD ROGERS. 2nd Edition. 2 vols. 8vo. 25s. With Portrait. Author's Popular Edition. Extra fcp. 8vo. 3s. 6d.

—— PUBLIC ADDRESSES. Edited by J. E. T. ROGERS. 8vo. 14s.

BRIGHT (H. A.)—THE ENGLISH FLOWER GARDEN. Crown 8vo. 3s. 6d.

BRIMLEY (George).—ESSAYS. Globe 8vo. 5s.

BRODIE (Sir Benjamin).—IDEAL CHEMISTRY. Crown 8vo. 2s.

BROOKE.—THE RAJA OF SARAWAK (Life of). By GERTRUDE L. JACOB. Portrait and Maps. 2 vols. 8vo. 25s.

BROOKE (Stopford A.).—PRIMER OF ENGLISH LITERATURE. 18mo. 1s. Large Paper Edition. 8vo. 7s. 6d.

—— RIQUET OF THE TUFT : A LOVE DRAMA. Extra crown 8vo. 6s.

—— POEMS. Globe 8vo. 6s.

—— MILTON. Fcp. 8vo. 1s. 6d. Large Paper Edition. 8vo. 21s.

—— POEMS OF SHELLEY. Edited by STOPFORD A. BROOKE, M.A. With Vignette. 18mo. 4s. 6d. Large Paper Edition. 12s. 6d.

BROOKS (Rev. Phillips).—THE CANDLE OF THE LORD, AND OTHER SERMONS. Cr. 8vo. 6s.

—— SERMONS PREACHED IN ENGLISH CHURCHES. Crown 8vo. 6s.

—— TWENTY SERMONS. Crown 8vo. 6s.

—— TOLERANCE. Crown 8vo. 2s. 6d.

BROOKSMITH (J.).—ARITHMETIC IN THEORY AND PRACTICE. Crown 8vo. 4s. 6d.

BROOKSMITH (J. and E. J.).—ARITHMETIC FOR BEGINNERS. Globe 8vo. 1s. 6d.

BROOKSMITH (E. J.).—WOOLWICH MATHEMATICAL PAPERS, for Admission in the Royal Military Academy for the years 1880—1888. Ed. by E. J. BROOKSMITH, B.A. Cr. 8vo. 6s.

BROWN (J. Allen).—PALÆOLITHIC MAN IN NORTH-WEST MIDDLESEX. 8vo. 7s. 6d.

BROWN (T. E.).—THE MANX WITCH: AND OTHER POEMS. Crown 8vo. 7s. 6d.

BROWNE (J. H. Balfour).—WATER SUPPLY. Crown 8vo. 2s. 6d.

BROWNE (Sir Thomas).—RELIGIO MEDICI ; LETTER TO A FRIEND, &c., AND CHRISTIAN MORALS. Edited by W. A. GREENHILL, M.D. With Portrait. 18mo. 4s. 6d.

BRUNTON (Dr. T. Lauder).—A TEXT-BOOK OF PHARMACOLOGY, THERAPEUTICS, AND MATERIA MEDICA. 3rd Edition. Medium 8vo. 21s.

—— DISORDERS OF DIGESTION : THEIR CONSEQUENCES AND TREATMENT. 8vo. 10s. 6d.

BRUNTON (Dr. T. Lauder).—PHARMACO-
LOGY AND THERAPEUTICS; OR, MEDICINE
PAST AND PRESENT. Crown 8vo. 6s.

—— TABLES OF MATERIA MEDICA: A COM-
PANION TO THE MATERIA MEDICA MU-
SEUM. 8vo. 5s.

—— THE BIBLE AND SCIENCE. With Illustrations. Crown 8vo. 10s. 6d.

BRYANS (Clement).—LATIN PROSE EXER-
CISES BASED UPON CAESAR'S "GALLIC
WAR." With a Classification of Caesar's
Phrases and Grammatical Notes on Caesar's
Chief Usages. Pott 8vo. 2s. 6d.
KEY (for Teachers only). 4s. 6d.

BRYCE (James, M.P., D.C.L.).—THE HOLY
ROMAN EMPIRE. 8th Ed. Cr. 8vo. 7s. 6d..
Library Edition. 8vo. 14s.

—— TRANSCAUCASIA AND ARARAT. 3rd
Edition. Crown 8vo. 9s.

—— THE AMERICAN COMMONWEALTH. 2nd
Edition. 2 vols. Extra Crown 8vo. 25s.

BUCHHEIM (Dr.).—DEUTSCHE LYRIK.
18mo. 4s. 6d.

BUCKLAND (Anna).—OUR NATIONAL IN-
STITUTIONS. 18mo. 1s.

BUCKLEY (Arabella).—HISTORY OF ENG-
LAND FOR BEGINNERS. With Coloured
Maps and Chronological and Genealogical
Tables. Globe 8vo. 3s.

BUCKNILL (Dr.).—THE CARE OF THE
INSANE AND THEIR LEGAL CONTROL.
Crown 8vo. 3s. 6d.

BUCKTON (G. B.).—MONOGRAPH OF THE
BRITISH CICADÆ, OR FETTIGIIDÆ. In 8
parts. Part I. 8vo. 8s.

BUMBLEBEE BOGO'S BUDGET. By a
RETIRED JUDGE. Illustrations by ALICE
HAVERS. Crown 8vo. 2s. 6d.

BUNYAN (John).—THE PILGRIM'S PROGRESS
FROM THIS WORLD TO THAT WHICH IS TO
COME. 18mo. 4s. 6d.

BUNYAN. By J. A. FROUDE. Crown 8vo.
1s. 6d.; sewed, 1s.

BURGON (Dean).—POEMS. Ex. fcp.8vo. 4s.6d.

BURKE (Edmund).—LETTERS, TRACTS, AND
SPEECHES ON IRISH AFFAIRS. Edited by
MATTHEW ARNOLD, with Preface. Cr. 8vo. 6s.

BURKE. By JOHN MORLEY. Globe 8vo.
5s. Crown 8vo. 1s. 6d.; sewed, 1s.

BURN (Robert).—ROMAN LITERATURE IN
RELATION TO ROMAN ART. With Illustrations. Extra Crown 8vo. 14s.

BURNETT (F. Hodgson).—"HAWORTH'S."
Globe 8vo. 2s.

—— LOUISIANA : AND THAT LASS O' LOWRIE'S.
Two Stories. Illustrated. Cr. 8vo. 3s. 6d.
Cheap Edition. Globe 8vo. 2s.

BURNS, THE COMPLETE WORKS OF. Edited
by ALEXANDER SMITH. Globe 8vo. 3s. 6d.

—— THE POETICAL WORKS. With a Biographical Memoir by ALEXANDER SMITH. In
2 vols. fcp. 8vo. 10s.

BURNS. By Principal SHAIRP. Crown 8vo.
1s. 6d.; sewed, 1s.

BURY (J. B.).—A HISTORY OF THE LATER
ROMAN EMPIRE FROM ARCADIUS TO IRENE,
A.D. 390—800. 2 vols. 8vo. 32s.

BUTCHER (Prof. S. H.).—DEMOSTHENES.
Fcp. 8vo. 1s. 6d.

BUTLER (Archer).—SERMONS, DOCTRINAL
AND PRACTICAL. 11th Edition. 8vo. 8s.

—— A SECOND SERIES OF SERMONS. Ninth
Edition. 8vo. 7s.

—— LETTERS ON ROMANISM. 2nd Ed., revised
by Archdeacon HARDWICK. 8vo. 10s. 6d.

BUTLER (George).—SERMONS PREACHED IN
CHELTENHAM COLLEGE CHAPEL. 8vo. 7s. 6d.

BUTLER'S HUDIBRAS. Edited by ALFRED
MILNES. Fcp. 8vo. Part I., 3s. 6d. Part
II. and III., 4s. 6d.

BYRON.—POETRY OF BYRON, chosen and
arranged by MATTHEW ARNOLD. 18mo.
4s. 6d.
Large Paper Edition. Crown 8vo. 9s.

BYRON. By Prof. NICHOL. Crown 8vo.
1s. 6d. ; sewed, 1s.

CAESAR.—THE GALLIC WAR. Book I.
Edited, with Notes and Vocabulary by
A. S. WALPOLE, M.A. 18mo. 1s. 6d.

—— THE GALLIC WAR.—Books II. and III.
Edited by W. G. RUTHERFORD, LL.D.
18mo. 1s. 6d.

—— THE INVASION OF BRITAIN. Being Selections from Books IV. and V. of the "De
Bello Gallico." With Notes, Vocabulary,
and Exercises, by W. WELCH, M.A., and
C. G. DUFFIELD, M.A. 18mo. 1s. 6d.

—— SCENES FROM THE FIFTH AND SIXTH
BOOKS OF THE GALLIC WAR. Selected and
Edited by C. COLBECK, M.A. 18mo. 1s. 6d.

—— THE HELVETIAN WAR. Selected from
Book I. of "The Gallic War," with Notes,
Vocabulary, and Exercises, by W. WELCH
and C. G. DUFFIELD. 18mo. 1s. 6d.

—— THE GALLIC WAR. Edited by the Rev.
J. BOND, M.A., and A. S. WALPOLE, M.A.
Fcp. 8vo. 6s.

—— THE GALLIC WAR.—Book IV. Edited,
with Introduction, Notes, and Vocabulary,
by CLEMENT BRYANS, M.A. 18mo. 1s. 6d.

—— THE GALLIC WAR.—Book V. Edited
with Notes and Vocabulary, by C. COLBECK,
M.A. 18mo. 1s. 6d.

—— THE GALLIC WAR—Book VI. By the
same Editor. With Notes and Vocabulary.
18mo. 1s. 6d.

—— THE GALLIC WAR—Book VII. Edited
by the Rev. J. BOND, M.A., and A. S.
WALPOLE, M.A. With Notes and Vocabulary. 18mo. 1s. 6d.

CAIRNES (Prof. J. E.).—POLITICAL ESSAYS.
8vo. 10s. 6d.

—— SOME LEADING PRINCIPLES OF POLITICAL
ECONOMY NEWLY EXPOUNDED. 8vo. 14s.

—— THE SLAVE POWER. 8vo. 10s. 6d.

—— THE CHARACTER AND LOGICAL METHOD
OF POLITICAL ECONOMY. Crown 8vo. 6s.

CALDERON.—SELECT PLAYS OF CALDERON.
Ed. by NORMAN MACCOLL, M.A. Cr. 8vo 14s.

CALDERWOOD (Prof. H.).—HAND-BOOK
OF MORAL PHILOSOPHY. 14th Edition.
Crown 8vo. 6s.

—— THE RELATIONS OF MIND AND BRAIN.
2nd Edition. 8vo. 12s.

CALDERWOOD (Prof. H.).—THE PARA-BLES OF OUR LORD. 2nd Edition. Crown 8vo. 6s.

—— THE RELATIONS OF SCIENCE AND RELIGION. Crown 8vo. 5s.

—— ON TEACHING. 4th Ed. Ex. fcp. 8vo. 2s.6d.

CALVERT.—SCHOOL-READINGS IN THE GREEK TESTAMENT. Edited, with Notes and Vocabulary, by A. CALVERT, M.A. Fcp. 8vo. 4s. 6d.

CAMBRIDGE.—COOPER'S LE KEUX'S MEMO-RIALS OF CAMBRIDGE. Illustrated with 90 Woodcuts in the Text, 154 Plates on Steel and Copper by LE KEUX, STORER, &c., in-cluding 20 Etchings by R. FARREN. 3 vols. Medium 8vo. Cloth, gilt tops.
A few copies, proofs, large paper, 4to, bound in half-levant morocco, with gilt tops.
Fifty copies of the Etchings by R. FARREN, from the "Memorials of Cambridge." Proofs, signed, in a Portfolio.

CAMBRIDGE SENATE-HOUSE PROBLEMS AND RIDERS, WITH SOLUTIONS:
1848—51. RIDERS. By JAMESON. 8vo. 7s. 6d.
1875. PROBLEMS AND RIDERS. Edited by Prof. A. G. GREENHILL. Cr. 8vo. 8s. 6d.
1878. SOLUTIONS BY THE MATHEMATICAL MODERATORS AND EXAMINERS. Edited by J. W. L. GLAISHER, M.A. 8vo. 12s.

CAMEOS FROM ENGLISH HISTORY. By the Author of "The Heir of Redclyffe." 6 vols. Extra fcp. 8vo. 5s. each.
Vol. I. Rollo to Edward II. II. The Wars in France. III. The Wars of the Roses. IV. Reformation Times. V. England and Spain. VI. Forty Years of Stuart Rule (1603—43). VII. The Rebellion and Restoration (1642—78).
[In the Press.

CAMERON (V. L.).—OUR FUTURE HIGHWAY TO INDIA. 2 vols. Crown 8vo. 21s.

CAMPBELL (Dr. John M'Leod).—THE NA-TURE OF THE ATONEMENT. 6th Edition. Crown 8vo. 6s.

—— REMINISCENCES AND REFLECTIONS. Ed., with an Introductory Narrative, by his Son, DONALD CAMPBELL, M.A. Cr. 8vo. 7s. 6d.

—— RESPONSIBILITY FOR THE GIFT OF ETER-NAL LIFE. Compiled from Sermons preached at Row, in the years 1829—31. Cr. 8vo. 5s.

—— THOUGHTS ON REVELATION. 2nd Edition. Crown 8vo. 5s.

CAMPBELL (J. F.).—MY CIRCULAR NOTES. Cheaper issue. Crown 8vo. 6s.

CAMPBELL (Lord George).—LOG-LETTERS FROM THE "CHALLENGER." 7th Edition. Crown 8vo. 6s.

CAMPBELL (Prof. Lewis).—SOPHOCLES. Fcp. 8vo. 1s. 6d.

CANDLER (H.).—HELP TO ARITHMETIC. 2nd Edition. Globe 8vo. 2s. 6d.

CANTERBURY (His Grace Edward White, Archbishop of).—BOY-LIFE: ITS TRIAL, ITS STRENGTH, ITS FULNESS. Sundays in Wel-lington College, 1859—73. 4th Ed. Cr. 8vo. 6s.

—— THE SEVEN GIFTS. Addressed to the Diocese of Canterbury in his Primary Visita-tion. 2nd Edition. Crown 8vo. 6s.

CANTERBURY (Archbishop of).—CHRIST AND HIS TIMES. Addressed to the Diocese of Canterbury in his Second Visitation. Crown 8vo. 6s.

CAPES (Rev. W. W.)—LIVY. Fcp. 8vo. 1s. 6d.

CARLES (W. R.).—LIFE IN COREA. 8vo. 12s. 6d.

CARLYLE (Thomas).—REMINISCENCES. Ed. by CHARLES ELIOT NORTON. 2 vols. Crown 8vo. 12s.

—— EARLY LETTERS OF THOMAS CARLYLE. Edited by C. E. NORTON. 2 vols. 1814—26. Crown 8vo. 18s.

—— LETTERS OF THOMAS CARLYLE. Ed. by C. E. NORTON. 2 vols. 1826—36. Cr. 8vo. 18s.

—— GOETHE AND CARLYLE, CORRESPONDENCE BETWEEN. Ed. by C. E. NORTON. Cr. 8vo. 9s.

CARMARTHEN (Marchioness of). — A LOVER OF THE BEAUTIFUL. A Novel. Crown 8vo.

CARPENTER (Bishop W. Boyd).—TRUTH IN TALE. Addresses, chiefly to children. Cr. 8vo. 4s. 6d.

—— THE PERMANENT ELEMENTS OF RE-LIGION: Bampton Lectures, 1887. 8vo. 14s.

CARR (J. Comyns).—PAPERS ON ART. Cr. 8vo. 8s. 6d.

CARROLL (Lewis).—ALICE'S ADVENTURES IN WONDERLAND. With 42 Illustrations by TENNIEL. Crown 8vo. 6s.
People's Edition. With all the original Illustrations. Crown 8vo. 2s. 6d.
A GERMAN TRANSLATION OF THE SAME. Crown 8vo. gilt. 6s.
A FRENCH TRANSLATION OF THE SAME. Crown 8vo. gilt. 6s.
AN ITALIAN TRANSLATION OF THE SAME. Crown 8vo. gilt. 6s.

—— ALICE'S ADVENTURES UNDER-GROUND. Being a Facsimile of the Original MS. Book, afterwards developed into "Alice's Adven-tures in Wonderland." With 27 Illustrations by the Author. Crown 8vo. 4s.

—— THROUGH THE LOOKING-GLASS AND WHAT ALICE FOUND THERE. With 50 Illus-trations by TENNIEL. Crown 8vo. gilt. 6s.
People's Edition. With all the original Illustrations. Crown 8vo. 2s. 6d.
People's Edition of "Alice's Adventures in Wonderland," and "Through the Looking-Glass." 1 vol. Crown 8vo. 4s. 6d.

—— THE GAME OF LOGIC. Crown 8vo. 3s.

—— RHYME? AND REASON? With 65 Illus-trations by ARTHUR B. FROST, and 9 by HENRY HOLIDAY. Crown 8vo. 6s.

—— A TANGLED TALE. Reprinted from the "Monthly Packet." With 6 Illustrations by ARTHUR B. FROST. Crown 8vo. 4s. 6d.

—— SYLVIE AND BRUNO. With 46 Illustra-tions by HARRY FURNISS. Cr. 8vo. 7s. 6d.

CARSTARES (William).—A Character and Career of the Revolutionary Epoch (1649—1715). By R. H. STORY. 8vo. 12s.

CARTER (R. Brudenell, F.C.S.).—A PRAC-TICAL TREATISE ON DISEASES OF THE EYE. 8vo. 16s.

CARTER (R. Brudenell).—Eyesight, Good and Bad. Cr. 8vo. 6s.
—— Modern Operations for Cataract. 8vo. 6s.

CASSEL.—Manual of Jewish History and Literature. Translated by Mrs. Henry Lucas. Fcp. 8vo. 2s. 6d.

CATULLUS.—Select Poems. Edited by F. P. Simpson, B.A. Fcp. 8vo. 5s.

CAUCASUS : Notes on the. By "Wanderer." 8vo. 9s.

CAUTLEY (G. S.).—A Century of Emblems. With Illustrations by the Lady Marian Alford. Small 4to. 10s. 6d.

CAZENOVE (J. Gibson).—Concerning the Being and Attributes of God. 8vo. 5s.

CHALMERS (J. B.).—Graphical Determination of Forces in Engineering Structures. 8vo. 24s.

CHALMERS (M.D.).—Local Government. Crown 8vo. 3s. 6d. [English Citizen Series.

CHATTERTON : A Biographical Study. By Sir Daniel Wilson, LL.D. Cr.8vo. 6s. 6d.

CHAUCER. By Prof. A. W. Ward. Crown 8vo. 1s. 6d. ; sewed, 1s.

CHEYNE (C. H. H.).—An Elementary Treatise on the Planetary Theory. Crown 8vo. 7s. 6d.

CHEYNE (T. K.).—The Book of Isaiah Chronologically Arranged. Crown 8vo. 7s. 6d.

CHILDREN'S GARLAND FROM THE BEST POETS. Selected and arranged by Coventry Patmore. 18mo. 4s. 6d.
Globe Readings Edition for Schools. 2s.

CHOICE NOTES ON THE FOUR GOSPELS, drawn from Old and New Sources. Crown 8vo. 4 vols. 4s. 6d. each. (St. Matthew and St. Mark in 1 vol. 9s.)

CHRISTIE (J.).—Cholera Epidemics in East Africa. 8vo. 15s.

CHRISTIE (J. R.).—Elementary Test Questions in Pure and Mixed Mathematics. Crown 8vo. 8s. 6d.

CHRISTMAS CAROL, A. Printed in Colours, with Illuminated Borders from MSS. of the 14th and 15th Centuries. 4to. 21s.

CHRISTY CAREW. By the Author of "Hogan, M.P." Globe 8vo. 2s.

CHURCH (Very Rev. R. W.).—The Sacred Poetry of Early Religions. 2nd Edition. 18mo. 1s.
—— St. Anselm. Crown 8vo. 6s.
—— Human Life and its Conditions. Cr. 8vo. 6s.
—— The Gifts of Civilisation, and other Sermons and Lectures. Crown 8vo. 7s. 6d.
—— Discipline of the Christian Character, and other Sermons. Crown 8vo. 4s. 6d.
—— Advent Sermons. 1885. Cr. 8vo. 4s. 6d.
—— Miscellaneous Writings. Collected Edition. 5 vols. Globe 8vo. 5s. each.
Vol. I. Miscellaneous Essays. II. St. Anselm. III. Dante: and other Essays. IV. Spenser. V. Bacon.

CHURCH (Very Rev. R. W.).—Spenser. Globe 8vo. 5s.; Crown 8vo. 1s. 6d.; swd., 1s.
—— Bacon. Globe 8vo. 5s.; Cr. 8vo. 1s. 6d.; sewed, 1s.

CHURCH (Rev. A. J.).—Latin Version of Selections from Tennyson. By Prof. Conington, Prof. Seeley, Dr. Hessey, T. E. Kebbel, &c. Edited by A. J. Church, M.A. Extra fcp. 8vo. 6s.

CHURCH (A. J.) and BRODRIBB (W. J.).—Tacitus. Fcp. 8vo. 1s. 6d.

CICERO.—The Life and Letters of Marcus Tullius Cicero. Being a New Translation of the Letters included in Mr. Watson's Selection. By the Rev. G. E. Jeans, M.A. 2nd Edition. Crown 8vo. 10s. 6d.
—— The Academica. The Text revised and explained by J. S. Reid, M.L. 8vo. 15s.
—— The Academics. Translated by J. S. Reid, M.L. 8vo. 5s. 6d.
—— De Amicitia. Edited by E. S. Shuckburgh, M.A. With Notes, Vocabulary, and Biographical Index. 18mo. 1s. 6d.
—— De Senectute. Edited, with Notes, Vocabulary, and Biographical Index, by E. S. Shuckburgh, M.A. 18mo. 1s. 6d.
—— Select Letters. Edited by Rev. G. E. Jeans, M.A. 18mo. 1s. 6d.
—— The Second Philippic Oration. Edited by Prof. John E. B. Mayor. New Edition, revised. Fcp. 8vo. 5s.
—— Pro Publio Sestio. Edited by Rev. H. A. Holden, M.A., LL.D. Fcp. 8vo. 5s.
—— The Catiline Orations. Edited by Prof. A. S. Wilkins, Litt.D. New Edition. Fcp. 8vo. 3s. 6d.
—— Pro Lege Manilia. Edited by Prof. A. S. Wilkins, Litt.D. Fcp. 8vo. 2s. 6d.
—— Pro Roscio Amerino. Edited by E. H. Donkin, M.A. Fcp. 8vo. 4s. 6d.
—— Stories of Roman History. With Notes, Vocabulary, and Exercises by G. E. Jeans, M.A., and A. V. Jones. 18mo. 1s. 6d.

CLARK.—Memorials from Journals and Letters of Samuel Clark, M.A. Edited by his Wife. Crown 8vo. 7s. 6d.

CLARK (L.) and SADLER (H.).—The Star Guide. Roy. 8vo. 5s.

CLARKE (C. B.).—A Geographical Reader and Companion to the Atlas. Cr. 8vo. 2s.
—— A Class-Book of Geography. With 18 Coloured Maps. Fcp. 8vo. 3s. 6d.; swd., 3s.
—— Speculations from Political Economy. Crown 8vo. 3s. 6d.

CLARKE (F. W.).—A Table of Specific Gravity for Solids and Liquids. (Constants of Nature, Part I.) 8vo. 12s. 6d.

CLASSICAL WRITERS. Edited by John Richard Green. Fcp. 8vo. 1s. 6d. each.
Euripides. By Prof. Mahaffy.
Milton. By the Rev. Stopford A. Brooke.
Livy. By the Rev. W. W. Capes, M.A.
Vergil. By Prof. Nettleship, M.A.
Sophocles. By Prof. L. Campbell, M.A.
Demosthenes. By Prof. Butcher, M.A.
Tacitus. By Church and Brodribb.

CLAUSIUS(R.).—THE MECHANICAL THEORY OF HEAT. Translated by WALTER R. BROWNE. Crown 8vo. 10s. 6d.

CLERGYMAN'S SELF-EXAMINATION CONCERNING THE APOSTLES' CREED. Extra fcp. 8vo. 1s. 6d.

CLIFFORD (Prof. W. K.).—ELEMENTS OF DYNAMIC. An Introduction to the Study of Motion and Rest in Solid and Fluid Bodies. Crown 8vo. Part I. Kinematic. Books I.—III., 7s. 6d. Book IV. and Appendix, 6s.

—— LECTURES AND ESSAYS. Ed. by LESLIE STEPHEN and Sir F. POLLOCK. Cr. 8vo. 8s. 6d.

—— SEEING AND THINKING. With Diagrams. Crown 8vo. 3s. 6d.

—— MATHEMATICAL PAPERS. Edited by R. TUCKER. With an Introduction by H. J. STEPHEN SMITH, M.A. 8vo. 30s.

CLIFFORD(Mrs. W. K.).—ANYHOW STORIES. With Illustrations by DOROTHY TENNANT. Crown 8vo. 1s. 6d. ; paper covers, 1s.

CLOUGH (A. H.).—POEMS. New Edition. Crown 8vo. 7s. 6d.

—— PROSE REMAINS. With a Selection from his Letters, and a Memoir by his Wife. Crown 8vo. 7s. 6d.

COAL: ITS HISTORY AND ITS USES. By Profs. GREEN, MIALL, THORPE, RÜCKER, and MARSHALL. Crown 8vo. 12s. 6d.

COBDEN (Richard.).—SPEECHES ON QUESTIONS OF PUBLIC POLICY. Edited by JOHN BRIGHT and J. E. THOROLD ROGERS. Globe 8vo. 3s. 6d.

COCKSHOTT (A.) and WALTERS (F. B.). —A TREATISE ON GEOMETRICAL CONICS. Crown 8vo. 5s.

COHEN (D. Julius B.).—THE OWENS COLLEGE COURSE OF PRACTICAL ORGANIC CHEMISTRY. Fcp. 8vo. 2s. 6d.

COLBECK (C.).—FRENCH READINGS FROM ROMAN HISTORY. Selected from various Authors, with Notes. 18mo. 4s. 6d.

COLENSO.— THE COMMUNION SERVICE FROM THE BOOK OF COMMON PRAYER, WITH SELECT READINGS FROM THE WRITINGS OF THE REV. F. D. MAURICE. Edited by the late BISHOP COLENSO. 6th Ed. 16mo. 2s. 6d.

COLERIDGE.—THE POETICAL AND DRAMATIC WORKS OF SAMUEL TAYLOR COLERIDGE. 4 vols. Fcp. 8vo. 31s. 6d. Also an Edition on Large Paper, at 12s. 6d.

COLERIDGE. By H. D. TRAILL. Crown 8vo. 1s. 6d. ; sewed, 1s.

COLLECTS OF THE CHURCH OF ENGLAND. With a Coloured Floral Design to each Collect. Crown 8vo. 12s.

COLLIER (John).—A PRIMER OF ART. 18mo. 1s.

COLQUHOUN.—RHYMES AND CHIMES. By F. S. COLQUHOUN (née F. S. FULLER MAITLAND). Extra fcp. 8vo. 2s. 6d.

COLSON (F. H.).—FIRST GREEK READER. Stories and Legends. With Notes, Vocabulary, and Exercises. Globe 8vo. 3s.

COLVIN (S.).—LANDOR. Crown 8vo. 1s. 6d. ; sewed, 1s.

COLVIN (S.).—SELECTIONS FROM THE WRITINGS OF WALTER SAVAGE LANDOR. 18mo. 4s. 6d.

—— KEATS. Crown 8vo. 1s. 6d. ; sewed, 1s.

COMBE.—LIFE OF GEORGE COMBE. By CHARLES GIBBON. 2 vols. 8vo. 32s.

—— EDUCATION : ITS PRINCIPLES AND PRACTICE AS DEVELOPED BY GEORGE COMBE. Edited by WILLIAM JOLLY. 8vo. 15s.

CONGREVE (Rev. John).—HIGH HOPES AND PLEADINGS FOR A REASONABLE FAITH, NOBLER THOUGHTS, LARGER CHARITY. Crown 8vo. 5s.

CONSTABLE (Samuel).—GEOMETRICAL EXERCISES FOR BEGINNERS. Cr. 8vo. 3s. 6d.

CONWAY (Hugh).— A FAMILY AFFAIR. Globe 8vo. 2s.

—— LIVING OR DEAD. Globe 8vo. 2s.

COOKE (E. T.).—A POPULAR HANDBOOK TO THE NATIONAL GALLERY. Including, by special permission, Notes collected from the Works of Mr. RUSKIN. With a Preface by JOHN RUSKIN, LL.D., D.C.L. Crown 8vo, half morocco. 14s. Also an Edition on Large Paper, limited to 250 copies. 2 vols. 8vo.

COOKE (Josiah P., jun.).—PRINCIPLES OF CHEMICAL PHILOSOPHY. New Ed. 8vo. 16s.

—— RELIGION AND CHEMISTRY. Cr. 8vo. 7s. 6d.

—— ELEMENTS OF CHEMICAL PHYSICS. 4th Edition. Royal 8vo. 21s.

COOKERY. MIDDLE CLASS BOOK. Compiled for Manchester School of Cookery. Fcp. 8vo. 1s. 6d.

CO-OPERATION IN THE UNITED STATES : HISTORY OF. Edited by H. B. ADAMS. 8vo. 15s.

COPE (E. M.).—AN INTRODUCTION TO ARISTOTLE'S RHETORIC. 8vo. 14s.

COPE (E. D.).—THE ORIGIN OF THE FITTEST. Essays on Evolution. 8vo. 12s. 6d.

CORBETT (Julian).—THE FALL OF ASGARD : A Tale of St. Olaf's Day. 2 vols. 12s.

—— FOR GOD AND GOLD. Crown 8vo. 6s.

—— KOPHETUA THE THIRTEENTH. 2 vols. Globe 8vo. 12s.

—— MONK. With Portrait. Cr. 8vo. 2s. 6d. [English Men of Action.

CORE (T. H.).—QUESTIONS ON BALFOUR STEWART'S "LESSONS IN ELEMENTARY PHYSICS." Fcp. 8vo. 2s.

CORFIELD (Dr. W. H.).—THE TREATMENT AND UTILIZATION OF SEWAGE. 3rd Edition, Revised by the Author, and by LOUIS C. PARKES, M.D. 8vo. 16s.

CORNAZ (S.).—NOS ENFANTS ET LEURS AMIS. Edited by EDITH HARVEY. Globe 8vo. 1s. 6d.

CORNELL UNIVERSITY STUDIES IN CLASSICAL PHILOLOGY. Edited by I. FLAGG, W. G. HALE, and B. I. WHEELER. I. The C U M-Constructions : their History and Functions. Part I. Critical. 1s. 8d. nett. Part II. Constructive. By W. G. HALE. 3s. 4d. nett. II. Analogy and the Scope of its Application in Language. By B. I. WHEELER. 1s. 3d. nett.

CORNEILLE.—LE CID. Ed. by G. EUGÈNE FASNACHT. 18mo. 1s.

COSSA.—GUIDE TO THE STUDY OF POLITICAL ECONOMY. From the Italian of Dr. LUIGI COSSA. Crown 8vo. 4s. 6d.

COTTERILL (Prof. James H.).—APPLIED MECHANICS : An Introduction to the Theory of Structures and Machines. 2nd Edition. Med. 8vo. 18s.

COTTON (Bishop).—SERMONS PREACHED TO ENGLISH CONGREGATIONS IN INDIA. Crown 8vo. 7s. 6d.

COTTON and PAYNE.—COLONIES AND DEPENDENCIES. Part I. INDIA. By J. S. COTTON. Part II. THE COLONIES. By E. J. PAYNE. Crown 8vo. 3s. 6d.

COUES (Elliott).—KEY TO NORTH AMERICAN BIRDS. Illustrated. 8vo. 2l. 2s.

COWELL (George).—LECTURES ON CATA-RACT : ITS CAUSES, VARIETIES, AND TREAT-MENT. Crown 8vo. 4s. 6d.

COWPER. —COWPER'S POETICAL WORKS. Ed. by Rev. W. BENHAM. Globe 8vo. 3s. 6d.

—— THE TASK : An Epistle to Joseph Hill, Esq. ; TIROCINIUM, or a Review of the Schools ; and the HISTORY OF JOHN GILPIN. Edited by WILLIAM BENHAM. Globe 8vo. 1s.

—— LETTERS OF WILLIAM COWPER. Edited by the Rev. W. BENHAM. 18mo. 4s. 6d.

—— SELECTIONS FROM COWPER'S POEMS. In-troduction by Mrs. OLIPHANT. 18mo. 4s. 6d.

COWPER. By GOLDWIN SMITH. Crown 8vo. 1s. 6d. ; sewed, 1s.

COX (G. V.).—RECOLLECTIONS OF OXFORD. 2nd Edition. Crown 8vo, 6s.

CRAIK (Mrs.).—OLIVE. Illustrated. Crown 8vo. 6s.—Cheap Edition. Globe 8vo. 2s.

—— THE OGILVIES. Illustrated. Crown 8vo. 6s.—Cheap Edition. Globe 8vo. 2s.

—— AGATHA'S HUSBAND. Illustrated. Crown 8vo. 6s.—Cheap Edition. Globe 8vo. 2s.

—— THE HEAD OF THE FAMILY. Illustrated. Cr. 8vo. 6s.—Cheap Edition. Gl. 8vo. 2s.

—— TWO MARRIAGES. Globe 8vo. 2s.

—— THE LAUREL BUSH. Crown 8vo. 6s.

—— MY MOTHER AND I. Illust. Cr. 8vo. 6s.

—— MISS TOMMY : A MEDIÆVAL ROMANCE. Illustrated. Crown 8vo. 6s.

—— KING ARTHUR: NOT A LOVE STORY. Crown 8vo. 6s.

   ₊ Beginning on March 1st, 1890, and con-tinued monthly, a uniform edition of Mrs. Craik's Novels will be issued, price 3s. 6d. each.

—— POEMS. New and Enlarged Edition. Extra fcp. 8vo. 6s.

—— CHILDREN'S POETRY. Ex. fcp. 8vo. 4s. 6d.

—— SONGS OF OUR YOUTH. Small 4to. 6s.

—— CONCERNING MEN : AND OTHER PAPERS. Crown 8vo. 4s. 6d.

—— ABOUT MONEY: AND OTHER THINGS. Crown 8vo. 6s.

—— SERMONS OUT OF CHURCH. Cr. 8vo. 6s.

—— AN UNKNOWN COUNTRY. Illustrated by F. Noel Paton. Royal 8vo. 7s. 6d.

CRAIK (Mrs.).—ALICE LEARMONT : A FAIRY TALE. With Illustrations. 4s. 6d.

—— AN UNSENTIMENTAL JOURNEY THROUGH CORNWALL. Illustrated. 4to. 12s. 6d.

—— OUR YEAR : A CHILD'S BOOK IN PROSE AND VERSE. Illustrated. 2s. 6d.

—— LITTLE SUNSHINE'S HOLIDAY. Globe 8vo. 2s. 6d.

—— THE ADVENTURES OF A BROWNIE. Illus-trated by Mrs. ALLINGHAM. 4s. 6d.

—— THE LITTLE LAME PRINCE AND HIS TRAVELLING CLOAK. A Parable for Old and Young. With 24 Illustrations by J. McL. RALSTON. Crown 8vo. 4s. 6d.

—— THE FAIRY BOOK : THE BEST POPULAR FAIRY STORIES. Selected and rendered anew. With a Vignette by Sir NOEL PATON. 18mo. 4s. 6d.

CRAIK (Henry).—THE STATE IN ITS RELA-TION TO EDUCATION. Crown 8vo. 3s. 6d.

CRANE (Lucy).—LECTURES ON ART AND THE FORMATION OF TASTE. Cr. 8vo. 6s.

CRANE (Walter).—THE SIRENS THREE. A Poem. Written and Illustrated by WALTER CRANE. Royal 8vo. 10s. 6d.

CRAVEN (Mrs. Dacre).—A GUIDE TO DIS-TRICT NURSES. Crown 8vo. 2s. 6d.

CRAWFORD (F. Marion).—MR. ISAACS : A TALE OF MODERN INDIA. Cr. 8vo. 3s. 6d.

—— DOCTOR CLAUDIUS : A TRUE STORY. Crown 8vo. 3s. 6d.

—— A ROMAN SINGER. Crown 8vo. 3s. 6d.

—— ZOROASTER. Crown 8vo. 3s. 6d.

—— A TALE OF A LONELY PARISH. Crown 8vo. 3s. 6d.

—— MARZIO'S CRUCIFIX. Crown 8vo. 3s. 6d.

—— PAUL PATOFF. Crown 8vo. 3s. 6d.

—— WITH THE IMMORTALS. 2 vols. Globe 8vo. 12s. 1 vol. Crown 8vo. 3s. 6d.

—— GREIFENSTEIN. Crown 8vo. 6s.

—— SANT ILARIO. Crown 8vo. 6s.

CREIGHTON (M.).—ROME. 18mo. 1s.
                                    [Literature Primers.
—— CARDINAL WOLSEY. Crown 8vo. 2s. 6d.

CROSS (Rev. J. A.).—BIBLE READINGS SE-LECTED FROM THE PENTATEUCH AND THE BOOK OF JOSHUA. 2nd Ed. Globe 8vo. 2s. 6d.

CROSSLEY (E.), GLEDHILL (J.), and WILSON (J. M.).—A HANDBOOK OF DOU-BLE STARS. 8vo. 21s.

   CORRECTIONS TO THE HANDBOOK OF DOUBLE STARS. 8vo. 1s.

CUMMING (Linnæus).—ELECTRICITY. An Introduction to the Theory of Electricity. With numerous Examples. Cr. 8vo. 8s. 6d.

CUNNINGHAM (Sir H. S.).—THE CŒRU-LEANS : A VACATION IDYLL. Cr. 8vo. 3s. 6d.

—— THE HERIOTS. 3 vols. Cr. 8vo. 31s. 6d.

CUNNINGHAM (Rev. W.).—THE EPISTLE OF ST. BARNABAS. A Dissertation, including a Discussion of its Date and Authorship. Together with the Greek Text, the Latin Version, and a New English Translation and Commentary. Crown 8vo. 7s. 6d.

CUNNINGHAM (Rev. W.).—CHRISTIAN CIVILISATION, WITH SPECIAL REFERENCE TO INDIA. Crown 8vo. 5s.

—— THE CHURCHES OF ASIA: A METHODICAL SKETCH OF THE SECOND CENTURY. Crown 8vo. 6s.

CUNNINGHAM (Rev. John). — THE GROWTH OF THE CHURCH IN ITS ORGANISATION AND INSTITUTIONS. Being the Croall Lectures for 1886. 8vo. 9s.

CUNYNGHAME (Gen. Sir A. T.).—MY COMMAND IN SOUTH AFRICA, 1874—78. 8vo. 12s. 6d.

CURTEIS (Rev. G. H.).—DISSENT IN ITS RELATION TO THE CHURCH OF ENGLAND. Bampton Lectures for 1871. Cr. 8vo. 7s. 6d.

—— THE SCIENTIFIC OBSTACLES TO CHRISTIAN BELIEF. The Boyle Lectures, 1884. Cr. 8vo. 6s.

CUTHBERTSON (Francis). — EUCLIDIAN GEOMETRY. Extra fcp. 8vo. 4s. 6d.

DAGONET THE JESTER. Cr. 8vo. 4s. 6d.

DAHN (Felix).—FELICITAS. Translated by M. A. C. E. Crown 8vo. 4s. 6d.

"DAILY NEWS."—CORRESPONDENCE OF THE WAR BETWEEN RUSSIA AND TURKEY, 1877. TO THE FALL OF KARS. Cr. 8vo. 6s.

—— CORRESPONDENCE OF THE RUSSO-TURKISH WAR. FROM THE FALL OF KARS TO THE CONCLUSION OF PEACE. Crown 8vo. 6s.

DALE (A. W. W.).—THE SYNOD OF ELVIRA, AND CHRISTIAN LIFE IN THE FOURTH CENTURY. Crown 8vo. 10s. 6d.

DALTON (Rev. T.).—RULES AND EXAMPLES IN ARITHMETIC. New Edition. 18mo. 2s. 6d.

—— RULES AND EXAMPLES IN ALGEBRA. Part I. New Ed. 18mo. 2s. Part II. 2s. 6d. KEY TO ALGEBRA. Part I. Cr. 8vo. 7s. 6d.

DAMIEN (Father).—A JOURNEY FROM CASHMERE TO HIS HOME IN HAWAII. By EDWARD CLIFFORD. Crown 8vo. 2s. 6d.

DAMPIER.—By W. CLARK RUSSELL. With Portrait. Crown 8vo. 2s. 6d.

DANIELL (Alfred).—A TEXT-BOOK OF THE PRINCIPLES OF PHYSICS. With Illustrations. 2nd Edition. Medium 8vo. 21s.

DANTE.—THE PURGATORY OF DANTE ALIGHIERI. Edited, with Translations and Notes, by A. J. BUTLER. Cr. 8vo. 12s. 6d.

—— THE PARADISO OF DANTE. Edited, with a Prose Translation and Notes, by A. J. BUTLER. Crown 8vo. 12s. 6d.

—— DE MONARCHIA. Translated by F. J. CHURCH. 8vo. 4s. 6d.

—— DANTE: AND OTHER ESSAYS. By the DEAN OF ST. PAUL'S. Globe 8vo. 5s.

—— READINGS ON THE PURGATORIO OF DANTE. Chiefly based on the Commentary of Benvenuto Da Imola. By the Hon. W. W. VERNON, M.A. With an Introduction by the Very Rev. the DEAN OF ST. PAUL'S. 2 vols. Crown 8vo. 24s.

DARWIN (Charles).—MEMORIAL NOTICES, reprinted from *Nature*. By T. H. HUXLEY, G. J. ROMANES, ARCHIBALD GEIKIE, and W. T. THISELTON DYER. With a Portrait. Crown 8vo. 2s. 6d. [*Nature* Series.

DAVIES (Rev. J. Llewelyn).—THE GOSPEL AND MODERN LIFE. 2nd Edition, to which is added MORALITY ACCORDING TO THE SACRAMENT OF THE LORD'S SUPPER. Extra fcp. 8vo. 6s.

—— WARNINGS AGAINST SUPERSTITION. Ex. fcp. 8vo. 2s. 6d.

—— THE CHRISTIAN CALLING. Ex.fcp. 8vo. 6s.

—— THE EPISTLES OF ST. PAUL TO THE EPHESIANS, THE COLOSSIANS, AND PHILEMON. With Introductions and Notes. 2nd Edition. 8vo. 7s. 6d.

—— SOCIAL QUESTIONS FROM THE POINT OF VIEW OF CHRISTIAN THEOLOGY. 2nd Ed. Crown 8vo. 6s.

DAVIES (J. Ll.) and VAUGHAN (D. J.).— THE REPUBLIC OF PLATO. Translated into English. 18mo. 4s. 6d.

DAWKINS (Prof. W. Boyd).—EARLY MAN IN BRITAIN AND HIS PLACE IN THE TERTIARY PERIOD. Medium 8vo. 25s.

DAWSON (Sir J. W.).—ACADIAN GEOLOGY, THE GEOLOGICAL STRUCTURE, ORGANIC REMAINS, AND MINERAL RESOURCES OF NOVA SCOTIA, NEW BRUNSWICK, AND PRINCE EDWARD ISLAND. 3rd Ed. 8vo. 21s.

DAWSON (James).—AUSTRALIAN ABORIGINES. Small 4to. 14s.

DAY (Rev. Lal Behari).—BENGAL PEASANT LIFE. Crown 8vo. 6s.

—— FOLK TALES OF BENGAL. Cr. 8vo. 4s. 6d.

DAY (R. E.).—ELECTRIC LIGHT ARITHMETIC. Pott 8vo. 2s.

DAY (H. G.).—PROPERTIES OF CONIC SECTIONS PROVED GEOMETRICALLY. Crown 8vo. 3s. 6d.

DAYS WITH SIR ROGER DE COVERLEY. From the *Spectator*. With Illustrations by HUGH THOMSON. Fcp. 4to. 6s.

DEÁK (Francis).—HUNGARIAN STATESMAN. A Memoir. 8vo. 12s. 6d.

DEFOE (Daniel). — THE ADVENTURES OF ROBINSON CRUSOE. Ed. by HENRY KINGSLEY. Globe 8vo. 3s. 6d. [*Globe Series.*

Golden Treasury Series Edition. Edited by J. W. CLARK, M.A. 18mo. 4s. 6d.

DEFOE. By W. MINTO. Crown 8vo. 1s. 6d.; sewed, 1s. [*English Men of Letters Series.*

DELAMOTTE (Prof. P. H.).—A BEGINNER'S DRAWING-BOOK. Progressively arranged. With upwards of 50 Plates. 3rd Edition. Crown 8vo. 3s. 6d.

DEMOCRACY: AN AMERICAN NOVEL. Crown 8vo. 4s. 6d.

DEMOSTHENES.—ADVERSUS LEPTINEM. Ed. Rev. J. R. KING, M.A. Fcp. 8vo. 4s. 6d.

—— THE ORATION ON THE CROWN. Edited by B. DRAKE, M.A. 7th Ed. Fcp. 8vo. 4s. 6d.

—— THE FIRST PHILIPPIC. Edited by Rev. T. GWATKIN, M.A. Fcp. 8vo. 2s. 6d.

DEMOSTHENES.—By Prof. S. H. BUTCHER, M.A. Fcp. 8vo. 1s. 6d.

DE MAISTRE.—LA JEUNE SIBÉRIENNE ET LE LÉPREUX DE LA CITÉ D'AOSTE. Edited, with Notes and Vocabulary, by S. BARLET, B.Sc. Globe 8vo. 1s. 6d.

DE MORGAN (Mary).—THE NECKLACE OF PRINCESS FIORIMONDE, AND OTHER STORIES. Illustrated by WALTER CRANE. Extra fcp. 8vo. 3s. 6d. Also a Large Paper Edition, with the Illustrations on India Paper. 100 copies only printed.

DE QUINCEY. By Prof. MASSON. Crown 8vo. 1s. 6d. ; sewed, 1s.

DEUTSCHE LYRIK.—THE GOLDEN TREASURY OF THE BEST GERMAN LYRICAL POEMS. Selected and arranged by Dr. BUCHHEIM. 18mo. 4s. 6d.

DE VERE (Aubrey).—ESSAYS CHIEFLY ON POETRY. 2 vols. Globe 8vo. 12s.

—— ESSAYS, CHIEFLY LITERARY AND ETHICAL. Globe 8vo. 6s.

DE WINT.—MEMOIR OF PETER DE WINT. By WALTER ARMSTRONG, B.A. Oxon. Illustrated by 24 Photogravures from the Artist's pictures. Super-Royal 4to. 31s. 6d.

DICEY (Prof. A. V.).—LECTURES INTRODUCTORY TO THE STUDY OF THE LAW OF THE CONSTITUTION. 3rd Edition. 8vo. 12s. 6d.

—— LETTERS ON UNIONIST DELUSIONS. Crown 8vo. 2s. 6d.

—— THE PRIVY COUNCIL. Crown 8vo. 3s. 6d.

DICKENS (Charles). — THE POSTHUMOUS PAPERS OF THE PICKWICK CLUB. With Notes and numerous Illustrations. Edited by CHARLES DICKENS the younger. 2 vols. Extra crown 8vo. 21s.

DICKENS. By A. W. WARD. Crown 8vo. 1s. 6d. ; sewed, 1s.

DIDEROT AND THE ENCYCLOPÆDISTS. By JOHN MORLEY. 2 vols. Globe 8vo. 10s.

DIGGLE (Rev. J. W.). — GODLINESS AND MANLINESS. A Miscellany of Brief Papers touching the Relation of Religion to Life. Crown 8vo. 6s.

DILETTANTI SOCIETY'S PUBLICATIONS.—ANTIQUITIES OF IONIA. Vols. I. II. and III. 2l. 2s. each, or 5l. 5s. the set. Part IV., folio, half morocco, 3l. 13s. 6d.

—— PENROSE (Francis C.). An Investigation of the Principles of Athenian Architecture. Illustrated by numerous engravings. New Edition. Enlarged. Folio. 7l. 7s.

—— SPECIMENS OF ANCIENT SCULPTURE: EGYPTIAN, ETRUSCAN, GREEK, AND ROMAN. Selected from different Collections in Great Britain by the Society of Dilettanti. Vol. II. Folio. 5l. 5s.

DILKE (Sir C. W.).—GREATER BRITAIN. A Record of Travel in English-Speaking Countries during 1866-67. (America, Australia, India.) 9th Edition. Crown 8vo. 6s.

—— PROBLEMS OF GREATER BRITAIN. Maps. 2 vols. 8vo. 36s.

DILLWYN (E. A.).—JILL. Crown 8vo. 6s.

—— JILL AND JACK. 2 vols. Globe 8vo. 12s.

DOBSON (Austin).—FIELDING. Crown 8vo. 1s. 6d. ; sewed, 1s.

DODGSON (C. L.).—EUCLID. Books I. and II. With Words substituted for the Algebraical Symbols used in the first edition. 4th Edition. Crown 8vo. 2s.

DODGSON (C. L.).—EUCLID AND HIS MODERN RIVALS. 2nd Edition. Cr. 8vo. 6s.

—— SUPPLEMENT TO FIRST EDITION "EUCLID AND HIS MODERN RIVALS." Crown 8vo. Sewed, 1s.

—— CURIOSA MATHEMATICA. Part I. A New Theory of Parallels. 2nd Ed. Cr. 8vo. 2s.

DONALDSON (Prof. James).—THE APOSTOLICAL FATHERS. A CRITICAL ACCOUNT OF THEIR GENUINE WRITINGS, AND OF THEIR DOCTRINES. 2nd Ed. Cr. 8vo. 7s. 6d.

DONISTHORPE (Wordsworth). — INDIVIDUALISM : A SYSTEM OF POLITICS. 8vo. 14s.

DOWDEN (Prof. E.).—SHAKSPERE. 18mo. 1s.

—— SOUTHEY. Crown 8vo. 1s. 6d. ; sewed, 1s.

DOYLE (J. A.).—HISTORY OF AMERICA. With Maps. 18mo. 4s. 6d.

DOYLE (Sir F. H.).—THE RETURN OF THE GUARDS: AND OTHER POEMS. Cr. 8vo. 7s. 6d.

DREW (W. H.).—A GEOMETRICAL TREATISE ON CONIC SECTIONS. 8th Ed. Cr. 8vo. 5s.

DRUMMOND (Prof. James).—INTRODUCTION TO THE STUDY OF THEOLOGY. Crown 8vo. 5s.

DRYDEN : ESSAYS OF. Edited by Prof. C. D. YONGE. Fcp. 8vo. 2s. 6d.

—— POETICAL WORKS. Edited, with Memoir, Revised Text, and Notes, by W. D. CHRISTIE, C.B. Globe 8vo. 3s. 6d. [Globe Edition.

DRYDEN. By G. SAINTSBURY. Crown 8vo. 1s. 6d. ; sewed, 1s.

DU CANE (Col. Sir E. F.).—THE PUNISHMENT AND PREVENTION OF CRIME. Crown 8vo. 3s. 6d.

DUFF (Right Hon. Sir M. E. Grant).—NOTES OF AN INDIAN JOURNEY. 8vo. 10s. 6d.

—— MISCELLANIES, POLITICAL AND LITERARY. 8vo. 10s. 6d.

DUMAS.—LES DEMOISELLES DE ST. CYR. Comédie par ALEXANDRE DUMAS. Edited by VICTOR OGER. 18mo. 1s. 6d.

DÜNTZER.—LIFE OF GOETHE. Translated by T. W. LYSTER. With Illustrations. 2 vols. Crown 8vo. 21s.

—— LIFE OF SCHILLER. Translated by P. E. PINKERTON. Illustrations. Cr. 8vo. 10s. 6d.

DU PRÉ (A. M. D.).—OUTLINES OF ENGLISH HISTORY. Globe 8vo. In 2 Parts.

DUPUIS (Prof. N. F.).—ELEMENTARY SYNTHETIC GEOMETRY OF THE POINT, LINE, AND CIRCLE IN THE PLANE. Gl. 8vo. 4s. 6d.

DYER (J. M.).—EXERCISES IN ANALYTICAL GEOMETRY. Crown 8vo. 4s. 6d.

EADIE (Prof. John).—THE ENGLISH BIBLE: AN EXTERNAL AND CRITICAL HISTORY OF THE VARIOUS ENGLISH TRANSLATIONS OF SCRIPTURE. 2 vols. 8vo. 28s.

—— ST. PAUL'S EPISTLES TO THE THESSALONIANS, COMMENTARY ON THE GREEK TEXT. 8vo. 12s.

—— LIFE OF JOHN EADIE, D.D., LL.D. By JAMES BROWN, D.D. 2nd Ed. Cr. 8vo. 7s. 6d.

EAGLES (T. H.).—CONSTRUCTIVE GEOMETRY OF PLANE CURVES. Crown 8vo. 12s.

EASTLAKE (Lady).—FELLOWSHIP: LETTERS ADDRESSED TO MY SISTER-MOURNERS. Cr. 8vo. 2s. 6d.

EBERS (Dr. George).—THE BURGOMASTER'S WIFE. Translated by CLARA BELL. Crown 8vo. 4s. 6d.

—— ONLY A WORD. Translated by CLARA BELL. Crown 8vo. 4s. 6d.

ECCE HOMO. A SURVEY OF THE LIFE AND WORK OF JESUS CHRIST. 20th Edition. Crown 8vo. 6s.

ECONOMICS, THE QUARTERLY JOURNAL OF. Vol. II. Part II. January, 1888. 8vo. 2s. 6d. Part III. 2s. 6d. Part IV. 2s. 6d. Vol. III. 4 parts, 2s. 6d. each. Vol. IV. Part I. 2s. 6d.

EDGAR (J. H.) and PRITCHARD (G. S.).— NOTE-BOOK ON PRACTICAL SOLID OR DESCRIPTIVE GEOMETRY, CONTAINING PROBLEMS WITH HELP FOR SOLUTION. 4th Edition, Enlarged. By ARTHUR G. MEEZE. Globe 8vo. 4s. 6d.

EDWARDS (Joseph). — AN ELEMENTARY TREATISE ON THE DIFFERENTIAL CALCULUS. Crown 8vo. 10s. 6d.

EDWARDS-MOSS (J. E.).—A SEASON IN SUTHERLAND. Crown 8vo. 4s. 6d.

EGGLESTON (E.). — THE HOUSEHOLD HISTORY OF THE UNITED STATES AND ITS PEOPLE. Illustrations and Maps. 4to. 12s.

EICKE (K. M.).—FIRST LESSONS IN LATIN. Extra fcp. 8vo. 2s.

EIMER (G. H. T.).—ORGANIC EVOLUTION. Translated by J. T. CUNNINGHAM, M.A. 8vo.

ELDERTON (W. A.).—MAP DRAWING AND MAP MAKING. Globe 8vo.

ELLERTON (Rev. John).—THE HOLIEST MANHOOD, AND ITS LESSONS FOR BUSY LIVES. Crown 8vo. 6s.

ELLIOT (Hon. A.).—THE STATE AND THE CHURCH. Crown 8vo. 3s. 6d.

ELLIOTT.—LIFE OF HENRY VENN ELLIOTT, OF BRIGHTON. By JOSIAH BATEMAN, M.A. 3rd Edition. Extra fcp. 8vo. 6s.

ELLIS (A. J.).—PRACTICAL HINTS ON THE QUANTITATIVE PRONUNCIATION OF LATIN. Extra fcp. 8vo. 4s. 6d.

ELLIS (Tristram).—SKETCHING FROM NATURE. With Illustrations by H. STACY MARKS, R.A., and the Author. 2nd Edition. Crown 8vo. 3s. 6d.

EMERSON.—THE LIFE OF RALPH WALDO EMERSON. By J. L. CABOT. 2 vols. Crown 8vo. 18s.

—— THE COLLECTED WORKS OF RALPH WALDO EMERSON. 6 vols. (1) MISCELLANIES. With an Introductory Essay by JOHN MORLEY. (2) ESSAYS. (3) POEMS. (4) ENGLISH TRAITS; AND REPRESENTATIVE MEN. (5) CONDUCT OF LIFE; AND SOCIETY AND SOLITUDE. (6) LETTERS; AND SOCIAL AIMS, &c. Globe 8vo. 5s. each.

ENGLAND (E. B.).—EXERCISES IN LATIN SYNTAX AND IDIOM. Arranged with reference to Roby's School Latin Grammar. Crown 8vo. 2s. 6d.
KEY to the above. Crown 8vo. 2s. 6d.

ENGLISH CITIZEN, THE.—A Series of Short Books on his Rights and Responsibilities. Edited by HENRY CRAIK, C.B. Crown 8vo. 3s. 6d. each.

CENTRAL GOVERNMENT. By H. D. TRAILL, D.C.L.

THE ELECTORATE AND THE LEGISLATURE. By SPENCER WALPOLE.

THE POOR LAW. By the Rev. T. W. FOWLE.

THE NATIONAL BUDGET; THE NATIONAL DEBT; TAXES AND RATES. By A. J. WILSON.

THE STATE IN RELATION TO LABOUR. By W. STANLEY JEVONS, LL.D., F.R.S.

THE STATE AND THE CHURCH. By the Hon. ARTHUR ELLIOTT, M.P.

FOREIGN RELATIONS. By SPENCER WALPOLE.

THE STATE IN ITS RELATION TO TRADE. By Sir T. H. FARRER, Bart.

LOCAL GOVERNMENT. By M. D. CHALMERS.

THE STATE IN ITS RELATION TO EDUCATION. By HENRY CRAIK, C.B.

THE LAND LAWS. By Sir F. POLLOCK, Bart. 2nd Edition.

COLONIES AND DEPENDENCIES.
Part I. INDIA. By J. S. COTTON, M.A.
II. THE COLONIES. By E. J. PAYNE.

JUSTICE AND POLICE. By F. W. MAITLAND.

THE PUNISHMENT AND PREVENTION OF CRIME. By Colonel Sir EDMUND DU CANE.

ENGLISH HISTORY, READINGS IN.— Selected and Edited by JOHN RICHARD GREEN. 3 Parts. Fcp. 8vo. 1s. 6d. each. Part I. Hengist to Cressy. II. Cressy to Cromwell. III. Cromwell to Balaklava.

ENGLISH ILLUSTRATED MAGAZINE, THE.—Profusely Illustrated. Published Monthly. Number I. October, 1883. 6d. Vol. I. 1884. 7s. 6d. Vols. II.—VI. Super royal 8vo, extra cloth, coloured edges. 8s. each. Cloth Covers for binding Volumes, 1s. 6d. each.

—— Proof Impressions of Engravings originally published in The English Illustrated Magazine. 1884. In Portfolio 4to. 21s.

ENGLISH MEN OF ACTION. —Crown 8vo. With Portraits. 2s. 6d. each.
The following Volumes are Ready:
GENERAL GORDON. By Col. Sir W. BUTLER.
HENRY V. By the Rev. A. J. CHURCH.
LIVINGSTONE. By THOMAS HUGHES.
LORD LAWRENCE. By Sir RICHARD TEMPLE.
WELLINGTON. By GEORGE HOOPER.
DAMPIER. By W. CLARK RUSSELL.
MONK. By JULIAN CORBETT.
STRAFFORD. By H. D. TRAILL.
WARREN HASTINGS. By Sir ALFRED LYALL.
PETERBOROUGH. By W. STEBBING.
The undermentioned are in the Press or in Preparation:
WARWICK, THE KING-MAKER. By C. W. OMAN.
DRAKE. By JULIAN CORBETT.

ENGLISH MEN OF ACTION—*contd.*
MONTROSE. By MOWBRAY MORRIS.
MARLBOROUGH. By Col. Sir WM. BUTLER.
CAPTAIN COOK. By WALTER BESANT.
RODNEY. By DAVID HANNAY.
CLIVE. By Colonel Sir CHARLES WILSON.
SIR JOHN MOORE. By Colonel MAURICE.
SIR CHARLES NAPIER. By Col. BUTLER.
SIR HENRY HAVELOCK. By ARCHIBALD FORBES.
ENGLISH MEN OF LETTERS.—Edited by JOHN MORLEY. Crown 8vo. 2s. 6d. each. Cheap Edition. 1s. 6d. ; sewed, 1s.
JOHNSON. By LESLIE STEPHEN.
SCOTT. By R. H. HUTTON.
GIBBON. By J. COTTER MORISON.
HUME. By T. H. HUXLEY.
GOLDSMITH. By WILLIAM BLACK.
SHELLEY. By J. A. SYMONDS.
DEFOE. By W. MINTO.
BURNS. By Principal SHAIRP.
SPENSER. By the DEAN OF ST. PAUL'S.
THACKERAY. By ANTHONY TROLLOPE.
MILTON. By MARK PATTISON.
BURKE. By JOHN MORLEY.
HAWTHORNE. By HENRY JAMES.
SOUTHEY. By Prof. DOWDEN.
BUNYAN. By J. A. FROUDE.
CHAUCER. By Prof. A. W. WARD.
COWPER. By GOLDWIN SMITH.
POPE. By LESLIE STEPHEN.
BYRON. By Prof. NICHOL.
DRYDEN. By G. SAINTSBURY.
LOCKE. By Prof. FOWLER.
WORDSWORTH. By F. W. H. MYERS.
LANDOR. By SIDNEY COLVIN.
DE QUINCEY. By Prof. MASSON.
CHARLES LAMB. By Rev. ALFRED AINGER.
BENTLEY. By Prof. JEBB.
DICKENS. By A. W. WARD.
GRAY. By EDMUND GOSSE.
SWIFT. By LESLIE STEPHEN.
STERNE. By H. D. TRAILL.
MACAULAY. By J. COTTER MORISON.
FIELDING. By AUSTIN DOBSON.
SHERIDAN. By Mrs. OLIPHANT.
ADDISON. By W. J. COURTHOPE.
BACON. By the DEAN OF ST. PAUL'S.
COLERIDGE. By H. D. TRAILL.
SIR PHILIP SIDNEY. By J. A. SYMONDS.
KEATS. By SIDNEY COLVIN.
ENGLISH POETS. Selections, with Critical Introductions by various Writers, and a General Introduction by MATTHEW ARNOLD. Edited by T. H. WARD, M.A. 4 vols. Crown 8vo. 7s. 6d. each.
Vol. I. CHAUCER TO DONNE. II. BEN JONSON TO DRYDEN. III. ADDISON TO BLAKE. IV. WORDSWORTH TO ROSSETTI.

ENGLISH STATESMEN (TWELVE). Crown 8vo. 2s. 6d. each.
WILLIAM THE CONQUEROR. By EDWARD A. FREEMAN, D.C.L., LL.D. [*Ready.*
HENRY II. By Mrs. J. R. GREEN. [*Ready.*
EDWARD I. By F. YORK POWELL.
HENRY VII. By JAMES GARDINER. [*Ready.*
CARDINAL WOLSEY. By Prof. M. CREIGHTON. [*Ready.*
ELIZABETH. By E. S. BEESLEY.
OLIVER CROMWELL. By FREDERIC HARRISON. [*Ready.*
WILLIAM III. By H. D. TRAILL. [*Ready.*
WALPOLE. By JOHN MORLEY. [*Ready.*
CHATHAM. By JOHN MORLEY.
PITT. By JOHN MORLEY.
PEEL. By J. R. THURSFIELD.
ESSEX FIELD CLUB MEMOIRS. Vol. I. REPORT ON THE EAST ANGLIAN EARTHQUAKE OF 22ND APRIL, 1884. By RAPHAEL MELDOLA, F.R.S., and WILLIAM WHITE, F.E.S. Maps and Illustrations. 8vo. 3s. 6d.
ETON COLLEGE, HISTORY OF, 1440—1884. By H. C. MAXWELL LYTE, C.B. Illustrations. 2nd Ed. Med. 8vo. Cloth, 21s.
EURIPIDES.—MEDEA. Edited by A. W. VERRALL, Litt.D. 8vo. 7s. 6d.
—— HIPPOLYTUS. Edited by J. P. MAHAFFY, M.A., and J. B. BURY. Fcp. 8vo. 3s. 6d.
—— HECUBA. Edited by Rev. JOHN BOND, M.A., and A. S. WALPOLE, M.A. 18mo. 1s. 6d.
—— IPHIGENIA IN TAURIS. Edited by E. B. ENGLAND, M.A. Fcp. 8vo. 4s. 6d.
—— MEDEA. Edited by A. W. VERRALL, Litt.D. Fcp. 8vo. 3s. 6d.
—— ION. Edited by M. A. BAYFIELD, M.A. Fcp. 8vo. 3s. 6d.
EURIPIDES. By Prof. MAHAFFY. Fcp. 8vo. 1s. 6d.
EUROPEAN HISTORY, NARRATED IN A SERIES OF HISTORICAL SELECTIONS FROM THE BEST AUTHORITIES. Edited and arranged by E. M. SEWELL and C. M. YONGE. 2 vols. 3rd Edition. Crown 8vo. 6s. each.
EUTROPIUS. Adapted for the Use of Beginners. With Notes, Exercises, and Vocabularies. By W. WELCH, M.A., and C. G. DUFFIELD, M.A. 18mo. 1s. 6d.
EVANS (Sebastian).—BROTHER FABIAN'S MANUSCRIPT, AND OTHER POEMS. Fcp. 8vo, cloth. 6s.
—— IN THE STUDIO: A DECADE OF POEMS. Extra fcp. 8vo. 5s.
EVERETT (Prof. J. D.).—UNITS AND PHYSICAL CONSTANTS. 2nd Ed. Globe 8vo. 5s.
FAIRFAX.—LIFE OF ROBERT FAIRFAX OF STEETON, Vice-Admiral, Alderman, and Member for York, A.D. 1666—1725. By CLEMENTS R. MARKHAM, C.B. 8vo. 12s. 6d.
FAITH AND CONDUCT: AN ESSAY ON VERIFIABLE RELIGION. Crown 8vo. 7s. 6d.
FARRAR (Archdeacon).—THE FALL OF MAN, AND OTHER SERMONS. 5th Ed. Cr. 8vo. 6s.

FARRAR (Archdeacon).—THE WITNESS OF HISTORY TO CHRIST. Being the Hulsean Lectures for 1870. 7th Edit. Cr. 8vo. 5s.

—— SEEKERS AFTER GOD. THE LIVES OF SENECA, EPICTETUS, AND MARCUS AURELIUS. 12th Edition. Crown 8vo. 6s.

—— THE SILENCE AND VOICES OF GOD. University and other Sermons. 7th Ed. Cr. 8vo. 6s.

—— IN THE DAYS OF THY YOUTH. Sermons on Practical Subjects, preached at Marlborough College. 9th Edition. Cr. 8vo. 9s.

—— ETERNAL HOPE. Five Sermons, preached in Westminster Abbey. 28th Thousand. Crown 8vo. 6s.

—— SAINTLY WORKERS. Five Lenten Lectures, delivered at St. Andrew's, Holborn. 3rd Edition. Crown 8vo. 6s.

—— EPHPHATHA; OR, THE AMELIORATION OF THE WORLD. Sermons preached at Westminster Abbey. Crown 8vo. 6s.

—— MERCY AND JUDGMENT. A few Last Words on Christian Eschatology. 2nd Ed. Crown 8vo. 10s. 6d.

—— THE MESSAGES OF THE BOOKS. Being Discourses and Notes on the Books of the New Testament. 8vo. 14s.

—— SERMONS AND ADDRESSES DELIVERED IN AMERICA. Crown 8vo. 7s. 6d.

—— THE HISTORY OF INTERPRETATION. Being the Bampton Lectures, 1885. 8vo. 16s.

FARREN (Robert).—THE GRANTA AND THE CAM, FROM BYRON'S POOL TO ELY. Thirty-six Etchings. Large Imperial, cloth gilt. A few Copies, Proofs, Large Paper, of which but 50 were printed, half morocco.

—— CAMBRIDGE AND ITS NEIGHBOURHOOD. A Series of Etchings. With an Introduction by JOHN WILLIS CLARK, M.A. Imp. 4to.

—— A ROUND OF MELODIES. A Series of Etched Designs. Oblong folio, half morocco.

—— THE BIRDS OF ARISTOPHANES. 13s. net. Proofs.

—— THE BATTLE GROUND OF THE EIGHTS. THE THAMES, THE ISIS, AND THE CAM. Oblong 4to, cloth.

—— CATHEDRAL CITIES : ELY AND NORWICH. With Introduction by E.A. FREEMAN, D.C.L. Col. 4to. Proofs on Japanese paper.

—— —— PETERBOROUGH. WITH THE ABBEYS OF CROWLAND AND THORNEY. With Introduction by EDMUND VENABLES, M.A. Col. 4to. 2l. 2s. net. Proofs, folio, 5l. 5s. net. The Edition is limited to 125 Small Paper and 45 Large.

—— THE EUMENIDES OF ÆSCHYLUS. As performed by Members of the University at the Theatre Royal, Cambridge. Oblong 4to. Small size, 10s. 6d. net. Large size, India Proofs, 21s. net. On Whatman paper, 27s. net.

—— THE OEDIPUS TYRANNUS OF SOPHOCLES. As performed at Cambridge. Oblong 4to. Prints, 10s. 6d. net. Proofs, 21s. net.

FASNACHT (G. Eugène).—THE ORGANIC METHOD OF STUDYING LANGUAGES. I. FRENCH. Extra fcp. 8vo. 3s. 6d.

—— A SYNTHETIC FRENCH GRAMMAR FOR SCHOOLS. Crown 8vo. 3s. 6d.

FAWCETT (Rt. Hon. Henry).—MANUAL OF POLITICAL ECONOMY. 7th Edition, revised. Crown 8vo. 12s.

—— AN EXPLANATORY DIGEST OF PROFESSOR FAWCETT'S MANUAL OF POLITICAL ECONOMY. By CYRIL A. WATERS. Cr. 8vo. 2s. 6d.

—— SPEECHES ON SOME CURRENT POLITICAL QUESTIONS. 8vo. 10s. 6d.

—— FREE TRADE AND PROTECTION. 9th Edition. Crown 8vo. 3s. 6d.

FAWCETT (Mrs. H.).—POLITICAL ECONOMY FOR BEGINNERS, WITH QUESTIONS. 7th Edition. 18mo. 2s. 6d.

—— SOME EMINENT WOMEN OF OUR TIMES. Short Biographical Sketches. Cr. 8vo. 2s. 6d.

FAWCETT (Rt. Hon. Henry and Mrs. H.).— ESSAYS AND LECTURES ON POLITICAL AND SOCIAL SUBJECTS. 8vo. 10s. 6d.

FAY (Amy.).—MUSIC-STUDY IN GERMANY. With a Preface by Sir GEORGE GROVE, D.C.L. Crown 8vo. 4s. 6d.

FEARNLEY (W.).—A MANUAL OF ELEMENTARY PRACTICAL HISTOLOGY. Cr. 8vo. 7s. 6d.

FEARON (D. R.).—SCHOOL INSPECTION. 6th Edition. Crown 8vo. 2s. 6d.

FERREL (Prof. W.).—A POPULAR TREATISE ON THE WINDS. 8vo. 18s.

FERRERS (Rev. N. M.).—A TREATISE ON TRILINEAR CO-ORDINATES, THE METHOD OF RECIPROCAL POLARS, AND THE THEORY OF PROJECTIONS. 3rd Ed. Cr. 8vo. 6s. 6d.

—— SPHERICAL HARMONICS AND SUBJECTS CONNECTED WITH THEM. Crown 8vo. 7s. 6d.

FIELDING.—By AUSTIN DOBSON. Crown 8vo. 1s. 6d. ; sewed, 1s.

FINCK (Henry T.).—ROMANTIC LOVE AND PERSONAL BEAUTY. 2 vols. Cr. 8vo. 18s.

FIRST LESSONS IN BUSINESS MATTERS. By a BANKER'S DAUGHTER. 2nd Edition. 18mo. 1s.

FISHER (Rev. Osmond).—PHYSICS OF THE EARTH'S CRUST. 2nd Edition. 8vo. 12s.

FISKE (John).—OUTLINES OF COSMIC PHILOSOPHY, BASED ON THE DOCTRINE OF EVOLUTION. 2 vols. 8vo. 25s.

—— DARWINISM, AND OTHER ESSAYS. Crown 8vo. 7s. 6d.

—— MAN'S DESTINY VIEWED IN THE LIGHT OF HIS ORIGIN. Crown 8vo. 3s. 6d.

—— AMERICAN POLITICAL IDEAS VIEWED FROM THE STAND-POINT OF UNIVERSAL HISTORY. Crown 8vo. 4s.

—— THE CRITICAL PERIOD IN AMERICAN HISTORY, 1783–89. Ex. Cr. 8vo. 10s. 6d.

—— THE BEGINNINGS OF NEW ENGLAND; OR, THE PURITAN THEOCRACY IN ITS RELATIONS TO CIVIL AND RELIGIOUS LIBERTY. Crown 8vo. 7s. 6d.

FISON (L.) and HOWITT (A. W.).—KAMILAROI AND KURNAI GROUP. Group-Marriage and Relationship and Marriage by Elopement, drawn chiefly from the usage of the Australian Aborigines, also the Kurnai Tribe, their Customs in Peace and War. With an Introduction by LEWIS H. MORGAN, LL.D. 8vo. 15s.

FITZGERALD (Edward). — LETTERS AND
LITERARY REMAINS OF. Ed. by W. ALDIS
WRIGHT, M.A. 3 vols. Crown 8vo. 31s. 6d.

FITZ GERALD (Caroline). — VENETIA VIC-
TRIX, AND OTHER POEMS. Ex. fcp. 8vo. 3s. 6d.

FLEAY (Rev. F. G.). — A SHAKESPEARE
MANUAL. Extra fcp. 8vo. 4s. 6d.

FLEISCHER (Dr. Emil). — A SYSTEM OF
VOLUMETRIC ANALYSIS. Translated by M.
M. PATTISON MUIR, F.R.S.E. Cr. 8vo. 7s. 6d.

FLEMING (George). — A NILE NOVEL. GL
8vo. 2s.

—— MIRAGE. A Novel. Globe 8vo. 2s.

—— THE HEAD OF MEDUSA. Globe 8vo. 2s.

—— VESTIGIA. Globe 8vo. 2s.

FLITTERS, TATTERS, AND THE
COUNSELLOR; WEEDS; AND OTHER
SKETCHES. By the Author of "Hogan,
M.P." Globe 8vo. 2s.

FLORIAN'S FABLES. Selected and Edited
by Rev. CHARLES YELD, M.A. Illustrated.
Globe 8vo. 1s. 6d.
[Primary French and German Readers.

FLOWER (Prof. W. H.). — AN INTRODUCTION
TO THE OSTEOLOGY OF THE MAMMALIA.
With numerous Illustrations. 3rd Edition,
revised with the assistance of HANS GADOW,
Ph.D., M.A. Crown 8vo. 10s. 6d.

FLÜCKIGER (F. A.) and HANBURY (D.).
— PHARMACOGRAPHIA. A History of the
principal Drugs of Vegetable Origin met
with in Great Britain and India. 2nd Edition,
revised. 8vo. 21s.

FO'C'SLE YARNS, including "Betsy Lee,"
and other Poems. Crown 8vo. 7s. 6d.

FORBES (Archibald). — SOUVENIRS OF SOME
CONTINENTS. Crown 8vo. 6s.

FORBES (Edward). — MEMOIR OF. By
GEORGE WILSON, M.D., and ARCHIBALD
GEIKIE, F.R.S., &c. Demy 8vo. 14s.

FORBES (Rev. Granville). — THE VOICE OF
GOD IN THE PSALMS. Crown 8vo. 6s 6d.

FORBES (George). — THE TRANSIT OF VENUS.
Crown 8vo. 3s. 6d. [Nature Series.

FORSYTH (A. R.). — A TREATISE OF DIF-
FERENTIAL EQUATIONS. Demy 8vo. 14s.

FOSTER (Prof. Michael). — A TEXT-BOOK OF
PHYSIOLOGY. With Illustrations. 5th Ed.
3 Parts. Part I., comprising Book I. Blood—
The Tissues of Movement, the Vascular Me-
chanism. 8vo. 10s. 6d. — Part II., comprising Book II. The Tissues of Chemical Action, with their Respective Mechan-
isms—Nutrition. 10s. 6d.
4th Edition. Part III., comprising Book
III. The Central Nervous System and its Instruments. Book IV. The Tissues and Mech-
anisms of Reproduction. 8vo. 7s. 6d.

—— PRIMER OF PHYSIOLOGY. New Edition.
18mo. 1s. [Science Primers.

FOSTER (Prof. Michael) and BALFOUR
(F. M.) (the late). — THE ELEMENTS OF EM-
BRYOLOGY. Edited by ADAM SEDGWICK,
M.A., and WALTER HEAPE. With Illustra-
tions. 3rd Edition, revised and enlarged.
Crown 8vo. 10s. 6d.

FOSTER (Michael) and LANGLEY (J. N.).
— A COURSE OF ELEMENTARY PRACTICAL
PHYSIOLOGY AND HISTOLOGY. 6th Edition,
enlarged. Crown 8vo. 7s. 6d.

FOTHERGILL (Dr. J. Milner). — THE PRAC-
TITIONER'S HANDBOOK OF TREATMENT;
OR, THE PRINCIPLES OF THERAPEUTICS.
3rd Edition, enlarged. 8vo. 16s.

—— THE ANTAGONISM OF THERAPEUTIC
AGENTS, AND WHAT IT TEACHES. Crown
8vo. 6s.

—— FOOD FOR THE INVALID, THE CONVALES-
CENT, THE DYSPEPTIC, AND THE GOUTY.
2nd Edition. Crown 8vo. 3s. 6d.

FOWLE (Rev. T. W.). — THE POOR LAW.
Cr. 8vo. 3s. 6d. [English Citizen Series.

—— A NEW ANALOGY BETWEEN REVEALED
RELIGION AND THE COURSE AND CONSTI-
TUTION OF NATURE. Crown 8vo. 6s.

FOWLER (Rev. Thomas). — LOCKE. Crown
8vo. 1s. 6d.; sewed, 1s.

—— PROGRESSIVE MORALITY: AN ESSAY IN
ETHICS. Crown 8vo. 5s.

FOWLER (W. W.). — TALES OF THE BIRDS.
Illustrated. Crown 8vo. 3s. 6d.

—— A YEAR WITH THE BIRDS. Illustrated.
Crown 8vo. 3s. 6d.

FOX (Dr. Wilson). — ON THE ARTIFICIAL
PRODUCTION OF TUBERCLE IN THE LOWER
ANIMALS. With Plates. 4to. 5s. 6d.

—— ON THE TREATMENT OF HYPERPYREXIA,
AS ILLUSTRATED IN ACUTE ARTICULAR
RHEUMATISM BY MEANS OF THE EXTERNAL
APPLICATION OF COLD. 8vo. 2s. 6d.

FRAMJI (Dosabhai). — HISTORY OF THE
PARSIS: INCLUDING THEIR MANNERS, CUS-
TOMS, RELIGION, AND PRESENT POSITION.
With Illustrations. 2 vols. Med. 8vo. 36s.

FRANKLAND (Prof. Percy). — A HANDBOOK
OF AGRICULTURAL CHEMICAL ANALYSIS.
Founded upon "Leitfaden für die Agricultur-
Chemische Analyse," von Dr. F. KROCKER.
Crown 8vo. 7s. 6d.

FRASER. — SERMONS. By the Right Rev.
JAMES FRASER, D.D., Second Bishop of
Manchester. Edited by Rev. JOHN W.
DIGGLE. 2 vols. Crown 8vo. 6s. each.

FRASER — HUGHES. — JAMES FRASER,
SECOND BISHOP OF MANCHESTER: A Memoir. By T. HUGHES. Crown 8vo. 6s.

FRASER-TYTLER. — SONGS IN MINOR
KEYS. By C. C. FRASER-TYTLER (Mrs.
EDWARD LIDDELL). 2nd Ed. 18mo. 6s.

FRATERNITY: A Romance. 2 vols. Cr.
8vo. 21s.

FREDERICK (Mrs.). — HINTS TO HOUSE-
WIVES ON SEVERAL POINTS, PARTICULARLY
ON THE PREPARATION OF ECONOMICAL AND
TASTEFUL DISHES. Crown 8vo. 1s.

FREEMAN (Prof. E. A.). — HISTORY OF THE
CATHEDRAL CHURCH OF WELLS. Crown
8vo. 3s. 6d.

—— OLD ENGLISH HISTORY. With 5 Col.
Maps. 9th Edition. revised. Extra fcp.
8vo. 6s.

—— HISTORICAL ESSAYS. First Series. 4th
Edition. 8vo. 10s. 6d.

FREEMAN (Prof. E. A.). — HISTORICAL ESSAYS. Second Series. 3rd Edition. With Additional Essays. 8vo. 10s. 6d.
—— —— Third Series. 8vo. 12s.
—— THE GROWTH OF THE ENGLISH CONSTITUTION FROM THE EARLIEST TIMES. 5th Edition. Crown 8vo. 5s.
—— GENERAL SKETCH OF EUROPEAN HISTORY. With Maps, &c. 18mo. 3s. 6d.
—— EUROPE. 18mo. 1s. [Literature Primers.
—— COMPARATIVE POLITICS. Lectures at the Royal Institution. To which is added "The Unity of History." 8vo. 14s.
—— HISTORICAL AND ARCHITECTURAL SKETCHES : CHIEFLY ITALIAN. Illustrated by the Author. Crown 8vo. 10s. 6d.
—— SUBJECT AND NEIGHBOUR LANDS OF VENICE. Illustrated. Crown 8vo. 10s. 6d.
—— ENGLISH TOWNS AND DISTRICTS. A Series of Addresses and Essays. 8vo. 14s.
—— THE OFFICE OF THE HISTORICAL PROFESSOR. Inaugural Lecture at Oxford. Cr. 8vo. 2s.
—— DISESTABLISHMENT AND DISENDOWMENT. WHAT ARE THEY? 4th Ed. Cr. 8vo. 1s.
—— GREATER GREECE AND GREATER BRITAIN : GEORGE WASHINGTON THE EXPANDER OF ENGLAND. With an Appendix on IMPERIAL FEDERATION. Cr. 8vo. 3s. 6d.
—— THE METHODS OF HISTORICAL STUDY. Eight Lectures at Oxford. 8vo. 10s. 6d.
—— THE CHIEF PERIODS OF EUROPEAN HISTORY. Six Lectures read in the University of Oxford, with an Essay on GREEK CITIES UNDER ROMAN RULE. 8vo. 10s. 6d.
—— FOUR OXFORD LECTURES, 1887. FIFTY YEARS OF EUROPEAN HISTORY—TEUTONIC CONQUEST IN GAUL AND BRITAIN. 8vo. 5s.
—— WILLIAM THE CONQUEROR. Crown 8vo. 2s. 6d. [Twelve English Statesmen.
FRENCH COURSE.—See Macmillan's Progressive French Course.
FRENCH READINGS FROM ROMAN HISTORY. Selected from various Authors. With Notes by C. COLBECK. 18mo. 4s. 6d.
FRIEDMANN (Paul).—ANNE BOLEYN. A Chapter of English History, 1527—36. 2 vols. 8vo. 28s.
FROST (Percival).—AN ELEMENTARY TREATISE ON CURVE TRACING. 8vo. 12s.
—— THE FIRST THREE SECTIONS OF NEWTON'S PRINCIPIA. 3rd Edition. 8vo. 12s.
—— SOLID GEOMETRY. 3rd Edition. 8vo. 16s.
—— HINTS FOR THE SOLUTION OF PROBLEMS IN THE THIRD EDITION OF SOLID GEOMETRY. 8vo. 8s. 6d.
FROUDE (J. A.).—BUNYAN. Crown 8vo. 1s. 6d. ; sewed, 1s.
FURNIVALL (F. J.).—LE MORTE ARTHUR. Edited from the Harleian MS. 2252, in the British Museum. Fcp. 8vo. 7s. 5d.
FYFFE (C. A.).—GREECE. 18mo. 1s.
GALTON (Francis). — METEOROGRAPHICA ; OR, METHODS OF MAPPING THE WEATHER. 4to. 9s.

GALTON (F.).—ENGLISH MEN OF SCIENCE : THEIR NATURE AND NURTURE. 8vo. 8s. 6d.
—— INQUIRIES INTO HUMAN FACULTY AND ITS DEVELOPMENT. 8vo. 16s.
—— RECORD OF FAMILY FACULTIES. Consisting of Tabular Forms and Directions for Entering Data. 4to. 2s. 6d.
—— LIFE HISTORY ALBUM : Being a Personal Note-book, combining the chief advantages of a Diary, Photograph Album, a Register of Height, Weight, and other Anthropometrical Observations, and a Record of Illnesses. 4to. 3s. 6d.—Or, with Cards of Wools for Testing Colour Vision. 4s. 6d.
—— NATURAL INHERITANCE. 8vo. 9s.
GAMGEE (Prof. Arthur).—A TEXT-BOOK OF THE PHYSIOLOGICAL CHEMISTRY OF THE ANIMAL BODY, including an account of the Chemical Changes occurring in Disease. Vol. I. Med. 8vo. 18s. [Vol. II. in the Press.
GANGUILLET (E.) and KUTTER (W. R.). —A GENERAL FORMULA FOR THE UNIFORM FLOW OF WATER IN RIVERS AND OTHER CHANNELS. Translated by RUDOLPH HERING and JOHN C. TRAUTWINE, Jun. 8vo. 17s.
GARDNER (Percy).—SAMOS AND SAMIAN COINS. An Essay. 8vo. 7s. 6d.
GARNETT (R.).—IDYLLS AND EPIGRAMS. Chiefly from the Greek Anthology. Fcp. 8vo. 2s. 6d.
GASKOIN (Mrs. Herman). — CHILDREN'S TREASURY OF BIBLE STORIES. 18mo. 1s. each. —Part I. Old Testament ; II. New Testament ; III. Three Apostles.
GEDDES (Prof. William D.).—THE PROBLEM OF THE HOMERIC POEMS. 8vo. 14s.
—— FLOSCULI GRÆCI BOREALES, SIVE ANTHOLOGIA GRÆCA ABERDONENSIS CONTEXUIT GULIELMUS D. GEDDES. Cr. 8vo. 6s.
—— THE PHAEDO OF PLATO. Edited with Introduction and Notes. 2nd Ed. 8vo. 8s. 6d.
GEIKIE (Archibald).—PRIMER OF PHYSICAL GEOGRAPHY. With Illustrations. 18mo. 1s.
—— PRIMER OF GEOLOGY. Illust. 18mo. 1s.
—— ELEMENTARY LESSONS IN PHYSICAL GEOGRAPHY. With Illustrations. Fcp. 8vo. 4s. 6d.—QUESTIONS ON THE SAME. 1s. 6d.
—— OUTLINES OF FIELD GEOLOGY. With numerous Illustrations. Crown 8vo. 3s. 6d.
—— TEXT-BOOK OF GEOLOGY. Illustrated. 2nd Edition. 7th Thousand. Med. 8vo. 28s.
—— CLASS-BOOK OF GEOLOGY. With upwards of 200 New Illustrations. Cr. 8vo. 10s. 6d.
—— GEOLOGICAL SKETCHES AT HOME AND ABROAD. With Illustrations. 8vo. 10s. 6d.
—— THE SCENERY OF SCOTLAND. Viewed in connection with its Physical Geology. 2nd Edition. Crown 8vo. 12s. 6d.
—— THE TEACHING OF GEOGRAPHY. A Practical Handbook for the use of Teachers. Globe 8vo. 2s.
—— GEOGRAPHY OF THE BRITISH ISLES. 18mo. 1s.
GEOMETRY, SYLLABUS OF PLANE. Corresponding to Euclid I.—VI. Prepared by the Association for the Improvement of Geometrical Teaching. 9th Ed. Cr. 8vo. 1s.

2

GIBBON. By J. C. Morison. Crown 8vo. 1s. 6d. ; sewed, 1s.

GILMAN (N. P.).—Profit-Sharing between Employer and Employé. A Study in the Evolution of the Wages System. Crown 8vo. 7s. 6d.

GILMORE (Rev. John).—Storm Warriors ; or, Lifeboat Work on the Goodwin Sands. Crown 8vo. 3s. 6d.

GLADSTONE (Rt. Hon. W. E.).—Homeric Synchronism. An Inquiry into the Time and Place of Homer. Crown 8vo. 6s.
—— Primer of Homer. 18mo. 1s.

GLADSTONE (J. H.).—Spelling Reform from an Educational Point of View. 3rd Edition. Crown 8vo. 1s. 6d.

GLADSTONE (J. H.) and TRIBE (A.).— The Chemistry of the Secondary Batteries of Planté and Fauré. Crown 8vo. 2s. 6d.

GLAISTER (Elizabeth). — Needlework. Crown 8vo. 2s. 6d.

GLOBE EDITIONS. Gl. 8vo. 3s. 6d. each.
The Complete Works of William Shakespeare. Edited by W. G. Clark and W. Aldis Wright.

Morte d'Arthur. Sir Thomas Malory's Book of King Arthur and of his Noble Knights of the Round Table. The Edition of Caxton, revised for modern use. By Sir E. Strachey, Bart.

The Poetical Works of Sir Walter Scott. With Essay by Prof. Palgrave.

The Poetical Works and Letters of Robert Burns. Edited, with Life and Glossarial Index, by Alexander Smith.

The Adventures of Robinson Crusoe. With Introduction by Henry Kingsley.

Goldsmith's Miscellaneous Works. Edited by Prof. Masson.

Pope's Poetical Works. Edited, with Memoir and Notes, by Prof. Ward.

Spenser's Complete Works. Edited by R. Morris. Memoir by J. W. Hales.

Dryden's Poetical Works. A revised Text and Notes. By W. D. Christie.

Cowper's Poetical Works. Edited by the Rev. W. Benham, B.D.

Virgil's Works. Rendered into English by James Lonsdale and S. Lee.

Horace's Works. Rendered into English by James Lonsdale and S. Lee.

Milton's Poetical Works. Edited, with Introduction, &c., by Prof. Masson.

GLOBE READERS, The.—A New Series of Reading Books for Standards I.—VI. Selected, arranged, and Edited by A. F. Murison, sometime English Master at Aberdeen Grammar School. With Original Illustrations. Globe 8vo.

Primer I.	...	...	(48 pp.)	3d.
Primer II.	...	...	(48 pp.)	3d.
Book I.	...	...	(96 pp.)	6d.
Book II.	...	...	(136 pp.)	9d.
Book III.	...	...	(232 pp.)	1s. 3d.
Book IV.	...	...	(328 pp.)	1s. 9d.
Book V.	...	...	(416 pp.)	2s.
Book VI.	...	...	(448 pp.)	2s. 6d.

GLOBE READERS, The Shorter.—A New Series of Reading Books for Standards I.—VI. Edited by A. F. Murison. Gl. 8vo.

Primer I.	...	...	(48 pp.)	3d.
Primer II.	...	...	(48 pp.)	3d.
Standard I.	...	...	(92 pp.)	6d.
Standard II.	...	...	(124 pp.)	9d.
Standard III.	...	...	(178 pp.)	1s.
Standard IV.	...	...	(182 pp.)	1s.
Standard V.	...	...	(216 pp.)	1s. 3d.
Standard VI.	...	...	(228 pp.)	1s. 6d.

** This Series has been abridged from the "Globe Readers" to meet the demand for smaller reading books.

GLOBE READINGS FROM STANDARD AUTHORS. Globe 8vo.

Cowper's Task : An Epistle to Joseph Hill, Esq. ; Tirocinium, or a Review of the Schools ; and the History of John Gilpin. Edited, with Notes, by Rev. William Benham, B.D. 1s.

Goldsmith's Vicar of Wakefield. With a Memoir of Goldsmith by Prof. Masson. 1s.

Lamb's (Charles) Tales from Shakspeare. Edited, with Preface, by Rev. Alfred Ainger, M.A. 2s.

Scott's (Sir Walter) Lay of the Last Minstrel ; and the Lady of the Lake. Edited by Prof. F. T. Palgrave. 1s.

Marmion ; and The Lord of the Isles. By the same Editor. 1s.

The Children's Garland from the Best Poets. Selected and arranged by Coventry Patmore. 2s.

A Book of Golden Deeds of all Times and all Countries. Gathered and narrated anew by Charlotte M. Yonge. 2s.

GODFRAY (Hugh). — An Elementary Treatise on Lunar Theory. 2nd Edition. Crown 8vo. 5s. 6d.
—— A Treatise on Astronomy, for the use of Colleges and Schools. 8vo. 12s. 6d.

GOETHE—CARLYLE.—Correspondence between Goethe and Carlyle. Edited by C. E. Norton. Crown 8vo. 9s.

GOETHE'S LIFE. By Prof. Heinrich Düntzer. Translated by T. W. Lyster. 2 vols. Crown 8vo. 21s.

GOETHE.—Faust. Translated into English Verse by John Stuart Blackie. 2nd Edition. Crown 8vo. 9s.
—— Part I. Edited, with Introduction and Notes; followed by an Appendix on Part II., by Jane Lee. 18mo. 4s. 6d.
—— Reynard the Fox. Translated into English Verse by A. Douglas Ainslie. Crown 8vo. 7s. 6d.
—— Götz von Berlichingen. Edited by H. A. Bull, M.A. 18mo. 2s.

GOLDEN TREASURY SERIES. — Uniformly printed in 18mo, with Vignette Titles by Sir J. E. Millais, Sir Noel Paton, T. Woolner, W. Holman Hunt, Arthur Hughes, &c. Engraved on Steel. Bound in extra cloth. 4s. 6d. each.

The Golden Treasury of the Best Songs and Lyrical Poems in the English Language. Selected and arranged, with Notes, by Prof. F. T. Palgrave.

GOLDEN TREASURY SERIES—*contd.*

THE CHILDREN'S GARLAND FROM THE BEST POETS. Selected by COVENTRY PATMORE.

THE BOOK OF PRAISE. From the best English Hymn Writers. Selected by ROUNDELL, EARL OF SELBORNE.

THE FAIRY BOOK: THE BEST POPULAR FAIRY STORIES. Selected by the Author of "John Halifax, Gentleman."

THE BALLAD BOOK. A Selection of the Choicest British Ballads. Edited by WILLIAM ALLINGHAM.

THE JEST BOOK. The Choicest Anecdotes and Sayings. Arranged by MARK LEMON.

BACON'S ESSAYS AND COLOURS OF GOOD AND EVIL. With Notes and Glossarial Index by W. ALDIS WRIGHT, M.A.

THE PILGRIM'S PROGRESS FROM THIS WORLD TO THAT WHICH IS TO COME. By JOHN BUNYAN.

THE SUNDAY BOOK OF POETRY FOR THE YOUNG. Selected by C. F. ALEXANDER.

A BOOK OF GOLDEN DEEDS OF ALL TIMES AND ALL COUNTRIES. By the Author of "The Heir of Redclyffe."

THE ADVENTURES OF ROBINSON CRUSOE. Edited by J. W. CLARK, M.A.

THE REPUBLIC OF PLATO. Translated by J. LL. DAVIES, M.A., and D. J. VAUGHAN.

THE SONG BOOK. Words and Tunes Selected and arranged by JOHN HULLAH.

LA LYRE FRANÇAISE. Selected and arranged, with Notes, by G. MASSON.

TOM BROWN'S SCHOOL DAYS. By AN OLD BOY.

A BOOK OF WORTHIES. By the Author of "The Heir of Redclyffe."

GUESSES AT TRUTH. By TWO BROTHERS.

THE CAVALIER AND HIS LADY. Selections from the Works of the First Duke and Duchess of Newcastle. With an Introductory Essay by EDWARD JENKINS.

SCOTTISH SONG. Compiled by MARY CARLYLE AITKEN.

DEUTSCHE LYRIK. The Golden Treasury of the best German Lyrical Poems. By Dr. BUCHHEIM.

CHRYSOMELA. A Selection from the Lyrical Poems of Robert Herrick. By FRANCIS TURNER PALGRAVE.

POEMS OF PLACES—ENGLAND AND WALES. Edited by H. W. LONGFELLOW. 2 vols.

SELECTED POEMS OF MATTHEW ARNOLD.

THE STORY OF THE CHRISTIANS AND MOORS IN SPAIN. By CHARLOTTE M. YONGE.

LAMB'S TALES FROM SHAKSPEARE. Edited by Rev. ALFRED AINGER, M.A.

SHAKESPEARE'S SONGS AND SONNETS. Ed. with Notes, by Prof. F. T. PALGRAVE.

POEMS OF WORDSWORTH. Chosen and Edited by MATTHEW ARNOLD.
Large Paper Edition. 9s.

POEMS OF SHELLEY. Edited by STOPFORD A. BROOKE.
Large Paper Edition. 12s. 6d.

GOLDEN TREASURY SERIES—*contd.*

THE ESSAYS OF JOSEPH ADDISON. Chosen and Edited by JOHN RICHARD GREEN.

POETRY OF BYRON. Chosen and arranged by MATTHEW ARNOLD.
Large Paper Edition. 9s.

SIR THOMAS BROWNE'S RELIGIO MEDICI; LETTER TO A FRIEND, &C., AND CHRISTIAN MORALS. Ed. by W. A. GREENHILL, M.D.

THE SPEECHES AND TABLE-TALK OF THE PROPHET MOHAMMAD. Translated by STANLEY LANE-POOLE.

SELECTIONS FROM WALTER SAVAGE LANDOR. Edited by SIDNEY COLVIN.

SELECTIONS FROM COWPER'S POEMS. With an Introduction by Mrs. OLIPHANT.

LETTERS OF WILLIAM COWPER. Edited, With Introduction, by Rev. W. BENHAM.

THE POETICAL WORKS OF JOHN KEATS. Edited by Prof. F. T. PALGRAVE.

LYRICAL POEMS OF LORD TENNYSON. Selected and Annotated by Prof. FRANCIS T. PALGRAVE.
Large Paper Edition. 8vo. 9s.

IN MEMORIAM. By LORD TENNYSON, Poet Laureate.
Large Paper Edition. 8vo. 9s.

THE TRIAL AND DEATH OF SOCRATES. Being the Euthyphron, Apology, Crito, and Phaedo of Plato. Translated by F. J. CHURCH.

A BOOK OF GOLDEN THOUGHTS. By HENRY ATTWELL.

PLATO.—PHAEDRUS, LYSIS, AND PROTAGORAS. A New Translation, by J. WRIGHT.

THEOCRITUS, BION, AND MOSCHUS. Rendered into English Prose by ANDREW LANG.
Large Paper Edition. 8vo. 9s.

BALLADS, LYRICS, AND SONNETS. From the Works of HENRY W. LONGFELLOW.

GOLDEN TREASURY PSALTER.—THE STUDENT'S EDITION. Being an Edition with briefer Notes of "The Psalms Chronologically Arranged by Four Friends." 18mo. 3s. 6d.

GOLDSMITH. By WILLIAM BLACK. Crown 8vo. 1s. 6d.; sewed, 1s.

GOLDSMITH. — THE MISCELLANEOUS WORKS OF OLIVER GOLDSMITH. With Biographical Essay by Prof. MASSON. Globe 8vo. 3s. 6d.

—— ESSAYS OF OLIVER GOLDSMITH. Edited by C. D. YONGE, M.A. Fcp. 8vo. 2s. 6d.

—— THE TRAVELLER AND THE DESERTED VILLAGE. With Notes by J. W. HALES, M.A. Crown 8vo. 6d.

—— THE VICAR OF WAKEFIELD. With a Memoir of Goldsmith by Prof. MASSON. Globe 8vo. 1s.

——THE TRAVELLER AND THE DESERTED VILLAGE. Edited, with Introduction and Notes, by ARTHUR BARRETT, M.A. Gl. 8vo. 1s. 6d.

GONE TO TEXAS.—LETTERS FROM OUR BOYS. Edited, with Preface, by THOMAS HUGHES, Q.C. Crown 8vo. 4s. 6d.

GOODWIN (Prof. W. W.).—SYNTAX OF THE GREEK MOODS AND TENSES. New Edition. 8vo. 14s.

GOODWIN (Prof.).—A GREEK GRAMMAR. New Revised Edition. Crown 8vo. 6s.

— A SCHOOL GREEK GRAMMAR. Crown 8vo. 3s. 6d.

GORDON (General). A SKETCH. By REGINALD H. BARNES. Crown 8vo. 1s.

— LETTERS OF GENERAL C. G. GORDON TO HIS SISTER, M. A. GORDON. 4th Edition. Crown 8vo. 3s. 6d.

GORDON. By Colonel Sir WILLIAM BUTLER. With Portrait. Crown 8vo. 2s. 6d.

GORDON (Lady Duff).—LAST LETTERS FROM EGYPT, TO WHICH ARE ADDED LETTERS FROM THE CAPE. 2nd Edition. Cr. 8vo. 9s.

GOSCHEN (Rt. Hon. George J.).—REPORTS AND SPEECHES ON LOCAL TAXATION. 8vo. 5s.

GOSSE (E.).—GRAY. Cr. 8vo. 1s. 6d.; swd., 1s.

GOW (Dr. James).—A COMPANION TO SCHOOL CLASSICS. Illustrated. 2nd Ed. Cr. 8vo. 6s.

GOYEN (P.).—HIGHER ARITHMETIC AND ELEMENTARY MENSURATION, for the Senior Classes of Schools and Candidates preparing for Public Examinations. Globe 8vo. 5s.

GRAHAM (David).—KING JAMES I. An Historical Tragedy. Globe 8vo. 7s.

GRAHAM (John W.).—NEÆRA : A TALE OF ANCIENT ROME. Crown 8vo. 6s.

GRAND'HOMME. — CUTTING OUT AND DRESSMAKING. From the French of Mdlle. E. GRAND'HOMME. 18mo. 1s.

GRAY (Prof. Andrew).—THE THEORY AND PRACTICE OF ABSOLUTE MEASUREMENTS IN ELECTRICITY AND MAGNETISM. 2 vols. Crown 8vo. Vol. I. 12s. 6d.

— ABSOLUTE MEASUREMENTS IN ELECTRICITY AND MAGNETISM. 2nd Edition, revised. Fcp. 8vo. 5s. 6d.

GRAY (Prof. Asa).—STRUCTURAL BOTANY ; OR, ORGANOGRAPHY ON THE BASIS OF MORPHOLOGY. Crown 8vo. 10s. 6d.

— THE SCIENTIFIC PAPERS OF ASA GRAY. Selected by CHARLES S. SARGENT. 2 vols. 8vo. 21s.

GRAY (Thomas).—Edited by EDMUND GOSSE. In 4 vols. Globe 8vo. 20s.—Vol. I. POEMS, JOURNALS, AND ESSAYS.—II. LETTERS.—III. LETTERS. — IV. NOTES ON ARISTOPHANES ; AND PLATO.

GRAY. By EDMUND GOSSE. Crown 8vo. 1s. 6d. ; sewed, 1s.

GREAVES (John).—A TREATISE ON ELEMENTARY STATICS. 2nd Ed. Cr. 8vo. 6s. 6d.

— STATICS FOR BEGINNERS. Gl. 8vo. 3s. 6d.

GREEK ELEGIAC POETS. FROM CALLINUS TO CALLIMACHUS. Selected and Edited by Rev. H. KYNASTON. 18mo. 1s. 6d.

GREEK TESTAMENT.—THE NEW TESTAMENT IN THE ORIGINAL GREEK. The Text revised by Prof. B. F. WESTCOTT, D.D., and Prof. F. J. A. HORT, D.D. 2 vols. Crown 8vo. 10s. 6d. each.—Vol. I. Text; II. Introduction and Appendix.

THE NEW TESTAMENT IN THE ORIGINAL GREEK, FOR SCHOOLS. The Text Revised by B. F. WESTCOTT, D.D., and F. J. A. HORT, D.D. 12mo. cloth. 4s. 6d.—18mo. roan, red edges. 5s. 6d.

GREEK TESTAMENT—continued.

SCHOOL READINGS IN THE GREEK TESTAMENT. Being the Outlines of the Life of our Lord as given by St. Mark, with additions from the Text of the other Evangelists. Edited, with Notes and Vocabulary, by A. CALVERT, M.A. Fcp. 8vo. 4s. 6d.

THE GREEK TESTAMENT AND THE ENGLISH VERSION, A COMPANION TO. By PHILIP SCHAFF, D.D. Crown 8vo. 12s.

THE ACTS OF THE APOSTLES. Being the Greek Text as Revised by Drs. WESTCOTT and HORT. With Explanatory Notes by T. E. PAGE, M.A. Fcp. 8vo. 4s. 6d.

THE GOSPEL ACCORDING TO ST. MATTHEW. Being the Greek Text as Revised by Drs. WESTCOTT and HORT. With Introduction and Notes by Rev. A. SLOMAN, M.A. Fcp. 8vo. 2s. 6d.

GREEN (John Richard).—A SHORT HISTORY OF THE ENGLISH PEOPLE. With Coloured Maps, Genealogical Tables, and Chronological Annals. New Edition, thoroughly revised. Cr. 8vo. 8s. 6d. 150th Thousand. Also the same in Four Parts. With the corresponding portion of Mr. Tait's "Analysis." 3s. each. Part I. 607–1265. II. 1204–1553. III. 1540–1689. IV. 1660–1873.

— STRAY STUDIES FROM ENGLAND AND ITALY. Crown 8vo. 8s. 6d.

— HISTORY OF THE ENGLISH PEOPLE. In 4 vols. 8vo.—Vol. I. With 8 Coloured Maps. 16s.—II. 16s.—III. With 4 Maps. 16s.—IV. With Maps and Index. 16s.

— THE MAKING OF ENGLAND. With Maps. 8vo. 16s.

— THE CONQUEST OF ENGLAND. With Maps and Portrait. 8vo. 18s.

— READINGS IN ENGLISH HISTORY. In 3 Parts. Fcp. 8vo. 1s. 6d. each.

— ESSAYS OF JOSEPH ADDISON. 18mo. 4s. 6d.

GREEN (J. R.) and GREEN (Alice S.).— A SHORT GEOGRAPHY OF THE BRITISH ISLANDS. With 28 Maps. Fcp. 8vo. 3s. 6d.

GREEN (W. S.). — AMONG THE SELKIRK GLACIERS. Crown 8vo.

GREENHILL (Prof. A. G.).—DIFFERENTIAL AND INTEGRAL CALCULUS. Cr. 8vo. 7s. 6d.

GREENWOOD (Jessy E.). — THE MOON MAIDEN: AND OTHER STORIES. Cr. 8vo. 3s. 6d.

GREENWOOD (Principal J. G.).—THE ELEMENTS OF GREEK GRAMMAR. Cr. 8vo. 5s. 6d.

GRIFFITHS (W. H.).—LESSONS ON PRESCRIPTIONS AND THE ART OF PRESCRIBING. New Edition. 18mo. 3s. 6d.

GRIMM'S FAIRY TALES. A Selection from the Household Stories. Translated from the German by LUCY CRANE, and done into Pictures by WALTER CRANE. Crown 8vo. 6s.

GRIMM.—KINDER-UND-HAUSMÄRCHEN. Selected and Edited, with Notes and Vocabulary, by G. E. FASNACHT. Gl. 8vo. 2s. 6d.

GUEST (M. J.).—LECTURES ON THE HISTORY OF ENGLAND. Crown 8vo. 6s.

GUEST (Dr. E.).—ORIGINES CELTICÆ (A Fragment) and other Contributions to the History of Britain. Maps. 2 vols. 8vo. 32s.

LIST OF PUBLICATIONS. 21

GROVE (Sir George).—A DICTIONARY OF MUSIC AND MUSICIANS, A.D. 1450—1889. Edited by Sir GEORGE GROVE, D.C.L. In 4 vols. 8vo, 21s. each. With Illustrations in Music Type and Woodcut.— Also published in Parts. Parts I.—XIV., XIX.—XXII. 3s. 6d. each; XV. XVI. 7s.; XVII. XVIII. 7s.; XXIII.—XXV., Appendix, Edited by J. A. FULLER MAITLAND, M.A. 9s. [Cloth cases for binding the volumes, 1s. each.]

—— PRIMER OF GEOGRAPHY. Maps. 18mo. 1s.

GUILLEMIN (Amédée).—THE FORCES OF NATURE. A Popular Introduction to the Study of Physical Phenomena. 455 Woodcuts. Royal 8vo. 21s.

—— THE APPLICATIONS OF PHYSICAL FORCES. With Coloured Plates and Illustrations. Royal 8vo. 21s.

—— ELECTRICITY AND MAGNETISM. A Popular Treatise. Translated and Edited, with Additions and Notes, by Prof. SILVANUS P. THOMPSON. Royal 8vo. [In the Press.

GUIDE TO THE UNPROTECTED, In Every-day Matters relating to Property and Income. 5th Ed. Extra fcp. 8vo. 3s. 6d.

GUIZOT.—GREAT CHRISTIANS OF FRANCE. ST. LOUIS AND CALVIN. Crown 8vo. 6s.

GUNTON (George).—WEALTH AND PROGRESS. Crown 8vo. 6s.

HADLEY (Prof. James).—ESSAYS, PHILOLOGICAL AND CRITICAL. 8vo. 14s.

HADLEY—ALLEN.—A GREEK GRAMMAR FOR SCHOOLS AND COLLEGES. By Prof. JAMES HADLEY. Revised and in part Rewritten by Prof. FREDERIC DE FOREST ALLEN. Crown 8vo. 6s.

HAILSTONE (H.).—NOVAE ARUNDINES; OR, NEW MARSH MELODIES. Fcp. 8vo. 3s. 6d.

HALES (Prof. J. W.).—LONGER ENGLISH POEMS, with Notes, Philological and Explanatory, and an Introduction on the Teaching of English. 12th Ed. Ex. fcp. 8vo. 4s. 6d.

HALL (H. S.) and KNIGHT (S. R.).—ELEMENTARY ALGEBRA FOR SCHOOLS. 5th Ed., revised. Gl. 8vo. 3s. 6d. With Answers, 4s. 6d.

—— ALGEBRAICAL EXERCISES AND EXAMINATION PAPERS to accompany "Elementary Algebra." 2nd Edition. Globe 8vo. 2s. 6d.

—— ARITHMETICAL EXERCISES AND EXAMINATION PAPERS. Globe 8vo. 2s. 6d.

—— HIGHER ALGEBRA. A Sequel to "Elementary Algebra for Schools." 3rd Edition. Crown 8vo. 7s. 6d.

—— SOLUTIONS OF THE EXAMPLES IN "HIGHER ALGEBRA." Crown 8vo. 10s. 6d.

HALL (H. S.) and STEVENS (F. H.).— A TEXT-BOOK OF EUCLID'S ELEMENTS. Globe 8vo. Book I. 1s.; I. II. 1s. 6d.; I.— IV. 3s.; III.—VI. 3s.; I.—VI. and XI. 4s. 6d.; XI. 1s.

HALLWARD (R. F.).—FLOWERS OF PARADISE. Music, Verse, Design, Illustration. Royal 4to. 6s.

HALSTEAD (G. B.).—THE ELEMENTS OF GEOMETRY. 8vo. 12s. 6d.

HAMERTON (P. G.).—THE INTELLECTUAL LIFE. 4th Edition. Crown 8vo. 10s. 6d.

HAMERTON (P. G.). — ETCHING AND ETCHERS. 3rd Edition, revised. With 48 Plates. Colombier 8vo.

—— THOUGHTS ABOUT ART. New Edition. Crown 8vo. 8s. 6d.

—— HUMAN INTERCOURSE. 4th Edition. Crown 8vo. 8s. 6d.

—— FRENCH AND ENGLISH: A COMPARISON. Crown 8vo. 10s. 6d.

HAMILTON (John). — ON TRUTH AND ERROR. Crown 8vo. 5s.

—— ARTHUR'S SEAT; OR, THE CHURCH OF THE BANNED. Crown 8vo. 6s.

—— ABOVE AND AROUND: THOUGHTS ON GOD AND MAN. 12mo. 2s. 6d.

HAMILTON (Prof. D. J.).—ON THE PATHOLOGY OF BRONCHITIS, CATARRHAL PNEUMONIA, TUBERCLE, AND ALLIED LESIONS OF THE HUMAN LUNG. 8vo. 8s. 6d.

—— A TEXT-BOOK OF PATHOLOGY, SYSTEMATIC AND PRACTICAL. Illustrated. Vol. I. 8vo. 25s.

HANBURY (Daniel). — SCIENCE PAPERS, CHIEFLY PHARMACOLOGICAL AND BOTANICAL. Medium 8vo. 14s.

HANDEL.—LIFE OF GEORGE FREDERICK HANDEL. By W. S. ROCKSTRO. Crown 8vo. 10s. 6d.

HARDWICK (Ven. Archdeacon). — CHRIST AND OTHER MASTERS. 6th Edition. Crown 8vo. 10s. 6d.

—— A HISTORY OF THE CHRISTIAN CHURCH. Middle Age. 6th Edition. Edited by Prof. STUBBS. Crown 8vo. 10s. 6d.

—— A HISTORY OF THE CHRISTIAN CHURCH DURING THE REFORMATION. 9th Edition. Revised by Prof. STUBBS. Cr. 8vo. 10s. 6d.

HARDY (Arthur Sherburne).—BUT YET A WOMAN. A Novel. Crown 8vo. 4s. 6d.

—— THE WIND OF DESTINY. 2 vols. Globe 8vo. 12s.

HARDY (H. J.).—A LATIN READER FOR THE LOWER FORMS IN SCHOOLS. Gl. 8vo. 2s. 6d.

HARDY (Thomas). — THE WOODLANDERS. Crown 8vo. 3s. 6d.

—— WESSEX TALES: STRANGE, LIVELY, AND COMMONPLACE. Crown 8vo. 3s. 6d.

HARE (Julius Charles).—THE MISSION OF THE COMFORTER. New Edition. Edited by Prof. E. H. PLUMPTRE. Crown 8vo. 7s. 6d.

—— THE VICTORY OF FAITH. Edited by Prof. PLUMPTRE, with Introductory Notices by the late Prof. MAURICE and by the late Dean STANLEY. Crown 8vo. 6s. 6d.

—— GUESSES AT TRUTH. By Two Brothers, AUGUSTUS WILLIAM HARE and JULIUS CHARLES HARE. With a Memoir and Two Portraits. 18mo. 4s. 6d.

HARMONIA. By the Author of "Estelle Russell." 3 vols. Crown 8vo. 31s. 6d.

HARPER (Father Thomas). — THE METAPHYSICS OF THE SCHOOL. In 5 vols. Vols. I. and II. 8vo. 18s. each; Vol. III., Part I. 12s.

HARRIS (Rev. G. C.).—SERMONS. With a Memoir by CHARLOTTE M. YONGE, and Portrait. Extra fcp. 8vo. 6s.

HARRISON (Frederic).—THE CHOICE OF BOOKS. Globe 8vo. 6s.
Large Paper Edition. Printed on hand-made paper. 8vo. 15s.
—— OLIVER CROMWELL. Crown 8vo. 2s. 6d.

HARRISON (Miss Jane) and VERRALL (Mrs. A. W.).—CULTS AND MONUMENTS OF ANCIENT ATHENS. Illustrated. Cr. 8vo.

HARTE (Bret).—CRESSY: A Novel. Crown 8vo. 3s. 6d.
—— THE HERITAGE OF DEDLOW MARSH: AND OTHER TALES. 2 vols. Globe 8vo. 12s.

HARTLEY (Prof. W. Noel).—A COURSE OF QUANTITATIVE ANALYSIS FOR STUDENTS. Globe 8vo. 5s.

HARWOOD (George).—DISESTABLISHMENT; OR, A DEFENCE OF THE PRINCIPLE OF A NATIONAL CHURCH. 8vo. 12s.
—— THE COMING DEMOCRACY. Cr. 8vo. 6s.
—— FROM WITHIN. Crown 8vo. 6s.

HASTINGS (Warren). By Sir ALFRED LYALL. With Portrait. Crown 8vo. 2s. 6d.

HAUFF.—DIE KARAVANE. Edited, with Notes and Vocabulary, by HERMAN HAGER, Ph. D. Globe 8vo. 3s.

HAWTHORNE (Nathaniel). By HENRY JAMES. Crown 8vo. 1s. 6d.; sewed, 1s.

HEARD (Rev. W. A.).—A SECOND GREEK EXERCISE BOOK. Globe 8vo.

HEINE. SELECTIONS FROM THE REISEBILDER AND OTHER PROSE WORKS. Edited by C. COLBECK, M.A. 18mo. 2s. 6d.

HELLENIC STUDIES, THE JOURNAL OF.—Vol. I. 8vo. With Plates of Illustrations. 30s.—Vol. II. 8vo. 30s. With Plates of Illustrations. Or in 2 Parts, 15s. each.—Vol. III. 2 Parts. 8vo. With Plates of Illustrations. 15s. each.—Vol. IV. 2 Parts. With Plates. Part I. 21s. Part II. 15s. Or complete, 30s.—Vol. V. With Plates. 30s.—Vol. VI. With Plates. Part I. 15s. Part II. 15s. Or complete, 30s.—Vol. VII. Part I. 15s. Part II. 15s. Or complete, 30s.—Vol. VIII. Part I. 15s. Part II. 15s.—Vol. IX. 2 Parts. 15s. each.—Vol. X. 30s.
The Journal will be sold at a reduced price to Libraries wishing to subscribe, but official application must in each case be made to the Council. Information on this point, and upon the conditions of Membership, may be obtained on application to the Hon. Secretary, Mr. George Macmillan, 29, Bedford Street, Covent Garden.

HELPS.—ESSAYS WRITTEN IN THE INTERVALS OF BUSINESS. Edited by F. J. ROWE, M.A., and W. T. WEBB, M.A. Gl. 8vo. 2s. 6d.

HENRY II. By Mrs. J. R. GREEN. Crown 8vo. 2s. 6d.

HENRY V. By the Rev. A. J. CHURCH. With Portrait. Crown 8vo. 2s. 6d.

HENRY VII. By JAMES GAIRDNER. Crown 8vo. 2s. 6d.

HENSLOW (Rev. G.).—THE THEORY OF EVOLUTION OF LIVING THINGS, AND THE APPLICATION OF THE PRINCIPLES OF EVOLUTION TO RELIGION. Crown 8vo. 6s.

HERODOTOS.—Books I.—III. Edited by A. H. SAYCE, M.A. 8vo. 16s.

HERODOTOS.—SELECTIONS FROM BOOKS VII. & VIII. THE EXPEDITION OF XERXES. Edited by A. H. COOKE, M.A. 18mo. 1s. 6d.
—— THE HISTORY. Translated into English, with Notes and Indices, by G. C. MACAULAY, M.A. 2 vols. Crown 8vo. 18s.

HERRICK. — CHRYSOMELA. A Selection from the Lyrical Poems of ROBERT HERRICK. Arranged, with Notes, by Prof. F. T. PALGRAVE. 18mo. 4s. 6d.

HERTEL (Dr.).—OVERPRESSURE IN HIGH SCHOOLS IN DENMARK. With Introduction by Sir J. CRICHTON-BROWNE. Cr. 8vo. 3s. 6d.

HERVEY (Rt. Rev. Lord Arthur).—THE GENEALOGIES OF OUR LORD AND SAVIOUR JESUS CHRIST. 8vo. 10s. 6d.

HICKS (W. M.).—DYNAMICS OF PARTICLES AND SOLIDS. Crown 8vo. 6s. 6d.

HILL (Florence D.).—CHILDREN OF THE STATE. Ed. by FANNY FOWKE. Cr. 8vo. 6s.

HILL (Octavia).—OUR COMMON LAND, AND OTHER ESSAYS. Extra fcp. 8vo. 3s. 6d.
—— HOMES OF THE LONDON POOR. Sewed. Crown 8vo. 1s.

HIORNS (Arthur H.).—PRACTICAL METALLURGY AND ASSAYING. A Text-Book for the use of Teachers, Students, and Assayers. With Illustrations. Globe 8vo. 6s.
—— A TEXT-BOOK OF ELEMENTARY METALLURGY FOR THE USE OF STUDENTS. Gl. 8vo 4s.
—— IRON AND STEEL MANUFACTURE. A Text-Book for Beginners. With Illustrations. Globe 8vo. 3s. 6d.

HISTORICAL COURSE FOR SCHOOLS. Edited by EDWARD A. FREEMAN, D.C.L.

Vol. I. GENERAL SKETCH OF EUROPEAN HISTORY. By E. A. FREEMAN. With Maps, &c. 18mo. 3s. 6d.
II. HISTORY OF ENGLAND. By EDITH THOMPSON. Col. Maps. 18mo. 2s. 6d.
III. HISTORY OF SCOTLAND. By MARGARET MACARTHUR. 18mo. 2s.
IV. HISTORY OF ITALY. By the Rev. W. HUNT, M.A. With Coloured Maps. 18mo. 3s. 6d.
V. HISTORY OF GERMANY. By JAMES SIME, M.A. 18mo. 3s.
VI. HISTORY OF AMERICA. By J. A. DOYLE. With Maps. 18mo. 4s. 6d.
VII. HISTORY OF EUROPEAN COLONIES. By E. J. PAYNE, M.A. With Maps. 18mo. 4s. 6d.
VIII. HISTORY OF FRANCE. By CHARLOTTE M. YONGE. With Maps. 18mo. 3s. 6d.

HOBART. — ESSAYS AND MISCELLANEOUS WRITINGS OF VERE HENRY, LORD HOBART. With a Biographical Sketch. Edited by MARY, LADY HOBART. 2 vols. 8vo. 25s.

HOBDAY (E.). — VILLA GARDENING. A Handbook for Amateur and Practical Gardeners. Extra crown 8vo. 6s.

HODGSON (F.).—MYTHOLOGY FOR LATIN VERSIFICATION. 6th Edition. Revised by F. C. HODGSON, M.A. 18mo. 3s.

HODGSON. — MEMOIR OF REV. FRANCIS HODGSON, B.D., SCHOLAR, POET, AND DIVINE. By his Son, the Rev. JAMES T. HODGSON, M.A. 2 vols. Crown 8vo. 18s.

HOFMANN (Prof. A. W.).—THE LIFE WORK OF LIEBIG IN EXPERIMENTAL AND PHILOSOPHIC CHEMISTRY. 8vo. 5*s.*

HOGAN, M.P. Globe 8vo. 2*s.*

HOLE (Rev. C.).—GENEALOGICAL STEMMA OF THE KINGS OF ENGLAND AND FRANCE. On a Sheet. 1*s.*

—— A BRIEF BIOGRAPHICAL DICTIONARY. 2nd Edition. 18mo. 4*s.* 6*d.*

HOLLAND (Prof. T. E.).—THE TREATY RELATIONS OF RUSSIA AND TURKEY, FROM 1774 TO 1853. Crown 8vo. 2*s.*

HOLMES (O. W., Jun.).—THE COMMON LAW. 8vo. 12*s.*

HOMER.—THE ODYSSEY OF HOMER DONE INTO ENGLISH PROSE. By S. H. BUTCHER, M.A., and A. LANG, M.A. 7th Edition. Crown 8vo. 6*s.*

—— ODYSSEY. Book I. Edited, with Notes and Vocabulary, by Rev. J. BOND, M.A., and A. S. WALPOLE, M.A. 18mo. 1*s.* 5*d.*

—— ODYSSEY. Book IX. Edited by JOHN E. B. MAYOR, M.A. Fcp. 8vo. 2*s.* 6*d.*

—— ODYSSEY. THE TRIUMPH OF ODYSSEUS. Books XXI.—XXIV. Edited by S. G. HAMILTON, B.A. Fcp. 8vo. 3*s.* 6*d.*

—— THE ODYSSEY OF HOMER. Books I.—XII. Translated into English Verse by the EARL OF CARNARVON. Crown 8vo. 7*s.* 6*d.*

—— THE ILIAD. Edited, with English Notes and Introduction, by WALTER LEAF, Litt.D. 2 vols. 8vo. 14*s.* each.—Vol. I. Books I.—XII; Vol. II. Books XIII.—XXIV.

—— ILIAD. THE STORY OF ACHILLES. Edited by J. H. PRATT, M.A., and WALTER LEAF, Litt.D. Fcap. 8vo. 6*s.*

—— ILIAD. Book I. Edited by Rev. J. BOND, M.A., and A. S. WALPOLE, M.A. With Notes and Vocabulary. 18mo. 1*s.* 6*d.*

—— ILIAD. Book XVIII. THE ARMS OF ACHILLES. Edited by S. R. JAMES, M.A. 18mo. 1*s.* 6*d.*

—— ILIAD. Translated into English Prose. By ANDREW LANG, WALTER LEAF, and ERNEST MYERS. Crown 8vo. 12*s.* 6*d.*

HON. MISS FERRARD, THE. By the Author of "Hogan, M.P." Globe 8vo. 2*s.*

HOOKER (Sir J. D.).—THE STUDENT'S FLORA OF THE BRITISH ISLANDS. 3rd Edition. Globe 8vo. 10*s.* 6*d.*

—— PRIMER OF BOTANY. 18mo. 1*s.*

HOOKER (Sir Joseph D.) and BALL (J.).— JOURNAL OF A TOUR IN MAROCCO AND THE GREAT ATLAS. 8vo. 21*s.*

HOOLE (C. H.).—THE CLASSICAL ELEMENT IN THE NEW TESTAMENT. Considered as a Proof of its Genuineness, with an Appendix on the Oldest Authorities used in the Formation of the Canon. 8vo. 10*s.* 6*d.*

HOOPER (W. H.) and PHILLIPS (W. C.)— A MANUAL OF MARKS ON POTTERY AND PORCELAIN. 16mo. 4*s.* 6*d.*

HOPE (Frances J.).—NOTES AND THOUGHTS ON GARDENS AND WOODLANDS. Crown 8vo. 6*s.*

HOPKINS (Ellice).—AUTUMN SWALLOWS: A Book of Lyrics. Extra fcp. 8vo. 6*s.*

HOPPUS (Mary).—A GREAT TREASON: A Story of the War of Independence. 2 vols. Crown 8vo. 9*s.*

HORACE.—THE WORKS OF HORACE RENDERED INTO ENGLISH PROSE. By J. LONSDALE, M.A., and S. LEE, M.A. 3*s.* 6*d.*

—— STUDIES, LITERARY AND HISTORICAL, IN THE ODES OF HORACE. By A. W. VERRALL, Litt.D. 8vo. 8*s.* 6*d.*

—— THE ODES OF HORACE IN A METRICAL PARAPHRASE. By R. M. HOVENDEN, B.A. Extra fcap. 8vo. 4*s.* 6*d.*

—— LIFE AND CHARACTER: AN EPITOME OF HIS SATIRES AND EPISTLES. By R. M. HOVENDEN, B.A. Extra fcp. 8vo. 4*s.* 6*d.*

—— WORD FOR WORD FROM HORACE: The Odes Literally Versified. By W. T. THORNTON, C.B. Crown 8vo. 7*s.* 6*d.*

—— ODES. Books I. II. III. and IV. Edited by T. E. PAGE, M.A. With Vocabularies. 18mo. 1*s.* 6*d.* each.

—— ODES. Books I.—IV. and CARMEN SECULARE. Edited by T. E. PAGE. Fcap. 8vo. 6*s.*; or separately, 2*s.* each.

—— THE SATIRES. Edited by ARTHUR PALMER, M.A. Fcap. 8vo. 6*s.*

—— THE EPISTLES AND ARS POETICA. Edited by A. S. WILKINS, Litt.D. Fcp. 8vo. 6*s.*

—— SELECTIONS FROM THE EPISTLES AND SATIRES. Edited by Rev. W. J. F. V. BAKER, B.A. 18mo. 1*s.* 6*d.*

—— SELECT EPODES AND ARS POETICA. Edited by Rev. H. A. DALTON, M.A. 18mo. 1*s.* 6*d.*

HORT.—TWO DISSERTATIONS. I. On MONOΓΕΝΗΣ ΘΕΟΣ in Scripture and Tradition. II. On the "Constantinopolitan" Creed and other Eastern Creeds of the Fourth Century. By FENTON JOHN ANTHONY HORT, D.D. 8vo. 7*s.* 6*d.*

HORTON (Hon. S. Dana).—THE SILVER POUND AND ENGLAND'S MONETARY POLICY SINCE THE RESTORATION. With a History of the Guinea. 8vo. 14*s.*

HOWES (Prof. G. B.).—AN ATLAS OF PRACTICAL ELEMENTARY BIOLOGY. With a Preface by Prof. HUXLEY. 4to. 14*s.*

HOWSON (Very Rev. J. S.).—BEFORE THE TABLE: AN INQUIRY, HISTORICAL AND THEOLOGICAL, INTO THE MEANING OF THE CONSECRATION RUBRIC IN THE COMMUNION SERVICE OF THE CHURCH OF ENGLAND. 8vo. 7*s.* 6*d.*

HOZIER (Lieut.-Colonel H. M.).—THE SEVEN WEEKS' WAR. 3rd Edition. Crown 8vo. 6*s.*

—— THE INVASIONS OF ENGLAND. 2 vols. 8vo. 28*s.*

HÜBNER (Baron von).—A RAMBLE ROUND THE WORLD. Crown 8vo. 6*s.*

HUGHES (Thomas).—ALFRED THE GREAT. Crown 8vo. 6*s.*

—— THE MANLINESS OF CHRIST. Cr. 8vo. 4*s.* 6*d.*

—— MEMOIR OF DANIEL MACMILLAN. With Portrait. Cr. 8vo. 4*s.* 6*d.*—Popular Edition. Sewed. Crown 8vo. 1*s.*

HUGHES (Thomas).—RUGBY, TENNESSEE. Crown 8vo. 4s. 6d.

—— TOM BROWN'S SCHOOL DAYS. By AN OLD BOY. Illustrated Edition. Crown 8vo. 6s.—Golden Treasury Edition. 4s. 6d.—Uniform Edition. 3s. 6d.—People's Edition. 2s.—People's Sixpenny Edition, Illustrated. Med. 4to. 6d.

—— TOM BROWN AT OXFORD. Crown 8vo. 6s.—Uniform Edition. 3s. 6d.

—— GONE TO TEXAS. Edited by THOMAS HUGHES, Q.C. Crown 8vo. 4s. 6d.

—— JAMES FRASER, Second Bishop of Manchester. A Memoir, 1818—85. Cr. 8vo. 6s.

—— THE SCOURING OF THE WHITE HORSE, AND THE ASHEN FAGGOT. Uniform Ed. 3s. 6d.

—— LIVINGSTONE. With Portrait and Map. Cr. 8vo. 2s. 6d. [English Men of Action.

HULL (E.).—A TREATISE ON ORNAMENTAL AND BUILDING STONES OF GREAT BRITAIN AND FOREIGN COUNTRIES. 8vo. 12s.

HULLAH (John).—THE SONG BOOK. Words and Tunes from the best Poets and Musicians. With Vignette. 18mo. 4s. 6d.

—— MUSIC IN THE HOUSE. 4th Edition. Crown 8vo. 2s. 6d.

HULLAH (M. E.).—HANNAH TARNE. A Story for Girls. Globe 8vo. 2s. 6d.

HUME. By THOMAS H. HUXLEY. Crown 8vo. 1s. 6d. ; sewed, 1s.

HUMPHRY (Prof. G. M.).—THE HUMAN SKELETON (INCLUDING THE JOINTS). With 260 Illustrations drawn from Nature. Med. 8vo. 14s.

—— THE HUMAN FOOT AND THE HUMAN HAND. With Illustrations. Fcp. 8vo. 4s. 6d.

—— OBSERVATIONS IN MYOLOGY. 8vo. 6s.

—— OLD AGE. The Results of Information received respecting nearly nine hundred persons who had attained the age of eighty years, including seventy-four centenarians. Crown 8vo. 4s. 6d.

HUNT (Rev. W.).—HISTORY OF ITALY. Maps. 3rd Edition. 18mo. 3s. 6d.

HUNT (W.).—TALKS ABOUT ART. With a Letter from Sir J. E. MILLAIS, Bart., R.A. Crown 8vo. 3s. 6d.

HUSS (Hermann).—A SYSTEM OF ORAL INSTRUCTION IN GERMAN. Crown 8vo. 5s.

HUTTON (R. H.).—ESSAYS ON SOME OF THE MODERN GUIDES OF ENGLISH THOUGHT IN MATTERS OF FAITH. Globe 8vo. 6s.

—— SCOTT. Crown 8vo. 1s. 6d. ; sewed, 1s.

—— ESSAYS. 2 vols. Globe 8vo. 6s. each.—Vol. I. Literary Essays ; II. Theological Essays.

HUXLEY (Thomas Henry). — LESSONS IN ELEMENTARY PHYSIOLOGY. With numerous Illustrations. New Edit. Fcp. 8vo. 4s. 6d.

—— LAY SERMONS, ADDRESSES, AND REVIEWS. 9th Edition. 8vo. 7s. 6d.

—— ESSAYS SELECTED FROM LAY SERMONS, ADDRESSES, AND REVIEWS. 3rd Edition. Crown 8vo. 1s.

—— CRITIQUES AND ADDRESSES. 8vo. 10s. 6d.

HUXLEY (T. H.). — PHYSIOGRAPHY. AN INTRODUCTION TO THE STUDY OF NATURE. 13th Edition. Crown 8vo. 6s.

—— AMERICAN ADDRESSES, WITH A LECTURE ON THE STUDY OF BIOLOGY. 8vo. 6s. 6d.

—— SCIENCE AND CULTURE, AND OTHER ESSAYS. 8vo. 10s. 6d.

—— INTRODUCTORY PRIMER. 18mo. 1s. [Science Primers.

—— HUME. Crown 8vo. 1s. 6d. ; sewed, 1s.

HUXLEY'S PHYSIOLOGY, QUESTIONS ON, FOR SCHOOLS. By T. ALCOCK, M.D. 5th Edition. 18mo. 1s. 6d.

HUXLEY (T. H.) and MARTIN (H. N.).—A COURSE OF PRACTICAL INSTRUCTION IN ELEMENTARY BIOLOGY. New Edition, Revised and Extended by Prof. G. B. HOWES and D. H. SCOTT, M.A., Ph.D. With Preface by T. H. HUXLEY, F.R.S. Cr. 8vo. 10s. 6d.

IBBETSON (W. J.). — AN ELEMENTARY TREATISE ON THE MATHEMATICAL THEORY OF PERFECTLY ELASTIC SOLIDS. 8vo. 21s.

ILLINGWORTH (Rev. J. R.).—SERMONS PREACHED IN A COLLEGE CHAPEL. Crown 8vo. 5s.

IMITATIO CHRISTI, LIBRI IV. Printed in Borders after Holbein, Dürer, and other old Masters, containing Dances of Death, Acts of Mercy, Emblems, &c. Cr. 8vo. 7s. 6d.

INDIAN TEXT-BOOKS.—PRIMER OF ENGLISH GRAMMAR. By R. MORRIS, LL.D. 18mo. 1s.

EASY SELECTIONS FROM MODERN ENGLISH LITERATURE. For the use of the Middle Classes in Indian Schools. With Notes. By Sir ROPER LETHBRIDGE. Cr. 8vo. 1s. 6d.

SELECTIONS FROM MODERN ENGLISH LITERATURE. For the use of the Higher Classes in Indian Schools. By Sir ROPER LETHBRIDGE, M.A. Crown 8vo. 3s. 6d.

SERIES OF SIX ENGLISH READING BOOKS FOR INDIAN CHILDREN. By P. C. SIRCAR. Revised by Sir ROPER LETHBRIDGE. Cr. 8vo. Book I. 5d. ; Book II. 6d. ; Book III. 8d. ; Book IV. 1s. ; Book V. 1s. 2d. ; Book VI. 1s. 3d.

A GEOGRAPHICAL READER AND COMPANION TO THE ATLAS. By C. B. CLARKE, F.R.S. Crown 8vo. 2s.

A CLASS-BOOK OF GEOGRAPHY. By the same. Fcap. 8vo. 3s. 6d. ; sewed, 3s.

THE WORLD'S HISTORY. Compiled under direction of Sir ROPER LETHBRIDGE. Crown 8vo. 1s.

EASY INTRODUCTION TO THE HISTORY OF INDIA. By Sir ROPER LETHBRIDGE. Crown 8vo. 1s. 6d.

HISTORY OF ENGLAND. Compiled under direction of Sir ROPER LETHBRIDGE. Crown 8vo. 1s. 6d.

EASY INTRODUCTION TO THE HISTORY AND GEOGRAPHY OF BENGAL. By Sir ROPER LETHBRIDGE. Crown 8vo. 1s. 6d.

ARITHMETIC. With Answers. By BARNARD SMITH. 18mo. 2s.

ALGEBRA. By I. TODHUNTER, F.R.S. 18mo. 2s. 6d.

INDIAN TEXT-BOOKS—*continued*.

EUCLID. First Four Books. With Notes, &c. By the same Author. 18mo. 2s.

ELEMENTARY MENSURATION AND LAND SURVEYING. By the same Author. 18mo. 2s.

EUCLID. Books I.—IV. By H. S. HALL and F. H. STEVENS. Gl. 8vo. 3s.; sewed, 2s.6d.

PHYSICAL GEOGRAPHY. By H. F. BLANFORD. Crown 8vo. 2s. 6d.

ELEMENTARY GEOMETRY AND CONIC SECTIONS. By J. M. WILSON. Ex. fcp. 8vo. 6s.

INGRAM (T. Dunbar).—A HISTORY OF THE LEGISLATIVE UNION OF GREAT BRITAIN AND IRELAND. 8vo. 10s. 6d.

—— TWO CHAPTERS OF IRISH HISTORY : I. The Irish Parliament of James II. ; II. The Alleged Violation of the Treaty of Limerick. 8vo. 6s.

IONIA.—ANTIQUITIES OF IONIA. Folio. Vols. I. II. and III. 2l. 2s. each, or 5l. 5s. the set.—Part IV. 3l. 13s. 6d.

IRVING (Joseph).—ANNALS OF OUR TIME. A Diurnal of Events, Social and Political, Home and Foreign. From the Accession of Queen Victoria to Jubilee Day, being the First Fifty Years of Her Majesty's Reign. In 2 vols. 8vo.—Vol. I. June 20th, 1837, to February 28th, 1871. Vol. II. February 24th, 1871, to June 24th, 1887. 18s. each. The Second Volume may also be had in Three Parts : Part I. February 24th, 1871, to March 19th, 1874, 4s. 6d. Part II. March 20th, 1874, to July 22nd, 1878, 4s. 6d. Part III. July 23rd, 1878, to June 24th, 1887, 9s.

IRVING (Washington).—OLD CHRISTMAS. From the Sketch Book. With upwards of 100 Illustrations by RANDOLPH CALDECOTT. Cloth elegant, gilt edges. Crown 8vo. 6s. Also with uncut edges, paper label. Crown 8vo. 6s.

People's Edition. Medium 4to. 6d.

—— BRACEBRIDGE HALL. With 120 Illustrations by RANDOLPH CALDECOTT. Cloth elegant, gilt edges. Crown 8vo. 6s. Also with uncut edges, paper label Crown 8vo. 6s.

People's Edition. Medium 4to. 6d.

—— OLD CHRISTMAS AND BRACEBRIDGE HALL. Illustrations by RANDOLPH CALDECOTT. *Edition de Luxe*. Royal 8vo. 21s.

ISMAY'S CHILDREN. By the Author of "Hogan, M.P." Globe 8vo. 2s.

JACK AND THE BEAN-STALK. English Hexameters by the Honourable HALLAM TENNYSON. With 40 Illustrations by RANDOLPH CALDECOTT. Fcp. 4to. 3s. 6d.

JACKSON (Rev. Blomfield).—FIRST STEPS TO GREEK PROSE COMPOSITION. 12th Edit. 18mo. 1s. 6d.

KEY (supplied to Teachers only). 3s. 6d.

—— SECOND STEPS TO GREEK PROSE COMPOSITION. 18mo. 2s. 6d.

KEY (supplied to Teachers only). 3s. 6d.

JACKSON (Helen).—RAMONA : A Story. Globe 8vo. 2s.

JACOB (Rev. J. A.).—BUILDING IN SILENCE, AND OTHER SERMONS. Extra fcp. 8vo. 6s.

JAMES (Henry).—THE EUROPEANS : A Novel. Crown 8vo. 6s.

JAMES (Henry). — DAISY MILLER, AND OTHER STORIES. Crown 8vo. 6s. — Globe 8vo. 2s.

—— THE AMERICAN. Crown 8vo. 6s.

—— RODERICK HUDSON. Crown 8vo. 6s.— Globe 8vo. 2s.

—— THE MADONNA OF THE FUTURE, AND OTHER TALES. Crown 8vo. 6s. — Globe 8vo. 2s.

—— WASHINGTON SQUARE : THE PENSION BEAUREPAS. Crn. 8vo. 6s.—Globe 8vo. 2s.

—— THE PORTRAIT OF A LADY. Cr. 8vo. 6s.

—— STORIES REVIVED. In Two Series. Crown 8vo. 6s. each.

—— THE BOSTONIANS. Crown 8vo. 6s.

—— NOVELS AND TALES. Pocket Edition. 18mo. 14 vols. 2s. each volume : THE PORTRAIT OF A LADY. 3 vols.—RODERICK HUDSON. 2 vols.—THE AMERICAN. 2 vols. —WASHINGTON SQUARE. 1 vol.—THE EUROPEANS. 1 vol.—CONFIDENCE. 1 vol. —THE SIEGE OF LONDON ; MADAME DE MAUVES. 1 vol.—AN INTERNATIONAL EPISODE ; THE PENSION BEAUREPAS ; THE POINT OF VIEW. 1 vol.—DAISY MILLER, A STUDY ; FOUR MEETINGS ; LONGSTAFF'S MARRIAGE ; BENVOLIO. 1 vol.—THE MADONNA OF THE FUTURE ; A BUNDLE OF LETTERS ; THE DIARY OF A MAN OF FIFTY ; EUGENE PICKERING. 1 vol.

—— HAWTHORNE. Cr. 8vo. 1s. 6d. ; swd. 1s.

—— FRENCH POETS AND NOVELISTS. New Edition. Crown 8vo. 4s. 6d.

—— TALES OF THREE CITIES. Cr. 8vo. 4s.6d.

—— PORTRAITS OF PLACES. Cr. 8vo. 7s.6d.

—— THE PRINCESS CASAMASSIMA. Crown 8vo. 6s.—Globe 8vo. 2s.

—— PARTIAL PORTRAITS. Crown 8vo. 6s.

—— THE REVERBERATOR. Crown 8vo. 6s.

—— THE ASPERN PAPERS ; LOUISA PALLANT ; THE MODERN WARNING. 2 vols. Globe 8vo. 12s.

—— A LONDON LIFE. Crown 8vo. 3s. 6d.

JAMES (Right Hon. Sir William Milbourne). —THE BRITISH IN INDIA. 8vo. 12s. 6d.

JARDINE (Rev. Robert).—THE ELEMENTS OF THE PSYCHOLOGY OF COGNITION. Third Edition. Crown 8vo. 6s. 6d.

JEANS (Rev. G. E.).—HAILEYBURY CHAPEL, AND OTHER SERMONS. Fcp. 8vo. 3s. 6d.

—— THE LIFE AND LETTERS OF MARCUS TULLIUS CICERO. Being a Translation of the Letters included in Mr. Watson's Selection. Crown 8vo. 10s. 6d.

JEBB (Prof. R. C.).—THE ATTIC ORATORS, FROM ANTIPHON TO ISAEOS. 2 vols. 8vo. 25s.

—— THE ATTIC ORATORS. Selections from Antiphon, Andocides, Lysias, Isocrates, and Isaeos. Ed., with Notes. 2nd Ed. Fcp.8vo. 6s.

—— MODERN GREECE. Two Lectures. Crown 8vo. 5s.

—— PRIMER OF GREEK LITERATURE. 18mo. 1s.

—— BENTLEY. Crown 8vo. 1s. 6d. ; sewed, 1s.

JELLETT (Rev. Dr.).—THE ELDER SON, AND OTHER SERMONS. Crown 8vo. 6s.

JELLETT (Rev. Dr.).—THE EFFICACY OF PRAYER. 3rd Edition. Crown 8vo. 5s.

JENNINGS (A. C.).—CHRONOLOGICAL TABLES OF ANCIENT HISTORY. With Index. 8vo. 5s.

JENNINGS (A. C.) and LOWE (W. H.).—THE PSALMS, WITH INTRODUCTIONS AND CRITICAL NOTES. 2 vols. 2nd Edition. Crown 8vo. 10s 6d. each.

JEVONS (W. Stanley).—THE PRINCIPLES OF SCIENCE: A TREATISE ON LOGIC AND SCIENTIFIC METHOD. Crown 8vo. 12s. 6d.

—— ELEMENTARY LESSONS IN LOGIC: DEDUCTIVE AND INDUCTIVE. 18mo. 3s. 6d.

—— PRIMER OF LOGIC. 18mo. 1s.

—— THE THEORY OF POLITICAL ECONOMY. 3rd Edition. 8vo. 10s. 6d.

—— PRIMER OF POLITICAL ECONOMY. 18mo. 1s.

—— STUDIES IN DEDUCTIVE LOGIC. 2nd Edition. Crown 8vo. 6s.

—— INVESTIGATIONS IN CURRENCY AND FINANCE. Edited, with an Introduction, by H. S. FOXWELL, M.A. Illustrated by 20 Diagrams. 8vo. 21s.

—— METHODS OF SOCIAL REFORM. 8vo. 10s.6d.

—— THE STATE IN RELATION TO LABOUR. Crown 8vo. 3s. 6d.

—— LETTERS AND JOURNAL. Edited by HIS WIFE. 8vo. 14s.

JEX-BLAKE (Dr. Sophia).—THE CARE OF INFANTS: A Manual for Mothers and Nurses. 18mo. 1s.

JOHNSON (W. E.).—A TREATISE ON TRIGONOMETRY. Crown 8vo. 8s. 6d.

JOHNSON (Prof. W. Woolsey).—CURVE TRACING IN CARTESIAN CO-ORDINATES. Crown 8vo. 4s. 6d.

—— A TREATISE ON ORDINARY AND DIFFERENTIAL EQUATIONS. Crown 8vo. 15s.

—— AN ELEMENTARY TREATISE ON THE INTEGRAL CALCULUS. Crown 8vo. 9s.

JOHNSON'S LIVES OF THE POETS. The Six Chief Lives, with Macaulay's "Life of Johnson." Edited by MATTHEW ARNOLD. Crown 8vo. 4s. 6d.

JOHNSON. By LESLIE STEPHEN. Crown 8vo. 1s. 6d.; sewed, 1s.

JONES (D. E.).—EXAMPLES IN PHYSICS. Fcp. 8vo. 3s. 6d.

—— SOUND, LIGHT, AND HEAT. An Elementary Text-Book. Fcp. 8vo.

JONES (F.).—THE OWENS COLLEGE JUNIOR COURSE OF PRACTICAL CHEMISTRY. With Preface by Sir HENRY E. ROSCOE. New Edition. 18mo. 2s. 6d.

—— QUESTIONS ON CHEMISTRY. A Series of Problems and Exercises in Inorganic and Organic Chemistry. 18mo. 3s.

JONES (Rev. C. A.) and CHEYNE (C. H.).—ALGEBRAICAL EXERCISES. Progressively arranged. 18mo. 2s. 6d.

—— SOLUTIONS OF SOME OF THE EXAMPLES IN THE ALGEBRAICAL EXERCISES OF MESSRS. JONES AND CHEYNE. By the Rev. W. FAILES. Crown 8vo. 7s. 6d.

JUVENAL. THIRTEEN SATIRES OF JUVENAL. With a Commentary by Prof. J. E. B. MAYOR, M.A. 4th Edition. Vol. I. Crown 8vo. 10s. 6d.—Vol. II. Crown 8vo. 10s. 6d.

SUPPLEMENT to Third Edition, containing the Principal Changes made in the Fourth Edition. 5s.

—— THIRTEEN SATIRES. Edited, for the Use of Schools, with Notes, Introduction, and Appendices, by E. G. HARDY, M.A. Fcp. 8vo. 5s.

—— SELECT SATIRES. Edited by Prof. JOHN E. B. MAYOR. Satires X. and XI. 3s. 6d.—Satires XII. and XVI. Fcp. 8vo. 4s. 6d.

—— THIRTEEN SATIRES. Translated into English after the Text of J. E. B. MAYOR by ALEX. LEEPER, M.A. Cr. 8vo. 3s. 6d.

KANT.—KANT'S CRITICAL PHILOSOPHY FOR ENGLISH READERS. By JOHN P. MAHAFFY, D.D., and JOHN H. BERNARD, B.D. New Edition. 2 vols. Crown 8vo. Vol. I. THE KRITIK OF PURE REASON EXPLAINED AND DEFENDED. 7s. 6d.—Vol. II. THE "PROLEGOMENA." Translated, with Notes and Appendices. 6s.

KANT—MAX MÜLLER.—CRITIQUE OF PURE REASON BY IMMANUEL KANT. Translated by F. MAX MÜLLER. With Introduction by LUDWIG NOIRÉ. 2 vols. 8vo. 16s. each.—Sold separately. Vol. I. HISTORICAL INTRODUCTION, by LUDWIG NOIRÉ, etc., etc.; Vol. II. CRITIQUE OF PURE REASON.

KAY (Rev. W.).—A COMMENTARY ON ST. PAUL'S TWO EPISTLES TO THE CORINTHIANS. Greek Text, with Commentary. 8vo. 9s.

KEARY (Annie).—JANET'S HOME. Globe 8vo. 2s.

—— CLEMENCY FRANKLYN. Globe 8vo. 2s.

—— OLDBURY. Globe 8vo. 2s.

—— A YORK AND A LANCASTER ROSE. Globe 8vo. 2s.

—— CASTLE DALY: THE STORY OF AN IRISH HOME THIRTY YEARS AGO. Cr. 8vo. 3s.6d.

—— A DOUBTING HEART. Crown 8vo. 6s.

—— NATIONS AROUND. Crown 8vo. 4s. 6d.

KEARY (Eliza).—THE MAGIC VALLEY; OR, PATIENT ANTOINE. With Illustrations by "E.V.B." Globe 8vo. 4s. 6d.

KEATS.—THE POETICAL WORKS OF JOHN KEATS. With Notes, by Prof. PALGRAVE. 18mo. 4s. 6d.

KEATS. By SIDNEY COLVIN. Crown 8vo. 1s. 6d.; sewed, 1s.

KELLAND (P.) and TAIT (P. G.).—INTRODUCTION TO QUATERNIONS, WITH NUMEROUS EXAMPLES. 2nd Edition. Cr. 8vo. 7s. 6d.

KELLOGG (Rev. S. H.).—THE LIGHT OF ASIA AND THE LIGHT OF THE WORLD. Cr. 8vo. 7s. 6d.

KEMPE (A. B.).—HOW TO DRAW A STRAIGHT LINE. A Lecture on Linkages. Cr. 8vo. 1s.6d.

KENNEDY (Prof. Alex. W. B.).—THE MECHANICS OF MACHINERY. With Illustrations. Crown 8vo. 12s. 6d.

KERNEL AND THE HUSK (THE): LETTERS ON SPIRITUAL CHRISTIANITY. By the Author of "Philochristus." Crown 8vo. 5s.

KEYNES (J. N.).—STUDIES AND EXERCISES IN FORMAL LOGIC. 2nd Edition. Crown 8vo. 10s. 6d.

KIEPERT (H.).—MANUAL OF ANCIENT GEOGRAPHY. Crown 8vo. 5s.

KILLEN (W. D.).—ECCLESIASTICAL HISTORY OF IRELAND, FROM THE EARLIEST DATE TO THE PRESENT TIME. 2 vols. 8vo. 25s.

KINGSLEY (Charles).—NOVELS AND POEMS. Eversley Edition. 13 vols. Gl. 8vo. 5s. each.
WESTWARD HO! 2 vols.—TWO YEARS AGO. 2 vols.—HYPATIA. 2 vols.—YEAST. 1 vol.—ALTON LOCKE. 2 vols.—HEREWARD THE WAKE. 2 vols.—POEMS. 2 vols.

—— Complete Edition OF THE WORKS OF CHARLES KINGSLEY. Cr. 8vo. 3s. 6d. each.
WESTWARD HO! With a Portrait.
HYPATIA.
YEAST.
ALTON LOCKE.
TWO YEARS AGO.
HEREWARD THE WAKE.
POEMS.
THE HEROES; OR, GREEK FAIRY TALES FOR MY CHILDREN.
THE WATER BABIES: A FAIRY TALE FOR A LAND-BABY.
MADAM HOW AND LADY WHY; OR, FIRST LESSONS IN EARTH-LORE FOR CHILDREN.
AT LAST: A CHRISTMAS IN THE WEST INDIES.
PROSE IDYLLS.
PLAYS AND PURITANS.
THE ROMAN AND THE TEUTON. With Preface by Professor MAX MÜLLER.
SANITARY AND SOCIAL LECTURES.
HISTORICAL LECTURES AND ESSAYS.
SCIENTIFIC LECTURES AND ESSAYS.
LITERARY AND GENERAL LECTURES.
THE HERMITS.
GLAUCUS; OR, THE WONDERS OF THE SEA-SHORE. With Coloured Illustrations.
VILLAGE AND TOWN AND COUNTRY SERMONS.
SERMONS ON NATIONAL SUBJECTS, AND THE KING OF THE EARTH.
SERMONS FOR THE TIMES.
GOOD NEWS OF GOD.
THE GOSPEL OF THE PENTATEUCH, AND DAVID.
THE WATER OF LIFE, AND OTHER SERMONS.
DISCIPLINE, AND OTHER SERMONS.
WESTMINSTER SERMONS.

—— A Sixpenny Edition OF CHARLES KINGSLEY'S NOVELS. Med. 8vo. 6d. each.
WESTWARD HO!—HYPATIA. — YEAST. — ALTON LOCKE. — TWO YEARS AGO. — HEREWARD THE WAKE.

KINGSLEY (Charles).—THE WATER BABIES: A FAIRY TALE FOR A LAND BABY. New Edition, with a Hundred New Pictures by LINLEY SAMBOURNE; engraved by J. SWAIN. Fcp. 4to. 12s. 6d.

—— HEALTH AND EDUCATION. Cr. 8vo. 6s.

—— POEMS. Pocket Edition. 18mo. 1s. 6d.

—— SELECTIONS FROM SOME OF THE WRITINGS OF CHARLES KINGSLEY. Cr. 8vo. 6s.

—— OUT OF THE DEEP: WORDS FOR THE SORROWFUL. From the Writings of CHARLES KINGSLEY. Extra fcp. 8vo. 3s. 6d.

—— DAILY THOUGHTS. Selected from the Writings of CHARLES KINGSLEY. By HIS WIFE. Crown 8vo. 6s.

—— THE HEROES; OR, GREEK FAIRY TALES FOR MY CHILDREN. Extra cloth, gilt edges. Presentation Edition. Crown 8vo. 7s. 6d.

—— GLAUCUS; OR, THE WONDERS OF THE SEA SHORE. With Coloured Illustrations, extra cloth, gilt edges. Presentation Edition. Crown 8vo. 7s. 6d.

—— FROM DEATH TO LIFE. Fragments of Teaching to a Village Congregation. With Letters on the "Life after Death." Edited by HIS WIFE. Fcp. 8vo. 2s. 6d.

—— HIS LETTERS AND MEMOIRS. Edited by HIS WIFE. Crown 8vo. 6s.—2 vols. 12s.

—— ALL SAINTS' DAY, AND OTHER SERMONS. Crown 8vo. 7s. 6d.

—— TRUE WORDS FOR BRAVE MEN. Crown 8vo. 2s. 6d.

KINGSLEY (H.).—TALES OF OLD TRAVEL. Re-narrated by HENRY KINGSLEY. Crown 8vo, cloth, extra gilt. 5s.

KITCHENER (F. E.). — GEOMETRICAL NOTE-BOOK. Containing Easy Problems in Geometrical Drawing, preparatory to the Study of Geometry. 4to. 2s.

KLEIN (Dr. E.).—MICRO-ORGANISMS AND DISEASE. An Introduction into the Study of Specific Micro-Organisms. With 121 Engravings. 3rd Edition. Crown 8vo. 6s.

—— THE BACTERIA IN ASIATIC CHOLERA. Crown 8vo. 5s.

KNOX (A.).—DIFFERENTIAL CALCULUS FOR BEGINNERS. Fcp. 8vo. 3s. 6d.

KTESIAS. THE FRAGMENTS OF THE PERSIKA OF KTESIAS. Edited, with Introduction and Notes, by J. GILMORE, M.A. 8vo. 8s. 6d.

KUENEN.—AN HISTORICO-CRITICAL INQUIRY INTO THE ORIGIN AND COMPOSITION OF THE HEXATEUCH (PENTATEUCH AND BOOK OF JOSHUA). By Prof. A. KUENEN, Leiden. Translated by PHILIP H. WICKSTEED, M.A. 8vo. 14s.

KYNASTON (Herbert, D.D.). — SERMONS PREACHED IN THE COLLEGE CHAPEL, CHELTENHAM. Crown 8vo. 6s.

—— PROGRESSIVE EXERCISES IN THE COMPOSITION OF GREEK IAMBIC VERSE. Extra fcp. 8vo. 5s.
KEY (supplied to Teachers only). 4s. 6d.

—— EXEMPLARIA CHELTONIENSIA. Sive quae discipulis suis Carmina identidem Latine reddenda proposuit ipse reddidit ex cathedra dictavit HERBERT KYNASTON, M.A. Extra fcp. 8vo. 5s.

LABBERTON (R. H.).—NEW HISTORICAL ATLAS AND GENERAL HISTORY. New Edition. Demy 4to. 15*s*.

LAFARGUE (Philip).—THE NEW JUDGMENT OF PARIS: A Novel. 2 vols. Gl. 8vo. 12*s*.

LA FONTAINE'S FABLES. A Selection, with Introduction, Notes, and Vocabulary, by L. M. MORIARTY, B.A. Illustrations by RANDOLPH CALDECOTT. Globe 8vo. 2*s*.6*d*.

LAMB.—COLLECTED WORKS. Edited, with Introduction and Notes, by the Rev. ALFRED AINGER, M.A. Globe 8vo. 5*s*. each volume. I. ESSAYS OF ELIA.—II. PLAYS, POEMS, AND MISCELLANEOUS ESSAYS.—III. MRS. LEICESTER'S SCHOOL; THE ADVENTURES OF ULYSSES; AND OTHER ESSAYS.—IV. TALES FROM SHAKESPEARE.—V. and VI. LETTERS. Newly arranged, with additions.

—— THE LIFE OF CHARLES LAMB. By Rev. ALFRED AINGER, M.A. Uniform with above. Globe 8vo. 5*s*.

TALES FROM SHAKSPEARE. 18mo. 4*s*. 6*d*. *Globe Readings Edition.* For Schools. Globe 8vo. 2*s*.

LAMB. By Rev. ALFRED AINGER, M.A. Crown 8vo. 1*s*. 6*d*. ; sewed, 1*s*.

LANCIANI (Prof. R.).—ANCIENT ROME IN THE LIGHT OF RECENT DISCOVERIES. 4to. 24*s*.

LAND OF DARKNESS (THE). Along with some further Chapters in the Experiences of The Little Pilgrim. By the Author of "A Little Pilgrim in the Unseen." Crown 8vo. 5*s*.

LANDAUER (J.).—BLOWPIPE ANALYSIS. Authorised English Edition by JAMES TAYLOR and WM. E. KAY. Ext. fcp. 8vo. 4*s*. 6*d*.

LANDOR.—SELECTIONS FROM THE WRITINGS OF WALTER SAVAGE LANDOR. Arranged and Edited by SIDNEY COLVIN. 18mo. 4*s*. 6*d*.

LANDOR. By SIDNEY COLVIN. Crown 8vo, 1*s*. 6*d*. ; sewed, 1*s*.

LANE-POOLE. — SELECTIONS FROM THE SPEECHES AND TABLE-TALK OF MOHAMMAD. By S. LANE-POOLE. 18mo. 4*s*. 6*d*.

LANG (Andrew).—THE LIBRARY. With a Chapter on Modern Illustrated Books, by AUSTIN DOBSON. Crown 8vo. 3*s*. 6*d*.

LANKESTER (Prof. E. Ray).—A CHAPTER IN DARWINISM, AND OTHER ESSAYS AND ADDRESSES. 8vo.

LASLETT (Thomas).—TIMBER AND TIMBER TREES, NATIVE AND FOREIGN. Crown 8vo. 8*s*. 6*d*.

LATIN ACCIDENCE AND EXERCISES ARRANGED FOR BEGINNERS. By WILLIAM WELCH, M.A., and C. G. DUFFIELD, M.A. 18mo. 1*s*. 6*d*.

LAWRENCE (LORD). By Sir RICHARD TEMPLE. With Portrait. Crown 8vo. 2*s*. 6*d*.

LEAHY (Sergeant).—THE ART OF SWIMMING IN THE ETON STYLE. Edited by Two Etonians, with Preface by Mrs. OLIPHANT. Crown 8vo. 2*s*.

LECTURES ON ART. By REGD. STUART POOLE, Professor W. B. RICHMOND, E. J. POYNTER, R.A., J. T. MICKLETHWAITE, and WILLIAM MORRIS. Crown 8vo. 4*s*. 6*d*.

LEE (Margaret).—FAITHFUL AND UNFAITHFUL. Crown 8vo. 3*s*. 6*d*.

LEGGE (Alfred O.).—THE GROWTH OF THE TEMPORAL POWER OF THE PAPACY. Crown 8vo. 8*s*. 6*d*.

LEMON.—THE JEST BOOK. The Choicest Anecdotes and Sayings. Selected by MARK LEMON. 18mo. 4*s*. 6*d*.

LETHBRIDGE (Sir Roper). — A SHORT MANUAL OF THE HISTORY OF INDIA. With Maps. Crown 8vo. 5*s*. For other Works by this Author, see *Indian Text-Books Series*, p. 24.

LEVY (Amy).—REUBEN SACHS: A SKETCH. Crown 8vo. 3*s*. 6*d*.

LEWIS (Richard).—HISTORY OF THE LIFEBOAT AND ITS WORK. Crown 8vo. 5*s*.

LIECHTENSTEIN (Princess Marie).—HOLLAND HOUSE. With Steel Engravings, Woodcuts, and nearly 40 Illustrations by the Woodburytype Permanent Process. 2 vols. Medium 4to. Half mor., elegant. 4*l*. 4*s*.

LIGHTFOOT (The Right Rev. Bishop).— ST. PAUL'S EPISTLE TO THE GALATIANS. A Revised Text, with Introduction, Notes, and Dissertations. 9th Edition. 8vo. 12*s*.

—— ST. PAUL'S EPISTLE TO THE PHILIPPIANS. A Revised Text, with Introduction, Notes and Dissertations. 9th Edition. 8vo. 12*s*.

—— ST. CLEMENT OF ROME. An Appendix, containing the newly-recovered portions. With Introductions, Notes, and Translations. 8vo. 8*s*. 6*d*.

—— ST. PAUL'S EPISTLES TO THE COLOSSIANS AND TO PHILEMON. A Revised Text, with Introductions, Notes, and Dissertations. 9th Edition. 8vo. 12*s*.

—— PRIMARY CHARGE. Two Addresses delivered to the Clergy of the Diocese of Durham, 1882. 8vo. 2*s*.

—— THE APOSTOLIC FATHERS. Part II. S. IGNATIUS to St. POLYCARP. Revised Texts, with Introductions, Notes, Dissertations, and Translations. 3 vols. 2nd Edition. Demy 8vo. 48*s*.

—— APOSTOLIC FATHERS. Abridged Edition. With Short Introductions, Greek Text, and English Translation. 8vo.

—— ST. CLEMENT OF ROME: THE TWO EPISTLES TO THE CORINTHIANS. A Revised Text, with Introduction and Notes. New Edition. 2 vols. 8vo.

—— A CHARGE DELIVERED TO THE CLERGY OF THE DIOCESE OF DURHAM, NOV. 25TH, 1886. Demy 8vo. 2*s*.

—— ESSAYS ON THE WORK ENTITLED "SUPERNATURAL RELIGION." 8vo. 10*s*. 6*d*.

LIGHTWOOD (J. M.)—THE NATURE OF POSITIVE LAW. 8vo. 12*s*. 6*d*.

LINDSAY (Dr. J. A.). — THE CLIMATIC TREATMENT OF CONSUMPTION. Cr. 8vo. 5*s*.

LITTLE PILGRIM IN THE UNSEEN. 24th Thousand. Crown 8vo. 2*s*. 6*d*.

LIVINGSTONE. By THOMAS HUGHES. With Portrait and Map. Crown 8vo. 2*s*. 6*d*.

LIVY.—By Rev. W. W. CAPES, Fcp. 8vo. 1*s*. 6*d*.

LIVY.—HANNIBAL'S FIRST CAMPAIGN IN ITALY. Books XXI. and XXII. Edited by Rev. W. W. CAPES, M.A. Fcp. 8vo. 5*.

—— BOOK I. Edited, with Notes and Vocabulary, by H. M. STEPHENSON, M.A. 18mo. 1*. 6d.

—— BOOKS II. AND III. Edited by H. M. STEPHENSON, M.A. Fcp. 8vo. 5*.

—— THE HANNIBALIAN WAR. Being part of the 21st and 22nd Books of Livy, adapted for the Use of Beginners. By G. C. MACAULAY, M.A. 18mo. 1*. 6d.

—— BOOK XXI. Adapted from Mr. Capes' Edition. With Notes and Vocabulary by W. W. CAPES, M.A., and J. E. MELHUISH, M.A. 18mo. 1*. 6d.

—— BOOKS XXI.—XXV. THE SECOND PUNIC WAR. Translated by A. J. CHURCH, M.A., and W. J. BRODRIBB, M.A. With Maps. Crown 8vo. 7*. 6d.

—— BOOKS XXIII. AND XXIV. Edited by G. C. MACAULAY. Maps. Fcp. 8vo. 5*.

—— THE SIEGE OF SYRACUSE. Being part of Books XXIV. and XXV. of Livy. Adapted for the Use of Beginners, with Notes, Exercises, and Vocabulary, by G. RICHARDS, M.A., and A. S. WALPOLE, M.A. 18mo. 1*. 6d.

—— THE LAST TWO KINGS OF MACEDON. Extracts from the fourth and fifth Decades of Livy. Selected and Edited, with Introduction and Notes, by F. H. RAWLINS, M.A. With Maps. Fcp. 8vo. 3*. 6d.

—— LEGENDS OF ANCIENT ROME, FROM LIVY. Adapted and Edited, with Notes, Exercises, and Vocabularies, by H. WILKINSON, M.A. 18mo. 1*. 6d.

LOCK (Rev. J. B.)—TRIGONOMETRY. Globe 8vo. Part I. ELEMENTARY TRIGONOMETRY. 4*. 6d.—Part II. HIGHER TRIGONOMETRY. 4*. 6d. Complete, 7*. 6d.

—— KEY TO "ELEMENTARY TRIGONOMETRY." By H. CARR, B.A. Crown 8vo. 8*. 6d.

—— TRIGONOMETRY FOR BEGINNERS. As far as the Solution of Triangles. Gl. 8vo. 2*. 6d.

—— KEY TO "TRIGONOMETRY FOR BEGINNERS." Crown 8vo. 6*. 6d.

—— ARITHMETIC FOR SCHOOLS. 4th Edition, revised. Globe 8vo. Complete with Answers, 4*. 6d. Without Answers, 4*. 6d. Part I., with Answers, 2*. Part II., with Answers, 3*.

—— KEY TO "ARITHMETIC FOR SCHOOLS." By the Rev. R. G. WATSON. Cr. 8vo. 10*. 6d.

—— DYNAMICS FOR BEGINNERS. 2nd Edit. Globe 8vo. 4*. 6d.

—— ARITHMETIC FOR BEGINNERS. A School Class-Book of COMMERCIAL ARITHMETIC. Globe 8vo. 2*. 6d.

—— KEY TO "ARITHMETIC FOR BEGINNERS." By Rev. R. G. WATSON. Crown 8vo. 8*. 6d.

—— ELEMENTARY STATICS. Gl. 8vo. 4*. 6d.

—— A SHILLING CLASS-BOOK OF ARITHMETIC ADAPTED FOR USE IN ELEMENTARY SCHOOLS. 18mo.

LOCKE. By Prof. FOWLER. Crown 8vo. 1*. 6d.; sewed, 1*.

LOCKYER (J. Norman, F.R.S.).—ELEMENTARY LESSONS IN ASTRONOMY. With numerous Illustrations and Coloured Diagram. New Edition. 18mo. 5*. 6d.

—— CONTRIBUTIONS TO SOLAR PHYSICS. With Illustrations. Royal 8vo. 31*. 6d.

—— PRIMER OF ASTRONOMY. Illustrated. New Edition. 18mo. 1*.

—— OUTLINES OF PHYSIOGRAPHY: THE MOVEMENTS OF THE EARTH. Crown 8vo. 1*. 6d.

—— THE CHEMISTRY OF THE SUN. 8vo. 14*.

LOCKYER'S ASTRONOMY, QUESTIONS ON. By J. FORBES-ROBERTSON. 18mo. 1*. 6d.

LOCKYER—SEABROKE.—STAR-GAZING PAST AND PRESENT. By J. NORMAN LOCKYER, F.R.S. Expanded from Shorthand Notes with the assistance of G. M. SEABROKE, F.R.A.S. Illustrated. Royal 8vo. 21*.

LODGE (Prof. Oliver J.).—MODERN VIEWS OF ELECTRICITY. Illustrated. Crown 8vo. 6*. 6d.

LOEWY (B.).—QUESTIONS AND EXAMPLES IN EXPERIMENTAL PHYSICS, SOUND, LIGHT, HEAT, ELECTRICITY, AND MAGNETISM. Fcp. 8vo. 2*.

—— A GRADUATED COURSE OF NATURAL SCIENCE, EXPERIMENTAL AND THEORETICAL, FOR SCHOOLS AND COLLEGES. Part I. FIRST YEAR'S COURSE FOR ELEMENTARY SCHOOLS AND THE JUNIOR CLASSES OF TECHNICAL SCHOOLS AND COLLEGES. Globe 8vo. 2*.

LOFTIE (Mrs.).—THE DINING-ROOM. With Illustrations. Crown 8vo. 2*. 6d.

LONGFELLOW.—POEMS OF PLACES: ENGLAND AND WALES. Edited by H. W. LONGFELLOW. 2 vols. 9*.

—— BALLADS, LYRICS, AND SONNETS. From the Poetic Works of HENRY WADSWORTH LONGFELLOW. 18mo. 4*. 6d.

LOWE (W. H.).—THE HEBREW STUDENT'S COMMENTARY ON ZECHARIAH HEBREW AND LXX. 8vo. 10*. 6d.

LOWELL (James Russell). — COMPLETE POETICAL WORKS. 18mo. 4*. 6d.

—— HEARTSEASE AND RUE. Crown 8vo. 5*.

—— POLITICAL ESSAYS. Ext. cr. 8vo. 7*. 6d.

LUBBOCK (Sir John, Bart.).—THE ORIGIN AND METAMORPHOSES OF INSECTS. With Illustrations. Crown 8vo. 3*. 6d.

—— ON BRITISH WILD FLOWERS CONSIDERED IN THEIR RELATION TO INSECTS. With Illustrations. Crown 8vo. 4*. 6d.

—— FLOWERS, FRUITS, AND LEAVES. With Illustrations. Crown 8vo. 4*. 6d.

—— SCIENTIFIC LECTURES. With Illustrations. New Edition, revised. 8vo. 8*. 6d.

—— POLITICAL AND EDUCATIONAL ADDRESSES. 8vo. 8*. 6d.

—— THE PLEASURES OF LIFE. New Edition. Globe 8vo. 1*. 6d.; sewed, 1*.
Library Edition. Globe 8vo. 3*. 6d.
Part II. Globe 8vo. 1*. 6d.; sewed, 1*.
Library Edition. Globe 8vo. 3*. 6d.

LUCAS (F.).—SKETCHES OF RURAL LIFE. Poems. Globe 8vo. 5s.

LUCIAN.—EXTRACTS FROM LUCIAN. Edited, with Introduction, Exercises, Notes, and Vocabulary, by the Rev. J. BOND, M.A., and A. S. WALPOLE, M.A. 18mo. 1s. 6d.

LUCRETIUS.—BOOKS I.—III. Edited by J. H. WARBURTON LEE. Fcp. 8vo. 4s. 6d.

LUPTON (J. H.).—AN INTRODUCTION TO LATIN ELEGIAC VERSE COMPOSITION. Globe 8vo. 2s. 6d.

—— LATIN RENDERING OF THE EXERCISES IN PART II. (XXV.-C.) TO LUPTON'S "INTRODUCTION TO LATIN ELEGIAC VERSE COMPOSITION." Globe 8vo. 3s. 6d.

—— AN INTRODUCTION TO LATIN LYRIC VERSE COMPOSITION. Globe 8vo. 3s.—Key, 4s. 6d.

LUPTON (Sydney).—CHEMICAL ARITHMETIC. With 1200 Examples. 2nd Edition. Fcp. 8vo. 4s. 6d.

—— NUMERICAL TABLES AND CONSTANTS IN ELEMENTARY SCIENCE. Ex. fcp. 8vo. 2s. 6d.

LYSIAS.—SELECT ORATIONS. Edited by E. S. SHUCKBURGH, M.A. Fcp. 8vo. 6s.

LYRE FRANÇAISE (LA). Selected and arranged, with Notes, by GUSTAVE MASSON. With Vignette. 18mo. 4s. 6d.

LYTE (H. C. Maxwell).—ETON COLLEGE, HISTORY OF, 1440—1884. With Illustrations. New and Cheaper Issue. 8vo. 21s.

—— THE UNIVERSITY OF OXFORD, A HISTORY OF, FROM THE EARLIEST TIMES TO THE YEAR 1530. 8vo. 16s.

LYTTON (Rt. Hon. Earl of).—THE RING OF AMASIS: A ROMANCE. Crown 8vo.

MACARTHUR (Margaret). — HISTORY OF SCOTLAND. 18mo. 2s.

MACAULAY. By J. C. MORISON. Crown 8vo. 1s. 0d.; sewed, 1s.

M'CLELLAND (W. J.) and PRESTON (T.). —A TREATISE ON SPHERICAL TRIGONOMETRY. With numerous Examples. Crown 8vo. 8s. 6d.—Or Part I. 4s. 6d.; Part II. 5s.

McCOSH (Rev. Dr. James).—THE METHOD OF THE DIVINE GOVERNMENT, PHYSICAL AND MORAL. 8vo. 10s. 6d.

—— THE SUPERNATURAL IN RELATION TO THE NATURAL. Crown 8vo. 7s. 6d.

—— THE INTUITIONS OF THE MIND. New Edition. 8vo. 10s. 6d.

—— AN EXAMINATION OF MR. J. S. MILL'S PHILOSOPHY. 8vo. 10s. 6d.

—— THE LAWS OF DISCURSIVE THOUGHT. Being a Text-Book of Formal Logic. Crown 8vo. 5s.

—— CHRISTIANITY AND POSITIVISM. Lectures on Natural Theology and Apologetics. Crown 8vo. 7s. 6d.

—— THE SCOTTISH PHILOSOPHY, FROM HUTCHESON TO HAMILTON, BIOGRAPHICAL, EXPOSITORY, CRITICAL. Royal 8vo. 16s.

—— THE EMOTIONS. 8vo. 9s.

—— REALISTIC PHILOSOPHY DEFENDED IN A PHILOSOPHIC SERIES. 2 vols. Vol. I. EXPOSITORY. Vol. II. HISTORICAL AND CRITICAL. Crown 8vo. 14s.

McCOSH (Rev. Dr.).—PSYCHOLOGY. Crown 8vo. I. THE COGNITIVE POWERS. 6s. 6d.— II. THE MOTIVE POWERS. 6s. 6d.

—— FIRST AND FUNDAMENTAL TRUTHS. Being a Treatise on Metaphysics. 8vo. 9s.

MACDONALD (George).—ENGLAND'S ANTIPHON. Crown 8vo. 4s. 6d.

MACDONELL (Joh).—THE LAND QUESTION. 8vo. 10s. 6d.

MACFARLANE (Alexander). — PHYSICAL ARITHMETIC. Crown 8vo. 7s. 6d.

MACGREGOR (James Gordon).—AN ELEMENTARY TREATISE ON KINEMATICS AND DYNAMICS. Crown 8vo. 10s. 6d.

MACKENZIE (Sir Morell).—THE HYGIENE OF THE VOCAL ORGANS. A Practical Handbook for Singers and Speakers. With Illustrations. 6th Edition. Crown 8vo. 6s.

MACKIE (Rev. Ellis).—PARALLEL PASSAGES FOR TRANSLATION INTO GREEK AND ENGLISH. Globe 8vo. 4s. 6d.

MACLAGAN (Dr. T.).—THE GERM THEORY. 8vo. 10s. 6d.

MACLAREN (Rev. Alexander).—SERMONS PREACHED AT MANCHESTER. 11th Edition. Fcp. 8vo. 4s. 6d.

—— A SECOND SERIES OF SERMONS. 7th Edition. Fcp. 8vo. 4s. 6d.

—— A THIRD SERIES. 6th Edition. Fcp. 8vo. 4s. 6d.

—— WEEK-DAY EVENING ADDRESSES. 4th Edition. Fcp. 8vo. 2s. 6d.

—— THE SECRET OF POWER, AND OTHER SERMONS. Fcp. 8vo. 4s. 6d.

MACLAREN (Arch.).—THE FAIRY FAMILY. A Series of Ballads and Metrical Tales. Crown 8vo, gilt. 5s.

MACLEAN (Surgeon-General W. C.).— DISEASES OF TROPICAL CLIMATES. Crown 8vo. 10s. 6d.

MACLEAR (Rev. Canon).—A CLASS-BOOK OF OLD TESTAMENT HISTORY. With Four Maps. 18mo. 4s. 6d.

—— A CLASS-BOOK OF NEW TESTAMENT HISTORY. Including the connection of the Old and New Testament. 18mo. 5s. 6d.

—— A CLASS-BOOK OF THE CATECHISM OF THE CHURCH OF ENGLAND. 18mo. 1s. 6d.

—— A SHILLING BOOK OF OLD TESTAMENT HISTORY. 18mo. 1s.

—— A SHILLING BOOK OF NEW TESTAMENT HISTORY. 18mo. 1s.

—— A FIRST CLASS-BOOK OF THE CATECHISM OF THE CHURCH OF ENGLAND, WITH SCRIPTURE PROOFS FOR JUNIOR CLASSES AND SCHOOLS. 18mo. 6d.

—— A MANUAL OF INSTRUCTION FOR CONFIRMATION AND FIRST COMMUNION, WITH PRAYERS AND DEVOTIONS. 32mo. 2s.

—— FIRST COMMUNION, WITH PRAYERS AND DEVOTIONS FOR THE NEWLY CONFIRMED. 32mo. 6d.

—— THE ORDER OF CONFIRMATION, WITH PRAYERS AND DEVOTIONS. 32mo. 6d.

—— THE HOUR OF SORROW; OR, THE OFFICE FOR THE BURIAL OF THE DEAD. 32mo. 2s.

MACLEAR (Rev. Dr.).—APOSTLES OF MEDI-
ÆVAL EUROPE. Crown 8vo. 4s. 6d.

—— AN INTRODUCTION TO THE CREEDS.
18mo. 2s. 6d.

—— AN INTRODUCTION TO THE THIRTY-NINE
ARTICLES. 18mo.

M'LENNAN (J. F.).—THE PATRIARCHAL
THEORY. Edited and completed by DONALD
M'LENNAN, M.A. 8vo. 14s.

—— STUDIES IN ANCIENT HISTORY. Comprising a Reprint of "Primitive Marriage."
New Edition. 8vo. 16s.

MACMILLAN (D.). MEMOIR OF DANIEL
MACMILLAN. By THOMAS HUGHES, Q.C.
Crown 8vo. 4s. 6d.

Popular Edition. Crown 8vo, sewed. 1s.

MACMILLAN (Rev. Hugh).—BIBLE TEACH-
INGS IN NATURE. 15th Ed. Gl. 8vo. 6s.

—— HOLIDAYS ON HIGH LANDS; OR, RAM-
BLES AND INCIDENTS IN SEARCH OF ALPINE
PLANTS. 2nd Edition. Globe 8vo. 6s.

—— THE TRUE VINE; OR, THE ANALOGIES
OF OUR LORD'S ALLEGORY. 5th Edition.
Globe 8vo. 6s.

—— THE MINISTRY OF NATURE. 8th Edition.
Globe 8vo. 6s.

—— THE SABBATH OF THE FIELDS. Being a
Sequel to "Bible Teachings in Nature."
6th Edition. Globe 8vo. 6s.

—— THE MARRIAGE IN CANA. Globe 8vo. 6s.

—— TWO WORLDS ARE OURS. 3rd Edition.
Globe 8vo. 6s.

—— THE OLIVE LEAF. Globe 8vo. 6s.

—— ROMAN MOSAICS; OR, STUDIES IN ROME
AND ITS NEIGHBOURHOOD. Globe 8vo. 6s.

MACMILLAN (M. C.)—FIRST LATIN GRAM-
MAR. Extra fcp. 8vo. 1s. 6d.

MACMILLAN'S MAGAZINE. Published
Monthly. 1s.—Vols. I.—LX. 7s. 6d. each.

MACMILLAN'S SIX-SHILLING NO-
VELS. 6s. each vol. Crown 8vo, cloth.

By the Rev. Charles Kingsley.
WESTWARD HO!
HYPATIA.
HEREWARD THE WAKE.
TWO YEARS AGO.
YEAST.
ALTON LOCKE. With Portrait.

By William Black.
A PRINCESS OF THULE.
STRANGE ADVENTURES OF A PHAETON.
Illustrated.
THE MAID OF KILLEENA, AND OTHER
TALES.
MADCAP VIOLET.
GREEN PASTURES AND PICCADILLY.
THE BEAUTIFUL WRETCH; THE FOUR
MACNICOLS; THE PUPIL OF AURELIUS.
MACLEOD OF DARE. Illustrated.
WHITE WINGS: A YACHTING ROMANCE.
SHANDON BELLS.
YOLANDE.

MACMILLAN'S SIX - SHILLING NO-
VELS—*continued.*

By William Black.
JUDITH SHAKESPEARE.
THE WISE WOMEN OF INVERNESS, A TALE;
AND OTHER MISCELLANIES.
WHITE HEATHER.
SABINA ZEMBRA.

*By Mrs. Craik, Author of "John Halifax,
Gentleman."*
THE OGILVIES. Illustrated.
THE HEAD OF THE FAMILY. Illustrated.
OLIVE. Illustrated.
AGATHA'S HUSBAND. Illustrated.
MY MOTHER AND I. Illustrated.
MISS TOMMY: A MEDIÆVAL ROMANCE.
Illustrated.
KING ARTHUR: NOT A LOVE STORY.

By J. H. Shorthouse.
JOHN INGLESANT.
SIR PERCIVAL.
A TEACHER OF THE VIOLIN, AND OTHER
TALES.
THE COUNTESS EVE.

By Annie Keary.
A DOUBTING HEART.

By Henry James.
THE AMERICAN.
THE EUROPEANS.
DAISY MILLER; AN INTERNATIONAL EPI-
SODE; FOUR MEETINGS.
THE MADONNA OF THE FUTURE, AND
OTHER TALES.
RODERICK HUDSON.
WASHINGTON SQUARE; THE PENSION BEAU-
REPAS; A BUNDLE OF LETTERS.
THE PORTRAIT OF A LADY.
STORIES REVIVED. Two Series. 6s. each.
THE BOSTONIANS.
THE REVERBERATOR.

By F. Marion Crawford.
SANT' ILARIO.
GREIFENSTEIN.

REALMAH. By the Author of "Friends in
Council."
OLD SIR DOUGLAS. By the Hon. Mrs.
NORTON.
VIRGIN SOIL. By TOURGENIEF.
THE HARBOUR BAR.
BENGAL PEASANT LIFE. By LAL BEHARI
DAY.
VIDA: STUDY OF A GIRL. By AMY DUNS-
MUIR.
JILL. By E. A. DILLWYN.
NEÆRA: A TALE OF ANCIENT ROME. By
J. W. GRAHAM.
THE NEW ANTIGONE: A ROMANCE.

MACMILLAN'S THREE-AND-SIX-PENNY NOVELS. Crown 8vo. 3s. 6d.

ROBBERY UNDER ARMS : A Story of Life and Adventure in the Bush and in the Gold-fields of Australia. By ROLF BOLDREWOOD.

SCHWARTZ. By D. CHRISTIE MURRAY.

NEIGHBOURS ON THE GREEN. By Mrs. OLIPHANT.

THE WEAKER VESSEL. By D. CHRISTIE MURRAY.

JOYCE. By Mrs. OLIPHANT.

CRESSY. By BRET HARTE.

FAITHFUL AND UNFAITHFUL. By MARGARET LEE.

REUBEN SACHS. By AMY LEVY.

WESSEX TALES: STRANGE, LIVELY, AND COMMONPLACE. By THOMAS HARDY.

MISS BRETHERTON. By Mrs. HUMPHRY WARD.

A LONDON LIFE. By HENRY JAMES.

A BELEAGUERED CITY. By Mrs. OLIPHANT.

CASTLE DALY. By ANNIE KEARY.

THE WOODLANDERS. By THOMAS HARDY.

AUNT RACHEL. By D. CHRISTIE MURRAY.

LOUISIANA, AND THAT LASS O' LOWRIE'S. By FRANCES HODGSON BURNETT.

THE CŒRULEANS. By Sir H. CUNNINGHAM.

Uniform with the above.

STORM WARRIORS ; OR, LIFEBOAT WORK ON THE GOODWIN SANDS. By the Rev. JOHN GILMORE.

TALES OF OLD JAPAN. By A. B. MITFORD.

A YEAR WITH THE BIRDS. By W. WARDE FOWLER. Illustrated by BRYAN HOOK.

TALES OF THE BIRDS. By the same. Illustrated by BRYAN HOOK.

MACMILLAN'S TWO SHILLING NOVELS. Globe 8vo. 2s. each.

By Mrs. Craik, Author of "John Halifax, Gentleman."

TWO MARRIAGES.

AGATHA'S HUSBAND.

THE OGILVIES.

By Mrs. Oliphant.

THE CURATE IN CHARGE.

A SON OF THE SOIL.

YOUNG MUSGRAVE.

HE THAT WILL NOT WHEN HE MAY.

A COUNTRY GENTLEMAN.

HESTER. | SIR TOM.

THE SECOND SON.

THE WIZARD'S SON.

By the Author of "Hogan, M.P."

HOGAN, M.P.

THE HONOURABLE MISS FERRARD.

FLITTERS, TATTERS, AND THE COUNSELLOR, WEEDS, AND OTHER SKETCHES.

CHRISTY CAREW.

ISMAY'S CHILDREN.

MACMILLAN'S TWO-SHILLING NOVELS—*continued.*

By George Fleming.

A NILE NOVEL.

MIRAGE.

THE HEAD OF MEDUSA.

VESTIGIA.

By Mrs. Macquoid.

PATTY.

By Annie Keary.

JANET'S HOME.

OLDBURY.

CLEMENCY FRANKLYN.

A YORK AND A LANCASTER ROSE.

By W. E. Norris.

MY FRIEND JIM. | CHRIS.

By Henry James.

DAISY MILLER ; AN INTERNATIONAL EPISODE ; FOUR MEETINGS.

RODERICK HUDSON.

THE MADONNA OF THE FUTURE, AND OTHER TALES.

WASHINGTON SQUARE.

PRINCESS CASAMASSIMA.

By Frances Hodgson Burnett.

LOUISIANA, AND THAT LASS O' LOWRIE'S. Two Stories.

HAWORTH'S.

By Hugh Conway.

A FAMILY AFFAIR.

LIVING OR DEAD.

By D. Christie Murray.

AUNT RACHEL.

By Helen Jackson.

RAMONA : A STORY.

A SLIP IN THE FENS.

MACMILLAN'S HALF-CROWN SERIES OF JUVENILE BOOKS. Globe 8vo, cloth, extra. 2s. 6d.

OUR YEAR. By the Author of "John Halifax, Gentleman."

LITTLE SUNSHINE'S HOLIDAY. By the Author of "John Halifax, Gentleman."

WHEN I WAS A LITTLE GIRL. By the Author of "St. Olave's."

NINE YEARS OLD. By the Author of "When I was a Little Girl," etc.

A STOREHOUSE OF STORIES. Edited by CHARLOTTE M. YONGE. 2 vols.

AGNES HOPETOUN'S SCHOOLS AND HOLIDAYS. By Mrs. OLIPHANT.

THE STORY OF A FELLOW SOLDIER. By FRANCES AWDRY. (A Life of Bishop Patteson for the Young.)

RUTH AND HER FRIENDS : A STORY FOR GIRLS.

THE HEROES OF ASGARD : TALES FROM SCANDINAVIAN MYTHOLOGY. By A. and E. KEARY.

MACMILLAN'S HALF-CROWN SERIES OF JUVENILE BOOKS—*continued.*

THE RUNAWAY. By the Author of "Mrs. Jerningham's Journal."

WANDERING WILLIE. By the Author of "Conrad the Squirrel."

PANSIE'S FLOUR BIN. Illustrated by ADRIAN STOKES.

MILLY AND OLLY. By Mrs. T. H. WARD. Illustrated by Mrs. ALMA TADEMA.

HANNAH TARNE. By MARY E. HULLAH. Illustrated by W. J. HENNESSY.

"CARROTS," JUST A LITTLE BOY. By Mrs. MOLESWORTH. Illust. by WALTER CRANE.

TELL ME A STORY. By Mrs. MOLESWORTH. Illustrated by WALTER CRANE.

THE CUCKOO CLOCK. By Mrs. MOLESWORTH. Illustrated by WALTER CRANE.

A CHRISTMAS CHILD. By Mrs. MOLESWORTH. Illustrated by WALTER CRANE.

ROSY. By Mrs. MOLESWORTH. Illustrated by WALTER CRANE.

THE TAPESTRY ROOM. by Mrs. MOLESWORTH. Illustrated by WALTER CRANE.

GRANDMOTHER DEAR. By Mrs. MOLESWORTH. Illustrated by WALTER CRANE.

HERR BABY. By Mrs. MOLESWORTH. Illustrated by WALTER CRANE.

"US": AN OLD-FASHIONED STORY. By Mrs. MOLESWORTH. Illust. by W. CRANE.

THE POPULATION OF AN OLD PEAR TREE; OR, STORIES OF INSECT LIFE. From the French of E. VAN BRUYSSEL. Edited by CHARLOTTE M. YONGE. Illustrated.

LITTLE MISS PEGGY. By Mrs. MOLESWORTH. Illustrated by WALTER CRANE.

TWO LITTLE WAIFS. By Mrs. MOLESWORTH. Illustrated by WALTER CRANE.

CHRISTMAS-TREE LAND. By Mrs. MOLESWORTH. Illustrated by WALTER CRANE.

MACMILLAN'S READING BOOKS.

Adapted to the English and Scotch Codes.

Primer	(48 pp.) 18mo, 2d.
Book I. for Standard I.	(96 pp.) 18mo, 4d.
Book II. for Standard II.	(144 pp.) 18mo, 5d.
Book III. for Standard III.	(160 pp.) 18mo, 6d.
Book IV. for Standard IV.	(176 pp.) 18mo, 8d.
Book V. for Standard V.	(380 pp.) 18mo, 1s.
Book VI. for Standard VI.	(430 pp.) Cr. 8vo, 2s.

MACMILLAN'S COPY-BOOKS

*1. Initiatory Exercises and Short Letters.

*2. Words consisting of Short Letters.

*3. Long Letters, with words containing Long Letters. Figures.

*4. Words containing Long Letters.

4A. Practising and Revising Copybook for Nos. 1 to 4.

*5. Capitals, and Short Half-text Words beginning with a Capital.

*6. Half-text Words beginning with a Capital. Figures.

*7. Small-hand and Half-text, with Capitals and Figures.

*8. Small-hand and Half-text, with Capitals and Figures.

MACMILLAN'S COPY-BOOKS—*contd.*

8A. Practising and Revising Copybook for Nos. 5 to 8.

*9. Small-hand Single Head Lines. Figures.

10. Small-hand Single Head Lines. Figures.

*11. Small-hand Double Head Lines. Figures.

12. Commercial and Arithmetical Examples, etc.

12A. Practising and Revising Copybook for Nos. 8 to 12.

The Copybooks may be had in two sizes:
(1) Large Post 4to, 4d. each;
(2) Post oblong, 2d. each.

The numbers marked * may also be had in Large Post 4to, with GOODMAN'S PATENT SLIDING COPIES. 6d. each.

MACMILLAN'S LATIN COURSE. Part I.

By A. M. COOK, M.A. 2nd Edition, enlarged. Globe 8vo. 3s. 6d.

Part II. Globe 8vo. 2s. 6d.

MACMILLAN'S SHORTER LATIN COURSE. By A. M. COOK, M.A. Being an Abridgment of "Macmillan's Latin Course, Part I." Globe 8vo. 1s. 6d.

MACMILLAN'S LATIN READER. A Latin Reader for the Lower Forms in Schools. By H. J. HARDY. Gl. 8vo. 2s. 6d.

MACMILLAN'S GREEK COURSE. Edit. by Rev. W. G. RUTHERFORD, M.A. Gl. 8vo.

I. FIRST GREEK GRAMMAR. By the Rev. W. G. RUTHERFORD, M.A. 2s.

II. EASY EXERCISES IN GREEK ACCIDENCE. By H. G. UNDERHILL, M.A. 2s.

III. SECOND GREEK EXERCISE BOOK. By Rev. W. A. HEARD, M.A.

MACMILLAN'S GREEK READER. Stories and Legends. A First Greek Reader. With Notes, Vocabulary, and Exercises, by F. H. COLSON, M.A. Globe 8vo. 3s.

MACMILLAN'S ELEMENTARY CLASSICS. 18mo. 1s. 6d. each.

This Series falls into two classes:—

(1) First Reading Books for Beginners, provided not only with *Introductions and Notes,* but with *Vocabularies,* and in some cases with *Exercises* based upon the Text.

(2) Stepping-stones to the study of particular authors, intended for more advanced students, who are beginning to read such authors as Terence, Plato, the Attic Dramatists, and the harder parts of Cicero, Horace, Virgil, and Thucydides.

These are provided with Introductions and Notes, but no *Vocabulary.* The Publishers have been led to provide the more strictly Elementary Books with Vocabularies by the representations of many teachers, who hold that beginners do not understand the use of a Dictionary, and of others who, in the case of middle-class schools where the cost of books is a serious consideration, advocate the Vocabulary system on grounds of economy. It is hoped that the two parts of the Series, fitting into one another, may together fulfil all the requirements of Elementary and Preparatory Schools, and the Lower Forms of Public Schools.

3

MACMILLAN'S ELEMENTARY CLASSICS—*continued.*

The following Elementary Books, *with Introductions, Notes, and Vocabularies,* and in some cases with *Exercises,* are either ready or in preparation:

LATIN ACCIDENCE AND EXERCISES ARRANGED FOR BEGINNERS. By WILLIAM WELCH, M.A., and C. G. DUFFIELD, M.A.

ÆSCHYLUS.—PROMETHEUS VINCTUS. Edit. by Rev. H. M. STEPHENSON, M.A.

ARRIAN.—SELECTIONS. Edited by JOHN BOND, M.A., and A. S. WALPOLE, M.A.

AULUS GELLIUS, STORIES FROM. By Rev. G. H. NALL, M.A.

CÆSAR.—THE GALLIC WAR. Book I. Edit. by A. S. WALPOLE, M.A.

— THE INVASION OF BRITAIN. Being Selections from Books IV. and V. of the "De Bello Gallico." Adapted for the use of Beginners by W. WELCH, M.A., and C. G. DUFFIELD, M.A.

— THE HELVETIAN WAR. Selected from Book I. of "The Gallic War," arranged for the use of Beginners by W. WELCH, M.A., and C. G. DUFFIELD, M.A.

— THE GALLIC WAR. Books II. and III. Ed. by Rev. W. G. RUTHERFORD, M.A.

— THE GALLIC WAR. Book IV. Edited by C. BRYANS, M.A.

— THE GALLIC WAR. Scenes from Books V. and VI. Edited by C. COLBECK, M.A.

— THE GALLIC WAR. Books V. and VI. (separately). By the same Editor.

— THE GALLIC WAR. Book VII. Ed. by J. BOND, M.A., and A. S. WALPOLE, M.A.

CICERO.—DE SENECTUTE. Edited by E. S. SHUCKBURGH, M.A.

— DE AMICITIA. Edited by E. S. SHUCKBURGH, M.A.

— STORIES OF ROMAN HISTORY. Edited by Rev. G. E. JEANS, M.A., and A. V. JONES, M.A.

EURIPIDES.—HECUBA. Edited by Rev. J. BOND, M.A., and A. S. WALPOLE, M.A.

EUTROPIUS. Adapted for the use of Beginners by W. WELCH, M.A., and C. G. DUFFIELD, M.A.

HOMER.—ILIAD. Book I. Ed. by Rev. J. BOND, M.A., and A. S. WALPOLE, M.A.

— ILIAD. Book XVIII. THE ARMS OF ACHILLES. Edited by S. R. JAMES, M.A.

— ODYSSEY. Book I. Edited by Rev. J. BOND, M.A., and A. S. WALPOLE, M.A.

HORACE.—ODES. Books I.—IV. Edited by T. E. PAGE, M.A. *1s. 6d.* each.

LIVY. Book I. Edited by H. M. STEPHENSON, M.A.

— THE HANNIBALIAN WAR. Being part of the 21st and 22nd Books of Livy. Adapted for the use of Beginners by G. C. MACAULAY, M.A.

— THE SIEGE OF SYRACUSE. Being part of the 24th and 25th Books of Livy. Adapted for the use of Beginners by G. RICHARDS, M.A., and A. S. WALPOLE, M.A.

MACMILLAN'S ELEMENTARY CLASSICS—*continued.*

LIVY, Book XXI. With Notes adapted from Mr. Capes' Edition for the Use of Junior Students, by W. W. CAPES, M.A., and J. E. MELHUISH, M.A.

— LEGENDS OF ANCIENT ROME, FROM LIVY. Adapted for the Use of Beginners. With Notes, Exercises, and Vocabulary, by H. WILKINSON, M.A.

LUCIAN, EXTRACTS FROM. Edited by J. BOND, M.A., and A. S. WALPOLE, M.A.

NEPOS.—SELECTIONS ILLUSTRATIVE OF GREEK AND ROMAN HISTORY. Edited by G. S. FARNELL, B.A.

OVID.—SELECTIONS. Edited by E. S. SHUCKBURGH, M.A.

— EASY SELECTIONS FROM OVID IN ELEGIAC VERSE. Arranged for the use of Beginners by H. WILKINSON, M.A.

— STORIES FROM THE METAMORPHOSES. Arranged for the use of Beginners by J. BOND, M.A., and A. S. WALPOLE, M.A.

PHÆDRUS.—SELECT FABLES. Adapted for use of Beginners by A. S. WALPOLE, M.A.

THUCYDIDES.—THE RISE OF THE ATHENIAN EMPIRE. Book I. Chaps. lxxxix.—cxvii. and cxxviii.—cxxxviii. Edited by F. H. COLSON, M.A.

VIRGIL.—GEORGICS. Book I. Edited by T. E. PAGE, M.A.

— ÆNEID. Book I. Edited by A. S. WALPOLE, M.A.

— ÆNEID. Book II. Ed. by T. E. PAGE.

— ÆNEID. Book III. Edited by T. E. PAGE, M.A.

— ÆNEID. Book IV. Edit. by Rev. H. M. STEPHENSON, M.A.

— ÆNEID. Book V. Edited by Rev. A. CALVERT, M.A.

— ÆNEID. Book VI. Ed. by T. E. PAGE.

— ÆNEID. Book VII. THE WRATH OF TURNUS. Edited by A. CALVERT, M.A.

— ÆNEID. Book IX. Edited by Rev. H. M. STEPHENSON, M.A.

— SELECTIONS. Edited by E. S. SHUCKBURGH, M.A.

XENOPHON.—ANABASIS. Book I. Edited by A. S. WALPOLE, M.A.

— ANABASIS. Book I., Chaps. i.—viii. Edit. by E. A. WELLS, M.A.

— ANABASIS. Book II. Edited by A. S. WALPOLE, M.A.

— SELECTIONS FROM BOOK IV. OF "THE ANABASIS." Edit. by Rev. E. D. STONE.

— SELECTIONS FROM THE CYROPAEDIA. Edited by Rev. A. H. COOKE, M.A.

The following more advanced books have *Introductions, Notes,* but no *Vocabularies*:

CICERO.—SELECT LETTERS. Edit. by Rev. G. E. JEANS, M.A.

HERODOTUS.—SELECTIONS FROM BOOKS VII. AND VIII. THE EXPEDITION OF XERXES. Edited by A. H. COOKE, M.A.

MACMILLAN'S ELEMENTARY CLAS-
SICS—*continued.*

HORACE.—SELECTIONS FROM THE SATIRES
AND EPISTLES. Edited by Rev. W. J. V.
BAKER, M.A.

— SELECT EPODES AND ARS POETICA.
Edited by H. A. DALTON, M.A.

PLATO.—EUTHYPHRO AND MENEXENUS.
Edited by C. E. GRAVES, M.A.

TERENCE.—SCENES FROM THE ANDRIA.
Edited by F. W. CORNISH, M.A.

THE GREEK ELEGIAC POETS, FROM CAL-
LINUS TO CALLIMACHUS. Selected and
Edited by Rev. H. KYNASTON.

THUCYDIDES. Book IV., Chaps. i.—lxi.
THE CAPTURE OF SPHACTERIA. Edited
by C. E. GRAVES, M.A.

VIRGIL.—GEORGICS. Book II. Edited by
Rev. J. H. SKRINE, M.A.

Other Volumes to follow.

MACMILLAN'S CLASSICAL SERIES
FOR COLLEGES AND SCHOOLS.
Fcp. 8vo. Being select portions of Greek
and Latin authors, edited, with Introductions
and Notes, for the use of Middle and Upper
Forms of Schools, or of Candidates for Public
Examinations at the Universities and else-
where.

ÆSCHINES.—IN CTESIPHONTEM. Edited by
Rev. T. GWATKIN, M.A., and E. S.
SHUCKBURGH, M.A. [*In the Press.*

ÆSCHYLUS. — PERSÆ. Edited by A. O.
PRICKARD, M.A. With Map. 3s. 6d.

— THE "SEVEN AGAINST THEBES." Edit.
by A. W. VERRALL, Litt.D., and M. A.
BAYFIELD, M.A. 3s. 6d.

ANDOCIDES.—DE MYSTERIIS. Edited by
W. J. HICKIE, M.A. 2s. 6d.

ATTIC ORATORS, SELECTIONS FROM THE.
Antiphon, Andocides, Lysias, Isocrates,
and Isæus. Ed. by R. C. JEBB, Litt.D. 6s.

CÆSAR.—THE GALLIC WAR. Edited after
Kraner by Rev. J. BOND, M.A., and A. S.
WALPOLE, M.A. With Maps. 6s.

CATULLUS.—SELECT POEMS. Edited by F.
P. SIMPSON, B.A. 5s. [The Text of this
Edition is carefully adapted to School use.]

CICERO.—THE CATILINE ORATIONS. From
the German of Karl Halm. Edited by
A. S. WILKINS, Litt.D. 3s. 6d.

— PRO LEGE MANILIA. Edited, after Halm,
by Prof. A. S. WILKINS, Litt.D. 2s. 6d.

— THE SECOND PHILIPPIC ORATION. From
the German of Karl Halm. Edited, with
Corrections and Additions, by Prof. J. E. B.
MAYOR. 5s.

— PRO ROSCIO AMERINO. Edited, after
Halm, by E. H. DONKIN, M.A. 4s. 6d.

— PRO P. SESTIO. Edited by Rev. H. A.
HOLDEN, M.A. 5s.

DEMOSTHENES.—DE CORONA. Edited by B.
DRAKE, M.A. New and revised edit. 4s. 6d.

— ADVERSUS LEPTINEM. Edited by Rev.
J. R. KING, M.A. 4s. 6d.

— THE FIRST PHILIPPIC. Edited, after C.
Rehdantz, by Rev. T. GWATKIN. 2s. 6d.

MACMILLAN'S CLASSICAL SERIES—
continued.

EURIPIDES.—HIPPOLYTUS. Edited by Prof.
J. P. MAHAFFY and J. B. BURY. 3s. 6d.

— MEDEA. Edited by A. W. VERRALL,
Litt.D. 3s. 6d.

— IPHIGENIA IN TAURIS. Edited by E. B.
ENGLAND, M.A. 4s. 6d.

— ION. Ed. by M. A. BAYFIELD, M.A. 3s. 6d.

HERODOTUS. Books VII. and VIII. Edit.
by Mrs. MONTAGU BUTLER.

HOMER.—ILIAD. Books I. IX. XI. XVI.-
XXIV. THE STORY OF ACHILLES. Ed. by
J. H. PRATT, M.A., and W. LEAF, Litt.D. 6s.

— ODYSSEY. Book IX. Edited by Prof.
J. E. B. MAYOR, M.A. 2s. 6d.

— ODYSSEY. Books XXI.—XXIV. THE
TRIUMPH OF ODYSSEUS. Edited by S. G.
HAMILTON, B.A. 3s. 6d.

HORACE.—THE ODES. Edited by T. E.
PAGE, M.A. 6s. (Books I. II. III. and
IV. separately, 2s. each.)

— THE SATIRES. Edited by Prof. A.
PALMER, M.A. 6s.

— THE EPISTLES AND ARS POETICA. Edit.
by Prof. A. S. WILKINS, Litt.D. 6s.

JUVENAL.—THIRTEEN SATIRES. Edited, for
the use of Schools, by E. G. HARDY, M.A.
5s. [The Text of this Edition is carefully
adapted to School use.]

— SELECT SATIRES. Edited by Prof. JOHN
E. B. MAYOR. X. and XI. 3s. 6d. ; XII.—
XVI. 4s. 6d.

LIVY. Books II. and III. Edited by Rev.
H. M. STEPHENSON, M.A. 5s.

— Books XXI. and XXII. Edited by Rev.
W. W. CAPES, M.A. 5s.

— Books XXIII. and XXIV. Ed. by G. C.
MACAULAY. With Maps. 5s.

— THE LAST TWO KINGS OF MACEDON.
Extracts from the Fourth and Fifth De-
cades of Livy. Selected and Edit. by F. H.
RAWLINS, M.A. With Maps. 3s. 6d.

LUCRETIUS. Books I.—III. Edited by
J. H. WARBURTON LEE, M.A. 4s. 6d.

LYSIAS.—SELECT ORATIONS. Edited by
E. S. SHUCKBURGH, M.A. 6s.

MARTIAL.—SELECT EPIGRAMS. Edited by
Rev. H. M. STEPHENSON, M.A. 6s. 6d.

OVID.—FASTI. Edited by G. H. HALLAM,
M.A. With Maps. 5s.

— HEROIDUM EPISTULÆ XIII. Edited by
E. S. SHUCKBURGH, M.A. 4s. 6d.

— METAMORPHOSES. Books XIII. and XIV.
Edited by C. SIMMONS, M.A. 4s. 6d.

PLATO.—THE REPUBLIC. Books I.—V.
Edited by T. H. WARREN, M.A. 6s.

— LACHES. Edited by M. T. TATHAM,
M.A. 2s. 6d.

PLAUTUS.—MILES GLORIOSUS. Edited by
Prof. R. Y. TYRRELL, M.A. 5s.

— AMPHITRUO. Ed. by A. PALMER, M.A. 5s.

PLINY.—LETTERS. Books I. and II. Edited
by J. COWAN, M.A. 5s.

MACMILLAN'S CLASSICAL SERIES—
continued.

PLINY.—LETTERS. Book III. Edited by Prof.
J. E. B. MAYOR. With Life of Pliny by
G. H. RENDALL. 5*s.*

PLUTARCH.—LIFE OF THEMISTOKLES. Ed.
by Rev. H. A. HOLDEN, M.A., LL.D. 5*s.*

— LIVES OF GALBA AND OTHO. Edited by
E. G. HARDY, M.A.

POLYBIUS. The History of the Achæan
League as contained in the remains of
Polybius. Edited by W. W. CAPES. 6*s.* 6*d.*

PROPERTIUS.—SELECT POEMS. Edited by
Prof. J. P. POSTGATE, M.A. 6*s.*

SALLUST.—CATILINE AND JUGURTHA. Ed.
by C. MERIVALE, D.D. 4*s.* 6*d.*—Or separately, 2*s.* 6*d.* each.

— BELLUM CATULINAE. Edited by A. M.
COOK, M.A. 4*s.* 6*d.*

TACITUS.—AGRICOLA AND GERMANIA. Ed.
by A. J. CHURCH, M.A., and W. J.
BRODRIBB, M.A. 3*s.* 6*d.*—Or separately,
2*s.* each.

— THE ANNALS. Book VI. By the same
Editors. 2*s.* 6*d.*

— THE HISTORIES. Books I. and II.
Edited by A. D. GODLEY, M.A. 5*s.*

— THE HISTORIES. Books III.—V. By
the same Editor. 5*s.*

TERENCE.—HAUTON TIMORUMENOS. Edit.
by E. S. SHUCKBURGH, M.A. 3*s.*—With
Translation, 4*s.* 6*d.*

— PHORMIO. Ed. by Rev. J. BOND, M.A.,
and A. S. WALPOLE, M.A. 4*s.* 6*d.*

THUCYDIDES. Book IV. Edited by C. E.
GRAVES, M.A. 5*s.*

— Book V. By the same Editor.

— Books VI. and VII. THE SICILIAN EX-
PEDITION. Edited by Rev. P. FROST,
M.A. With Map. 5*s.*

VIRGIL.—ÆNEID. Books I. and II. THE
NARRATIVE OF ÆNEAS. Edited by E. W.
HOWSON, M.A. 3*s.*

XENOPHON.—HELLENICA. Books I. and II.
Edited by H. HAILSTONE, M.A. 4*s.* 6*d.*

— CYROPÆDIA. Books VII. and VIII. Ed.
by Prof. A. GOODWIN, M.A. 5*s.*

— MEMORABILIA SOCRATIS. Edited by
A. R. CLUER, B.A. 6*s.*

— THE ANABASIS. Books I.—IV. Edited
by Professors W. W. GOODWIN and J. W.
WHITE. Adapted to Goodwin's Greek
Grammar. With a Map. 5*s.*

— HIERO. Edited by Rev. H. A. HOLDEN,
M.A., LL.D. 3*s.* 6*d.*

— OECONOMICUS. By the same Editor.
With Introduction, Explanatory Notes,
Critical Appendix, and Lexicon. 6*s.*

The following are in preparation:

DEMOSTHENES.—IN MIDIAM. Edited by
Prof. A. S. WILKINS, Litt.D., and HER-
MAN HAGER, Ph.D.

HERODOTUS. Books V. and VI. Edited
by Prof. J. STRACHAN, M.A.

ISÆOS.—THE ORATIONS. Edited by Prof.
WM. RIDGEWAY, M.A.

MACMILLAN'S CLASSICAL SERIES—
continued.

OVID.—METAMORPHOSES. Books I.—III.
Edited by C. SIMMONS, M.A.

SALLUST.—JUGURTHA. Edited by A. M.
COOK, M.A.

TACITUS.—THE ANNALS. Books I. and II.
Edited by J. S. REID, Litt.D.

Other Volumes will follow.

MACMILLAN'S GEOGRAPHICAL
SERIES. Edited by ARCHIBALD GEIKIE,
F.R.S., Director-General of the Geological
Survey of the United Kingdom.

THE TEACHING OF GEOGRAPHY. A Practical
Handbook for the use of Teachers. Cr.
8vo. 2*s.*

GEOGRAPHY OF THE BRITISH ISLES. By
ARCHIBALD GEIKIE, F.R.S. 18mo. 1*s.*

THE ELEMENTARY SCHOOL ATLAS. 24 Maps
in Colours. By JOHN BARTHOLOMEW,
F.R.G.S. 4to. 1*s.*

AN ELEMENTARY CLASS-BOOK OF GENERAL
GEOGRAPHY. By HUGH ROBERT MILL,
D.Sc. Edin. Illustrated. Cr. 8vo. 3*s.* 6*d.*

MAP DRAWING AND MAP MAKING. By
W. A. ELDERTON.

GEOGRAPHY OF THE BRITISH COLONIES. By
G. M. DAWSON and ALEX. SUTHERLAND.

GEOGRAPHY OF EUROPE. By JAMES SIME,
M.A. With Illustrations. Globe 8vo.

GEOGRAPHY OF NORTH AMERICA. By Prof.
N. S. SHALER.

GEOGRAPHY OF INDIA. By H. F. BLAN-
FORD, F.G.S.

MACMILLAN'S SCIENTIFIC CLASS-
BOOKS. Fcp. 8vo.

ELEMENTARY LESSONS IN THE SCIENCE OF
AGRICULTURAL PRACTICE. By Prof. H.
TANNER. 3*s.* 6*d.*

POPULAR ASTRONOMY. By Sir G. B. AIRY,
K.C.B., late Astronomer-Royal. 4*s.* 6*d.*

ELEMENTARY LESSONS IN PHYSIOLOGY. By
T. H. HUXLEY, F.R.S. 4*s.* 6*d.* (Questions on, 1*s.* 6*d.*)

LESSONS IN LOGIC, INDUCTIVE AND DEDUC-
TIVE. By W. S. JEVONS, LL.D. 3*s.* 6*d.*

LESSONS IN ELEMENTARY CHEMISTRY. By
Sir H. ROSCOE, F.R.S. 4*s.* 6*d.*—Problems
adapted to the same, by Prof. THORPE.
With Key. 2*s.*

OWENS COLLEGE JUNIOR COURSE OF PRAC-
TICAL CHEMISTRY. By F. JONES. With
Preface by Sir H. ROSCOE, F.R.S. 2*s.* 6*d.*

EXPERIMENTAL PROOFS OF CHEMICAL
THEORY FOR BEGINNERS. By WILLIAM
RAMSAY, Ph.D. 2*s.* 6*d.*

NUMERICAL TABLES AND CONSTANTS IN
ELEMENTARY SCIENCE. By SYDNEY
LUPTON, M.A. 2*s.* 6*d.*

LESSONS IN ELEMENTARY ANATOMY. By
ST. G. MIVART, F.R.S. 6*s.* 6*d.*

POLITICAL ECONOMY FOR BEGINNERS. By
Mrs. FAWCETT. With Questions. 2*s.* 6*d.*

DISEASES OF FIELD AND GARDEN CROPS.
By W. G. SMITH. 4*s.* 6*d.*

MACMILLAN'S SCIENTIFIC CLASS-BOOKS—*continued.*

LESSONS IN ELEMENTARY BOTANY. By Prof. OLIVER, F.R.S. 4s. 6d.

LESSONS IN ELEMENTARY PHYSICS. By Prof. BALFOUR STEWART, F.R.S. New Edition. 4s. 6d. (Questions on, 2s.)

ELEMENTARY LESSONS ON ASTRONOMY. By J. N. LOCKYER, F.R.S. New Edition. 5s. 6d. (Questions on, 1s. 6d.)

AN ELEMENTARY TREATISE ON STEAM. By Prof. J. PERRY, C.E. 4s. 6d.

QUESTIONS AND EXAMPLES ON EXPERI-MENTAL PHYSICS: Sound, Light, Heat, Electricity, and Magnetism. By B. LOEWY, F.R.A.S. Fcp. 8vo. 2s.

A GRADUATED COURSE OF NATURAL SCI-ENCE FOR ELEMENTARY AND TECHNICAL SCHOOLS AND COLLEGES. Part I. First Year's Course. By the same. Gl. 8vo. 2s.

PHYSICAL GEOGRAPHY, ELEMENTARY LES-SONS IN. By ARCHIBALD GEIKIE, F.R.S. 4s. 6d. (Questions, 1s. 6d.)

SOUND, ELEMENTARY LESSONS ON. By Dr. W. H. STONE. 3s. 6d.

CLASS-BOOK OF GEOGRAPHY. By C. B. CLARKE, F.R.S. 3s. 6d. ; sewed, 3s.

QUESTIONS ON CHEMISTRY. A Series of Problems and Exercises in Inorganic and Organic Chemistry. By F. JONES. 3s.

ELECTRICITY AND MAGNETISM. By Prof. SILVANUS THOMPSON. 4s. 6d.

ELECTRIC LIGHT ARITHMETIC. By R. E. DAY, M.A. 2s

THE ECONOMICS OF INDUSTRY. By Prof. A. MARSHALL and M. P. MARSHALL. 2s. 6d.

SHORT GEOGRAPHY OF THE BRITISH IS-LANDS. By J. R. GREEN and ALICE S. GREEN. With Maps. 3s. 6d.

A COLLECTION OF EXAMPLES OF HEAT AND ELECTRICITY. By H. H. TURNER. 2s. 6d.

OWENS COLLEGE COURSE OF PRACTICAL ORGANIC CHEMISTRY. By JULIUS B. COHEN, Ph.D. With Preface by Sir H. ROSCOE and Prof. SCHORLEMMER. 2s. 6d.

ELEMENTS OF CHEMISTRY. By Prof. IRA REMSEN. 2s. 6d.

EXAMPLES IN PHYSICS. By Prof. D. E. JONES, B.Sc. 3s. 6d.

MACMILLAN'S PROGRESSIVE FRENCH COURSE. By G. EUGÈNE FASNACHT. Extra fcp. 8vo.

I. FIRST YEAR, CONTAINING EASY LESSONS IN THE REGULAR ACCIDENCE. Thoroughly revised Edition. 1s.

II. SECOND YEAR, CONTAINING AN ELE-MENTARY GRAMMAR. With copious Exer-cises, Notes, and Vocabularies. New Edition, enlarged. 2s.

III. THIRD YEAR, CONTAINING A SYSTEM-ATIC SYNTAX AND LESSONS IN COMPO-SITION. 2s. 6d.

THE TEACHER'S COMPANION TO THE SAME. With copious Notes, Hints for different renderings, Synonyms, Philological Re-marks, etc. 1st Year, 4s. 6d. 2nd Year, 4s. 6d. 3rd Year, 4s. 6d.

MACMILLAN'S PROGRESSIVE FRENCH READERS. By G. EUGÈNE FASNACHT. Extra fcp. 8vo.

I. FIRST YEAR, CONTAINING TALES, HIS-TORICAL EXTRACTS, LETTERS, DIA-LOGUES, FABLES, BALLADS, NURSERY SONGS, etc. With Two Vocabularies: (1) In the Order of Subjects ; (2) In Alpha-betical Order. 2s. 6d.

II. SECOND YEAR, CONTAINING FICTION IN PROSE AND VERSE, HISTORICAL AND DESCRIPTIVE EXTRACTS, ESSAYS, LET-TERS, etc. 2s. 6d.

MACMILLAN'S FRENCH COMPOSI-TION. By G. EUGÈNE FASNACHT. Extra fcp. 8vo.

Part I. ELEMENTARY. 2s. 6d. — Part II. ADVANCED.

THE TEACHER'S COMPANION TO THE SAME. Part I. 4s. 6d.

MACMILLAN'S PROGRESSIVE GERMAN COURSE. By G. EUGÈNE FASNACHT. Extra fcp. 8vo.

I. FIRST YEAR, CONTAINING EASY LESSONS ON THE REGULAR ACCIDENCE. 1s. 6d.

II. SECOND YEAR, CONTAINING CONVERSA-TIONAL LESSONS ON SYSTEMATIC ACCI-DENCE AND ELEMENTARY SYNTAX, WITH PHILOLOGICAL ILLUSTRATIONS AND ETY-MOLOGICAL VOCABULARY. New Edition, enlarged. 3s. 6d.

THE TEACHER'S COMPANION TO THE SAME. 1st Year, 4s. 6d. 2nd Year, 4s. 6d.

MACMILLAN'S PROGRESSIVE GERMAN READERS. By G. EUGÈNE FASNACHT. Extra fcap. 8vo.

I. FIRST YEAR, CONTAINING AN INTRODUC-TION TO THE GERMAN ORDER OF WORDS, WITH COPIOUS EXAMPLES, EXTRACTS FROM GERMAN AUTHORS IN PROSE AND POETRY, NOTES, VOCABULARIES. 2s. 6d.

MACMILLAN'S SERIES OF FOREIGN SCHOOL CLASSICS. Edited by G. E. FASNACHT. 18mo.

Select works of the best foreign Authors, with suitable Notes and Introductions based on the latest researches of French and German Scholars by practical masters and teachers.

FRENCH.

CORNEILLE.—LE CID. Edited by G. E. FASNACHT. 1s.

DUMAS.—LES DEMOISELLES DE ST. CYR. Edited by VICTOR OGER. 1s. 6d.

LA FONTAINE'S FABLES. Books I.—VI. Edit. by L. M. MORIARTY. [*In the Press.*

MOLIÈRE.—LES FEMMES SAVANTES. By G. E. FASNACHT. 1s.

— LE MISANTHROPE. By the same. 1s.

— LE MÉDECIN MALGRÉ LUI. By the same. 1s.

— L'AVARE. Ed. by L. M. MORIARTY. 1s.

— LE BOURGEOIS GENTILHOMME. By the same. 1s. 6d.

RACINE.—BRITANNICUS. Edited by EUGÈNE PELLISSIER. 2s.

MACMILLAN'S FOREIGN SCHOOL CLASSICS—continued.

FRENCH.

FRENCH READINGS FROM ROMAN HISTORY. Selected from various Authors. Edited by C. COLBECK, M.A. 4s. 6d.

SAND (George).—LA MARE AU DIABLE. Edited by W. E. RUSSELL, M.A. 1s.

SANDEAU (Jules).—MADEMOISELLE DE LA SEIGLIÈRE. Edit. by H. C. STEEL. 1s. 6d.

THIERS'S HISTORY OF THE EGYPTIAN EXPEDITION. Edit. by Rev. H. A. BULL, M.A.

VOLTAIRE.—CHARLES XII. Edited by G. E. FASNACHT. 3s. 6d.

GERMAN.

FREYTAG.—DOKTOR LUTHER. Edited by FRANCIS STORR, M.A. [In the Press.

GOETHE.—GÖTZ VON BERLICHINGEN. Edit. by H. A. BULL, M.A. 2s.

— FAUST. Part I. Ed. by Miss J. LEE. 4s.6d.

HEINE.—SELECTIONS FROM THE REISE-BILDER AND OTHER PROSE WORKS. Edit. by C. COLBECK, M.A. 2s. 6d.

LESSING.—MINNA VON BARNHELM. Edited by J. SIME, M.A.

SCHILLER.—DIE JUNGFRAU VON ORLEANS. Edited by JOSEPH GOSTWICK. 2s. 6d.

— MARIA STUART. Edited by C. SHELDON, M.A., D.Lit. 2s. 6d.

— WALLENSTEIN. Part I. DAS LAGER. Edited by H. B. COTTERILL, M.A. 2s.

— WILHELM TELL. Edited by G. E. FAS-NACHT. 2s. 6d.

— SELECTIONS FROM SCHILLER'S LYRICAL POEMS. Edited by E. J. TURNER, M.A., and E. D. A. MORSHEAD, M.A. 2s. 6d.

UHLAND.—SELECT BALLADS. Adapted as a First Easy Reading Book for Beginners. Edited by G. E. FASNACHT. 1s.

MACMILLAN'S PRIMARY SERIES OF FRENCH AND GERMAN READING BOOKS. Edited by G. EUGÈNE FASNACHT. With Illustrations. Globe 8vo.

CORNAZ.—NOS ENFANTS ET LEURS AMIS. Edited by EDITH HARVEY. 1s. 6d.

DE MAISTRE.—LA JEUNE SIBÉRIENNE ET LE LÉPREUX DE LA CITÉ D'AOSTE. Edit. by S. BARLET, B.Sc. 1s. 6d.

FLORIAN.—SELECT FABLES. Edited by CHARLES YELD, M.A. 1s. 6d.

GRIMM.—KINDER- UND HAUSMÄRCHEN. Selected and Edited by G. E. FASNACHT. Illustrated. 2s. 6d.

HAUFF.—DIE KARAVANE. Edited by HERMAN HAGER, Ph.D. With Exercises by G. E. FASNACHT. 3s.

LA FONTAINE.—FABLES. A Selection, by L. M. MORIARTY, M.A. With Illustrations by RANDOLPH CALDECOTT. 2s. 6d.

MOLESWORTH.—FRENCH LIFE IN LETTERS. By Mrs. MOLESWORTH. 1s. 6d.

PERRAULT.—CONTES DE FÉES. Edited by G. E. FASNACHT. 1s. 6d.

SCHMID.—HEINRICH VON EICHENFELS. Ed. by G. E. FASNACHT. 2s. 6d.

SCHWAB (G.).—ODYSSEUS. By same Editor.

MACNAMARA (C.).—A HISTORY OF ASIATIC CHOLERA. Crown 8vo. 10s. 6d.

MACQUOID (K. S.).—PATTY. Globe 8vo. 2s.

MADAGASCAR : AN HISTORICAL AND DESCRIPTIVE ACCOUNT OF THE ISLAND AND ITS FORMER DEPENDENCIES. By Captain S. OLIVER, F.S.A. 2 vols. Med. 8vo. 2l.12s.6d.

MADAME TABBY'S ESTABLISHMENT. By KARI. Illustrated by L. WAIN. Crown 8vo. 4s. 6d.

MADOC (Fayr).—THE STORY OF MELICENT. Crown 8vo. 4s. 6d.

— MARGARET JERMINE. 3 vols. Crown 8vo. 31s. 6d.

MAGUIRE (J. F.).—YOUNG PRINCE MARIGOLD. Illustrated. Globe 8vo. 4s. 6d.

MAHAFFY (Rev. Prof. J. P.).—SOCIAL LIFE IN GREECE, FROM HOMER TO MENANDER. 6th Edition. Crown 8vo. 9s.

— GREEK LIFE AND THOUGHT FROM THE AGE OF ALEXANDER TO THE ROMAN CONQUEST. Crown 8vo. 12s. 6d.

— RAMBLES AND STUDIES IN GREECE. Illustrated. 3rd Edition. Crown 8vo. 10s. 6d.

— A HISTORY OF CLASSICAL GREEK LITERATURE. 2 vols. Cr. 8vo. 9s. each.—Vol. I. The Poets. With an Appendix on Homer by Prof. SAYCE.—Vol. II. The Prose Writers.

— GREEK ANTIQUITIES. Illust. 18mo. 1s.

— EURIPIDES. 18mo. 1s. 6d.

— THE DECAY OF MODERN PREACHING: AN ESSAY. Crown 8vo. 3s. 6d.

— THE PRINCIPLES OF THE ART OF CONVERSATION. 2nd Ed. Crown 8vo. 4s. 6d.

MAHAFFY (Rev. Prof. J. P.) and ROGERS (J. E.).—SKETCHES FROM A TOUR THROUGH HOLLAND AND GERMANY. Illustrated by J. E. ROGERS. Extra crown 8vo. 10s. 6d.

MAHAFFY (Prof. J. P.) and BERNARD (J. H.).—KANT'S CRITICAL PHILOSOPHY FOR ENGLISH READERS. A new and completed Edition in 2 vols. Crown 8vo.—Vol. I. The KRITIK OF PURE REASON EXPLAINED AND DEFENDED. 7s. 6d.—Vol. II. The "PROLEGOMENA." Translated, with Notes and Appendices. 6s.

MAITLAND (F. W.).—PLEAS OF THE CROWN FOR THE COUNTY OF GLOUCESTER, A.D. 1221. Edited by F. W. MAITLAND. 8vo. 7s. 6d.

— JUSTICE AND POLICE. Cr. 8vo. 3s. 6d.

MALET (Lucas).—MRS. LORIMER : A SKETCH IN BLACK AND WHITE. Cr. 8vo. 4s. 6d.

MANCHESTER SCIENCE LECTURES FOR THE PEOPLE. Eighth Series, 1876—77. With Illustrations. Cr. 8vo. 2s.

MANSFIELD (C. B.).—A THEORY OF SALTS. Crown 8vo. 14s.

— AERIAL NAVIGATION. Cr. 8vo. 10s. 6d.

MARKHAM (C. R.).—LIFE OF ROBERT FAIRFAX, OF STEETON. 8vo. 12s. 6d.

MARLBOROUGH. By Col. Sir W. BUTLER. With Portrait. Crown 8vo. 2s. 6d.

MARRIOTT (J. A. R.).—THE MAKERS OF MODERN ITALY : MAZZINI, CAVOUR, GARIBALDI. Three Oxford Lectures. Cr. 8vo. 1s.6d.

MARSHALL (J. M.).—A TABLE OF IRREGU-LAR GREEK VERBS. 8vo. 1*s.*

MARSHALL (Prof. A. and Mary P.).—THE ECONOMICS OF INDUSTRY. Ex. fcp. 8vo. 2*s.* 6*d.*

MARTEL (Chas.).—MILITARY ITALY. With Map. 8vo. 12*s.* 6*d.*

MARTIAL.—SELECT EPIGRAMS FOR ENG-LISH READERS. Translated by W. T. WEBB, M.A. Extra fcp. 8vo. 4*s.* 6*d.*

—— SELECT EPIGRAMS. Edit. by Rev. H. M. STEPHENSON, M.A. Fcp. 8vo. 6*s.* 6*d.*

MARTIN (Frances).—THE POET'S HOUR. Poetry Selected and Arranged for Children. 12mo. 2*s.* 6*d.*

—— SPRING-TIME WITH THE POETS. 18mo. 3*s.* 6*d.*

—— ANGELIQUE ARNAULD, Abbess of Port Royal. Crown 8vo. 4*s.* 6*d.*

MARTIN (Frederick)—THE HISTORY OF LLOYD'S, AND OF MARINE INSURANCE IN GREAT BRITAIN. 8vo. 14*s.*

MARTINEAU (Harriet).—BIOGRAPHICAL SKETCHES, 1852–75. Crown 8vo. 6*s.*

MARTINEAU (Dr. James).—SPINOZA. 2nd Edition. Crown 8vo. 6*s.*

MARTINEAU (Miss C. A.).—EASY LESSONS ON HEAT. Globe 8vo. 2*s.* 6*d.*

MASSON (Prof. David).—RECENT BRITISH PHILOSOPHY. 3rd Edition. Cr. 8vo. 6*s.*

—— DRUMMOND OF HAWTHORNDEN. Crown 8vo. 10*s.* 6*d.*

—— WORDSWORTH, SHELLEY, KEATS, AND OTHER ESSAYS. Crown 8vo. 5*s.*

—— CHATTERTON : A STORY OF THE YEAR 1770. Crown 8vo. 5*s.*

—— LIFE OF MILTON. See "Milton."

—— MILTON'S POEMS. See "Milton."

—— DE QUINCEY. Cr. 8vo. 1*s.* 6*d.* ; sewed, 1*s.*

MASSON (Gustave).—A COMPENDIOUS DIC-TIONARY OF THE FRENCH LANGUAGE (FRENCH-ENGLISH AND ENGLISH-FRENCH). Crown 8vo. 6*s.*

—— LA LYRE FRANÇAISE. Selected and ar-ranged, with Notes. Vignette. 18mo. 4*s.* 6*d.*

MASSON (Mrs.).—THREE CENTURIES OF ENGLISH POETRY. Being Selections from Chaucer to Herrick. Globe 8vo. 3*s.* 6*d.*

MATHEWS.—THE LIFE OF CHARLES J. MATHEWS. Edited by CHARLES DICKENS. With Portraits. 2 vols. 8vo. 25*s.*

MATURIN (Rev. W.).—THE BLESSEDNESS OF THE DEAD IN CHRIST. Cr. 8vo. 7*s.* 6*d.*

MAUDSLEY (Dr. Henry).—THE PHYSIOLOGY OF MIND. Crown 8vo. 10*s.* 6*d.*

—— THE PATHOLOGY OF MIND. 8vo. 18*s.*

—— BODY AND MIND. Crown 8vo. 6*s.* 6*d.*

MAURICE.—LIFE OF FREDERICK DENISON MAURICE. By his Son, FREDERICK MAURICE, With Two Portraits. 3rd Edition. 2 vols. Demy 8vo. 36*s.* Popular Edition (4th Thousand) 2 vols. Crown 8vo. 16*s.*

MAURICE (Frederick Denison).—THE KING-DOM OF CHRIST. 3rd Ed. 2 vols. Cr. 8vo. 12*s.*

—— SOCIAL MORALITY. 3rd Ed. Cr. 8vo. 6*s.*

MAURICE (F. D.).—LECTURES ON THE APOCALYPSE. 2nd Edition. Cr. 8vo. 6*s.*

—— THE CONSCIENCE. Lectures on Casuistry. 3rd Edition. Crown 8vo. 4*s.* 6*d.*

—— DIALOGUES ON FAMILY WORSHIP. Crown 8vo. 4*s.* 6*d.*

—— THE PATRIARCHS AND LAWGIVERS OF THE OLD TESTAMENT. 7th Ed. Cr. 8vo. 4*s.* 6*d.*

—— THE PROPHETS AND KINGS OF THE OLD TESTAMENT. 5th Edition. Crown 8vo. 6*s.*

—— THE GOSPEL OF THE KINGDOM OF HEAVEN. 3rd Edition. Crown 8vo. 6*s.*

—— THE GOSPEL OF ST. JOHN. 8th Edition. Crown 8vo. 6*s.*

—— THE EPISTLES OF ST. JOHN. 4th Edition. Crown 8vo. 6*s.*

—— EXPOSITORY SERMONS ON THE PRAYER-BOOK ; AND ON THE LORD'S PRAYER. New Edition. Crown 8vo. 6*s.*

—— THEOLOGICAL ESSAYS. 4th Ed. Cr. 8vo. 6*s.*

—— THE DOCTRINE OF SACRIFICE DEDUCED FROM THE SCRIPTURES. 2nd Ed. Cr. 8vo. 6*s.*

—— MORAL AND METAPHYSICAL PHILOSOPHY. 4th Edition. 2 vols. 8vo. 16*s.*

—— THE RELIGIONS OF THE WORLD. 6th Edition. Crown 8vo. 4*s.* 6*d.*

—— ON THE SABBATH DAY ; THE CHARACTER OF THE WARRIOR ; AND ON THE INTERPRE-TATION OF HISTORY. Fcp. 8vo. 2*s.* 6*d.*

—— LEARNING AND WORKING. Cr. 8vo. 4*s.* 6*d.*

—— THE LORD'S PRAYER, THE CREED, AND THE COMMANDMENTS. 18mo. 1*s.*

—— SERMONS PREACHED IN COUNTRY CHURCHES. 2nd Edition. Crown 8vo. 6*s.*

—— THE FRIENDSHIP OF BOOKS, AND OTHER LECTURES. 3rd Edition. Cr. 8vo. 4*s.* 6*d.*

—— THE UNITY OF THE NEW TESTAMENT. 2nd Edition. 2 vols. Crown 8vo. 12*s.*

—— LESSONS OF HOPE. Readings from the Works of F. D. MAURICE. Selected by Rev. J. LL. DAVIES, M.A. Crown 8vo. 5*s.*

—— THE COMMUNION SERVICE FROM THE BOOK OF COMMON PRAYER, WITH SELECT READINGS FROM THE WRITINGS OF THE REV. F. D. MAURICE. Edited by the Right Rev. Bishop COLENSO. 16mo. 2*s.* 6*d.*

MAXWELL.—PROFESSOR CLERK MAXWELL, A LIFE OF. By Prof. L. CAMPBELL, M.A., and W. GARNETT, M.A. 2nd Edition. Crown 8vo. 7*s.* 6*d.*

MAYER (Prof. A. M.).—SOUND. A Series of Simple, Entertaining, and Inexpensive Ex-periments in the Phenomena of Sound. With Illustrations. Crown 8vo. 3*s.* 6*d.*

MAYER (Prof. A. M.) and BARNARD (C.)—LIGHT. A Series of Simple, Entertaining, and Useful Experiments in the Phenomena of Light. Illustrated. Crown 8vo. 2*s.* 6*d.*

MAYOR (Prof. John E. B.).—A FIRST GREEK READER. New Edition. Fcp. 8vo. 4*s.* 6*d.*

—— AUTOBIOGRAPHY OF MATTHEW ROBIN-SON. Fcp. 8vo. 5*s.*

—— A BIBLIOGRAPHICAL CLUE TO LATIN LITERATURE. Crown 8vo. 10*s.* 6*d.* See also under "Juvenal."

MAYOR (Prof. Joseph B.).—GREEK FOR BE-GINNERS. Fcp. 8vo. Part I. 1s. 6d.—Parts II. and III. 3s. 6d.—Complete, 4s. 6d.

MAZINI (Linda).—IN THE GOLDEN SHELL. With Illustrations. Globe 8vo. 4s. 6d.

MELBOURNE.—MEMOIRS OF VISCOUNT MELBOURNE. By W. M. TORRENS. With Portrait. 2nd Edition. 2 vols. 8vo. 32s.

MELDOLA (Prof. R.).—THE CHEMISTRY OF PHOTOGRAPHY. Crown 8vo. 6s.

MELDOLA (Prof. R.) and WHITE (Wm.).—REPORT ON THE EAST ANGLIAN EARTH-QUAKE OF 22ND APRIL, 1884. 8vo. 3s. 6d.

MENDENHALL (T. C.).—A CENTURY OF ELECTRICITY. Crown 8vo. 4s. 6d.

MERCIER (Dr. C.).—THE NERVOUS SYSTEM AND THE MIND. 8vo. 12s. 6d.

MERCUR (Prof. J.).—ELEMENTS OF THE ART OF WAR. 8vo. 17s.

MEREDITH (George).—A READING OF EARTH. Extra fcp. 8vo. 5s.

—— POEMS AND LYRICS OF THE JOY OF EARTH. Extra fcp. 8vo. 6s.

—— BALLADS AND POEMS OF TRAGIC LIFE. Crown 8vo. 6s.

MIALL.—LIFE OF EDWARD MIALL. By his Son, ARTHUR MIALL. 8vo. 10s. 6d.

MILL (H. R.).—AN ELEMENTARY CLASS-BOOK OF GENERAL GEOGRAPHY. Crown 8vo. 3s. 6d.

MILLAR (J.B.).—ELEMENTS OF DESCRIPTIVE GEOMETRY. 2nd Edition. Crown 8vo. 6s.

MILLER (R. Kalley).—THE ROMANCE OF ASTRONOMY. 2nd Ed. Cr. 8vo. 4s. 6d.

MILLIGAN (Rev. Prof. W.).—THE RESUR-RECTION OF OUR LORD. 2nd Ed. Cr. 8vo. 5s.

—— THE REVELATION OF ST. JOHN. 2nd Edition. Crown 8vo. 7s. 6d.

MILNE (Rev. John J.).—WEEKLY PROBLEM PAPERS. Fcp. 8vo. 4s. 6d.

—— COMPANION TO WEEKLY PROBLEMS. Cr. 8vo. 10s. 6d.

—— SOLUTIONS OF WEEKLY PROBLEM PAPERS. Crown 8vo. 10s. 6d.

MILNE (Rev. J. J.) and DAVIS (R. F.).—GEOMETRICAL CONICS. Part I. THE PARA-BOLA. Crown 8vo.

MILTON.—THE LIFE OF JOHN MILTON. By Prof. DAVID MASSON. Vol. I., 21s.; Vol. III., 18s.; Vols. IV. and V., 32s.; Vol. VI., with Portrait, 21s.

—— POETICAL WORKS. Edited, with Intro-duction and Notes, by Prof. DAVID MASSON, M.A. 3 vols. 8vo. (Uniform with the Cam-bridge Shakespeare.)

—— POETICAL WORKS. Ed. by Prof. MASSON. 3 vols. Fcp. 8vo. 15s.

—— POETICAL WORKS. (Globe Edition.) Ed. by Prof. MASSON. Globe 8vo. 3s. 6d.

—— PARADISE LOST. Books I. and II. Ed., with Introduction and Notes, by Prof. M. MACMILLAN. Globe 8vo. 2s. 6d. (Or sepa-rately, 1s. 6d. each Book.)

—— L'ALLEGRO, IL PENSEROSO, LYCIDAS, ARCADES, SONNETS, ETC. Edited by Prof. WM. BELL, M.A. Globe 8vo. 2s.

MILTON.—COMUS. Edited by Prof. WM. BELL, M.A. Globe 8vo. 1s. 6d.

—— SAMSON AGONISTES. By H. M. PER-CIVAL, M.A. Globe 8vo. 2s. 6d.

MILTON. By MARK PATTISON. Cr. 8vo. 1s. 6d.; sewed, 1s.

MILTON. By Rev. STOPFORD A. BROOKE, M.A. Fcp. 8vo. 1s. 6d.

Large Paper Edition. 21s.

MINCHIN (Rev. Prof. G. M.).—NATURÆ VERITAS. Fcp. 8vo. 2s. 6d.

MINTO (W.).—THE MEDIATION OF RALPH HARDELOT. 3 vols. Crown 8vo. 31s. 6d.

—— DEFOE. Crown 8vo. 1s. 6d.; sewed, 1s.

MITFORD (A. B.).—TALES OF OLD JAPAN. With Illustrations. Crown 8vo. 3s. 6d.

MIVART (St. George).—LESSONS IN ELE-MENTARY ANATOMY. 18mo. 6s. 6d.

MIXTER (Prof. W. G.).—AN ELEMENTARY TEXT-BOOK OF CHEMISTRY. 2nd Edition. Crown 8vo. 7s. 6d.

MIZ MAZE (THE); OR, THE WINKWORTH PUZZLE. A Story in Letters by Nine Authors. Crown 8vo. 4s. 6d.

MOHAMMAD. THE SPEECHES AND TABLE-TALK OF THE PROPHET. Translated by STANLEY LANE-POOLE. 18mo. 4s. 6d.

MOLESWORTH (Mrs.).—HERR BABY. Il-lustrated by WALTER CRANE. Gl. 8vo. 2s. 6d.

—— GRANDMOTHER DEAR. Illustrated by WALTER CRANE. Globe 8vo. 2s. 6d.

—— THE TAPESTRY ROOM. Illustrated by WALTER CRANE. Globe 8vo. 2s. 6d.

—— A CHRISTMAS CHILD. Illustrated by WALTER CRANE. Globe 8vo. 2s. 6d.

—— SUMMER STORIES. Crown 8vo. 4s. 6d.

—— ROSY. Illustrated by WALTER CRANE. Globe 8vo. 2s. 6d.

—— TWO LITTLE WAIFS. Illustrated by WALTER CRANE. Globe 8vo. 2s. 6d.

—— CHRISTMAS TREE LAND. Illustrated by WALTER CRANE. Globe 8vo. 2s. 6d.

—— "US": AN OLD-FASHIONED STORY. Il-lustrated by WALTER CRANE. Gl. 8vo. 2s. 6d.

—— "CARROTS," JUST A LITTLE BOY. Illus-trated by WALTER CRANE. Gl. 8vo. 2s. 6d.

—— TELL ME A STORY. Illustrated by WALTER CRANE. Globe 8vo. 2s. 6d.

—— THE CUCKOO CLOCK. Illustrated by WALTER CRANE. Globe 8vo. 2s. 6d.

—— FOUR WINDS FARM. Illustrated by WALTER CRANE. Globe 8vo. 2s. 6d.

—— LITTLE MISS PEGGY. Illustrated by WALTER CRANE. Globe 8vo. 2s. 6d.

—— FOUR GHOST STORIES. Crown 8vo. 6s.

—— A CHRISTMAS POSY. Illustrated by WALTER CRANE. Crown 8vo. 4s. 6d.

—— FRENCH LIFE IN LETTERS. With Notes on Idioms, etc. Globe 8vo. 1s. 6d.

—— THE RECTORY CHILDREN. Illustrated by WALTER CRANE. Crown 8vo. 4s. 6d.

MOLIÈRE.—LE MALADE IMAGINAIRE. Edit. by F. TARVER, M.A. Fcp. 8vo. 2s. 6d.

MOLIÈRE.—LES FEMMES SAVANTES. Edit. by G. E. FASNACHT. 18mo. 1s.
—— LE MÉDECIN MALGRÉ LUI. By the same Editor. 18mo. 1s.
—— LE MISANTHROPE. By the same Editor. 18mo. 1s.
—— L'AVARE. Edited by L. M. MORIARTY, M.A. 18mo. 1s.
—— LE BOURGEOIS GENTILHOMME. By the same Editor. 1s. 6d.

MOLLOY (Rev. G.).—GLEANINGS IN SCIENCE: A SERIES OF POPULAR LECTURES ON SCIENTIFIC SUBJECTS. 8vo. 7s. 6d.

MONAHAN (James H.).—THE METHOD OF LAW. Crown 8vo. 6s.

MONK. By JULIAN CORBETT. With Portrait. Crown 8vo. 2s. 6d.

MONTELIUS—WOODS.—THE CIVILISATION OF SWEDEN IN HEATHEN TIMES. By Prof. OSCAR MONTELIUS. Translated by Rev. F. H. WOODS, B.D. With Illustrations. 8vo. 14s.

MONTROSE. By MOWBRAY MORRIS. Cr. 8vo. 2s. 6d.

MOORE (Prof. C. H.).—THE DEVELOPMENT AND CHARACTER OF GOTHIC ARCHITECTURE. Illustrated. Medium 8vo. 18s.

MOORE (SIR JOHN). By Col. MAURICE. Crown 8vo. 2s. 6d.

MOORHOUSE (Rt. Rev. Bishop).—JACOB: THREE SERMONS. Extra fcp. 8vo. 3s. 6d.

MORISON (J. C.).—THE LIFE AND TIMES OF SAINT BERNARD. 4th Ed. Cr. 8vo. 6s.
—— GIBBON. Cr. 8vo. 1s. 6d.; sewed, 1s.
—— MACAULAY. Cr. 8vo. 1s. 6d.; sewed, 1s.

MORISON (Jeanie).—THE PURPOSE OF THE AGES. Crown 8vo. 9s.

MORLEY (John).—WORKS. Collected Edit. In 10 vols. Globe 8vo. 5s. each.
VOLTAIRE. 1 vol.—ROUSSEAU. 2 vols.—DIDEROT AND THE ENCYCLOPÆDISTS. 2 vols.—ON COMPROMISE. 1 vol.—MISCELLANIES. 3 vols.—BURKE. 1 vol.
—— ON THE STUDY OF LITERATURE. Crown 8vo. 1s. 6d.
Also a Popular Edition for distribution, 2d.
—— BURKE. Crown 8vo. 1s. 6d.; sewed, 1s.
—— WALPOLE. Crown 8vo. 2s. 6d.
—— APHORISMS. An Address before the Philosophical Society of Edinburgh. Globe 8vo. 1s. 6d.

MORRIS (Rev. Richard, LL.D.).—HISTORICAL OUTLINES OF ENGLISH ACCIDENCE. Fcp. 8vo. 6s.
—— ELEMENTARY LESSONS IN HISTORICAL ENGLISH GRAMMAR. 18mo. 2s. 6d.
—— PRIMER OF ENGLISH GRAMMAR. 18mo, cloth. 1s.

MORRIS (R.) and BOWEN (H. C.).—ENGLISH GRAMMAR EXERCISES. 18mo. 1s.

MORTE D'ARTHUR. THE EDITION OF CAXTON REVISED FOR MODERN USE. By Sir EDWARD STRACHEY. Gl. 8vo. 3s. 6d.

MOULTON (Louise Chandler).—SWALLOW-FLIGHTS. Extra fcp. 8vo. 4s. 6d.

MOULTON (Louise Chandler).—IN THE GARDEN OF DREAMS: LYRICS AND SONNETS. Crown 8vo. 6s.

MOULTRIE (J.).—POEMS. Complete Edition. 2 vols. Crown 8vo. 7s. each.

MUDIE (C. E.).—STRAY LEAVES: POEMS. 4th Edition. Extra fcp. 8vo. 3s. 6d.

MUIR (Thomas).—A TREATISE ON THE THEORY OF DETERMINANTS. Cr. 8vo. 7s. 6d.

MUIR (M. M. Pattison).—PRACTICAL CHEMISTRY FOR MEDICAL STUDENTS. Fcp. 8vo. 1s. 6d.

MUIR (M. M. P.) and WILSON (D. M.).—THE ELEMENTS OF THERMAL CHEMISTRY. 8vo. 12s. 6d.

MÜLLER—THOMPSON.—THE FERTILISATION OF FLOWERS. By Prof. HERMANN MÜLLER. Translated by D'ARCY W. THOMPSON. With a Preface by CHARLES DARWIN, F.R.S. Medium 8vo. 21s.

MULLINGER (J. B.).—CAMBRIDGE CHARACTERISTICS IN THE SEVENTEENTH CENTURY. Crown 8vo. 4s. 6d.

MURPHY (J. J.).—HABIT AND INTELLIGENCE. 2nd Ed. Illustrated. 8vo. 16s.

MURRAY (E. C. Grenville).—ROUND ABOUT FRANCE. Crown 8vo. 7s. 6d.

MURRAY (D. Christie). — AUNT RACHEL. Crown 8vo. 3s. 6d.
—— SCHWARTZ. Crown 8vo. 3s. 6d.
—— THE WEAKER VESSEL. Cr. 8vo. 3s. 6d.
—— JOHN VALE'S GUARDIAN. 3 vols. Crown 8vo. 31s. 6d.

MUSIC.—A DICTIONARY OF MUSIC AND MUSICIANS, A.D. 1450—1889. Edited by Sir GEORGE GROVE, D.C.L. In 4 vols. 8vo. 21s. each.—Parts I.—XIV. XIX.—XXII. 3s. 6d. each.—Parts XV. XVI. 7s.—Parts XVII. XVIII. 7s.—Parts XXIII.—XXV. APPENDIX. Edited by J. A. FULLER MAITLAND, M.A. 9s. [Cloth cases for binding, 1s. each.]

MYERS (F. W. H.).—THE RENEWAL OF YOUTH, AND OTHER POEMS. Cr. 8vo. 7s. 6d.
—— ST. PAUL: A POEM. Ex. fcp. 8vo. 2s. 6d.
—— WORDSWORTH. Cr. 8vo. 1s. 6d.; sewed, 1s.
—— ESSAYS. 2 vols. — I. Classical. II. Modern. Crown 8vo. 4s. 6d. each.

MYERS (E.).—THE PURITANS: A POEM. Extra fcap. 8vo. 2s. 6d.
—— PINDAR'S ODES. Translated, with Introduction and Notes. Crown 8vo. 5s.
—— POEMS. Extra fcp. 8vo. 4s. 6d.
—— THE DEFENCE OF ROME, AND OTHER POEMS. Extra fcp. 8vo. 5s.
—— THE JUDGMENT OF PROMETHEUS, AND OTHER POEMS. Extra fcp. 8vo. 3s. 6d.

MYLNE (The Rt. Rev. Bishop).—SERMONS PREACHED IN ST. THOMAS'S CATHEDRAL, BOMBAY. Crown 8vo. 6s.

NADAL (E. S.).—ESSAYS AT HOME AND ELSEWHERE. Crown 8vo. 6s.

NAPOLEON I., HISTORY OF. By P. LANFREY. 4 vols. Crown 8vo. 30s.

NATURAL RELIGION. By the Author of "Ecce Homo." 2nd Edition. 8vo. 9s.

NATURE : A WEEKLY ILLUSTRATED JOUR-
NAL OF SCIENCE. Published every Thursday.
Price 6*d*. Monthly Parts, 2*s*. and 2*s*. 6*d*. ;
Current Half-yearly vols., 15*s*. each. Vols.
I.—XL. [Cases for binding vols. 1*s*. 6*d*. each.]

NATURE PORTRAITS. A Series of Portraits of Scientific Worthies engraved by
JEENS and others in Portfolio. India Proofs,
5*s*. each. [Portfolio separately, 6*s*.]

NATURE SERIES. Crown 8vo :

THE ORIGIN AND METAMORPHOSES OF
INSECTS. By Sir JOHN LUBBOCK, M.P.,
F.R.S. With Illustrations. 3*s*. 6*d*.

THE TRANSIT OF VENUS. By Prof. G.
FORBES. With Illustrations. 3*s*. 6*d*.

POLARISATION OF LIGHT. By W. SPOTTIS-
WOODE, LL.D. Illustrated. 3*s*. 6*d*.

ON BRITISH WILD FLOWERS CONSIDERED
IN RELATION TO INSECTS. By Sir JOHN
LUBBOCK, M.P., F.R.S. Illustrated. 4*s*.6*d*.

FLOWERS, FRUITS, AND LEAVES. By Sir
JOHN LUBBOCK. Illustrated. 4*s*. 6*d*.

HOW TO DRAW A STRAIGHT LINE ; A LEC-
TURE ON LINKAGES. By A. B. KEMPE,
B.A. Illustrated. 1*s*. 6*d*.

LIGHT : A SERIES OF SIMPLE, ENTERTAIN-
ING, AND USEFUL EXPERIMENTS. By A. M.
MAYER and C. BARNARD. Illust. 2*s*. 6*d*.

SOUND : A SERIES OF SIMPLE, ENTERTAIN-
ING, AND INEXPENSIVE EXPERIMENTS.
By A. M. MAYER. 3*s*. 6*d*.

SEEING AND THINKING. By Prof. W. K.
CLIFFORD, F.R.S. Diagrams. 3*s*. 6*d*.

CHARLES DARWIN. Memorial Notices re-
printed from "Nature." By THOMAS H.
HUXLEY, F.R.S., G. J. ROMANES, F.R.S.,
ARCHIBALD GEIKIE, F.R.S., and W. T.
DYER, F.R.S. 2*s*. 6*d*.

ON THE COLOURS OF FLOWERS. By GRANT
ALLEN. Illustrated. 3*s*. 6*d*.

THE CHEMISTRY OF THE SECONDARY BAT-
TERIES OF PLANTÉ AND FAURÉ. By J.
H. GLADSTONE and A. TRIBE. 2*s*. 6*d*.

A CENTURY OF ELECTRICITY. By T. C.
MENDENHALL. 4*s*. 6*d*.

ON LIGHT. The Burnett Lectures. By Sir
GEORGE GABRIEL STOKES, M.P., P.R.S.
Three Courses : I. On the Nature of Light.
II. On Light as a Means of Investigation.
III. On Beneficial Effects of Light. 7*s*. 6*d*.

THE SCIENTIFIC EVIDENCES OF ORGANIC
EVOLUTION. By GEORGE J. ROMANES,
M.A., LL.D. 2*s*. 6*d*.

POPULAR LECTURES AND ADDRESSES. By
Sir WM. THOMSON. In 3 vols. Vol. I.
Constitution of Matter. Illustrated. 6*s*.

THE CHEMISTRY OF PHOTOGRAPHY. By Prof.
R. MELDOLA, F.R.S. Illustrated. 6*s*.

MODERN VIEWS OF ELECTRICITY. By Prof.
O. J. LODGE, LL.D. Illustrated. 6*s*. 6*d*.

TIMBER AND SOME OF ITS DISEASES. By
Prof. H. M. WARD, M.A. Illustrated. 6*s*.

NEPOS. SELECTIONS ILLUSTRATIVE OF
GREEK AND ROMAN HISTORY, FROM COR-
NELIUS NEPOS. Edited by G. S. FARNELL,
M.A. 18mo. 1*s*. 6*d*.

NETTLESHIP.—VIRGIL. By Prof. NETTLE-
SHIP, M.A. Fcap. 8vo. 1*s*. 6*d*.

NEW ANTIGONE, THE : A ROMANCE.
Crown 8vo. 6*s*.

NEWCOMB (Prof. Simon).—POPULAR AS-
TRONOMY. With 112 Engravings and Maps
of the Stars. 2nd Edition. 8vo. 18*s*.

NEWMAN (F. W.). — MATHEMATICAL
TRACTS. Part I. 8vo. 5*s*.—Part II. 4*s*.

—— ELLIPTIC INTEGRALS. 8vo. 9*s*.

NEWTON (Sir C. T.).—ESSAYS ON ART AND
ARCHÆOLOGY. 8vo. 12*s*. 6*d*.

NEWTON'S PRINCIPIA. Edited by Prof.
Sir W. THOMSON and Prof. BLACKBURN.
4to. 31*s*. 6*d*.

—— FIRST BOOK. Sections I. II. III. With
Notes, Illustrations, and Problems. By
P. FROST, M.A. 3rd Edition. 8vo. 12*s*.

NICHOL (Prof. John).—PRIMER OF ENGLISH
COMPOSITION. 18mo. 1*s*.

—— EXERCISES IN ENGLISH COMPOSITION.
18mo. 1*s*.

—— BYRON. Crown 8vo. 1*s*. 6*d*. ; sewed, 1*s*.

NINE YEARS OLD. By the Author of
"St. Olave's." Illustrated by FRÖLICH. New
Edition. Globe 8vo. 2*s*. 6*d*.

NIXON (J. E.).—PARALLEL EXTRACTS. Arranged for Translation into English and
Latin, with Notes on Idioms. Part I. Historical and Epistolary. 2nd Ed. Cr.8vo. 3*s*.6*d*.

—— PROSE EXTRACTS. Arranged for Translation into English and Latin, with General
and Special Prefaces on Style and Idiom.
I. Oratorical. II. Historical. III. Philosophical. IV. Anecdotes and Letters. 2nd
Ed., enlarged to 280 pp. Cr. 8vo. 4*s*. 6*d*.

—— SELECTIONS FROM PROSE EXTRACTS. Including Anecdotes and Letters, with Notes
and Hints, pp. 120. Globe 8vo. 3*s*.

NOEL (Lady Aug.).—WANDERING WILLIE.
Globe 8vo. 2*s*. 6*d*.

—— HITHERSEA MERE. 3 vols. Cr.8vo. 31*s*.6*d*.

NORDENSKIÖLD. — VOYAGE OF THE
"VEGA" ROUND ASIA AND EUROPE. By
Baron A. E. VON NORDENSKIÖLD. Translated by ALEXANDER LESLIE. 400 Illustrations, Maps, etc. 2 vols. Medium 8vo. 45*s*.
Popular Edition. With Portrait, Maps,
and Illustrations. Crown 8vo. 6*s*.

—— THE ARCTIC VOYAGES OF ADOLPH ERIC
NORDENSKIÖLD, 1858—79. By ALEXANDER
LESLIE. 8vo. 16*s*.

NORGATE (Kate).—ENGLAND UNDER THE
ANGEVIN KINGS. In 2 vols. With Maps
and Plans. 8vo. 32*s*.

NORRIS (W. E.).—MY FRIEND JIM. Globe
8vo. 2*s*.

—— CHRIS. Globe 8vo. 2*s*.

NORTON (the Hon. Mrs.).—THE LADY OF
LA GARAYE. 9th Ed. Fcp. 8vo. 4*s*. 6*d*.

—— OLD SIR DOUGLAS. Crown 8vo. 6*s*.

O'BRIEN (Bishop J. T.).—PRAYER. Five
Sermons. 8vo. 6*s*.

OLD SONGS. With Drawings by E. A.
ABBEY and A. PARSONS. 4to. Morocco
gilt. 1*l*. 11*s*. 6*d*.

OLIPHANT (Mrs. M. O. W.).—A Son of
the Soil. Globe 8vo. 2s.
—— The Curate in Charge. Globe 8vo. 2s.
—— Francis of Assisi. Crown 8vo. 6s.
—— Young Musgrave. Globe 8vo. 2s.
—— He that will not when He may.
Globe 8vo. 2s.
—— Sir Tom. Globe 8vo. 2s.
—— Hester. Globe 8vo. 2s.
—— The Wizard's Son. Globe 8vo. 2s.
—— A Country Gentleman and his
Family. Globe 8vo. 2s.
—— The Second Son. Globe 8vo. 2s.
—— Neighbours on the Green. Crown
8vo. 3s. 6d.
—— Joyce. Crown 8vo. 3s. 6d.
—— A Beleaguered City. Cr. 8vo. 3s. 6d.
—— The Makers of Venice. With nume-
rous Illustrations. Crown 8vo. 10s. 6d.
—— The Makers of Florence: Dante,
Giotto, Savonarola, and their City.
With Illustrations. Cr. 8vo, cloth. 10s. 6d.
—— Agnes Hopetoun's Schools and Holi-
days. Illustrated. Globe 8vo. 2s. 6d.
—— The Literary History of England in
the End of the Eighteenth and Begin-
ning of the Nineteenth Century. 3
vols. 8vo. 21s.
—— Sheridan. Cr. 8vo. 1s. 6d. ; sewed, 1s.
—— Selections from Cowper's Poems.
18mo. 4s. 6d.
OLIPHANT (T. L. Kington).—The Old and
Middle English. Globe 8vo. 9s.
—— The Duke and the Scholar, and
other Essays. 8vo. 7s. 6d.
—— The New English. 2 vols. Cr. 8vo. 21s.
OLIVER (Prof. Daniel).—Lessons in Ele-
mentary Botany. Illust. Fcp. 8vo. 4s.6d.
—— First Book of Indian Botany. Illus-
trated. Extra fcp. 8vo. 6s. 6d.
OLIVER (Capt. S. P.).—Madagascar: An
Historical and Descriptive Account of
the Island and its former Dependen-
cies. 2 vols. Medium 8vo. 2l. 12s. 6d.
ORCHIDS: Being the Report on the
Orchid Conference held at South Ken-
sington, 1885. 8vo. 2s. 6d.
OTTÉ (E. C.).—Scandinavian History.
With Maps. Globe 8vo. 6s.
OVID. —Selections. Edited by E. S.
Shuckburgh, M.A. 18mo. 1s. 6d.
—— Fasti. Edited by G. H. Hallam,
M.A. Fcp. 8vo. 5s.
—— Heroidum Epistulæ XIII. Edited by
E. S. Shuckburgh, M.A. Fcp. 8vo. 4s. 6d.
—— Metamorphoses. Books I. — III.
Edited by C. Simmons, M.A.
—— Stories from the Metamorphoses.
Edited by the Rev. J. Bond, M.A., and
A. S. Walpole, M.A. With Notes,
Exercises, and Vocabulary. 18mo. 1s. 6d.
—— Metamorphoses. Books XIII. and
XIV. Ed. by C. Simmons. Fcp 8vo. 4s.6d.

OVID.—Easy Selections from Ovid in
Elegiac Verse. Arranged and Edited by
H. Wilkinson, M.A. 18mo. 1s. 6d.
OWENS COLLEGE CALENDAR, 1889—
90. Crown 8vo. 3s.
OWENS COLLEGE ESSAYS AND AD-
DRESSES. By Professors and Lecturers
of the College. 8vo. 14s.
OXFORD, A HISTORY OF THE UNI-
VERSITY OF. From the Earliest Times
to the Year 1530. By H. C. Maxwell
Lyte, M.A. 8vo. 16s.
PALGRAVE (Sir Francis). — History of
Normandy and of England. 4 vols.
8vo. 4l. 4s.
PALGRAVE (William Gifford).—A Narra-
tive of a Year's Journey through Cen-
tral and Eastern Arabia, 1862—63. 9th
Edition. Crown 8vo. 6s.
—— Essays on Eastern Questions. 8vo.
10s. 6d.
—— Dutch Guiana. 8vo. 9s.
—— Ulysses; or, Scenes and Studies in
many Lands. 8vo. 12s. 6d.
PALGRAVE (Prof. Francis Turner).—The
Five Days' Entertainments at Went-
worth Grange. A Book for Children.
Small 4to, cloth extra. 9s.
—— Essays on Art. Extra fcp. 8vo. 6s.
—— Original Hymns. 3rd Ed. 18mo. 1s.6d.
—— Lyrical Poems. Extra fcp. 8vo. 6s.
—— Visions of England: A Series of
Lyrical Poems on Leading Events and
Persons in English History. Crown
8vo. 7s. 6d.
—— The Golden Treasury of the best
Songs and Lyrical Poems in the Eng-
lish Language. 18mo. 4s. 6d.
—— Sonnets and Songs of Shakespeare.
Edited by F. T. Palgrave. 18mo. 4s. 6d.
—— The Children's Treasury of Lyrical
Poetry. 18mo. 2s. 6d.—Or in Two Parts,
1s. each.
—— Herrick: Selections from the Lyri-
cal Poems. 18mo. 4s. 6d.
—— The Poetical Works of John Keats.
With Notes. 18mo. 4s. 6d.
—— Lyrical Poems of Lord Tennyson.
Selected and Annotated. 18mo. 4s. 6d.
Large Paper Edition. 8vo. 9s.
PALGRAVE (Reginald F. D.).—The House
of Commons: Illustrations of its His-
tory and Practice. New Edition. Cr.
8vo. 2s. 6d.
PALMER (Lady Sophia),—Mrs. Penicott's
Lodger, and other Stories. Cr.8vo. 2s.6d.
PALMER (J. H.).—Text-Book of Practi-
cal Logarithms and Trigonometry.
Crown 8vo. 4s. 6d.
PANSIE'S FLOUR BIN. By the Author
of "When I was a Little Girl," etc. Illus-
trated. Globe 8vo. 2s. 6d.
PANTIN (W. E. P.).—A First Latin Verse
Book. Globe 8vo. 1s. 6d.
PARADOXICAL PHILOSOPHY: A Se-
quel to "The Unseen Universe." Cr.
8vo. 7s. 6d.

PARKER (H.).—THE NATURE OF THE FINE ARTS. Crown 8vo. 10s. 6d.

PARKER (Prof. W. K.) and BETTANY (G. T.).—THE MORPHOLOGY OF THE SKULL. Crown 8vo. 10s. 6d.

PARKER (Prof. T. Jeffrey).—A COURSE OF INSTRUCTION IN ZOOTOMY (VERTEBRATA). With 74 Illustrations. Crown 8vo. 8s. 6d.

PARKINSON (S.).—A TREATISE ON ELEMENTARY MECHANICS. Crown 8vo. 9s. 6d.

—— A TREATISE ON OPTICS. 4th Edition, revised. Crown 8vo. 10s. 6d.

PARKMAN (Francis).— MONTCALM AND WOLFE. Library Edition. Illustrated with Portraits and Maps. 2 vols. 8vo. 12s. 6d. each.

—— THE COLLECTED WORKS OF FRANCIS PARKMAN. Popular Edition. In 10 vols. Crown 8vo. 7s. 6d. each; or complete, 3l. 13s. 6d.—PIONEERS OF FRANCE IN THE NEW WORLD. 1 vol.—THE JESUITS IN NORTH AMERICA. 1 vol.—LA SALLE AND THE DISCOVERY OF THE GREAT WEST. 1 vol.—THE OREGON TRAIL. 1 vol.—THE OLD RÉGIME IN CANADA UNDER LOUIS XIV. 1 vol.—COUNT FRONTENAC AND NEW FRANCE UNDER LOUIS XIV. 1 vol.—MONTCALM AND WOLFE. 2 vols.—THE CONSPIRACY OF PONTIAC. 2 vols.

PASTEUR — FAULKNER. — STUDIES ON FERMENTATION: THE DISEASES OF BEER, THEIR CAUSES, AND THE MEANS OF PREVENTING THEM. By L. PASTEUR. Translated by FRANK FAULKNER. 8vo. 21s.

PATER (W.).—THE RENAISSANCE : STUDIES IN ART AND POETRY. 4th Ed. Cr. 8vo. 10s. 6d.

—— MARIUS THE EPICUREAN : HIS SENSATIONS AND IDEAS. 3rd Edition. 2 vols. 8vo. 12s.

—— IMAGINARY PORTRAITS. Crown 8vo. 6s.

—— APPRECIATIONS. With an Essay on Style. Crown 8vo. 8s. 6d.

PATERSON (James).—COMMENTARIES ON THE LIBERTY OF THE SUBJECT, AND THE LAWS OF ENGLAND RELATING TO THE SECURITY OF THE PERSON. 2 vols. Cr. 8vo. 21s.

—— THE LIBERTY OF THE PRESS, SPEECH, AND PUBLIC WORSHIP. Crown 8vo. 12s.

PATMORE (C.).— THE CHILDREN'S GARLAND FROM THE BEST POETS. With a Vignette. 18mo. 4s. 6d.
Globe Readings Edition. For Schools. Globe 8vo. 2s.

PATTESON.—LIFE AND LETTERS OF JOHN COLERIDGE PATTESON, D.D., MISSIONARY BISHOP. By CHARLOTTE M. YONGE. 8th Edition. 2 vols. Crown 8vo. 12s.

PATTISON (Mark).—MILTON. Crown 8vo. 1s. 6d. ; sewed, 1s.

—— MEMOIRS. Crown 8vo. 8s. 6d.

—— SERMONS. Crown 8vo. 6s.

PAUL OF TARSUS. 8vo. 10s. 6d.

PAYNE (E. J.).—HISTORY OF EUROPEAN COLONIES. 18mo. 4s. 6d.

PEABODY (Prof. C. H.).—THERMODYNAMICS OF THE STEAM ENGINE AND OTHER HEAT-ENGINES. 8vo. 21s.

PEDLEY (S.).—EXERCISES IN ARITHMETIC. With upwards of 7000 Examples and Answers. Cr. 8vo. 5s.—Also in Two Parts. 2s. 6d. each.

PEEL (Edmund).—ECHOES FROM HOREB, AND OTHER POEMS. Crown 8vo. 3s. 6d.

PEILE (John).—PHILOLOGY. 18mo. 1s.

PELLISSIER (Eugène).—FRENCH ROOTS AND THEIR FAMILIES. Globe 8vo. 6s.

PENNELL (Joseph).—PEN DRAWING AND PEN DRAUGHTSMEN : Their Work and Methods, a Study of the Art to-day, with Technical Suggestions. With 158 Illustrations, 12 of which are photogravure. 4to. 3l. 13s. 6d. net.

PENNINGTON (Rooke).—NOTES ON THE BARROWS AND BONE CAVES OF DERBYSHIRE. 8vo. 6s.

PENROSE (Francis).—ON A METHOD OF PREDICTING, BY GRAPHICAL CONSTRUCTION, OCCULTATIONS OF STARS BY THE MOON AND SOLAR ECLIPSES FOR ANY GIVEN PLACE. 4to. 12s.

—— AN INVESTIGATION OF THE PRINCIPLES OF ATHENIAN ARCHITECTURE. Illustrated. Folio. 7l. 7s.

PEOPLE'S EDITIONS. Price 6d. each; or complete in One Volume, medium 4to, cloth binding, price 3s. Contents : TOM BROWN'S SCHOOL DAYS. By an OLD BOY. With upwards of 60 Illustrations.—WATERTON'S WANDERINGS IN SOUTH AMERICA. With 100 Illustrations.—OLD CHRISTMAS. From WASHINGTON IRVING'S Sketch Book. With 100 Illustrations by RANDOLPH CALDECOTT. —— BRACEBRIDGE HALL. From WASHINGTON IRVING'S Sketch Book. With 100 Illustrations by RANDOLPH CALDECOTT.

PERRAULT.—CONTES DE FÉES. Edited by G. EUGÈNE FASNACHT. Globe 8vo. 1s. 6d.

PERRY (Prof. John).—AN ELEMENTARY TREATISE ON STEAM. 18mo. 4s. 6d.

PERSIA, EASTERN. AN ACCOUNT OF THE JOURNEYS OF THE PERSIAN BOUNDARY COMMISSION, 1870—71—72. 2 vols. 8vo. 42s.

PETERBOROUGH. By W. STEBBING. With Portrait. Crown 8vo. 2s. 6d.

PETTIGREW (J. Bell).—THE PHYSIOLOGY OF THE CIRCULATION. 8vo. 12s.

PHAEDRUS.—SELECT FABLES. Edited by A. S. WALPOLE, M.A. With Notes, Exercises, and Vocabularies. 18mo. 1s. 6d.

PHILLIMORE (John G.).—PRIVATE LAW AMONG THE ROMANS. From the Pandects. 8vo. 16s.

PHILLIPS (J. A.).—A TREATISE ON ORE DEPOSITS. Illustrated. Medium 8vo. 25s.

PHILOCHRISTUS.—MEMOIRS OF A DISCIPLE OF THE LORD. 3rd Ed. 8vo. 12s.

PHILOLOGY.—THE JOURNAL OF SACRED AND CLASSICAL PHILOLOGY. 4 vols. 8vo. 12s. 6d. each.

—— THE JOURNAL OF PHILOLOGY. New Series. Edited by W. A. WRIGHT, M.A., I. BYWATER, M.A., and H. JACKSON, M.A. 4s. 6d. each number (half-yearly).

—— THE AMERICAN JOURNAL OF PHILOLOGY. Edited by Prof. BASIL L. GILDERSLEEVE. 4s. 6d. each (quarterly).

PHRYNICHUS. THE NEW PHRYNICHUS. A revised text of "The Ecloga" of the Grammarian PHRYNICHUS. With Introductions and Commentary. By W. GUNION RUTHERFORD, M.A. 8vo. 18s.

PICKERING (Prof. Edward C.).—ELEMENTS OF PHYSICAL MANIPULATION. Medium 8vo. Part I., 12s. 6d.; Part II., 14s.

PICTON (J. A.).—THE MYSTERY OF MATTER, AND OTHER ESSAYS. Crown 8vo. 6s.

PIFFARD (H. G.).—AN ELEMENTARY TREATISE ON DISEASES OF THE SKIN. With Illustrations. 8vo. 16s.

PINDAR'S EXTANT ODES. Translated by ERNEST MYERS, M.A. 3rd Edition. Crown 8vo. 5s.

PIRIE (Prof. G.).—LESSONS ON RIGID DYNAMICS. Crown 8vo. 6s.

PLATO.—PHÆDO. Edited by R. D. ARCHER-HIND, M.A. 8vo. 8s. 6d.

—— TIMÆUS. With Introduction, Notes, and Translation, by the same Editor. 8vo. 16s.

—— PHÆDO. Ed. by Principal W. D. GEDDES, LL.D. 2nd Edition. 8vo. 8s. 6d.

—— THE TRIAL AND DEATH OF SOCRATES: BEING THE EUTHYPHRON, APOLOGY, CRITO, AND PHÆDO OF PLATO. Translated by F. J. CHURCH. 18mo. 4s. 6d.

—— EUTHYPHRO AND MENEXENUS. Ed. by C. E. GRAVES, M.A. 18mo. 1s. 6d.

—— THE REPUBLIC. Books I.—V. Edited by T. H. WARREN, M.A. Fcp. 8vo. 6s.

—— THE REPUBLIC OF PLATO. Translated by J. Ll. DAVIES, M.A., and D. J VAUGHAN, M.A. 18mo. 4s. 6d.

—— LACHES. Edited by M. T. TATHAM, M.A. Fcap. 8vo. 2s. 6d.

—— PHAEDRUS, LYSIS, AND PROTAGORAS. A New Translation, by J. WRIGHT, M.A. 18mo. 4s. 6d.

PLAUTUS. — THE MOSTELLARIA. With Notes, Prolegomena, and Excursus. By the late Prof. RAMSAY. Ed. by G. G. RAMSAY, M.A. 8vo. 14s.

—— MILES GLORIOSUS. Edit. by Prof. R. Y. TYRRELL, M.A. 2nd Ed. Fcp. 8vo. 5s.

—— AMPHITRUO. Edited by Prof. A. PALMER, M.A. Fcp. 8vo. 5s.

PLINY.—LETTERS. Books I. and II. Edit. by JAMES COWAN, M.A. Fcp. 8vo. 5s.

—— LETTERS. Book III. Edited by Prof. JOHN E. B. MAYOR. Fcp. 8vo. 5s.

—— CORRESPONDENCE WITH TRAJAN. C. Plinii Caecilii Secundi Epistulæ ad Traianum Imperatorem cum Eiusdem Responsis. Ed., with Notes and Introductory Essays, by E. G. HARDY, M.A. 8vo. 10s. 6d.

PLUMPTRE (Prof. E. H.).—MOVEMENTS IN RELIGIOUS THOUGHT. Fcp. 8vo. 3s. 6d.

PLUTARCH. Being a Selection from the Lives in North's Plutarch which illustrate Shakespeare's Plays. Edited by Rev. W. W. SKEAT, M.A. Crown 8vo. 6s.

—— LIFE OF THEMISTOKLES. Edited by Rev. H. A. HOLDEN, M.A. Fcp. 8vo. 5s.

—— LIVES OF GALBA AND OTHO. Edited by E. G. HARDY, M.A. Fcp. 8vo.

POLLOCK (Prof. Sir F., Bart.).—ESSAYS IN JURISPRUDENCE AND ETHICS. 8vo. 10s. 6d.

—— THE LAND LAWS. 2nd Ed. Cr. 8vo. 3s. 6d.

POLLOCK (W. H. and Lady).—AMATEUR THEATRICALS. Crown 8vo. 2s. 6d.

POLLOCK (Sir Frederick).—PERSONAL REMEMBRANCES. 2 vols. Crown 8vo. 16s.

POLYBIUS.—THE HISTORY OF THE ACHÆAN LEAGUE. As contained in the "Remains of Polybius." Edited by Rev. W. W. CAPES. Fcp. 8vo. 6s. 6d.

—— THE HISTORIES OF POLYBIUS. Transl. by E. S. SHUCKBURGH. 2 vols. Cr. 8vo. 24s.

POOLE (M. E.).—PICTURES OF COTTAGE LIFE IN THE WEST OF ENGLAND. 2nd Ed. Crown 8vo. 3s. 6d.

POOLE (Reginald Lane).—A HISTORY OF THE HUGUENOTS OF THE DISPERSION AT THE RECALL OF THE EDICT OF NANTES. Crown 8vo. 6s.

POOLE, THOMAS, AND HIS FRIENDS. By Mrs. SANDFORD. With Portrait. 2 vols. Crown 8vo. 15s.

POPE.—THE POETICAL WORKS OF ALEX. POPE. Ed. by Prof. WARD. Globe 8vo. 3s. 6d.

—— POPE. By LESLIE STEPHEN. Crown 8vo. 1s. 6d.; sewed, 1s.

POPULATION OF AN OLD PEAR TREE; OR, STORIES OF INSECT LIFE. From the French of E. VAN BRUYSSEL. Ed. by C. M. YONGE. Illustrated. Globe 8vo. 2s. 6d.

POSTGATE (Prof. J. P.).—SERMO LATINUS. A Short Guide to Latin Prose Composition. Part I. Introduction. Part II. Selected Passages for Translation. Gl. 8vo. 2s. 6d.—Key to "Selected Passages." Cr. 8vo. 3s. 6d.

POTTER (Louisa).—LANCASHIRE MEMORIES. Crown 8vo. 6s.

POTTER (R.).—THE RELATION OF ETHICS TO RELIGION. Crown 8vo. 2s. 6d.

POTTS (A. W.).—HINTS TOWARDS LATIN PROSE COMPOSITION. 8th Edition. Extra fcp. 8vo. 3s.

—— PASSAGES FOR TRANSLATION INTO LATIN PROSE. 4th Ed. Extra fcp. 8vo. 2s. 6d.

—— LATIN VERSIONS OF PASSAGES FOR TRANSLATION INTO LATIN PROSE. Extra fcp. 8vo. 2s. 6d. (For Teachers only.)

PRACTICAL POLITICS. Published under the auspices of the National Liberal Federation. 8vo. 6s.

PRACTITIONER (THE): A MONTHLY JOURNAL OF THERAPEUTICS AND PUBLIC HEALTH. Edited by T. LAUDER BRUNTON, M.D., F.R.C.P., F.R.S., Assistant Physician to St. Bartholomew's Hospital, etc., etc.; DONALD MACALISTER, M.A., M.D., B.Sc., F.R.C.P., Fellow and Medical Lecturer, St. John's College, Cambridge, Physician to Addenbrooke's Hospital and University Lecturer in Medicine; and J. MITCHELL BRUCE, M.A., M.D., F.R.C.P., Physician and Lecturer on Therapeutics at Charing Cross Hospital. 1s. 6d. monthly. Vols. I.—XLIII. Half-yearly vols. 10s. 6d.

PRESTON (Rev. G.).—EXERCISES IN LATIN VERSE OF VARIOUS KINDS. Globe 8vo. 2s. 6d.—Key. Globe 8vo. 5s.

PRESTON (T.).—A TREATISE ON THE THEORY OF LIGHT. Illustrated. 8vo.

PRICE (L. L. F. R.).—INDUSTRIAL PEACE: ITS ADVANTAGES, METHODS, AND DIFFICULTIES. Medium 8vo. 6s.

PRIMERS.—HISTORY. Edited by JOHN R. GREEN, Author of "A Short History of the English People," etc. 18mo. 1s. each:
EUROPE. By E. A. FREEMAN, M.A.
GREECE. By C. A. FYFFE, M.A.
ROME. By Prof. CREIGHTON.
GREEK ANTIQUITIES. By Prof. MAHAFFY.
ROMAN ANTIQUITIES. By Prof. WILKINS.
CLASSICAL GEOGRAPHY. By H. F. TOZER.
FRANCE. By CHARLOTTE M. YONGE.
GEOGRAPHY. By Sir GEO. GROVE, D.C.L.

PRIMERS.—LITERATURE. Edited by JOHN R. GREEN, M.A., LL.D. 18mo. 1s. each:
ENGLISH GRAMMAR. By Rev. R. MORRIS.
ENGLISH GRAMMAR EXERCISES. By Rev. R. MORRIS and H. C. BOWEN.
EXERCISES ON MORRIS'S PRIMER OF ENGLISH GRAMMAR. By J. WETHERELL, M.A.
ENGLISH COMPOSITION. By Prof. NICHOL.
EXERCISES IN ENGLISH COMPOSITION. By Prof. NICHOL.
PHILOLOGY. By J. PEILE, M.A.
ENGLISH LITERATURE. By Rev. STOPFORD BROOKE, M.A.
CHILDREN'S TREASURY OF LYRICAL POETRY. Selected by Prof. F. T. PALGRAVE. In 2 parts. 1s. each.
SHAKSPERE. By Prof. DOWDEN.
GREEK LITERATURE. By Prof. JEBB.
HOMER. By Right Hon. W. E. GLADSTONE.
ROMAN LITERATURE. By A. S. WILKINS.

PRIMERS.—SCIENCE. Under the joint Editorship of Prof. HUXLEY, Sir H. E. ROSCOE, and Prof. BALFOUR STEWART. 18mo. 1s. each:
INTRODUCTORY. By Prof. HUXLEY.
CHEMISTRY. By Sir HENRY ROSCOE, F.R.S. With Illustrations, and Questions.
PHYSICS. By BALFOUR STEWART, F.R.S. With Illustrations, and Questions.
PHYSICAL GEOGRAPHY. By A. GEIKIE, F.R.S. With Illustrations, and Questions.
GEOLOGY. By ARCHIBALD GEIKIE, F.R.S.
PHYSIOLOGY. By MICHAEL FOSTER, F.R.S.
ASTRONOMY. By J. N. LOCKYER, F.R.S.
BOTANY. By Sir J. D. HOOKER, C.B.
LOGIC. By W. STANLEY JEVONS, F.R.S.
POLITICAL ECONOMY. By W. STANLEY JEVONS, LL.D., M.A., F.R.S.

PROCTER (Rev. F.).—A HISTORY OF THE BOOK OF COMMON PRAYER. 18th Edition. Crown 8vo. 10s. 6d.

PROCTER (Rev. F.) and MACLEAR (Rev. Canon).—AN ELEMENTARY INTRODUCTION TO THE BOOK OF COMMON PRAYER. 18mo. 2s. 6d.

PROPERT (J. Lumsden).—A HISTORY OF MINIATURE ART. With Illustrations. Super royal 4to. 3l. 13s. 6d.
Also bound in vellum. 4l. 14s. 6d.

PROPERTIUS.—SELECT POEMS. Edited by J. P. POSTGATE, M.A. Fcp. 8vo. 6s.

PSALMS (THE). With Introductions and Critical Notes. By A. C. JENNINGS, M.A., and W. H. LOWE, M.A. In 2 vols. 2nd Edition. Crown 8vo. 10s. 6d. each.

PUCKLE (G. H.).—AN ELEMENTARY TREATISE ON CONIC SECTIONS AND ALGEBRAIC GEOMETRY, WITH NUMEROUS EXAMPLES AND HINTS FOR THEIR SOLUTION. 6th Ed. Crown 8vo. 7s. 6d.

PYLODET (L.).—NEW GUIDE TO GERMAN CONVERSATION. 18mo. 2s. 6d.

RACINE.—BRITANNICUS. Ed. by EUGÈNE PELLISSIER, M.A. 18mo. 2s.

RADCLIFFE (Charles B.).—BEHIND THE TIDES. 8vo. 6s.

RAMSAY (Prof. William).—EXPERIMENTAL PROOFS OF CHEMICAL THEORY FOR BEGINNERS. 18mo. 2s. 6d.

RAY (Prof. P. K.).—A TEXT-BOOK OF DEDUCTIVE LOGIC. 4th Ed. Globe 8vo. 4s. 6d.

RAYLEIGH (Lord).—THEORY OF SOUND. 8vo. Vol. I. 12s. 6d.—Vol. II. 12s. 6d.—Vol. III. (in preparation.)

RAYS OF SUNLIGHT FOR DARK DAYS. With a Preface by C. J. VAUGHAN, D.D. New Edition. 18mo. 3s. 6d.

REALMAH. By the Author of "Friends in Council." Crown 8vo. 6s.

REASONABLE FAITH: A SHORT RELIGIOUS ESSAY FOR THE TIMES. By "THREE FRIENDS." Crown 8vo. 1s.

RECOLLECTIONS OF A NURSE. By E. D. Crown 8vo. 2s.

REED.—MEMOIR OF SIR CHARLES REED. By his Son, CHARLES E. B. REED, M.A. With Portrait. Crown 8vo. 4s. 6d.

REMSEN (Prof. Ira).—AN INTRODUCTION TO THE STUDY OF ORGANIC CHEMISTRY. Crown 8vo. 6s. 6d.

—— AN INTRODUCTION TO THE STUDY OF CHEMISTRY (INORGANIC CHEMISTRY). Cr. 8vo. 6s. 6d.

—— THE ELEMENTS OF CHEMISTRY. A Text-Book for Beginners. Fcp. 8vo. 2s. 6d.

—— TEXT-BOOK OF INORGANIC CHEMISTRY. 8vo. 16s.

RENDALL (Rev. Frederic).—THE EPISTLE TO THE HEBREWS IN GREEK AND ENGLISH. With Notes. Crown 8vo. 6s.

—— THE THEOLOGY OF THE HEBREW CHRISTIANS. Crown 8vo. 5s.

—— THE EPISTLE TO THE HEBREWS. English Text, with Commentary. Crown 8vo. 7s. 6d.

RENDALL (Prof. G. H.).—THE CRADLE OF THE ARYANS. 8vo. 3s.

RENDU.—THE THEORY OF THE GLACIERS OF SAVOY. By M. LE CHANOINE RENDU. Translated by A. WILLS, Q.C. 8vo. 7s. 6d.

REULEAUX.— THE KINEMATICS OF MA-CHINERY: OUTLINES OF A THEORY OF MACHINES. By Prof. F. REULEAUX. Translated by Prof. A. B. W. KENNEDY, F.R.S., C.E. Medium 8vo. 21s.

REYNOLDS (J. R.).—A SYSTEM OF MEDI-CINE. Edited by J. RUSSELL REYNOLDS, M.D., F.R.C.P. London. In 5 vols. Vols. I. II. III. and V. 8vo. 25s. each.—Vol. IV. 21s.

REYNOLDS (H. R.).— NOTES OF THE CHRISTIAN LIFE. Crown 8vo. 7s. 6d.

REYNOLDS (Prof. Osborne).—SEWER GAS, AND HOW TO KEEP IT OUT OF HOUSES. 3rd Edition. Crown 8vo. 1s. 6d.

RICE (Prof. J. M.) and JOHNSON (W. W.).— AN ELEMENTARY TREATISE ON THE DIF-FERENTIAL CALCULUS. New Edition. 8vo. 18s. Abridged Edition. 9s.

RICHARDSON (Dr. B. W.).—ON ALCOHOL. Crown 8vo. 1s.

—— DISEASES OF MODERN LIFE. Crown 8vo. 6s.

—— HYGEIA: A CITY OF HEALTH. Crown 8vo. 1s.

—— THE FUTURE OF SANITARY SCIENCE. Crown 8vo. 1s.

RICHEY (Alex. G.).—THE IRISH LAND LAWS. Crown 8vo. 3s. 6d.

ROBINSON CRUSOE. Edited after the Original Editions, with Introduction by HENRY KINGSLEY. Globe 8vo. 3s. 6d.— Golden Treasury Edition. Edit. by J. W. CLARK, M.A. 18mo. 4s. 6d.

ROBINSON (Prebendary H. G.).—MAN IN THE IMAGE OF GOD, AND OTHER SERMONS. Crown 8vo. 7s. 6d.

ROBINSON (Rev. J. L.).—MARINE SURVEY-ING: AN ELEMENTARY TREATISE ON. Pre-pared for the Use of Younger Naval Officers. With Illustrations. Crown 8vo. 7s. 6d.

ROBY (H. J.).—A GRAMMAR OF THE LATIN LANGUAGE FROM PLAUTUS TO SUETONIUS. In Two Parts.—Part I. containing Sounds, Inflexions, Word Formation, Appendices, etc. 5th Edition. Crown 8vo. 9s.—Part II. Syntax, Prepositions, etc. 6th Edition. Crown 8vo. 10s. 6d.

—— A LATIN GRAMMAR FOR SCHOOLS. Cr. 8vo. 5s.

—— EXERCISES IN LATIN SYNTAX AND IDIOM. Arranged with reference to Roby's School Latin Grammar. By E. B. ENGLAND, M.A. Crown 8vo. 2s. 6d.—Key, 2s. 6d.

ROCKSTRO (W. S.).—LIFE OF GEORGE FREDERICK HANDEL. Crown 8vo. 10s. 6d.

RODNEY. By D. HANNAY. Cr. 8vo. 2s. 6d.

ROGERS (Prof. J. E. T.).—HISTORICAL GLEANINGS.—First Series. Cr. 8vo. 4s. 6d. —Second Series. Crown 8vo. 6s.

—— COBDEN AND POLITICAL OPINION. 8vo. 10s. 6d.

ROMANES (George J.).—THE SCIENTIFIC EVIDENCES OF ORGANIC EVOLUTION. Cr. 8vo. 2s. 6d.

ROSCOE (Sir Henry E., M.P., F.R.S.).— LESSONS IN ELEMENTARY CHEMISTRY. With Illustrations. Fcp. 8vo. 4s. 6d.

—— PRIMER OF CHEMISTRY. With Illustra-tions. 18mo, cloth. With Questions. 1s.

ROSCOE (Sir H. E.) and SCHORLEMMER (C.).—A TREATISE ON CHEMISTRY. With Illustrations. 8vo.—Vols. I. and II. INOR-GANIC CHEMISTRY: Vol. I. THE NON-METALLIC ELEMENTS. With a Portrait of DALTON. 21s.—Vol. II. Part I. METALS. 18s.; Part II. METALS. 18s.—Vol. III. OR-GANIC CHEMISTRY: Parts I. II. and IV. 21s. each; Parts III. and V. 18s. each.

ROSCOE—SCHUSTER.—SPECTRUM ANA-LYSIS. By Sir HENRY E. ROSCOE, LL.D., F.R.S. 4th Edition, revised and consider-ably enlarged by the Author and A. SCHUSTER, Ph.D., F.R.S. With Illustrations and Plates. Medium 8vo. 21s.

ROSENBUSCH (H.).—MICROSCOPICAL PHY-SIOGRAPHY OF THE ROCK-MAKING MINE-RALS. Translated by J. P. IDDINGS. Illus-trated. 8vo. 24s.

ROSS (Percy).—A MISGUIDIT LASSIE. Crown 8vo. 4s. 6d.

ROSSETTI (Dante Gabriel). — A RECORD AND A STUDY. By W. SHARP. Crown 8vo. 10s. 6d.

ROSSETTI (Christina).—POEMS. Complete Edition. Extra fcp. 8vo. 6s.

—— A PAGEANT, AND OTHER POEMS. Extra fcp. 8vo. 6s.

—— SPEAKING LIKENESSES. Illustrated by ARTHUR HUGHES. Crown 8vo. 4s. 6d.

ROUSSEAU. By JOHN MORLEY. 2 vols. Globe 8vo. 10s.

ROUTH (E. J.).— A TREATISE ON THE DYNAMICS OF A SYSTEM OF RIGID BODIES. 4th Edition, revised and enlarged. 8vo. In Two Parts.—Part I. ELEMENTARY. 14s.— Part II. ADVANCED. 14s.

—— STABILITY OF A GIVEN STATE OF MO-TION, PARTICULARLY STEADY MOTION. 8vo. 8s. 6d.

ROUTLEDGE (James).— POPULAR PRO-GRESS IN ENGLAND. 8vo. 16s.

RUMFORD (Count).—COMPLETE WORKS OF COUNT RUMFORD. With Memoir by GEORGE ELLIS, and Portrait. 5 vols. 8vo. 4l. 14s. 6d.

RUNAWAY (THE). By the Author of "Mrs. Jerningham's Journal." Globe 8vo. 2s. 6d.

RUSH (Edward).—THE SYNTHETIC LATIN DELECTUS. A First Latin Construing Book. Extra fcp. 8vo. 2s. 6d.

RUSHBROOKE (W. G.).—SYNOPTICON: AN EXPOSITION OF THE COMMON MATTER OF THE SYNOPTIC GOSPELS. Printed in Colours. In Six Parts, and Appendix. 4to.—Part I. 3s. 6d.—Parts II. and III. 7s.—Parts IV. V. and VI., with Indices. 10s. 6d.—Appen-dices. 10s. 6d.—Complete in 1 vol. 35s.

RUSSELL (W. Clark).—MAROONED. 3 vols. Crown 8vo. 31s. 6d.

—— DAMPIER. Portrait. Cr. 8vo. 2s. 6d.

RUSSELL (Sir Charles).—NEW VIEWS ON IRELAND. Crown 8vo. 2s. 6d.

—— THE PARNELL COMMISSION : THE OPEN-ING SPEECH FOR THE DEFENCE. 8vo. 10s.6d. *Popular Edition.* Sewed. 2s.

RUST (Rev. George).—FIRST STEPS TO LATIN PROSE COMPOSITION. 18mo. 1s. 6d.

—— A KEY TO RUST'S FIRST STEPS TO LATIN PROSE COMPOSITION. By W. YATES. 18mo. 3s. 6d.

RUTH AND HER FRIENDS : A STORY FOR GIRLS. Illustrated. Gl. 8vo. 2s. 6d.

RUTHERFORD (W. Gunion, M.A., LL.D.). —FIRST GREEK GRAMMAR. New Edition, enlarged. Globe 8vo. 2s.

—— THE NEW PHRYNICHUS. Being a revised Text of the Ecloga of the Grammarian Phry-nichus, with Introduction and Commentary. 8vo. 18s.

—— BABRIUS. With Introductory Disserta-tions, Critical Notes, Commentary, and Lexicon. 8vo. 12s. 6d.

—— THUCYDIDES. Book IV. A Revision of the Text, illustrating the Principal Causes of Corruption in the Manuscripts of this Author. 8vo. 7s. 6d.

RYLAND (F.).—CHRONOLOGICAL OUTLINES OF ENGLISH LITERATURE. Cr. 8vo.

ST. JOHNSTON (A.).—CAMPING AMONG CANNIBALS. Crown 8vo. 4s. 6d.

SAINTSBURY (George).—A HISTORY OF ELIZABETHAN LITERATURE. Cr. 8vo. 7s.6d.

—— DRYDEN. Crown 8vo. 1s. 6d. ; sewed, 1s.

SALLUST.—CAII SALLUSTII CRISPI CATI-LINA ET JUGURTHA. For Use in Schools. By C. MERIVALE, D.D. New Edition. Fcp. 8vo. 4s. 6d.

The JUGURTHA and the CATILINE may be had separately, 2s. 6d. each.

—— THE CONSPIRACY OF CATILINE AND THE JUGURTHINE WAR. Translated into English by A. W. POLLARD, B.A. Crown 8vo. 6s.

CATILINE separately. Crown 8vo. 3s.

—— BELLUM CATULINAE. Edited, with In-troduction and Notes, by A. M. COOK, M.A. Fcp. 8vo. 4s. 6d.

SALMON (Rev. Prof. George). — NON-MIRACULOUS CHRISTIANITY, AND OTHER SERMONS. 2nd Edition. Crown 8vo. 6s.

—— GNOSTICISM AND AGNOSTICISM, AND OTHER SERMONS. Crown 8vo. 7s. 6d.

SAND (G.).—LA MARE AU DIABLE. Edited by W. E. RUSSELL, M.A. 18mo. 1s.

SANDEAU (Jules).—MADEMOISELLE DE LA SEIGLIÈRE. Ed. H. C. STEEL. 18mo. 1s. 6d.

SANDERSON (F. W.).—HYDROSTATICS FOR BEGINNERS. Globe 8vo. 4s. 6d.

SANDYS (J. E.).—AN EASTER VACATION IN GREECE. Crown 8vo. 3s. 6d.

SAYCE (Prof. A. H.).—THE ANCIENT EM-PIRES OF THE EAST. Crown 8vo. 6s.

—— HERODOTOS. Books I.—III. The An-cient Empires of the East. Edited, with Notes, and Introduction. 8vo. 16s.

SCHILLER.—DIE JUNGFRAU VON ORLEANS. Edited by JOSEPH GOSTWICK. 18mo. 2s. 6d.

—— MARIA STUART. Edited, with Introduc-tion and Notes, by C. SHELDON. 18mo. 2s.6d.

—— SELECTIONS FROM SCHILLER'S LYRICAL POEMS. Edit. E. J. TURNER and E. D. A. MORSHEAD. 18mo. 2s. 6d.

—— WALLENSTEIN. Part I. DAS LÄGER. Edit. by H. B. COTTERILL, M.A. 18mo. 2s.

—— WILHELM TELL. Edited by G. E. FAS-NACHT. 18mo. 2s. 6d.

SCHILLER'S LIFE. By Prof. HEINRICH DÜNTZER. Translated by PERCY E. PIN-KERTON. Crown 8vo. 10s. 6d.

SCHMID. — HEINRICH VON EICHENFELS. Edited by G. E. FASNACHT. 2s. 6d.

SCHMIDT—WHITE.—AN INTRODUCTION TO THE RHYTHMIC AND METRIC OF THE CLASSICAL LANGUAGES. By Dr. J. H. HEINRICH SCHMIDT. Translated by JOHN WILLIAMS WHITE, Ph.D. 8vo. 10s. 6d.

SCIENCE LECTURES AT SOUTH KEN-SINGTON. With Illustrations.—Vol. I. Containing Lectures by Capt. ABNEY, R.E., F.R.S. ; Prof. STOKES ; Prof. A. B. W. KENNEDY, F.R.S., C.E. ; F. J. BRAMWELL, C.E., F.R.S. ; Prof. F. FORBES ; H. C. SORBY, F.R.S. ; J. T. BOTTOMLEY, F.R.S.E.; S. H. VINES, D.Sc. ; Prof. CAREY FORSTER. Crown 8vo. 6s.

Vol. II. Containing Lectures by W. SPOT-TISWOODE, F.R.S. ; Prof. FORBES ; H. W. CHISHOLM ; Prof. T. F. PIGOT ; W. FROUDE, LL.D., F.R.S ; Dr. SIEMENS ; Prof. BAR-RETT ; Dr. BURDON-SANDERSON ; Dr. LAUDER BRUNTON, F.R.S. ; Prof. McLEOD; Sir H. E. ROSCOE, F.R.S. Illust. Cr.8vo. 6s.

SCOTCH SERMONS, 1880. By Principal CAIRD and others. 3rd Edit. 8vo. 10s. 6d.

SCOTT.—THE POETICAL WORKS OF SIR WALTER SCOTT. Edited by Prof. F. T. PALGRAVE. Globe 8vo. 3s. 6d.

—— THE LAY OF THE LAST MINSTREL, and THE LADY OF THE LAKE. Edited, with Introductions and Notes, by Prof. F. T. PALGRAVE. Globe 8vo. 1s.

—— MARMION, and THE LORD OF THE ISLES. By the same Editor. Globe 8vo. 1s.

—— MARMION. A Tale of Flodden Field in Six Cantos. Edited, with Introduction and Notes, by Prof. M. MACMILLAN, B.A. Globe 8vo. 3s. 6d.

—— ROKEBY. By the same. Gl. 8vo. 3s. 6d.

—— THE LAY OF THE LAST MINSTREL. Cantos I.—III. Edited, with Introduction and Notes, by Prof. G. H. STUART, M.A. Globe 8vo. 1s. 6d.

—— THE LADY OF THE LAKE. By the same Editor. Globe 8vo.

SCOTT (Sir Walter). By R. H. HUTTON. Crown 8vo. 1s. 6d. ; sewed, 1s.

SCOTTISH SONG : A SELECTION OF THE LYRICS OF SCOTLAND. Compiled by MARY CARLYLE AITKEN. 18mo. 4s. 6d.

SCRATCHLEY — KINLOCH COOKE.—
AUSTRALIAN DEFENCES AND NEW GUINEA.
Compiled from the Papers of the late Major-
General Sir PETER SCRATCHLEY, R.E.,
K.C.M.G., by C. KINLOCH COOKE, B.A.
8vo. 14s.

SCULPTURE, SPECIMENS OF AN-
CIENT. Egyptian, Etruscan, Greek, and
Roman. Selected from different Collections
in Great Britain by the SOCIETY OF DILET-
TANTI. Vol. II. 5l. 5s.

SEATON (Dr. Edward C.).—A HAND-BOOK
OF VACCINATION. Extra fcp. 8vo. 8s. 6d.

SEELEY (Prof. J. R.).—LECTURES AND
ESSAYS. 8vo. 10s. 6d.

—— THE EXPANSION OF ENGLAND. Two
Courses of Lectures. Crown 8vo. 4s. 6d.

—— OUR COLONIAL EXPANSION. Extracts
from "The Expansion of England." Crown
8vo. 1s.

SEILER.—MICRO-PHOTOGRAPHS IN HIS-
TOLOGY, NORMAL AND PATHOLOGICAL. By
CARL SEILER, M.D. 4to. 31s. 6d.

SELBORNE (Roundell, Earl of).—A DE-
FENCE OF THE CHURCH OF ENGLAND
AGAINST DISESTABLISHMENT. Cr.8vo. 2s.6d.

—— ANCIENT FACTS AND FICTIONS CONCERN-
ING CHURCHES AND TITHES. Cr.8vo. 7s. 6d.

—— THE BOOK OF PRAISE. From the Best
English Hymn Writers. 18mo. 4s. 6d.

—— A HYMNAL. Chiefly from "The Book of
Praise." In various sizes.—A. In Royal
32mo, cloth limp. 6d.—B. Small 18mo,
larger type, cloth limp. 1s.—C. Same
Edition, fine paper, cloth. 1s. 6d.—An
Edition with Music, Selected, Harmonised,
and Composed by JOHN HULLAH. Square
18mo. 3s. 6d.

SERVICE (Rev. John).—SERMONS. With
Portrait. Crown 8vo. 6s.

—— PRAYERS FOR PUBLIC WORSHIP. Crown
8vo. 4s. 6d.

SHAIRP (John Campbell).—GLEN DESSERAY,
AND OTHER POEMS, LYRICAL AND ELEGIAC.
Ed. by F. T. PALGRAVE. Crown 8vo. 6s.

—— BURNS. Crown 8vo. 1s. 6d. ; sewed, 1s.

SHAKESPEARE.—THE WORKS OF WILLIAM
SHAKESPEARE. Cambridge Edition. Edit.
by WM. GEORGE CLARK, M.A., and W.
ALDIS WRIGHT, M.A. 9 vols. 8vo. 10s. 6d.
each.

—— SHAKESPEARE. By the same Editors.
Globe 8vo. 3s. 6d.

—— THE WORKS OF WILLIAM SHAKESPEARE.
Victoria Edition.—Vol. I. Comedies.—Vol.
II. Histories.—Vol. III. Tragedies. In
Three Vols. Crown 8vo. 6s. each.

—— SHAKESPEARE'S SONGS AND SONNETS.
Edited, with Notes, by F. T. PALGRAVE.
18mo. 4s. 6d.

—— CHARLES LAMB'S TALES FROM SHAKS-
PEARE. Edited, with Preface, by the Rev.
A. AINGER, M.A. 18mo. 4s. 6d.
    Globe Readings Edition. For Schools.
    Globe 8vo. 2s.—*Library Edition.* Globe
    8vo. 5s.

—— SHAKSPERE. By Prof. DOWDEN. 18mo. 1s.

SHAKESPEARE.—MUCH ADO ABOUT NO-
THING. Edited by K. DEIGHTON. Globe
8vo. 2s.

—— RICHARD III. Edited by Prof. C. H.
TAWNEY, M.A. Globe 8vo. 2s. 6d.

—— THE WINTER'S TALE. Edited by K.
DEIGHTON. Globe 8vo. 2s. 6d.

—— HENRY V. By the same Editor. Globe
8vo. 2s.

—— OTHELLO. By the same Editor. Globe
8vo. 2s. 6d.

—— CYMBELINE. By the same Editor. Globe
8vo. 2s. 6d.

—— THE TEMPEST. By the same Editor.
Globe 8vo. 1s. 6d.

—— TWELFTH NIGHT ; OR, WHAT YOU WILL.
By the same Editor. Globe 8vo. 1s. 6d.

—— MACBETH. By same Editor. Gl. 8vo. 1s. 6d.

SHANN (G.).—AN ELEMENTARY TREATISE
ON HEAT IN RELATION TO STEAM AND THE
STEAM-ENGINE. Illustr. Cr. 8vo. 4s. 6d.

SHARP (W.).—DANTE GABRIEL ROSSETTI.
Crown 8vo. 10s. 6d.

SHELBURNE.—LIFE OF WILLIAM, EARL
OF SHELBURNE. By Lord EDMOND FITZ-
MAURICE. In 3 vols.—Vol. I. 8vo. 12s.—
Vol. II. 8vo. 12s.—Vol. III. 8vo. 16s.

SHELLEY. SELECTIONS. Edited by STOP-
FORD A. BROOKE. 18mo. 4s. 6d.
    Large Paper Edition. Crown 8vo. 12s. 6d.

SHELLEY. By J. A. SYMONDS, M.A.
Crown 8vo. 1s. 6d. ; sewed, 1s.

SHERIDAN. By Mrs. OLIPHANT. Crown
8vo. 1s. 6d. ; sewed, 1s.

SHIRLEY (W. N.).—ELIJAH : FOUR UNI-
VERSITY SERMONS. Fcp. 8vo. 2s. 6d.

SHORTHOUSE (J. H.).—JOHN INGLESANT :
A ROMANCE. Crown 8vo. 6s.

—— THE LITTLE SCHOOLMASTER MARK : A
SPIRITUAL ROMANCE. Two Parts. Crown
8vo. 2s. 6d. each : or complete, in one
volume, 4s. 6d.

—— SIR PERCIVAL : A STORY OF THE PAST
AND OF THE PRESENT. Crown 8vo. 6s.

—— A TEACHER OF THE VIOLIN, AND OTHER
TALES. Crown 8vo. 6s.

—— THE COUNTESS EVE. Crown 8vo. 6s.

SHORTLAND (Admiral).—NAUTICAL SUR-
VEYING. 8vo.

SHUCKBURGH (E. S.).—PASSAGES FROM
LATIN AUTHORS FOR TRANSLATION INTO
ENGLISH. Crown 8vo. 2s.

SIBSON.— DR. FRANCIS SIBSON'S COL-
LECTED WORKS. Edited by W. M. ORD,
M.D. Illustrated. 4 vols. 8vo. 3l. 3s.

SIDGWICK (Prof. Henry).—THE METHODS
OF ETHICS. 3rd Edit., revised. 8vo. 14s.

—— A SUPPLEMENT TO THE SECOND EDITION.
Containing all the important Additions and
Alterations in the 3rd Edit. 8vo. 6s.

—— THE PRINCIPLES OF POLITICAL ECONOMY.
2nd Edition. 8vo. 16s.

—— OUTLINES OF THE HISTORY OF ETHICS
FOR ENGLISH READERS. Cr. 8vo. 3s. 6d.

—— THE ELEMENTS OF POLITICS. 8vo.

4

SIDNEY, SIR PHILIP. By JOHN ADDINGTON SYMONDS. Cr. 8vo. 1s.6d.; sewed, 1s

SIME (James).—HISTORY OF GERMANY. 2nd Edition. Maps. 18mo. 3s.

—— GEOGRAPHY OF EUROPE. Globe 8vo.

SIMPSON (F. P.).—LATIN PROSE AFTER THE BEST AUTHORS.—Part I. CÆSARIAN PROSE. Extra fcp. 8vo. 2s. 6d.

KEY (for Teachers only). Ex. fcp. 8vo. 5s.

SIMPSON (W.).—AN EPITOME OF THE HISTORY OF THE CHRISTIAN CHURCH. Fcp. 8vo. 3s. 6d.

SKRINE (J. H.).—UNDER TWO QUEENS. Crown 8vo. 3s.

—— A MEMORY OF EDWARD THRING. Crown 8vo. 6s.

SLIP IN THE FENS (A). Globe 8vo. 2s.

SMITH (Barnard).—ARITHMETIC AND ALGEBRA. New Edition. Crown 8vo. 10s. 6d.

—— ARITHMETIC FOR THE USE OF SCHOOLS. New Edition. Crown 8vo. 4s. 6d.

—— KEY TO ARITHMETIC FOR SCHOOLS. New Edition. Crown 8vo. 8s. 6d.

—— EXERCISES IN ARITHMETIC. Crown 8vo, 2 Parts, 1s. each, or complete, 2s.—With Answers, 2s. 6d.—Answers separately, 6d.

—— SCHOOL CLASS-BOOK OF ARITHMETIC. 18mo. 3s.—Or, sold separately, in Three Parts. 1s. each.

—— KEY TO SCHOOL CLASS-BOOK OF ARITHMETIC. In Parts I. II. and III. 2s. 6d. each.

—— SHILLING BOOK OF ARITHMETIC FOR NATIONAL AND ELEMENTARY SCHOOLS. 18mo, cloth.—Or separately, Part I. 2d.; II. 3d.; III. 7d.—With Answers, 1s. 6d.

—— ANSWERS TO THE SHILLING BOOK OF ARITHMETIC. 18mo. 6d.

—— KEY TO THE SHILLING BOOK OF ARITHMETIC. 18mo. 4s. 6d.

—— EXAMINATION PAPERS IN ARITHMETIC. In Four Parts. 18mo. 1s. 6d.—With Answers, 2s.—Answers, 6d.

—— KEY TO EXAMINATION PAPERS IN ARITHMETIC. 18mo. 4s. 6d.

—— THE METRIC SYSTEM OF ARITHMETIC. 3d.

—— A CHART OF THE METRIC SYSTEM OF ARITHMETIC. On a Sheet size, 42 by 34 in., on Roller mounted and varnished. 3s. 6d.

—— EASY LESSONS IN ARITHMETIC. Combining Exercises in Reading, Writing, Spelling, and Dictation. Part I. for Standard I. in National Schools. Crown 8vo. 9d.

—— EXAMINATION CARDS IN ARITHMETIC. With Answers and Hints. Standards I. and II. In box. 1s.—Standards III. IV. and V. In boxes. 1s. each.—Standard VI. in Two Parts. In boxes. 1s. each.

SMITH (Catherine Barnard).—POEMS. Fcp. 8vo. 5s.

SMITH (Charles).—AN ELEMENTARY TREATISE ON CONIC SECTIONS. 7th Edition. Crown 8vo. 7s. 6d.

—— SOLUTIONS OF THE EXAMPLES IN "AN ELEMENTARY TREATISE ON CONIC SECTIONS." Crown 8vo. 10s. 6d.

SMITH (Charles).—AN ELEMENTARY TREATISE ON SOLID GEOMETRY. 2nd Edition. Crown 8vo. 9s. 6d.

—— ELEMENTARY ALGEBRA. Gl 8vo. 4s. 6d.

—— A TREATISE ON ALGEBRA. Cr. 8vo. 7s. 6d.

—— SOLUTIONS OF THE EXAMPLES IN "A TREATISE ON ALGEBRA." Cr. 8vo. 10s. 6d.

SMITH (Goldwin).—THREE ENGLISH STATESMEN. New Edition. Crown 8vo. 5s.

—— COWPER. Crown 8vo. 1s. 6d.; sewed, 1s.

—— PROHIBITIONISM IN CANADA AND THE UNITED STATES. 8vo, sewed. 6d.

SMITH (Horace).—POEMS. Globe 8vo. 5s.

SMITH (J.).—ECONOMIC PLANTS, DICTIONARY OF POPULAR NAMES OF: THEIR HISTORY, PRODUCTS, AND USES. 8vo. 14s.

SMITH (W. Saumarez).—THE BLOOD OF THE NEW COVENANT: A THEOLOGICAL ESSAY. Crown 8vo. 2s. 6d.

SMITH (Rev. Travers).—MAN'S KNOWLEDGE OF MAN AND OF GOD. Crown 8vo. 6s.

SMITH (W. G.).—DISEASES OF FIELD AND GARDEN CROPS, CHIEFLY SUCH AS ARE CAUSED BY FUNGI. With 143 new Illustrations. Fcp. 8vo, 4s. 6d.

SNOWBALL (J. C.).—THE ELEMENTS OF PLANE AND SPHERICAL TRIGONOMETRY. 14th Edition. Crown 8vo. 7s. 6d.

SONNENSCHEIN (A.) and MEIKLEJOHN (J. M. D.).—THE ENGLISH METHOD OF TEACHING TO READ. Fcp. 8vo. Comprising—

THE NURSERY BOOK, containing all the Two Letter Words in the Language. 1d.—Also in Large Type on Four Sheets, with Roller. 1s.

THE FIRST COURSE, consisting of Short Vowels with Single Consonants. 7d.

THE SECOND COURSE, with Combinations and Bridges, consisting of Short Vowels with Double Consonants. 7d.

THE THIRD AND FOURTH COURSES, consisting of Long Vowels and all the Double Vowels in the Language. 7d.

SOPHOCLES.—ŒDIPUS THE KING. Translated into Greek from the English Verse by E. D. A. MORSHEAD, M.A. Fcp. 8vo. 3s.6d.

—— ŒDIPUS TYRANNUS. A Record by L. SPEED and F. R. PRYOR of the performance at Cambridge. Illustr. Small folio. 12s. 6d.

—— By Prof. L. CAMPBELL. Fcp. 8vo. 1s. 6d.

SOUTHEY. By Prof. DOWDEN. Crown 8vo. 1s. 6d.; sewed, 1s.

SPENDER (J. Kent).—THERAPEUTIC MEANS FOR THE RELIEF OF PAIN. 8vo. 8s. 6d.

SPENSER.—COMPLETE WORKS OF EDMUND SPENSER. Ed. by R. MORRIS, with Memoir by J. W. HALES. Globe 8vo. 3s. 6d.

SPENSER. By the Very Rev. Dean CHURCH. Cr. 8vo. 1s. 6d.; swd., 1s.—Library Ed., 5s.

SPINOZA: A STUDY OF. By JAMES MARTINEAU, LL.D. 2nd Ed. Cr. 8vo. 6s.

SPOTTISWOODE (W.).—POLARISATION OF LIGHT. Illustrated. Crown 8vo. 3s. 6d.

STANLEY (Very Rev. A. P.).—THE ATHA-
NASIAN CREED. Crown 8vo. 2s.

—— THE NATIONAL THANKSGIVING. Sermons
preached in Westminster Abbey. 2nd Ed.
Crown 8vo. 2s. 6d.

—— ADDRESSES AND SERMONS DELIVERED AT
ST. ANDREWS IN 1872—75 and 1877. Crown
8vo. 5s.

—— ADDRESSES AND SERMONS DELIVERED
DURING A VISIT TO THE UNITED STATES
AND CANADA IN 1878. Crown 8vo. 6s.

STANLEY (Hon. Maude).—CLUBS FOR
WORKING GIRLS. Crown 8vo. 6s.

STATESMAN'S YEAR-BOOK (THE). A
Statistical and Historical Annual of the
States of the Civilised World for the year
1890. Twenty-seventh Annual Publication.
Revised after Official Returns. Edited by
J. SCOTT KELTIE. Crown 8vo. 10s. 6d.

STATHAM (R.).—BLACKS, BOERS, AND
BRITISH. Crown 8vo. 6s.

STEPHEN (Sir J. Fitzjames, Q.C., K.C.S.I.).
—A DIGEST OF THE LAW OF EVIDENCE.
5th Edition. Crown 8vo. 6s.

—— A DIGEST OF THE CRIMINAL LAW:
CRIMES AND PUNISHMENTS. 4th Edition.
8vo. 16s.

—— A DIGEST OF THE LAW OF CRIMINAL
PROCEDURE IN INDICTABLE OFFENCES. By
Sir JAMES F. STEPHEN, K.C.S.I., etc., and
HERBERT STEPHEN, LL.M. 8vo. 12s. 6d.

—— A HISTORY OF THE CRIMINAL LAW OF
ENGLAND. 3 vols. 8vo. 48s.

—— THE STORY OF NUNCOMAR AND THE IM-
PEACHMENT OF SIR ELIJAH IMPEY. 2 vols.
Crown 8vo. 15s.

—— A GENERAL VIEW OF THE CRIMINAL
LAW OF ENGLAND. 2nd Edition. 8vo.

STEPHEN (J. K.).—INTERNATIONAL LAW
AND INTERNATIONAL RELATIONS. Crown
8vo. 6s.

STEPHEN (Leslie).—JOHNSON. Crown 8vo.
1s. 6d. ; sewed, 1s.

—— SWIFT. Crown 8vo. 1s. 6d. ; sewed, 1s.

—— POPE. Crown 8vo. 1s. 6d. ; sewed, 1s.

STEPHEN (Caroline E.).—THE SERVICE OF
THE POOR. Crown 8vo. 6s. 6d.

STEPHENS (J. B.).—CONVICT ONCE, AND
OTHER POEMS. Crown 8vo. 7s. 6d.

STERNE. By H. D. TRAILL. Crown 8vo.
1s. 6d. ; sewed, 1s.

STEVENS (F. H.).—ELEMENTARY MEN-
SURATION. With Exercises in the Mensuration of Plane and Solid Figures. Globe 8vo.

STEVENSON (J. J.).—HOUSE ARCHITEC-
TURE. With Illustrations. 2 vols. Royal
8vo. 18s. each. Vol. I. ARCHITECTURE. Vol.
II. HOUSE PLANNING.

STEWART (Aubrey).—THE TALE OF TROY.
Done into English. Globe 8vo. 3s. 6d.

STEWART (Prof. Balfour).—LESSONS IN
ELEMENTARY PHYSICS. With Illustrations
and Coloured Diagram. New Edition. Fcp.
8vo. 4s. 6d.

—— PRIMER OF PHYSICS. Illustrated. New
Edition, with Questions. 18mo. 1s.

STEWART (Prof. Balfour).—QUESTIONS ON
STEWART'S LESSONS ON ELEMENTARY
PHYSICS. By T. H. CORE. 12mo. 2s.

STEWART (Prof. Balfour) and GEE (W. W.
Haldane).—LESSONS IN ELEMENTARY PRAC-
TICAL PHYSICS. Crown 8vo. Illustrated.
Vol. I. GENERAL PHYSICAL PROCESSES. 6s.
—Vol. II. ELECTRICITY AND MAGNETISM.
Cr. 8vo. 7s. 6d.—Vol. III. OPTICS, HEAT,
AND SOUND.

—— PRACTICAL PHYSICS FOR SCHOOLS AND
THE JUNIOR STUDENTS OF COLLEGES. Globe
8vo. Vol. I. ELECTRICITY AND MAGNETISM.
2s. 6d.—Vol. II. HEAT, LIGHT, AND SOUND.

STEWART (Prof. Balfour) and TAIT (P. G.).
—THE UNSEEN UNIVERSE ; OR, PHYSICAL
SPECULATIONS ON A FUTURE STATE. 15th
Edition. Crown 8vo. 6s.

STEWART (S. A.) and CORRY (T. H.).—
A FLORA OF THE NORTH-EAST OF IRELAND.
Crown 8vo. 5s. 6d.

STOKES (Sir George G.).—ON LIGHT. The
Burnett Lectures. Crown 8vo. 7s. 6d.

STONE (W. H.).—ELEMENTARY LESSONS ON
SOUND. Illustrated. Fcap. 8vo. 3s. 6d.

STRACHAN (J. S.) and WILKINS (A. S.).—
ANALECTA. Passages for Translation. Cr.
8vo. 5s.

STRACHEY (Lieut.-Gen. R.).—LECTURES
ON GEOGRAPHY. Crown 8vo. 4s. 6d.

STRAFFORD. By H. D. TRAILL. With
Portrait. Crown 8vo. 2s. 6d.

STRANGFORD (Viscountess). — EGYPTIAN
SEPULCHRES AND SYRIAN SHRINES. New
Edition. Crown 8vo. 7s. 6d.

STRETTELL (Alma).—SPANISH AND ITAL-
IAN FOLK SONGS. Illust. Roy. 16mo. 12s. 6d.

STUBBS (Rev. C. W.).—FOR CHRIST AND
CITY. Sermons and Addresses. Cr. 8vo.

SURGERY, THE INTERNATIONAL
ENCYCLOPAEDIA OF. A Systematic
Treatise on the Theory and Practice of Surgery by Authors of Various Nations. Edited
by JOHN ASHHURST, Jun., M.D., Professor
of Clinical Surgery in the University of Penn-
sylvania. 6 vols. Royal 8vo. 31s. 6d. each.

SWIFT. By LESLIE STEPHEN. Crown 8vo.
1s. 6d. ; sewed, 1s.

SYLLABUS OF PLANE GEOMETRY, A.
Corresponding to Euclid, Books I. to VI.
Prepared by the Association for the Improvement of Geometrical Teaching. 9th Edition,
revised. 12mo. 1s.

SYLLABUS OF MODERN PLANE GEO-
METRY. Association for the Improvement
of Geometrical Teaching. Crown 8vo. 1s.

SYLLABUS OF ELEMENTARY DYNA-
MICS. With an Appendix on the Alterna-
tive Mode of regarding symbols in Physical
Equations. 4to. 1s.

SYMONS (Arthur).—DAYS AND NIGHTS:
POEMS. Globe 8vo. 6s.

SYMONDS (J. A.).—SHELLEY. Crown 8vo.
1s. 6d. ; sewed, 1s.

—— SIR PHILIP SIDNEY. 1s. 6d. ; sewed, 1s.

TACITUS, The Works of. Transl. by A. J. Church, M.A., and W. J. Brodribb, M.A. The History of Tacitus. 4th Edition. Crown 8vo. 6s.

The Agricola and Germania. A Revised Text. With Notes. Fcp. 8vo. 3s. 6d. The Agricola and Germania may be had separately. 2s. each.

The Annals. Book VI. With Introduction and Notes. Fcp. 8vo. 2s. 6d.

The Agricola and Germania. With the Dialogue on Oratory. Translated. Crown 8vo. 4s. 6d.

Annals of Tacitus. Translated. 5th Ed. Crown 8vo. 7s. 6d.

—— The Annals. Edited by Prof. G. O. Holbrooke, M.A. 8vo. 16s.

—— The Histories. Books I. and II. Ed. by A. D. Godley, M.A. Fcp. 8vo. 5s.

—— The Histories. Books III.—V. Edited by A. D. Godley, M.A. Fcp. 8vo. 5s.

TACITUS. By A. J. Church, M.A., and W. J. Brodribb, M.A. Fcp. 8vo. 1s. 6d.

TAIT (Archbishop).—The Present Position of the Church of England. Being the Charge delivered at his Primary Visitation. 3rd Edition. 8vo. 3s. 6d.

—— Duties of the Church of England. Being Seven Addresses delivered at his Second Visitation. 8vo. 4s. 6d.

—— The Church of the Future. Charges delivered at his Third Quadrennial Visitation. 2nd Edition. Crown 8vo. 3s. 6d.

TAIT.—The Life of Archibald Campbell Tait, Archbishop of Canterbury. By the Very Rev. the Dean of Windsor and Rev. W. Benham, B.D. 8vo.

TAIT.—Catharine and Crawford Tait, Wife and Son of Archibald Campbell, Archbishop of Canterbury: A Memoir. Edited by the Rev. W. Benham, B.D. Crown 8vo. 6s. Popular Edition, abridged. Cr. 8vo. 2s. 6d.

TAIT (C. W. A.).—Analysis of English History, based on Green's "Short History of the English People." Crown 8vo. 3s. 6d.

TAIT (Prof. P. G.).—Lectures on some Recent Advances in Physical Science. 3rd Edition. Crown 8vo. 9s.

—— Heat. With Illustrations. Cr. 8vo. 6s.

TAIT (P. G.) and STEELE (W. J.).—A Treatise on Dynamics of a Particle. 6th Edition. Crown 8vo. 12s.

TANNER (Prof. Henry).—First Principles of Agriculture. 18mo. 1s.

—— The Abbott's Farm ; or, Practice with Science. Crown 8vo. 3s. 6d.

—— The Alphabet of the Principles of Agriculture. Extra fcp. 8vo. 6d.

—— Further Steps in the Principles of Agriculture. Extra fcp. 8vo. 1s.

—— Elementary School Readings in the Principles of Agriculture for the Third Stage. Extra fcp. 8vo. 1s.

—— Elementary Lessons in the Science of Agricultural Practice. Fcp. 8vo. 3s. 6d.

TAYLOR (Franklin).—Primer of Pianoforte Playing. 18mo. 1s.

TAYLOR (Isaac).—The Restoration of Belief. Crown 8vo. 8s. 6d.

TAYLOR (Isaac). —Words and Places. 9th Edition. Maps. Globe 8vo. 6s.

—— Etruscan Researches. With Woodcuts. 8vo. 14s.

—— Greeks and Goths : A Study of the Runes. 8vo. 9s.

TAYLOR (Sedley).—Sound and Music. 2nd Edition. Extra Crown 8vo. 8s. 6d.

—— A System of Sight-Singing from the Established Musical Notation. 8vo.

TEBAY (S.).—Elementary Mensuration for Schools. Extra fcp. 8vo. 3s. 6d.

TEGETMEIER (W. B.).—Household Management and Cookery. 18mo. 1s.

TEMPLE (Right Rev. Frederick, D.D., Bishop of London).—Sermons preached in the Chapel of Rugby School. 3rd and Cheaper Edition. Extra fcp. 8vo. 4s. 6d.

—— Second Series. 3rd Ed. Ex. fcp. 8vo. 6s.

—— Third Series. 4th Ed. Ex. fcp. 8vo. 6s.

—— The Relations between Religion and Science. Bampton Lectures, 1884. 7th and Cheaper Edition. Crown 8vo. 6s.

TENNYSON (Lord).—Complete Works. New and enlarged Edition, with Portrait. Crown 8vo. 7s. 6d. School Edition. In Four Parts. Crown 8vo. 2s. 6d. each.

—— Works. Library Edition. In 8 vols. Globe 8vo. 5s. each. Each volume may be had separately.—Poems. 2 vols.—Idylls of the King.—The Princess, and Maud. —Enoch Arden, and In Memoriam.— Ballads, and other Poems. — Queen Mary, and Harold.—Becket, and other Plays.

—— Works. Extra Fcp. 8vo. Edition, on Hand-made Paper. In 7 volumes (supplied in sets only). 3l. 13s. 6d. — Vol. I. Early Poems ; II. Lucretius, and other Poems ; III. Idylls of the King ; IV. The Princess, and Maud ; V. Enoch Arden, and In Memoriam ; VI. Queen Mary, and Harold ; VII. Ballads, and other Poems.

—— The Collected Works. Miniature Edition, in 14 volumes, namely, "The Poetical Works," 10 vols. in a box. 21s. —"The Dramatic Works," 4 vols. in a box. 10s. 6d.

—— Lyrical Poems. Selected and Annotated by Prof. F. T. Palgrave. 18mo. 4s. 6d. Large Paper Edition. 8vo. 9s.

—— In Memoriam. 18mo. 4s. 6d. Large Paper Edition. 8vo. 9s.

—— The Tennyson Birthday Book. Edit. by Emily Shakespear. 18mo. 2s. 6d.

—— The Brook. With 20 Illustrations by A. Woodruff. 32mo. 2s. 6d.

—— Selections from Tennyson. With Introduction and Notes, by F. J. Rowe, M.A., and W. T. Webb, M.A. Globe 8vo. 3s. 6d.

TENNYSON.—A COMPANION TO "IN MEMORIAM." By ELIZABETH R. CHAPMAN. Globe 8vo. 2s.

—— *The Original Editions.* Fcp. 8vo.
POEMS. 6s.
MAUD, AND OTHER POEMS. 3s. 6d.
THE PRINCESS. 3s. 6d.
IDYLLS OF THE KING. (Collected.) 6s.
ENOCH ARDEN, etc. 3s. 6d.
THE HOLY GRAIL, AND OTHER POEMS. 4s.6d.
IN MEMORIAM. 4s.
BALLADS, AND OTHER POEMS. 5s.
HAROLD: A DRAMA. 6s.
QUEEN MARY: A DRAMA. 6s.
THE CUP, AND THE FALCON. 6s.
BECKET. 6s.
TIRESIAS, AND OTHER POEMS. 6s.
LOCKSLEY HALL, SIXTY YEARS AFTER, etc. 6s.
DEMETER, AND OTHER POEMS. 6s.
—— THE ROYAL EDITION. 1 vol. 8vo. 16s.
—— SELECTIONS FROM TENNYSON'S WORKS. Square 8vo. 3s. 6d.; gilt, square 8vo, 4s.
—— SONGS FROM TENNYSON'S WRITINGS. Square 8vo. 2s. 6d.

TENNYSON (Hallam). — JACK AND THE BEAN-STALK. With 40 Illustrations by RANDOLPH CALDECOTT. Fcp. 4to. 3s. 6d.

TERENCE.—HAUTON TIMORUMENOS. Edit. by E. S. SHUCKBURGH, M.A. Fcp. 8vo. 3s.—With Translation, 4s. 6d.

—— PHORMIO. Edited by Rev. JOHN BOND, and A. S. WALPOLE. Fcp. 8vo. 4s. 6d.

—— SCENES FROM THE ANDRIA. Edited by F. W. CORNISH, M.A. 18mo. 1s. 6d.

TERESA (ST.), LIFE OF. By the Author of "Devotions before and after Holy Communion." Crown 8vo. 8s. 6d.

THACKERAY. By ANTHONY TROLLOPE. Crown 8vo. 1s. 6d.; sewed, 1s.

THEOCRITUS, BION, AND MOSCHUS. Rendered into English Prose, with Introductory Essay, by A. LANG, M.A. 18mo. 4s.6d.
Large Paper Edition. 8vo. 9s.

THOMPSON (Edith).—HISTORY OF ENGLAND. New Edit., with Maps. 18mo. 2s.6d.

THOMPSON (Prof. Silvanus P.).—ELECTRICITY AND MAGNETISM, ELEMENTARY. Illustrated. New Edition. Fcp. 8vo. 4s. 6d.

THOMPSON (G. Carslake)—PUBLIC OPINION AND LORD BEACONSFIELD, 1875—80. 2 vols. 8vo. 36s.

THOMSON (J. J.).—A TREATISE ON THE MOTION OF VORTEX RINGS. 8vo. 6s.

—— APPLICATIONS OF DYNAMICS TO PHYSICS AND CHEMISTRY. Crown 8vo. 7s. 6d.

THOMSON (Sir Wm.)—REPRINT OF PAPERS ON ELECTROSTATICS AND MAGNETISM. 2nd Edition. 8vo. 18s.

—— POPULAR LECTURES AND ADDRESSES. In 3 vols.—Vol. I. CONSTITUTION OF MATTER. Illustrated. Crown 8vo. 6s.

THOMSON (Sir C. Wyville).—THE DEPTHS OF THE SEA. An Account of the General Results of the Dredging Cruises of H.M.SS. "Lightning" and "Porcupine" during the Summers of 1868-69-70. With Illustrations, Maps, and Plans. 2nd Edit. 8vo. 31s. 6d.

—— THE VOYAGE OF THE "CHALLENGER": THE ATLANTIC. With Illustrations, Coloured Maps, Charts, etc. 2 vols. 8vo. 45s.

THORNTON (W. T.).—A PLEA FOR PEASANT PROPRIETORS. New Edit. Cr. 8vo. 7s. 6d.

—— OLD-FASHIONED ETHICS AND COMMON-SENSE METAPHYSICS. 8vo. 10s. 6d.

—— INDIAN PUBLIC WORKS, AND COGNATE INDIAN TOPICS. Crown 8vo. 8s. 6d.

—— WORD FOR WORD FROM HORACE: THE ODES LITERALLY VERSIFIED. Cr.8vo. 7s.6d.

THORNTON (J.).—FIRST LESSONS IN BOOK-KEEPING. New Edition. Crown 8vo. 2s. 6d.

—— KEY TO "FIRST LESSONS IN BOOK-KEEPING." Containing all the Exercises fully worked out, with brief Notes. Oblong 4to. 10s. 6d.

THORPE (Prof. T. E.)—A SERIES OF PROBLEMS, FOR USE IN COLLEGES AND SCHOOLS. New Edition, with Key. 18mo. 2s.

THRING (Rev. Edward).—A CONSTRUING BOOK. Fcp. 8vo. 2s. 6d.

—— A LATIN GRADUAL. 2nd Ed. 18mo. 2s.6d

—— THE ELEMENTS OF GRAMMAR TAUGHT IN ENGLISH. 5th Edition. 18mo. 2s.

—— EDUCATION AND SCHOOL. 2nd Edition. Crown 8vo. 6s.

—— A MANUAL OF MOOD CONSTRUCTIONS. Extra fcp. 8vo. 1s. 6d.

—— THOUGHTS ON LIFE SCIENCE. 2nd Edit. Crown 8vo. 7s. 6d.

—— A MEMORY OF EDWARD THRING. By J. H. SKRINE. Portrait. Crown 8vo. 6s.

THROUGH THE RANKS TO A COMMISSION. New Edit. Cr. 8vo. 2s. 6d.

THRUPP (Rev. J. F.)—INTRODUCTION TO THE STUDY AND USE OF THE PSALMS. 2nd Edition. 2 vols. 8vo. 25s.

THUCYDIDES.--THE SICILIAN EXPEDITION. Books VI. and VII. Edited by the Rev. PERCIVAL FROST, M.A. Fcp. 8vo. 5s.

—— THE CAPTURE OF SPHACTERIA. Book IV. Chaps. 1—41. Edit. by C. E. GRAVES, M.A. 18mo. 1s. 6d.

—— BOOK IV. By the same. Fcp. 8vo. 5s.

—— THE RISE OF THE ATHENIAN EMPIRE. Being Selections from Book I. Edited by F. H. COLSON, M.A. 18mo. 1s. 6d.

—— BOOK IV. A Revision of the Text, illustrating the Principal Causes of Corruption in the Manuscripts of this Author. By WILLIAM G. RUTHERFORD, M.A., LL.D. 8vo. 7s.6d.

THUDICHUM (J. L. W.) and DUPRÉ (A.). —TREATISE ON THE ORIGIN, NATURE, AND VARIETIES OF WINE. Medium 8vo. 25s.

TODHUNTER (Isaac).—EUCLID FOR COLLEGES AND SCHOOLS. 18mo. 3s. 6d.

—— KEY TO EXERCISES IN EUCLID. Crown 8vo. 6s. 6d.

TODHUNTER (I.). — MENSURATION FOR BEGINNERS. With Examples. 18mo. 2*s.* 6*d.*

—— KEY TO MENSURATION FOR BEGINNERS. By Rev. FR. L. MCCARTHY. Cr. 8vo. 7*s.* 6*d.*

—— ALGEBRA FOR BEGINNERS. With numerous Examples. 18mo. 2*s.* 6*d.*

—— KEY TO ALGEBRA FOR BEGINNERS. Cr. 8vo. 6*s.* 6*d.*

—— TRIGONOMETRY FOR BEGINNERS. With numerous Examples. 18mo. 2*s.* 6*d.*

—— KEY TO TRIGONOMETRY FOR BEGINNERS. Crown 8vo. 8*s.* 6*d.*

—— MECHANICS FOR BEGINNERS. With numerous Examples. 18mo. 4*s.*

—— KEY TO MECHANICS FOR BEGINNERS. 6*s.* 6*d.*

—— ALGEBRA FOR THE USE OF COLLEGES AND SCHOOLS. Crown 8vo. 7*s.* 6*d.*

—— KEY TO ALGEBRA FOR COLLEGES AND SCHOOLS. Crown 8vo. 10*s.* 6*d.*

—— A TREATISE ON THE THEORY OF EQUATIONS. Crown 8vo. 7*s.* 6*d.*

—— PLANE TRIGONOMETRY FOR COLLEGES AND SCHOOLS. Crown 8vo. 5*s.*

—— KEY TO PLANE TRIGONOMETRY. Crown 8vo. 10*s.* 6*d.*

—— A TREATISE ON SPHERICAL TRIGONOMETRY FOR THE USE OF COLLEGES AND SCHOOLS. Crown 8vo. 4*s.* 6*d.*

—— A TREATISE ON PLANE CO-ORDINATE GEOMETRY. Crown 8vo. 7*s.* 6*d.*

—— SOLUTIONS AND PROBLEMS CONTAINED IN A TREATISE ON PLANE CO-ORDINATE GEOMETRY. By C. W. BOURNE, M.A. Crown 8vo. 10*s.* 6*d.*

—— A TREATISE ON THE DIFFERENTIAL CALCULUS. Crown 8vo. 10*s.* 6*d.*

—— KEY TO TREATISE ON THE DIFFERENTIAL CALCULUS. By H. ST. J. HUNTER, M.A. Crown 8vo. 10*s.* 6*d.*

—— A TREATISE ON THE INTEGRAL CALCULUS. Crown 8vo. 10*s.* 6*d.*

—— KEY TO TREATISE ON THE INTEGRAL CALCULUS AND ITS APPLICATIONS. By H. ST. J. HUNTER, M.A. Cr. 8vo. 10*s.* 6*d.*

—— EXAMPLES OF ANALYTICAL GEOMETRY OF THREE DIMENSIONS. Crown 8vo. 4*s.*

—— THE CONFLICT OF STUDIES. 8vo. 10*s.* 6*d.*

—— AN ELEMENTARY TREATISE ON LAPLACE'S, LAMÉ'S, AND BESSEL'S FUNCTIONS. Crown 8vo. 10*s.* 6*d.*

—— A TREATISE ON ANALYTICAL STATICS. Edited by J. D. EVERETT, M.A., F.R.S. 5th Edition. Crown 8vo. 10*s.* 6*d.*

TOM BROWN'S SCHOOL-DAYS. By AN OLD BOY.
Golden Treasury Edition. 18mo. 4*s.* 6*d.*
Illustrated Edition. Crown 8vo. 6*s.*
Uniform Edition. Crown 8vo. 3*s.* 6*d.*
People's Edition. 18mo. 2*s.*
People's Sixpenny Edition. With Illustrations. Medium 4to. 6*d.*—Also uniform with the Sixpenny Edition of Charles Kingsley's Novels. Medium 8vo. 6*d.*

TOM BROWN AT OXFORD. By the Author of "Tom Brown's School-days." Illustrated. Crown 8vo. 6*s.*
Uniform Edition. Crown 8vo. 3*s.* 6*d.*

TOURGÉNIEF.—VIRGIN SOIL. Translated by ASHTON W. DILKE. Crown 8vo. 6*s.*

TOZER (H. F.).—CLASSICAL GEOGRAPHY. 18mo. 1*s.*

TRAIL (H. D.).—STERNE. Crown 8vo. 1*s.* 6*d.* ; sewed, 1*s.*

—— CENTRAL GOVERNMENT. Cr. 8vo. 3*s.* 6*d.*

—— WILLIAM III. Crown 8vo. 2*s.* 6*d.*

—— STRAFFORD. Portrait. Cr. 8vo. 2*s.* 6*d.*

—— COLERIDGE. Cr. 8vo. 1*s.* 6*d.* ; sewed, 1*s.*

TRENCH (R. Chenevix).—HULSEAN LECTURES. 8vo. 7*s.* 6*d.*

TRENCH (Capt. F.).—THE RUSSO-INDIAN QUESTION. Crown 8vo. 7*s.* 6*d.*

TREVELYAN (Sir Geo. Otto).—CAWNPORE. Crown 8vo. 6*s.*

TRISTRAM (W. Outram).—COACHING DAYS AND COACHING WAYS. Illustrated by HERBERT RAILTON and HUGH THOMSON. Extra Crown 4to. 21*s.*

TROLLOPE (Anthony).—THACKERAY. Cr. 8vo. 1*s.* 6*d.* ; sewed, 1*s.*

TRUMAN (Jos.).—AFTER-THOUGHTS: POEMS. Crown 8vo. 3*s.* 6*d.*

TULLOCH (Principal).—THE CHRIST OF THE GOSPELS AND THE CHRIST OF MODERN CRITICISM. Extra fcp. 8vo. 4*s.* 6*d.*

TURNER'S LIBER STUDIORUM. A Description and a Catalogue. By W. G. RAWLINSON. Medium 8vo. 12*s.* 6*d.*

TURNER (Charles Tennyson).—COLLECTED SONNETS, OLD AND NEW. Ex. fcp. 8vo. 7*s.* 6*d.*

TURNER (Rev. Geo.).—SAMOA, A HUNDRED YEARS AGO AND LONG BEFORE. Preface by E. B. TYLOR, F.R.S. Crown 8vo. 9*s.*

TURNER (H. H.).—A COLLECTION OF EXAMPLES ON HEAT AND ELECTRICITY. Cr. 8vo. 2*s.* 6*d.*

TYLOR (E. B.).—ANTHROPOLOGY. With Illustrations. Crown 8vo. 7*s.* 6*d.*

TYRWHITT (Rev. R. St. John). — OUR SKETCHING CLUB. 4th Ed. Cr. 8vo. 7*s.* 6*d.*

—— FREE FIELD. Lyrics, chiefly Descriptive. Globe 8vo. 3*s.* 6*d.*

—— BATTLE AND AFTER: Concerning Sergt. Thomas Atkins, Grenadier Guards; and other Verses. Globe 8vo. 3*s.* 6*d.*

UHLAND.—SELECT BALLADS. Edited by G. E. FASNACHT. 18mo. 1*s.*

UNDERHILL (H. G.).—EASY EXERCISES IN GREEK ACCIDENCE. Globe 8vo. 2*s.*

UPPINGHAM BY THE SEA. By J. H. S. Crown 8vo. 3*s.* 6*d.*

VAUGHAN (Very Rev. Charles J.).—NOTES FOR LECTURES ON CONFIRMATION. 14th Edition. Fcp. 8vo. 1*s.* 6*d.*

—— MEMORIALS OF HARROW SUNDAYS. 5th Edition. Crown 8vo. 10*s.* 6*d.*

—— LECTURES ON THE EPISTLE TO THE PHILIPPIANS. 4th Edition. Cr. 8vo. 7*s.* 6*d.*

VAUGHAN (Very Rev. C. J.).—LECTURES ON THE REVELATION OF ST. JOHN. 5th Edition. Crown 8vo. 10s. 6d.

—— EPIPHANY, LENT, AND EASTER. 3rd Edition. Crown 8vo. 10s. 5d.

—— HEROES OF FAITH. 2nd Ed. Cr. 8vo. 6s.

—— THE BOOK AND THE LIFE, AND OTHER SERMONS. 3rd Edition. Fcp. 8vo. 4s. 6d.

—— ST. PAUL'S EPISTLE TO THE ROMANS. The Greek Text with English Notes. 6th Edition. Crown 8vo. 7s. 6d.

—— TWELVE DISCOURSES ON SUBJECTS CONNECTED WITH THE LITURGY AND WORSHIP OF THE CHURCH OF ENGLAND. 4th Edition. Fcp. 8vo. 6s.

—— WORDS FROM THE GOSPELS. 3rd Edition. Fcp. 8vo. 4s. 6d.

—— THE EPISTLES OF ST. PAUL. For English Readers. Part I. containing the First Epistle to the Thessalonians. 2nd Ed. 8vo. 1s. 6d.

—— THE CHURCH OF THE FIRST DAYS. Series I. THE CHURCH OF JERUSALEM. 3rd Edition. 4s. 6d.—II. THE CHURCH OF THE GENTILES. 4s. 6d.—III. THE CHURCH OF THE WORLD. Fcp. 8vo. 4s. 6d.

—— LIFE'S WORK AND GOD'S DISCIPLINE. 3rd Edition. Extra fcp. 8vo. 2s. 6d.

—— THE WHOLESOME WORDS OF JESUS CHRIST. 2nd Edition. Fcp. 8vo. 3s. 6d.

—— FOES OF FAITH. 2nd Ed. Fcp. 8vo. 3s. 6d.

—— CHRIST SATISFYING THE INSTINCTS OF HUMANITY. 2nd Ed. Extra fcp. 8vo. 3s. 6d.

—— COUNSELS FOR YOUNG STUDENTS. Fcp. 8vo. 2s. 6d.

—— THE TWO GREAT TEMPTATIONS. 2nd Edition. Fcp. 8vo. 3s. 6d.

—— ADDRESSES FOR YOUNG CLERGYMEN. Extra fcp. 8vo. 4s. 6d.

—— "MY SON, GIVE ME THINE HEART." Extra fcp. 8vo. 5s.

—— REST AWHILE. Addresses to Toilers in the Ministry. Extra fcp. 8vo. 5s.

—— TEMPLE SERMONS. Crown 8vo. 10s. 6d.

—— AUTHORISED OR REVISED? Sermons on some of the Texts in which the Revised Version differs from the Authorised. Crown 8vo. 7s. 6d.

—— ST. PAUL'S EPISTLE TO THE PHILIPPIANS. With Translation, Paraphrase, and Notes for English Readers. Crown 8vo. 5s.

—— LESSONS OF THE CROSS AND PASSION. WORDS FROM THE CROSS. THE REIGN OF SIN. THE LORD'S PRAYER. Four Courses of Lent Lectures. Crown 8vo. 10s. 6d.

—— UNIVERSITY SERMONS, NEW AND OLD. Crown 8vo. 10s. 6d.

—— THE EPISTLE TO THE HEBREWS. With Notes. Crown 8vo.

VAUGHAN (D. J.).—THE PRESENT TRIAL OF FAITH. Crown 8vo. 9s.

VAUGHAN (E. T.).—SOME REASONS OF OUR CHRISTIAN HOPE. Hulsean Lectures for 1875. Crown 8vo. 6s. 6d.

VELEY (Marg.).—A GARDEN OF MEMORIES; MRS. AUSTIN; LIZZIE'S BARGAIN. Three Stories. 2 vols. Globe 8vo. 12s.

VENN (Rev. John).—ON SOME CHARACTERISTICS OF BELIEF, SCIENTIFIC AND RELIGIOUS. Hulsean Lectures, 1869. 8vo. 7s. 6d.

—— THE LOGIC OF CHANCE. 2nd Edition. Crown 8vo. 10s. 6d.

—— SYMBOLIC LOGIC. Crown 8vo. 10s. 6d.

—— THE PRINCIPLES OF EMPIRICAL OR INDUCTIVE LOGIC. 8vo. 18s.

VERNEY (Lady).—HOW THE PEASANT OWNER LIVES IN PARTS OF FRANCE, GERMANY, ITALY, AND RUSSIA. Cr. 8vo. 3s. 6d.

VERRALL (A. W.).—STUDIES, LITERARY AND HISTORICAL, IN THE ODES OF HORACE. 8vo. 8s. 6d.

VICTORIA UNIVERSITY CALENDAR, 1890. Crown 8vo. 1s.

VICTOR EMMANUEL II., FIRST KING OF ITALY. By G. S. GODKIN. 2nd Edition. Crown 8vo. 6s.

VIDA: STUDY OF A GIRL. By AMY DUNSMUIR. 3rd Edition. Crown 8vo. 6s.

VINCENT (Sir E.) and DICKSON (T. G.).—HANDBOOK TO MODERN GREEK. 3rd Ed. Crown 8vo. 6s.

VIRGIL.—THE WORKS OF VIRGIL RENDERED INTO ENGLISH PROSE. By JAS. LONSDALE, M.A., and S. LEE, M.A. Globe 8vo. 3s. 6d.

—— THE ÆNEID. Translated into English Prose by J. W. MACKAIL, M.A. Crown 8vo. 7s. 6d.

—— GEORGICS, I. Edited by T. E. PAGE, M.A. 18mo. 1s. 6d.

—— GEORGICS II. Edited by Rev. J. H. SKRINE, M.A. 18mo. 1s. 6d.

—— ÆNEID, I. Edited by A. S. WALPOLE, M.A. 18mo. 1s. 6d.

—— ÆNEID, II. Edit. by T. E. PAGE, M.A. 18mo. 1s. 6d.

—— ÆNEID, II. and III.: THE NARRATIVE OF ÆNEAS. Edit. by E. W. HOWSON, M.A. Fcp. 8vo. 3s.

—— ÆNEID, III. Edited by T. E. PAGE, M.A. 18mo. 1s. 6d.

—— ÆNEID, IV. Edited by Rev. H. M. STEPHENSON, M.A. 18mo. 1s. 6d.

—— ÆNEID, V.: THE FUNERAL GAMES. Ed. by Rev. A. CALVERT, M.A. 18mo. 1s. 6d.

—— ÆNEID, VI. Edit. by T. E. PAGE, M.A. 18mo. 1s. 6d.

—— ÆNEID, VII.: THE WRATH OF TURNUS. Ed. by Rev. A. CALVERT, M.A. 18mo. 1s. 6d.

—— ÆNEID, IX. Edited by Rev. H. M. STEPHENSON, M.A. 18mo. 1s. 6d.

—— SELECTIONS. Edited by E. S. SHUCKBURGH, M.A. 18mo. 1s. 6d.

VIRGIL. By Prof. NETTLESHIP, M.A. Fcp. 8vo. 1s. 6d.

VITA.—LINKS AND CLUES. By VITA (the Hon. Lady WELBY-GREGORY). 2nd Edition. Crown 8vo. 6s.

VOICES CRYING IN THE WILDERNESS. A New Novel. Cr. 8vo. 7s. 6d.

VOLTAIRE.—HISTOIRE DE CHARLES XII., ROI DE SUÈDE. Edited by G. EUGÈNE FASNACHT. 18mo. 3s. 6d.

VOLTAIRE. By JOHN MORLEY. Gl. 8vo. 5s.

WALDSTEIN (C.).—CATALOGUE OF CASTS IN THE MUSEUM OF CLASSICAL ARCHÆOLOGY, CAMBRIDGE. Crown 8vo. 1s. 6d.
Large Paper Edition. Small 4to. 5s.

WALKER (Prof. Francis A.).—THE WAGES QUESTION. 8vo. 14s.
—— MONEY. 8vo. 16s.
—— MONEY IN ITS RELATION TO TRADE AND INDUSTRY. Crown 8vo. 7s. 6d.
—— POLITICAL ECONOMY. 2nd Ed. 8vo. 12s.6d.
—— A BRIEF TEXT-BOOK OF POLITICAL ECONOMY. Crown 8vo. 6s. 6d.
—— LAND AND ITS RENT. Fcp. 8vo. 3s. 6d.

WALLACE (Alfred Russel).—THE MALAY ARCHIPELAGO : THE LAND OF THE ORANG UTANG AND THE BIRD OF PARADISE. Maps and Illustrations. 9th Ed. Cr. 8vo. 7s. 6d.
—— THE GEOGRAPHICAL DISTRIBUTION OF ANIMALS. With Illustrations and Maps. 2 vols. Medium 8vo. 42s.
—— ISLAND LIFE. With Illustrations and Maps. Demy 8vo. 18s.
—— BAD TIMES. An Essay on the present Depression of Trade. Crown 8vo. 2s. 6d.
—— DARWINISM. An Exposition of the Theory of Natural Selection, with some of its Applications. Illustrated. 3rd Ed. Cr. 8vo. 9s.

WALLACE (Sir D. Mackenzie).—EGYPT AND THE EGYPTIAN QUESTION. 8vo. 14s.

WALPOLE (Spencer).—FOREIGN RELATIONS. Crown 8vo. 3s. 6d.
—— THE ELECTORATE AND LEGISLATURE. Crown 8vo. 3s. 6d.

WALPOLE. By JOHN MORLEY. Cr. 8vo. 2s.6d.

WALTON and COTTON—LOWELL.—THE COMPLETE ANGLER ; OR, THE CONTEMPLATIVE MAN'S RECREATION OF IZAAK WALTON AND THOMAS COTTON. With an Introduction by JAS. RUSSELL LOWELL. Illustrated. Extra crown 8vo. 2l. 12s. 6d. net.
Also an Edition on large paper, Proofs on Japanese paper. 3l. 13s. 6d. net.

WANDERING WILLIE. By the Author of "Conrad the Squirrel." Globe 8vo. 2s. 6d.

WARD (Prof. A. W.).—A HISTORY OF ENGLISH DRAMATIC LITERATURE, TO THE DEATH OF QUEEN ANNE. 2 vols. 8vo. 32s.
—— CHAUCER. Cr. 8vo. 1s. 6d. ; sewed, 1s.
—— DICKENS. Cr. 8vo. 1s. 6d. ; sewed, 1s.

WARD (Prof. H. M.).—TIMBER AND SOME OF ITS DISEASES. Illustrated. Cr. 8vo. 6s.

WARD (John).—EXPERIENCES OF A DIPLOMATIST. 8vo. 10s. 6d.

WARD (T. H.).—ENGLISH POETS. Selections, with Critical Introductions by various Writers, and a General Introduction by MATTHEW ARNOLD. Edited by T. H. WARD, M.A. 4 vols. 2nd Ed. Crown 8vo. 7s. 6d. each.—Vol. I. CHAUCER TO DONNE. – II. BEN JONSON TO DRYDEN. – III. ADDISON TO BLAKE.—IV. WORDSWORTH TO ROSSETTI.

WARD (Mrs. T. Humphry).—MILLY AND OLLY. With Illustrations by Mrs. ALMA TADEMA. Globe 8vo. 2s. 6d.

WARD (Mrs. T. H.).—MISS BRETHERTON. Crown 8vo. 3s. 6d.
—— THE JOURNAL INTIME OF HENRIFRÉDÉRIC AMIEL. Translated, with an Introduction and Notes. 2nd Ed. Cr. 8vo. 6s.

WARD (Samuel).—LYRICAL RECREATIONS. Fcp. 8vo. 6s.

WARD (Wilfrid).—WILLIAM GEORGE WARD AND THE OXFORD MOVEMENT. With Portrait. 8vo. 14s.

WARINGTON (G.).—THE WEEK OF CREATION. Crown 8vo. 4s. 6d.

WARWICK, THE KING-MAKER. By C. W. OMAN. Crown 8vo. 2s. 6d.

WATERTON (Charles).—WANDERINGS IN SOUTH AMERICA, THE NORTH-WEST OF THE UNITED STATES, AND THE ANTILLES. Edited by Rev. J. G. WOOD. With 100 Illustrations. Crown 8vo. 6s.
People's Edition. With 100 Illustrations. Medium 4to. 6d.

WATSON.—A RECORD OF ELLEN WATSON. Arranged and Edited by ANNA BUCKLAND. With Portrait. Crown 8vo. 6s.

WATSON (R. Spence).—A VISIT TO WAZAN, THE SACRED CITY OF MOROCCO. 8vo. 10s.6d.

WEBSTER (Augusta).—DAFFODIL AND THE CROÄXAXICANS. Crown 8vo. 6s.

WELBY-GREGORY (The Hon. Lady).—LINKS AND CLUES. 2nd Ed. Cr. 8vo. 6s.

WELCH (Wm.) and DUFFIELD (C. G.).—LATIN ACCIDENCE AND EXERCISES ARRANGED FOR BEGINNERS. 18mo. 1s. 6d.

WELLDON (Rev. J. E. C.).—THE SPIRITUAL LIFE, AND OTHER SERMONS. Cr. 8vo. 6s.

WELLINGTON. By GEO. HOOPER. With Portrait. Crown 8vo. 2s. 6d.

WESTBURY (Hugh).—FREDERICK HAZZLEDEN. 3 vols. Crown 8vo. 31s. 6d.

WESTCOTT (Rev. Prof. B. F.)—A GENERAL SURVEY OF THE HISTORY OF THE CANON OF THE NEW TESTAMENT DURING THE FIRST FOUR CENTURIES. 6th Edition. Cr. 8vo. 10s. 6d.
—— INTRODUCTION TO THE STUDY OF THE FOUR GOSPELS. 7th Ed. Cr. 8vo. 10s. 6d.
—— THE GOSPEL OF THE RESURRECTION. 6th Edition. Crown 8vo. 6s.
—— THE BIBLE IN THE CHURCH. 10th Edit. 18mo. 4s. 6d.
—— THE CHRISTIAN LIFE, MANIFOLD AND ONE. Crown 8vo. 2s. 6d.
—— ON THE RELIGIOUS OFFICE OF THE UNIVERSITIES. Sermons. Cr. 8vo. 4s. 6d.
—— THE REVELATION OF THE RISEN LORD. 4th Edition. Crown 8vo. 6s.
—— THE HISTORIC FAITH. 3rd Edition. Cr. 8vo. 6s.
—— THE EPISTLES OF ST. JOHN. The Greek Text, with Notes. 2nd Edition. 8vo. 12s. 6d.
—— THE REVELATION OF THE FATHER. Cr. 8vo. 6s.
—— CHRISTUS CONSUMMATOR. 2nd Edition. Crown 8vo. 6s.
—— SOME THOUGHTS FROM THE ORDINAL. Crown 8vo. 1s. 6d.

WESTCOTT (Rev. Prof.).—SOCIAL ASPECTS OF CHRISTIANITY. Crown 8vo. 6s.

—— GIFTS FOR MINISTRY. Addresses to Candidates for Ordination. Crown 8vo. 1s. 6d.

—— THE EPISTLE TO THE HEBREWS. The Greek Text, with Notes and Essays. 8vo. 14s.

—— THE VICTORY OF THE CROSS. Sermons preached during Holy Week, 1888, in Hereford Cathedral. Crown 8vo. 3s. 6d.

—— FROM STRENGTH TO STRENGTH. Three Sermons (In Memoriam J. B. D.) Cr. 8vo. 2s.

—— THOUGHTS ON REVELATION AND LIFE. Selections from the Writings of Canon WESTCOTT. Edited by Rev. S. PHILLIPS. Crown 8vo. 6s.

WESTCOTT (Rev. B. F.) and HORT (F. J. A.).—THE NEW TESTAMENT IN THE ORIGINAL GREEK. Revised Text. 2 vols. Crown 8vo. 10s. 6d. each.—Vol. I. Text. —Vol. II. The Introduction and Appendix.

—— THE NEW TESTAMENT IN THE ORIGINAL GREEK. An Edition for Schools. The Text revised by Professors WESTCOTT and HORT. 12mo, 4s. 6d. ; 18mo, 5s. 6d.

WETHERELL (J.).—EXERCISES ON MORRIS' PRIMER OF ENGLISH GRAMMAR. 18mo. 1s.

WHEELER (J. Talboys).—A SHORT HISTORY OF INDIA. With Maps. Crown 8vo. 12s.

—— INDIA UNDER BRITISH RULE. 8vo. 12s. 6d.

—— COLLEGE HISTORY OF INDIA. Asiatic and European. Crown 8vo. 3s. 6d.

WHEN I WAS A LITTLE GIRL. By the Author of "St. Olave's." With Illustrations. Globe 8vo. 2s. 6d.

WHEN PAPA COMES HOME. By the Author of "When I was a Little Girl." With Illustrations. Globe 8vo. 4s. 6d.

WHEWELL.—DR. WILLIAM WHEWELL, late Master of Trinity College, Cambridge. An Account of his Writings, with Selections from his Literary and Scientific Correspondence. By I. TODHUNTER, M.A. 2 vols. 8vo. 25s.

WHITE (Gilbert).—NATURAL HISTORY AND ANTIQUITIES OF SELBORNE. Edited by FRANK BUCKLAND. With a Chapter on Antiquities by Lord SELBORNE. 6s.

WHITE (John Williams).—A SERIES OF FIRST LESSONS IN GREEK. Adapted to GOODWIN's Greek Grammar. Crown 8vo. 3s. 6d.

WHITE (Dr. W. Hale).—A TEXT-BOOK OF GENERAL THERAPEUTICS. Illustrated. Cr. 8vo. 8s. 6d.

WHITNEY (Prof. W. D.).—A COMPENDIOUS GERMAN GRAMMAR. Crown 8vo. 4s. 6d.

—— A GERMAN READER IN PROSE AND VERSE. With Notes and Vocabulary. Cr. 8vo. 5s.

—— A COMPENDIOUS GERMAN AND ENGLISH DICTIONARY. Crown 8vo. 7s. 6d.—German-English Part separately. 5s.

WHITTIER.—COMPLETE POETICAL WORKS OF JOHN GREENLEAF WHITTIER. With Portrait. 18mo. 4s. 6d.

WHITTIER.—THE COMPLETE WORKS OF JOHN GREENLEAF WHITTIER. 7 vols. Crown 8vo. 6s. each.—Vol. I. NARRATIVE AND LEGENDARY POEMS.—II. POEMS OF NATURE; POEMS SUBJECTIVE AND REMINISCENT; RELIGIOUS POEMS.—III. ANTI-SLAVERY POEMS; SONGS OF LABOUR AND REFORM.—IV. PERSONAL POEMS; OCCASIONAL POEMS; THE TENT ON THE BEACH; with the Poems of ELIZABETH H. WHITTIER, and an Appendix containing early and Uncollected Verses.—V. MARGARET SMITH's JOURNAL; TALES AND SKETCHES.—VI. OLD PORTRAITS AND MODERN SKETCHES; PERSONAL SKETCHES AND TRIBUTES; HISTORICAL PAPERS.—VII. THE CONFLICT WITH SLAVERY, POLITICS AND REFORM; THE INNER LIFE, CRITICISM.

WICKHAM (Rev. E. C.)—WELLINGTON COLLEGE SERMONS. Crown 8vo. 6s.

WICKSTEED (Philip H.).—ALPHABET OF ECONOMIC SCIENCE.—I. ELEMENTS OF THE THEORY OF VALUE OR WORTH. Gl.8vo. 2s.6d.

WIEDERSHEIM—PARKER.— ELEMENTS OF THE COMPARATIVE ANATOMY OF VERTEBRATES. Adapted from the German of Prof. ROBERT WIEDERSHEIM, by Prof. W. NEWTON PARKER. Illustrated. Med. 8vo. 12s.6d.

WILBRAHAM (Frances M.).—IN THE SERE AND YELLOW LEAF: THOUGHTS AND RECOLLECTIONS FOR OLD AND YOUNG. Globe 8vo. 3s. 6d.

WILKINS (Prof. A. S.).—THE LIGHT OF THE WORLD: AN ESSAY. 2nd Ed. Cr.8vo. 3s.6d.

—— ROMAN ANTIQUITIES. Illustr. 18mo. 1s.

—— ROMAN LITERATURE. 18mo. 1s.

WILKINSON (S.). — THE BRAIN OF AN ARMY. A Popular Account of the German General Staff. Crown 8vo. 2s. 6d.

WILLIAMS (Montagu).—LEAVES OF A LIFE. 2 vols. 8vo. 30s.

WILLIAMS (S. E.).—FORENSIC FACTS AND FALLACIES. Globe 8vo. 4s. 6d.

WILLOUGHBY (F.).—FAIRY GUARDIANS. Illustr. by TOWNLEY GREEN. Cr. 8vo. 5s.

WILLS (W. G.).—MELCHIOR; A POEM. Cr. 8vo. 9s.

WILSON (A. J.).—THE NATIONAL BUDGET; THE NATIONAL DEBT; RATES AND TAXES. Crown 8vo. 3s. 6d.

WILSON (Dr. George).—RELIGIO CHEMICI. Crown 8vo. 8s. 6d.

—— THE FIVE GATEWAYS OF KNOWLEDGE. 9th Edition. Extra fcp. 8vo. 2s. 6d.

WILSON.—MEMOIR OF PROF. GEORGE WILSON, M.D. By His SISTER. With Portrait. 2nd Edition. Crown 8vo. 6s.

WILSON (Rev. Canon)—THE BIBLE STUDENT'S GUIDE. 2nd Edition. 4to. 25s.

WILSON (Sir Daniel, LL.D.).—PREHISTORIC ANNALS OF SCOTLAND. With Illustrations. 2 vols. Demy 8vo. 36s.

—— PREHISTORIC MAN: RESEARCHES INTO THE ORIGIN OF CIVILISATION IN THE OLD AND NEW WORLD. 3rd Edition. With Illustrations. 2 vols. Medium 8vo. 36s.

www.ingramcontent.com/pod-product-compliance
Lightning Source LLC
Chambersburg PA
CBHW031818270326
41932CB00008B/462